Stephen Walther

ONE WEEK LOAN

ork

SHED

SAMS | 800 East 96th Street, Indianapolis, Indiana 46240 USA

ASP.NET MVC Framework Unleashed

Copyright © 2010 by Pearson Education, Inc.

ISBN-13: 978-0-672-32998-2

ISBN-10: 0-672-32998-0

Library of Congress Cataloging-in-Publication data

Walther, Stephen.

  ASP.NET MVP framework unleashed / Stephen Walther.

    p. cm.

  ISBN 978-0-672-32998-2

  1. Active server pages. 2. Microsoft .NET Framework. 3. Web site development. I. Title.

  TK5105.8885.A26W3522 2010

  006.7'882–dc22

                                        2009021084

Printed in the United States of America

First Printing July 2009

Trademarks

All terms mentioned in this book that are known to be trademarks or service marks have been appropriately capitalized. Sams Publishing cannot attest to the accuracy of this information. Use of a term in this book should not be regarded as affecting the validity of any trademark or service mark.

Warning and Disclaimer

Every effort has been made to make this book as complete and as accurate as possible, but no warranty or fitness is implied. The information provided is on an "as is" basis. The author and the publisher shall have neither liability nor responsibility to any person or entity with respect to any loss or damages arising from the information contained in this book.

Bulk Sales

Sams Publishing offers excellent discounts on this book when ordered in quantity for bulk purchases or special sales. For more information, please contact

> **U.S. Corporate and Government Sales**
> **1-800-382-3419**
> **corpsales@pearsontechgroup.com**

For sales outside of the U.S., please contact

> **International Sales**
> **international@pearson.com**

Editor-in-Chief
Karen Gettman

Executive Editor
Neil Rowe

Development Editor
Mark Renfrow

Managing Editor
Kristy Hart

Project Editor
Betsy Harris

Copy Editor
Apostrophe Editing Services

Indexer
Erika Millen

Proofreader
Keith Cline

Technical Editor
Rebecca Riordan

Publishing Coordinator
Cindy Teeters

Book Designer
Gary Adair

Compositor
Jake McFarland

Contents at a Glance

Table of Contents

About the Author

Stephen Walther has lived a year in Borneo, taught classes on metaphysics at Harvard and MIT, helped found two successful startups, and has run a training and consulting company. He currently is a Program Manager on the Microsoft ASP.NET team where he works on the Microsoft Ajax framework. He has spoken at numerous conferences including PDC, MIX, TechEd, ASP.NET Connections, and VSLive.

Dedication

This book is dedicated to Athena,
Ada, and Jon (who are too small to read!).

Acknowledgments

I took on this book at the same time that I was hired at Microsoft. Completing the book while navigating the requirements of a new job was, umm, not an experience that I ever want to repeat. I want to thank Simon Muzio and Scott Guthrie, who encouraged me to finish the book.

I also want to thank Charlie Poole, who is one of the primary developers behind NUnit, for doing a technical review of the chapters concerning test-driven development.

I also want to thank Neil Rowe, who demonstrated incredible patience over the lifetime of this book. Yikes, this book took a long time to write.

Finally, I owe a huge debt of gratitude to my wife—Ruth.

We Want to Hear from You!

As the reader of this book, *you* are our most important critic and commentator. We value your opinion and want to know what we're doing right, what we could do better, what areas you'd like to see us publish in, and any other words of wisdom you're willing to pass our way.

You can email or write me directly to let me know what you did or didn't like about this book—and what we can do to make our books stronger.

Please note that I cannot help you with technical problems related to the topic of this book, and that due to the high volume of mail I receive, I might not be able to reply to every message.

When you write, please be sure to include this book's title and author, and your name and phone or email address. I will carefully review your comments and share them with the author and editors who worked on the book.

Email: feedback@samspublishing.com

Mail: Neil Rowe
Executive Editor
Sams Publishing
800 East 96th Street
Indianapolis, IN 46240 USA

Reader Services

Visit our website and register this book at informit.com/register for convenient access to any updates, downloads, or errata that might be available for this book.

Introduction

ASP.NET MVC is Microsoft's newest technology for building web applications. Although ASP.NET MVC is new, there are already several large and successful websites that are built on the ASP.NET MVC framework including StackOverflow.com and parts of CodePlex.com.

ASP.NET MVC was created to appeal to several different audiences. If you are the type of developer who wants total control over every HTML tag and pixel that appears in a web page, the ASP.NET MVC framework will appeal to you.

ASP.NET MVC also enables you to expose intuitive URLs to the world. Exposing intuitive URLs is important for getting your website indexed by search engines. If you care about Search Engine Optimization, you will be happy with ASP.NET MVC.

The ASP.NET MVC framework enables you to build web applications that are easier to maintain and extend over time. The Model View Controller pattern encourages a clear separation of concerns. The framework encourages good software design patterns.

Finally, the ASP.NET MVC framework was designed from the ground up to support testability. In particular, the ASP.NET MVC framework enables you to practice test-driven development. You are not required to practice test-driven development when building an ASP.NET MVC application, but the ASP.NET MVC framework makes test-driven development possible.

How This Book Is Organized

The book is divided into two parts. The first part of the book describes the ASP.NET MVC framework feature-by-feature. For example, there are chapters devoted to the subject of controllers, caching, and validation.

The second part of this book contains a walkthrough of building a full ASP.NET MVC application: We build a simple blog application. We implement features such as data access and validation.

Because one of the primary benefits of the ASP.NET MVC framework is that it enables test-driven development, we build the blog application by using test-driven development. The blog application illustrates how you can overcome many challenges that you face when writing real-world applications with the ASP.NET MVC framework.

You can approach this book in two ways. Some readers might want to read through the first chapters of this book before reading the chapters on building the blog application. Other readers might want to read the walkthrough of building the blog application before reading anything else.

What You Should Know Before Reading This Book

I make few assumptions about your technical background. I assume that you know either the C# or the Visual Basic .NET programming language—all the code samples are included in both languages in the body of the book. I also assume that you know basic HTML.

ASP.NET MVC uses many advanced features of the C# and Visual Basic .NET language. The first appendix of this book, Appendix A, "C# and VB.NET Language Features," contains an overview of these new features. For example, if you are not familiar with anonymous types or LINQ to SQL, you should take a look at Appendix A.

The other two appendixes, Appendix B, "Using a Unit Testing Framework," and Appendix C, "Using a Mock Object Framework," are devoted to explaining how to use the main tools of test-driven development. In Appendix B, you learn how to use both the Visual Studio Unit Test framework and how to use the NUnit Unit Test framework. Appendix C is devoted to Mock Object Frameworks.

Throughout the book, when a line of code is too long for the printed page, a code-continuation arrow (➡) has been used to mark the continuation. For example:

```
ReallyLongClassName.ReallyLongMethodName("Here is a value",
➡"Here is another value")
```

What Software Do You Need?

You can download all the software that you need to build ASP.NET MVC applications by visiting the www.ASP.net/mvc website. You need to install three software components:

1. **Microsoft .NET Framework 3.5 Service Pack 1**—The Microsoft .NET framework includes the Microsoft ASP.NET framework.
2. **Microsoft ASP.NET MVC 1.0**—The actual ASP.NET MVC framework that runs on top of the ASP.NET framework.
3. **Microsoft Visual Web Developer 2008 Service Pack 1 or Microsoft Visual Studio 2008 Service Pack 1**—The development environment for creating ASP.NET applications. Also includes the option of installing Microsoft SQL Server Express.

The Microsoft .NET framework, Microsoft ASP.NET MVC, and Microsoft Visual Web Developer are all free. You can build ASP.NET MVC applications without paying a single cent.

Instead of downloading and installing each of these software components one-by-one, you can take advantage of the Microsoft Web Platform Installer to manage the download and installation of all these components. You can launch the Microsoft Web Platform Installer from the www.ASP.net/mvc site.

Where Do You Download the Code Samples?

The code samples for the book are located on the book's product page, www.informit.com/title/9780672329982.

If You Like This Book

After you read this book, if you discover that this book helped you to understand and build ASP.NET MVC applications, please post a review of this book at the www.Amazon.com website.

To get the latest information on ASP.NET MVC, I encourage you to visit the official Microsoft ASP.NET MVC website at www.ASP.net/mvc. I also encourage you to subscribe to my blog at StephenWalther.com that contains ASP.NET MVC tips and tutorials. I also use my blog to post any errata that is discovered after the book is published.

PART I

Building ASP.NET MVC Applications

IN THIS PART

An Introduction to ASP.NET MVC

"There is nothing permanent except change."
Heraclitus

This chapter provides you with an overview and introduction to the Microsoft ASP.NET MVC framework. The goal of this chapter is to explain why you should build web applications using ASP.NET MVC.

Because the ASP.NET MVC framework was designed to enable you to write good software applications, the first part of this chapter is devoted to a discussion of the nature of good software. You learn about the software design principles and patterns that enable you to build software that is resilient to change.

Finally, we discuss the architecture of an ASP.NET MVC application and how this architecture enables you to write good software applications. We provide you with an overview of the different parts of an MVC application including models, views, and controllers and also introduce you to the sample application that you get when you create a new ASP.NET MVC project.

A Story with a Moral

I still remember the day that my manager came to my office and asked me to build the *Single Button Application*. He explained that he needed a simple call manager application to help interviewers dial phone numbers while conducting a health survey. The call manager application would load a list of phone numbers and dial each number one-by-one when you hit a button. What could be simpler?

I said, with great earnestness and confidence, that I would have the call manager application done that same afternoon. I closed my office door, put on my cowboy hat, turned up the music, and pounded out some code. By the end of the day, I had completed the application. My manager was happy, and I went home that night with the happy thought that I had done a good day of work.

The next morning, my manager appeared again at my office door. Worried, I asked if there was a problem with the call manager application. He reassured me that the application worked fine. In fact, he liked it so much that he wanted me to add another feature. He wanted the call manager application to display a survey form when a number is dialed. That way, survey answers could be stored in the database.

With heroic determination, I once again spent the day knocking out code. By the end of the day, I had finished updating the call manager and I proudly presented the finished application to my manager.

I won't continue this story, because anyone who builds software for a living knows how this story ends. The story never ends. When a software project is brought to life, it is almost impossible to kill it. A software application needs to be continuously fed with new features, bug fixes, and performance enhancements.

Being asked to change software that you have created is a compliment. Only useless software goes stagnant. When people care about software, when software is actively used, it undergoes constant change.

I no longer work at the company where I created the call manager application. (I am currently sitting in an office at Microsoft.) But I still have friends at the company and every once in a while I get a report on how the application has changed. Needless to say, it has turned into a massively complex application that supports different time zones, complicated calling rules, and advanced reporting with charts. It can no longer be described as the Single Button Application.

What Is Good Software?

I dropped out of graduate school at MIT to launch an Internet startup in the earliest days of the Web. At that time, building a website was difficult. This was before technologies such as Active Server Pages or ASP.NET existed. (We had only stone knives.) Saving the contents of an HTML form to a database table was a major accomplishment. Blinking text was the height of cool.

When I first started writing software, simply getting the software to do what I wanted was the goal. Adding as many features to a website in the shortest amount of time was the key to survival in the ferociously competitive startup world of the '90s. I used to sleep in my office under my desk.

During my startup phase, I would define good software like this:

Good software is software that works as you intended.

If I was feeling particularly ambitious, I would worry about performance. And maybe, just maybe, if I had extra time, I would add a comment or two to my code. But really, at the end of the day, my criterion for success was simply that the software worked.

For the past 8 years, I've provided training and consulting to large companies and organizations such as Boeing, NASA, Lockheed Martin, and the National Science Foundation. Large organizations are not startups. In a large organization, the focus is not on building software applications as fast as possible; the focus is on building software applications that can be easily maintained over time.

Over the years, my definition of good software has shifted substantially. As I have been faced with the scary prospect of maintaining my own monsters, I've changed my definition of good software to this:

Good software is software that works as you intended and that is easy to change.

There are many reasons that software changes over time. Michael Feathers, in his excellent book *Working Effectively with Legacy Code*, offers the following reasons:

1. You might need to add a new feature to existing software.
2. You might need to fix a bug in existing software.
3. You might need to optimize existing software.
4. You might need to improve the design of existing software.

For example, you might need to add a new feature to an application. The call manager application started as a Single Button Application. However, each day, more and more features were added to the application.

You also need to change software when you discover a bug in the software. For instance, in the case of the call manager, we discovered that it did not calculate daylight savings time correctly. (It was waking some people up in the morning!) We rushed to change the broken code.

You also might need to modify a software application to make the application run faster. At one point, the call manager application took as long as 12 seconds to dial a new phone number. The business rules were getting complex. We had to rewrite the code to get the phone number retrieval time down to the millisecond range.

Finally, you might need to modify software to improve its design. In other words, you might need to take badly written code and convert it into good code. You might need to make your code more resilient to change.

Avoiding Code Smells

Unless you are careful, a software application quickly becomes difficult to change. We all have had the experience of inheriting an application that someone else has written and being asked to modify it. Think of the fear that strikes your heart just before you make your first change.

In the game of Pick-Up Sticks, you must remove stick after stick from a pile of sticks without disturbing the other sticks. The slightest mistake and the whole pile of sticks might scatter.

Modifying an existing software application is similar to the game of Pick-Up Sticks. You bump the wrong piece of code and you introduce a bug.

Bad software is software that is difficult to change. Robert and Micah Martin describe the markers of bad software as *code smells*. The following code smells indicate that software is badly written:

▸ **Rigidity**—Rigid software is software that requires a cascade of changes when you make a change in one place.

▸ **Fragility**—Fragile software is software that breaks in multiple places when you make a change.

▸ **Needless complexity**—Needlessly complex software is software that is overdesigned to handle any possible change.

▸ **Needless repetition**—Needlessly repetitious software contains duplicate code.

▸ **Opacity**—Opaque software is difficult to understand.

> **NOTE**
>
> These code smells are described by Micah and Robert Martin in their book *Agile Principles, Patterns, and Practices in C#* on page 104. This book is strongly recommended!

Notice that these code smells are all related to change. Each of these code smells is a barrier to change.

Software Design Principles

Software does not need to be badly written. A software application can be designed from the beginning to survive change.

The best strategy for making software easy to change is to make the components of the application *loosely coupled*. In a loosely coupled application, you can make a change to one component of an application without making changes to other parts.

Over the years, several principles have emerged for writing good software. These principles enable you to reduce the dependencies between different parts of an application. These software principles have been collected together in the work of Robert Martin (AKA Uncle Bob).

Robert Martin did not invent all the principles; however, he was the first one to gather the principles into a single list. Here is his list of software design principles:

▸ **SRP**—Single Responsibility Principle

▸ **OCP**—Open Closed Principle

- ▶ **LSP**—Liskov Substitution Principle

- ▶ **ISP**—Interface Segregation Principle

- ▶ **DIP**—Dependency Inversion Principle

This collection of principles is collectively known by the acronym SOLID. (Yes, SOLID is an acronym of acronyms.)

For example, according to the Single Responsibility Principle, a class should have one, and only one, reason to change. Here's a concrete example of how this principle is applied: If you know that you might need to modify your application's validation logic separately from its data access logic, then you should not mix validation and data access logic in the same class.

> **NOTE**
>
> There are other lists of software design principles. For example, the *Head First Design Patterns* book has a nice list. You should also visit the C2.com website.

Software Design Patterns

Software design patterns represent strategies for applying software design principles. In other words, a software design principle is a good idea and a software design pattern is the tool that you use to implement the good idea. (It's the hammer.)

The idea behind software design patterns was originally promoted by the book *Design Patterns: Elements of Reusable Object-Oriented Software*. (This book is known as the Gang of Four book.) This book has inspired many other books that describe software design patterns.

The *Head First Design Pattern* book provides a more user-friendly introduction to the design patterns from the Gang of Four book. The *Head First Design* book devotes chapters to 14 patterns with names like Observer, Façade, Singleton, and Adaptor.

Another influential book on software design patterns is Martin Fowler's book *Patterns of Enterprise Application Architecture.* This book has a companion website that lists the patterns from the book: www.martinfowler.com/eaaCatalog.

Software design patterns provide you with patterns for making your code more resilient to change. For example, in many places in this book, we take advantage of a software design pattern named the Repository pattern. Eric Evans, in his book *Domain-Driven Design*, describes the Repository pattern like this:

"A REPOSITORY represents all objects of a certain type as a conceptual set (usually emulated). It acts like a collection, except with more elaborate querying capability. Objects of the appropriate type are added and removed, and the machinery behind the REPOSITORY inserts them or deletes them from the database" (see page 151).

According to Evans, one of the major benefits of the Repository pattern is that it enables you to "decouple application and domain design from persistence technology, multiple database strategies, or even multiple data sources." In other words, the Repository pattern enables you to shield your application from changes in how you perform database access.

For example, when we write our blog application at the end of this book, we take advantage of the Repository pattern to isolate our blog application from a particular persistence technology. The blog application will be designed in such a way that we could switch between different data access technologies such as LINQ to SQL, the Entity Framework, or even NHibernate.

Writing Unit Tests for Your Code

By taking advantage of software design principles and patterns, you can build software that is more resilient to change. Software design patterns are architectural patterns. They focus on the gross architecture of your application.

If you want to make your applications more change proof on a more granular level, then you can build unit tests for your application. A unit test enables you to verify whether a particular method in your application works as you intend it to work.

There are many benefits that result from writing unit tests for your code:

1. Building tests for your code provides you with a safety net for change.
2. Building tests for your code forces you to write loosely coupled code.
3. Building tests for your code forces you to take a user perspective on the code.

First, unit tests provide you with a safety net for change. This is a point that Michael Feathers emphasizes again and again in his book *Working Effectively with Legacy Code*. In fact, he defines legacy code as "simply code without tests" (see xvi).

When your application code is covered by unit tests, you can modify the code without the fear that the modifications will break the functionality of your code. Unit tests make your code safe to refactor. If you can refactor, then you can modify your code using software design patterns and thus produce better code that is more resilient to change.

> **NOTE**
>
> *Refactoring* is the process of modifying code without changing the functionality of the code.

Second, writing unit tests for your code forces you to write code in a particular way. Testable code tends to be loosely coupled code. A unit test performs a test on a unit of code in isolation. To build your application so that it is testable, you need to build the application in such a way that it has isolatable components.

One class is loosely coupled to a second class when you can change the first class without changing the second class. Test-driven development often forces you to write loosely coupled code. Loosely coupled code is resistant to change.

Finally, writing unit tests forces you to take a user's perspective on the code. When writing a unit test, you take on the same perspective as a developer who will use your code in the future. Because writing tests forces you to think about how a developer (perhaps, your future self) will use your code, the code tends to be better designed.

Test-Driven Development

In the previous section, we discussed the importance of building unit tests for your code. Test-driven development is a software design methodology that makes unit tests central to the process of writing software applications. When you practice test-driven development, you write tests first and then write code against the tests.

More precisely, when practicing test-driven development, you complete three steps when creating code (Red/Green/Refactor):

1. Write a unit test that fails (Red).
2. Write code that passes the unit test (Green).
3. Refactor your code (Refactor).

First, you write the unit test. The unit test should express your intention for how you expect your code to behave. When you first create the unit test, the unit test should fail. The test should fail because you have not yet written any application code that satisfies the test.

Next, you write just enough code for the unit test to pass. The goal is to write the code in the laziest, sloppiest, and fastest possible way. You should not waste time thinking about the architecture of your application. Instead, you should focus on writing the minimal amount of code necessary to satisfy the intention expressed by the unit test.

Finally, after you write enough code, you can step back and consider the overall architecture of your application. In this step, you rewrite (refactor) your code by taking advantage of software design patterns—such as the Repository pattern—so that your code is more maintainable. You can fearlessly rewrite your code in this step because your code is covered by unit tests.

There are many benefits that result from practicing test-driven development. First, test-driven development forces you to focus on code that actually needs to be written. Because you are constantly focused on just writing enough code to pass a particular test, you are prevented from wandering into the weeds and writing massive amounts of code that you will never use.

Second, a "test first" design methodology forces you to write code from the perspective of how your code will be used. In other words, when practicing test-driven development, you constant write your tests from a user perspective. Therefore, test-driven development can result in cleaner and more understandable APIs.

Finally, test-driven development forces you to write unit tests as part of the normal process of writing an application. As a project deadline approaches, testing is typically the first thing that goes out the window. When practicing test-driven development, on the other hand, you are more likely to be virtuous about writing unit tests because test-driven development makes unit tests central to the process of building an application.

Short-Term Pain, Long-Term Gain

Building software designed for change requires more upfront effort. Implementing software design principles and patterns takes thought and effort. Writing tests takes time. However, the idea is that the initial effort required to build software the right way will pay huge dividends in the future.

There are two ways to be a developer. You can be a cowboy or you can be a craftsman. A cowboy jumps right in and starts coding. A cowboy can build a software application quickly. The problem with being a cowboy is that software must be maintained over time.

A craftsman is patient. A craftsman builds software carefully by hand. A craftsman is careful to build unit tests that cover all the code in an application. It takes longer for a craftsman to create an application. However, after the application is created, it is easier to fix bugs in the application and add new features to the application.

Most software developers start their programming careers as cowboys. At some point, however, you must hang up your saddle and start building software that can stand the test of time.

What Is ASP.NET MVC?

The Microsoft ASP.NET MVC framework is Microsoft's newest framework for building web applications. The ASP.NET MVC framework was designed from the ground up to make it easier to build good software in the sense of good software discussed in this chapter.

The ASP.NET MVC framework was created to support *pattern-based* software development. In other words, the framework was designed to make it easier to implement software design principles and patterns when building web applications.

Furthermore, the ASP.NET MVC framework was designed to its core to support unit tests. Web applications written with the ASP.NET MVC framework are highly testable.

Because ASP.NET MVC applications are highly testable, this makes the ASP.NET MVC framework a great framework to use when practicing test-driven development.

ASP.NET MVC Is Part of the ASP.NET Framework

Microsoft's framework for building software applications—any type of application including desktop, web, and console applications—is called the *.NET framework*. The .NET framework consists of a vast set of classes, tens of thousands of classes, which you can use when building any type of software application. For example, the .NET framework includes classes for working with the file system, accessing a database, using regular expressions, and generating images.

The ASP.NET framework is one part of the .NET framework. The ASP.NET framework is Microsoft's framework for building web applications. It contains a set of classes that were created specifically to support building web applications. For example, the ASP.NET framework includes classes for implementing web page caching, authentication, and authorization.

Microsoft has two frameworks for building web applications built on top of the ASP.NET framework: ASP.NET Web Forms and ASP.NET MVC (see Figure 1.1).

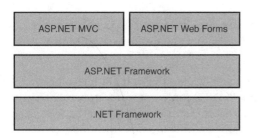

FIGURE 1.1   The ASP.NET frameworks

ASP.NET MVC is an alternative to, but not a replacement for, ASP.NET Web Forms. Some developers find the style of programming represented by ASP.NET Web Forms more compelling, and some developers find ASP.NET MVC more compelling. Microsoft continues to make heavy investments in both technologies.

NOTE

This book is devoted to the topic of ASP.NET MVC. If you want to learn about ASP.NET Web Forms, buy my book *ASP.NET Unleashed*.

The Origins of MVC

The ASP.NET MVC framework is new; however, the MVC software design pattern itself has a long history. The MVC pattern was invented by Trygve Reenskaug while he was a visiting scientist at the Smalltalk group at the famed Xerox Palo Alto Research Center. He wrote his first paper on MVC in 1978. He originally called it the Thing Model View Editor pattern, but he quickly changed the name of the pattern to the Model View Controller pattern.

NOTE

Trygve Reenskaug, the inventor of the MVC pattern, currently works as a professor of informatics at the University of Oslo in Norway.

The MVC pattern was first implemented as part of the Smalltalk-80 class library. It was originally used as an architectural pattern for creating graphical user interfaces (GUIs).

The meaning of MVC shifted radically when the pattern was adapted to work with web applications. In the context of web applications, the MVC pattern is sometimes referred to as the Model 2 MVC pattern.

The MVC pattern has proven to be very successful. Today, the MVC pattern is used by several popular web application frameworks including Ruby on Rails, Merb, and Django. The MVC pattern is also popular in the Java world. In the Java world, MVC is used in the Struts, Spring, and Tapestry frameworks.

The first major MVC framework for ASP.NET was the open source MonoRail project (see CastleProject.org). There continues to be an active developer community around this project.

The Microsoft ASP.NET MVC framework was originally created by Scott Guthrie on an airplane trip to Austin, Texas, to speak at the first Alt.NET conference in October 2007. (Scott Guthrie was one of the creators of ASP.NET.) Scott Guthrie's talk generated so much excitement that the ASP.NET MVC framework became an official Microsoft product. ASP.NET MVC 1.0 was released in the first part of 2009.

The Architecture of an ASP.NET MVC Application

An MVC application, a Model View Controller application, is divided into the following three parts:

- **Model**—An MVC model contains all of an application's logic that is not contained in a view or controller. The model includes all of an application's validation logic, business logic, and data access logic. The MVC model contains model classes that model objects in the application's domain.

- **View**—An MVC view contains HTML markup and view logic.

- **Controller**—An MVC controller contains control-flow logic. An MVC controller interacts with MVC models and views to control the flow of application execution.

Enforcing this separation of concerns among models, views, and controllers has proven to be a useful way of structuring a web application.

First, sharply separating views from the remainder of a web application enables you to redesign the appearance of your application without touching any of the core logic. A web page designer (the person who wears the black beret) can modify the views independently of the software engineers who build the business and data access logic. People with different skills and roles can modify different parts of the application without stepping on each other's toes.

Furthermore, separating the views from the remainder of your application logic enables you to easily change the view technology in the future. One fine day, you might decide to re-implement the views in your application using Silverlight instead of HTML. If you entangle your view logic with the rest of your application logic, migrating to a new view technology will be difficult.

Separating controller logic from the remainder of your application logic has also proven to be a useful pattern for building web applications. You often need to modify the way that a user interacts with your application. You don't want to touch your view logic or model logic when modifying the flow of execution of your application.

Understanding the Sample ASP.NET MVC Application

A good way to get a firmer grasp on the three logical parts of an MVC application is to take a look at the sample application that is created automatically when you create a new ASP.NET MVC project with Visual Studio.

> **NOTE**
>
> We discuss installing ASP.NET MVC in the Introduction.

Follow these steps:

1. Launch Visual Studio.
2. Select the menu option File, New Project.
3. In the New Project dialog, select your favorite programming language (C# or VB.NET) and select the ASP.NET MVC Web Application template. Give your project the name MyFirstMvcApp and click the OK button (see Figure 1.2).

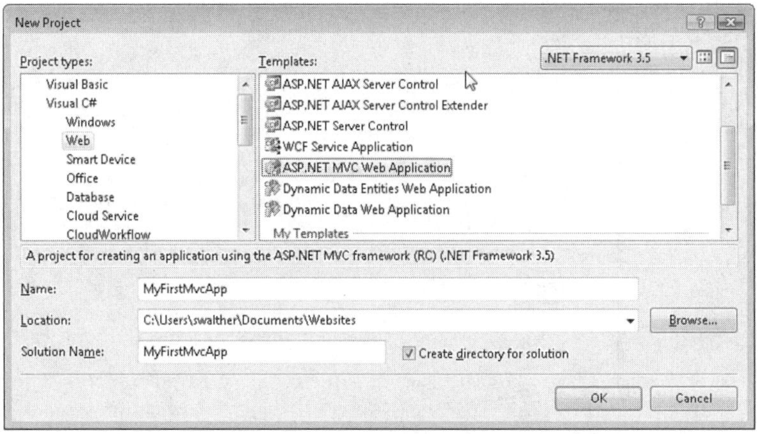

FIGURE 1.2   Creating a new ASP.NET MVC project

Immediately after you click the OK button to create a new ASP.NET MVC project, you see the Create Unit Test Project dialog in Figure 1.3. Leave the default option selected—**Yes, Create a Unit Test Project**—and click the OK button.

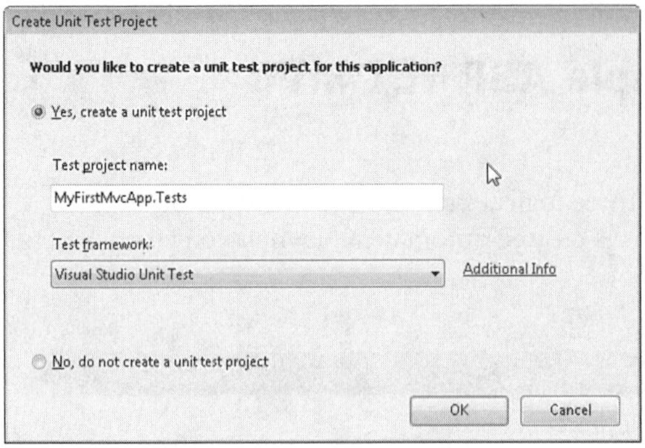

FIGURE 1.3   Creating a unit test project

Your computer hard drive will churn for a few seconds while Visual Studio creates the default files for a new ASP.NET MVC project. After all the files are created, the Solution Explorer window should contain the files in Figure 1.4.

The Solution Explorer window in Figure 1.4 contains two separate projects: the ASP.NET MVC project and the Test project. The Test project contains all the unit tests for your application.

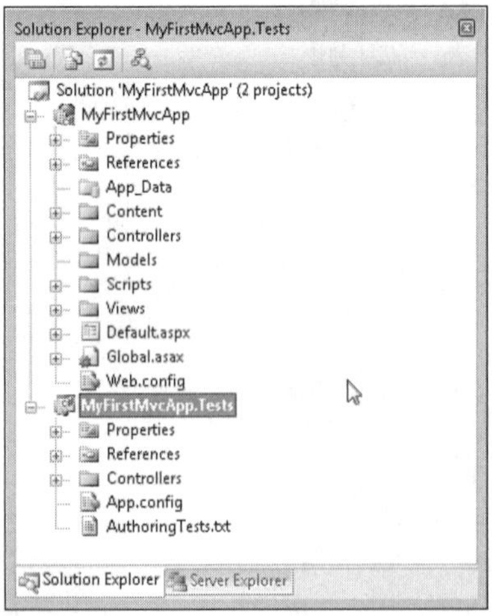

FIGURE 1.4   Files in a new ASP.NET MVC project

ASP.NET MVC Folder Conventions

The ASP.NET MVC framework emphasizes convention over configuration. There are standard locations for each type of file in an ASP.NET MVC project. The ASP.NET MVC application project contains the following folders:

- **App_Data**—Contains database files. For example, the App_Data folder might contain a local instance of a SQL Server Express database.

- **Content**—Contains static content such as images and Cascading Style Sheet files.

- **Controllers**—Contains ASP.NET MVC controller classes.

- **Models**—Contains ASP.NET MVC model classes.

- **Scripts**—Contains JavaScript files including the ASP.NET AJAX Library and jQuery.

- **Views**—Contains ASP.NET MVC views.

When building an ASP.NET MVC application, you should place controllers only in the Controllers folder, JavaScript scripts only in the Scripts folder, ASP.NET MVC views only in the Views folder, and so on. By following these conventions, your application is more easily maintained, and it can be more easily understood by others.

Running the Sample ASP.NET MVC Application

When you create a new ASP.NET MVC application, you get a simple sample application. You can run this sample application by selecting the menu option Debug, Start Debugging (or press the F5 key).

> **NOTE**
>
> When running an ASP.NET MVC application, make sure that the ASP.NET MVC project and not the Test project is selected in the Solution Explorer window.

The first time that you run a new ASP.NET MVC application in Visual Studio, you receive a dialog asking if you want to enable debugging. Simply click the OK button.

When you run the application, your browser opens with the page in Figure 1.5.

You can use the tabs that appear at the top of the page to navigate to either the Home or the About page. You also can click the Login link to register or log in to the application. And, that is all you can do with the application.

This sample application is implemented with one ASP.NET MVC controller and two ASP.NET MVC views. The sample application does not contain any business or data access logic, so it does not contain any ASP.NET MVC model classes.

The controller is located in the Controllers folder:

(C#)

\Controllers\HomeController.cs

(VB)

\Controllers\HomeController.vb

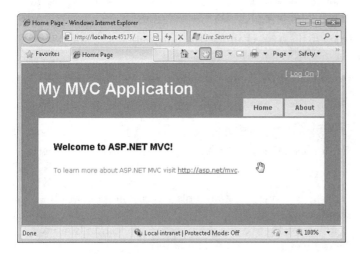

FIGURE 1.5   The sample application

If you open the HomeController in the Code Editor window, you see the file in Listing 1.1.

LISTING 1.1   Controllers\HomeController.cs (C#)

```
using System;
using System.Collections.Generic;
using System.Linq;
using System.Web;
using System.Web.Mvc;

namespace MyFirstMvcApp.Controllers
{
    [HandleError]
    public class HomeController : Controller
    {
        public ActionResult Index()
        {
            ViewData["Message"] = "Welcome to ASP.NET MVC!";

            return View();
        }

        public ActionResult About()
        {
            return View();
        }
```

```
    }
}
```

LISTING 1.1   Controllers\HomeController.vb (VB)

```vb
<HandleError()> _
Public Class HomeController
    Inherits System.Web.Mvc.Controller

    Function Index() As ActionResult
        ViewData("Message") = "Welcome to ASP.NET MVC!"

        Return View()
    End Function

    Function About() As ActionResult
        Return View()
    End Function
End Class
```

The file in Listing 1.1 contains a class with two methods named Index() and About().
Methods exposed by a controller are called actions. Both the Index() and About() actions
return a view.

When you first run the sample application, the Index() action is invoked and this action
returns the Index view. If you click the About tab, the About() action is invoked and this
action returns the About view.

The two views can be found in the Views folder at the following location:

\Views\Home\About.aspx

\Views\Home\Index.aspx

The content of the Index view is contained in Listing 1.2.

LISTING 1.2   Views\Home\Index.aspx (C#)

```csharp
<%@ Page Language="C#" MasterPageFile="~/Views/Shared/Site.Master"
➥Inherits="System.Web.Mvc.ViewPage" %>


<asp:Content ID="indexTitle" ContentPlaceHolderID="TitleContent" runat="server">
    Home Page
</asp:Content>


<asp:Content ID="indexContent" ContentPlaceHolderID="MainContent" runat="server">
```

```
<h2><%= Html.Encode(ViewData["Message"]) %></h2>
<p>
    To learn more about ASP.NET MVC visit <a href="http://asp.net/mvc"
➥title="ASP.NET MVC Website">http://asp.net/mvc</a>.
</p>
</asp:Content>
```

LISTING 1.2   Views\Home\Index.aspx (VB)

```
<%@ Page Language="VB" MasterPageFile="~/Views/Shared/Site.Master"
➥Inherits="System.Web.Mvc.ViewPage" %>

<asp:Content ID="indexTitle" ContentPlaceHolderID="TitleContent" runat="server">
    Home Page
</asp:Content>

<asp:Content ID="indexContent" ContentPlaceHolderID="MainContent" runat="server">
    <h2><%= Html.Encode(ViewData("Message")) %></h2>
    <p>
        To learn more about ASP.NET MVC visit <a href="http://asp.net/mvc"
➥title="ASP.NET MVC Website">http://asp.net/mvc</a>.
    </p>
</asp:Content>
```

Notice that a view consists mostly of standard HTML content. For example, the view contains standard <h2> and <p> tags. A view generates a page that is sent to the browser.

Summary

The goal of this chapter was to provide you with an overview of the ASP.NET MVC framework. The first part of this chapter was devoted to a discussion of a definition of good software. You were provided with a brief introduction to software design principles and patterns and the importance of unit tests. You learned how software design principles and patterns and unit tests enable you to create software that is resilient to change.

Next, you were provided with an introduction to the Model View Controller software design pattern. You learned about the history and benefits of this pattern. You learned how the ASP.NET MVC framework implements the Model View Controller pattern and how ASP.NET MVC enables you to perform pattern-based software development.

Finally, we explored the sample ASP.NET MVC application that is created when you create a new ASP.NET MVC project. We took our first look at an ASP.NET MVC controller and an ASP.NET MVC view.

CHAPTER 2

Building a Simple ASP.NET MVC Application

In the previous chapter, we discussed all the lofty goals of the ASP.NET MVC framework. In this chapter, we completely ignore them. In this chapter, we build a simple database-driven ASP.NET MVC application in the easiest way possible. We ignore design principles and patterns. We don't create a single unit test. The goal is to clarify the basic mechanics of building an ASP.NET MVC application.

Over the course of this chapter, we build a simple Toy Store application. Our Toy Store application enables us to display a list of toys and create new toys. In other words, it illustrates how to build a web application that performs basic database operations.

> **NOTE**
>
> The third part of this book is devoted to an extended walkthrough of building an ASP.NET MVC application in the "right" way. We build a blog application by using test-driven development and software design principles and patterns.

Starting with a Blank Slate

Let's start by creating a new ASP.NET MVC application and removing all the sample files. Follow these steps to create a new ASP.NET MVC Web Application project:

1. Launch Visual Studio 2008.
2. Select the menu option File, New Project.

3. In the New Project dialog, select your preferred programming language and select the ASP.NET MVC Web Application template (see Figure 2.1).

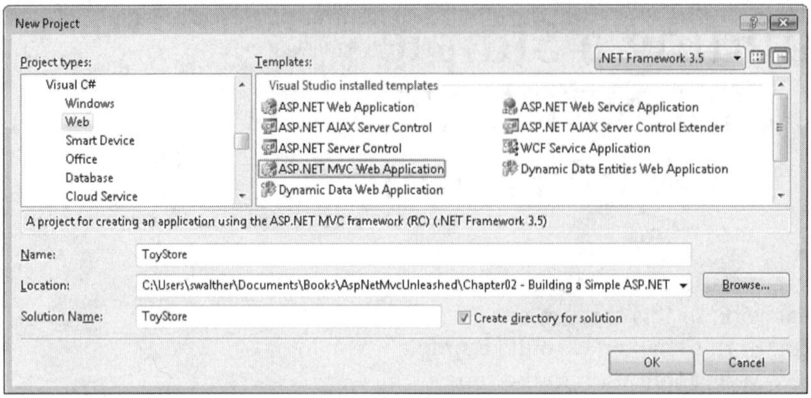

FIGURE 2.1   Creating a new ASP.NET MVC application

4. Name your new project ToyStore and click the OK button.

When you create a new ASP.NET MVC project, the Create Unit Test Project dialog appears automatically (see Figure 2.2). When asked whether you want to create a unit test project, select the option Yes, Create a Unit Test Project. (In general, you should always select this option because it is a pain to add a new unit test project to your solution after your ASP.NET MVC project is already created).

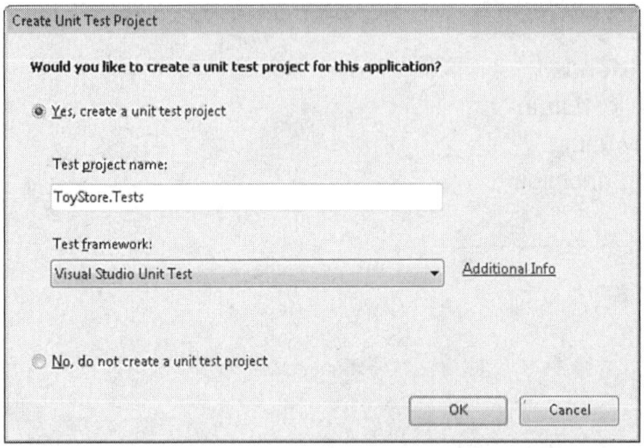

FIGURE 2.2   The Create Unit Test Project dialog

NOTE

The Create Unit Test Project dialog won't appear when you create an ASP.NET MVC application in Microsoft Visual Web Developer. Visual Web Developer does not support Test projects.

As we discussed in the previous chapter, when you create a new ASP.NET MVC application, you get several sample files by default. These files get in our way as we build a new application. Delete the following files from your ASP.NET MVC project:

(C#)

\Controllers\HomeController.cs

\Views\Home\About.aspx

\Views\Home\Index.aspx

(VB)

\Controllers\HomeController.vb

\Views\Home\About.aspx

\Views\Home\Index.aspx

Delete the following file from your Test project:

(C#)

\Controllers\HomeControllerTest.cs

(VB)

\Controllers\HomeControllerTest.vb

TIP

If you always want to start with an empty ASP.NET MVC project, you can create a new Visual Studio project template after deleting the sample files. Create a new project template by selecting the menu option File, Export Template.

Creating the Database

We need to create a database and database table to contain our list of toys for our toy store. The ASP.NET MVC framework is compatible with any modern database including Oracle 11g, MySQL, and Microsoft SQL Server.

In this book, we use Microsoft SQL Server Express for our database. Microsoft SQL Server Express is the free version of Microsoft SQL Server. It includes all the basic functionality of the full version of Microsoft SQL Server. (It uses the same database engine.)

NOTE

You can install Microsoft SQL Server Express when you install Visual Studio or Visual Web Developer. (It is an installation option.) You also can download Microsoft SQL Server Express by using the Web Platform Installer that you can download from the following website: www.asp.net/downloads/.

Follow these steps to create a new database from within Visual Studio:

1. Right-click the App_Data folder in the Solution Explorer window and select the menu option Add, New Item.
2. In the Add New Item dialog, select the SQL Server Database template (see Figure 2.3).

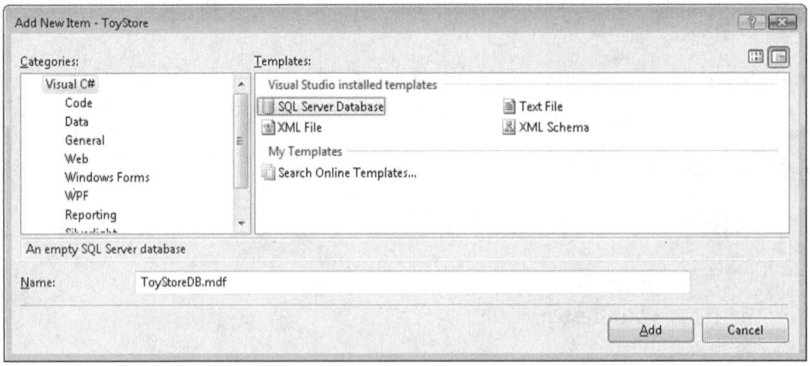

FIGURE 2.3   Adding a new SQL Server database

3. Give the new database the name ToyStoreDB.
4. Click the Add button.

After you create the database, you need to create the database table that will contain the list of toys. Follow these steps to create the Products database table:

1. Double-click the ToyStoreDB.mdf file in the App_Data folder to open the Server Explorer window and connect to the ToyStoreDB database.
2. Right-click the Tables folder and select the menu option Add New Table.
3. Enter the columns listed in Table 2.1 into the Table Designer (see Figure 2.4).

TABLE 2.1   Columns in the Products Table

Column Name	Data Type	Allow Nulls
Id	int	False
Name	nvarchar(100)	False
Description	nvarchar(MAX)	False
Price	money	False

4. Set the Id column as an Identity column by expanding the Identity Specification node under Column Properties and setting the (Is Identity) property to the value Yes.
5. Set the Id column as the primary key column by selecting this column in the Table Designer and clicking the Set Primary Key button (the button with an icon of a key).

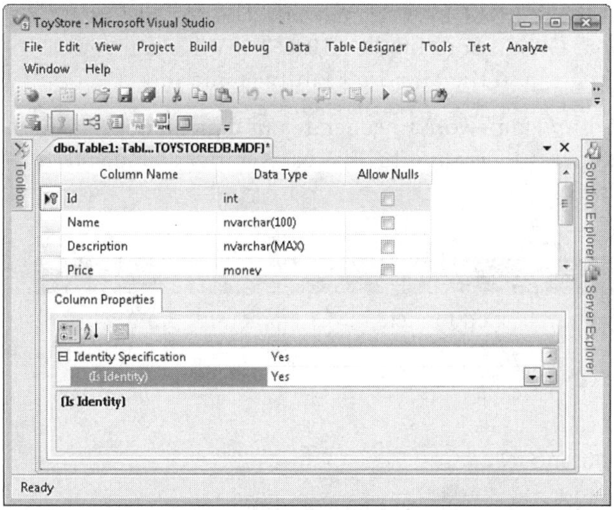

FIGURE 2.4   Creating the Products table

6. Save the new table by clicking the Save button (the button with the anachronistic icon of a floppy disk).

7. In the Choose Name dialog, enter the table name Products and click OK.

NOTE

The Server Explorer window is called the Database Explorer window in Visual Web Developer.

After you finish creating the Products database table, you should add some database records to the table. Right-click the Products table in the Server Explorer window and select the menu option Show Table Data. Enter two or three products—you can enter anything you want (see Figure 2.5).

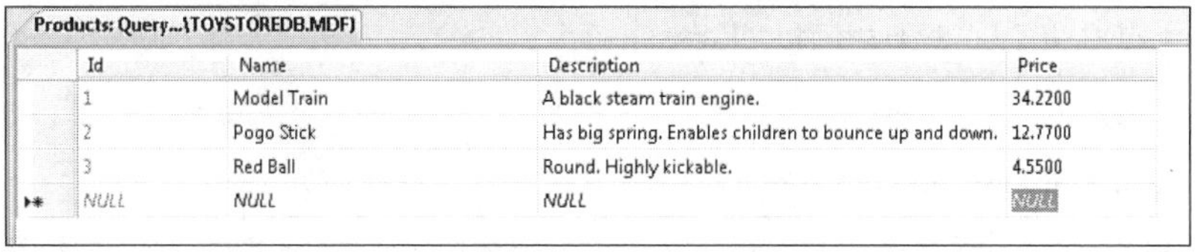

FIGURE 2.5   Entering sample data in the Products database table

Creating the Model

We need to create model classes to represent our database tables in our ASP.NET MVC application. The easiest way to create the data model classes is to use an *Object Relational Mapping* (ORM) tool to generate the classes from a database automatically.

You can use your favorite ORM with the ASP.NET MVC framework. The ASP.NET MVC framework is not tied to any particular ORM. For example, ASP.NET MVC is compatible with Microsoft LINQ to SQL, NHibernate, and the Microsoft Entity Framework.

In this book, we use the Microsoft Entity Framework to generate our data model classes. We focus on the Microsoft Entity Framework because the Microsoft Entity Framework is Microsoft's recommended data access solution.

NOTE

To use the Microsoft Entity Framework, you need to install .NET Framework 3.5 Service Pack 1.

Follow these steps to generate the data model classes:

1. Right-click the Models folder in the Solution Explorer window and select the menu option Add, New Item.
2. Select the Data category and the ADO.NET Entity Data Model template (see Figure 2.6).

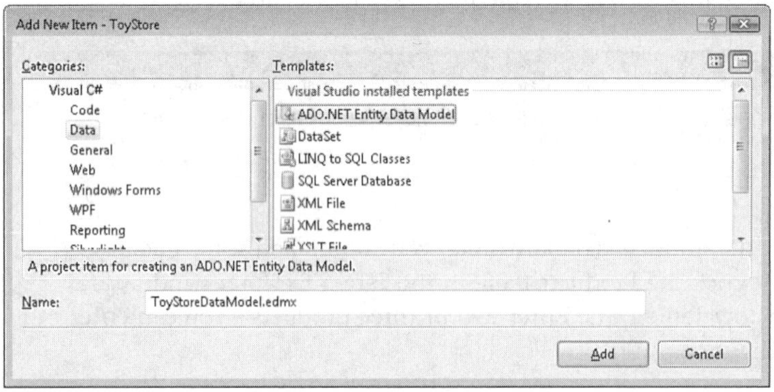

FIGURE 2.6   Adding ADO.NET Entity Data Model classes

3. Name the data model ToyStoreDataModel.edmx and click the Add button.

After you complete these steps, the Entity Model Data Wizard launches. Complete these wizard steps:

1. In the Choose Model Contents step, select the Generate From database option.
2. In the Choose Your Data Connection step, select the ToyStoreDB.mdf data connection and name the entity connection ToyStoreDBEntities (see Figure 2.7).
3. In the Choose Your Database Objects step, select the Products database table and enter Models for the namespace (see Figure 2.8).

FIGURE 2.7   Choose your data connection

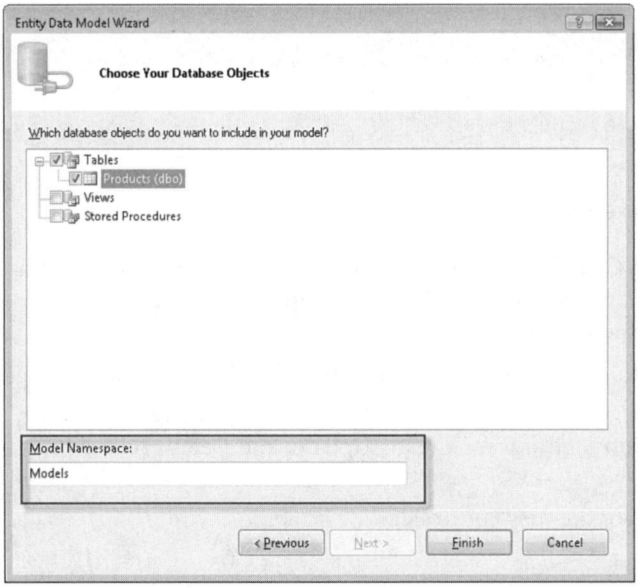

FIGURE 2.8   Entering the model namespace

4. Click the Finish button to complete the wizard.

After you complete the Entity Data Model Wizard, the Entity Designer appears with a single entity named Products (see Figure 2.9). The Entity Framework has generated a class named Products that represents your Products database table.

FIGURE 2.9   The Entity Designer

Most likely, you want to rename the classes generated by the Entity Framework. The Entity Framework simply names its entities with the same names as the database tables. Because the Products class represents a particular product, you want to change the name of the class to Product (singular instead of plural).

Right-click the Products entity in the Entity Designer and select the menu option Rename. Provide the new name Product.

At this point, we have successfully created our data model classes. We can use these classes to represent our ToyStoreDB database within our ASP.NET MVC application.

> **NOTE**
>
> You can open the Entity Designer at any time in the future by double-clicking the ToyStoreDataModel.edmx file in the Models folder.

Creating the Controller

The controllers in an ASP.NET MVC application control the flow of application execution. The controller that is invoked by default is named the Home controller. We need to create the Home controller by following these steps:

1. Right-click the Controllers folder and select the menu option Add Controller.
2. In the Add Controller dialog, enter the controller name HomeController and select the option labeled Add Action Methods for Create, Update, and Details scenarios (see Figure 2.10).
3. Click the Add button to create the new controller.

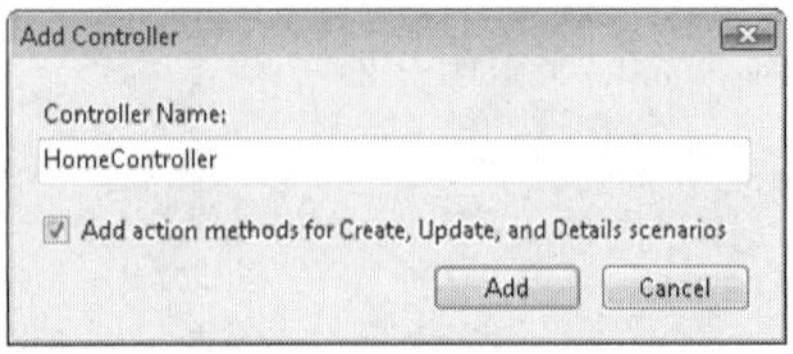

FIGURE 2.10   Adding a new controller

The Home controller is contained in Listing 2.1.

LISTING 2.1   Controllers\HomeController.cs (C#)

```csharp
using System;
using System.Collections.Generic;
using System.Linq;
using System.Web;
using System.Web.Mvc;
using System.Web.Mvc.Ajax;

namespace ToyStore.Controllers
{
    public class HomeController : Controller
    {
        //
        // GET: /Home/

        public ActionResult Index()
        {
            return View();
        }

        //
        // GET: /Home/Details/5

        public ActionResult Details(int id)
        {
            return View();
        }

        //
        // GET: /Home/Create

        public ActionResult Create()
        {
            return View();
        }

        //
        // POST: /Home/Create

        [AcceptVerbs(HttpVerbs.Post)]
        public ActionResult Create(FormCollection collection)
```

```
        {
            try
            {
                // TODO: Add insert logic here

                return RedirectToAction("Index");
            }
            catch
            {
                return View();
            }
        }


        //
        // GET: /Home/Edit/5

        public ActionResult Edit(int id)
        {
            return View();
        }


        //
        // POST: /Home/Edit/5

        [AcceptVerbs(HttpVerbs.Post)]
        public ActionResult Edit(int id, FormCollection collection)
        {
            try
            {
                // TODO: Add update logic here

                return RedirectToAction("Index");
            }
            catch
            {
                return View();
            }
        }
    }
}
```

LISTING 2.1   Controllers\HomeController.vb (VB)

```
Public Class HomeController
    Inherits System.Web.Mvc.Controller
```

```vbnet
'
' GET: /Home/

Function Index() As ActionResult
    Return View()
End Function


' GET: /Home/Details/5

Function Details(ByVal id As Integer) As ActionResult
    Return View()
End Function


' GET: /Home/Create

Function Create() As ActionResult
    Return View()
End Function


' POST: /Home/Create

<AcceptVerbs(HttpVerbs.Post)> _
Function Create(ByVal collection As FormCollection) As ActionResult
    Try
        ' TODO: Add insert logic here
        Return RedirectToAction("Index")
    Catch
        Return View()
    End Try
End Function


' GET: /Home/Edit/5

Function Edit(ByVal id As Integer) As ActionResult
    Return View()
End Function


' POST: /Home/Edit/5

<AcceptVerbs(HttpVerbs.Post)> _
```

```
    Function Edit(ByVal id As Integer, ByVal collection As FormCollection) As
↪ActionResult
        Try
            ' TODO: Add update logic here

            Return RedirectToAction("Index")
        Catch
            Return View()
        End Try
    End Function
End Class
```

Because we selected the option to generate Create, Update, and Details methods when creating the Home controller, the Home controller in Listing 2.1 includes these actions. In particular, the Home controller exposes the following actions:

▶ Index()—This is the default action of the controller. Typically, this action displays a list of items.

▶ Details(id)—This action displays details for a particular item.

▶ Create()—This action displays a form for creating a new item.

▶ Create(collection)—This action inserts the new item into the database.

▶ Edit(id)—This action displays a form for editing an existing item.

▶ Edit(id, collection)—This action update the existing item in the database.

Currently, the Home controller contains only stubs for these actions. Let's go ahead and take advantage of the data model classes that we created with the Entity Framework to implement the Index() and Create() actions. The updated Home controller is contained in Listing 2.2.

LISTING 2.2   Controllers\HomeController.cs (C#)

```
using System.Linq;
using System.Web.Mvc;
using ToyStore.Models;

namespace ToyStore.Controllers
{
    public class HomeController : Controller
    {
        private ToyStoreDBEntities _dataModel = new ToyStoreDBEntities();

        //
        // GET: /Home/
```

```csharp
public ActionResult Index()
{
    return View(_dataModel.ProductSet.ToList());
}

//
// GET: /Home/Create

public ActionResult Create()
{
    return View();
}

//
// POST: /Home/Create


[AcceptVerbs(HttpVerbs.Post)]
public ActionResult Create([Bind(Exclude="Id")]Product productToCreate)
{
    if (!ModelState.IsValid)
        return View();

    try

    {
        _dataModel.AddToProductSet(productToCreate);
        _dataModel.SaveChanges();

        return RedirectToAction("Index");
    }
    catch
    {
        return View();
    }
}


}
}
```

LISTING 2.2   Controllers\HomeController.vb (VB)

```vbnet
Public Class HomeController
    Inherits System.Web.Mvc.Controller
```

```vbnet
    Private _dataModel As New ToyStoreDBEntities()


    '
    ' GET: /Home/

    Function Index() As ActionResult
        Return View(_dataModel.ProductSet.ToList())
    End Function

    '
    ' GET: /Home/Create

    Function Create() As ActionResult
        Return View()
    End Function


    '
    ' POST: /Home/Create

    <AcceptVerbs(HttpVerbs.Post)> _
    Function Create(<Bind(Exclude:="Id")> ByVal productToCreate As Product) As
➥ActionResult

        If Not ModelState.IsValid Then
            Return View()
        End If

        Try
            _dataModel.AddToProductSet(productToCreate)
            _dataModel.SaveChanges()

            Return RedirectToAction("Index")
        Catch
            Return View()
        End Try
    End Function


End Class
```

Notice that a private field named _dataModel of type DBStoreEntities is defined at the top of the controller in Listing 2.2. The DBStoreEntities class was one of the classes that was generated by the Entity Model Data Wizard. We use this class to communicate with the database.

The `Index()` action has been modified to return a list of products. The expression `_dataModel.ProductSet.ToList()` returns a list of products from the Products database table.

There are two `Create()` actions. The first `Create()` action displays the form for creating a new product. The form is submitted to the second `Create()` action that actually performs the database insert of the new product.

Notice that the second `Create()` action has been modified to accept a `Product` parameter. The Product class also was generated by the Entity Model Data Wizard. The `Product` class has properties that correspond to each column in the underlying Products database table.

Finally, the `Create()` action calls the following methods to add the new product to the database:

(C#)

```
_dataModel.AddToProductSet(productToCreate);
_dataModel.SaveChanges();
```

(VB)

```
_dataModel.AddToProductSet(productToCreate)
_dataModel.SaveChanges()
```

Our `Home` controller now contains all the necessary database logic. We can use the controller to return a set of products, and we can use the controller to create a new product.

Notice that both the `Index()` action and the first `Create()` action return a view. The next and final step is to create these views.

Creating the Views

An MVC view contains all the HTML markup and view logic required to generate an HTML page. The set of views exposed by an ASP.NET MVC application is the public face of the application.

NOTE

A view does not need to be HTML. For example, you can create Silverlight views.

Our simple application needs two views: the Index view and the Create view. We use the Index view to displays the list of products and the Create view to display a form for creating new products.

Adding the Index View

Let's start by creating the Index view. Follow these steps:

1. Build your application by selecting the menu option Build, Build Solution.
2. Right-click the `Index()` action in the Code Editor window and select the menu option Add View (see Figure 2.11).

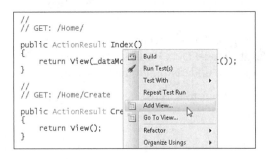

FIGURE 2.11   Adding a view

3. In the Add View dialog, select the option Create a Strongly Typed View.
4. In the Add View dialog, from the drop-down list labeled View Data Class, select the ToyStore.Models.Product class.
5. In the Add View dialog, from the drop-down list labeled View Content, select List.
6. Click the Add button to add the new view to your project (see Figure 2.12).

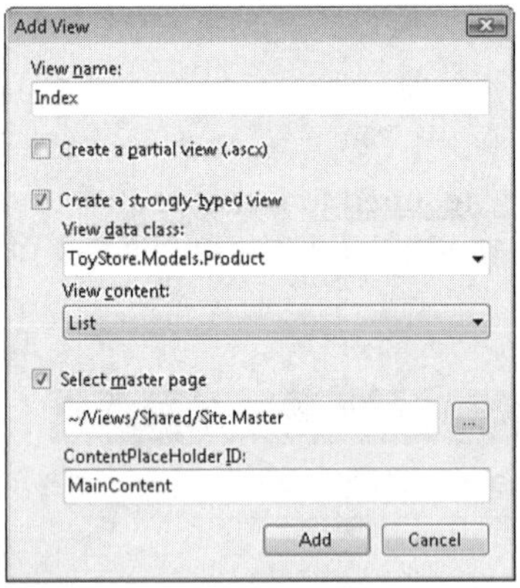

FIGURE 2.12   The Add View dialog

> **NOTE**
>
> You need to build your ASP.NET MVC application before adding a view with the Add View dialog to build the classes displayed by the View Data Class drop-down list. If your application has build errors, this list will be blank.

Views are added to the Views folder. Views follow a particular naming convention. A view returned by the Index() action exposed by the Home controller class is located at the following path:

\Views\Home\Index.aspx

In general, views adhere to the following naming convention:

\Views\Controller Name\Action Name.aspx

The contents of the Index view are contained in Listing 2.3. This view loops through all the products and displays the products in an HTML table (see Figure 2.13).

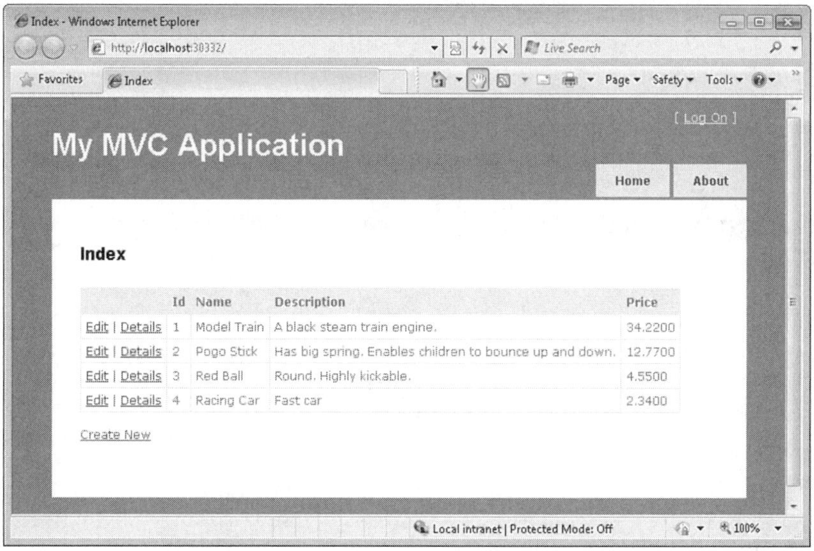

FIGURE 2.13   The Index view

LISTING 2.3   Views\Home\Index.aspx (C#)

```
<%@ Page Title="" Language="C#" MasterPageFile="~/Views/Shared/Site.Master"
➥Inherits="System.Web.Mvc.ViewPage<IEnumerable<ToyStore.Models.Product>>" %>
```

```
<asp:Content ID="Content1" ContentPlaceHolderID="TitleContent" runat="server">
        Home Page
</asp:Content>

<asp:Content ID="Content2" ContentPlaceHolderID="MainContent" runat="server">

    <h2>Index</h2>

    <table>
        <tr>
            <th></th>
            <th>
                Id
            </th>
            <th>
                Name
            </th>
            <th>
                Description
            </th>
            <th>
                Price
            </th>
        </tr>

    <% foreach (var item in Model) { %>

        <tr>
            <td>
                <%= Html.ActionLink("Edit", "Edit", new { /* id=item.PrimaryKey */
➥}) %> ¦
                <%= Html.ActionLink("Details", "Details", new { /*
➥id=item.PrimaryKey */ })%>
            </td>
            <td>
                <%= Html.Encode(item.Id) %>
            </td>
            <td>
                <%= Html.Encode(item.Name) %>
            </td>
            <td>
                <%= Html.Encode(item.Description) %>
            </td>
            <td>
                <%= Html.Encode(item.Price) %>
            </td>
```

```
        </tr>

    <% } %>

    </table>

    <p>
        <%= Html.ActionLink("Create New", "Create") %>
    </p>

</asp:Content>
```

LISTING 2.3   Views\Home\Index.aspx (VB)

```
<%@ Page Title="" Language="VB" MasterPageFile="~/Views/Shared/Site.Master"
➥Inherits="System.Web.Mvc.ViewPage(Of IEnumerable(Of ToyStore.Product))" %>


<asp:Content ID="indexTitle" ContentPlaceHolderID="TitleContent" runat="server">
    Home Page
</asp:Content>

<asp:Content ID="Content2" ContentPlaceHolderID="MainContent" runat="server">

    <h2>Index</h2>

    <p>
        <%=Html.ActionLink("Create New", "Create")%>
    </p>

    <table>
        <tr>
            <th></th>
            <th>
                Id
            </th>
            <th>
                Name
            </th>
            <th>
                Description
            </th>
            <th>
                Price
            </th>
```

```
        </tr>

    <% For Each item In Model%>

        <tr>
            <td>
                <%--<%=Html.ActionLink("Edit", "Edit", New With
➡{.id = item.PrimaryKey})%> ¦
                <%=Html.ActionLink("Details", "Details", New With
➡{.id = item.PrimaryKey})%>--%>
            </td>
            <td>
                <%=Html.Encode(item.Id)%>
            </td>
            <td>
                <%=Html.Encode(item.Name)%>
            </td>
            <td>
                <%=Html.Encode(item.Description)%>
            </td>
            <td>
                <%=Html.Encode(item.Price)%>
            </td>
        </tr>

    <% Next%>

    </table>

</asp:Content>
```

Notice that the Index view includes a link labeled Create New that appears at the bottom of the view. We add the Create view in the next section.

Adding the Create View

The Create view displays the HTML form for adding a new product. We can follow a similar set of steps to add the Create view:

1. Right-click the first Create() action in the Code Editor window and select the menu option Add View.
2. In the Add View dialog, select the option Create a Strongly Typed View.
3. In the Add View dialog, from the drop-down list labeled View Data Class, select the ToyStore.Models.Product class.
4. In the Add View dialog, from the drop-down list labeled View Content, select Create.

5. Click the Add button to add the new view to your project (see Figure 2.14).

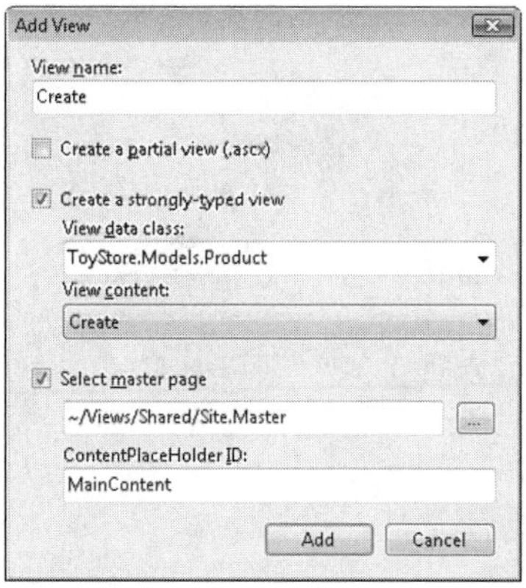

FIGURE 2.14   Adding the Create view

The Create view is added to your project at the following location:

\Views\Home\Create.aspx

The contents of the Create view are contained in Listing 2.4.

LISTING 2.4   Views\Home\Create.aspx (C#)

```
<%@ Page Title="" Language="C#" MasterPageFile="~/Views/Shared/Site.Master"
➥Inherits="System.Web.Mvc.ViewPage<ToyStore.Models.Product>" %>


<asp:Content ID="indexTitle" ContentPlaceHolderID="TitleContent" runat="server">
    Create
</asp:Content>

<asp:Content ID="Content2" ContentPlaceHolderID="MainContent" runat="server">

    <h2>Create</h2>

    <%= Html.ValidationSummary() %>

    <% using (Html.BeginForm()) {%>

        <fieldset>
            <legend>Fields</legend>
            <p>
                <label for="Id">Id:</label>
                <%= Html.TextBox("Id") %>
```

```
            <%= Html.ValidationMessage("Id", "*") %>
        </p>
        <p>
            <label for="Name">Name:</label>
            <%= Html.TextBox("Name") %>
            <%= Html.ValidationMessage("Name", "*") %>
        </p>
        <p>
            <label for="Description">Description:</label>
            <%= Html.TextBox("Description") %>
            <%= Html.ValidationMessage("Description", "*") %>
        </p>
        <p>
            <label for="Price">Price:</label>
            <%= Html.TextBox("Price") %>
            <%= Html.ValidationMessage("Price", "*") %>
        </p>
        <p>
            <input type="submit" value="Create" />
        </p>
    </fieldset>

<% } %>

<div>
    <%=Html.ActionLink("Back to List", "Index") %>
</div>

</asp:Content>
```

LISTING 2.4   Views\Home\Create.aspx (VB)

```
<%@ Page Title="" Language="VB" MasterPageFile="~/Views/Shared/Site.Master"
➥Inherits="System.Web.Mvc.ViewPage(Of ToyStore.Product)" %>


<asp:Content ID="indexTitle" ContentPlaceHolderID="TitleContent" runat="server">
    Create
</asp:Content>

<asp:Content ID="Content2" ContentPlaceHolderID="MainContent" runat="server">

    <h2>Create</h2>
```

```
<%= Html.ValidationSummary() %>

<% Using Html.BeginForm()%>

    <fieldset>
        <legend>Fields</legend>
        <p>
            <label for="Id">Id:</label>
            <%= Html.TextBox("Id") %>
            <%= Html.ValidationMessage("Id", "*") %>
        </p>
        <p>
            <label for="Name">Name:</label>
            <%= Html.TextBox("Name") %>
            <%= Html.ValidationMessage("Name", "*") %>
        </p>
        <p>
            <label for="Description">Description:</label>
            <%= Html.TextBox("Description") %>
            <%= Html.ValidationMessage("Description", "*") %>
        </p>
        <p>
            <label for="Price">Price:</label>
            <%= Html.TextBox("Price") %>
            <%= Html.ValidationMessage("Price", "*") %>
        </p>
        <p>
            <input type="submit" value="Create" />
        </p>
    </fieldset>

<% End Using %>

<div>
    <%=Html.ActionLink("Back to List", "Index") %>
</div>

</asp:Content>
```

The Create view displays an HTML form for creating new products (see Figure 2.15). The Add View dialog generates HTML form fields that correspond to each of the properties of the Product class. If you complete the HTML form and submit it, a new product will be created in the database.

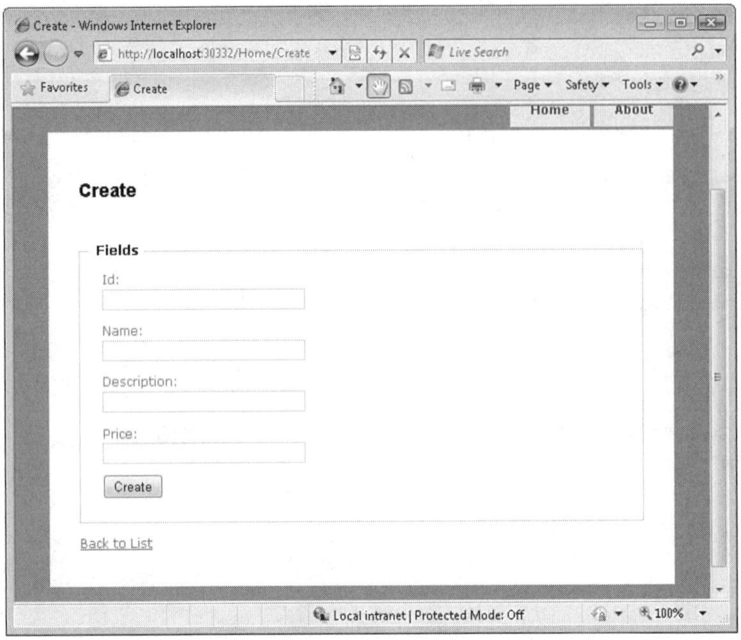

FIGURE 2.15   The Create view

Summary

In this chapter, we used the ASP.NET MVC framework to build a simple database-driven web application. We created models, views, and controllers.

First, we created a database and a database model. We used Microsoft SQL Server Express for our database. We created our database model classes by taking advantage of the Microsoft Entity Framework.

Next, we created the Home controller. We used Visual Studio to generate the actions for our Home controller automatically. We added a few lines of data access logic to interact with our database.

Finally, we created two views. We created an Index view that displays a list of all the products in an HTML table. We also added a Create view that displays an HTML form for adding a new product to the database.

Understanding Controllers and Actions

ASP.NET MVC controllers are responsible for controlling the flow of application execution. When you make a browser request against an ASP.NET MVC application, a controller is responsible for returning a response to that request.

Controllers expose one or more actions. A controller action can return different types of action results to a browser. For example, a controller action might return a view, a controller action might return a file, or a controller action might redirect you to another controller action.

In this chapter, you learn how to create controllers and controller actions. You learn how to return different types of controller action results. You also learn how to use attributes to control when a particular controller action gets invoked. We complete this chapter by discussing how you can write unit tests for your controllers and actions.

Creating a Controller

The easiest way to create a controller is to right-click the Controllers folder in the Visual Studio Solution Explorer window and select the menu option Add, Controller. Selecting this menu option displays the Add Controller dialog (see Figure 3.1). If you enter the name ProductController, you get the code in Listing 3.1.

> **WARNING**
>
> A controller name must end with the suffix *Controller*. If you forget to include the Controller suffix, you can't invoke the controller.

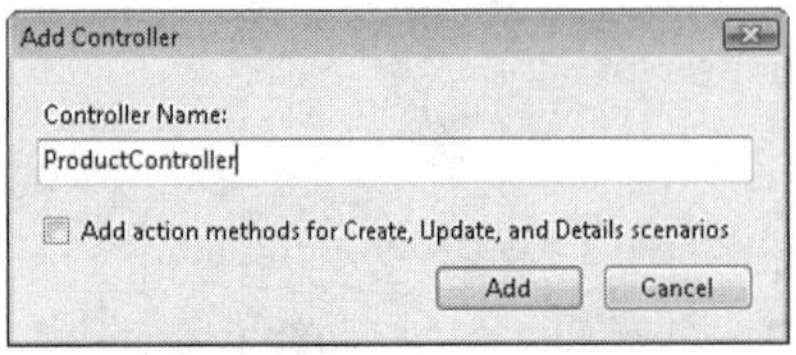

FIGURE 3.1   The Add Controller dialog

LISTING 3.1   Controllers\ProductController.cs (C#)

```csharp
using System;
using System.Collections.Generic;
using System.Linq;
using System.Web;
using System.Web.Mvc;
using System.Web.Mvc.Ajax;

namespace MvcApplication1.Controllers
{
    public class ProductController : Controller
    {
        //
        // GET: /Product/

        public ActionResult Index()
        {
            return View();
        }

    }
}
```

LISTING 3.1   Controllers\ProductController.vb (VB)

```vb
Public Class ProductController
    Inherits System.Web.Mvc.Controller

    '

    ' GET: /Product/

    Function Index() As ActionResult
        Return View()
    End Function

End Class
```

Notice that a controller is just a class (a Visual Basic or C# class) that inherits from the base `System.Web.Mvc.Controller` class.

Any public method exposed by a controller is exposed as a controller action. The controller class in Listing 3.1 exposes one action named `Index()`. The `Index()` action is the default action that is invoked on a controller when no explicit action is specified.

WARNING

By default, any public method contained in a controller class can be invoked by anyone located anywhere on the Internet. Be careful about the methods that you publicly expose from a controller. If you want to prevent a public controller method from being invoked, you can decorate the method with the `NonAction` attribute.

Notice that the `Index()` action returns an `ActionResult`. A controller action always returns an `ActionResult` (even if it doesn't appear to be returning an `ActionResult`). The `ActionResult` determines the response returned to the browser. The `Index()` controller returns a view as its `ActionResult`.

A controller typically exposes multiple actions. You add actions to a controller by adding new methods to the controller. For example, the modified `Product` controller in Listing 3.2 exposes three actions named `Index()`, `Help()`, and `Details()`.

LISTING 3.2   Controllers\ProductController.cs with Additional Methods (C#)

```
using System.Web.Mvc;

namespace MvcApplication1.Controllers
{
    public class ProductController : Controller
    {
        //
        // GET: /Product/

        public ActionResult Index()
        {
            return View();
        }

        //
        // GET: /Product/Help

        public ActionResult Help()
```

```
    {
        return View();
    }


    //
    // GET: /Details/1

    public ActionResult Details(int Id)
    {
        return View();
    }



    }
}
```

LISTING 3.2   Controllers\ProductController.vb with Additional Methods (VB)

```
Public Class ProductController
    Inherits System.Web.Mvc.Controller

    '
    ' GET: /Product/

    Function Index() As ActionResult
        Return View()
    End Function


    '
    ' GET: /Product/Help

    Function Help() As ActionResult
        Return View()
    End Function


    '
    ' GET: /Details/1

    Function Details(ByVal id As Integer) As ActionResult
        Return View()
    End Function


End Class
```

Here's what you would type into a browser address bar to invoke the different actions:

- ▶ /Product/Index—Invokes the ProductController Index() action

- ▶ /Product—Invokes the ProductController Index() action

- ▶ /Product/Help—Invokes the ProductController Help() action

- ▶ /Product/Details/34—Invokes the ProductController Details() action with the value 34 for the Id parameter

You invoke a controller action by following a particular pattern that looks like this:

{controller}/{action}/{id}

Notice that when you invoke a controller, you don't include the Controller suffix in the URL. For example, you invoke the Product controller with the URL /Product/Index and not the URL /ProductController/Index.

The default controller action is the Index() action. Therefore, the URL /Product/Index and the URL /Product both invoke the Product controller Index() action.

When you invoke a controller, you can supply an optional Id parameter. For example, the Details() action accepts an Id parameter. The URL /Product/Details/2 invokes the Details() action and passes the value 2 for the Id parameter. The name of the parameter is important. You must name the parameter Id.

NOTE

The default pattern for invoking controller actions is defined by the default route in the Global.asax file. If you want to modify the URL pattern for invoking actions, you can modify this default route. To learn more about creating custom routes, see Chapter 9, "Understanding Routing."

Returning Action Results

A controller action always returns an ActionResult. The ASP.NET MVC framework includes the following types of ActionResults:

- ▶ ViewResult—Represents an ASP.NET MVC view.

- ▶ PartialViewResult—Represents a fragment of an ASP.NET MVC view.

▶ `RedirectResult`—Represents a redirection to another controller action or URL.

▶ `ContentResult`—Represents raw content sent to the browser.

▶ `JsonResult`—Represents a JavaScript Object Notation result (This is useful in Ajax scenarios).

▶ `FileResult`—Represents a file to be downloaded.

▶ `EmptyResult`—Represents no result returned by an action.

▶ `HttpUnauthorizedResult`—Represents an HTTP Unauthorized status code.

▶ `JavaScriptResult`—Represents a JavaScript file.

▶ `RedirectToRouteResult`—Represents a redirection to another controller action or URL using route values.

Typically, you don't directly return an `ActionResult` from a controller action. Instead, you call a controller method that returns an `ActionResult`. For example, if you want to return a `ViewResult`, you call the controller `View()` method.

Here's a list of controller methods that return `ActionResults`:

▶ `View()`—Returns a `ViewResult`

▶ `PartialView()`—Returns a `PartialViewResult`

▶ `RedirectToAction()`—Returns a `RedirectToRouteResult`

▶ `Redirect()`—Returns a `RedirectResult`

▶ `Content()`—Returns a `ContentResult`

▶ `Json()`—Returns a `JsonResult`

▶ `File()`—Returns a `FileResult`

▶ `JavaScript()`—Returns a `JavaScriptResult`

▶ `RedirectToRoute()`—Returns a `RedirectToRouteResult`

In the following sections, we examine several of these `ActionResults` in more detail.

> **NOTE**
>
> We examine partial view results (AKA view user controls or partials) in Chapter 10, "Understanding View Master Pages and View User Controls."

Returning a View Result

The most common `ActionResult` returned by a controller action is a `ViewResult`. A `ViewResult` represents an ASP.NET MVC view. You return a `ViewResult` when you want to return HTML to the browser.

The `Details()` action exposed by the `Customer` controller in Listing 3.3 returns a `ViewResult`.

LISTING 3.3   Controllers\CustomerController.cs (C#)

```csharp
using System.Web.Mvc;

namespace MvcApplication1.Controllers
{
    public class CustomerController : Controller
    {

        public ActionResult Details()
        {
            return View();
        }

    }
}
```

LISTING 3.3   Controllers\CustomerController.vb (VB)

```vb
Public Class CustomerController
    Inherits System.Web.Mvc.Controller

    Function Details() As ActionResult
        Return View()
    End Function

End Class
```

The Details() method calls the View() method to return a ViewResult. There are two ways that you can specify a view when calling the View() method: You can specify a view *implicitly* or *explicitly*.

In Listing 3.3, the name of the view is specified implicitly. The ASP.NET MVC framework determines the name of the view from the name of the action. In this case, the action returns a view at the following location:

\Views\Customer\Details.aspx

The ASP.NET MVC framework follows this pattern to determine the location of a view:

\Views\{controller}\{action}.aspx

If you prefer, you can specify the name of a view explicitly. In Listing 3.4, the View() method includes an explicit view name.

LISTING 3.4   Controllers\CustomerController.cs with Explicit View (C#)

```csharp
using System.Web.Mvc;

namespace MvcApplication1.Controllers
{
    public class CustomerController : Controller
    {

        public ActionResult Details()
        {
            return View("Details");
        }


    }
}
```

LISTING 3.4   Controllers\CustomerController.vb with Explicit View (VB)

```vb
Public Class CustomerController
    Inherits System.Web.Mvc.Controller

    Function Details() As ActionResult
        Return View("Details")
    End Function

End Class
```

The View() method in Listing 3.4 returns the same view. However, it is explicit about the view name. Notice that you don't include the .aspx extension when providing the name of the view.

TIP

If you plan to build unit tests for your ASP.NET MVC application, it is a good idea to be explicit about your view names. Otherwise, you cannot test to see if the view with the right view name has been returned from a controller action.

A view name can contain a relative or absolute path. If you specify a relative path, then the location of the view is calculated relative to its normal location. For example, calling View("Subfolder/Details") from the Details() action would return a view from this location:

\Views\Details\Subfolder\Details.aspx

You also can provide an absolute path to a view. If you call View("~/Details.aspx") from the Details() action, then a view from the following location is returned:

\Details.aspx

Notice that when you provide an absolute path, you provide the .aspx extension.

There are multiple overloads of the View() method that accept different parameters. Here is a list of all the possible parameters that you can pass to the View() method:

- ▶ viewName—The name of the view (or path to the view)
- ▶ masterName—The name of a view master page
- ▶ model—The model class passed to the view

We discuss view master pages in Chapter 10. We discuss passing models to views in Chapter 4, "Understanding Views."

Returning a Redirect Result

Often, you need to redirect from one controller action to a second controller action. You can use the RedirectToAction() method to return a RedirectResult that redirects a user from one controller action to another.

For example, the Widget controller in Listing 3.5 contains a Details() action. If the Details() action is invoked without a value for the id parameter, the user is redirected to the Index() action.

LISTING 3.5   Controllers\WidgetController.cs (C#)

```csharp
using System.Web.Mvc;

namespace MvcApplication1.Controllers
{
    public class WidgetController : Controller
    {
        //
        // GET: /Widget/

        public ActionResult Index()
        {
            return View();
        }


        //
```

```csharp
// POST: /Widget/Create

public ActionResult Details(int? id)
{
    if (!id.HasValue)
        return RedirectToAction("Index");

    return View();
}


    }
}
```

LISTING 3.5   Controllers\WidgetController.cs (VB)

```vb
Public Class WidgetController
    Inherits System.Web.Mvc.Controller

    Function Index() As ActionResult
        Return View()
    End Function


    Function Details(ByVal id As Integer?) As ActionResult
        If Not id.HasValue Then
            Return RedirectToAction("Index")
        End If

        Return View()
    End Function


End Class
```

NOTE

The id parameter in Listing 3.5 is a nullable type. A nullable integer can have any value of an integer or the value null. You create a nullable type by placing a question mark (?) after the type keyword.

There are multiple overloads of the `RedirectToAction()` method. Here's a list of all the possible parameters that you can use with the `RedirectToAction()` method:

- ▶ `actionName`—The name of a controller action
- ▶ `controllerName`—The name of a controller
- ▶ `routeValues`—The route values passed to the action

You can use the `controllerName` parameter to redirect from an action in one controller to another controller. When you specify the `controllerName`, you do not include the Controller suffix. For example, use `Product` and not `ProductController` like this:

(C#)

```
return RedirectToAction("Index", "Product");
```

(VB)

```
Return RedirectToAction("Index", "Product")
```

Providing a value for `routeValues` is particularly important when you need to pass an id to an action. For example, imagine that you want to redirect to the `Details()` action from another action and pass a value for the id parameter. In that case, you can call the `RedirectToAction()` method like this:

(C#)

```
return RedirectToAction("Details", new {id=53});
```

(VB)

```
Return RedirectToAction("Details", New With {.id=53})
```

This call to the `RedirectToAction()` method passes the value 53 as the id parameter to the `Index()` action.

> **NOTE**
>
> The `RedirectToAction()` method returns a 302 Found HTTP status code to the browser to perform the redirect to the new action. One advantage of performing a browser redirect is that it updates the browser address bar with the new URL. The disadvantage is that a browser must do a second request.

Returning a Content Result

The `Say()` action exposed by the `Hello` controller in Listing 3.6 does not return an `ActionResult`. Instead, the action returns a string. If you invoke this action, the string is rendered to your browser (see Figure 3.2).

FIGURE 3.2   Results of invoking Say() action

LISTING 3.6   Controllers\HelloController.cs (C#)

```csharp
using System.Web.Mvc;

namespace MvcApplication1.Controllers
{
    public class HelloController : Controller
    {

        public string Say()
        {
            return "Hello";
        }

    }
}
```

LISTING 3.6   Controllers\HelloController.vb (VB)

```vb
Public Class HelloController
    Inherits System.Web.Mvc.Controller

    Function Say() As String
        Return "Hello!"
    End Function

End Class
```

An action method can also return DateTime values, integer values, or any type of values from the .NET framework.

Behind the scenes, the ASP.NET MVC framework converts any value that is not an ActionResult into an ActionResult. In particular, the ASP.NET MVC framework converts any value that is not an `ActionResult` into a `ContentResult`. The ASP.NET MVC frame-work calls the `ToString()` method on the value and wraps the resulting value in a `ContentResult`.

If you prefer, you can explicitly return a `ContentResult` like this:

(C#)

```
public ActionResult Say()
{
  return Content("Hello!");
}
```

(VB)

```
Function Say() As ActionResult
   Return Content("Hello!")
End Function
```

There are multiple overloads of the `Content()` method. Here is a list of all the possible parameters that you can pass to this method:

- ▶ string—The string to render to the browser
- ▶ contentype—The MIME type of the content (defaults to text/html)
- ▶ contentEncoding—The text encoding of the content (for example, Unicode or ASCII)

Returning a JSON Result

JavaScript Object Notation (JSON) was invented by Douglas Crockford as a lightweight alter-native to XML appropriate for sending data across the Internet in Ajax applications. For example, you can convert a set of database records into a JSON representation and pass the data from the server to the browser.

> **NOTE**
>
> You can learn more about JSON by visiting JSON.org.

You return JSON from an action by calling the `Json()` method. For example, the controller in Listing 3.7 returns a collection of quotations.

LISTING 3.7   Controllers\QuotationController.cs (C#)

```
using System.Collections.Generic;
using System.Web.Mvc;

namespace MvcApplication1.Controllers
{
```

```csharp
public class QuotationController : Controller
{

    public ActionResult Index()
    {
        return View();
    }


    public ActionResult List()
    {
        var quotes = new List<string>
        {
            "Look before you leap",
            "The early bird gets the worm",
            "All hat, no cattle"
        };

        return Json(quotes);
    }

}
}
```

LISTING 3.7   Controllers\QuotationController.vb (VB)

```vbnet
Public Class QuotationController
    Inherits System.Web.Mvc.Controller

    Function Index() As ActionResult
        Return View()
    End Function


    Function List() As ActionResult
        Dim quotes As New List(Of String)()
        quotes.Add("Look before you leap")
        quotes.Add("The early bird gets the worm")
        quotes.Add("All hat, no cattle")

        Return Json(quotes)
    End Function


End Class
```

NOTE

Behind the scenes, the Json() method uses a class in the .NET framework called the JavaScriptSerializer class to serialize an object into a JSON representation. You can control how this class serializes objects by registering custom converters.

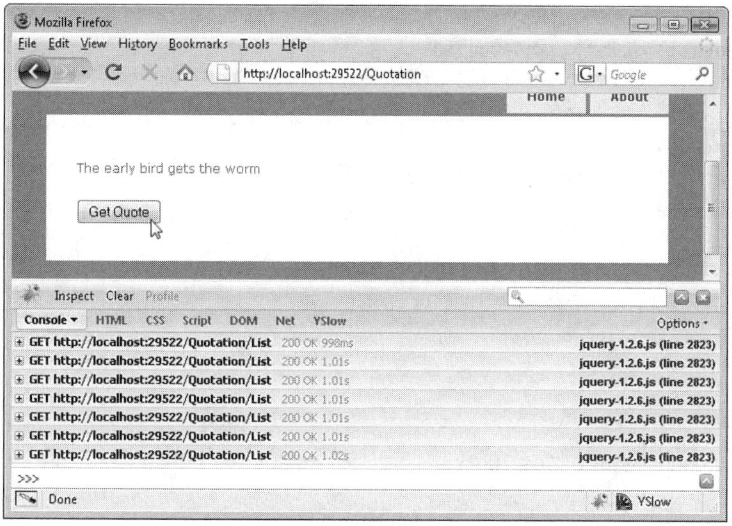

FIGURE 3.3   Using JSON to retrieve quotations

When the List() action is invoked, the action returns the following JSON representation of the collection of quotations:

```
["Look before you leap", "The early bird gets the worm", "All hat, no cattle"]
```

You can invoke the Index() method from a view by performing an Ajax call against the server. The view in Listing 3.8 grabs the collection of quotations and randomly displays one of them.

LISTING 3.8   Views\Quotation\Index.aspx

```
<%@ Page Title="" Language="C#" MasterPageFile="~/Views/Shared/Site.Master"
➥Inherits="System.Web.Mvc.ViewPage" %>


<asp:Content ID="Content2" ContentPlaceHolderID="MainContent" runat="server">
```

```
<script src="../../Scripts/jquery-1.2.6.js" type="text/javascript"></script>

<script type="text/javascript">

    $.ajaxSetup({ cache: false });
    $(getQuote);

    function getQuote() {
        $.getJSON("Quotation/List", showQuote);
    }

    function showQuote(data) {
        var index = Math.floor(Math.random() * 3);
        $("#quote").text(data[index]);
    }

</script>


<p id="quote"></p>

<button onclick="getQuote()">Get Quote</button>


</asp:Content>
```

NOTE

The view in Listing 3.8 uses jQuery to retrieve the JSON result from the server. We discuss jQuery in detail in Chapter 15, "Using jQuery."

The Json() method has several overloads and supports the following parameters:

▶ data—The content to serialize

▶ contentType—The MIME type of the content (defaults to application/json)

▶ contentEncoding—The text encoding of the content (for example, Unicode or ASCII)

Returning a File Result

You can return a file from an action. For example, you can return an image file, a Microsoft Word file, or a Microsoft Excel file.

For example, the controller in Listing 3.9 exposes two actions named `Index()` and `Download()`. The `Index()` action displays a view with a link to the `Download()` action. When you click the link, you are prompted with a dialog to view or save the file (see Figure 3.4).

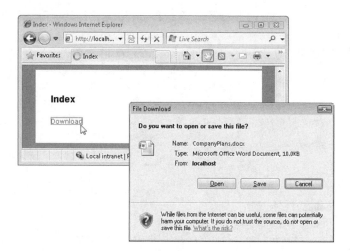

FIGURE 3.4   Downloading a file

LISTING 3.9   Controllers\ContentManagerController.cs (C#)

```csharp
using System.Web.Mvc;

namespace MvcApplication1.Controllers
{
    public class ContentManagerController : Controller
    {

        public ActionResult Index()
        {
            return View();
        }


        public ActionResult Download()
```

```
        {

            return File("~/Content/CompanyPlans.docx",
➥"application/vnd.openxmlformats-officedocument.wordprocessingml.document",
➥"CompanyPlans.docx");
        }


    }
}
```

LISTING 3.9   Controllers\ContentManagerController.vb (VB)

```vb
Public Class ContentManagerController
    Inherits System.Web.Mvc.Controller


    Function Index()
        Return View()
    End Function

    Function Download() As ActionResult
        Return File("~/Content/CompanyPlans.docx",
➥"application/vnd.openxmlformats-officedocument.wordprocessingml.document",
➥"CompanyPlans.docx")
    End Function

End Class
```

The Download() action returns a Microsoft Word document named CompanyPlans.docx. Notice that the File() method requires three parameters: the path to the file, the content type of the file, and the name of the file. The proper MIME type for a Microsoft Word DOCX file is

```
application/vnd.openxmlformats-officedocument.wordprocessingml.document
```

The File() method has multiple overloads and accepts the following parameters:

- ▶ filename—The path to the file to download.

- ▶ contentType—The MIME type of the file to download.

- ▶ fileDownloadName—The name of the file as it appears in the browser dialog.

- ▶ fileContents—Instead of providing the path to the file to download, you can provide the actual file contents as a byte array.

- ▶ fileStream—Instead of providing the path to the file to download, you can provide the actual file contents as a file stream.

NOTE

The File() method uses the HTTP Content-Disposition header to set the file download name.

Controlling How Actions Are Invoked

The default algorithm for how the ASP.NET MVC framework invokes actions is quite simple. If you type /Product/Details, for example, the Details() method of the ProductController class is executed.

However, things can quickly become more complicated. What happens when you have multiple methods with the same name? How do you invoke an action when posting form data but not otherwise? How do you invoke a particular action when an Ajax request is made?

In this section, you learn how to use the AcceptVerbs, ActionName, and ActionMethodSelector attributes to specify when a particular action gets invoked.

Using AcceptVerbs

The AcceptVerbs attribute enables you to prevent an action from being invoked unless a particular HTTP operation is performed. For example, you can use the AcceptVerbs attribute to prevent an action from being invoked unless an HTTP POST operation is performed.

The Employee controller in Listing 3.10 exposes two actions named Create(). The first Create() action is used to display an HTML form for creating a new employee. The second Create() action inserts the new employee into the database.

Both Create() methods are decorated with the AcceptVerbs attribute. The first Create() action can be invoked only by an HTTP GET operation and the second Create() action can be invoked only by an HTTP POST operation.

LISTING 3.10   Controllers\EmployeeController.cs (C#)

```csharp
using System.Web.Mvc;
using MvcApplication1.Models;

namespace MvcApplication1.Controllers
{
    public class EmployeeController : Controller
    {
        private EmployeeRepository _repository = new EmployeeRepository();

        // GET: /Employee/
        public ActionResult Index()
        {
```

```csharp
        return View();
    }

    // GET: /Employee/Create
    [AcceptVerbs(HttpVerbs.Get)]
    public ActionResult Create()
    {
        return View();
    }

    // POST: /Employee/Create
    [AcceptVerbs(HttpVerbs.Post)]
    public ActionResult Create(Employee employeeToCreate)
    {
        try
        {
            _repository.InsertEmployee(employeeToCreate);
            return RedirectToAction("Index");
        }
        catch
        {
            return View();
        }
    }

    // DELETE: /Employee/Delete/1
    [AcceptVerbs(HttpVerbs.Delete)]
    public ActionResult Delete(int id)
    {
        _repository.DeleteEmployee(id);
        return Json(true);
    }

}
}
```

LISTING 3.10   Controllers\EmployeeController.vb (VB)

```vb
Public Class EmployeeController
    Inherits System.Web.Mvc.Controller

    Private _repository As New EmployeeRepository()

    ' GET: /Employee/Create
    Function Index() As ActionResult
```

```vb
        Return View()
    End Function


    ' GET: /Employee/Create
    <AcceptVerbs(HttpVerbs.Get)> _
    Function Create() As ActionResult
        Return View()
    End Function

    ' POST: /Employee/Create
    <AcceptVerbs(HttpVerbs.Post)> _
    Function Create(ByVal employeeToCreate As Employee) As ActionResult
        Try
            _repository.InsertEmployee(employeeToCreate)
            Return RedirectToAction("Index")
        Catch
            Return View()
        End Try
    End Function


    ' DELETE: /Employee/Create
    <AcceptVerbs(HttpVerbs.Delete)> _
    Function Delete(ByVal id As Integer) As ActionResult
        _repository.DeleteEmployee(id)
        Return Json(True)
    End Function



End Class
```

Most people are familiar with HTTP GET and HTTP POST operations. You perform an HTTP GET operation whenever you request a page from a website by typing the address of the page in your web browser. You perform an HTTP POST operation when you submit an HTML form that has a method="post" attribute.

Most people don't realize that the HTTP protocol supports a number of additional types of HTTP operations:

▶ OPTIONS—Returns information about the communication options available

▶ GET—Returns whatever information is identified by the request

▶ HEAD—Performs the same operation as GET without returning the message body

▶ POST—Posts new information or updates existing information

▶ PUT—Posts new information or updates existing information

▶ DELETE—Deletes information

▶ TRACE—Performs a message loop back

▶ CONNECT—Used for SSL tunneling

NOTE

The HTTP operations are defined as part of the HTTP 1.1 standard that you can read about at www.w3.org/Protocols/rfc2616/rfc2616-sec9.html.

You can perform these additional HTTP operations when performing Ajax requests. The controller in Listing 3.10 includes a Delete() action that can be invoked only with an HTTP DELETE operation. The view in Listing 3.11 includes a delete link that uses Ajax to perform an HTTP DELETE operation.

LISTING 3.11   Views\Employee\Delete.aspx (C#)

```
<%@ Page Title="" Language="C#" MasterPageFile="~/Views/Shared/Site.Master"
➡Inherits="System.Web.Mvc.ViewPage" %>


<asp:Content ID="Content2" ContentPlaceHolderID="MainContent" runat="server">

    <script src="../../Scripts/MicrosoftAjax.js" type="text/javascript"></script>
    <script src="../../Scripts/MicrosoftMvcAjax.js"
type="text/javascript"></script>

    <h2>Index</h2>

    <%= Ajax.ActionLink
        (
            "Delete",   // link text
            "Delete",   // action name
            new {id=39}, // route values
            new AjaxOptions {HttpMethod="DELETE", Confirm="Delete Employee?"}
        ) %>

</asp:Content>
```

LISTING 3.11   Views\Employee\Delete.aspx (VB)

```
<%@ Page Title="" Language="VB" MasterPageFile="~/Views/Shared/Site.Master"
➡Inherits="System.Web.Mvc.ViewPage" %>
```

```
<asp:Content ID="Content2" ContentPlaceHolderID="MainContent" runat="server">

    <script src="../../Scripts/MicrosoftAjax.js" type="text/javascript"></script>
    <script src="../../Scripts/MicrosoftMvcAjax.js"
type="text/javascript"></script>

    <h2>Index</h2>

    <%=Ajax.ActionLink( _
        "Delete", _
        "Delete", _
        New With {.id = 39}, _
        New AjaxOptions With {.HttpMethod = "DELETE", .Confirm = "Delete
Employee?"} _
    )%>

    <%=DateTime.Now%>

</asp:Content>
```

In Listing 3.11, the Ajax.ActionLink() helper renders a link that performs an HTTP
DELETE operation. The link deletes the employee with ID 39. You can verify that the link
performs an HTTP DELETE operation in Firebug (see Figure 3.5).

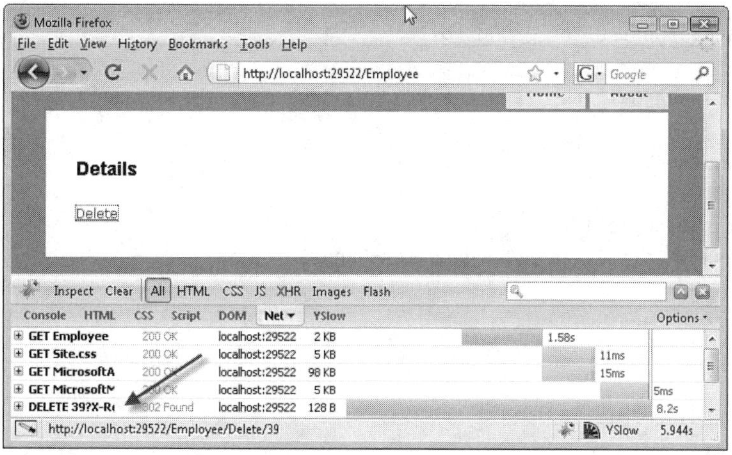

FIGURE 3.5   Performing an HTTP DELETE operation

NOTE

Firebug is an essential tool for debugging Ajax applications. Firebug is a Mozilla Firefox
extension that you can download from http://getFirebug.com.

Using `ActionName`

The `ActionName` attribute enables you to expose an action with a different name than its method name. There are two situations in which the `ActionName` attribute is useful.

First, when a controller has overloaded methods, you can use the `ActionName` attribute to distinguish the two methods. In other words, you can use the `ActionName` attribute to expose two methods with the same name as actions with different names.

For example, imagine that you have created a `Product` controller that has two overloaded methods named `Details()`. The first `Details()` method accepts an `id` parameter, and the second `Details()` method does not. In that case, you can use the `ActionName` attribute to distinguish the two `Details()` methods by exposing the two `Details()` methods with different action names.

Second, using the `ActionName` attribute is useful when a controller has methods with different names and you want to expose these methods as actions with the same name. For example, the controller in Listing 3.12 exposes two actions named `Edit()` that accept the same parameter.

LISTING 3.12   Controllers\MerchandiseController.cs (C#)

```
using System.Web.Mvc;
using MvcApplication1.Models;

namespace MvcApplication1.Controllers
{
    public class MerchandiseController : Controller
    {
        private MerchandiseRepository _repository = new MerchandiseRepository();

        // GET: /Merchandise/Edit
        [ActionName("Edit")]
        [AcceptVerbs(HttpVerbs.Get)]
        public ActionResult Edit_GET(Merchandise merchandiseToEdit)
        {
            return View(merchandiseToEdit);
        }

        // POST: /Merchandise/Edit
        [ActionName("Edit")]
        [AcceptVerbs(HttpVerbs.Post)]
        public ActionResult Edit_POST(Merchandise merchandiseToEdit)
        {
            try
            {
                _repository.Edit(merchandiseToEdit);
```

```
                return RedirectToAction("Edit");
            }
            catch
            {
                return View();
            }
        }
    }
}
```

LISTING 3.12   Controllers\MerchandiseController.vb (VB)

```
Public Class MerchandiseController
    Inherits System.Web.Mvc.Controller

    Private _repository As New MerchandiseRepository()

    ' GET: /Merchandise/Edit
    <ActionName("Edit")> _
    <AcceptVerbs(HttpVerbs.Get)> _
    Function Edit_GET(ByVal merchandiseToEdit As Merchandise) As ActionResult
        Return View(merchandiseToEdit)
    End Function

    ' POST: /Merchandise/Edit
    <ActionName("Edit")> _
    <AcceptVerbs(HttpVerbs.Post)> _
    Function Edit_POST(ByVal merchandiseToEdit As Merchandise) As ActionResult
        Try
            _repository.Edit(merchandiseToEdit)
            Return RedirectToAction("Edit")
        Catch
            Return View()
        End Try
    End Function

End Class
```

You can't have two *methods* with the same name and the same parameters in the same class. However, you can have two *actions* that have the same name and the same parameters.

The two Edit() actions in Listing 3.12 are distinguished by the AcceptVerbs attribute. The first Edit() action can be invoked only by an HTTP GET operation, and the second Edit() action can be invoked only by an HTTP POST operation. The ActionName attribute enables you to expose these two actions with the same name.

Using `ActionMethodSelector`

You can build your own attributes that you can apply to controller actions to control when the controller actions are invoked. You build your own attributes by deriving a new attribute from the abstract `ActionMethodSelectorAttribute` class.

This is an extremely simple class. It has a single method that you must implement named `IsValidForRequest()`. If this method returns false, the action method won't be invoked.

You can use any criteria that you want when implementing the `IsValidForRequest()` method including the time of day, a random number generator, or the current temperature outside. The `AjaxMethod` attribute in Listing 3.13 is a more practical sample of how you can use the `ActionMethod` attribute. This attribute prevents a method from being called in cases in which the request is not an Ajax request.

LISTING 3.13   Selectors\AjaxMethodAttribute.cs (C#)

```csharp
using System.Reflection;
using System.Web.Mvc;

namespace MvcApplication1.Selectors
{
    public class AjaxMethod : ActionMethodSelectorAttribute
    {
        public override bool IsValidForRequest(ControllerContext controllerContext,
➥MethodInfo methodInfo)
        {
            return controllerContext.HttpContext.Request.IsAjaxRequest();
        }
    }
}
```

LISTING 3.13   Selectors\AjaxMethodAttribute.vb (VB)

```vbnet
Imports System.Reflection


Public Class AjaxMethodAttribute
    Inherits ActionMethodSelectorAttribute

    Public Overrides Function IsValidForRequest(ByVal controllerContext
➥As ControllerContext, ByVal methodInfo As MethodInfo) As Boolean
        Return controllerContext.HttpContext.Request.IsAjaxRequest
    End Function

End Class
```

The selector in Listing 3.13 simply returns the value of the `IsAjaxRequest()` method as its selection criterion.

The controller in Listing 3.14 illustrates how you can use the `AjaxMethod` attribute.

LISTING 3.14   Controllers\NewsController.cs (C#)

```csharp
using System;
using System.Collections.Generic;
using System.Web.Mvc;
using MvcApplication1.Selectors;

namespace MvcApplication1.Controllers
{
    public class NewsController : Controller
    {
        private readonly List<string> _news = new List<string>();
        private Random _rnd = new Random();

        public NewsController()
        {
            _news.Add("Moon explodes!");
            _news.Add("Stock market up 200 percent!");
            _news.Add("Talking robot created!");
        }

        public ActionResult Index()
        {
            var selectedIndex = _rnd.Next(_news.Count);
            ViewData.Model = _news[selectedIndex];
            return View();
        }


        [AjaxMethod]
        [ActionName("Index")]
        public string Index_AJAX()
        {
            var selectedIndex = _rnd.Next(_news.Count);
            return _news[selectedIndex];
        }


    }
}
```

LISTING 3.14   Controllers\NewsController.vb (VB)

```vb
Public Class NewsController
    Inherits System.Web.Mvc.Controller

    Private ReadOnly _news As New List(Of String)
    Private _rnd As New Random()

    Sub New()
        _news.Add("Moon explodes!")
        _news.Add("Stock market up 200 percent!")
        _news.Add("Talking robot created!")
    End Sub

    Function Index() As ActionResult
        Dim selectedIndex = _rnd.Next(_news.Count)
        ViewData.Model = _news(selectedIndex)
        Return View()
    End Function


    <AjaxMethod()> _
    <ActionName("Index")> _
    Function Index_AJAX() As String
        Dim selectedIndex = _rnd.Next(_news.Count)
        Return _news(selectedIndex)
    End Function


End Class
```

The controller in Listing 3.14 exposes two actions named Index(). The first Index() action is intended to be invoked by a normal browser request. The second action is intended to be invoked by an Ajax request.

The AjaxMethod attribute is applied to the second Index() action. If this action were not decorated with the AjaxMethod attribute, you would get an Ambiguous Match exception because the ASP.NET MVC framework could not decide which of the two actions to execute (see Figure 3.6).

The view in Listing 3.15 uses the Ajax.ActionLink() helper method to render a Get News link for displaying the news. If you use an uplevel browser—a browser that supports basic JavaScript—then clicking the link performs an Ajax request against the server. The Index() method decorated with the AjaxMethod attribute is invoked, and the page is updated without performing a postback.

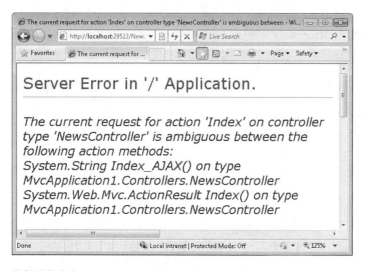

FIGURE 3.6   An Ambiguous Match exception

If, on the other hand, you use a downlevel browser—a browser that does not support basic JavaScript—then clicking the Get News link performs a normal postback. The page still gets updated with a news item, but the user must undergo the awful experience of a postback (see Figure 3.7).

FIGURE 3.7   Displaying the news

LISTING 3.15   Views\News\Index.aspx (C#)

```
<%@ Page Title="" Language="C#" MasterPageFile="~/Views/Shared/Site.Master"
➥Inherits="System.Web.Mvc.ViewPage" %>


<asp:Content ID="Content2" ContentPlaceHolderID="MainContent" runat="server">
```

```
    <script src="../../Scripts/MicrosoftAjax.js" type="text/javascript"></script>
    <script src="../../Scripts/MicrosoftMvcAjax.js"
type="text/javascript"></script>

    <%=Ajax.ActionLink("Get News", "Index", new AjaxOptions {UpdateTargetId =
➥"news"})%>

    <span id="news"></span>

</asp:Content>
```

LISTING 3.15   Views\News\Index.aspx (VB)

```
<%@ Page Title="" Language="VB" MasterPageFile="~/Views/Shared/Site.Master"
➥Inherits="System.Web.Mvc.ViewPage" %>

<asp:Content ID="Content2" ContentPlaceHolderID="MainContent" runat="server">

    <script src="../../Scripts/MicrosoftAjax.js" type="text/javascript"></script>
    <script src="../../Scripts/MicrosoftMvcAjax.js"
➥type="text/javascript"></script>

    <%=Ajax.ActionLink("Get News", "Index", New AjaxOptions With {.UpdateTargetId
➥= "news"})%>

    <span id="news"></span>

</asp:Content>
```

Handling Unknown Actions

A controller has a special method named HandleUnknownAction(). This method is called automatically when a controller cannot find an action that matches a browser request. For example, if you request the URL /Product/DoSomethingCrazy and the Product controller does not have an action named DoSomethingCrazy(), then the Product controller HandleUnknownAction() method is invoked.

By default, this method throws a 404 Resource Not Found HTTP exception. However, you can override this method and do anything you want. For example, the controller in Listing 3.16 displays a custom error message.

LISTING 3.16   Controllers\CatalogController.cs (C#)

```csharp
using System.Web.Mvc;

namespace MvcApplication1.Controllers
{
    public class CatalogController : Controller
    {

        public ActionResult Create()
        {
            return View();
        }

        public ActionResult Delete(int id)
        {
            return View();
        }


        protected override void HandleUnknownAction(string actionName)
        {
            ViewData["actionName"] = actionName;
            View("Unknown").ExecuteResult(this.ControllerContext);
        }


    }
}
```

LISTING 3.16   Controllers\CatalogController.vb (VB)

```vbnet
Public Class CatalogController
    Inherits System.Web.Mvc.Controller


    Function Create() As ActionResult
        Return View()
    End Function

    Function Delete() As ActionResult
        Return View()
```

```
    End Function

    Protected Overrides Sub HandleUnknownAction(ByVal actionName As String)
        ViewData("actionName") = actionName
        View("Unknown").ExecuteResult(Me.ControllerContext)
    End Sub


End Class
```

If you request the URL /Catalog/Create or /Catalog/Delete, then the Catalog controller returns the Create or Delete view. If you request a URL that contains an unknown action such as /Catalog/Wow or /Catalog/Eeeks, then the HandleUnknownAction() method executes.

In Listing 3.16, the HandleUnknownAction() method adds the name of the action to view data and then renders a view named Unknown (see Figure 3.8).

FIGURE 3.8   Displaying the Unknown view

Testing Controllers and Actions

The ASP.NET MVC team worked hard to make sure that controller actions were extremely easy to test. If you want to test a controller action, you simply need to instantiate the controller and call the action method.

For example, the controller in Listing 3.17 exposes two actions named Index() and Details(). If you invoke the Details() action without passing a value for the id parameter, you should be redirected to the Index() action.

LISTING 3.17   Controllers\PersonController.cs (C#)

```
using System.Web.Mvc;


namespace MvcApplication1.Controllers
{
```

```
public class PersonController : Controller
{
    public ActionResult Index()
    {
        return View("Index");
    }

    public ActionResult Details(int? id)
    {
        if (!id.HasValue)
            return RedirectToAction("Index");
        return View("Details");
    }

}
}
```

LISTING 3.17   Controllers\PersonController.vb (VB)

```
Public Class PersonController
    Inherits System.Web.Mvc.Controller


    Function Index() As ActionResult
        Return View("Index")
    End Function

    Function Details(ByVal id As Integer?) As ActionResult
        If Not id.HasValue Then
            Return RedirectToAction("Index")
        End If

        Return View("Details")
    End Function

End Class
```

WARNING

When returning a view, you must be explicit about the view name, or you can't verify the name of the view in a unit test. For example, in Listing 3.17, the `Index()` method returns `View("Index")` and not `View()`.

The unit tests in Listing 3.18 illustrate how you can test the actions exposed by the Person controller. The first unit test, named DetailsWithId(), verifies that calling the Details() method with a value for the id parameter returns the Details view.

The second unit test, named DetailsWithoutId(), verifies that calling the Details() method with no value for the id parameter causes a RedirectToRouteResult to be returned that redirects to the Index view.

LISTING 3.18   Controllers\PersonControllerTest.cs (C#)

```csharp
using System.Web.Mvc;
using Microsoft.VisualStudio.TestTools.UnitTesting;
using MvcApplication1.Controllers;

namespace MvcApplication1.Tests.Controllers
{
    [TestClass]
    public class PersonControllerTest
    {
        [TestMethod]
        public void DetailsWithId()
        {
            // Arrange
            var controller = new PersonController();

            // Act
            var result = (ViewResult)controller.Details(33);

            // Assert
            Assert.AreEqual("Details", result.ViewName);
        }


        [TestMethod]
        public void DetailsWithoutId()
        {
            // Arrange
            var controller = new PersonController();

            // Act
            var result = (RedirectToRouteResult)controller.Details(null);

            // Assert
            Assert.AreEqual("Index", result.RouteValues["action"]);
        }
```

```
        }
}
```

LISTING 3.18   Controllers\PersonControllerTest.vb (VB)

```vb
Imports Microsoft.VisualStudio.TestTools.UnitTesting
Imports System.Web.Mvc

<TestClass()> Public Class PersonControllerTest

    <TestMethod()> _
    Public Sub DetailsWithId()
        ' Arrange
        Dim controller As New PersonController()

        ' Act
        Dim result As ViewResult = controller.Details(33)

        ' Assert
        Assert.AreEqual("Details", result.ViewName)
    End Sub

    <TestMethod()> _
    Public Sub DetailsWithoutId()
        ' Arrange
        Dim controller As New PersonController()

        ' Act
        Dim result As RedirectToRouteResult = controller.Details(Nothing)

        ' Assert
        Assert.AreEqual("Index", result.RouteValues("action"))
    End Sub

End Class
```

NOTE

To learn more about creating and running unit tests, see Appendix B, "Using a Unit Testing Framework," in this book.

Summary

This chapter was devoted to the topic of ASP.NET MVC controllers. The goal of this chapter was to provide an in-depth explanation of how you can create controllers and controller actions.

In the first part of this chapter, you were provided with an overview of the different types of `ActionResults` that can be returned from a controller action. You learned how to returns views, redirect users to other actions, return JSON, and return downloadable files.

Next, we examined the different attributes that you can apply to a controller action to control when the controller action is invoked. You learned how to use the `AcceptVerbs` and `ActionName` attributes. You also learned how to create a custom `ActionSelect` attribute that enables you to execute an action only within the context of an Ajax request.

Finally, you learned how to build unit tests for your controllers. You learned how to test whether a controller returns different `ActionResults` such as a `ViewResult` or a `RedirectToRouteResult`.

CHAPTER 4

Understanding Views

The set of views in an ASP.NET MVC application is the public face of the application. ASP.NET MVC views are responsible for rendering the HTML pages that people see when they visit your website.

In this chapter, you learn how to create and work with views. You learn how to pass information from a controller to a view. You also learn how to create both typed and untyped views. Finally, you learn strategies for testing your views.

Creating a View

The easiest way to create a new view is to create the view from an existing controller action. You can right-click any controller action within the Visual Studio Code Editor window and select the menu option Add View to create a new view automatically (see Figure 4.1).

When you select the Add View menu option, the Add View dialog opens (see Figure 4.2). This dialog enables you to set various view options. For example, you can specify whether a view uses a view master page.

NOTE

We discuss view master pages in detail in Chapter 10, "Understanding View Master Pages and View User Controls." A view master page provides you with a way to create a common page layout for all of the content pages in your application.

For example, if you open a controller named `Customer` and right-click the `Index()` action to add a view, and you leave the default options selected in the Add View dialog, you'll get the view in Listing 4.1.

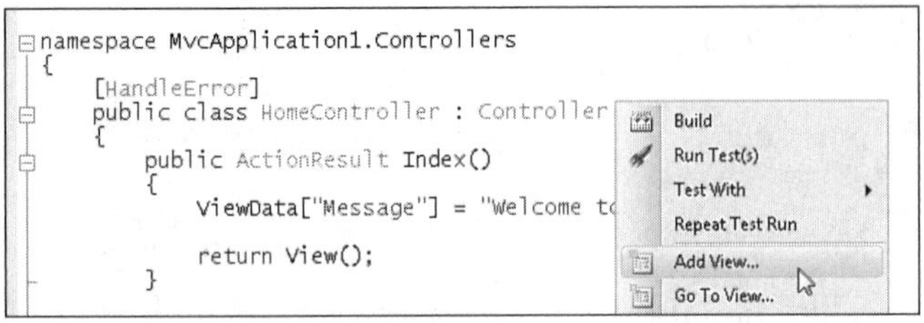

FIGURE 4.1   Adding a new view from a controller action

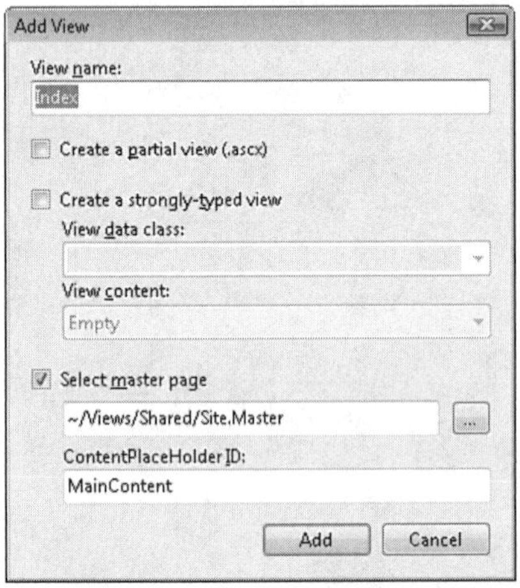

FIGURE 4.2   Using the Add View dialog

LISTING 4.1   Views\Customer\Index.aspx

```
<%@ Page Title="" Language="C#" MasterPageFile="~/Views/Shared/Site.Master"
➥Inherits="System.Web.Mvc.ViewPage" %>


<asp:Content ID="Content1" ContentPlaceHolderID="TitleContent" runat="server">
        Index
</asp:Content>


<asp:Content ID="Content2" ContentPlaceHolderID="MainContent" runat="server">
```

```
        <h2>Index</h2>

</asp:Content>
```

The file in Listing 4.1 looks *almost* like a standard HTML document. This view contains two <asp:Content> tags. Any content that you place within the first <asp:Content> tag appears in the <title> tag of the resulting HTML document. Any content that you place within the second <asp:Content> tag appears in the <body> tag of the resulting HTML document.

For example, the modified Index view in Listing 4.2 has been modified to display the current time.

NOTE

Notice that the first <asp:Content> tag has been removed from the view in Listing 4.2. If you don't need to modify the contents of the <title> tag, you don't need the first <asp:Content> tag.

LISTING 4.2   Views\Product\Index.aspx with the Time

```
<%@ Page Title="" Language="C#" MasterPageFile="~/Views/Shared/Site.Master"
➥Inherits="System.Web.Mvc.ViewPage" %>


<asp:Content ID="Content2" ContentPlaceHolderID="MainContent" runat="server">

    <h1>Time</h1>

    <p>
    At the tone, the time will be
    <%= DateTime.Now.ToString("T") %>.
    </p>

</asp:Content>
```

The view in Listing 4.2 contains familiar HTML tags such as the <h1> and <p> tags. You can put anything that you would put in a normal HTML page within a view including images, iframes, Java applets, Flash, and Silverlight.

The view also contains a script that displays the time. The expression DateTime.Now.ToString("T") returns the current time (see Figure 4.3).

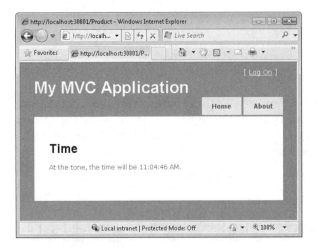

FIGURE 4.3   Displaying the current time

You embed a script in a view by using the <% %> script delimiters. For example, if for some bizarre reason you want to display the string Hello World! 999 times in a page, you could embed the following script in a page (see Figure 4.4):

(C#)

```
<%
    for (var i = 1; i < 999; i++)
        Response.Write("Hello World!");
%>
```

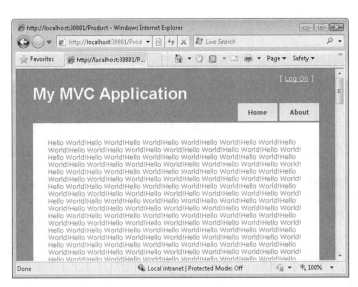

FIGURE 4.4   Displaying Hello World! 999 times

(VB)

```
<%
    For i = 1 to 999
        Response.Write("Hello World!")
    Next
%>
```

The <%= %> script delimiters are shorthand for <% Response.Write %>. You can use the <%= %> script delimiters to write the value of an expression to the browser. The following two scripts do exactly the same thing:

(C#)

```
<%= DateTime.Now.ToString("T") %>
<% Response.Write(DateTime.Now.ToString("T")); %>
```

(VB)

```
<%= DateTime.Now.ToString("T") %>
<% Response.Write(DateTime.Now.ToString("T")) %>
```

TIP

You can create views that contain Visual Basic scripts in a C# ASP.NET MVC application, and you can create views that contain C# scripts in a Visual Basic ASP.NET MVC application. However, you cannot mix both C# and Visual Basic scripts within the same view.

Using View Data

You pass information between a controller and a view by taking advantage of something called *view data*. You can use view data to represent any type of information including strings, objects, and database records.

For example, imagine that you want to display a set of database records in a view. In that case, you would use view data to pass the set of records from a controller action to a view.

NOTE

I like to think of view data as a UPS truck delivering a package from a controller to a view.

You add an item to view data within a controller by adding the item to the view data dictionary exposed by the controller's ViewData property. For example, you could add the following code to a controller action to add a new item to view data named message:

(C#)

```
ViewData["message"] = "Hello World!";
```

(VB)

```
ViewData("message") = "Hello World!"
```

View data works like a dictionary. You can add any key and value pair that you want to the view data dictionary. The key must be a string, but the value can be any type of data whatsoever.

After you add one or more items to view data, you can display these items in a view by accessing the view data dictionary exposed by the view's ViewData property. For example, the view in Listing 4.3 displays the value of the message item from view data.

LISTING 4.3   Views\Person\Index.aspx (C#)

```
<%@ Page Title="" Language="C#" MasterPageFile="~/Views/Shared/Site.Master"
➥Inherits="System.Web.Mvc.ViewPage" %>


<asp:Content ID="Content2" ContentPlaceHolderID="MainContent" runat="server">

    <%= ViewData["message"] %>


</asp:Content>
```

LISTING 4.3   Views\Person\Index.aspx (VB)

```
<%@ Page Title="" Language="VB" MasterPageFile="~/Views/Shared/Site.Master"
➥Inherits="System.Web.Mvc.ViewPage" %>


<asp:Content ID="Content2" ContentPlaceHolderID="MainContent" runat="server">

    <%= ViewData("message") %>


</asp:Content>
```

Typed and Untyped Views

In the previous section, you learned how to add items to the view data dictionary. One problem with the view data dictionary is that it represents everything as untyped objects. This means that you must cast items to a particular data type before you can use the items in a view.

Consider, for example, the controller action in Listing 4.4. This action adds a set of database records representing products to view data.

LISTING 4.4   Controllers\HomeController.cs (C#)

```csharp
public ActionResult Index()
{
    ViewData["products"] = _dataModel.ProductSet.ToList();
    return View();
}
```

LISTING 4.4   Controllers\HomeController.cs (VB)

```vb
Public Function Index() As ActionResult
    ViewData("products") = _dataModel.ProductSet.ToList()
    Return View()
End Function
```

The view in Listing 4.5 illustrates how you can display the records from the database table in an HTML table.

LISTING 4.5   Views\Home\Index.aspx (C#)

```aspx
<%@ Page Title="" Language="C#" MasterPageFile="~/Views/Shared/Site.Master"
➥Inherits="System.Web.Mvc.ViewPage" %>
<%@ Import Namespace="ToyStore.Models" %>

<asp:Content ID="Content2" ContentPlaceHolderID="MainContent" runat="server">


    <table>

    <% foreach (var item in (IEnumerable<Product>)ViewData["products"]) { %>

        <tr>
            <td>
                <%= Html.Encode(item.Id) %>
            </td>
            <td>
                <%= Html.Encode(item.Name) %>
            </td>
            <td>
                <%= Html.Encode(item.Description) %>
            </td>
```

```
            <td>
                <%= Html.Encode(item.Price) %>
            </td>
        </tr>

    <% } %>

    </table>

</asp:Content>
```

LISTING 4.5   Views\Home\Index.aspx (VB)

```
<%@ Page Title="" Language="VB" MasterPageFile="~/Views/Shared/Site.Master"
➥Inherits="System.Web.Mvc.ViewPage" %>
<%@ Import Namespace="ToyStore" %>
<asp:Content ID="Content2" ContentPlaceHolderID="MainContent" runat="server">

    <table>

    <% For Each item In CType(ViewData("products"), IEnumerable(Of Product))%>


        <tr>
            <td>
                <%=Html.Encode(item)%>
            </td>
            <td>
                <%=Html.Encode(item.Name)%>
            </td>
            <td>
                <%=Html.Encode(item.Description)%>
            </td>
            <td>
                <%=Html.Encode(item.Price)%>
            </td>
        </tr>

    <% Next%>

    </table>

</asp:Content>
```

In Listing 4.5, notice that the `products` item from view data is cast to an `IEnumerable` of `Product`. An `IEnumerable` is something that you can enumerate over—something you can loop through. If you write your view with C#, then you must cast the products item to an `IEnumerable` or you get an error (see Figure 4.5). Regardless of whether you use C# or VB.NET, you won't get Intellisense for `Product` properties unless you cast.

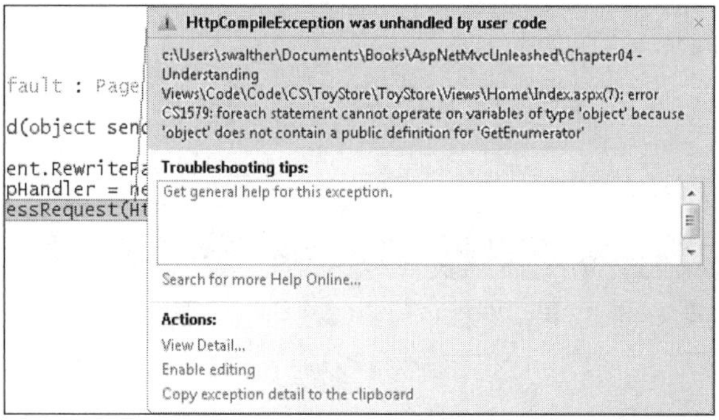

FIGURE 4.5   Failing to cast to `IEnumerable`

> **NOTE**
>
> If you have Option Strict enabled, Visual Basic, like C#, generates an error when you don't cast the product item to an `IEnumerable`.

If you don't want to clutter your views by casting the view data, you can create a strongly typed view.

The view data dictionary exposes a property named `Model`. Within a controller you can assign anything you want to the view data model. For example, the controller action in Listing 4.6 assigns the Product database records to the `Model` property.

> **NOTE**
>
> The `ViewDataDictionary` class derives from the standard generic `Dictionary` class (more precisely, `IDictionary`) and adds additional properties. So, you can use all of the standard generic `Dictionary` methods with the `ViewDataDictionary` class.

LISTING 4.6   Controllers\HomeController.cs Using Model (C#)

```
public ActionResult Index()
{
    ViewData.Model = _dataModel.ProductSet.ToList();
```

```
    return View();
}
```

LISTING 4.6   Controllers\HomeController.vb Using Model (VB)

```
Function Index() As ActionResult
    ViewData.Model = _dataModel.ProductSet.ToList()
    Return View()
End Function
```

> **NOTE**
>
> The following code does the exact same thing as the code in Listing 4.6:
>
> (C#)
>
> ```
> public ActionResult Index()
> {
>     return View(_dataModel.ProductSet.ToList());
> }
> ```
>
> (VB)
>
> ```
> Function Index() As ActionResult
>     Return View(_dataModel.ProductSet.ToList())
> End Function
> ```

The advantage of assigning a value to the ViewData.Model property is that you can cast the Model property automatically in a view. In a view, you can specify the type of object that the Model represents with the <%@ Page %> directive Inherits attribute.

For example, the strongly typed view in Listing 4.7 renders the exact same page as the previous untyped view.

LISTING 4.7   Views\Home\Index.aspx with Model (C#)

```
<%@ Page Title="" Language="C#" MasterPageFile="~/Views/Shared/Site.Master"
➥Inherits="System.Web.Mvc.ViewPage<IEnumerable<ToyStore.Models.Product>>" %>
<%@ Import Namespace="ToyStore.Models" %>

<asp:Content ID="Content2" ContentPlaceHolderID="MainContent" runat="server">

    <table>

        <% foreach (var item in ViewData.Model) { %>
```

```
            <tr>
                <td>
                    <%= Html.Encode(item.Id) %>
                </td>
                <td>
                    <%= Html.Encode(item.Name) %>
                </td>
                <td>
                    <%= Html.Encode(item.Description) %>
                </td>
                <td>
                    <%= Html.Encode(item.Price) %>
                </td>
            </tr>

    <% } %>

    </table>

</asp:Content>
```

LISTING 4.7   Views\Home\Index.aspx with Model (VB)

```
<%@ Page Title="" Language="VB" MasterPageFile="~/Views/Shared/Site.Master"
➥Inherits="System.Web.Mvc.ViewPage(Of IEnumerable(Of ToyStore.Product))" %>
<%@ Import Namespace="ToyStore" %>
<asp:Content ID="Content2" ContentPlaceHolderID="MainContent" runat="server">

    <table>

    <% For Each item In ViewData.Model %>

        <tr>
            <td>
                <%=Html.Encode(item)%>
            </td>
            <td>
                <%=Html.Encode(item.Name)%>
            </td>
            <td>
                <%=Html.Encode(item.Description)%>
            </td>
            <td>
                <%=Html.Encode(item.Price)%>
            </td>
```

```
    </tr>

  <% Next%>

  </table>

</asp:Content>
```

Notice the `Inherits` attribute in Listing 4.7. The view inherits from the following class:

(C#)

```
System.Web.Mvc.ViewPage<IEnumerable<ToyStore.Models.Product>>
```

(VB)

```
System.Web.Mvc.ViewPage(Of IEnumerable(Of ToyStore.Product))
```

This `Inherits` attribute casts the `ViewData.Model` property to an `IEnumerable` of `Product`. For this reason, in the body of the view, you do not need to cast the `ViewData.Model` property before looping through its items.

The `ViewPage` class is the base class for all ASP.NET MVC views. There is both a generic and nongeneric version of this class. When you use the generic `ViewPage` class, you must supply a generic type parameter that represents the type of the model class.

Creating Strongly Typed Views

Providing the proper value for the `Inherits` attribute for a typed view can be tricky. Because you don't get any Intellisense for the `Inherits` attribute, you can easily make a mistake, and your view generates an error.

Instead of creating a strongly typed view by hand, you can take advantage of the Visual Studio Add View dialog to create a strongly typed view automatically (see Figure 4.6). You open this dialog by right-clicking a controller action and selecting the menu option Add View. Alternatively, you can right-click a folder located in the Views folder and select the menu option Add, View.

The Add View dialog includes a check box labeled Create a Strongly Typed View. If you check this check box, you can specify the view data class and the view content.

> **WARNING**
>
> The View Data Class drop-down list will be empty until you successfully build your application. It is a good idea to select the menu option Build, Build Solution before opening the Add View dialog.

The View Data Class drop-down list enables you to pick a class from your project. The `Inherits` directive uses this class. For example, you can pick the `Product` class.

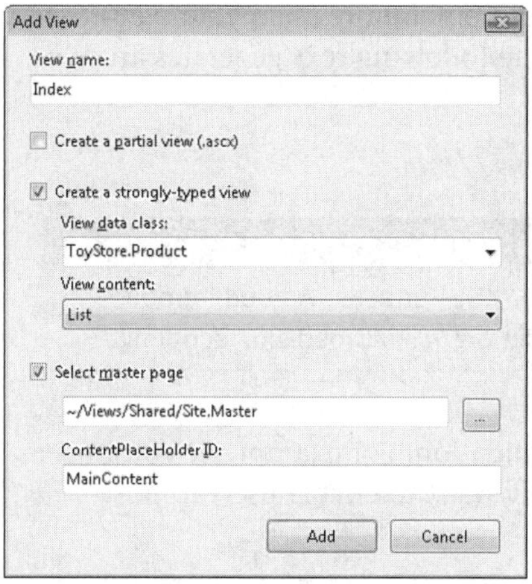

FIGURE 4.6   Creating a strongly typed view

The View Content drop-down list enables you to pick the type of view that you want to create. Your options are Create, Details, Edit, Empty, and List. If you pick List, your view data model is cast to an IEnumerable of Products. Otherwise, if you pick any of the other options, your view data model is cast to a Product.

Preventing JavaScript Injection Attacks

When you submit form data using a view, the ASP.NET MVC framework validates the form data automatically. If the framework identifies potentially malicious markup, the framework throws an exception (see Figure 4.7).

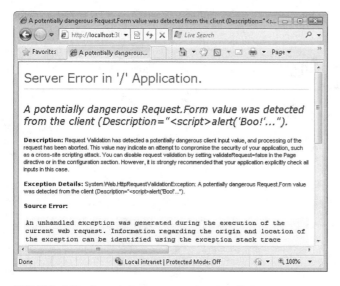

FIGURE 4.7   Preventing an attacking JavaScript

What counts as malicious markup? Anything that could potentially open your website to a JavaScript injection attack. For example, submitting the following text generates an error:

```
<script>alert('Boo!')</script>
```

> **NOTE**
>
> JavaScript injection attacks include cross-site scripting (XSS) attacks. A good introduction to XSS attacks can be found at http://en.wikipedia.org/wiki/Cross-site_scripting.

In some situations, you don't want to perform this validation. For example, if you host a discussion forum on building websites, you most likely want to enable users to post messages that contain HTML tags.

You disable request validation with the [ValidateInput] attribute. You apply this attribute to the controller action that accepts the HTML form input. For example, the Create() action in Listing 4.8 has request validation disabled.

LISTING 4.8   Controllers\HomeController.cs (C#)

```csharp
//
// POST: /Home/Create
[ValidateInput(false)]
[AcceptVerbs(HttpVerbs.Post)]
public ActionResult Create([Bind(Exclude="Id")]Product productToCreate)
{
    if (!ModelState.IsValid)
        return View();

    try
    {
        _dataModel.AddToProductSet(productToCreate);
        _dataModel.SaveChanges();

        return RedirectToAction("Index");
    }
    catch
    {
        return View();
    }
}
```

LISTING 4.8   Controllers\HomeController.vb (VB)

```
'
' POST: /Home/Create
<ValidateInput(false)> _
<AcceptVerbs(HttpVerbs.Post)> _
Function Create(<Bind(Exclude:="Id")> ByVal productToCreate As Product) As
➥ActionResult

    If Not ModelState.IsValid Then
        Return View()
    End If

    Try
        _dataModel.AddToProductSet(productToCreate)
        _dataModel.SaveChanges()

        Return RedirectToAction("Index")
    Catch
        Return View()
    End Try
End Function
```

> **NOTE**
>
> Unlike ASP.NET Web Forms, you cannot disable request validation with the `<%@ Page ValidateRequest="false" %>` directive, and you cannot disable request validation in the web configuration (web.config) file. In an ASP.NET MVC application, the only way to disable request validation is with the `ValidateInput` attribute.

If you disable request validation, ensure that you never display user-submitted content without first HTML encoding the content. HTML encoding text converts potentially dangerous characters such as < and > into safe entities such as < and >. Use the `Html.Encode()` helper to HTML encode all user-submitted content in your views.

Using Alternative View Engines

The default view engine for the ASP.NET MVC framework is the Web Forms view engine. The Web Forms view engine uses ASP.NET pages as views.

The ASP.NET MVC framework was designed to support alternative view engines, and there are already several open source alternatives to the Web Forms view engine. Here's a list of some of the more interesting and popular ones:

▶ **NHaml (pronounced enamel)**—NHaml is an implementation of the popular RAILS Haml view engine for the ASP.NET MVC framework. Distributed under the open source MIT license.

http://code.google.com/p/nhaml

▶ **Spark**—The idea behind the Spark view engine is to allow "the HTML to dominate the flow and the code to fit seamlessly."

http://dev.dejardin.org

▶ **Brail**—A port of the Brail view engine from MonoRail to the ASP.NET MVC framework. The Brail view engine is part of the MVCContrib project.

www.codeplex.com/MVCContrib

▶ **nVelocity**—The nVelocity view engine is a port of the Java Apache Software Foundation Velocity project to the .NET framework. The nVelocity view engine is part of the MVCContrib project.

http://www.codeplex.com/MVCContrib

The different view engines enable you to write your views in radically different ways. For example, Listing 4.9 contains a sample of a view written with the NHaml view engine.

LISTING 4.9   Views\Home\Index.haml

```
!!!
%html{xmlns="http://www.w3.org/1999/xhtml"}
  %head
    %title My Index View
  %body
  %h1 Product List
  %ul
    - foreach (var p in ViewData.Model)
      %li =m.Name
```

The NHaml view in Listing 4.9 loops through all the products represented by the ViewData.Model property and renders the value of the Product Name property. Just like the Web Forms view engine, the NHaml view engine renders HTML. However, notice the terseness of the syntax. You can render a valid and complete HTML page that displays a set of database records with a minimum of effort.

You can use multiple view engines in the same ASP.NET MVC application by registering multiple engines in the Global.asax file. Each view engine can handle a file with a different extension. For example, all .aspx files can be rendered by the Web Forms view engine, whereas all .haml files can be rendered by the NHaml view engine. We look at a concrete example of registering alternative view engines in the next section.

Creating a Custom View Engine

Creating a simple custom view engine for the ASP.NET MVC framework is not difficult. When you create a custom view engine, you get to decide how you want to write your views.

The easiest approach to create a custom view engine is to derive a new view engine from the abstract `VirtualPathProviderViewEngine` class. This is the base class of the `WebFormsViewEngine` (the default view engine). The `VirtualPathProviderViewEngine` class takes care of all the low-level mechanics of finding and caching views.

The view engine in Listing 4.10 is the simplest view engine that I could imagine. (That's why I call it the Simple View Engine.) The Simple View Engine derives from the `VirtualPathProviderViewEngine` class and returns simple views.

LISTING 4.10   MyViewEngines\SimpleViewEngine.cs (C#)

```csharp
using System.Web.Mvc;

namespace MvcApplication1.MyViewEngines
{
    public class SimpleViewEngine : VirtualPathProviderViewEngine
    {
        public SimpleViewEngine()
        {
            this.ViewLocationFormats = new string[] { "~/Views/{1}/{0}.simple",
"~/Views/Shared/{0}.simple"};
            this.PartialViewLocationFormats = new string[] {
"~/Views/{1}/{0}.simple", "~/Views/Shared/{0}.simple" };
        }

        protected override IView CreateView(ControllerContext controllerContext,
string viewPath, string masterPath)
        {
            var physicalPath = controllerContext.HttpContext.Server.
MapPath(viewPath);
            return new SimpleView(physicalPath);
        }

        protected override IView CreatePartialView(ControllerContext
controllerContext, string partialPath)
        {
            var physicalPath = controllerContext.HttpContext.Server.MapPath
(partialPath);
            return new SimpleView(physicalPath);
        }
    }
}
```

LISTING 4.10   MyViewEngines\SimpleViewEngine.vb (VB)

```vb
Public Class SimpleViewEngine
    Inherits VirtualPathProviderViewEngine

    Public Sub New()
        Me.ViewLocationFormats = New String() { "~/Views/{1}/{0}.simple",
➥"~/Views/Shared/{0}.simple"}
        Me.PartialViewLocationFormats = New String() { "~/Views/{1}/{0}.simple",
➥"~/Views/Shared/{0}.simple" }
    End Sub

    Protected Overrides Function CreateView(ByVal controllerContext As
➥ControllerContext, ByVal viewPath As String, ByVal masterPath As String)
➥As IView
        Dim physicalPath = controllerContext.HttpContext.Server.MapPath(viewPath)
        Return New SimpleView(physicalPath)
    End Function

    Protected Overrides Function CreatePartialView(ByVal controllerContext As
➥ControllerContext, ByVal partialPath As String) As IView
        Dim physicalPath = controllerContext.HttpContext.Server.MapPath
➥(partialPath)
        Return New SimpleView(physicalPath)
    End Function
End Class
```

When you implement the `VirtualPathProviderViewEngine` class, you are required to implement two methods named `CreateView()` and `CreatePartialView()`. In Listing 4.10, these methods simply return an instance of the `SimpleView` class.

Notice that two properties of the base `VirtualPathProviderViewEngine` class are set in the constructor. These properties indicate where the view engine should search to find a matching view or partial view. The parameter {1} represents the name of the controller and the parameter (0) represents the name of the action. Therefore, if you request the URL /Product/Index, the Simple View Engine searches in the following locations for a matching view:

> \Views\Product\Index.simple

> \Views\Shared\Index.simple

The `SimpleView` class implements the `IView` interface. The `SimpleView` class is responsible for actually rendering the view. This class is contained in Listing 4.11.

LISTING 4.11   MyViewEngines\SimpleView.cs (C#)

```csharp
using System.IO;
using System.Text.RegularExpressions;
using System.Web.Mvc;
```

```
namespace MvcApplication1.MyViewEngines
{
    public class SimpleView : IView
    {
        private string _viewPhysicalPath;

        public SimpleView(string viewPhysicalPath)
        {
            _viewPhysicalPath = viewPhysicalPath;
        }

        #region IView Members

        public void Render(ViewContext viewContext, TextWriter writer)
        {
            // Load file
            string rawContents = File.ReadAllText(_viewPhysicalPath);

            // Perform replacements
            string parsedContents = Parse(rawContents, viewContext.ViewData);

            // Write results to HttpContext
            writer.Write(parsedContents);
        }

        #endregion

        public string Parse(string contents, ViewDataDictionary viewData)
        {
            return Regex.Replace(contents, "\\{(.+)\\}",m => GetMatch(m, viewData));
        }

        protected virtual string GetMatch(Match m, ViewDataDictionary viewData)
        {
            if (m.Success)
            {
                string key = m.Result("$1");
                if (viewData.ContainsKey(key))
                {
                    return viewData[key].ToString();
                }
            }
            return string.Empty;
        }

    }
}
```

LISTING 4.11   MyViewEngines\SimpleView.vb (VB)

```vb
Imports System.IO


Public Class SimpleView
    Implements IView

    Private _viewPhysicalPath As String

    Public Sub New(ByVal viewPhysicalPath As String)
        _viewPhysicalPath = viewPhysicalPath
    End Sub

#Region "IView Members"

    Public Sub Render(ByVal viewContext As ViewContext, ByVal writer As
➥TextWriter) Implements IView.Render
        ' Load file
        Dim rawContents As String = File.ReadAllText(_viewPhysicalPath)

        ' Perform replacements
        Dim parsedContents As String = Parse(rawContents, viewContext.ViewData)

        ' Write results to HttpContext
        writer.Write(parsedContents)
    End Sub

#End Region

    Public Function Parse(ByVal contents As String, ByVal viewData As
➥ViewDataDictionary) As String
        Return Regex.Replace(contents, "\{(.+)\}", Function(m) GetMatch(m, viewData))
    End Function

    Protected Overridable Function GetMatch(ByVal m As Match, ByVal viewData As
➥ViewDataDictionary) As String
        If m.Success Then
            Dim key As String = m.Result("$1")
            If viewData.ContainsKey(key) Then
                Return viewData(key).ToString()
            End If
        End If
```

```
        Return String.Empty
    End Function

End Class
```

In Listing 4.11, the `Render()` method loads the file that contains the view, performs regular expression replacements in the file, and writes the result to a text writer.

The regular expression replacements inject view data into the view. For example, if the view contains the expression {message}, the message item from view data is injected into that location in the view.

To use a custom view engine, you must register the view engine in the Global.asax file. The `SimpleViewEngine` is registered in the `Application_Start()` method in Listing 4.12.

LISTING 4.12   Global.asax.cs (C#)

```
protected void Application_Start()
{
    RegisterRoutes(RouteTable.Routes);

    ViewEngines.Engines.Add(new SimpleViewEngine());
}
```

LISTING 4.12   Global.asax.vb (VB)

```
Sub Application_Start()
    RegisterRoutes(RouteTable.Routes)
    ViewEngines.Engines.Add(new SimpleViewEngine())
End Sub
```

You don't need to make any changes to your controllers to use a custom view engine. For example, the `Index` action in Listing 4.13 adds an item named message to view data and returns a view.

LISTING 4.13   Controllers\SimpleController.cs (C#)

```
using System.Web.Mvc;

namespace MvcApplication1.Controllers
{
    public class SimpleController : Controller
    {
        public ActionResult Index()
        {
```

```
        ViewData["message"] = "Hello World!";
        return View();
    }
  }
}
```

LISTING 4.13   Controllers\SimpleController.vb (VB)

```
Public Class SimpleController
    Inherits System.Web.Mvc.Controller

    Function Index() As ActionResult
        ViewData("message") = "Hello World!"
        Return View()
    End Function

End Class
```

The view in Listing 4.14 is named Index.simple. This view is returned by the Simple controller when you request the URL /Simple/Index.

LISTING 4.14   Views\Simple\Index.simple

```
<html>
<head><title>Index Simple View</title></head>
<body>

<h1>{message}</h1>

</body>
</html>
```

The SimpleView class loads the Index.simple file, replaces {message} with Hello World!, and renders the HTML page in Figure 4.8.

NOTE

Of course, Visual Studio does not contain a template for .simple files because we just made up this type of file. To add the file in Listing 4.14 to your project, add an HTML file and then change its extension.

FIGURE 4.8   The Index.simple view

Testing Views

You might want to build unit tests for the views in your ASP.NET MVC application. For example, you might want to test whether a particular view renders an HTML page that contains a particular string. After all, the more you can test, the stronger the safety net for your code.

Unfortunately, there is no easy way to build unit tests for views created with the default Web Forms view engine. The default Web Forms view engine relies on classes such as the VirtualPathProvider class and the HttpRuntime class down to its bones.

Therefore, if you want to test the views in your ASP.NET MVC application, you must seek an alternative. In this section, we discuss three methods to test your views that do not depend on the default Web Forms view engine.

Test the View Result

In many cases, what you actually need to test is not the view, but the view result. In particular, you need to test whether a controller returns the view and view data expected.

Consider the controller in Listing 4.15. This controller returns a view named Index and an item in view data named message.

LISTING 4.15   Controllers\HomeController.cs (C#)

```
using System.Web.Mvc;

namespace MvcApplication1.Controllers
{
    [HandleError]
    public class HomeController : Controller
```

```
    {
        public ActionResult Index()
        {
            ViewData["message"] = "Hello World!";
            return View("Index");
        }
    }
}
```

LISTING 4.15   Controllers\HomeController.vb (VB)

```
<HandleError()> _
Public Class HomeController
    Inherits System.Web.Mvc.Controller

    Function Index() As ActionResult
        ViewData("message") = "Hello World!"
        Return View("Index")
    End Function

End Class
```

You can write unit tests that verify several properties of the view result returned by the Index action in Listing 4.15. The unit test in Listing 4.16 verifies the type of action result returned by the controller, the name of the view result, and the view data associated with the view result.

LISTING 4.16   Controllers\HomeControllerTest.cs (C#)

```
using System.Web.Mvc;
using Microsoft.VisualStudio.TestTools.UnitTesting;
using MvcApplication1.Controllers;

namespace MvcApplication1.Tests.Controllers
{
    [TestClass]
    public class HomeControllerTest
    {
        [TestMethod]
        public void Index()
        {
            // Arrange
            var controller = new HomeController();
```

```
        // Act
        var result = controller.Index();

        // Did we get a view result?
        Assert.IsInstanceOfType(result, typeof(ViewResult));

        // Did we get a view named Index?
        var indexResult = (ViewResult)result;
        Assert.AreEqual("Index", indexResult.ViewName);

        // Did we get message in view data?
        Assert.AreEqual("Hello World!", indexResult.ViewData["message"]);
    }

    }
}
```

LISTING 4.16   Controllers\HomeControllerTest.vb (VB)

```
Imports Microsoft.VisualStudio.TestTools.UnitTesting
Imports System.Web.Mvc

<TestClass()> _
Public Class HomeControllerTest
    <TestMethod()> _
    Public Sub Index()
        ' Arrange
        Dim controller = New HomeController()

        ' Act
        Dim result = controller.Index()

        ' Did we get a view result?
        Assert.IsInstanceOfType(result, GetType(ViewResult))

        ' Did we get a view named Index?
        Dim indexResult = CType(result, ViewResult)
        Assert.AreEqual("Index", indexResult.ViewName)

        ' Did we get message in view data?
        Assert.AreEqual("Hello World!", indexResult.ViewData("message"))
    End Sub

End Class
```

> **NOTE**
>
> You can test the view name (the `ViewResult.ViewName` property) only when a controller action returns a view with an explicit name. In other words, you need to return a view explicitly with `View("Index")` instead of implicitly with `View()`.

Test HTML Helpers

When using the default Web Forms view engine, the best option for testing your views is to move any view logic that you want to test into an HTML helper. Although you cannot easily write unit tests for views, you can easily write unit tests for HTML helpers.

> **NOTE**
>
> We discuss HTML helpers in detail in Chapter 6, "Understanding HTML Helpers." Roughly speaking, an HTML helper is a method that renders HTML content to the browser.

For example, imagine that you want to display a list of products from a database in a view (see Figure 4.9). You could create the view in Listing 4.17. The problem with this view, however, is that it is not easily testable.

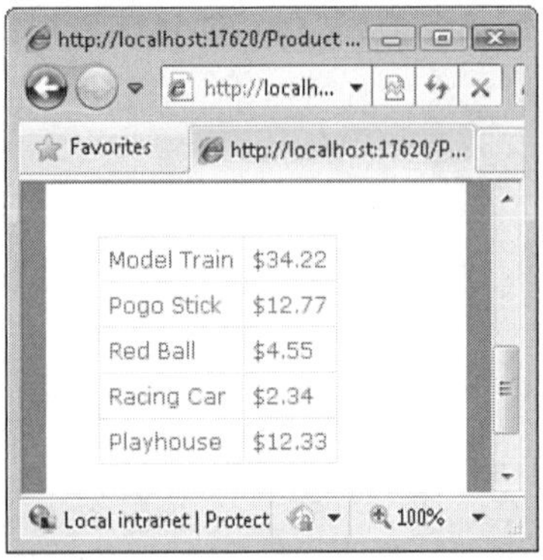

FIGURE 4.9   Displaying a list of products

LISTING 4.17   Views\Product\Index.aspx (C#)

```
<%@ Page Title="" Language="C#" MasterPageFile="~/Views/Shared/Site.Master"
➡Inherits="System.Web.Mvc.ViewPage<IEnumerable<MvcApplication1.Models.Product>>" %>


<asp:Content ID="Content2" ContentPlaceHolderID="MainContent" runat="server">

    <table>
```

```
    <% foreach (var item in Model) { %>
      <tr>
        <td>
          <%= Html.Encode(item.Name) %>
        </td>
        <td>
          <%= Html.Encode(String.Format("{0:c}", item.Price)) %>
        </td>
      </tr>
    <% } %>

    </table>

</asp:Content>
```

LISTING 4.17   Views\Product\Index.aspx (VB)

```
<%@ Page Title="" Language="VB" MasterPageFile="~/Views/Shared/Site.Master"
➥Inherits="System.Web.Mvc.ViewPage(Of IEnumerable (Of MvcApplication1.Product))" %>

<asp:Content ID="Content2" ContentPlaceHolderID="MainContent" runat="server">

    <table>

    <% For Each item In Model%>

      <tr>
        <td>
          <%= Html.Encode(item.Name) %>
        </td>
        <td>
          <%= Html.Encode(String.Format("{0:c}", item.Price)) %>
        </td>
      </tr>

    <% Next%>

    </table>

</asp:Content>
```

Instead of placing the logic to display the database records in a view, you can place the logic in an HTML helper. The HTML helper in Listing 4.18 displays the set of products.

LISTING 4.18   Helpers\ProductHelper.cs (C#)

```csharp
using System.Collections.Generic;
using System.IO;
using System.Web.Mvc;
using System.Web.UI;
using MvcApplication1.Models;

namespace MvcApplication1.Helpers
{
    public static class ProductHelper
    {
        public static string ProductList(this HtmlHelper helper)
        {
            // Get products from view data
            var products = (IEnumerable<Product>)helper.ViewData.Model;

            // Create HTML TextWriter
            var html = new HtmlTextWriter(new StringWriter());

            // Open table
            html.RenderBeginTag(HtmlTextWriterTag.Table);

            // Render product rows
            foreach (var product in products)
            {
                // Open tr
                html.RenderBeginTag(HtmlTextWriterTag.Tr);

                // Render name
                html.RenderBeginTag(HtmlTextWriterTag.Td);
                html.Write(product.Name);
                html.RenderEndTag();

                // Render price
                html.RenderBeginTag(HtmlTextWriterTag.Td);
                html.Write("{0:c}", product.Price);
                html.RenderEndTag();

                // Close tr
                html.RenderEndTag();
            }

            // Close table
            html.RenderEndTag();
```

```
            return html.InnerWriter.ToString();
        }


    }
}
```

LISTING 4.18   Helpers\ProductHelper.vb (VB)

```vb
Imports System.IO


Public Module ProductHelper

    <System.Runtime.CompilerServices.Extension()> _
    Function ProductList(ByVal helper As HtmlHelper) As String
        ' Get products from view data
        Dim products = CType(helper.ViewData.Model, IEnumerable(Of Product))

        ' Create HTML TextWriter
        Dim html = New HtmlTextWriter(New StringWriter())

        ' Open table
        html.RenderBeginTag(HtmlTextWriterTag.Table)

        ' Render product rows
        For Each product In products
            ' Open tr
            html.RenderBeginTag(HtmlTextWriterTag.Tr)

            ' Render name
            html.RenderBeginTag(HtmlTextWriterTag.Td)
            html.Write(product.Name)
            html.RenderEndTag()

            ' Render price
            html.RenderBeginTag(HtmlTextWriterTag.Td)
            html.Write("{0:c}", product.Price)
            html.RenderEndTag()

            ' Close tr
            html.RenderEndTag()
        Next

        ' Close table
```

```
        html.RenderEndTag()

        Return html.InnerWriter.ToString()
    End Function


End Module
```

The view in Listing 4.19 uses the `Html.ProductList()` helper to render the list of products. All the view logic for rendering the HTML table is now encapsulated within the helper method.

LISTING 4.19   Views\Product\Index2.aspx (C#)

```
<%@ Page Title="" Language="C#" MasterPageFile="~/Views/Shared/Site.Master"
➥Inherits="System.Web.Mvc.ViewPage" %>
<%@ Import Namespace="MvcApplication1.Helpers" %>

<asp:Content ID="Content2" ContentPlaceHolderID="MainContent" runat="server">

    <%= Html.ProductList() %>

</asp:Content>
```

LISTING 4.19   Views\Product\Index2.aspx (VB)

```
<%@ Page Title="" Language="VB" MasterPageFile="~/Views/Shared/Site.Master"
➥Inherits="System.Web.Mvc.ViewPage" %>
<%@ Import Namespace="MvcApplication1" %>

<asp:Content ID="Content2" ContentPlaceHolderID="MainContent" runat="server">

    <%= Html.ProductList() %>

</asp:Content>
```

Unlike a view, an HTML helper can be tested. The unit test in Listing 4.20 verifies that the first row of the HTML table rendered by the `ProductList()` helper matches the string `"<td>Laptop</td><td>$878.23</td>"`.

LISTING 4.20   Helpers\ProductHelperTest.cs (C#)

```
using System.Collections.Generic;
using Microsoft.VisualStudio.TestTools.UnitTesting;
```

```csharp
using MvcApplication1.Helpers;
using MvcApplication1.Models;
using MvcFakes;

namespace MvcApplication1.Tests.Helpers
{
    [TestClass]
    public class ProductHelperTest
    {
        [TestMethod]
        public void ContainsHtmlRow()
        {
            // Arrange products
            var products = new List<Product>();
            products.Add(Product.CreateProduct(-1, "Laptop", "A laptop", 878.23m));
            products.Add(Product.CreateProduct(-1, "Telescope", "A telescope",
➥200.19m));

            // Arrange HTML helper
            var helper = new FakeHtmlHelper();
            helper.ViewData.Model = products;

            // Act
            var result = ProductHelper.ProductList(helper);

            // Assert
            StringAssert.Contains(result, "<td>Laptop</td><td>$878.23</td>");
        }
    }
}
```

LISTING 4.20   Helpers\ProductHelperTest.vb (VB)

```vb
Imports Microsoft.VisualStudio.TestTools.UnitTesting
Imports MvcFakes

<TestClass()> _
Public Class ProductHelperTest
    <TestMethod()> _
    Public Sub ContainsHtmlRow()
        ' Arrange products
        Dim products = New List(Of Product)()
        products.Add(Product.CreateProduct(-1, "Laptop", "A laptop", 878.23D))
        products.Add(Product.CreateProduct(-1, "Telescope", "A telescope", 200.19D))
```

```
        ' Arrange HTML helper
        Dim helper = New FakeHtmlHelper()
        helper.ViewData.Model = products

        ' Act
        Dim result = ProductHelper.ProductList(helper)

        ' Assert
        StringAssert.Contains(result, "<td>Laptop</td><td>$878.23</td>")
    End Sub
End Class
```

> **NOTE**
>
> The unit test in Listing 4.20 takes advantage of the MvcFakes project. The
> FakeHtmlHelper class is defined in the MvcFakes project included with the code that is
> on the book's website (www.informit.com/title/9780672329982). The FakeHtmlHelper
> class simplifies the work that you must perform to test a helper method.

Whenever you need to build unit tests for your view logic, consider moving the view logic into a separate HTML helper. You can't easily unit test the page rendered by a view, but you can easily test the content rendered by an HTML helper.

Test a Custom View Engine

The final option for building unit tests for view is (most likely) the least appealing option. You can easily test views when you use a view engine other than the default Web Forms view engine. I claim that this is the least appealing option because I expect the vast majority of developers to use the default Web Forms view engine.

For example, earlier in this chapter, we created a Simple View Engine (see Listing 4.11). The Simple View Engine returns simple views (see Listing 4.10). Simple views are easy to test, as illustrated by the unit test in Listing 4.21.

LISTING 4.21   Controllers\SimpleControllerTest.cs (C#)

```csharp
using System.IO;
using System.Web.Mvc;
using Microsoft.VisualStudio.TestTools.UnitTesting;
using MvcApplication1.MyViewEngines;

namespace MvcApplication1.Tests.Controllers
{
```

```
[TestClass]
public class SimpleControllerTest
{
    private TestContext testContextInstance;

    public TestContext TestContext
    {
        get
        {
            return testContextInstance;
        }
        set
        {
            testContextInstance = value;
        }
    }


    [TestMethod]
    public void IndexView()
    {
        // Create simple view
        var viewPhysicalPath = testContextInstance.TestDir + @"\..\..\
➥MvcApplication1\Views\Simple\Index.simple";
        var indexView = new SimpleView(viewPhysicalPath);

        // Create view context
        var viewContext = new ViewContext();

        // Create view data
        var viewData = new ViewDataDictionary();
        viewData["message"] = "Hello World!";
        viewContext.ViewData = viewData;

        // Render simple view
        var writer = new StringWriter();
        indexView.Render(viewContext, writer);

        // Assert
        StringAssert.Contains(writer.ToString(), "<h1>Hello World!</h1>");
    }
}
}
```

LISTING 4.21   Controllers\SimpleControllerTest.vb (VB)

```vb
Imports Microsoft.VisualStudio.TestTools.UnitTesting
Imports System.Web.Mvc
Imports System.IO

<TestClass()> _
Public Class SimpleControllerTest

    Private testContextInstance As TestContext

    Public Property TestContext() As TestContext
        Get
            Return testContextInstance
        End Get
        Set(ByVal value As TestContext)
            testContextInstance = value
        End Set
    End Property


    <TestMethod()> _
    Public Sub IndexView()
        ' Create simple view
        Dim viewPhysicalPath = testContextInstance.TestDir & "\..\..\
➥MvcApplication1\Views\Simple\Index.simple"
        Dim indexView = New SimpleView(viewPhysicalPath)

        ' Create view context
        Dim context = New ViewContext()

        ' Create view data
        Dim viewData = New ViewDataDictionary()
        viewData("message") = "Hello World!"
        context.ViewData = viewData

        ' Render simple view
        Dim writer = New StringWriter()
        indexView.Render(context, writer)

        ' Assert
        StringAssert.Contains(writer.ToString(), "<h1>Hello World!</h1>")
    End Sub

End Class
```

The unit test in Listing 4.21 instantiates a simple view by passing the physical path to the view to the `SimpleView` class constructor. Next, the `SimpleView.Render()` method is called to render the view to a string writer. Finally, an assertion is made that the writer contains the text "`<h1>Hello World!</h1>`".

Summary

This chapter was devoted to the subject of ASP.NET MVC views. First, you learned how to create views, and you learned about the distinction between typed and untyped views. You learned how to pass data from a controller to a view by using view data.

Next, we discussed the important subject of preventing JavaScript injection attacks. You learned how to disable request validation by using the `[ValidateInput]` attribute.

You also were provided with an overview of alternative view engines, and you learned how to create a custom view engine of your own. You learned how to create the Simple View Engine and simple views.

Finally, we leapt into the important topic of testing your views. You learned several different strategies for building unit tests for your views. You learned how to test view results, how to test HTML helpers, and how to test custom views.

CHAPTER 5

Understanding Models

An ASP.NET MVC model contains all the business, validation, and data access logic required by your application. In other words, a model contains all your application logic except the view logic and controller logic. When building an ASP.NET MVC application, the bulk of your time and effort is devoted to building your model classes.

The focus of this chapter is on creating model classes for data access. In particular, you learn how to build model classes by using the Microsoft Entity Framework.

This chapter is divided into four parts. The first part provides you with an overview of the Microsoft Entity Framework. You learn how to perform basic database operations such as listing, inserting, updating, and deleting records.

Next, you learn about the Repository software design pattern. Things change. New technologies for data access are introduced every few years. The Repository pattern enables you to isolate your data access logic from the remainder of your application so that your application can adapt gracefully to change.

In the next section—and this is my favorite section of this chapter—you learn how to create a generic repository. I show you how you can avoid writing a new repository class each time you build a new application. I explain how you can create a single generic repository that works with both the Microsoft Entity Framework and LINQ to SQL (and other new data access technologies that might be introduced in the future).

Finally, we discuss how you write units tests for application logic that interacts with data access logic. You learn how to both mock and fake a repository layer.

Creating a Data Model

In this book, we focus on using the Microsoft Entity Framework to build our data model. The Microsoft Entity Framework is Microsoft's recommended data access technology.

It is important to emphasize, however, that the ASP.NET MVC framework is not tied to the Microsoft Entity Framework. You can use your favorite data access technology with ASP.NET MVC. For example, ASP.NET MVC is entirely compatible with alternative data access technologies such as Microsoft LINQ to SQL or NHibernate.

The Microsoft Entity Framework (in part) is an *Object Relational Mapping* (ORM) tool. You can use the Microsoft Entity Framework to generate data model classes from a database automatically. That way, you do not have to undergo the tedious process of building these data model classes by hand.

For example, if you have a database table named Products, you can use the Microsoft Entity Framework to generate a class named `Product` that represents a particular row from the table. In your code, instead of interacting with the Products database directly, you interact with the Entity Framework object context and the `Product` class.

The Entity Framework shields you from needing to interact directly with the database. By taking advantage of the Entity Framework, you never need to write SQL queries again. You can write all your data access code in C# or VB.NET instead of SQL.

NOTE

To use the Microsoft Entity Framework, you need .NET Framework 3.5 Service Pack 1. The Entity Framework is included in Service Pack 1.

Creating a Data Model with the Microsoft Entity Framework

Imagine that you created a database named ProductsDB and a database table named Products. The columns for the Products table are listed in Figure 5.1. This table has four columns. The first column, the Id column, is a primary key column and an identity column.

	Column Name	Data Type	Allow Nulls
🔑	Id	int	☐
	Name	nvarchar(100)	☐
	Description	nvarchar(MAX)	☐
▶	Price	money	☐
			☐

FIGURE 5.1   Products database table

Now, imagine that you want to access this table from an ASP.NET MVC application. The first step is to use the Microsoft Entity Framework to generate a data model. Follow these steps:

1. Right-click the Models folder in the Solution Explorer window and select the menu option Add, New Item.

2. In the Add New Item dialog, pick the Data category and the ADO.NET Entity Data Model template (see Figure 5.2). Name your data model `DataModel.edmx` and click the Add button. After you click the Add button, the Entity Data Model Wizard appears (see Figure 5.3).

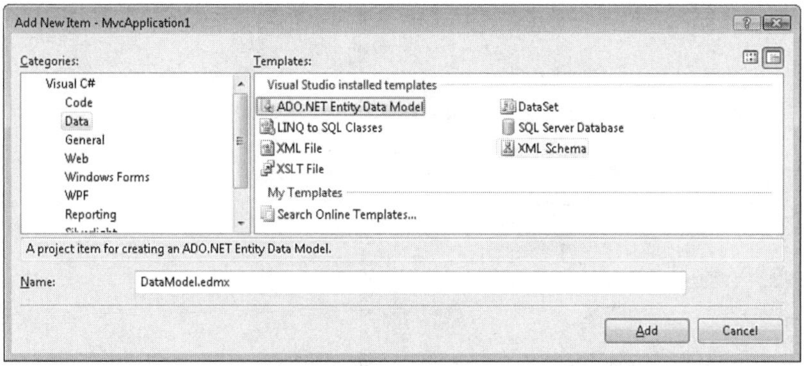

FIGURE 5.2   Adding an ADO.NET entity data model

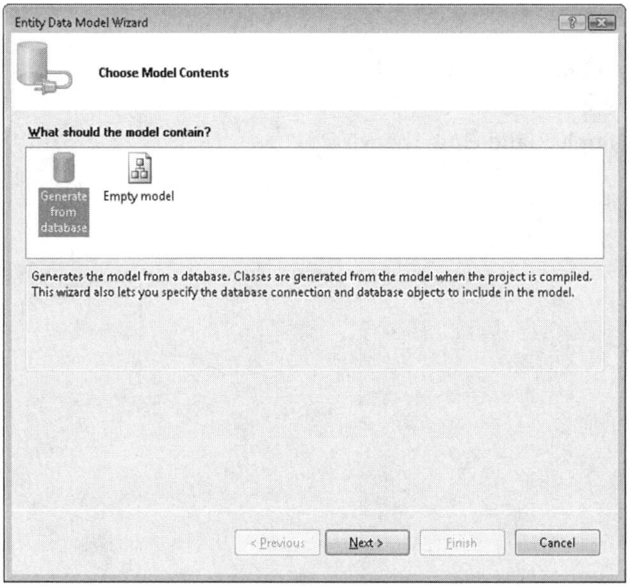

FIGURE 5.3   Using the Entity Data Model Wizard

3. In the Choose Model Contents step, select Generate from database.
4. In the Choose Your Data Connection step, pick the ProductsDB.mdf database for the data connection and use `ProductsDBEntities` for the connection settings name (see Figure 5.4).

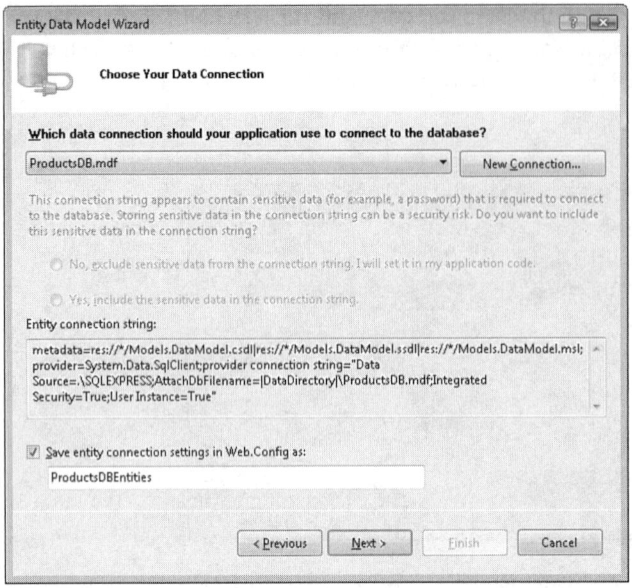

FIGURE 5.4   Choosing your data connection

5. In the Choose Your Database Objects step, select the Products table and enter the namespace Models (see Figure 5.5).

6. Click the Finish button to complete and close the wizard.

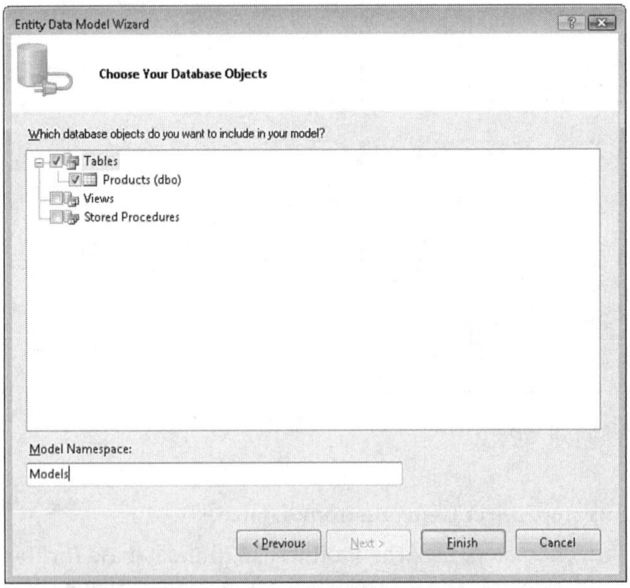

FIGURE 5.5   Choosing your database objects

After you complete the wizard, the ADO.NET Entity Designer appears (see Figure 5.6). The designer displays a single entity class named Products that corresponds to the Products database table. The class contains a property that corresponds to each column from the database.

FIGURE 5.6   The ADO.NET Entity Designer

Notice that the name of the entity class is Products. The wizard generates an entity class with the same name as the corresponding database table. Because we want to use the entity class to represent a particular product, you should change the name of the entity class from Products to Product (singular). Right-click the entity on the designer surface and select the menu option Rename to rename the class. Click the Save button (the button with the anachronistic icon of a floppy disk) to save the renamed entity.

Each entity displayed in the ADO.NET Entity Designer corresponds to a C# or VB.NET class. When you modify entities in the designer and save the changes, the ADO.NET Entity Framework generates the C# or VB.NET classes in the background. You can see these classes by expanding the DataModel.edmx node in the Solution Explorer window and double-clicking the DataModel.Designer file to open the file in the Visual Studio Code Editor (see Figure 5.7).

NOTE

In a Visual Basic project, the DataModel.Designer file is hidden. To see the file, you need to select the menu option Project, Show All Files.

Currently, our Entity Framework designer file contains definitions for two classes named ProductsDBEntities and Product. The ProductsDBEntities class represents an Entity Framework object context class. The object context class is the class that you use to interact with the database in your code.

In the following sections, you learn how to use the ProductsDBEntities and the Product classes to list, insert, edit, and delete database records.

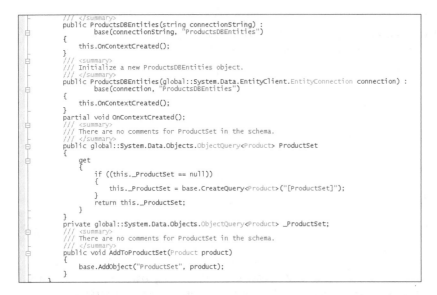

```
      /// </summary>
      public ProductsDBEntities(string connectionString) :
            base(connectionString, "ProductsDBEntities")
      {
          this.OnContextCreated();
      }
      /// <summary>
      /// Initialize a new ProductsDBEntities object.
      /// </summary>
      public ProductsDBEntities(global::System.Data.EntityClient.EntityConnection connection) :
            base(connection, "ProductsDBEntities")
      {
          this.OnContextCreated();
      }
      partial void OnContextCreated();
      /// <summary>
      /// There are no comments for ProductSet in the schema.
      /// </summary>
      public global::System.Data.Objects.ObjectQuery<Product> ProductSet
      {
          get
          {
              if ((this._ProductSet == null))
              {
                  this._ProductSet = base.CreateQuery<Product>("[ProductSet]");
              }
              return this._ProductSet;
          }
      }
      private global::System.Data.Objects.ObjectQuery<Product> _ProductSet;
      /// <summary>
      /// There are no comments for ProductSet in the schema.
      /// </summary>
      public void AddToProductSet(Product product)
      {
          base.AddObject("ProductSet", product);
      }
```

FIGURE 5.7   The DataModel.Designer file

WARNING

You never want to modify the Entity Framework designer file directly. The ADO.NET Entity Framework overwrites any changes that you make to this file the next time you save changes that you made in the ADO.NET Entity Designer.

Listing Records

You use the Entity Framework object context—in our case, the `ProductsDBEntities` class—to retrieve a set of database records. Instead of using a SQL SELECT command, you use LINQ to represent the query.

For example, the `Index()` action in Listing 5.1 illustrates how you can retrieve all the products from the Products database table.

LISTING 5.1   Controllers\HomeController.cs Index Action (C#)

```csharp
using System.Linq;
using System.Web.Mvc;
using MvcApplication1.Models;

namespace MvcApplication1.Controllers
{
    public class HomeController : Controller
    {
        private ProductsDBEntities _entities = new
```

```
ProductsDBEntities();


        //
        // GET: /Home/

        public ActionResult Index()
        {
            return View(_entities.ProductSet.ToList());
        }


    }
}
```

LISTING 5.1   Controllers\HomeController.vb Index Action (VB)

```
Public Class HomeController
    Inherits System.Web.Mvc.Controller

    Private _entities As New ProductsDBEntities()


    ' GET: /Home/

    Function Index() As ActionResult
        Return View(_entities.ProductSet.ToList())
    End Function

End Class
```

Notice that the Home controller has a private field named _entities that represents an Entity Framework object context. The expression _entities.ProductSet.ToList() returns a generic list of Product classes that represent all the records from the Products database table.

Of course, you can use LINQ to perform more complicated types of queries. The following query returns all the products that have a price greater than $10.00 and returns the products in order of the product name:

(C#)

```
var results = from p in _entities.ProductSet
              where p.Price > 10.00m
              orderby p.Name
              select p;
```

(VB)

```
Dim results = From p In _entities.ProductSet _
    Where p.Price > 10.0 _
    Order By p.Name _
    Select p
```

NOTE

To learn more about LINQ, see Appendix A, "C# and VB.NET Language Features."

Getting a Single Record

You use a different LINQ query when retrieving a single record. For example, the Details() action in Listing 5.2 retrieves the product record from the Products database that has an Id of 2.

LISTING 5.2   Controllers\HomeController.cs Details Action (C#)

```
//
// GET: /Home/Details/5

public ActionResult Details(int id)
{
    var result = (from p in _entities.ProductSet
                  where p.Id == id
                  select p).FirstOrDefault();
    return View(result);
}
```

LISTING 5.2   Controllers\HomeController.vb Details Action (VB)

```
'
' GET: /Home/Details/5

Function Details(ByVal id As Integer) As ActionResult
    Dim result = (From p In _entities.ProductSet _
                  Where p.Id = id _
                  Select p).FirstOrDefault()

    Return View(result)
End Function
```

Creating Records

You also use the Entity Framework object context to create new database records. For example, the second `Create()` action in Listing 5.3 adds a new product to the Products database table.

LISTING 5.3   Controllers\HomeController.cs Create Action (C#)

```
//
// GET: /Home/Create

public ActionResult Create()
{
    return View();
}

//
// POST: /Home/Create

[AcceptVerbs(HttpVerbs.Post)]
public ActionResult Create([Bind(Exclude="Id")]Product productToCreate)
{
    try
    {
        _entities.AddToProductSet(productToCreate);
        _entities.SaveChanges();

        return RedirectToAction("Index");
    }
    catch
    {
        return View();
    }
}
```

LISTING 5.3   Controllers\HomeController.vb Create Action (VB)

```
'
' GET: /Home/Create

Function Create() As ActionResult
    Return View()
End Function
```

```
' POST: /Home/Create

<AcceptVerbs(HttpVerbs.Post)> _
Function Create(<Bind(Exclude:="Id")>productToCreate As Product) As ActionResult
    Try
        _entities.AddToProductSet(productToCreate)
        _entities.SaveChanges()
        Return RedirectToAction("Index")
    Catch
        Return View()
    End Try
End Function
```

The first Create() action displays the HTML form for creating a new product. The HTML form is submitted to the second Create() action. This action actually adds the new product to the database.

Notice that two commands must be executed to add the new product to the database. First, the new product is added to the set of products represented by the Entity Framework object context by calling the AddToProductSet() method. Next, the SaveChanges() method is called to actually save the new record to the underlying database.

Editing Records

You can update a database record simply by modifying the properties of an entity and calling the SaveChanges() method. For example, the following three statements can be used to double the price for a product:

(C#)

```
var productToEdit = (from p in _entities.ProductSet
               where p.Id == 3
               select p).FirstOrDefault();
productToEdit.Price = productToEdit.Price * 2;
_entities.SaveChanges();
```

(VB)

```
Dim productToEdit = (From p In _entities.ProductSet _
                    Where p.Id = 3 _
                    Select p).FirstOrDefault()
productToEdit.Price = productToEdit.Price * 2
_entities.SaveChanges()
```

However, when creating an ASP.NET MVC action, you typically do not retrieve an entity before modifying it. Instead, an instance of the entity is handed to you as a parameter of the action method. For example, the second `Create()` action in Listing 5.4 accepts a `Product` parameter.

The object context can track changes to an entity only when the entity is attached to the context. When the ASP.NET MVC framework creates the entity as an action method parameter, the entity is not attached.

In this situation, you need to retrieve the original entity, apply any property changes to the original entity, and then call `SaveChanges()` to update the database. For example, the second `Edit()` action in Listing 5.4 updates a product in the database.

LISTING 5.4   Controllers\HomeController.cs Edit Action (C#)

```csharp
//
// GET: /Home/Edit/5

public ActionResult Edit(int id)
{
    var productToEdit = (from p in _entities.ProductSet
                where p.Id == id
                select p).FirstOrDefault();
    return View(productToEdit);
}


//
// POST: /Home/Edit/5

[AcceptVerbs(HttpVerbs.Post)]
public ActionResult Edit(Product productToEdit)
{
    try
    {
        var originalProduct = (from p in _entities.ProductSet
                            where p.Id == productToEdit.Id
                            select p).FirstOrDefault();
        _entities.ApplyPropertyChanges(originalProduct.EntityKey.EntitySetName,
➥productToEdit);
        _entities.SaveChanges();
        return RedirectToAction("Index");
    }
    catch
    {
        return View();
    }
}
```

LISTING 5.4   Controllers\HomeController.vb Edit Action (VB)

```vb
'
' GET: /Home/Edit/5

Function Edit(ByVal id As Integer) As ActionResult
    Dim productToEdit = (From p In _entities.ProductSet _
                Where p.Id = id _
                Select p).FirstOrDefault()
    Return View(productToEdit)
End Function


'
' POST: /Home/Edit/5

<AcceptVerbs(HttpVerbs.Post)> _
Function Edit(productToEdit As Product) As ActionResult
    Try
        Dim originalProduct = (From p In _entities.ProductSet _
                Where p.Id = productToEdit.Id _
                Select p).FirstOrDefault()
        _entities.ApplyPropertyChanges(originalProduct.EntityKey.EntitySetName,
➥productToEdit)
        _entities.SaveChanges()
        Return RedirectToAction("Index")
    Catch
        Return View()
    End Try
End Function
```

The first Edit() action in Listing 5.4 retrieves the product so that it can be displayed in an HTML form. The second Edit() action is invoked when the HTML form is submitted and this Edit() action performs the actual update in the database.

The second Edit() action

1. Retrieves the original product
2. Calls ApplyPropertyChanges() to update the original product with the changes from the modified product
3. Calls SaveChanges() to persist the changes to the database

WARNING

The ApplyChanges() method won't update navigation properties or related objects. It applies only to properties of the immediate object.

Deleting Records

Finally, you can use the Entity Framework object context to delete records. For example, the Delete() action in Listing 5.5 deletes a product record from the database.

In Listing 5.5, there are two actions named Delete(). The first Delete() action displays a delete confirmation page. The second Delete() action performs the actual delete against the database.

LISTING 5.5   Controllers\HomeController.cs Delete Action (C#)

```csharp
//
// GET: /Home/Delete/5

public ActionResult Delete(int id)
{
    var productToDelete = (from p in _entities.ProductSet
                        where p.Id == id
                        select p).FirstOrDefault();
    return View(productToDelete);
}


//
// POST: /Home/Delete

[AcceptVerbs(HttpVerbs.Post)]
public ActionResult Delete(Product productToDelete)
{
    try
    {
        var originalProduct = (from p in _entities.ProductSet
                            where p.Id == productToDelete.Id
                            select p).FirstOrDefault();

        _entities.DeleteObject(originalProduct);
        _entities.SaveChanges();
        return RedirectToAction("Index");
    }
    catch
    {
        return View();
    }
}
```

LISTING 5.5   Controllers\HomeController.vb Delete Action (VB)

```vb
'
' GET: /Home/Delete/5
Function Delete(ByVal id As Integer) As ActionResult
    Dim productToDelete = (From p In _entities.ProductSet _
                Where p.Id = id _
                Select p).FirstOrDefault()
    Return View(productToDelete)
End Function


'
' POST: /Home/Delete

<AcceptVerbs(HttpVerbs.Post)> _
Function Delete(productToDelete As Product) As ActionResult
    Try
        Dim originalProduct = (From p In _entities.ProductSet _
                Where p.Id = productToDelete.Id _
                Select p).FirstOrDefault()
        _entities.DeleteObject(originalProduct)
        _entities.SaveChanges()
        Return RedirectToAction("Index")
    Catch
        Return View()
    End Try
End Function
```

Using the Repository Pattern

Things change. When I originally wrote this chapter, I wrote all the code samples using Microsoft LINQ to SQL instead of the Microsoft Entity Framework. When Microsoft announced that the Entity Framework is the recommended data access technology, I rewrote this chapter.

When you build an application, you should build the application to gracefully adapt to change. If you believe that code is likely to change in the future, you should encapsulate the code into a separate class. That way, when the volatile code changes, you don't have to touch any of your other code.

In this section, you learn how to use a software design pattern named the *Repository pattern* to isolate your data access layer from the remainder of your application. By taking advantage of the Repository pattern, you can easily modify your application to take advantage of a different data access technology in the future.

Creating a Product Repository

Let's create a product repository that encapsulates all our data access logic for working with products. We need to create two objects:

▶ IProductRepository—This interface describes the methods for listing, getting, inserting, updating, and deleting products.

▶ ProductRepository—This class implements the IProductRepository interface.

Why do we need to create both an interface and a class? In our application code, we always program against the interface. We call methods of the IProductRepository interface instead of calling methods of the ProductRepository class. That way, we can change our implementation of the interface in the future without needing to rewrite any of the application code that interacts with the interface.

The IProductRepository interface is contained in Listing 5.6. This interface describes five methods named List(), Get(), Create(), Edit(), and Delete().

LISTING 5.6   Models\IProductRepository.cs (C#)

```csharp
using System.Collections.Generic;


namespace MvcApplication1.Models
{
    public interface IProductRepository
    {
        IEnumerable<Product> List();
        Product Get(int id);
        void Create(Product productToCreate);
        void Edit(Product productToEdit);
        void Delete(Product productToDelete);
    }
}
```

LISTING 5.6   Models\IProductRepository.vb (VB)

```vbnet
Public Interface IProductRepository
    Function List() As IEnumerable(Of Product)
    Function [Get](ByVal id As Integer) As Product
    Sub Create(ByVal productToCreate As Product)
    Sub Edit(ByVal productToEdit As Product)
    Sub Delete(ByVal productToDelete As Product)
End Interface
```

The `ProductRepository` class in Listing 5.7 implements the `IProductRepository` inter-face. This implementation of the `IProductRepository` interface uses the Microsoft Entity Framework. However, we could implement the `IProductRepository` interface with a class that uses Microsoft LINQ to SQL, NHibernate, or just about any other data access technology.

LISTING 5.7   Models\ProductRepository.cs (C#)

```
using System;
using System.Collections.Generic;
using System.Linq;
using System.Web;

namespace MvcApplication1.Models
{
    public class ProductRepository : IProductRepository
    {
        private ProductsDBEntities _entities = new ProductsDBEntities();

        #region IProductRepository Members
        public IEnumerable<Product> List()
        {
            return _entities.ProductSet.ToList();
        }

        public Product Get(int id)
        {
            return (from p in _entities.ProductSet
                        where p.Id == id
                        select p).FirstOrDefault();
        }

        public void Create(Product productToCreate)
        {
            _entities.AddToProductSet(productToCreate);
            _entities.SaveChanges();
        }

        public void Edit(Product productToEdit)
        {
            var originalProduct = Get(productToEdit.Id);
            _entities.ApplyPropertyChanges(originalProduct.EntityKey.EntitySetName,
➥productToEdit);
            _entities.SaveChanges();
        }

    }
```

```
        public void Delete(Product productToDelete)
        {
            var originalProduct = Get(productToDelete.Id);
            _entities.DeleteObject(originalProduct);
            _entities.SaveChanges();
        }


        #endregion
    }
}
```

LISTING 5.7   Models\ProductRepository.vb (VB)

```
Public Class ProductRepository
    Implements IProductRepository

    Private _entities As New ProductsDBEntities()

    #Region "IProductRepository Members"

    Public Function List() As IEnumerable(Of Product) Implements
➥IProductRepository.List
        Return _entities.ProductSet.ToList()
    End Function

    Public Function [Get](ByVal id As Integer) As Product Implements
➥IProductRepository.Get
        Return (From p In _entities.ProductSet _
                Where p.Id = id _
                Select p).FirstOrDefault()
    End Function

    Public Sub Create(ByVal productToCreate As Product) Implements
➥IProductRepository.Create
        _entities.AddToProductSet(productToCreate)
        _entities.SaveChanges()
    End Sub

    Public Sub Edit(ByVal productToEdit As Product) Implements
➥IProductRepository.Edit
        Dim originalProduct = [Get](productToEdit.Id)
        _entities.ApplyPropertyChanges(originalProduct.EntityKey.EntitySetName,
➥productToEdit)
        _entities.SaveChanges()
```

```vb
    End Sub

    Public Sub Delete(ByVal productToDelete As Product) Implements
➥IProductRepository.Delete
        Dim originalProduct = [Get](productToDelete.Id)
        _entities.DeleteObject(originalProduct)
        _entities.SaveChanges()
    End Sub

    #End Region

End Class
```

Finally, the Product controller in Listing 5.8 uses the product repository in its Index() and Create() actions.

LISTING 5.8   Models\ProductController.cs (C#)

```csharp
using System.Web.Mvc;
using MvcApplication1.Models;

namespace MvcApplication1.Controllers
{
    public class ProductController : Controller
    {
        private IProductRepository _repository;

        public ProductController()
            : this(new ProductRepository()) { }

        public ProductController(IProductRepository repository)
        {
            _repository = repository;
        }


        //
        // GET: /Product/

        public ActionResult Index()
        {
            return View(_repository.List());
        }
```

```
//
// GET: /Product/Create

public ActionResult Create()
{
    return View();
}

//
// POST: /Product/Create

[AcceptVerbs(HttpVerbs.Post)]
public ActionResult Create(Product productToCreate)
{
    try
    {
        _repository.Create(productToCreate);
        return RedirectToAction("Index");
    }
    catch
    {
        return View();
    }
}


    }
}
```

LISTING 5.8   Models\ProductController.vb (VB)

```
Public Class ProductController
    Inherits Controller

    Private _repository As IProductRepository

    Public Sub New()
        Me.New(New ProductRepository())
    End Sub

    Public Sub New(ByVal repository As IProductRepository)
        _repository = repository
    End Sub
```

```vb
'
' GET: /Product/

Public Function Index() As ActionResult
     Return View(_repository.List())
End Function


'
' GET: /Product/Create

Public Function Create() As ActionResult
     Return View()
End Function


'
' POST: /Product/Create

<AcceptVerbs(HttpVerbs.Post)> _
Public Function Create(ByVal productToCreate As Product) As ActionResult
     Try
          _repository.Create(productToCreate)
          Return RedirectToAction("Index")
     Catch
          Return View()
     End Try
End Function

End Class
```

Using the Dependency Injection Pattern

Notice that the Product controller in Listing 5.8 has two constructors. The first constructor, the parameterless constructor, calls the second constructor. The first constructor creates an instance of the ProductRepository class and passes the instance to the second constructor.

The only place in the Product controller that the ProductRepository class is used instead of the IProductRepository interface is in this first constructor. If you want to use a different class that implements the IProductRepository, you need to change only the code in the first constructor.

The Product controller uses a software design pattern called the *Dependency Injection pattern*. In particular, it uses a pattern named *Constructor Dependency Injection*.

> **NOTE**
>
> The Dependency Injection pattern, like many of the software design patterns dis-
> cussed in this book, was first described by Martin Fowler. Go to http://martinfowler.
> com/articles/injection.html.

The Constructor Dependency Injection pattern enables you to "loosely couple" two
classes. Class A is dependent on Class B. In our case, our `Product` controller class is dependent on a `product` repository class. Because we might need to change Class B in the future,
we want to change Class B with the minimum impact on the code in Class A.

The Constructor Dependency Injection pattern enables us to limit the contact between
the `Product` controller and the `product` repository to a single point of contact. A concrete
implementation of the `product` repository is used only in one place—within the `Product`
controller constructor. If we yank the two classes apart, the only part that would break
would be the constructor.

> **NOTE**
>
> If you want to eliminate any reference to the `ProductRepository` class within the
> `ProductController` class, you can take advantage of a Dependency Injection (DI)
> framework such as the Microsoft Managed Extensibility Framework (MEF) or
> StructureMap.

Later in this chapter—in the section titled "Testing Data Access"—you see another advantage of using the Dependency Injection pattern. The Dependency Injection pattern
enables us to easily unit test our application code.

Creating a Generic Repository

Whenever you discover that you are writing the same code over and over again, you
should step back and question your sanity. Most likely, you are wasting away precious
moments of your life that could be better spent seeing movies or taking a walk in the park.

Recently, I realized that I was writing pretty much the same repository class over and over
again. Therefore, I decided to create a generic repository. Creating a generic repository has
several benefits:

1. I can use the generic repository as a starting point for all my repository classes in
    the future.

2. I can use the generic repository with both the Microsoft Entity Framework and LINQ to SQL. Better yet, I can use the generic repository with some future and unknown data access technology.

3. I can use the generic repository in my unit tests.

In the code on the book's website (www.informit.com/title/9780672329982), you can find a GenericRepository solution. This solution contains four projects (see Figure 5.8). Here's a description of each project:

▶ GenericRepository project—Contains the `IGenericRepository` interface. Also contains the `FakeGenericRepository`.

▶ EFGenericRepository project—Contains the implementation of the `IGenericRepository` interface for the Microsoft Entity Framework.

▶ LSGenericRepository project—Contains the implementation of the `IGenericRepository` interface for Microsoft LINQ to SQL.

▶ GenericRepository.Tests project—Contains unit tests for the `FakeGenericRepository`.

▶ The `IGenericRepository` interface is contained in Listing 5.9.

LISTING 5.9   IGenericRepository.cs (C#)

```csharp
using System.Collections.Generic;
using System.Linq;

namespace GenericRepository
{
    public interface IGenericRepository
    {
        IQueryable<T> List<T>() where T:class;
        T Get<T>(int id) where T : class;
        void Create<T>(T entityToCreate) where T : class;
        void Edit<T>(T entityToEdit) where T : class;
        void Delete<T>(T entityToDelete) where T : class;
    }
}
```

LISTING 5.9   IGenericRepository.vb (VB)

```vb
Public Interface IGenericRepository
    Function List(Of T As Class)() As IQueryable(Of T)
    Function [Get](Of T As Class)(ByVal id As Integer) As T
    Sub Create(Of T As Class)(ByVal entityToCreate As T)
    Sub Edit(Of T As Class)(ByVal entityToEdit As T)
    Sub Delete(Of T As Class)(ByVal entityToDelete As T)
End Interface
```

FIGURE 5.8   The GenericRepository solution

Notice that each of the methods contained in the IGenericRepository interface is a
generic method. The methods contain an open generic type parameter for the entity. For
example, you can get a customer with a particular Id by executing the following code:

(C#)

```
var customerToEdit = _repository.Get<Customer>(3)
```

(VB)

```
Dim customerToEdit =_repository.Get(Of Customer)(3)
```

You can get a list of all products with a price less than $50.00 with the following code:

(C#)

```
var result = (from p in _repository.List<Product>()
            where p.Price < 50.00m
            select p).ToList();
```

(VB)

```
Dim result = (From p In _repository.List(Of Product)() _
            Where p.Price < 50.00D _
            Select p).ToList()
```

Using the Generic Repository with the Entity Framework

If you want to use the generic repository with the Microsoft Entity Framework, you need
to add references to two assemblies to your ASP.NET MVC project. You need to add a reference to the assembly generated by the GenericRepository project (the
GenericRepository.dll assembly), and you need to add a reference to the assembly generated by the EFGenericRepository project (the EFGenericRepository.dll assembly).

In your ASP.NET MVC project, you generate your data model classes with the Entity Framework Wizard in the normal way. After you generate the data model classes, you can use the classes with the generic repository.

The controller in Listing 5.10 uses the EF generic repository in its `Index()` and `Create()` actions.

NOTE

The code in Listing 5.10 is contained in the EFMvcApplication project included with the source code files on the book's website (www.informit.com/title/9780672329982).

LISTING 5.10   Controllers\HomeController.cs (C#)

```csharp
using System.Linq;
using System.Web.Mvc;
using EFMvcApplication.Models;
using GenericRepository;

namespace EFMvcApplication.Controllers
{
    public class HomeController : Controller
    {
        private IGenericRepository _repository;

        public HomeController()
        {
            _repository = new EFGenericRepository(new ToyStoreDBEntities());
        }

        //
        // GET: /Home/

        public ActionResult Index()
        {
            return View(_repository.List<Product>().ToList());
        }


        //
        // GET: /Home/Create

        public ActionResult Create()
        {
            return View();
```

```
        }

        //
        // POST: /Home/Create

        [AcceptVerbs(HttpVerbs.Post)]
        public ActionResult Create([Bind(Exclude="Id")]Product productToCreate)
        {
            try
            {
                _repository.Create<Product>(productToCreate);
                return RedirectToAction("Index");
            }
            catch
            {
                return View();
            }
        }


    }
}
```

LISTING 5.10   Controllers\HomeController.vb (VB)

```
Imports GenericRepository

Public Class HomeController
    Inherits Controller

    Private _repository As IGenericRepository

    Public Sub New()
        _repository = New EFGenericRepository(New ToyStoreDBEntities())
    End Sub


    '
    ' GET: /Home/

    Public Function Index() As ActionResult
        Return View(_repository.List(Of Product)().ToList())
    End Function
```

```
 '
 ' GET: /Home/Create

 Public Function Create() As ActionResult
     Return View()
 End Function
 '
 ' POST: /Home/Create

 <AcceptVerbs(HttpVerbs.Post)> _
 Public Function Create(<Bind(Exclude:="Id")> ByVal productToCreate As Product)
➥As ActionResult
     Try
         _repository.Create(Of Product)(productToCreate)
         Return RedirectToAction("Index")
     Catch
         Return View()
     End Try
 End Function



 End Class
```

Notice that an instance of the EFGenericRepository class is created in the controller's
constructor. The EFGenericRepository class is instantiated by passing an Entity
Framework object context to the constructor for the EFGenericRepository class.

Using the Generic Repository with LINQ to SQL

To use the generic repository with LINQ to SQL, you need to add references to two assemblies to your ASP.NET MVC project. You need to add a reference to the assembly generated
by the GenericRepository project (the GenericRepository.dll assembly), and you need to
add a reference to the assembly generated by the LSGenericRepository project (the
LSGenericRepository.dll assembly).

You generate your data model classes in the standard way: Drag your database tables onto
the LINQ to SQL designer.

The controller in Listing 5.11 uses the LS generic repository.

NOTE

The code in Listing 5.11 is contained in the LSMvcApplication project included on the
book's website (www.informit.com/title/9780672329982).

LISTING 5.11   Controllers\HomeController.cs (C#)

```csharp
using System.Linq;
using System.Web.Mvc;
using GenericRepository;
using LSMvcApplication.Models;

namespace LSMvcApplication.Controllers
{
    public class HomeController : Controller
    {
        private IGenericRepository _repository;


        public HomeController()
        {
            _repository = new LSGenericRepository(new DataModelDataContext());
        }
        //
        // GET: /Home/

        public ActionResult Index()
        {
            return View(_repository.List<Product>().ToList());
        }

        //
        // GET: /Home/Create

        public ActionResult Create()
        {
            return View();
        }

        //
        // POST: /Home/Create

        [AcceptVerbs(HttpVerbs.Post)]
        public ActionResult Create([Bind(Exclude="Id")]Product productToCreate)
        {
            try
            {
                _repository.Create<Product>(productToCreate);
                return RedirectToAction("Index");
            }
            catch
```

```
        {
            return View();
        }
    }



    }
}
```

LISTING 5.11   Controllers\HomeController.vb (VB)

```vb
Imports GenericRepository


Public Class HomeController
    Inherits Controller

    Private _repository As IGenericRepository


    Public Sub New()
        _repository = New LSGenericRepository(New DataModelDataContext())
    End Sub



    '
    ' GET: /Home/

    Public Function Index() As ActionResult
        Return View(_repository.List(Of Product)().ToList())
    End Function


    '
    ' GET: /Home/Create

    Public Function Create() As ActionResult
        Return View()
    End Function


    '
    ' POST: /Home/Create

    <AcceptVerbs(HttpVerbs.Post)> _
```

```
      Public Function Create(<Bind(Exclude:="Id")> ByVal productToCreate As Product)
➥As ActionResult
        Try
            _repository.Create(Of Product)(productToCreate)
            Return RedirectToAction("Index")
        Catch
            Return View()
        End Try
    End Function
```

```
End Class
```

The LSGenericRepository is created in the controller's constructor. You create an LSGenericRepository by passing a LINQ to SQL DataContext to the constructor for the LSGenericRepository class.

Extending the Generic Repository

The generic repository is meant to act only as a starting point. At some point, you need to add custom methods to the generic repository. The easiest way to extend the generic repository is to create two new types:

▶ IRepository—Create a custom interface that inherits from the IGenericRepository interface.

▶ Repository—Create a custom class that implements the IRepository interface and inherits from a GenericRepository class such as the EFGenericRepository or LSGenericRepository.

For example, imagine that you want to create a custom method named ProductCount() that returns a count of products in the database. You find it more intuitive to call the custom method than to call the generic method List<Product>().Count(). In that case, you can create the interface in Listing 5.12.

LISTING 5.12   IRepository.cs (C#)

```
using GenericRepository;


namespace EFMvcApplication.Models
{
    interface IRepository : IGenericRepository
    {
        int GetProductCount();
    }
}
```

LISTING 5.12   IRepository.vb (VB)

```vb
Imports GenericRepository


Public Interface IRepository
    Inherits IGenericRepository

    Function GetProductCount() As Integer

End Interface
```

Notice that the interface in Listing 5.12 inherits from the `IGenericRepository` interface. Any class that implements the `IRepository` interface must implement every method from the `IGenericRepository` interface.

The new repository class in Listing 5.13 inherits from the `EFGenericRepository` class. However, the new class includes a new method named `GetProductCount()`.

LISTING 5.13   Repository.cs (C#)

```csharp
using System.Data.Objects;
using System.Linq;
using GenericRepository;

namespace EFMvcApplication.Models
{
    public class Repository : EFGenericRepository, IRepository
    {
        public Repository(ObjectContext context)
            : base(context) { }


        #region IRepository Members

        public int GetProductCount()
        {
            return this.List<Product>().Count();
        }

        #endregion
    }
}
```

LISTING 5.13   Repository.vb (VB)

```vb
Imports GenericRepository
Imports System.Data.Objects

Public Class Repository
    Inherits EFGenericRepository
    Implements IRepository

    Sub New(ByVal context As ObjectContext)
        MyBase.New(context)
    End Sub

    Public Function GetProductCount() As Integer Implements
➥IRepository.GetProductCount
        Return Me.List(Of Product)().Count()
    End Function

End Class
```

After you create the IRepository and Repository types, you can use these types in your controllers in exactly the same way as you use the IGenericRepository and GenericRepository types. But now you are free to extend the generic repository as much as you please.

> **NOTE**
>
> Some people object to the idea of inheriting from a generic repository class because the repository class ends up exposing all sorts of methods that a developer should never call. For example, the repository would expose methods for updating tables that are intended as read-only lookup tables.
>
> If you are concerned about this issue then you can encapsulate the generic repository class within another class and selectively expose methods. That way, you can control exactly which generic methods get exposed to the world.

Testing Data Access

Normally, when you execute unit tests, you don't want to test code that interacts with an actual database. In other words, you want to avoid unit testing data access logic.

For unit tests to be useful, you need to execute them quickly. Unfortunately, accessing a database is one of the slowest operations that you can perform in a website. Therefore, you want to avoid interacting with a real database in your unit tests.

Instead of testing your data access logic, test all the business logic that interacts with the data access logic. For example, you definitely want to build unit tests for all the controller logic and all the validation logic in your application. The challenge is testing this business logic without testing the data access logic.

In this section, we discuss two approaches to overcoming this challenge. You learn how you can *mock* your repository and how you can *fake* your repository.

Testing with a Mock Repository

One approach to testing code that interacts with a repository is to mock the repository by using a Mock Object Framework such as Moq. You can use Moq to generate a mock class from any interface. For example, you can generate a mock generic repository from the IGenericRepository interface.

Consider the controller action in Listing 5.14. This action validates whether the product FirstName property has a value before creating the product in the database.

> **NOTE**
>
> We discuss validation in detail in Chapter 8, "Validating Form Data." We discuss Moq in Appendix C, "Using a Mock Object Framework."

LISTING 5.14   Controllers\HomeController.cs (C#)

```csharp
using System.Linq;
using System.Web.Mvc;
using EFMvcApplication.Models;
using GenericRepository;

namespace EFMvcApplication.Controllers
{
    public class HomeController : Controller
    {
        private IGenericRepository _repository;

        public HomeController()
            :this(new EFGenericRepository(new ToyStoreDBEntities())){}

        public HomeController(IGenericRepository repository)
        {
            _repository = repository;
        }
```

```csharp
//
// GET: /Home/

public ActionResult Index()
{
    return View(_repository.List<Product>().ToList());
}



//
// GET: /Home/Create

public ActionResult Create()
{
    return View();
}

//
// POST: /Home/Create

[AcceptVerbs(HttpVerbs.Post)]
public ActionResult Create([Bind(Exclude="Id")]Product productToCreate)
{
    if (productToCreate.Name.Trim().Length == 0)
    {
        ModelState.AddModelError("Name", "Product name is required.");
        return View();
    }
    try
    {
        _repository.Create<Product>(productToCreate);
        return RedirectToAction("Index");
    }
    catch
    {
        return View();
    }
}
```

LISTING 5.14   Controllers\HomeController.vb (VB)

```vb
Imports GenericRepository


Public Class HomeController
    Inherits Controller

    Private _repository As IGenericRepository

    Public Sub New()
        Me.New(New EFGenericRepository(New ToyStoreDBEntities()))
    End Sub

    Public Sub New(repository As IGenericRepository)
        _repository = repository
    End Sub


    '
    ' GET: /Home/

    Public Function Index() As ActionResult
        Return View(_repository.List(Of Product)().ToList())
    End Function


    '
    ' GET: /Home/Create

    Public Function Create() As ActionResult
        Return View()
    End Function

    '
    ' POST: /Home/Create

    <AcceptVerbs(HttpVerbs.Post)> _
    Public Function Create(<Bind(Exclude:="Id")> ByVal productToCreate As Product)
➥As ActionResult
        If productToCreate.Name.Trim().Length = 0 Then
            ModelState.AddModelError("Name", "Product name is required.")
            Return View()
        End If
        Try
            _repository.Create(Of Product)(productToCreate)
```

```
            Return RedirectToAction("Index")
        Catch
            Return View()
        End Try
    End Function

End Class
```

Imagine that you want to test the Create() action in Listing 5.14. You want to ensure that a validation error message is created when someone attempts to submit a new product without supplying a value for the Name property.

The unit test in Listing 5.15 contains two methods. The first method, named Initialize(), creates a mock generic repository. The Moq framework generates the mock generic repository from the IGenericRepository interface.

The second method, named NameIsRequired(), represents the unit test. This unit test creates an instance of the HomeController class with the mock generic repository. Next, the unit test invokes the Create() action and validates that an error message was, in fact, added to model state.

LISTING 5.15   Controllers\HomeControllerTestMock.cs (C#)

```csharp
using System;
using System.Web.Mvc;
using EFMvcApplication.Controllers;
using EFMvcApplication.Models;
using GenericRepository;
using Microsoft.VisualStudio.TestTools.UnitTesting;
using Moq;

namespace EFMvcApplication.Tests.Controllers
{
    [TestClass]
    public class HomeControllerTestMock
    {
        private Mock<IGenericRepository> _mockRepository;

        [TestInitialize]
        public void Initialize()
        {
            _mockRepository = new Mock<IGenericRepository>();
        }

        [TestMethod]
        public void NameIsRequired()
```

```csharp
        {
            // Arrange
            var controller = new HomeController(_mockRepository.Object);
            var productToCreate = new Product();
            productToCreate.Name = String.Empty;

            // Act
            var result = (ViewResult)controller.Create(productToCreate);

            // Assert
            var modelStateError = result.ViewData.ModelState
➡ ["Name"].Errors[0].ErrorMessage;
            Assert.AreEqual("Product name is required.", modelStateError);
        }
    }
}
```

LISTING 5.15   Controllers\HomeControllerTestMock.vb (VB)

```vbnet
Imports Microsoft.VisualStudio.TestTools.UnitTesting
Imports Moq
Imports System.Web.Mvc
Imports GenericRepository

<TestClass()> _
Public Class HomeControllerTestMock

    Private _mockRepository As Mock(Of IGenericRepository)

    <TestInitialize()> _
    Sub Initialize()
        _mockRepository = New Mock(Of IGenericRepository)()
    End Sub


    <TestMethod()> _
    Sub TestMethod1()
        ' Arrange
        Dim controller As New HomeController(_mockRepository.Object)
        Dim productToCreate As New Product()
        productToCreate.Name = String.Empty

        ' Act
        Dim result As ViewResult = controller.Create(productToCreate)
```

```
        ' Assert
        Dim modelStateError = result.ViewData.ModelState
➥("Name").Errors(0).ErrorMessage
        Assert.AreEqual("Product name is required.", modelStateError)
    End Sub

End Class
```

We are able to substitute the mock repository for the actual repository in our unit test because the Home controller uses dependency injection. We can take advantage of the second constructor that accepts any class that implements the IGenericRepository interface.

Testing with a Fake Generic Repository

When practicing test-driven development, you want your repository layer to behave just like a real repository layer in your tests. For example, if you create a new product by calling a repository method, you want to retrieve the new product by calling another repository method.

If you need to fake the behavior of the generic repository layer in a unit test, you can take advantage of the fake generic repository. The fake generic repository is an implementation of the IGenericRepository interface that works with a simple in-memory database.

For example, the unit test in Listing 5.16 verifies that when you invoke the List() action you can get back a product that you just created by invoking the Create() action.

LISTING 5.16   Controllers\HomeControllerTestFake.cs (C#)

```csharp
using System.Collections;
using System.Web.Mvc;
using EFMvcApplication.Controllers;
using EFMvcApplication.Models;
using GenericRepository;
using Microsoft.VisualStudio.TestTools.UnitTesting;

namespace EFMvcApplication.Tests.Controllers
{
    [TestClass]
    public class HomeControllerTestFake
    {
        IGenericRepository _fakeRepository;
        [TestInitialize]
        public void Initialize()
        {
            _fakeRepository = new FakeGenericRepository();
        }
```

```
[TestMethod]
public void CreateThenList()
{
    // Arrange
    var controller = new HomeController(_fakeRepository);
    var productToCreate = Product.CreateProduct(-1, "Test", "Test", 3.44m);

    // Act
    controller.Create(productToCreate);
    var results = (ViewResult)controller.Index();

    // Assert
    var products = (ICollection)results.ViewData.Model;
    CollectionAssert.Contains(products, productToCreate);
    }
  }
}
```

LISTING 5.16   Controllers\HomeControllerTestFake.vb (VB)

```
Imports Microsoft.VisualStudio.TestTools.UnitTesting
Imports GenericRepository
Imports System.Web.Mvc
Imports System.Collections

<TestClass()> _
Public Class HomeControllerTestFake

Private _fakeRepository As IGenericRepository

    <TestInitialize()> _
    Public Sub Initialize()
        _fakeRepository = New FakeGenericRepository()
    End Sub

    <TestMethod()> _
    Public Sub CreateThenList()
        ' Arrange
        Dim controller = New HomeController(_fakeRepository)
        Dim productToCreate = Product.CreateProduct(-1, "Test", "Test", 3.44D)

        ' Act
        controller.Create(productToCreate)
        Dim results = CType(controller.Index(), ViewResult)
```

```
    ' Assert
    Dim products = CType(results.ViewData.Model, ICollection)
    CollectionAssert.Contains(products, productToCreate)
  End Sub

End Class
```

Notice that a `FakeGenericRepository` class is created in the `Initialize()` method. The fake generic repository stores objects in memory instead of touching a real database server.

Summary

In this chapter, we concentrated on building data model classes. In the first section, you were provided with a brief introduction to the Microsoft Entity Framework. You learned how to perform basic database operations such as listing, creating, editing, and deleting database records.

Next, you learned how to implement the Repository software design pattern. You learned how to move database logic from your controllers into a separate repository layer. Moving your database logic into a repository layer makes your application more resilient to change.

We also discussed how you can create a generic repository layer, so you don't need to re-implement the same data access logic every time you create a new ASP.NET MVC project. You learned how to use the generic repository layer with both the Microsoft Entity Framework and Microsoft LINQ to SQL.

Finally, you learned how to unit test code that interacts with a repository layer. We discussed how you can mock a repository layer by taking advantage of the Moq Mock Object Framework. You also learned how to fake a repository layer by taking advantage of the `FakeGenericRepository` class.

CHAPTER 6

Understanding HTML Helpers

You use HTML helpers in a view to render HTML content. An HTML helper, in most cases, is just a method that returns a string.

You can build an entire ASP.NET MVC application without using a single HTML helper; however, HTML helpers make your life as a developer easier. By taking advantage of helpers, you can build your views with far less work.

In this chapter, you learn about the standard HTML helpers included with the ASP.NET MVC framework. You learn how to use the standard helpers to render HTML links and HTML form elements.

You also learn how to create custom helpers. We discuss the utility classes included in the ASP.NET framework that make it easier to build custom helpers. You learn how to work with the TagBuilder and the HtmlTextWriter classes.

Next, we tackle building a more complicated HTML helper: We build a DataGrid helper. The DataGrid helper enables you to easily display database records in an HTML table. It also supports paging and sorting.

Finally, we end this chapter with a discussion of how you can build unit tests for your custom HTML helpers.

> **NOTE**
>
> In the ASP.NET MVC world, HTML helpers are the equivalent of ASP.NET Web Form controls. Like a Web Form control, an HTML helper enables you to encapsulate the rendering of HTML. However, unlike a Web Form control, HTML helpers are extremely lightweight. For example, an HTML helper does not have an event model and does not use view state.

Using the Standard HTML Helpers

The ASP.NET MVC framework includes a standard set of helpers that you can use to render the most common types of HTML elements. For example, you can use the standard set of helpers to render HTML links and HTML text boxes.

Rendering Links

The easiest way to render an HTML link in a view is to use the `HTML.ActionLink()` helper. The `Html.ActionLink()` does not link to a view. Instead, you use the `Html.ActionLink()` helper to create a link to a controller action.

For example, the view in Listing 6.1 includes a link to an action named `About` (see Figure 6.1).

FIGURE 6.1   Link rendered by `Html.ActionLink()` helper

LISTING 6.1   Views\Home\About.aspx

```
<%@ Page Language="C#" MasterPageFile="~/Views/Shared/Site.Master"
➥Inherits="System.Web.Mvc.ViewPage" %>
<asp:Content ID="indexContent" ContentPlaceHolderID="MainContent" runat="server">
    <p>
        To learn more about this website, click the following link:
        <%= Html.ActionLink("About this Website", "About" ) %>
    </p>
</asp:Content>
```

In Listing 6.1, the first parameter passed to the `Html.ActionLink()` represents the link text, and the second parameter represents the name of the controller action. This `Html.ActionLink()` helper renders the following HTML:

```
<a href="/Home/About">About this Website</a>
```

The `Html.ActionLink()` helper has several overloads and supports several parameters:

- `linkText`—The label for the link.
- `actionName`—The action that is the target of the link.
- `routeValues`—The set of values passed to the action.
- `controllerName`—The controller that is the target of the link.
- `htmlAttributes`—The set of HTML attributes to add to the link.
- `protocol`—The protocol for the link (for example, HTTPS).
- `hostname`—The hostname for the link (for example, www.MyWebsite.com).
- `fragment`—The fragment (anchor target) for the link. For example, to link to a div in a view with an id of news, you would specify news for the fragment.

Notice that you can pass route values from an `Html.ActionLink()` to a controller action. For example, you might need to pass the Id of a database record that you want to edit. Here's how you pass an Id parameter to the `Edit()` action:

(C#)

```
<%= Html.ActionLink("Edit Record", "Edit", new {Id=3})
```

(VB)

```
<%= Html.ActionLink("Edit Record", "Edit", New With {.Id=3})%>
```

When this `Html.ActionLink()` is rendered to the browser, the following link is created:

```
<a href="/Home/Edit/3">Edit Record</a>
```

NOTE

Route values are URL encoded automatically. For example, the string `"Hello World!"` is encoded to `"Hello%20World!"`.

Rendering Image Links

Unfortunately, you can't use the `Html.ActionLink()` helper to render an image link. Because the `Html.ActionLink()` helper HTML encodes its link text automatically, you cannot pass an `<img>` tag to this method and expect the tag to render as an image.

Instead, you need to use the `Url.Action()` helper to generate the proper link. Here's how you can generate a delete link with an image:

```
<a href="<%= Url.Action("Delete") %>"><img src="../../Content/Delete.png"
➥alt="Delete" style="border:0px" /></a>
```

The `Url.Action()` helper supports a set of parameters that are similar to those supported by the `Html.ActionLink()` helper.

Rendering Form Elements

There are several HTML helpers that you can use to render HTML form elements:

▶ `BeginForm()`

▶ `CheckBox()`

▶ `DropDownList()`

▶ `EndForm()`

▶ `Hidden()`

▶ `ListBox()`

▶ `Password()`

▶ `RadioButton()`

▶ `TextArea()`

▶ `TextBox()`

The view in Listing 6.2 illustrates how you can use several of these HTML helpers. The view renders an HTML page with a simple user registration form (see Figure 6.2).

LISTING 6.2   Views\Customer\Register.aspx (C#)

```
<%@ Page Title="" Language="C#" MasterPageFile="~/Views/Shared/Site.Master"
➥Inherits="System.Web.Mvc.ViewPage<MvcApplication1.Models.Customer>" %>
<asp:Content ID="Content2" ContentPlaceHolderID="MainContent" runat="server">

    <%= Html.ValidationSummary("Create was unsuccessful. Please correct the errors
➥and try again.") %>

    <% using (Html.BeginForm()) {%>

        <fieldset>
            <legend>Register</legend>
            <p>
                <label for="FirstName">First Name:</label>
                <%= Html.TextBox("FirstName") %>
                <%= Html.ValidationMessage("FirstName", "*") %>
```

```
        </p>
        <p>
            <label for="LastName">Last Name:</label>
            <%= Html.TextBox("LastName") %>
            <%= Html.ValidationMessage("LastName", "*") %>
        </p>
        <p>
            <label for="Password">Password:</label>
            <%= Html.Password("Password") %>
            <%= Html.ValidationMessage("Password", "*") %>
        </p>
        <p>
            <label for="Password">Confirm Password:</label>
            <%= Html.Password("ConfirmPassword") %>
            <%= Html.ValidationMessage("ConfirmPassword", "*") %>
        </p>
        <p>
            <label for="Profile">Profile:</label>
            <%= Html.TextArea("Profile", new {cols=60, rows=10})%>
        </p>
        <p>
            <%= Html.CheckBox("ReceiveNewsletter") %>
            <label for="ReceiveNewsletter" style="display:inline">Receive
➥Newsletter?</label>
        </p>
        <p>
            <input type="submit" value="Register" />
        </p>
    </fieldset>

    <% } %>

</asp:Content>
```

FIGURE 6.2   The Register page

LISTING 6.2   Views\Customer\Register.aspx (VB)

```
<%@ Page Title="" Language="VB" MasterPageFile="~/Views/Shared/Site.Master"
➡Inherits="System.Web.Mvc.ViewPage(Of MvcApplication1.MvcApplication1.Models.
➡Customer)" %>
<asp:Content ID="Content2" ContentPlaceHolderID="MainContent" runat="server">

    <%= Html.ValidationSummary("Create was unsuccessful. Please correct the errors
➡and try again.") %>

    <% Using Html.BeginForm() %>

        <fieldset>
            <legend>Register</legend>
            <p>
                <label for="FirstName">First Name:</label>
                <%= Html.TextBox("FirstName") %>
                <%= Html.ValidationMessage("FirstName", "*") %>
            </p>
```

```
        <p>
            <label for="LastName">Last Name:</label>
            <%= Html.TextBox("LastName") %>
            <%= Html.ValidationMessage("LastName", "*") %>
        </p>
        <p>
            <label for="Password">Password:</label>
            <%= Html.Password("Password") %>
            <%= Html.ValidationMessage("Password", "*") %>
        </p>
        <p>
            <label for="Password">Confirm Password:</label>
            <%= Html.Password("ConfirmPassword") %>
            <%= Html.ValidationMessage("ConfirmPassword", "*") %>
        </p>
        <p>
            <label for="Profile">Profile:</label>
            <%= Html.TextArea("Profile", new With {.cols=60, .rows=10})%>
        </p>
        <p>
            <%= Html.CheckBox("ReceiveNewsletter") %>
            <label for="ReceiveNewsletter" style="display:inline">Receive
➥Newsletter?</label>
        </p>
        <p>
            <input type="submit" value="Register" />
        </p>
    </fieldset>

    <% End Using %>

</asp:Content>
```

You can try the page in Listing 6.2 by entering the address Customer/Register in the address bar of your web browser.

It is worth emphasizing, once again, that these form helpers are simply rendering strings. For example, the Html.TextBox() helper renders a string that includes an "<input>" tag. If you prefer, you can create the view in Listing 6.2 without using any of these helpers.

NOTE

You might have noticed that Listing 6.2 includes validation helpers. We discuss the validation helpers—Html.ValidationMessage() and Html.ValidationSummary—in Chapter 8, "Validating Form Data."

Rendering a Form

In Listing 6.2, the opening and closing <form> tags are created with a using statement. The opening and closing tags are created like this:

(C#)

```
<% using (Html.BeginForm()) {%>
    ... Form Contents ...
<% } %>
```

(VB)

```
<% Using Html.BeginForm() %>
    ... Form Contents ...
<% End Using %>
```

The advantage of opening and closing a <form> tag with a using statement is that you won't accidentally forget to close the <form> tag.

However, if you find this syntax confusing or otherwise disagreeable, you don't need to use a using statement. Instead, you can open the <form> tag with Html.BeginForm() and close the <form> with Html.EndForm() like this:

(C#)

```
<% Html.BeginForm(); %>
    ... Form Contents ...
<% Html.EndForm(); %>
```

(VB)

```
<% Html.BeginForm() %>
    ... Form Contents ...
<% Html.EndForm() %>
```

By default, the Html.BeginForm() method renders a form that posts back to the same controller action. In other words, if you retrieve the view by invoking the Customer controller Details() action, the Html.BeginForm() renders a <form> tag that looks like this:

```
<form action="/Customer/Details" method="post">
</form>
```

If you want to post to another action, or to modify any other property of the <form> tag, you can call the Html.BeginForm() helper with one or more parameters. The Html.BeginForm() helper accepts the following parameters:

▶ routeValues—The set of values passed to the action.

▶ actionName—The action that is the target of the form post.

▶ controllerName—The controller that is the target of the form post.

▶ Method—The HTTP method of the form post. The possible values are restricted to POST and GET. (You can't use other HTTP methods within HTML, you must use JavaScript.)

▶ htmlAttributes—The set of HTML attributes to add to the form.

Rendering a Drop-Down List

You can use the Html.DropDownList() helper to render a set of database records in an HTML <select> tag. You represent the set of database records with the SelectList class.

For example, the Index() action in Listing 6.3 creates an instance of the SelectList class that represents all the customers from the Customers database table. You can pass the following parameters to the constructor for a SelectList when creating a new SelectList:

▶ items—The items represented by the SelectList

▶ dataValueField—The name of the property to associate with each item in the SelectList as the value of the item

▶ dataTextField—The name of the property to display for each item in the SelectList as the label of the item

▶ selectedValue—The item to select in the SelectList

In Listing 6.3, the SelectList is assigned to ViewData with the name CustomerId.

LISTING 6.3   Controllers\CustomerController.cs (C#)

```csharp
public ActionResult Index()
{
    ViewData["CustomerId"] = new SelectList(_entities.CustomerSet.ToList(), "Id",
➥"LastName");
    return View();
}
```

LISTING 6.3   Controllers\CustomerController.vb (VB)

```vb
Function Index() As ActionResult
    ViewData("CustomerId") = New SelectList(_entities.CustomerSet.ToList(), "Id",
➥"LastName")
    Return View()
End Function
```

In a view, you can display a SelectList by calling the Html.DropDownList() helper with the name of the SelectList. The view in Listing 6.4 displays the CustomerId SelectList (see Figure 6.3).

FIGURE 6.3   Displaying the CustomerList

LISTING 6.4   Views\Customer\Index.aspx

```
<%@ Page Title="" Language="C#" MasterPageFile="~/Views/Shared/Site.Master"
➥Inherits="System.Web.Mvc.ViewPage" %>
<asp:Content ID="Content2" ContentPlaceHolderID="MainContent" runat="server">

    <p>
    <%= Html.DropDownList("CustomerId") %>
    </p>

</asp:Content>
```

The view in Listing 6.4 renders the following HTML `<select>` tag:

```
<select id="CustomerId" name="CustomerId">
 <option value="1">Walther</option>
 <option value="2">Henderson</option>
 <option value="3">Smith</option>
</select
```

The `Html.DropDownList()` helper also supports an `optionLabel` parameter. You can use this parameter to create a default option at the top of the drop-down list (see Figure 6.4). You add an `optionLabel` like this:

```
<%= Html.DropDownList("CustomerId", "Select a Customer") %>
```

If a user submits a form with the option label selected, an empty string is submitted to the server.

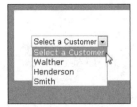

FIGURE 6.4   Displaying an option label

Encoding HTML Content

You should always HTML encode user-submitted content. Otherwise, an evil hacker can initiate a JavaScript injection attack and, potentially, steal sensitive information from your users, such as passwords and credit card numbers.

In a JavaScript injection attack, a hacker submits a JavaScript script when completing an HTML form. When the value of the form field is redisplayed, the script steals information from the page and sends the information to the hacker.

For example, because users typically select their own usernames, you should always HTML encode usernames that you display in a view like this:

```
<%= Html.Encode(UserName) %>
```

HTML encoding replaces characters with special meaning in an HTML document with safe characters:

- ▶ < becomes <
- ▶ > becomes >
- ▶ " becomes "
- ▶ & becomes &

Imagine that a hacker submits the following script as the value of a form field:

```
<script>alert('Boom!')</script>
```

When this script is HTML-encoded, the script no longer executes. The script gets encoded into the harmless string:

```
&lt;script&gt;alert('Boom!')&lt;/script&gt;
```

> **NOTE**
>
> The ASP.NET MVC framework prevents a hacker from submitting a form that contains suspicious characters automatically through a feature called request validation. We discussed request validation in Chapter 4, "Understanding Views."

Using Antiforgery Tokens

There is a particular type of JavaScript injection attack that is called a *cross-site request forgery* (CSRF) attack. In a CSRF attack, a hacker takes advantage of the fact that you are logged in to one website to steal or modify your information at another website.

> **NOTE**
>
> To learn more about CSRF attacks, see the Wikipedia entry at http://en.wikipedia.org/wiki/Csrf. The example discussed in this section is based on the example described in the Wikipedia entry.

For example, imagine that you have an online bank account. The bank website identifies and authenticates you with a cookie. Now, imagine that you visit a forums website. This forums website enables users to post messages that contain images. An evil hacker has posted an image to the forums that looks like this:

```
<img src="http://www.BigBank.com/withdraw?amount=9999" />
```

Notice that the src attribute of this image tag points to a URL at the bank website.

When you view this message in your browser, $9,999 dollars is withdrawn from your bank account. The hacker can withdraw money from your bank account because the bank website uses a browser cookie to identify you. The hacker has hijacked your browser.

If you create the bank website, you can prevent a CSRF attack by using the Html.AntiForgeryToken() helper. For example, the view in Listing 6.5 uses the Html.AntiForgeryToken() helper.

LISTING 6.5   Views\Bank\Withdraw.aspx (C#)

```
<%@ Page Title="" Language="C#" MasterPageFile="~/Views/Shared/Site.Master"
➥Inherits="System.Web.Mvc.ViewPage" %>
<asp:Content ID="Content2" ContentPlaceHolderID="MainContent" runat="server">

    <h2>Withdraw</h2>

    <% using (Html.BeginForm()) {%>

        <%= Html.AntiForgeryToken() %>

        <fieldset>
            <legend>Fields</legend>
            <p>
                <label for="Amount">Amount:</label>
                <%= Html.TextBox("Amount") %>
            </p>
            <p>
                <input type="submit" value="Withdraw" />
            </p>
        </fieldset>

    <% } %>

</asp:Content>
```

LISTING 6.5   Views\Bank\Withdraw.aspx (VB)

```
<%@ Page Title="" Language="VB" MasterPageFile="~/Views/Shared/Site.Master"
➥Inherits="System.Web.Mvc.ViewPage" %>
<asp:Content ID="Content2" ContentPlaceHolderID="MainContent" runat="server">
```

```
    <h2>Withdraw</h2>

    <% Using Html.BeginForm() %>

        <%= Html.AntiForgeryToken() %>

        <fieldset>
            <legend>Fields</legend>
            <p>
                <label for="Amount">Amount:</label>
                <%= Html.TextBox("Amount") %>
            </p>
            <p>
                <input type="submit" value="Withdraw" />
            </p>
        </fieldset>

    <% End Using %>

</asp:Content>
```

This helper creates a hidden input field that represents a cryptographically strong random value. Each time you request the view, you get a different random value in a hidden field that looks like this:

```
<input
  name="__RequestVerificationToken"
  type="hidden"
  value="6tbg3PWU9oAD3bhw6jZwxrYRyWPhKede87K/PFgaw
        6MI3huvHgpjlCcPzDzrTkn8" />
```

The helper also creates a cookie that represents the random value. The value in the cookie is compared against the value in the hidden form field to determine whether a CSRF attack is being performed.

The Html.AntiForgeryToken() helper accepts the following optional parameters:

▶ salt—Enables you to add a cryptographic salt to the random value to increase the security of the antiforgery token.

▶ domain—The domain associated with the antiforgery cookie. The cookie is sent only when requests originate from this domain.

▶ path—The virtual path associated with the antiforgery cookie. The cookie is sent only when requests originate from this path.

Generating the random value with the Html.AntiForgeryToken() helper is only half the story. To prevent CSRF attacks, you also must add a special attribute to the controller action that accepts the HTML form post. The Withdraw() controller action in Listing 6.6 is decorated with a ValidateAntiForgeryToken attribute.

LISTING 6.6   Controllers\BankController.cs (C#)

```csharp
using System.Web.Mvc;

namespace MvcApplication1.Controllers
{
    public class BankController : Controller
    {
        //
        // GET: /Bank/Withdraw

        public ActionResult Withdraw()
        {
            return View();
        }

        //
        // POST: /Bank/Withdraw
        [AcceptVerbs(HttpVerbs.Post)]
        [ValidateAntiForgeryToken]
        public ActionResult Withdraw(decimal amount)
        {
            // Perform withdrawal
            return View();
        }

    }
}
```

LISTING 6.6   Controllers\BankController.vb (VB)

```vbnet
Public Class BankController
    Inherits Controller
    '
    ' GET: /Bank/Withdraw

    Public Function Withdraw() As ActionResult
        Return View()
    End Function

    '
    ' POST: /Bank/Withdraw
    <AcceptVerbs(HttpVerbs.Post), ValidateAntiForgeryToken> _
    Public Function Withdraw(ByVal amount As Decimal) As ActionResult
```

```
        ' Perform withdrawal
        Return View()
    End Function

End Class
```

The `ValidateAntiForgeryToken` attribute compares the hidden form field to the cookie. If they don't match, the attribute throws the exception in Figure 6.5.

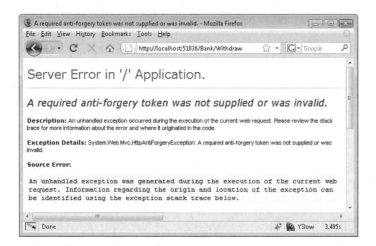

FIGURE 6.5   Antiforgery validation failure

WARNING

Visitors to your website must have cookies enabled or they get an AntiForgery exception when posting to a controller action that is decorated with the `ValidateAntiForgeryToken` attribute.

Creating Custom HTML Helpers

The ASP.NET MVC framework ships with a limited number of HTML helpers. The members of the ASP.NET MVC team identified the most common scenarios in which you would need a helper and focused on creating helpers for these scenarios.

Fortunately, creating new HTML helpers is an easy process. You create a new HTML helper by creating an extension method on the `HtmlHelper` class. For example, Listing 6.7 contains a new `Html.SubmitButton()` helper that renders an HTML form submit button.

NOTE

To learn about extension methods, see Appendix A, "C# and VB.NET Language Features."

LISTING 6.7   Helpers\SubmitButtonHelper.cs (C#)

```csharp
using System;
using System.Web.Mvc;

namespace Helpers
{
    public static class SubmitButtonHelper
    {
        /// <summary>
        /// Renders an HTML form submit button
        /// </summary>
        public static string SubmitButton(this HtmlHelper helper, string buttonText)
        {
            return String.Format("<input type=\"submit\" value=\"{0}\" />",
➥buttonText);
        }

    }
}
```

LISTING 6.7   Helpers\SubmitButtonHelper.cs (VB)

```vb
Public Module SubmitButtonHelper

    ''' <summary>
    ''' Renders an HTML form submit button
    ''' </summary>
    <System.Runtime.CompilerServices.Extension> _
    Function SubmitButton(ByVal helper As HtmlHelper, ByVal buttonText As String)
➥As String
        Return String.Format("<input type=""submit"" value=""{0}"" />", buttonText)
    End Function

End Module
```

Listing 6.7 contains an extension method named SubmitButton(). The SubmitButton() helper simply returns a string that represents an HTML <input type="submit" /> tag.

Because the SubmitButton() method extends the HtmlHelper class, this method appears as a method of the HtmlHelper class in Intellisense (see Figure 6.6).

The view in Listing 6.8 uses the new Html.SubmitButton() helper to render the submit button for a form. Make sure that you import the namespace associated with your helper, or the helper won't appear in Intellisense. The correct namespace is imported in Listing 6.8 with the help of the `<%@ Import %>` directive.

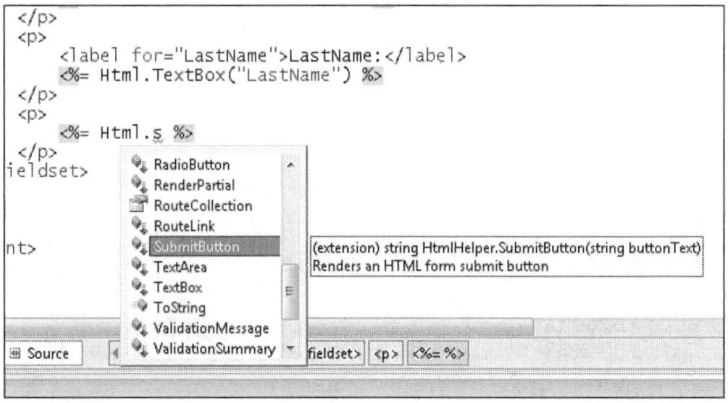

FIGURE 6.6   `Html.SubmitButton()` HTML helper included in Intellisense

> **NOTE**
>
> As an alternative to registering a namespace for a particular view with the `<%@ Import %>` directive, you can register a namespace for an entire application in the system.web.pages.namespaces section of the web configuration (web.config) file.

LISTING 6.8   Views\Customer\Create.aspx

```
<%@ Page Title="" Language="C#" MasterPageFile="~/Views/Shared/Site.Master"
➥Inherits="System.Web.Mvc.ViewPage<MvcApplication1.Models.Customer>" %>
<%@ Import Namespace="Helpers" %>
<asp:Content ID="Content2" ContentPlaceHolderID="MainContent" runat="server">

    <% using (Html.BeginForm()) {%>

        <fieldset>
            <legend>Fields</legend>
            <p>
                <label for="FirstName">FirstName:</label>
                <%= Html.TextBox("FirstName") %>
            </p>
            <p>
                <label for="LastName">LastName:</label>
                <%= Html.TextBox("LastName") %>
```

```
        </p>
        <p>
            <%= Html.SubmitButton("Create Customer") %>
        </p>
    </fieldset>

<% } %>

</asp:Content>
```

NOTE

All of the standard HTML helpers, such as the `Html.TextBox()` helper, are also implemented as extension methods. This means that you can swap the standard set of helpers for a custom set of helpers if you don't like the helpers that the ASP.NET team created.

Using the TagBuilder Class

The `TagBuilder` class is a utility class included in the ASP.NET MVC framework that you can use when building HTML helpers. The `TagBuilder` class, as it name suggests, makes it easier to build HTML tags.

Here's a list of the methods of the `TagBuilder` class:

▶ `AddCssClass()`—Enables you to add a new `class=""` attribute to a tag.

▶ `GenerateId()`—Enables you to add an `id` attribute to a tag. This method automatically replaces periods in the `id`. (By default, periods are replaced by underscores.)

▶ `MergeAttribute()`—Enables you to add attributes to a tag. There are multiple overloads of this method.

▶ `SetInnerText()`—Enables you to set the inner text of the tag. The inner text is HTML-encoded automatically.

▶ `ToString()`—Enables you to render the tag. You can specify whether you want to create a normal tag, a start tag, an end tag, or a self-closing tag.

The `TagBuilder` class has four important properties:

▶ `Attributes`—Represents all the attributes of the tag.

▶ `IdAttributeDotReplacement`—Represents the character used by the `GenerateId()` method to replace periods. (The default is an underscore.)

▶ `InnerHTML`—Represents the inner contents of the tag. Assigning a string to this property *does not* HTML-encode the string.

▶ `TagName`—Represents the name of the tag.

These methods and properties give you all the basic methods and properties that you need to build up an HTML tag. You don't actually need to use the `TagBuilder` class. You could use a `StringBuilder` class instead. However, the `TagBuilder` class makes your life a little easier.

The helper in Listing 6.9, the `Html.ImageLink()` helper, is created with a `TagBuilder`. The `Html.ImageLink()` helper renders an image link.

LISTING 6.9   Helpers\ImageLinkHelper.cs (C#)

```csharp
using System.Web.Mvc;
using System.Web.Routing;

namespace Helpers
{
    public static class ImageLinkHelper
    {
        public static string ImageLink(this HtmlHelper helper, string actionName,
➥string imageUrl, string alternateText)
        {
            return ImageLink(helper, actionName, imageUrl, alternateText, null,
➥null, null);
        }

        public static string ImageLink(this HtmlHelper helper, string actionName,
➥string imageUrl, string alternateText, object routeValues)
        {
            return ImageLink(helper, actionName, imageUrl, alternateText,
➥routeValues, null, null);
        }

        public static string ImageLink(this HtmlHelper helper, string actionName,
➥string imageUrl, string alternateText, object routeValues, object
➥linkHtmlAttributes, object imageHtmlAttributes)
        {
            var urlHelper = new UrlHelper(helper.ViewContext.RequestContext);
            var url = urlHelper.Action(actionName, routeValues);

            // Create link
            var linkTagBuilder = new TagBuilder("a");
            linkTagBuilder.MergeAttribute("href", url);
            linkTagBuilder.MergeAttributes(new RouteValueDictionary
➥(linkHtmlAttributes));

            // Create image
            var imageTagBuilder = new TagBuilder("img");
```

```
            imageTagBuilder.MergeAttribute("src", urlHelper.Content(imageUrl));
            imageTagBuilder.MergeAttribute("alt", urlHelper.Encode(alternateText));
            imageTagBuilder.MergeAttributes(new RouteValueDictionary
➥(imageHtmlAttributes));

            // Add image to link
            linkTagBuilder.InnerHtml = imageTagBuilder.ToString
➥(TagRenderMode.SelfClosing);

            return linkTagBuilder.ToString();
        }
    }
}
```

LISTING 6.9   Helpers\ImageLinkHelper.vb (C#)

```
Public Module ImageLinkHelper


    <System.Runtime.CompilerServices.Extension> _
    Function ImageLink(ByVal helper As HtmlHelper, ByVal actionName As String,
➥ByVal imageUrl As String, ByVal alternateText As String) As String
            Return ImageLink(helper, actionName, imageUrl, alternateText, Nothing,
➥Nothing, Nothing)
    End Function


    <System.Runtime.CompilerServices.Extension> _
    Function ImageLink(ByVal helper As HtmlHelper, ByVal actionName As String,
➥ByVal imageUrl As String, ByVal alternateText As String, ByVal routeValues As
➥Object) As String
            Return ImageLink(helper, actionName, imageUrl, alternateText, routeValues,
➥Nothing, Nothing)
    End Function


    <System.Runtime.CompilerServices.Extension> _
    Function ImageLink(ByVal helper As HtmlHelper, ByVal actionName As String, ByVal
➥imageUrl As String, ByVal alternateText As String, ByVal routeValues As Object,
➥ByVal linkHtmlAttributes As Object, ByVal imageHtmlAttributes As Object) As String
            Dim urlHelper = New UrlHelper(helper.ViewContext.RequestContext)
            Dim url = urlHelper.Action(actionName, routeValues)

        ' Create link
        Dim linkTagBuilder = New TagBuilder("a")
        linkTagBuilder.MergeAttribute("href", url)
```

```
          linkTagBuilder.MergeAttributes(New RouteValueDictionary
➥(linkHtmlAttributes))

          ' Create image
          Dim imageTagBuilder = New TagBuilder("img")
          imageTagBuilder.MergeAttribute("src", urlHelper.Content(imageUrl))
          imageTagBuilder.MergeAttribute("alt", urlHelper.Encode(alternateText))
          imageTagBuilder.MergeAttributes(New RouteValueDictionary
➥(imageHtmlAttributes))

          ' Add image to links
          linkTagBuilder.InnerHtml = imageTagBuilder.ToString
➥(TagRenderMode.SelfClosing)

          Return linkTagBuilder.ToString()
     End Function
End Module
```

The Html.ImageLink() helper in Listing 6.9 has three overloads. The helper accepts the following parameters:

- ▶ actionName—The controller action to invoke
- ▶ imageUrl—The URL of the image to display
- ▶ alternateText—The alt text to display for the image
- ▶ routeValues—The set of route values to pass to the controller action
- ▶ linkHtmlAttributes—The set of HTML attributes to apply to the link
- ▶ imageHtmlAttribute—The set of HTML attributes to apply to the image

For example, you can render a delete link by calling the Html.ImageLink() helper like this:

(C#)

```
<%= Html.ImageLink("Delete", "~/Content/Delete.png", "Delete Account", new
➥{AccountId=2}, null, new {border=0}) %>
```

(VB)

```
<%= Html.ImageLink("Delete", "~/Content/Delete.png", "Delete Account", New With
➥{.AccountId=2}, Nothing, New With {.border=0}) %>
```

Two instances of the TagBuilder class are used in Listing 6.9. The first TagBuilder builds up the <a> link tag. The second TagBuilder builds up the <img> image tag.

Notice that an instance of the UrlHelper class is created. Two methods of this class are called. First, the UrlHelper.Action() method generates the link to the controller action.

Second, the UrlHelper.Content() method converts an application relative path into a full relative path. For example, if your application is named MyApplication, the UrlHelper.Content() method would convert the application relative path "~/Content/Delete.png" into the relative path "/MyApplication/Content/Delete.png".

Using the `HtmlTextWriter` Class

As an alternative to using the TagBuilder class to build up HTML content in an HTML helper, you can use the HtmlTextWriter class. Like the TagBuilder class, the HtmlTextWriter class has specialized methods for building up a string of HTML.

Here is a list of some of the more interesting methods of the HtmlTextWriter class (this is not a comprehensive list):

- ▶ AddAttribute()—Adds an HTML attribute. When RenderBeginTag() is called, this attribute is added to the tag.

- ▶ AddStyleAttribute()—Adds a style attribute. When RenderBeginTag() is called, this style attribute is added to the tag.

- ▶ RenderBeginTag()—Renders an opening HTML tag to the output stream.

- ▶ RenderEndTag()—Closes the last tag opened with RenderBeginTag().

- ▶ Write()—Writes text to the output stream.

- ▶ WriteLine()—Writes a new line to the output stream (good for keeping your HTML readable when you do a browser View Source).

For example, the HTML helper in Listing 6.10 uses the HtmlTextWriter to create a bulleted list.

LISTING 6.10   Helpers\BulletedListHelper.cs (C#)

```csharp
using System;
using System.Collections;
using System.IO;
using System.Web.Mvc;
using System.Web.UI;

namespace Helpers
{
    public static class BulletedListHelper
    {
        public static string BulletedList(this HtmlHelper helper, string name)
        {
            var items = helper.ViewData.Eval(name) as IEnumerable;
            if (items == null)
```

```
                throw new NullReferenceException("Cannot find " + name + " in
➥view data");

            var writer = new HtmlTextWriter(new StringWriter());

            // Open UL
            writer.RenderBeginTag(HtmlTextWriterTag.Ul);
            foreach (var item in items)
            {
                writer.RenderBeginTag(HtmlTextWriterTag.Li);
                writer.Write(helper.Encode(item));
                writer.RenderEndTag();
                writer.WriteLine();
            }
            // Close UL
            writer.RenderEndTag();

            // Return the HTML string
            return writer.InnerWriter.ToString();
        }
    }

}
```

LISTING 6.10   Helpers\BulletedListHelper.vb (VB)

```
Imports System.IO

Public Module BulletedListHelper

    <System.Runtime.CompilerServices.Extension()> _
    Function BulletedList(ByVal helper As HtmlHelper, ByVal name As String) As String
        Dim items As IEnumerable = helper.ViewData.Eval(name)
        If items Is Nothing Then
            Throw New NullReferenceException("Cannot find " & name & " in view data")
        End If

        Dim writer = New HtmlTextWriter(New StringWriter())

        ' Open UL
        writer.RenderBeginTag(HtmlTextWriterTag.Ul)
        For Each item In items
            writer.RenderBeginTag(HtmlTextWriterTag.Li)
            writer.Write(helper.Encode(item))
```

```
        writer.RenderEndTag()
        writer.WriteLine()
    Next item
    ' Close UL
    writer.RenderEndTag()

    ' Return the HTML string
    Return writer.InnerWriter.ToString()
    End Function
End Module
```

The list of customers is retrieved from view state with the help of the `ViewData.Eval()` method. If you call `ViewData.Eval("Customers")`, the method attempts to retrieve an item from the view data dictionary named `Customers`. However, if the `Customers` item cannot be retrieved from the view data dictionary, the method attempts to retrieve the value of a property with the name `Customers` from the view data model. (The view data dictionary takes precedence over the view data model.)

The `HtmlTextWriter` class renders the HTML `<ul>` and `<li>` tags needed to create the bulleted list. Each item from the items collection is rendered into the list.

You can call the `Html.BulletedList()` helper in a view like this:

```
<%= Html.BulletedList("Customers") %>
```

You can add the list of customers to view data with the controller action in Listing 6.11.

LISTING 6.11   Controllers\CustomerController.cs (C#)

```
public ActionResult List()
{
    ViewData["Customers"] = from c in _entities.CustomerSet
                            select c.LastName;
    return View();
}
```

LISTING 6.11   Controllers\CustomerController.vb (VB)

```
Function List() As ActionResult
    ViewData("Customers") = From c In _entities.CustomerSet _
                           Select c.LastName
    Return View()
End Function
```

When you invoke the `List()` action, a list of customer last names are added to view state. When you call the `Html.BulletedList()` helper method, you get the bulleted list displayed in Figure 6.7.

All Customers

- Walther
- Johnson
- Smith

FIGURE 6.7   Using the `Html.BulletedList` HTML helper

There are multiple ways that you can build up HTML content within an HTML helper. You can use the `TagBuilder` class, the `HtmlTextWriter` class, or even the `StringBuilder` class. The choice is entirely a matter of preference.

Creating a `DataGrid` Helper

In this section, we tackle a more complicated HTML helper: We build an `Html.DataGrid()` helper that renders a list of database records in an HTML table. We start with the basics, and then we add sorting and paging to our `Html.DataGrid()` helper.

> **NOTE**
>
> In this section, we create multiple versions of the same `DataGrid` helper. To prevent conflicts, I commented out every version except the final version in the source code that accompanies this book. To use the DataGridHelperBasic version of the `DataGrid` helper, you need to uncomment the contents of the DataGridHelperBasic file and add comments to the DataGridHelperPaging file.

The basic `Html.DataGrid()` helper is contained in Listing 6.12.

LISTING 6.12   Helpers\DataGridHelperBasic.cs (C#)

```csharp
using System;
using System.Collections.Generic;
using System.IO;
```

```
using System.Linq;
using System.Web.Mvc;
using System.Web.UI;

namespace Helpers
{

    public static class DataGridHelper
    {
        public static string DataGrid<T>(this HtmlHelper helper)
        {
            return DataGrid<T>(helper, null, null);
        }

        public static string DataGrid<T>(this HtmlHelper helper, object data)
        {
            return DataGrid<T>(helper, data, null);
        }

        public static string DataGrid<T>(this HtmlHelper helper, object data,
➥string[] columns)
        {
            // Get items
            var items = (IEnumerable<T>)data;
            if (items == null)
                items = (IEnumerable<T>)helper.ViewData.Model;

            // Get column names
            if (columns == null)
                columns = typeof(T).GetProperties().Select(p => p.Name).ToArray();

            // Create HtmlTextWriter
            var writer = new HtmlTextWriter(new StringWriter());

            // Open table tag
            writer.RenderBeginTag(HtmlTextWriterTag.Table);

            // Render table header
            writer.RenderBeginTag(HtmlTextWriterTag.Thead);
            RenderHeader(helper, writer, columns);
            writer.RenderEndTag();

            // Render table body
            writer.RenderBeginTag(HtmlTextWriterTag.Tbody);
            foreach (var item in items)
                RenderRow<T>(helper, writer, columns, item);
```

```
            writer.RenderEndTag();

            // Close table tag
            writer.RenderEndTag();

            // Return the string
            return writer.InnerWriter.ToString();
        }

        private static void RenderHeader(HtmlHelper helper, HtmlTextWriter writer,
➥string[] columns)
        {
            writer.RenderBeginTag(HtmlTextWriterTag.Tr);
            foreach (var columnName in columns)
            {
                writer.RenderBeginTag(HtmlTextWriterTag.Th);
                writer.Write(helper.Encode(columnName));
                writer.RenderEndTag();
            }
            writer.RenderEndTag();
        }

        private static void RenderRow<T>(HtmlHelper helper, HtmlTextWriter writer,
➥string[] columns, T item)
        {
            writer.RenderBeginTag(HtmlTextWriterTag.Tr);
            foreach (var columnName in columns)
            {
                writer.RenderBeginTag(HtmlTextWriterTag.Td);
                var value = typeof(T).GetProperty(columnName).GetValue(item, null)
➥?? String.Empty;
                writer.Write(helper.Encode(value.ToString()));
                writer.RenderEndTag();
            }
            writer.RenderEndTag();
        }

    }

}
```

LISTING 6.12   Helpers\DataGridHelperBasic.vb (VB)

```vb
Imports System.IO


Public Module DataGridHelper

    <System.Runtime.CompilerServices.Extension()> _
    Function DataGrid(Of T)(ByVal helper As HtmlHelper) As String
        Return DataGrid(Of T)(helper, Nothing, Nothing)
    End Function



    <System.Runtime.CompilerServices.Extension()> _
    Function DataGrid(Of T)(ByVal helper As HtmlHelper, data As object) As String
        Return DataGrid(Of T)(helper, data, Nothing)
    End Function

    <System.Runtime.CompilerServices.Extension()> _
    Function DataGrid(Of T)(ByVal helper As HtmlHelper, ByVal data As IEnumerable
➥(Of T), ByVal columns() As String) As String
        ' Get items
        Dim items = CType(data, IEnumerable(Of T))
        If items Is Nothing Then
            items = CType(helper.ViewData.Model, IEnumerable(Of T))
        End If

        ' Get column names
        If columns Is Nothing Then
            columns = GetType(T).GetProperties().Select(Function(p) p.Name).ToArray()
        End If

        ' Create HtmlTextWriter
        Dim writer = New HtmlTextWriter(New StringWriter())

        ' Open table tag
        writer.RenderBeginTag(HtmlTextWriterTag.Table)

        ' Render table header
        writer.RenderBeginTag(HtmlTextWriterTag.Thead)
        RenderHeader(helper, writer, columns)
        writer.RenderEndTag()

        ' Render table body
        writer.RenderBeginTag(HtmlTextWriterTag.Tbody)
        For Each item In items
            RenderRow(Of T)(helper, writer, columns, item)
```

```
            Next item
        writer.RenderEndTag()

        ' Close table tag
        writer.RenderEndTag()

        ' Return the string
        Return writer.InnerWriter.ToString()
    End Function

    Private Sub RenderHeader(ByVal helper As HtmlHelper, ByVal writer As
➥HtmlTextWriter, ByVal columns() As String)
        writer.RenderBeginTag(HtmlTextWriterTag.Tr)
        For Each columnName In columns
            writer.RenderBeginTag(HtmlTextWriterTag.Th)
            writer.Write(helper.Encode(columnName))
            writer.RenderEndTag()
        Next columnName
        writer.RenderEndTag()
    End Sub

    Private Sub RenderRow(Of T)(ByVal helper As HtmlHelper, ByVal writer As
➥HtmlTextWriter, ByVal columns() As String, ByVal item As T)
        writer.RenderBeginTag(HtmlTextWriterTag.Tr)
        For Each columnName In columns
            writer.RenderBeginTag(HtmlTextWriterTag.Td)
              Dim value = GetType(T).GetProperty(columnName).GetValue(item, Nothing)
            if IsNothing(value) Then value = String.Empty
            writer.Write(helper.Encode(value.ToString()))
            writer.RenderEndTag()
        Next columnName
        writer.RenderEndTag()
    End Sub

End Module
```

In Listing 6.12, the Html.DataGrid() helper method has three overloads. All three overloads are generic overloads. You must supply the type of object—for example, Product—that the Html.DataGrid() should render.

Here are some examples of how you can call the html.DataGrid() helper:

(C#)

```
<%= Html.DataGrid<Product>()%>
<%= Html.DataGrid<Product>(ViewData["products"]) %>
<%= Html.DataGrid<Product>(Model, new string[] {"Id", "Name"})%>
```

(VB)

```
<%= Html.DataGrid(Of Product)()%>
<%= Html.DataGrid(Of Product)(ViewData("products")) %>
<%= Html.DataGrid(Of Product)(Model, New String() {"Id", "Name"})%>
```

In the first case, the Html.DataGrid() helper renders all the items in the view data model into an HTML table. All the public properties of the Product class are rendered in each row of the HTML table.

In the second case, the contents of the products item in view data is rendered into an HTML table. Again all the public properties of the Public class are rendered.

In the third case, once again, the contents of the view data model are rendered into an HTML table. However, only the Id and Name properties are rendered (see Figure 6.8).

Id	Name
1	Model Train
2	Pogo Stick
3	Red Ball
4	Racing Car
5	Playhouse

FIGURE 6.8   Rendering an HTML table with the Html.DataGrid() helper

The Html.DataGrid() helper uses an HtmlTextWriter to render the HTML table <table>, <thead>, <tr>, <tbody>, <th>, and <td> tags. Rendering these tags by taking advantage of the HtmlTextWriter results in cleaner and more readable code than using string concatenation. (Please try to avoid string concatenation whenever possible!)

A tiny bit of reflection is used in the DataGrid() helper. First, reflection is used in the second DataGrid() method to retrieve the list of columns to display when no explicit list of columns is supplied to the helper:

(C#)

```
columns = typeof(T).GetProperties().Select(p => p.Name).ToArray();
```

(VB)

```
columns = GetType(T).GetProperties().Select(Function(p) p.Name).ToArray()
```

Also, reflection is used to retrieve the value of a property to display within the RenderRow() method:

(C#)

```
var value = typeof(T).GetProperty(columnName).GetValue(item, null) ?? String.Empty;
```

(VB)

```
Dim value = GetType(T).GetProperty(columnName).GetValue(item, Nothing)
if IsNothing(value) Then value = String.Empty
```

NOTE

Reflection is a .NET framework feature that enables you get information about classes, methods, and properties at runtime. You can even use reflection to dynamically load assemblies and execute methods at runtime.

The Html.DataGrid() helper displays any collection of items that implements the IEnumerable<T> interface. For example, the controller action in Listing 6.13 assigns a set of products to the view data model property. This list of products can be displayed by the Html.DataGrid() helper.

LISTING 6.13   Controllers\ProductController.cs (C#)

```csharp
using System.Linq;
using System.Web.Mvc;
using MvcApplication1.Models;

namespace MvcApplication1.Controllers
{
    public class ProductController : Controller
    {
        private ToyStoreDBEntities _entities = new ToyStoreDBEntities();

        public ActionResult Index()
        {
            return View(_entities.ProductSet.ToList());
        }
    }
}
```

LISTING 6.13   Controllers\ProductController.vb (VB)

```vb
Public Class ProductController
    Inherits System.Web.Mvc.Controller
    Private _entities As New ToyStoreDBEntities()

    Function Index() As ActionResult
        Return View(_entities.ProductSet.ToList())
    End Function

End Class
```

Adding Sorting to the `DataGrid` Helper

Let's make our `Html.DataGrid()` helper just a little more fancy. In this section, we add sorting support. When you click a column header in the HTML table rendered by the `Html.DataGrid()` helper, the HTML table is sorted by the selected column (see Figure 6.9).

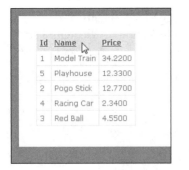

FIGURE 6.9   `Html.DataGrid()` with sorting support

To add the sorting support, we need to modify just one method of the existing `DataGridHelper` class. We need to modify the `RenderHeader()` method so that it renders links for headers. The modified `RenderHeader()` method is contained in Listing 6.14.

LISTING 6.14   Helpers\DataGridHelperSorting.cs (C#)

```csharp
private static void RenderHeader(HtmlHelper helper, HtmlTextWriter writer,
➥string[] columns)
{
    writer.RenderBeginTag(HtmlTextWriterTag.Tr);
    foreach (var columnName in columns)
    {
        writer.RenderBeginTag(HtmlTextWriterTag.Th);
        var currentAction = (string)helper.ViewContext.RouteData.Values["action"];
        var link = helper.ActionLink(columnName, currentAction, new {sort=
➥columnName});
        writer.Write(link);
        writer.RenderEndTag();
    }
    writer.RenderEndTag();

}
```

LISTING 6.14   Helpers\DataGridHelperSorting.vb (VB)

```vb
Private Sub RenderHeader(ByVal helper As HtmlHelper, ByVal writer As
➥HtmlTextWriter, ByVal columns() As String)
    writer.RenderBeginTag(HtmlTextWriterTag.Tr)
    For Each columnName In columns
        writer.RenderBeginTag(HtmlTextWriterTag.Th)
        Dim currentAction = CStr(helper.ViewContext.RouteData.Values("action"))
        Dim link = helper.ActionLink(columnName, currentAction, New With {Key .sort
➥= columnName})
        writer.Write(link)
        writer.RenderEndTag()
    Next columnName
    writer.RenderEndTag()
End Sub
```

The modified RenderHeader() method in Listing 6.14 creates a link for each header
column by calling the HtmlHelper.ActionLink() method. Notice that the name of the
header column is included as a route value in the link. For example, the following link is
rendered for the Price header:

```
/Product/SortProducts?sort=Price
```

The actual database sorting happens within the Product controller. The SortProducts
action in Listing 6.15 returns the products in different sort orders depending on the value
of the sort parameter passed to the action.

LISTING 6.15   Controllers\ProductController.cs with SortProducts (C#)

```csharp
public ActionResult SortProducts(string sort)
{
    IEnumerable<Product> products;
    sort = sort ?? string.Empty;
    switch (sort.ToLower())
    {
        case "name":
            products = from p in _entities.ProductSet
                        orderby p.Name select p;
            break;
        case "price":
            products = from p in _entities.ProductSet
                        orderby p.Price
                        select p;
            break;
```

```
        default:
            products = from p in _entities.ProductSet
                        orderby p.Id
                        select p;
            break;
    }

    return View(products);
}
```

LISTING 6.15   Controllers\ProductController.vb with SortProducts (VB)

```
Function SortProducts(ByVal sort As String) As ActionResult
    Dim products As IEnumerable(Of Product)
    sort = If((sort <> Nothing), sort, String.Empty)
    Select Case sort.ToLower()
        Case "name"
            products = From p In _entities.ProductSet _
                        Order By p.Name _
                        Select p
        Case "price"
            products = From p In _entities.ProductSet _
                        Order By p.Price _
                        Select p
        Case Else
            products = From p In _entities.ProductSet _
                        Order By p.Id _
                        Select p
    End Select

    Return View(products)
End Function
```

Adding Paging to the DataGrid Helper

It really wouldn't be a proper Html.DataGrid() helper unless the helper supported paging.
In this section, we modify our Html.DataGrid() helper so that it supports efficient paging
through a large set of database records (see Figure 6.10).

To add paging support, we need to create two new supporting classes:

▶ PagedList—An instance of this class is passed to the Html.DataGrid() helper to
represent a single page of records.

▶ PagingLinqExtensions—This class contains extension methods that extend the IQueryable<T> interface with ToPagedList() methods that return a PagedList from a query.

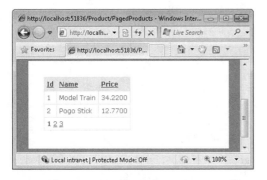

FIGURE 6.10   Paging through database records

The PagedList class is contained in Listing 6.16.

LISTING 6.16   Paging\PagedList.cs (C#)

```csharp
using System;
using System.Collections.Generic;

namespace Paging
{
    public class PagedList<T> : List<T>
    {
        public PagedList(IEnumerable<T> items, int pageIndex, int pageSize, int
➥totalItemCount, string sortExpression)
        {
            this.AddRange(items);
            this.PageIndex = pageIndex;
            this.PageSize = pageSize;
            this.SortExpression = sortExpression;
            this.TotalItemCount = totalItemCount;
            this.TotalPageCount = (int)Math.Ceiling(totalItemCount /
➥(double)pageSize);
        }

        public int PageIndex { get; set; }
        public int PageSize { get; set; }
        public string SortExpression { get; set; }
```

```
        public int TotalItemCount { get; set; }
        public int TotalPageCount { get; private set; }


    }
}
```

LISTING 6.16   Paging\PagedList.vb (VB)

```vb
Public Class PagedList(Of T)
    Inherits List(Of T)

    Private _pageIndex As Integer
    Private _pageSize As Integer
    Private _sortExpression As String
    Private _totalItemCount As Integer
    Private _totalPageCount As Integer

    Public Sub New(ByVal items As IEnumerable(Of T), ByVal pageIndex As Integer,
➡ByVal pageSize As Integer, ByVal totalItemCount As Integer, ByVal sortExpression
➡As String)
        Me.AddRange(items)
        Me.PageIndex = pageIndex
        Me.PageSize = pageSize
        Me.SortExpression = sortExpression
        Me.TotalItemCount = totalItemCount
        Me.TotalPageCount = CInt(Fix(Math.Ceiling(totalItemCount / CDbl
➡(pageSize))))
    End Sub

    Public Property PageIndex() As Integer
        Get
            Return _pageIndex
        End Get
        Set(ByVal value As Integer)
            _pageIndex = value
        End Set
    End Property
    Public Property PageSize() As Integer
        Get
            Return _pageSize
        End Get
        Set(ByVal value As Integer)
            _pageSize = value
        End Set
    End Property
```

```
Public Property SortExpression() As String
    Get
        Return _sortExpression
    End Get
    Set(ByVal value As String)
        _sortExpression = value
    End Set
End Property
Public Property TotalItemCount() As Integer
    Get
        Return _totalItemCount
    End Get
    Set(ByVal value As Integer)
        _totalItemCount = value
    End Set
End Property
Public Property TotalPageCount() As Integer
    Get
        Return _totalPageCount
    End Get
    Private Set(ByVal value As Integer)
        _totalPageCount = value
    End Set
End Property
```

End Class

The PagedList class inherits from the base generic List class and adds specialized properties for paging. The PageList class represents the following properties:

▶ PageIndex—The currently selected page (zero-based)

▶ PageSize—The number of records to display per page

▶ SortExpression—The column that determines the sort order of the records

▶ TotalItemCount—The total number of items in the database

▶ TotalPageCount—The total number of page numbers to display

The second class, the PagingLinqExtensions class, extends the IQueryable interface to make it easier to return a PagedList from a LINQ query. The PagingLinqExtensions class is contained in Listing 6.17.

LISTING 6.17   Paging\PagingLinqExtensions.cs (C#)

```csharp
using System;
using System.Linq;

namespace Paging
{
    public static class PageLinqExtensions
    {
        public static PagedList<T> ToPagedList<T>
            (
                this IQueryable<T> allItems,
                int? pageIndex,
                int pageSize
            )
        {
            return ToPagedList<T>(allItems, pageIndex, pageSize, String.Empty);

        }

        public static PagedList<T> ToPagedList<T>
            (
                this IQueryable<T> allItems,
                int? pageIndex,
                int pageSize,
                string sort
            )
        {
            var truePageIndex = pageIndex ?? 0;
            var itemIndex = truePageIndex * pageSize;
            var pageOfItems = allItems.Skip(itemIndex).Take(pageSize);
            var totalItemCount = allItems.Count();
            return new PagedList<T>(pageOfItems, truePageIndex, pageSize,
➥totalItemCount, sort);

        }
    }
}
```

LISTING 6.17   Paging\PagingLinqExtensions.vb (VB)

```vbnet
Public Module PageLinqExtensions


    <System.Runtime.CompilerServices.Extension> _
    Function ToPagedList(Of T)(ByVal allItems As IQueryable(Of T), ByVal pageIndex
➥As Integer?, ByVal pageSize As Integer) As PagedList(Of T)
```

```
        Return ToPagedList(Of T)(allItems, pageIndex, pageSize, String.Empty)
    End Function

    <System.Runtime.CompilerServices.Extension> _
    Function ToPagedList(Of T)(ByVal allItems As IQueryable(Of T), ByVal pageIndex
➥As Integer?, ByVal pageSize As Integer, ByVal sort As String) As PagedList(Of T)
        Dim truePageIndex = If(pageIndex.HasValue, pageIndex, 0)
        Dim itemIndex = truePageIndex * pageSize
        Dim pageOfItems = allItems.Skip(itemIndex).Take(pageSize)
        Dim totalItemCount = allItems.Count()
        Return New PagedList(Of T)(pageOfItems, truePageIndex, pageSize,
➥totalItemCount, sort)
    End Function
End Module
```

The `PagingLinqExtensions` class makes it possible to return a `PagedList` like this:

(C#)

```
var products = _entities.ProductSet
                        .OrderBy(p => p.Id)
                        .ToPagedList(page, 2);
```

(VB)

```
Dim products = _entities.ProductSet _
        .OrderBy(Function(p) p.Id) _
        .ToPagedList(page, 2)
```

Notice how you can call `ToPagedList()` directly on a LINQ query. The `PagingLinqExtensions` class simplifies your code.

Finally, we need to modify our `Html.DataGrid()` class to use the `PagedList` class to represent database records. The modified `Html.DataGrid()` class includes the new `RenderPagerRow()` method contained in Listing 6.18.

LISTING 6.18   Helpers\DataGridHelperPaging.cs (C#)

```
private static void RenderPagerRow<T>(HtmlHelper helper, HtmlTextWriter writer,
➥PagedList<T> items, int columnCount)
{
    // Don't show paging UI for only 1 page
    if (items.TotalPageCount == 1)
        return;

    // Render page numbers
    writer.RenderBeginTag(HtmlTextWriterTag.Tr);
    writer.AddAttribute(HtmlTextWriterAttribute.Colspan, columnCount.ToString());
```

```
    writer.RenderBeginTag(HtmlTextWriterTag.Td);
    var currentAction = (string)helper.ViewContext.RouteData.Values["action"];
    for (var i = 0; i < items.TotalPageCount; i++)
    {
        if (i == items.PageIndex)
        {
            writer.Write(String.Format("<strong>{0}</strong> ", i + 1));
        }
        else
        {
            var linkText = String.Format("{0}", i + 1);
            var link = helper.ActionLink(linkText, currentAction, new { page = i,
➥sort=items.SortExpression});
            writer.Write(link + " ");
        }
    }
    writer.RenderEndTag();
    writer.RenderEndTag();
}
```

LISTING 6.18   Helpers\DataGridHelperPaging.cs (VB)

```
    Private Sub RenderPagerRow(Of T)(ByVal helper As HtmlHelper, ByVal writer As
➥HtmlTextWriter, ByVal items As PagedList(Of T), ByVal columnCount As Integer)
        ' Don't show paging UI for only 1 page
        If items.TotalPageCount = 1 Then
            Return
        End If


        ' Render page numbers
        writer.RenderBeginTag(HtmlTextWriterTag.Tr)
        writer.AddAttribute(HtmlTextWriterAttribute.Colspan,
➥columnCount.ToString())
        writer.RenderBeginTag(HtmlTextWriterTag.Td)
        Dim currentAction = CStr(helper.ViewContext.RouteData.Values("action"))
        For i = 0 To items.TotalPageCount - 1
            If i = items.PageIndex Then
                writer.Write(String.Format("<strong>{0}</strong> ", i + 1))
            Else
                Dim linkText = String.Format("{0}", i + 1)
                Dim link = helper.ActionLink(linkText, currentAction, New With {Key
➥.page = i, Key .sort = items.SortExpression})
                writer.Write(link & " ")
            End If
        Next i
```

```
        writer.RenderEndTag()
        writer.RenderEndTag()


    End Sub
```

The RenderPagerRow() method in Listing 6.18 renders the user interface for paging. This method simply renders a list of page numbers that act as hyperlinks. The selected page number is highlighted with an HTML <strong> tag.

The modified Html.DataGrid() helper requires an instance of the PagedList class for its data parameter. You can use the controller action in Listing 6.19 to add the right data to view state.

LISTING 6.19   Controllers\ProductController.cs with PagedProducts (C#)

```
public ActionResult PagedProducts(int? page)
{
    var products = _entities.ProductSet
        .OrderBy(p => p.Id).ToPagedList(page, 2);

    return View(products);
}
```

LISTING 6.19   Controllers\ProductController.cs with PagedProducts (VB)

```
Function PagedProducts(ByVal page As Integer?) As ActionResult
    Dim products = _entities.ProductSet _
            .OrderBy(Function(p) p.Id) _
            .ToPagedList(page, 2)

    Return View(products)
End Function
```

WARNING

In Listing 6.19, notice that the ToPagedList() method is called on a LINQ query that includes a call to the OrderBy() method. When using the Entity Framework, you must order the results of a query before you can extract a page of records from the query.

If you want to both page *and sort* the products, you can use the controller action in Listing 6.20.

LISTING 6.20   Controllers\ProductController.cs with PagedSortedProducts (C#)

```csharp
public ActionResult PagedSortedProducts(string sort, int? page)
{
    IQueryable<Product> products;
    sort = sort ?? string.Empty;
    switch (sort.ToLower())
    {
        case "name":
            products = from p in _entities.ProductSet
                       orderby p.Name
                       select p;
            break;
        case "price":
            products = from p in _entities.ProductSet
                       orderby p.Price
                       select p;
            break;
        default:
            products = from p in _entities.ProductSet
                       orderby p.Id
                       select p;
            break;
    }

    ViewData.Model = products.ToPagedList(page, 2, sort);
    return View();
}
```

LISTING 6.20   Controllers\ProductController.cs with PagedSortedProducts (VB)

```vb
Function PagedSortedProducts(ByVal sort As String, ByVal page As Integer?) As
➥ActionResult
    Dim products As IQueryable(Of Product)
    sort = If((sort <> Nothing), sort, String.Empty)
    Select Case sort.ToLower()
        Case "name"
            products = From p In _entities.ProductSet _
                       Order By p.Name _
                       Select p
        Case "price"
            products = From p In _entities.ProductSet _
                       Order By p.Price _
                       Select p
        Case Else
```

```
              products = From p In _entities.ProductSet _
                         Order By p.Id _
                         Select p
        End Select

        ViewData.Model = products.ToPagedList(page, 2, sort)
        Return View()
End Function
```

Notice that when you want to support sorting, you must pass the current sort column to the `ToPageList()` method. If you don't pass the current sort column, clicking a page number causes the `Html.DataGrid()` to forget the sort order.

Testing Helpers

In general, you should place any complicated view logic in an HTML helper. There is a simple reason for this: You can test a helper, but you cannot test a view.

The `Html.DataGrid()` helper that we created in the previous section is a good example of a helper that requires unit tests. There are several things that I could have gotten wrong while writing this helper. You should never trust anything that you write!

Here are some expectations for our helper that we might want to test:

▶ The helper displays the right number of table rows. For example, if you specify that the page size is 2 rows, calling the `Html.DataGrid()` helper method should render an HTML table that contains 4 rows (1 header row + 2 data rows + 1 pager row).

▶ The helper selects the right page number. For example, if you specify that the current page index is 1, page number 2 should be highlighted in bold in the pager user interface.

The test class in Listing 6.21 contains unit tests for both of these expectations.

LISTING 6.21   Helpers\DataGridHelperTests.cs (C#)

```csharp
using System;
using System.Collections.Generic;
using System.Linq;
using System.Text.RegularExpressions;
using Helpers;
using Microsoft.VisualStudio.TestTools.UnitTesting;
using MvcFakes;
using Paging;

namespace MvcApplication1.Tests.Helpers
{
```

```
[TestClass]
public class DataGridHelperTests
{

    public List<Product> CreateItems(int count)
    {
        var items = new List<Product>();
        for (var i=0;i < count;i++)
        {
            var newProduct = new Product();
            newProduct.Id = i;
            newProduct.Name = String.Format("Product {0}", i);
            newProduct.Price = count - i;
            items.Add(newProduct);
        }
        return items;
    }

    [TestMethod]
    public void SecondPageNumberSelected()
    {
        // Arrange
        var items = CreateItems(5);
        var data = items.AsQueryable().ToPagedList(1, 2);

        // Act
        var fakeHtmlHelper = new FakeHtmlHelper();
        var results = DataGridHelper.DataGrid<Product>(fakeHtmlHelper, data);

        // Assert
        StringAssert.Contains(results, "<strong>2</strong>");

    }

    [TestMethod]
    public void CorrectNumberOfRows()
    {
        // Arrange
        var items = CreateItems(5);
        var data = items.AsQueryable().ToPagedList(1, 2);

        // Act
        var fakeHtmlHelper = new FakeHtmlHelper();
        var results = DataGridHelper.DataGrid<Product>(fakeHtmlHelper, data);

        // Assert (1 header row + 2 data rows + 1 pager row)
```

```
            Assert.AreEqual(4, Regex.Matches(results, "<tr>").Count);
        }
    }

    public class Product
    {
        public int Id { get; set; }
        public string Name { get; set; }
        public decimal Price { get; set; }
    }
}
```

LISTING 6.21   Helpers\DataGridHelperTests.vb (VB)

```
Imports Microsoft.VisualStudio.TestTools.UnitTesting
Imports MvcFakes
Imports System.Text.RegularExpressions

<TestClass()> _
Public Class DataGridHelperTests

    Public Function CreateItems(ByVal count As Integer) As List(Of Product)
        Dim items = New List(Of Product)()
        For i = 0 To count - 1
            Dim newProduct = New Product()
            newProduct.Id = i
            newProduct.Name = String.Format("Product {0}", i)
            newProduct.Price = count - i
            items.Add(newProduct)
        Next i
        Return items
    End Function

    <TestMethod()> _
    Public Sub SecondPageNumberSelected()
        ' Arrange
        Dim items = CreateItems(5)
        Dim data = items.AsQueryable().ToPagedList(1, 2)

        ' Act
        Dim fakeHtmlHelper = New FakeHtmlHelper()
        Dim results = DataGridHelper.DataGrid(Of Product)(fakeHtmlHelper, data)

        ' Assert
        StringAssert.Contains(results, "<strong>2</strong>")
```

```vb
    End Sub

    <TestMethod()> _
    Public Sub CorrectNumberOfRows()
        ' Arrange
        Dim items = CreateItems(5)
        Dim data = items.AsQueryable().ToPagedList(1, 2)

        ' Act
        Dim fakeHtmlHelper = New FakeHtmlHelper()
        Dim results = DataGridHelper.DataGrid(Of Product)(fakeHtmlHelper, data)

        ' Assert (1 header row + 2 data rows + 1 pager row)
        Assert.AreEqual(4, Regex.Matches(results, "<tr>").Count)
    End Sub
End Class

Public Class Product
    Private _id As Integer
    Private _name As String
    Private _price As Decimal

    Public Property Id() As Integer
        Get
            Return _id
        End Get
        Set(ByVal value As Integer)
            _id = value
        End Set
    End Property

    Public Property Name() As String
        Get
            Return _name
        End Get
        Set(ByVal value As String)
            _name = value
        End Set
    End Property

    Public Property Price() As Decimal
        Get
            Return _price
        End Get
        Set(ByVal value As Decimal)
```

```
            _price = value
        End Set
    End Property
End Class
```

If I want to feel completely confident about the Html.DataGrid() helper, I would need to write several more unit tests than the two tests contained in Listing 6.21. However, Listing 6.21 is a good start.

Both of the unit tests in Listing 6.21 take advantage of a utility method named CreateItems() that creates a list that contains a specific number of products.

Both unit tests also take advantage of the FakeHtmlHelper class from the MvcFakes project. When you call an HTML helper, you must supply an instance of the HtmlHelper class as the first parameter. The FakeHtmlHelper enables you to easily fake this helper.

> **NOTE**
>
> Before you can run the tests in Listing 6.21, you must add a reference to the MvcFakes project to your Test project. The MvcFakes project is included in the code on the book's website, www.informit.com/title/9780672329982.

Summary

This chapter was devoted to the topic of HTML helpers. You learned how to create views more easily by using HTML helpers to render HTML content.

In the first part of this chapter, you learned how to use the standard set of HTML helpers included with the ASP.NET MVC framework. For example, you learned how to create HTML links with the Html.ActionLink() and Url.Action() helpers. You also learned how to use the form helpers to render standard HTML form elements such as drop-down lists and text boxes.

We also discussed how you can make your websites more secure against JavaScript injection attacks by taking advantage of the Html.AntiForgeryToken() and Html.Encode() helpers.

In the next part of this chapter, we examined how you can create custom HTML helpers. We talked about the different utility classes that you can use when building a custom helper. In particular, you learned how to use the TagBuilder and HtmlTextWriter classes.

We then tackled building a real-world HTML helper. We created an Html.DataGrid() helper that renders database records in an HTML table. We added both sorting and paging support to our custom Html.DataGrid() helper.

In the final section of this chapter, you learned how to build unit tests for your custom HTML helpers. We created two unit tests for our Html.DataGrid() helper.

Understanding Model Binders and Action Filters

This chapter is devoted to the topic of model binders and action filters. First, we tackle the subject of model binders. You learn how to use a model binder to instantiate an object from a browser request.

For example, we already used the default model binder several times in this book. Whenever we use a class as a parameter for a controller action—such as a Product class—we are using the default model binder.

In some situations, you want to create a custom model binder. When you create a custom model binder, you get to decide how a new object is instantiated out of the ether.

In this chapter, you also learn how to create action filters. An action filter is a class that executes code before or after a controller action is invoked. You can use an action filter, for example, to log each time a controller action is invoked.

Understanding Model Binders

A model binder is responsible for mapping a browser request into an object. Consider the view in Listing 7.1. This view contains a simple HTML form for creating a new product (see Figure 7.1).

LISTING 7.1   Views\Product\Create.aspx (C#)

```
<%@ Page Title="" Language="C#"
➡MasterPageFile="~/Views/Shared/Site.Master"
➡Inherits="System.Web.Mvc.ViewPage" %>
```

```
<asp:Content ID="Content2" ContentPlaceHolderID="MainContent" runat="server">

    <h2>Create Product</h2>

    <% using (Html.BeginForm())
       { %>

        <label for="Name">Name:</label>
        <br /><%= Html.TextBox("Name") %>

        <br /><br />
        <label for="Price">Price:</label>
        <br /><%= Html.TextBox("Price") %>

        <br /><br />
        <input type="submit" value="Add Product" />

    <% } %>


</asp:Content>
```

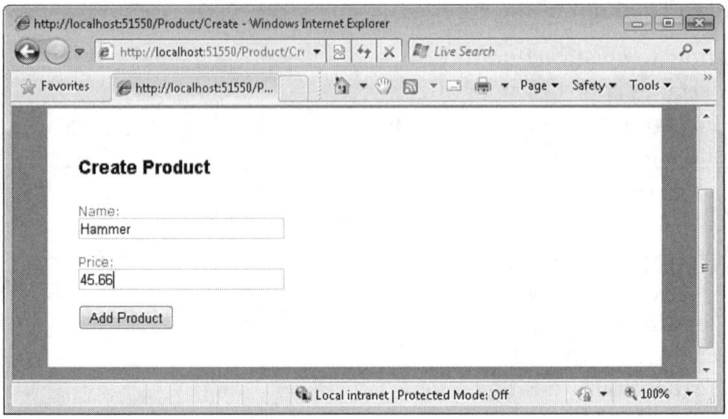

FIGURE 7.1   The Create view

LISTING 7.1   Views\Product\Create.aspx (VB)

```
<%@ Page Title="" Language="VB" MasterPageFile="~/Views/Shared/Site.Master"
➥Inherits="System.Web.Mvc.ViewPage" %>
<asp:Content ID="Content2" ContentPlaceHolderID="MainContent" runat="server">
```

```
<h2>Create Product</h2>

<% Using Html.BeginForm()%>

    <label for="Name">Name:</label>
    <br /><%= Html.TextBox("Name") %>

    <br /><br />
    <label for="Price">Price:</label>
    <br /><%= Html.TextBox("Price") %>

    <br /><br />
    <input type="submit" value="Add Product" />

<% End Using%>


</asp:Content>
```

When you submit the form in Listing 7.1, you submit the form to the controller action in Listing 7.2.

LISTING 7.2   Controllers\ProductController.cs (C#)

```
// POST: /Product/Create


[AcceptVerbs(HttpVerbs.Post)]
public ActionResult Create(Product productToCreate)
{
    // Add product to database
    return RedirectToAction("Index");
}
```

LISTING 7.2   Controllers\ProductController.vb (VB)

```
' POST: /Product/Create
<AcceptVerbs(HttpVerbs.Post)> _
Function Create(ByVal productToCreate As Product) As ActionResult

    ' Add product to database
    Return RedirectToAction("Index")
End Function
```

Notice that the controller action in Listing 7.2 accepts a `Product` parameter. A model binder—in this case, the default model binder—is responsible for instantiating a new `Product` class for the parameter. The default model binder also handles assigning the values of the HTML form fields to the properties of the new `Product` class.

The ASP.NET MVC framework ships with three model binders:

- Default model binder
- Form collection model binder
- HTTP posted file base model binder

In the following sections, you learn how to use each of these model binders. Later in this chapter, you learn how to extend the ASP.NET MVC framework by creating a custom model binder.

Using the Default Model Binder

The default model binder is smart enough to create a variety of different types of objects from a browser request including the following:

- A primitive type such as a `string`, `decimal`, or `DateTime`.
- A class such as a `Product` or `Customer` class.
- An array such as a `string` or `Product` array.
- A collections such as an `IEnumerable<T>`, `ICollection<T>`, `IList<T>`, `T[]`, `Collection<T>`, and `List<T>`.
- A dictionary such as an `IDictionary<TKey, TValue>` and `Dictionary<TKey, TValue>`.

For example, the view in Listing 7.3 contains a list of check boxes (see Figure 7.2). The check boxes all have the same name, and they are all part of the same check box group.

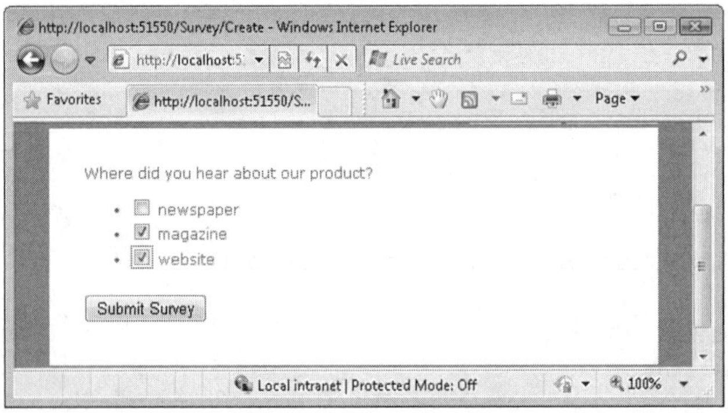

FIGURE 7.2   A view with check boxes

LISTING 7.3   Views\Survey\Create.aspx (C#)

```
<%@ Page Title="" Language="C#" MasterPageFile="~/Views/Shared/Site.Master"
➥Inherits="System.Web.Mvc.ViewPage" %>


<asp:Content ID="Content2" ContentPlaceHolderID="MainContent" runat="server">

<% using (Html.BeginForm()) { %>

 Where did you hear about our product?

 <ul>
    <li>
    <input name="source" type="checkbox" value="newspaper" /> newspaper
    </li>
    <li>
    <input name="source" type="checkbox" value="magazine" /> magazine
    </li>
    <li>
    <input name="source" type="checkbox" value="website" /> website
    </li>
 </ul>

 <input type="submit" value="Submit Survey" />

<% } %>

</asp:Content>
```

LISTING 7.3   Views\Survey\Create.aspx (VB)

```
<%@ Page Title="" Language="VB" MasterPageFile="~/Views/Shared/Site.Master"
➥Inherits="System.Web.Mvc.ViewPage" %>
<asp:Content ID="Content2" ContentPlaceHolderID="MainContent" runat="server">

<%  Using Html.BeginForm()%>

 Where did you hear about our product?

 <ul>
    <li>
    <input name="source" type="checkbox" value="newspaper" /> newspaper
    </li>
    <li>
```

```
    <input name="source" type="checkbox" value="magazine" /> magazine
    </li>
    <li>
    <input name="source" type="checkbox" value="website" /> website
    </li>
</ul>

<input type="submit" value="Submit Survey" />

<% End Using%>

</asp:Content>
```

The Create() action in Listing 7.4 accepts a collection parameter that represents a list of strings. The default model binder converts the input fields in the form post into this parameter automatically.

LISTING 7.4   Controllers\SurveyController.cs (C#)

```
[AcceptVerbs(HttpVerbs.Post)]
public ActionResult Create(List<string> source)
{
    return View();
}
```

LISTING 7.4   Controllers\SurveyController.vb (VB)

```
' POST: /Survey/Create
<AcceptVerbs(HttpVerbs.Post)> _
Function Create(ByVal source As List(Of String)) As ActionResult
    Return View()
End Function
```

So if a user selects the magazine and website check boxes, the source collection will contain these two strings automatically.

Binding to Complex Classes

The default model binder is smart enough to handle most complex classes. For example, the Customer class in Listing 7.5 includes an Address property that returns an instance of the Address class.

LISTING 7.5   Models\Customer.cs (C#)

```csharp
namespace MvcApplication1.Models
{
    public class Customer
    {
        public int Id { get; set; }
        public string FirstName { get; set; }
        public string LastName { get; set; }
        public Address Address { get; set; }
    }
    public class Address
    {
        public string Street { get; set; }
        public string City { get; set; }
        public string ZIP { get; set; }
    }
}
```

LISTING 7.5   Models\Customer.vb (VB)

```vb
Public Class Customer

    Private _id As Integer
    Private _firstName As String
    Private _lastName As String
    Private _address As Address

    Public Property Id() As Integer
        Get
            Return _id
        End Get
        Set(ByVal value As Integer)
            _id = value
        End Set
    End Property

    Public Property FirstName() As String
        Get
            Return _firstName
        End Get
        Set(ByVal value As String)
```

```vbnet
            _firstName = value
        End Set
    End Property


    Public Property LastName() As String
        Get
            Return _lastName
        End Get
        Set(ByVal value As String)
            _lastName = value
        End Set
    End Property


    Public Property Address() As Address
        Get
            Return _address
        End Get
        Set(ByVal value As Address)
            _address = value
        End Set
    End Property
End Class
Public Class Address

    Private _street As String
    Private _city As String
    Private _zip As String

    Public Property Street() As String
        Get
            Return _street
        End Get
        Set(ByVal value As String)
            _street = value
        End Set
    End Property
    Public Property City() As String
        Get
            Return _city
        End Get
        Set(ByVal value As String)
            _city = value
        End Set
    End Property
    Public Property ZIP() As String
        Get
```

```
            Return _zip
        End Get
        Set(ByVal value As String)
            _zip = value
        End Set
    End Property
End Class
```

The view in Listing 7.6 contains an HTML form for creating a new customer (see Figure 7.3). Notice that the form consists of two subforms: a form for the customer and a form for the customer address. The view that generates this form is contained in Listing 7.6.

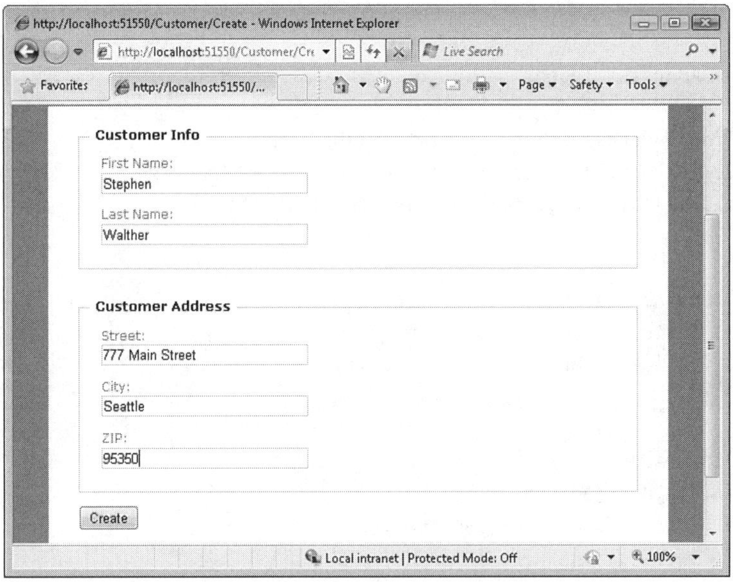

FIGURE 7.3   HTML form for creating a new customer.

LISTING 7.6   Views\Customer\Create.aspx (C#)

```
<%@ Page Title="" Language="C#" MasterPageFile="~/Views/Shared/Site.Master"
➥Inherits="System.Web.Mvc.ViewPage<MvcApplication1.Models.Widget>" %>


<asp:Content ID="Content2" ContentPlaceHolderID="MainContent" runat="server">

    <%= Html.ValidationSummary("Create was unsuccessful. Please correct the errors
➥and try again.") %>

    <% using (Html.BeginForm()) {%>
```

```
    <fieldset>
        <legend>Customer Info</legend>
        <p>
            <label for="FirstName">First Name:</label>
            <%= Html.TextBox("FirstName") %>
            <%= Html.ValidationMessage("FirstName", "*") %>
        </p>
        <p>
            <label for="LastName">Last Name:</label>
            <%= Html.TextBox("LastName") %>
            <%= Html.ValidationMessage("LastName", "*") %>
        </p>
    </fieldset>
    <fieldset>
    <legend>Customer Address</legend>
        <p>
            <label for="Address.Street">Street:</label>
            <%= Html.TextBox("Address.Street") %>
            <%= Html.ValidationMessage("Address.Street", "*") %>
        </p>
        <p>
            <label for="Address.City">City:</label>
            <%= Html.TextBox("Address.City") %>
            <%= Html.ValidationMessage("Address.City", "*") %>
        </p>
        <p>
            <label for="Address.ZIP">ZIP:</label>
            <%= Html.TextBox("Address.ZIP") %>
            <%= Html.ValidationMessage("Address.ZIP", "*") %>
        </p>
    </fieldset>
    <p>
        <input type="submit" value="Create" />
    </p>

    <% } %>


</asp:Content>
```

LISTING 7.6   Views\Customer\Create.aspx (VB)

```
<%@ Page Title="" Language="VB" MasterPageFile="~/Views/Shared/Site.Master"
➥Inherits="System.Web.Mvc.ViewPage" %>
<asp:Content ID="Content2" ContentPlaceHolderID="MainContent" runat="server">
```

```
    <%= Html.ValidationSummary("Create was unsuccessful. Please correct the errors
➥and try again.") %>

    <% Using Html.BeginForm()%>

        <fieldset>
            <legend>Customer Info</legend>
            <p>
                <label for="FirstName">First Name:</label>
                <%= Html.TextBox("FirstName") %>
                <%= Html.ValidationMessage("FirstName", "*") %>
            </p>
            <p>
                <label for="LastName">Last Name:</label>
                <%= Html.TextBox("LastName") %>
                <%= Html.ValidationMessage("LastName", "*") %>
            </p>
        </fieldset>
        <fieldset>
        <legend>Customer Address</legend>
            <p>
                <label for="Address.Street">Street:</label>
                <%= Html.TextBox("Address.Street") %>
                <%= Html.ValidationMessage("Address.Street", "*") %>
            </p>
            <p>
                <label for="Address.City">City:</label>
                <%= Html.TextBox("Address.City") %>
                <%= Html.ValidationMessage("Address.City", "*") %>
            </p>
            <p>
                <label for="Address.ZIP">ZIP:</label>
                <%= Html.TextBox("Address.ZIP") %>
                <%= Html.ValidationMessage("Address.ZIP", "*") %>
            </p>
        </fieldset>
        <p>
            <input type="submit" value="Create" />
        </p>

    <% End Using%>

</asp:Content>
```

Notice that each of the address form fields is qualified with an Address prefix. For example, the form field that corresponds to the Street property is named Address.Street. The default model binder maps the Address.Street property to the Street property automatically.

Finally, the Create() action in Listing 7.7 accepts an instance of the Customer class. The default model binder correctly populates the properties of the Customer.Address property.

LISTING 7.7   Controllers\CustomerController.cs (C#)

```
[AcceptVerbs(HttpVerbs.Post)]
public ActionResult Create(Customer customerToCreate)
{
    // Add customer and address to database
    return RedirectToAction("Index");
}
```

LISTING 7.7   Controllers\CustomerController.vb (VB)

```
    ' POST: /Customer/Create
    <AcceptVerbs(HttpVerbs.Post)> _
    Function Create(ByVal customerToCreate As Customer) As ActionResult
        ' Add customer to database
        Return RedirectToAction("Index")
    End Function
```

Using the Bind Attribute

You can use the Bind attribute to control how a model binder converts a request into an object. The Bind attribute has the following properties:

▶ Exclude—Enables you to exclude a comma-separated list of properties from binding

▶ Include—Enables you to include a comma-separated list of properties in binding

▶ Prefix—Enables you to associate a parameter with a particular form field prefix

The most common way that you use the Bind attribute is when you exclude an Id property from binding. For example, the Movies database table includes a column named Id that is an Identity column. Because the value of an Identity column is generated by the database automatically, you don't want to bind a form field to this property.

Consider the HTML form in Listing 7.8. The HTML form includes fields for the Title, Director, and DateReleased fields. However, it does not include a form field that corresponds to the Id column because the value of this column is generated automatically in the database.

LISTING 7.8   Views\Movie\Create.aspx (C#)

```
<%@ Page Title="" Language="C#" MasterPageFile="~/Views/Shared/Site.Master"
➥Inherits="System.Web.Mvc.ViewPage<MvcApplication1.Models.Movie>" %>


<asp:Content ID="Content2" ContentPlaceHolderID="MainContent" runat="server">

    <%= Html.ValidationSummary("Create was unsuccessful. Please correct the errors
➥and try again.") %>

    <% using (Html.BeginForm()) {%>

        <fieldset>
            <legend>Create Movie</legend>
            <p>
                <label for="Title">Title:</label>
                <%= Html.TextBox("Title") %>
                <%= Html.ValidationMessage("Title", "*") %>
            </p>
            <p>
                <label for="Director">Director:</label>
                <%= Html.TextBox("Director") %>
                <%= Html.ValidationMessage("Director", "*") %>
            </p>
            <p>
                <label for="DateReleased">DateReleased:</label>
                <%= Html.TextBox("DateReleased") %>
                <%= Html.ValidationMessage("DateReleased", "*") %>
            </p>
            <p>
                <input type="submit" value="Create" />
            </p>
        </fieldset>

    <% } %>

</asp:Content>
```

LISTING 7.8   Views\Movie\Create.aspx (VB)

```
<%@ Page Title="" Language="VB" MasterPageFile="~/Views/Shared/Site.Master"
➥Inherits="System.Web.Mvc.ViewPage(Of MvcApplication1.Movie)" %>


<asp:Content ID="Content2" ContentPlaceHolderID="MainContent" runat="server">
```

```
<h2>Create</h2>

<%= Html.ValidationSummary("Create was unsuccessful. Please correct the errors
➥and try again.") %>

<% Using Html.BeginForm()%>

    <fieldset>
        <legend>Fields</legend>
        <p>
            <label for="Title">Title:</label>
            <%= Html.TextBox("Title") %>
            <%= Html.ValidationMessage("Title", "*") %>
        </p>
        <p>
            <label for="Director">Director:</label>
            <%= Html.TextBox("Director") %>
            <%= Html.ValidationMessage("Director", "*") %>
        </p>
        <p>
            <label for="DateReleased">DateReleased:</label>
            <%= Html.TextBox("DateReleased") %>
            <%= Html.ValidationMessage("DateReleased", "*") %>
        </p>
        <p>
            <input type="submit" value="Create" />
        </p>
    </fieldset>

<% End Using %>

<div>
    <%=Html.ActionLink("Back to List", "Index") %>
</div>

</asp:Content>
```

The Create() method in Listing 7.9 illustrates how you can use the Bind attribute to exclude the Id property from binding. The Bind attribute is applied to the Movie parameter.

LISTING 7.9   Controllers\MovieController.cs (C#)

```
    //
    // POST: /Movie/Create
```

```
[AcceptVerbs(HttpVerbs.Post)]
public ActionResult Create([Bind(Exclude="Id")]Movie movieToCreate)
{
    if (!ModelState.IsValid)
        return View();

    // Add movie to database
    return RedirectToAction("Index");
}
```

LISTING 7.9   Controllers\MovieController.vb (VB)

```
' POST: /Movie/Create
<AcceptVerbs(HttpVerbs.Post)> _
Function Create(<Bind(Exclude:="Id")> ByVal movieToCreate As Movie) As
➥ActionResult
    If Not ModelState.IsValid Then
        Return View()
    End If

    ' Add movie to database
    Return RedirectToAction("Index")
End Function
```

If you neglect to use the Bind attribute to exclude the Id property, you get the (somewhat mysterious) validation error message in Figure 7.4. This validation error message results from the fact that the Movie Create() form does not have an Id form field.

Using Bind with Classes

In the previous section, we applied the Bind attribute to a method parameter. You also can apply the Bind attribute to a class.

For example, the class in Listing 7.10 represents an employee. Notice that the Bind attribute is applied to the class to exclude the Employee Id property from binding.

LISTING 7.10   Models\Employees.cs (C#)

```
using System.Web.Mvc;

namespace MvcApplication1.Models
{
    [Bind(Exclude="Id")]
    public class Employee
```

```
    {
        public int Id { get; set; }
        public string FirstName { get; set; }
        public string LastName { get; set; }
    }
}
```

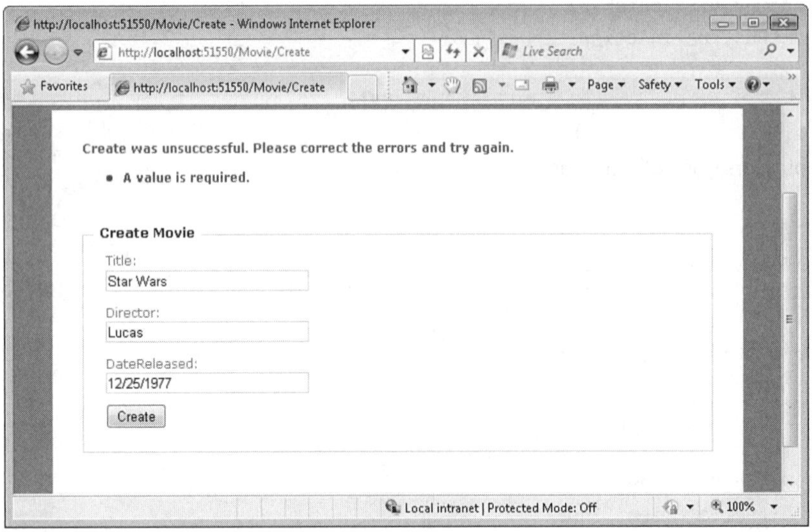

FIGURE 7.4   Use Bind to make this error go away.

LISTING 7.10   Models\Employees.vb (VB)

```vb
<Bind(Exclude:="Id")> _
Public Class Employee

    Private _id As Integer
    Private _firstName As String
    Private _lastName As String

    Public Property Id() As Integer
        Get
            Return _id
        End Get
        Set(ByVal value As Integer)
            _id = value
        End Set
    End Property

    Public Property FirstName() As String
```

```
        Get
            Return _firstName
        End Get
        Set(ByVal value As String)
            _firstName = value
        End Set
    End Property

    Public Property LastName() As String
        Get
            Return _lastName
        End Get
        Set(ByVal value As String)
            _lastName = value
        End Set
    End Property

End Class
```

After you apply the Bind attribute to a class, you no longer need to use the attribute in the controller. The Employee controller Create() action in Listing 7.11 does not use the Bind attribute. However, the default model binder respects the Bind attribute on the class and does not attempt to assign a value to the Employee Id property.

LISTING 7.11   Controllers\EmployeeController.cs (C#)

```csharp
[AcceptVerbs(HttpVerbs.Post)]
public ActionResult Create(Employee employeeToCreate)
{
    if (!ModelState.IsValid)
        return View();

    // Add employee to database

    return RedirectToAction("Index");
}
```

LISTING 7.11   Controllers\EmployeeController.vb (VB)

```vb
Public Class EmployeeController
    Inherits System.Web.Mvc.Controller

    ' GET: /Employee/Create
    Function Create() As ActionResult
```

```vb
        Return View()
    End Function


    ' POST: /Employee/Create
    <AcceptVerbs(HttpVerbs.Post)> _
    Function Create(ByVal employeeToCreate As Employee) As ActionResult
        If Not ModelState.IsValid Then
            Return View()
        End If


        ' Add employee to database
        Return RedirectToAction("Index")
    End Function

End Class
```

You can use the Bind attribute on a class even when the class is generated by the Microsoft Entity Framework (or LINQ to SQL). Entity Framework classes are partial classes. Therefore, you can create a partial class and apply the Bind attribute to the partial class.

Imagine, for example, that you create a data model for a database table named Widgets with the Entity Framework. Imagine that you have created the Widget entity in Figure 7.5.

FIGURE 7.5   Widget entity generated by Entity Framework

The Widget entity includes an Id property. You can exclude this Id property from binding by using the Bind attribute with a partial class. The partial class is contained in Listing 7.12.

LISTING 7.12   Models\Widget.cs (C#)

```csharp
using System.Web.Mvc;


namespace MvcApplication1.Models
{
    [Bind(Exclude="Id")]
    public partial class Widget
    {
```

```
        }
}
```

LISTING 7.12   Models\Widget.vb (VB)

```
<Bind(Exclude:="Id")> _
Partial Public Class Widget
End Class
```

> **WARNING**
>
> Do not apply the Bind attribute directly to the class generated by the Entity Framework Designer. The designer will delete the Bind attribute the next time that it generates the Entity Framework classes.

Using Prefixes When Binding

You can use the Bind attribute to map form fields with particular prefixes to particular classes. Use the Prefix property of the Bind attribute to associate a form field prefix with an action parameter. Using prefixes with form fields is particularly useful when you have the potential of naming conflicts in an HTML form.

In reality, you often won't need to use the Bind attribute to map prefixes to parameters because the default model binder is smart enough to do the correct mapping automatically. The default model binder will map form fields with a particular prefix to a parameter with the same name as the prefix.

For example, the form in Listing 7.13 includes both a billing address and a shipping address. Notice how the form fields are qualified with either the prefix Billing or Shipping.

LISTING 7.13   Views\Order\Create.aspx (C#)

```
<%@ Page Title="" Language="C#" MasterPageFile="~/Views/Shared/Site.Master"
➥Inherits="System.Web.Mvc.ViewPage" %>


<asp:Content ID="Content2" ContentPlaceHolderID="MainContent" runat="server">

    <% using (Html.BeginForm())
       {%>

        <fieldset>
            <legend>Billing Address</legend>

            <label for="Billing.Street">Street:</label>
```

```
                    <br /><%= Html.TextBox("Billing.Street")%>

                    <br /><br />
                    <label for="Billing.City">City:</label>
                    <br /><%= Html.TextBox("Billing.City")%>


                    <br /><br />
                    <label for="Billing.ZIP">ZIP:</label>
                    <br /><%= Html.TextBox("Billing.ZIP")%>
            </fieldset>

            <fieldset>
                <legend>Shipping Address</legend>

                <label for="Shipping.Street">Street:</label>
                <br /><%= Html.TextBox("Shipping.Street")%>

                <br /><br />
                <label for="Shipping.City">City:</label>
                <br /><%= Html.TextBox("Shipping.City")%>


                <br /><br />
                <label for="Shipping.ZIP">ZIP:</label>
                <br /><%= Html.TextBox("Shipping.ZIP")%>
            </fieldset>

            <input type="submit" value="Submit Addresses" />

            <% } %>


</asp:Content>
```

LISTING 7.13 Views\Order\Create.aspx (VB)

```
<%@ Page Title="" Language="VB" MasterPageFile="~/Views/Shared/Site.Master"
➥Inherits="System.Web.Mvc.ViewPage(Of MvcApplication1.Widget)" %>
<asp:Content ID="Content2" ContentPlaceHolderID="MainContent" runat="server">

    <% Using Html.BeginForm()%>

        <fieldset>
            <legend>Billing Address</legend>
```

```
            <label for="Billing.Street">Street:</label>
            <br /><%= Html.TextBox("Billing.Street")%>

            <br /><br />
            <label for="Billing.City">City:</label>
            <br /><%= Html.TextBox("Billing.City")%>


            <br /><br />
            <label for="Billing.ZIP">ZIP:</label>
            <br /><%= Html.TextBox("Billing.ZIP")%>
        </fieldset>

        <fieldset>
            <legend>Shipping Address</legend>

            <label for="Shipping.Street">Street:</label>
            <br /><%= Html.TextBox("Shipping.Street")%>

            <br /><br />
            <label for="Shipping.City">City:</label>
            <br /><%= Html.TextBox("Shipping.City")%>


            <br /><br />
            <label for="Shipping.ZIP">ZIP:</label>
            <br /><%= Html.TextBox("Shipping.ZIP")%>
        </fieldset>

        <input type="submit" value="Submit Addresses" />

        <% End Using%>

</asp:Content>
```

The Create() action in Listing 7.14 contains a shipping and billing parameter. The default model binder correctly associates the right form fields with the right parameters—even without the help of the Bind Prefix property. The default model binder matches the form field prefix to the parameter name.

LISTING 7.14   Controllers\OrderController.cs (C#)

```
[AcceptVerbs(HttpVerbs.Post)]
public ActionResult Create(Address shipping, Address billing)
{
```

```
// Insert into database
return RedirectToAction("Index");
}
```

LISTING 7.14   Controllers\OrderController.vb (VB)

```
' POST: /Order/Create
<AcceptVerbs(HttpVerbs.Post)> _
Function Create(ByVal shipping As Address, ByVal billing As Address) As
➥ActionResult
    ' Insert into database
    Return RedirectToAction("Index")
End Function
```

If the name of an action parameter did not match a form field prefix name, you must
use the Bind attribute's Prefix property to explicitly associate the right prefix with the
right parameter. However, in most cases, there is no need to use the Bind attribute's
Prefix property.

Using the Form Collection Model Binder

As an alternative to using the default model binder to pass strongly typed parameters to a
controller action, you can take advantage of the form collection model binder. The form
collection model binder represents an untyped collection of form fields.

For example, the Movie controller Create() action in Listing 7.15 accepts a form collection parameter. In the body of the Create() action, the form fields are bound to an
instance of the Movie class with the help of the UpdateModel() method.

When the second Create() action is invoked, the UpdateModel() method assigns the form
fields to an instance of the Movie class. The UpdateModel() method supports the following
parameters:

▶ model—The object that is the target of the binding.

▶ prefix—Only form fields with this prefix will be bound to the model.

▶ includeProperties—An array of properties to include when binding.

▶ excludeProperties—An array of properties to exclude when binding.

▶ valueProvider—The source of the information used during binding.

LISTING 7.15   Controllers\Movie2Controller.cs (C#)

```
using System.Web.Mvc;
using MvcApplication1.Models;
```

```
namespace MvcApplication1.Controllers
{
    public class Movie2Controller : Controller
    {
        // GET: /Movie2/Create
        public ActionResult Create()
        {
            return View();
        }

        // POST: /Movie2/Create
        [AcceptVerbs(HttpVerbs.Post)]
        public ActionResult Create(FormCollection collection)
        {
            var movieToCreate = new Movie();
            this.UpdateModel(movieToCreate, collection.ToValueProvider());

            // Insert movie into database
            return RedirectToAction("Index");
        }
    }
}
```

LISTING 7.15   Controllers\Movie2Controller.vb (VB)

```
Public Class Movie2Controller
    Inherits System.Web.Mvc.Controller

    ' GET: /Movie2/Create
    Function Create() As ActionResult
        Return View()
    End Function

    ' POST: /Movie2/Create
    <AcceptVerbs(HttpVerbs.Post)> _
    Function Create(ByVal collection As FormCollection) As ActionResult
        Dim movieToCreate As New Movie()
        Me.UpdateModel(movieToCreate, collection.ToValueProvider())
        ' Insert movie into database
        Return RedirectToAction("Index")
    End Function

End Class
```

NOTE

Behind the scenes, the UpdateModel() method uses the set of model binders registered for the application. For example, the UpdateModel() method uses the default
model binder and any custom model binders that you create.

You don't actually need to use the form collection model binder. You can use the
UpdateModel() method without passing the form collection to the UpdateModel()
method. For example, the Create() action in Listing 7.16 does not accept any parameters,
and the UpdateModel() method still works.

LISTING 7.16   Controllers\Movie3Controller.cs (C#)

```csharp
using System.Web.Mvc;
using MvcApplication1.Models;

namespace MvcApplication1.Controllers
{
    public class Movie3Controller : Controller
    {
        // GET: /Movie3/Create
        [ActionName("Create")]
        public ActionResult Create_GET()
        {
            return View();
        }

        // POST: /Movie3/Create
        [AcceptVerbs(HttpVerbs.Post)]
        [ActionName("Create")]
        public ActionResult Create_POST()
        {
            var movieToCreate = new Movie();
            this.UpdateModel(movieToCreate, new string[] {"Title", "Director",
➥"DateReleased"});
            // Add movie to database
            return RedirectToAction("Index");
        }

    }
}
```

LISTING 7.16   Controllers\Movie3Controller.vb (VB)

```vb
Public Class Movie3Controller
    Inherits System.Web.Mvc.Controller

    ' GET: /Movie3/Create
    <ActionName("Create")> _
    Function Create_GET() As ActionResult
        Return View()
    End Function

    ' POST: /Movie3/Create
    <AcceptVerbs(HttpVerbs.Post)> _
    <ActionName("Create")> _
    Function Create_POST() As ActionResult
        Dim movieToCreate As New Movie()
        Me.UpdateModel(movieToCreate, New String() {"Title", "Director",
➡"DateReleased"})
        ' Insert movie into database
        Return RedirectToAction("Index")
    End Function

End Class
```

In Listing 7.16, the UpdateModel() method is called with the model and includeProperties parameters. A form collection is not passed to the UpdateModel() method.

> **NOTE**
>
> The advantage of passing the form collection to the UpdateModel() method explicitly is that it makes your code more testable. You can easily fake the form collection in your tests.

Using the HTTP Posted File Base Model Binder

The third model binder included in the ASP.NET MVC framework is the HTTP posted file base model binder. This model binder enables you to pass uploaded files to a controller action.

The view in Listing 7.17 renders a form for uploading files (see Figure 7.6).

FIGURE 7.6   Uploading files

LISTING 7.17   Views\Content\Create.aspx

```
<%@ Page Title="" Language="C#" MasterPageFile="~/Views/Shared/Site.Master"
➥Inherits="System.Web.Mvc.ViewPage" %>


<asp:Content ID="Content2" ContentPlaceHolderID="MainContent" runat="server">

    <h2>Upload File</h2>

    <form method="post" enctype="multipart/form-data" action="<%= Url.Action
➥("Create") %>">
        <input name="upload" type="file" />
        <input type="submit" value="Upload File" />
    </form>

</asp:Content>
```

The controller action in Listing 7.18 illustrates how you can accept a file upload and save the file upload to the file system. Notice that the controller action accepts an HttpPostedFileBase parameter.

LISTING 7.18   Controllers\ContentController.cs (C#)

```
[AcceptVerbs(HttpVerbs.Post)]
public ActionResult Create(HttpPostedFileBase upload)
{
    // Save file
    var fileName = Path.GetFileName(upload.FileName);
    upload.SaveAs(Server.MapPath("~/Uploads/" + fileName));
```

```
        return RedirectToAction("Create");
}
```

LISTING 7.18 Controllers\ContentController.vb (VB)

```vb
    <AcceptVerbs(HttpVerbs.Post)> _
    Function Create(ByVal upload As HttpPostedFileBase) As ActionResult
        ' Save File
        Dim fileName = Path.GetFileName(upload.FileName)
        upload.SaveAs(Server.MapPath("~/Uploads/" & fileName))
        Return RedirectToAction("Create")
    End Function
```

Creating a Custom Model Binder

The default model binder is powerful. However, it cannot handle every object. If you need to handle a type of object that is beyond the power of the default model binder, you need to create a custom model binder.

You create a custom model binder by implementing the IModelBinder interface. This interface has a single method named BindModel().

> **NOTE**
>
> The user model binder example in Listing 7.19 is roughly based on an example original-ly created by Scott Hanselman, who is another member of my team at Microsoft. You can see his blog entry at www.hanselman.com/blog/ IPrincipalUserModelBinderInASPNETMVCForEasierTesting.aspx.

For example, Listing 7.19 contains a new model binder named the user model binder. This model binder enables you to pass a user parameter to a controller action that represents the current authenticated user automatically.

LISTING 7.19 CustomModelBinders\UserModelBinder.cs (C#)

```csharp
using System.Web.Mvc;


namespace MvcApplication1.CustomModelBinders
{
    public class UserModelBinder : IModelBinder
    {
        public object BindModel(ControllerContext controllerContext,
➥ModelBindingContext bindingContext)
```

```
    {
        return controllerContext.HttpContext.User;
    }

}
}
```

LISTING 7.19   CustomModelBinders\UserModelBinder.vb (VB)

```
Public Class UserModelBinder
    Implements IModelBinder

    Public Function BindModel(ByVal controllerContext As ControllerContext, ByVal
➥bindingContext As ModelBindingContext) As Object Implements IModelBinder.BindModel
        Return controllerContext.HttpContext.User
    End Function

End Class
```

After you create a custom model binder, there are two ways that you can use it. First, you can use the ModelBinder attribute and apply the custom model binder to a single parameter. This approach is illustrated by the GetSecret() action in Listing 7.20.

LISTING 7.20   Controllers\CompanyController.cs (C#)

```
using System.Web.Mvc;
using MvcApplication1.CustomModelBinders;
using System.Security.Principal;

namespace MvcApplication1.Controllers
{
    public class CompanyController : Controller
    {

        public string GetSecret([ModelBinder(typeof(UserModelBinder))] IPrincipal
➥user)
        {
            if (user.Identity.Name == "CEO")
                return "The secret is 42.";
            else
                return "You are not authorized!";
        }

    }
}
```

LISTING 7.20   Controllers\CompanyController.vb (VB)

```vb
Imports System.Security.Principal


Public Class CompanyController
    Inherits Controller

    Public Function GetSecret(<ModelBinder(GetType(UserModelBinder))> ByVal user As
➥IPrincipal) As String
        If user.Identity.Name = "CEO" Then
            Return "The secret is 42."
        Else
            Return "You are not authorized!"
        End If
    End Function

End Class
```

If you invoke the controller action in Listing 7.20, and you are not logged in with the username CEO, you cannot see the secret message. The user parameter gets its value automatically from the user model binder.

If you plan to use a custom model binder in multiple places within an application, you should register the custom model binder for the entire application. Listing 7.21 illustrates how you can register the user model binder in the Application_Start event handler in the Global.asax file.

LISTING 7.21   Global.asax.cs (C#)

```csharp
protected void Application_Start()
{
    RegisterRoutes(RouteTable.Routes);

    ModelBinders.Binders.Add(typeof(IPrincipal), new UserModelBinder());
}
```

LISTING 7.21   Global.asax.vb (VB)

```vb
Protected Sub Application_Start()
    RegisterRoutes(RouteTable.Routes)

    ModelBinders.Binders.Add(GetType(IPrincipal), New UserModelBinder())
End Sub
```

When you register a custom model binder, you associate the model binder with a particular type. In Listing 7.21, the user model binder is associated with the IPrincipal type.

> **NOTE**
>
> Another situation in which I discovered that I needed to create a custom model binder was when I was working with LINQ to SQL. The default model binder won't deserialize the LINQ to SQL Version property because it is a System.Data.Linq.Binary property. Luckily, you don't have to write this model binder yourself. The ASP.NET MVC Futures, available at CodePlex.com, includes a LinqBinaryModelBinder.

Understanding Action Filters

An action filter enables you to execute code in the following situations:

- ▶ Immediately before a controller action is executed
- ▶ Immediately after a controller action is executed
- ▶ Immediately before an action result is executed
- ▶ Immediately after an action result is executed

An action filter is an attribute that you apply to a controller action or entire controller. Several features of the ASP.NET MVC framework are implemented with action filters. For example, the OutputCache, HandleError, and Authorize attributes are all action filters.

> **NOTE**
>
> Technically, the Authorize and HandleError attributes are *filter attributes instead of action filter attributes*. (Action filters derive from filters.) Because you want certain types of filters to run before others, such as the Authorize filter, the ASP.NET MVC framework distinguishes these two types of filters.

You can do all manner of strange and interesting things in an action filter. For example, you can use an action filter to modify the view data that a controller action returns.

In this section, we create a simple custom action filter named the Log. This filter logs each action event to the Visual Studio output window.

> **NOTE**
>
> As an alternative to using an action filter, you can handle the OnActionExecuting(), OnActionExecuted(), OnResultExecuting(), or OnResultExecuted() methods on the controller class. These events are raised before and after a controller action and controller action result are executed.

Creating a Log Action Filter

In this section, we create a custom action filter that logs each action event to the Visual Studio Output window (see Figure 7.7). You can open the Visual Studio Output window by selecting the menu option Debug, Windows, Output.

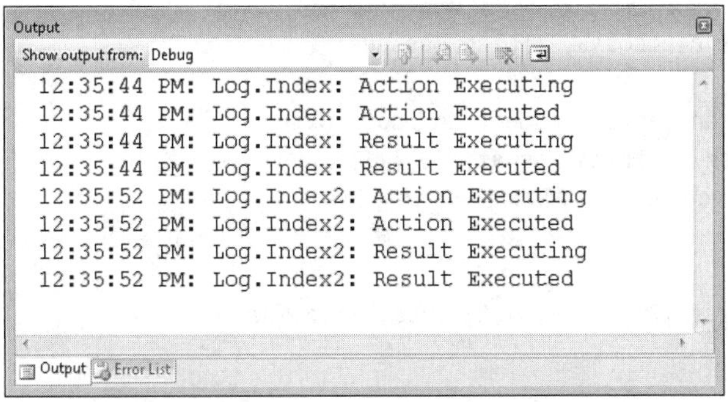

FIGURE 7.7   Output from the Log action filter

You can use the Log action filter to help debug your controllers. The Log action filter is contained in Listing 7.22.

LISTING 7.22   CustomActionFilters\LogActionFilter.cs (C#)

```csharp
using System;
using System.Web.Mvc;
using System.Web.Routing;

namespace MvcApplication1.CutomActionFilters
{
    public class LogAttribute: ActionFilterAttribute
    {
        public override void OnActionExecuting(ActionExecutingContext filterContext)
        {
            Log(filterContext.RouteData, "Action Executing");
        }

        public override void OnActionExecuted(ActionExecutedContext filterContext)
        {
            Log(filterContext.RouteData, "Action Executed");
        }

        public override void OnResultExecuting(ResultExecutingContext filterContext)
        {
            Log(filterContext.RouteData, "Result Executing");
```

```
        }

        public override void OnResultExecuted(ResultExecutedContext filterContext)
        {
            Log(filterContext.RouteData, "Result Executed");
        }

        private void Log(RouteData routeData, string message)
        {
            // Extract controller and action name from route data
            var controllerAndAction = String.Format("{0}.{1}",
➥routeData.Values["controller"], routeData.Values["action"]);

            // format message
            message = String.Format("{0:T}: {1}: {2}", DateTime.Now,
➥controllerAndAction, message);

            // write to console
            System.Diagnostics.Debug.WriteLine(message);
        }

    }
}
```

LISTING 7.22   CustomActionFilters\LogActionFilter.vb (VB)

```
Public Class LogAttribute
    Inherits ActionFilterAttribute

    Public Overrides Sub OnActionExecuting(ByVal filterContext As
➥ActionExecutingContext)
        Log(filterContext.RouteData, "Action Executing")
    End Sub

    Public Overrides Sub OnActionExecuted(ByVal filterContext As
➥ActionExecutedContext)
        Log(filterContext.RouteData, "Action Executed")
    End Sub

    Public Overrides Sub OnResultExecuting(ByVal filterContext As
➥ResultExecutingContext)
        Log(filterContext.RouteData, "Result Executing")
    End Sub
    Public Overrides Sub OnResultExecuted(ByVal filterContext As
➥ResultExecutedContext)
```

```
        Log(filterContext.RouteData, "Result Executed")
    End Sub

    Private Sub Log(ByVal routeData As RouteData, ByVal message As String)
        ' Extract controller and action name from route data
        Dim controllerAndAction = String.Format("{0}.{1}", routeData.Values
➥("controller"), routeData.Values("action"))

        ' format message
        message = String.Format("{0:T}: {1}: {2}", DateTime.Now,
➥controllerAndAction, message)

        ' write to console
        System.Diagnostics.Debug.WriteLine(message)
    End Sub

End Class
```

The `LogAttribute` class in Listing 7.22 inherits from the base `ActionFilterAttribute` class and the derived class overrides the `OnActionExecuting()`, `OnActionExecuted()`, `OnResultExecuting()`, and `OnResultExecuted()` method. Each of these methods writes a message to the Visual Studio Output window with the help of the `Log()` method.

You can apply the `Log` action filter to either a particular controller action or an entire controller. For example, the `Log` action filter is applied to the entire controller contained in Listing 7.23. When you call the `Index()` or `Index2()` action, the action events are logged to the Output window.

LISTING 7.23 Controllers\LogController.cs (C#)

```
using System.Web.Mvc;
using MvcApplication1.CutomActionFilters;

namespace MvcApplication1.Controllers
{
    [Log]
    public class LogController : Controller
    {

        public ActionResult Index()
        {
            return View();
        }

        public ActionResult Index2()
        {
```

```
            return View();
        }

    }
}
```

LISTING 7.23   Controllers\LogController.vb (VB)

```vb
<Log()> _
Public Class LogController
    Inherits System.Web.Mvc.Controller

    Function Index() As ActionResult
        Return View()
    End Function

    Function Index2() As ActionResult
        Return View()
    End Function

End Class
```

Summary

The bulk of this chapter was devoted to the topic of model binders. In this chapter, you learned how to work with the three model binders included with the ASP.NET MVC framework: the default model binder, the form collection model binder, and the HTTP posted file base model binder. You also learned how you can create a custom model binder.

In the final part of this chapter, we explored the topic of action filters. You learned how to create a custom action filter that logs action events to the Visual Studio Output window.

CHAPTER 8

Validating Form Data

This chapter is devoted to the topic of performing validation in an ASP.NET MVC application. For example, you learn how to validate whether a user has entered a required value into an HTML form field.

Over the course of this chapter, we examine alternative approaches to validation. You learn how to perform validation in a service layer and how to perform validation using the IDateErrorInfo interface.

Finally, at the end of this chapter, you learn how to test code that performs validation. You learn how to verify that the expected error message is generated from a controller.

Understanding Model State

You represent validation errors in an ASP.NET MVC application with something called the model state dictionary. The model state dictionary contains a collection of model state objects that represent the state of particular properties.

You pass validation errors from a controller action to a view by passing the model state dictionary from the controller to a view. Both the controller class and the view class have a property named ModelState that exposes the model state dictionary.

The controller in Listing 8.1 illustrates how you use model state. The Create() action validates the Title and Director properties of the movie passed to the action. If the movie fails validation, the ModelState.IsValid property returns the value false and the action redisplays the form for creating a movie (see Figure 8.1).

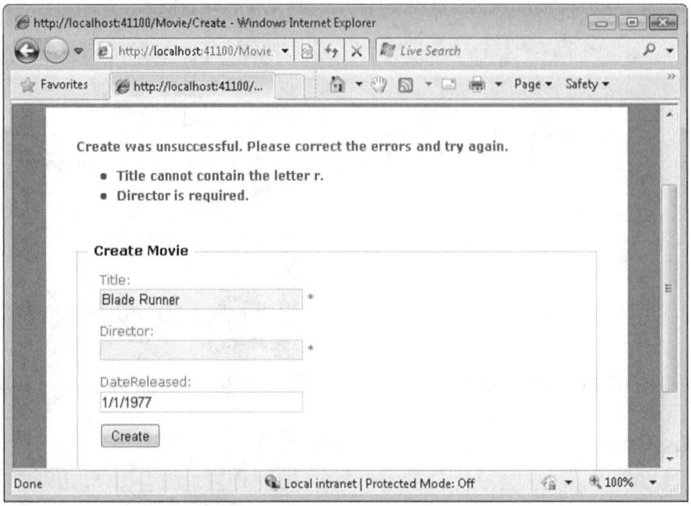

FIGURE 8.1   Validation errors generated from model state

LISTING 8.1   Controllers\MovieController.cs (C#)

```csharp
using System.Linq;
using System.Web.Mvc;
using MvcApplication1.Models;

namespace MvcApplication1.Controllers
{
    public class MovieController : Controller
    {
        private MoviesDBEntities _entities = new MoviesDBEntities();

        public ActionResult Index()
        {
            return View(_entities.MovieSet.ToList());
        }

        //
        // GET: /Movie/Create

        public ActionResult Create()
        {
            return View();
        }

        //
        // POST: /Movie/Create
```

```
        [AcceptVerbs(HttpVerbs.Post)]
        public ActionResult Create([Bind(Exclude="Id")]Movie movieToCreate)
        {
            // Validate
            if (movieToCreate.Title.Trim().Length == 0)
                ModelState.AddModelError("Title", "Title is required.");f
            if (movieToCreate.Title.IndexOf("r") > 0)

                ModelState.AddModelError("Title", "Title cannot contain the letter
➥r.");
            if (movieToCreate.Director.Trim().Length == 0)
                ModelState.AddModelError("Director", "Director is required.");
            if (!ModelState.IsValid)
                return View();

            // Add to database
            _entities.AddToMovieSet(movieToCreate);
            _entities.SaveChanges();

            // Redirect
            return RedirectToAction("Index");
        }


    }
}
```

LISTING 8.1   Controllers\MovieController.vb (VB)

```
Public Class MovieController
    Inherits Controller

    Private _entities As New MoviesDBEntities()

    Public Function Index() As ActionResult
        Return View(_entities.MovieSet.ToList())
    End Function

    '
    ' GET: /Movie/Create

    Public Function Create() As ActionResult
        Return View()
    End Function

    '
```

```
' POST: /Movie/Create

<AcceptVerbs(HttpVerbs.Post)> _
Public Function Create(<Bind(Exclude:="Id")> ByVal movieToCreate As Movie) As
➥ActionResult
    ' Validate
    If movieToCreate.Title.Trim().Length = 0 Then
        ModelState.AddModelError("Title", "Title is required.")
    End If
    If movieToCreate.Title.IndexOf("r") > 0 Then
        ModelState.AddModelError("Title", "Title cannot contain the letter r.")
    End If
    If movieToCreate.Director.Trim().Length = 0 Then
        ModelState.AddModelError("Director", "Director is required.")
    End If
    If (Not ModelState.IsValid) Then
        Return View()
    End If

    ' Add to database
    _entities.AddToMovieSet(movieToCreate)
    _entities.SaveChanges()

    ' Redirect
    Return RedirectToAction("Index")
End Function

End Class
```

Validation errors are added to model state with the help of the AddModelError() method. This method accepts two values: a key and an error message. The key (typically) corresponds to the property being validated.

If any errors have been added to model state, the ModelState.IsValid property returns false. In Listing 8.1, when ModelState.IsValid returns false, the original HTML form for creating a movie is redisplayed. Otherwise, if ModelState.IsValid returns true, the new movie is added to the database, and the user is redirected to the Index action.

NOTE

Notice the Bind attribute that is applied to the Movie parameter in Listing 8.1. This Bind attribute tells the model binder to ignore the Id property when binding. If you do not exclude the Id property and you do not include a form field for Id, you get a mysterious validation error in model state.

Understanding the Validation Helpers

The ASP.NET MVC framework includes two validation helpers: `Html.ValidationSummary()` and `Html.ValidationMessage()`. The `Html.ValidationSummary()` helper displays a bulleted list of all the validation error messages in model state. The `Html.ValidationMessage` helper displays a validation error message associated with a particular key (property).

When you generate a view by using the Visual Studio Add View command, the generated view contains both of these validation helpers automatically (see Listing 8.2). The `Html.ValidationSummary()` helper appears at the top of the form. The `Html.ValidationMessage()` helper appears next to each form field.

LISTING 8.2   Views\Movie\Create.aspx (C#)

```
<%@ Page Title="" Language="C#" MasterPageFile="~/Views/Shared/Site.Master"
➥Inherits="System.Web.Mvc.ViewPage<MvcApplication1.Models.Movie>" %>


<asp:Content ID="Content2" ContentPlaceHolderID="MainContent" runat="server">

    <%= Html.ValidationSummary("Create was unsuccessful. Please correct the errors
➥and try again.") %>

    <% using (Html.BeginForm()) {%>

        <fieldset>
            <legend>Create Movie</legend>
            <p>
                <label for="Title">Title:</label>
                <%= Html.TextBox("Title") %>
                <%= Html.ValidationMessage("Title", "*") %>
            </p>
            <p>
                <label for="Director">Director:</label>
                <%= Html.TextBox("Director") %>
                <%= Html.ValidationMessage("Director", "*") %>
            </p>
            <p>
                <label for="DateReleased">DateReleased:</label>
                <%= Html.TextBox("DateReleased") %>
                <%= Html.ValidationMessage("DateReleased", "*") %>
            </p>
            <p>
                <input type="submit" value="Create" />
```

```
            </p>
        </fieldset>

    <% } %>

    <div>
        <%=Html.ActionLink("Back to List", "Index") %>
    </div>

</asp:Content>
```

LISTING 8.2   Views\Movie\Create.aspx (VB)

```
<%@ Page Title="" Language="VB" MasterPageFile="~/Views/Shared/Site.Master"
➥Inherits="System.Web.Mvc.ViewPage(Of MvcApplication1.Movie)" %>


<asp:Content ID="Content2" ContentPlaceHolderID="MainContent" runat="server">

    <%= Html.ValidationSummary("Create was unsuccessful. Please correct the errors
➥and try again.") %>

    <% Using Html.BeginForm()%>

        <fieldset>
            <legend>Create Movie</legend>
            <p>
                <label for="Title">Title:</label>
                <%= Html.TextBox("Title") %>
                <%= Html.ValidationMessage("Title", "*") %>
            </p>
            <p>
                <label for="Director">Director:</label>
                <%= Html.TextBox("Director") %>
                <%= Html.ValidationMessage("Director", "*") %>
            </p>
            <p>
                <label for="DateReleased">DateReleased:</label>
                <%= Html.TextBox("DateReleased") %>
                <%= Html.ValidationMessage("DateReleased", "*") %>
            </p>
            <p>
                <input type="submit" value="Create" />
            </p>
        </fieldset>
```

```
    <% End Using %>

    <div>
        <%=Html.ActionLink("Back to List", "Index") %>
    </div>

</asp:Content>
```

The `Html.ValidationSummary()` helper accepts the following optional parameters:

▶ `message (optional)`—The message appears before the bulleted list of validation error messages.

▶ `htmlAttributes (optional)`—The HTML attributes are added to the `<span>` tag that surrounds the message and the `<ul>` tag that surrounds the list of validation error messages.

The `Html.ValidationMessage()` helper accepts the following parameters:

▶ `modelName`—The name of the key in model state that corresponds to the validation message.

▶ `validationMessage (optional)`—The error message displayed. If not supplied, the message from model state is displayed.

▶ `htmlAttributes`—The HTML attributes are added to the `<span>` tag that surrounds the error message.

Styling Validation Error Messages

There are several Cascading Style Sheets classes that you can modify to alter the appearance of the validation error messages. These classes are given default values in the Site.css file included in a new ASP.NET MVC project (located in the Content folder):

```
.field-validation-error
{
    color: #ff0000;
}


.input-validation-error
{
    border: 1px solid #ff0000;
    background-color: #ffeeee;
}


.validation-summary-errors
{
```

```
    font-weight: bold;
    color: #ff0000;
}
```

The `field-validation-error` class is applied to the error message rendered by the `Html.ValidationMessage()` helper.

The `input-validation-error` class is applied to form fields rendered by helpers such as the `Html.TextBox()` or `Html.TextArea()` helpers.

Finally, the `validation-summary-errors` class is applied to both the `<span>` and `<ul>` tags that are rendered by the `Html.ValidationSummary()` helper.

NOTE

The `HtmlHelper` class includes three static (shared) methods named `HtmlHelper.ValidationInputCssClassName()`, `HtmlHelper.ValidationMessageCssClassName()`, and `HtmlHelper.ValidationSummaryCssClassName()` that you can use to generate the CSS class names described in this section. These methods simply return CSS class names and nothing else.

Prebinding and Postbinding Validation

If you submit the form for creating a new movie, and you don't provide a value for the `DateReleased` property, you get the validation error message in Figure 8.2. Where does this error message come from?

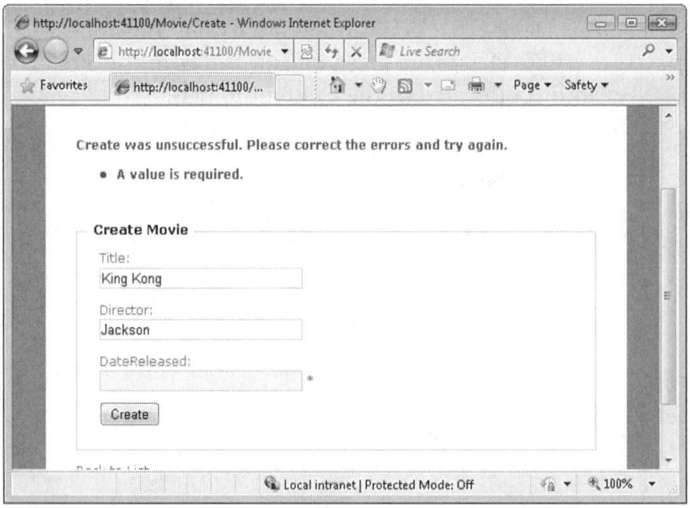

FIGURE 8.2   Mysterious error message

There are actually two types of validation error messages: prebinding and postbinding validation errors. Prebinding validation error messages are added to model state before a model binder creates an object and postbinding validation error messages are added to model state after an object is created.

In Chapter 7, "Understanding Model Binders and Action Filters," we discussed the default model binder. The default model binder is responsible for taking a browser request and converting it into a parameter passed to an action. For example, it takes a set of untyped form fields and converts them into an object.

However, the default model binder cannot always complete its task successfully. Imagine that a user types the string "apple" into the DateReleased form field. Because the default model binder cannot assign a string to a `DateTime` property, the default model binder adds an error message to model state.

There are two situations in which the default model binder generates a validation error message:

▶ **Property value required**—When you attempt to assign `null` to a property that does not accept `null` (for example, submitting a blank form field for a `DateTime` property)

▶ **Invalid property value**—When you attempt to assign the wrong type of value to a property (for example, submitting a form field with the value "apple" for an `Integer` property).

The only way to customize prebinding validation error messages is to create a custom resource string. Follow these steps:

1. Modify the `Application_Start` event handler in the Global.asax file so that it looks like Listing 8.3.

2. Create an `App_GlobalResources` folder by selecting the menu option Add, Add ASP.NET Folder, App_GlobalResources (see Figure 8.3).

3. Right-click the `App_GlobalResources` folder and select the menu option Add, Add New Item.

4. In the Add New Item dialog, select the Resource File template. Name the file MyResources.resx and click the Add button.

5. Add two resource strings named `InvalidPropertyValue` and `PropertyValueRequired` (see Figure 8.4).

LISTING 8.3   Global.asax.cs (C#)

```
protected void Application_Start()
{
    RegisterRoutes(RouteTable.Routes);

    DefaultModelBinder.ResourceClassKey = "MyResources";
    ValidationExtensions.ResourceClassKey = "MyResources";
}
```

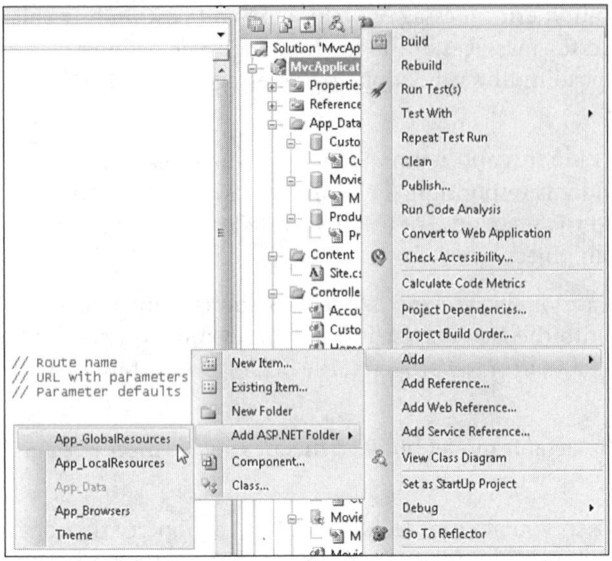

FIGURE 8.3   Adding the App_GlobalResources folder

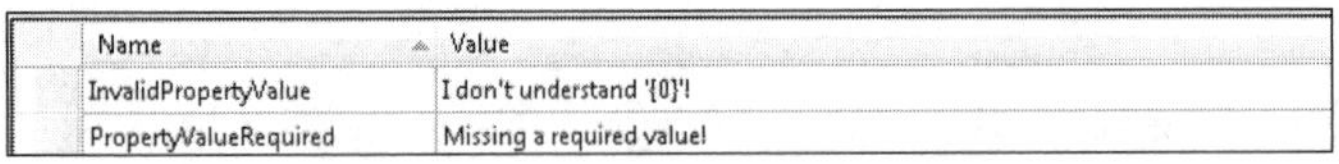

Name	Value
InvalidPropertyValue	I don't understand '{0}'!
PropertyValueRequired	Missing a required value!

FIGURE 8.4   Creating resources

LISTING 8.3   Global.asax.vb (VB)

```vb
Sub Application_Start()
    RegisterRoutes(RouteTable.Routes)

    DefaultModelBinder.ResourceClassKey = "MyResources"
    ValidationExtensions.ResourceClassKey = "MyResources"
End Sub
```

After you make these changes, the text defined in the MyResources.resx file will be used for the prebinding validation error messages. For example, Figure 8.5 illustrates what happens when you submit the value "eeek" for a DateTime field.

There are some limitations to customizing the prebinding error message. First, you cannot include the name of the property in the error message. Second, the Html.ValidationSummary() helper does not display the InvalidPropertyValue error message. If you need to completely customize a prebinding error message, you should consider creating a custom model binder or not using a model binder at all.

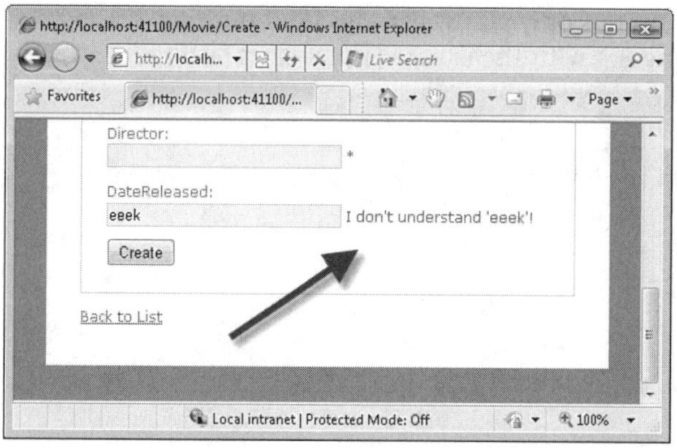

FIGURE 8.5   A customized prebinding error message

Validating with a Service Layer

From the perspective of good software design, the `Movie` controller is horrible. The `Movie` controller mixes controller logic, validation logic, and data access logic. It enthusiastically violates the Single Responsibility Principle (SRP).

In this section, we redeem ourselves by separating the controller, validation, and data access logic into separate layers. We create separate controller, service, and repository layers. That way, making changes in one layer does not jeopardize working code in another layer (see Figure 8.6).

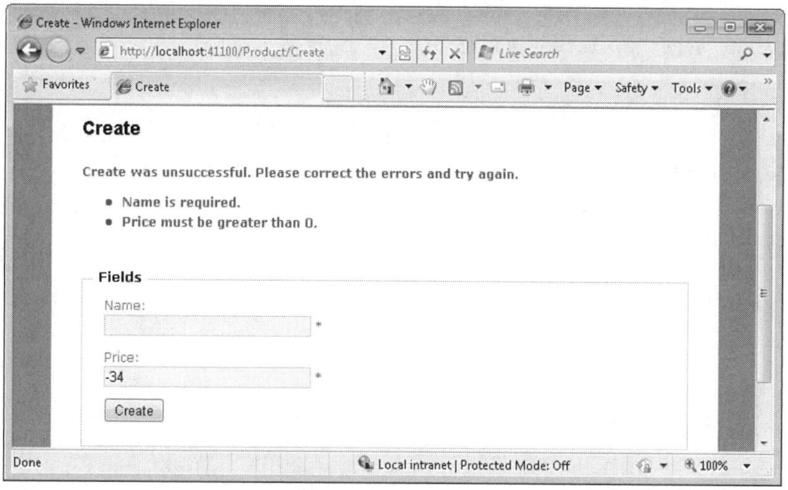

FIGURE 8.6   Dividing an application into separate layers

The `Movie2` controller in Listing 8.4 contains only controller logic and nothing else. Compare the `Create()` action in Listing 8.4 with the `Create()` action in Listing 8.1. The `Create()` action in Listing 8.4 has only a few lines of code.

LISTING 8.4   Controllers\Movie2Controller.cs (C#)

```csharp
using System.Linq;
using System.Web.Mvc;
using MvcApplication1.Models;

namespace MvcApplication1.Controllers
{
    public class Movie2Controller : Controller
    {
        private IMovieService _service;

        public Movie2Controller()
        {
            _service = new MovieService(this.ModelState);
        }

        public Movie2Controller(IMovieService service)
        {
            _service = service;
        }

        public ActionResult Index()
        {
            return View(_service.ListMovies());
        }

        //
        // GET: /Movie/Create

        public ActionResult Create()
        {
            return View();
        }

        //
        // POST: /Movie/Create

        [AcceptVerbs(HttpVerbs.Post)]
        public ActionResult Create([Bind(Exclude = "Id")]Movie movieToCreate)
        {
            if (_service.CreateMovie(movieToCreate))
```

```
                return RedirectToAction("Index");
            return View();
        }


    }
}
```

LISTING 8.4   Controllers\Movie2Controller.vb (VB)

```vb
Public Class Movie2Controller
    Inherits Controller

    Private _service As IMovieService

    Sub New()
        _service = New MovieService(Me.ModelState)
    End Sub

    Sub New(ByVal service As IMovieService)
        _service = service
    End Sub

    Function Index() As ActionResult
        Return View(_service.ListMovies())
    End Function

    ' GET: /Movie/Create

    Function Create() As ActionResult
        Return View()
    End Function

    ' POST: /Movie/Create

    <AcceptVerbs(HttpVerbs.Post)> _
 Function Create(<Bind(Exclude:="Id")> ByVal movieToCreate As Movie) As ActionResult
        If _service.CreateMovie(movieToCreate) Then
            Return RedirectToAction("Index")
        End If
        Return View()
    End Function

End Class
```

> **NOTE**
>
> The Movie2 controller uses a software pattern named Dependency Injection. Notice that the controller class uses the abstract IMovieService interface instead of the concrete MovieService class everywhere except the constructor.
>
> One benefit of the Dependency Injection pattern is that it makes the controller more testable. In the last section of this chapter, you learn how to test whether this controller class returns the right validation error messages.

The controller in Listing 8.4 uses a class named the MovieService in both its Index() and Create() action. The MovieService class is used in the Index() action to return the list of movies. The Movie service is used in the Create() action to create a new movie.

The MovieService class is created in the controller's constructor. Notice that the controller model state dictionary is passed to the Movie service when the service is created. The Movie service communicates validation error messages back to the controller through this model state dictionary.

The code for the MovieService class is included in Listing 8.5.

LISTING 8.5   Models\MovieService.cs (C#)

```
using System.Collections.Generic;
using System.Web.Mvc;

namespace MvcApplication1.Models
{
    public class MovieService : IMovieService
    {
        private ModelStateDictionary _modelState;
        private IMovieRepository _repository;

        public MovieService(ModelStateDictionary modelState)
            :this(modelState, new MovieRepository()){}

        public MovieService(ModelStateDictionary modelState, IMovieRepository
➥repository)
        {
            _modelState = modelState;
            _repository = repository;
        }

        public IEnumerable<Movie> ListMovies()
        {
            return _repository.ListMovies();
        }
```

```csharp
        public bool CreateMovie(Movie movieToCreate)
        {
            // validate
            if (movieToCreate.Title.Trim().Length == 0)
                _modelState.AddModelError("Title", "Title is required.");
            if (movieToCreate.Title.IndexOf("r") > 0)
                _modelState.AddModelError("Title", "Title cannot contain the letter
➥r.");
            if (movieToCreate.Director.Trim().Length == 0)
                _modelState.AddModelError("Director", "Director is required.");
            if (!_modelState.IsValid)
                return false;

            _repository.CreateMovie(movieToCreate);
            return true;
        }
    }

    public interface IMovieService
    {
        IEnumerable<Movie> ListMovies();
        bool CreateMovie(Movie movieToCreate);
    }
}
```

LISTING 8.5   Models\MovieService.vb (VB)

```vbnet
Public Class MovieService
    Implements IMovieService

    Private _modelState As ModelStateDictionary
    Private _repository As IMovieRepository

    Public Sub New(ByVal modelState As ModelStateDictionary)
        Me.New(modelState, New MovieRepository())
    End Sub

    Public Sub New(ByVal modelState As ModelStateDictionary, ByVal repository As
➥IMovieRepository)
        _modelState = modelState
        _repository = repository
    End Sub
```

```
    Public Function ListMovies() As IEnumerable(Of Movie) Implements
➥IMovieService.ListMovies
        Return _repository.ListMovies()
    End Function

    Public Function CreateMovie(ByVal movieToCreate As Movie) As Boolean Implements
➥IMovieService.CreateMovie
        ' validate
        If movieToCreate.Title.Trim().Length = 0 Then
            _modelState.AddModelError("Title", "Title is required.")
        End If
        If movieToCreate.Title.IndexOf("r") > 0 Then
            _modelState.AddModelError("Title", "Title cannot contain the letter r.")
        End If
        If movieToCreate.Director.Trim().Length = 0 Then
            _modelState.AddModelError("Director", "Director is required.")
        End If
        If (Not _modelState.IsValid) Then
            Return False
        End If

        _repository.CreateMovie(movieToCreate)
        Return True
    End Function
End Class

Public Interface IMovieService
    Function ListMovies() As IEnumerable(Of Movie)
    Function CreateMovie(ByVal movieToCreate As Movie) As Boolean
End Interface
```

The Movie service contains both a ListMovies() method and a CreateMovie() method.
The CreateMovie() method contains the validation logic that was previously located in the
controller class. The CreateMovie() method validates a new movie and, if the movie passes
validation, uses the MovieRepository class to insert the new movie into the database.

If there is a validation error, the error is added to the controller's model state. Because the
error message is added to model state, the error message is displayed by the Create() view
when the view is rendered to the browser.

The Movie service does not contain any data access logic. All the data access logic is
contained in a separate MovieRepository class. The code for the MovieRepository class is
contained in Listing 8.6.

LISTING 8.6   Models\MovieRepository.cs (C#)

```csharp
using System;
using System.Collections.Generic;
using System.Linq;
using System.Web;

namespace MvcApplication1.Models
{
    public class MovieRepository : IMovieRepository
    {
        private MoviesDBEntities _entities = new MoviesDBEntities();

        public IEnumerable<Movie> ListMovies()
        {
            return _entities.MovieSet.ToList();
        }

        public void CreateMovie(Movie movieToCreate)
        {
            _entities.AddToMovieSet(movieToCreate);
            _entities.SaveChanges();
        }
    }

    public interface IMovieRepository
    {
        IEnumerable<Movie> ListMovies();
        void CreateMovie(Movie movieToCreate);
    }
}
```

LISTING 8.6   Models\MovieRepository.vb (VB)

```vb
Public Class MovieRepository
    Implements IMovieRepository

    Private _entities As New MoviesDBEntities()

    Public Function ListMovies() As IEnumerable(Of Movie) Implements
➥IMovieRepository.ListMovies
        Return _entities.MovieSet.ToList()
    End Function
```

```
    Public Sub CreateMovie(ByVal movieToCreate As Movie) Implements
➥IMovieRepository.CreateMovie
        _entities.AddToMovieSet(movieToCreate)
        _entities.SaveChanges()
    End Sub
End Class

Public Interface IMovieRepository
    Function ListMovies() As IEnumerable(Of Movie)
    Sub CreateMovie(ByVal movieToCreate As Movie)
End Interface
```

Listing 8.6 uses the Microsoft Entity Framework to interact with the database. You could, of course, use a different data access technology. For example, you could implement the MovieRepository class using LINQ to SQL or NHibernate.

In this section, we fixed up our Movie controller so that the controller, validation, and data access logic is contained in separate classes. Creating this clear separation of concerns results in an application that is easier to maintain and modify over time.

Validating with the `IDataErrorInfo` Interface

In this section, we explore an alternative method of implementing validation logic. Instead of creating a separate service layer, we add the validation logic directly to the class being validated.

The default model binder respects an interface named the IDataErrorInfo interface. This interface is contained in Listing 8.7.

LISTING 8.7   IDataErrorInterface.cs (C#)

```
public interface IDataErrorInfo
{
    // Properties
    string Error { get; }
    string this[string columnName] { get; }
}
```

LISTING 8.7   IDataErrorInterface.vb (VB)

```
Public Interface IDataErrorInfo
    ' Properties
    ReadOnly Property [Error]() As String
    Default ReadOnly Property Item(ByVal columnName As String) As String
End Interface
```

The IDataErrorInfo interface provides you with a way of reporting validation error messages. The default model binder checks the indexer for each property. If the indexer returns a string, the model binder adds the validation error message string to model state.

For example, the controller in Listing 8.8 enables you to list and create products. Notice that the controller does not contain any validation logic. All the validation logic has been moved to the Product class.

LISTING 8.8   Controllers\ProductController.cs (C#)

```csharp
using System.Web.Mvc;
using MvcApplication1.Models;

namespace MvcApplication1.Controllers
{
    public class ProductController : Controller
    {
        private IProductRepository _repository;

        public ProductController()
            :this(new ProductRepository()){}

        public ProductController(IProductRepository repository)
        {
            _repository = repository;
        }

        public ActionResult Index()
        {
            return View(_repository.ListProducts());
        }

        //
        // GET: /Product/Create

        public ActionResult Create()
        {
            return View();
        }

        //
        // POST: /Product/Create

        [AcceptVerbs(HttpVerbs.Post)]
```

```csharp
        public ActionResult Create([Bind(Exclude="Id")]Product productToCreate)
        {
            if (!ModelState.IsValid)
                return View();
            _repository.CreateProduct(productToCreate);
            return RedirectToAction("Index");
        }

    }
}
```

LISTING 8.8   Controllers\ProductController.vb (VB)

```vb
Public Class ProductController
    Inherits Controller

    Private _repository As IProductRepository

    Public Sub New()
        Me.New(New ProductRepository())
    End Sub

    Public Sub New(ByVal repository As IProductRepository)
        _repository = repository
    End Sub

    Public Function Index() As ActionResult
        Return View(_repository.ListProducts())
    End Function

    '
    ' GET: /Product/Create

    Public Function Create() As ActionResult
        Return View()
    End Function

    '
    ' POST: /Product/Create

    <AcceptVerbs(HttpVerbs.Post)> _

    Public Function Create(<Bind(Exclude:="Id")> ByVal productToCreate As Product)
➥As ActionResult
        If (Not ModelState.IsValid) Then
```

```
            Return View()
        End If
        _repository.CreateProduct(productToCreate)
        Return RedirectToAction("Index")
    End Function

End Class
```

Because we use the Microsoft Entity Framework, the Product class is generated by the Entity Framework Designer. To implement the IDataErrorInfo interface, we must create a partial class. Our Product partial class is contained in Listing 8.9.

LISTING 8.9   Models\Product.cs (C#)

```
using System;
using System.Collections.Generic;
using System.ComponentModel;

namespace MvcApplication1.Models
{
    public partial class Product : IDataErrorInfo
    {

        private Dictionary<string, string> _errors = new Dictionary<string,
➥string>();

        partial void OnNameChanging(string value)
        {
            if (value.Trim() == String.Empty)
                _errors.Add("Name", "Name is required.");
        }

        partial void OnPriceChanging(decimal value)
        {
            if (value <= 0m)
                _errors.Add("Price", "Price must be greater than 0.");
        }

        #region IDataErrorInfo Members

        public string Error
        {
            get { return string.Empty; }
        }
```

```csharp
        public string this[string columnName]
        {
            get
            {
                if (_errors.ContainsKey(columnName))
                    return _errors[columnName];
                return string.Empty;
            }
        }

        #endregion


    }
}
```

LISTING 8.9   Models\Product.vb (VB)

```vb
Imports System.ComponentModel

Partial Public Class Product
    Implements IDataErrorInfo

    Private _errors As New Dictionary(Of String, String)()

    Private Sub OnNameChanging(ByVal value As String)
        If value.Trim() = String.Empty Then
            _errors.Add("Name", "Name is required.")
        End If
    End Sub

    Private Sub OnPriceChanging(ByVal value As Decimal)
        If value <= 0D Then
            _errors.Add("Price", "Price must be greater than 0.")
        End If
    End Sub

#Region "IDataErrorInfo Members"

    Public ReadOnly Property [Error]() As String Implements IDataErrorInfo.Error
        Get
            Return String.Empty
        End Get
    End Property
```

```vb
    Public ReadOnly Property Item(ByVal columnName As String) As String Implements
➥IDataErrorInfo.Item
        Get
            If _errors.ContainsKey(columnName) Then
                Return _errors(columnName)
            End If
            Return String.Empty
        End Get
    End Property

#End Region

End Class
```

The partial Product class in Listing 8.9 includes two event handlers named
OnNameChanging() and OnPriceChanging(). These event handlers are called when the
Product Name property or Product Price property is about to be changed. The
OnNameChanging() handler validates that the Name property has a value and the
OnPriceChanging() handler validates that the Price has a value greater than zero.

When there is a validation error, the OnNameChanging() or OnPriceChanging() handler
adds an error message to a dictionary named _errors. The _errors dictionary represents
all the validation errors associated with the Product class.

The class in Listing 8.9 implements the IDataErrorInfo interface. The default model
binder checks the IDataErrorInfo indexer for each property. If the indexer returns a value,
the model binder adds the error into model state. Because the error is added to model
state, the validation helpers display the error in a view automatically (see Figure 8.7).

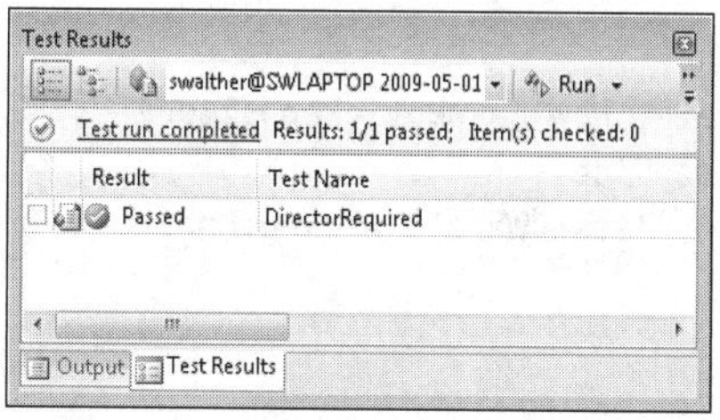

FIGURE 8.7   Validation using the IDataErrorInfo interface

NOTE

We don't use the Error property included in the IDataErrorInfo interface in Listing
8.9. You can use the Error property to represent a class wide error message. In other
words, you use the Error property to represent an error that is not associated with any
particular class property.

Testing Validation

Creating unit tests for validation is easy. Because validation error messages are represented in a standard location—model state—you can verify that the expected validation error messages get added to model state.

Imagine, for example, that you want to create a test that verifies that attempting to create a movie without a value for the Director property results in a validation error message. The test in Listing 8.10 verifies that the validation error message Director is required. gets added to model state when the Director property is missing a value.

LISTING 8.10   Controllers\Movie2ControllerTests.cs (C#)

```
using System;
using System.Web.Mvc;
using Microsoft.VisualStudio.TestTools.UnitTesting;
using MvcApplication1.Controllers;
using MvcApplication1.Models;
using MvcApplication1.Tests.Models;

namespace MvcApplication1.Tests.Controllers
{
    [TestClass]
    public class Movie2ControllerTests
    {

        [TestMethod]
        public void DirectorRequired()
        {
            // Arrange
            var modelState = new ModelStateDictionary();
            var service = new MovieService(modelState, new FakeMovieRepository());
            var controller = new Movie2Controller(service);
            var movieToCreate = Movie.CreateMovie(0, "Star Wars", String.Empty,
➥DateTime.Parse("1/1/1977"));

            // Act
            controller.Create(movieToCreate);

            // Assert
            Assert.IsTrue(HasErrorMessage(modelState["Director"], "Director is
➥required."));
        }

        private bool HasErrorMessage(ModelState modelState, string errorMessage)
        {
```

```
            foreach (var error in modelState.Errors)
            {
                if (error.ErrorMessage == errorMessage)
                    return true;
            }
            return false;
        }


    }
}
```

LISTING 8.10   Controllers\Movie2ControllerTests.vb (VB)

```
Imports Microsoft.VisualStudio.TestTools.UnitTesting
Imports System.Web.Mvc

<TestClass()> _
    Public Class Movie2ControllerTests

    <TestMethod()> _
    Public Sub DirectorRequired()
        ' Arrange
        Dim modelState = New ModelStateDictionary()
        Dim service = New MovieService(modelState, New FakeMovieRepository())
        Dim controller = New Movie2Controller(service)
        Dim movieToCreate = Movie.CreateMovie(0, "Star Wars", String.Empty,
➥DateTime.Parse("1/1/1977"))

        ' Act
        controller.Create(movieToCreate)

        ' Assert
        Assert.IsTrue(HasErrorMessage(modelState("Director"), "Director is
➥required."))
    End Sub

    Private Function HasErrorMessage(ByVal modelState As ModelState, ByVal
➥errorMessage As String) As Boolean
        For Each modelError In modelState.Errors
            If modelError.ErrorMessage = errorMessage Then
                Return True
            End If
        Next
        Return False
```

```
    End Function

End Class
```

Listing 8.10 contains a test for the `Movie2` controller that we created earlier in this chapter (see Listing 8.4). The test has three sections named `Arrange`, `Act`, and `Assert`.

In the `Arrange` section, four objects are created: a model state dictionary, a `Movie` service, a `Movie` controller, and a movie to create. Notice that the movie has an empty string for its `Director` property.

In the `Act` section, the controller `Create()` action is invoked with the movie to create.

Finally, in the `Assert` section, an assertion is made that the model state dictionary contains the validation error message `Director is required`. If the model state dictionary contains this message, the test passes (see Figure 8.8).

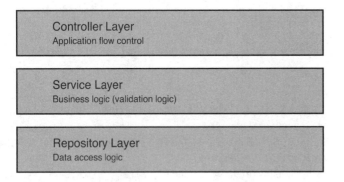

FIGURE 8.8   Passing validation test

The test takes advantage of a `helper` method named `HasErrorMessage()` that is also included in Listing 8.10. This `helper` method searches all the errors associated in model state for a particular error message string (a property might have multiple errors).

We don't want the test in Listing 8.10 to access the actual database. We want to avoid accessing the database because this would make the test too slow and possibly change the state of the database between tests. Therefore, we create a fake `Movie` repository that we can use in place of the real `Movie` repository. In the `Arrange` section, the `Movie` service is created with the fake `Movie` repository instead of the actual `Movie` repository.

The code for the fake `Movie` repository is contained in Listing 8.11. Notice that the fake `Movie` repository, just like the real one, implements the `IMovieRepository` interface. That way, because the `Movie` controller interacts with the `IMovieRepository` interface instead of a concrete Movie repository class, we can pass the fake Movie repository to the Movie controller and the Movie controller won't know the difference.

LISTING 8.11   Models\FakeMovieRepository.cs (C#)

```csharp
using System.Collections.Generic;
using MvcApplication1.Models;

namespace MvcApplication1.Tests.Models
{
    public class FakeMovieRepository : IMovieRepository
    {
        #region IMovieRepository Members

        public IEnumerable<Movie> ListMovies()
        {
            return null;
        }

        public void CreateMovie(Movie movieToCreate)
        {
        }

        #endregion
    }
}
```

LISTING 8.11   Models\FakeMovieRepository.vb (VB)

```vb
Public Class FakeMovieRepository
    Implements IMovieRepository

    Public Function ListMovies() As IEnumerable(Of Movie) Implements
➥IMovieRepository.ListMovies
        Return Nothing
    End Function

    Public Sub CreateMovie(ByVal movieToCreate As Movie) Implements
➥IMovieRepository.CreateMovie
    End Sub

End Class
```

> **NOTE**
>
> Another option here is to use a Mock Object Framework, such as Moq, to generate a
> FakeMovieRepository from the IMovieRepository interface. If the
> IMovieRepository had more than a few methods, I would have taken this approach.

Summary

In this chapter, you learned how to perform validation in an ASP.NET MVC application. First, you learned how to represent validation errors with model state. You learned how to add error messages to model state and display the errors in a view by taking advantage of the validation helpers.

Next, you learned how to move all your validation logic into a separate service layer. We separated our application code into a separate controller, service, and repository layer.

You also learned an alternative method of performing validation. You learned how to implement the IDataErrorInfo interface. This interface enables you to implement your validation logic within your model classes instead of within a service layer.

Finally, we discussed how you can create tests for your validation logic. We created a test that verifies that the expected error message is added to model state when a class property is missing a value.

Understanding Routing

When you request a page from an ASP.NET MVC application, the request gets routed to a particular controller. In this chapter, you learn how to use the ASP.NET Routing module to control how browser requests get mapped to controllers and controller actions.

In the first part of this chapter, you learn about the default route that you get when you create a new ASP.NET MVC application. You learn about the standard parts of any route.

Next, you learn how to debug the routes in your ASP.NET MVC applications. You learn how to use the Route Debugger project included with this book to see how browser requests get mapped to particular routes.

You also learn how to create custom routes. You learn how to extract custom parameters from a URL. You also learn how to create custom constraints that restrict the URLs that match a particular route.

Finally, you tackle the important topic of testing your routes. You learn how to build unit tests for custom routes and route constraints.

Using the Default Route

You configure ASP.NET Routing in an application's Global.asax file. This makes sense because the Global.asax file contains event handlers for application lifecycle events such as the application Start and application End events. Because you want your routes to be enabled when an application first starts, routing is set up in the application Start event.

When you create a new ASP.NET MVC application, you get the Global.asax file in
Listing 9.1.

NOTE

The default route defined in the Global.asax file works only with Internet Information
Server 7.0 and the ASP.NET Development Web Server. If you need to deploy your
ASP.NET MVC application to an older version of Internet Information Server, see
Chapter 13, "Deploying ASP.NET MVC Applications."

LISTING 9.1   Global.asax.cs (C#)

```
using System;
using System.Collections.Generic;
using System.Linq;
using System.Web;
using System.Web.Mvc;
using System.Web.Routing;

namespace MvcApplication1
{
    // Note: For instructions on enabling IIS6 or IIS7 classic mode,
    // visit http://go.microsoft.com/?LinkId=9394801

    public class MvcApplication : System.Web.HttpApplication
    {
        public static void RegisterRoutes(RouteCollection routes)
        {
            routes.IgnoreRoute("{resource}.axd/{*pathInfo}");

            routes.MapRoute(
                "Default", // Route name
                "{controller}/{action}/{id}", // URL with parameters
                new { controller = "Home", action = "Index", id = "" }  //
➥Parameter defaults
            );

        }

        protected void Application_Start()
        {
            RegisterRoutes(RouteTable.Routes);
        }
```

```
        }
}
```

LISTING 9.1   Global.asax.vb (VB)

```vb
' Note: For instructions on enabling IIS6 or IIS7 classic mode,
' visit http://go.microsoft.com/?LinkId=9394802

Public Class MvcApplication
    Inherits System.Web.HttpApplication

    Shared Sub RegisterRoutes(ByVal routes As RouteCollection)
        routes.IgnoreRoute("{resource}.axd/{*pathInfo}")

        ' MapRoute takes the following parameters, in order:
        ' (1) Route name
        ' (2) URL with parameters
        ' (3) Parameter defaults
        routes.MapRoute( _
            "Default", _
            "{controller}/{action}/{id}", _
            New With {.controller = "Home", .action = "Index", .id = ""} _
        )

    End Sub

    Sub Application_Start()
        RegisterRoutes(RouteTable.Routes)
    End Sub
End Class
```

The Global.asax file in Listing 9.1 includes two methods named Application_Start() and RegisterRoutes(). The Application_Start() method is called once, and only once, when an ASP.NET application first starts. In Listing 9.1, the Application_Start() method simply calls the RegisterRoutes() method.

NOTE

Why does the Global.asax file include a separate method called RegisterRoutes()? Why isn't the code in the RegisterRoutes() method simply contained in the Application_Start() method?

A separate method was created to improve testability. You can call the RegisterRoutes() method from your unit tests without instantiating the HttpApplication class.

The `RegisterRoutes()` method is used to configure all the routes in an application. The `RegisterRoutes()` method in Listing 9.1 configures the default route with the following code:

(C#)

```
routes.MapRoute(
    "Default",                      // Route name
    "{controller}/{action}/{id}",   // URL with parameters
    new { controller = "Home", action = "Index", id = "" }  // Parameter defaults
);
```

(VB)

```
routes.MapRoute( _
    "Default", _
    "{controller}/{action}/{id}", _
    New With {.controller = "Home", .action = "Index", .id = ""} _
)
```

You configure a new route by calling the `MapRoute()` method. This method accepts the following parameters:

▶ Name—The name of the route

▶ URL—The URL pattern for the route

▶ Defaults—The default values of the route parameters

▶ Constraints—A set of constraints that restrict the requests that match the route

▶ Namespaces—A set of namespaces that restrict the classes that match the route

The `MapRoute()` method has multiple overloads. You can call the `MapRoute()` method without supplying the `Defaults`, `Constraints`, or `Namespaces` parameters.

The default route configured in the Global.asax file in Listing 9.1 is named, appropriate enough, *Default*.

The URL parameter for the Default route matches URLs that satisfy the pattern `{controller}/{action}/{id}`. Therefore, the Default route matches URLs that look like this:

/Product/Insert/23

/Home/Index/1

/Do/Something/Useful

However, the Default route does not match a URL that looks like this:

/Product/Insert/Another/Item

The problem with this last URL is that it has too many segments. It has four different segments (four forward slashes) and the URL pattern `{controller}/{action}/{id}` matches only URLs that have three segments.

The URL pattern {controller}/{action}/{id} maps the first segment to a parameter named controller, the second segment to a parameter named action, and the final segment to a parameter named id.

The controller and action parameters are special. The ASP.NET MVC framework uses the controller parameter to determine which MVC controller to use to handle the request. The action parameter represents the action to call on the controller in response to the request.

If you create additional parameters that are not named controller or action, they are passed to an MVC controller action when the action is invoked. For example, the id parameter is passed as a parameter to a controller action.

Finally, the Default route includes a set of default values for the controller, action, and id parameters. By default, the controller parameter has the value Home, the action parameter has the value Index, and the id parameter has the value "" (empty string).

For example, imagine that you enter the following URL into the address bar of your browser:

    http://www.MySite.com/Product

In that case, the controller, action, and id parameters would have the following values:

    controller : Product
    action: Index
    id : ""

Now, imagine that you request the default page for a website:

    http://www.MySite.com/

In that case, the controller, action, and id parameters would have the following values:

    controller : Home
    action: Index
    id : ""

In this case, the ASP.NET MVC framework would invoke the Index() action method on the HomeController class.

NOTE

The code used to specify the defaults for a route might appear strange to you. This code is taking advantage of two new features of the Visual Basic .NET 9.0 and the C# 3.0 languages called anonymous types and property initializers. You can learn about these new language features by reading Appendix A, "C# and VB.NET Language Features."

Debugging Routes

In the next section, I show you how you can add custom routes to the Global.asax file. However, before we start creating custom routes, it is important to have some way to debug our routes. Otherwise, things quickly get confusing.

Included with the code that accompanies this book is a project named Route Debugger. If you add a reference to the assembly generated by this project, you can debug the routes configured within any ASP.NET MVC application.

Here's how you add a reference to the RouteDebugger assembly. Select the menu option Project, Add Reference to open the Add Reference dialog box (see Figure 9.1).

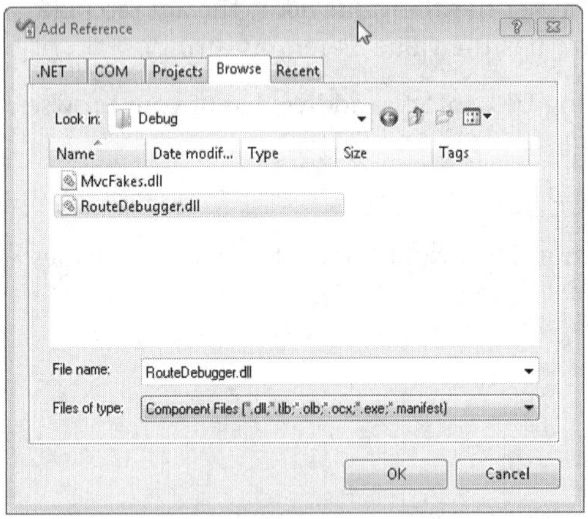

FIGURE 9.1   Using the Add Reference dialog box

Select the Browse tab and browse to the assembly named RouteDebugger.dll located in the RouteDebugger\Bin\Debug folder. Click the OK button to add the assembly to your project.

After you add the RouteDebugger assembly to an ASP.NET MVC project, you can debug the routes in the project by entering the following URL into the address bar of your browser:

    /RouteDebugger

Invoking the Route Debugger displays the page in Figure 9.2. You can enter any relative URL into the form field and view the routes that match the URL. The URL should be an *application-relative* URL and start with the tilde character (~).

Whenever you enter a URL into the Route Debugger, the Route Debugger displays all the routes from the application's route table. Each route that matches the URL is displayed

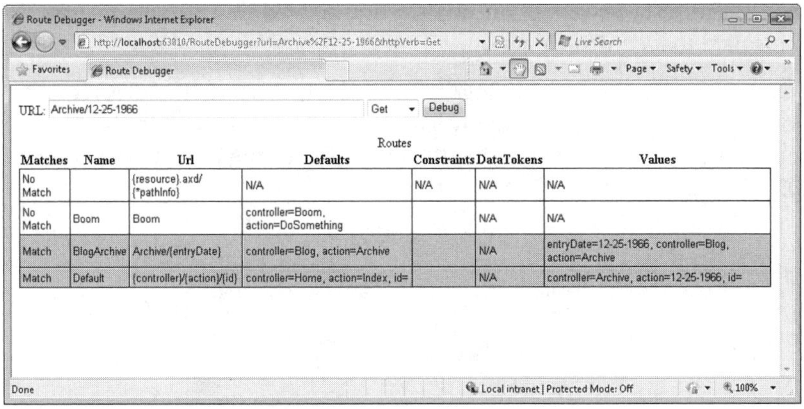

FIGURE 9.2   Using the Route Debugger

with a green background. The first route that matches the URL is the route that would actually be invoked when the application runs.

WARNING

Be warned that changing your routes might prevent you from using the Route Debugger. You cannot invoke the Route Debugger unless your application includes a route that maps to the `RouteDebugger` controller.

Creating Custom Routes

You can build an entire ASP.NET MVC application without creating a single custom route. However, there are situations in which it makes sense to create a new route. For example, imagine that you want to create a blog application and you want to route requests that look like this:

/Archive/12-25-2008

When someone requests this URL, you want to display blog entries for the date 12-25-2008.

The Default route defined in the Global.asax would extract the following parameters from this URL:

Controller: `Archive`

Action: `12-25-1966`

This is wrong. You don't want to invoke a controller action named 12-25-1966. Instead, you want to pass this date to a controller action.

Listing 9.2 contains a custom route, named BlogArchive, which correctly handles requests for blog entries. For example, a request for Archive/12-25-1966 gets mapped to the Blog controller and Archive action. The value 12/-25-1966 is passed as the entryDate parameter (see Figure 9.3).

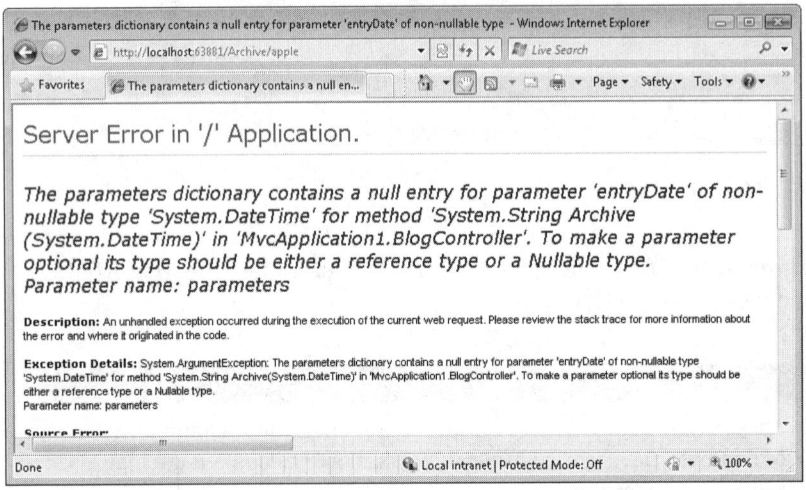

FIGURE 9.3   Invoking a custom route

LISTING 9.2   BlogArchive Route (C#)

```
routes.MapRoute(
  "BlogArchive",
  "Archive/{entryDate}",
  new { controller = "Blog", action = "Archive" }
);
```

LISTING 9.2   BlogArchive Route (VB)

```
routes.MapRoute( _
  "BlogArchive", _
  "Archive/{entryDate}", _
  New With {.controller = "Blog", .action = "Archive"} _
)
```

You can use the controller in Listing 9.3 with the BlogArchive route. This controller contains an Archive() action method that echoes back the value of the entryDate parameter.

LISTING 9.3   Controllers\BlogController.cs (C#)

```csharp
using System;
using System.Web.Mvc;

namespace MvcApplication1.Controllers
{
    public class BlogController : Controller
    {
        public string Archive(DateTime entryDate)
        {
            return entryDate.ToString();
        }


    }
}
```

LISTING 9.3   Controllers\BlogController.vb (VB)

```vb
Public Class BlogController
    Inherits System.Web.Mvc.Controller

    Function Archive(ByVal entryDate As DateTime) As String
        Return entryDate.ToString()
    End Function

End Class
```

The order that you add a custom route to the Global.asax file is important. The first route matched is used. For example, if you reverse the order of the BlogArchive and Default routes in Listing 9.2, then the Default route would always be executed instead of the BlogArchive route.

WARNING

The order of your routes in the Global.asax file matters.

Creating Route Constraints

When you create a custom route, you can include route constraints. A constraint restricts the requests that match a route. There are three basic types of constraints: regular expression constraints, the HttpMethod constraint, and custom constraints.

Using Regular Expression Constraints

You can use a regular expression constraint to prevent a request from matching a route unless a parameter extracted from the request matches a particular regular expression pattern. You can use regular expressions to match just about any string pattern including currency amounts, dates, times, and numeric formats.

For example, the BlogArchive custom route that we created in the previous section was created like this:

(C#)

```
routes.MapRoute(
  "BlogArchive",
  "Archive/{entryDate}",
  new { controller = "Blog", action = "Archive" }
);
```

(VB)

```
routes.MapRoute( _
   "BlogArchive", _
   "Archive/{entryDate}", _
   New With {.controller = "Blog", .action = "Archive"} _
)
```

This custom route matches the following URLs:

> /Archive/12-25-1966
>
> /Archive/02-09-1978

Unfortunately, the route also matches these URLs:

> /Archive/apple
>
> /Archive/blah

There is nothing to prevent you from entering something that is not a date in the URL. If you request a URL such as /Archive/apple, you get the error page in Figure 9.4.

We really need to prevent URLs that don't contain dates from matching our BlogArchive route. The easiest way to fix our route is to add a regular expression constraint. The following modified version of the BlogArchive route won't match URLs that don't contain dates in the format 01-01-0001:

(C#)

```
routes.MapRoute(
  "BlogArchive",
  "Archive/{entryDate}",
  new {controller = "Blog", action = "Archive"},
  new {entryDate = @"\d{2}-\d{2}-\d{4}"}
);
```

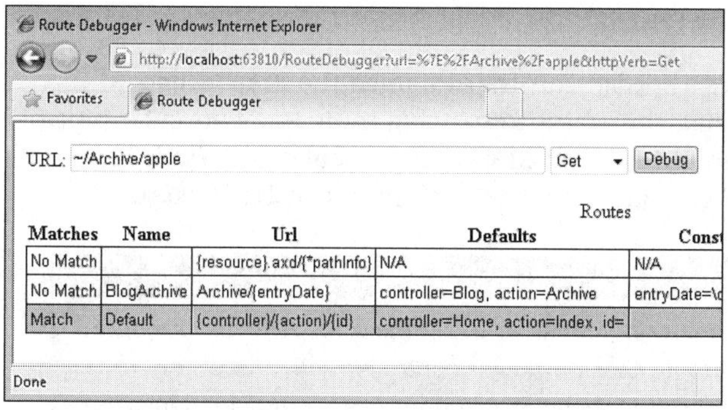

FIGURE 9.4   Entering a URL with an invalid date

(VB)

```
routes.MapRoute( _
  "BlogArchive", _
  "Archive/{entryDate}", _
  New With {.controller = "Blog", .action = "Archive"}, _
  New With {.entryDate = "\d{2}-\d{2}-\d{4}"} _
)
```

The fourth parameter passed to the MapRoute() method represents the constraints. This constraint prevents a request from matching this route when the entryDate parameter does not match the regular expression \d{2}-\d{2}-d{4}. In other words, the entryDate must match the pattern of two decimals followed by a dash followed by two decimals followed by a dash followed by four decimals.

You can quickly test your new version of the BlogArchive route with the Route Debugger. The page in Figure 9.5 shows the matched routes when an invalid date is entered. Notice that the BlogArchive route *is not* matched.

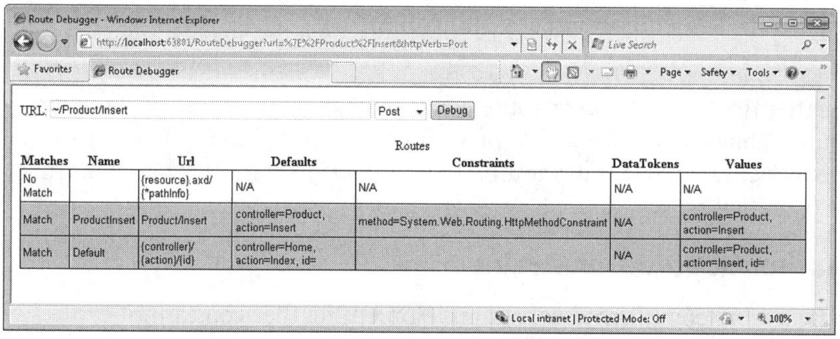

FIGURE 9.5   Using the Route Debugger with the modified BlogArchive route

Using the `HttpMethod` Constraint

The URL routing framework includes a special constraint named the `HttpMethod` constraint. You can use the `HttpMethod` constraint to match a route to a particular type of HTTP operation. For example, you might want to prevent a particular URL from being accessed when performing an HTTP `GET` but not when performing an HTTP `POST`.

NOTE

Instead of using the `HttpMethod` constraint, consider using the `AcceptVerbs` attribute. You can apply the `AcceptVerbs` attribute to a particular controller action or an entire controller to prevent a controller action from being invoked unless the action is invoked with the right HTTP method. We discuss the `AcceptVerbs` attribute in Chapter 3, "Understanding Controllers and Actions."

For example, the following route, named `ProductInsert`, can be called only when performing an HTTP `POST` operation:

(C#)

```
routes.MapRoute(
    "ProductInsert",
    "Product/Insert",
    new  {controller = "Product", action = "Insert"},
    new  {method = new HttpMethodConstraint("POST")}
);
```

(VB)

```
routes.MapRoute( _
    "ProductInsert", _
    "Product/Insert", _
    New With {.controller = "Product", .action = "Insert"}, _
    New With {.method = New HttpMethodConstraint("POST")} _
)
```

You can check whether the `ProductInsert` route works by taking advantage of the Route Debugger. The Route Debugger enables you to pick an HTTP method that you want to simulate. The page in Figure 9.6 illustrates testing the ProductInsert route when performing an HTTP `POST` operation.

Creating an Authenticated Constraint

If you need to create a more complicated constraint—something that you cannot easily represent with a regular expression—you can create a custom constraint. You create a custom constraint by creating a class that implements the `IRouteConstraint` interface. This interface is easy to implement because it includes only one method: the `Match()` method.

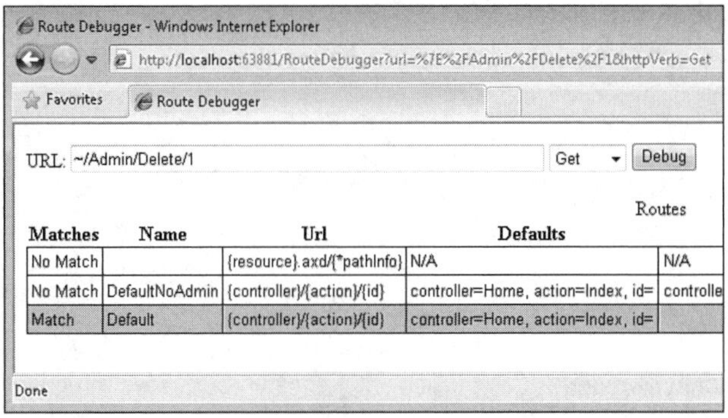

FIGURE 9.6   Matching the ProductInsert route when performing an HTTP POST

For example, Listing 9.4 contains a new constraint named the AuthenticatedConstraint. The AuthenticatedConstraint prevents a request from matching a route when the request is not made by an authenticated user.

LISTING 9.4   Constraints\AuthenticatedConstraint.cs (C#)

```csharp
using System.Web;
using System.Web.Routing;

namespace MvcApplication1.Constraints
{
    public class AuthenticatedConstraint : IRouteConstraint
    {

        public bool Match
            (
                HttpContextBase httpContext,
                Route route,
                string parameterName,
                RouteValueDictionary values,
                RouteDirection routeDirection
            )
        {
            return httpContext.Request.IsAuthenticated;
        }

    }
}
```

LISTING 9.4   Constraints\AuthenticatedConstraint.vb (VB)

```vb
Imports System.Web
Imports System.Web.Routing

Public Class AuthenticatedConstraint
    Implements IRouteConstraint

    Public Function Match _
    ( _
        ByVal httpContext As HttpContextBase, _
        ByVal route As Route, _
        ByVal parameterName As String, _
        ByVal values As RouteValueDictionary, _
        ByVal routeDirection As RouteDirection _
    ) As Boolean Implements IRouteConstraint.Match
        Return HttpContext.Request.IsAuthenticated
    End Function

End Class
```

In Listing 9.4, the `Match()` method simply returns the value of the `HttpContext.Request.IsAuthenticated` property to determine whether the current request is an authenticated request. If the `Match()` method returns the value `False`, the request fails to match the constraint and the route is not matched.

After you create the `AuthenticatedConstraint`, you can use it with a route like this:

(C#)

```csharp
routes.MapRoute(
    "Admin",
    "Admin/{action}",
    new {controller = "Admin"},
    new {Auth = new AuthenticatedConstraint()}
);
```

(VB)

```vb
routes.MapRoute( _
    "Admin", _
    "Admin/{action}", _
    New With {.controller = "Admin"}, _
    New With {.Auth = New AuthenticatedConstraint()} _
)
```

It is important to understand that the `AuthenticatedConstraint` prevents only a particular route from matching a request. Another route, that does not include the `AuthenticatedConstraint`, might match the same request and invoke the same controller action. In the next section, I show you how to create a constraint that prevents a route from ever invoking a particular controller.

> **NOTE**
>
> The ASP.NET MVC framework includes an `Authorize` attribute that you can apply to either a particular action or entire controller to prevent access from unauthorized users. We discuss the `Authorize` attribute in Chapter 3.

Creating a `NotEqual` Constraint

If you want to create a route that never matches a particular controller action—or more generally, that never matches a particular route parameter value—you can create a `NotEqual` constraint.

The code for the `NotEqual` constraint is contained in Listing 9.5.

LISTING 9.5   Constraints\NotEqual.cs (C#)

```csharp
using System;
using System.Web;
using System.Web.Routing;

namespace MvcApplication1.Constraints
{
    public class NotEqual:IRouteConstraint
    {
        private string _value;

        public NotEqual(string value)
        {
            _value = value;
        }

        public bool Match
            (
                HttpContextBase httpContext,
                Route route,
                string parameterName,
                RouteValueDictionary values,
```

```
            RouteDirection routeDirection
        )
    {
        var paramValue = values[parameterName].ToString();
        return String.Compare(paramValue, _value, true) != 0;
    }

    }
}
```

LISTING 9.5   Constraints\NotEqual.vb (VB)

```
Public Class NotEqual
    Implements IRouteConstraint

    Private _value As String

    Sub New(ByVal value As String)
        _value = value
    End Sub

    Public Function Match( _
        ByVal httpContext As HttpContextBase, _
        ByVal route As Route, _
        ByVal parameterName As String, _
        ByVal values As RouteValueDictionary, _
        ByVal routeDirection As RouteDirection _
    ) As Boolean Implements IRouteConstraint.Match
        Dim paramValue = values(parameterName).ToString()
        Return String.Compare(paramValue, _value, True) <> 0
    End Function

End Class
```

The NotEqual constraint performs a case-insensitive match of the value of a parameter against a field named _value. If there is a match, the constraint fails and the route is skipped.

After you create the NotEqual constraint, you can create a route that uses the constraint like this:

(C#)

```
routes.MapRoute(
    "DefaultNoAdmin",
```

```
    "{controller}/{action}/{id}",
    new {controller = "Home", action = "Index", id = ""},
    new {controller = new NotEqual("Admin")}
);
```

(VB)

```
routes.MapRoute( _
    "DefaultNoAdmin", _
    "{controller}/{action}/{id}", _
    New With {.controller = "Home", .action = "Index", .id = ""}, _
    New With {.controller = New NotEqual("Admin")} _
)
```

This route works just like the Default route except that it never matches when the
controller parameter has the value Admin. You can test the NotEqual constraint with the
Route Debugger. In Figure 9.7, the URL /Admin/Delete matches the Default route, but it
does not match the DefaultNoAdmin route.

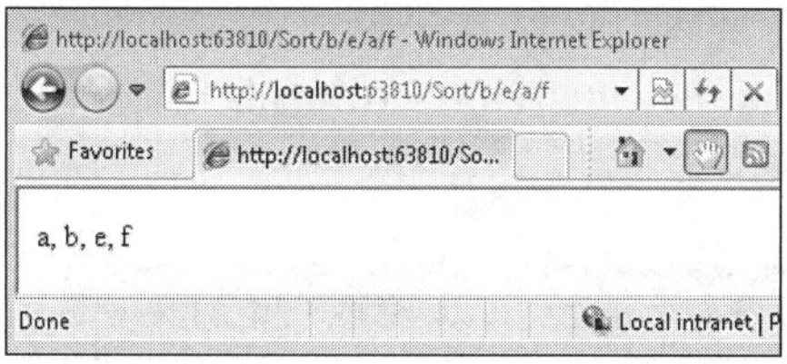

FIGURE 9.7   Using the NotEqual Constraint

Using Catch-All Routes

Normally, to match a route, a URL must contain a particular number of segments. For
example, the URL /Product/Details matches the following route:

(C#)

```
routes.MapRoute(

    "Product1",
    "Product/{action}",
    new {controller = "Product"}
);
```

(VB)

```
routes.MapRoute( _
    "Product1", _
```

```
    "Product/{action}", _
    New With {.controller = "Product"} _
)
```

However, it does not match the following route:

(C#)

```
routes.MapRoute(
    "Product2",
    "Product/{action}/{id}",
    new {controller = "Product"}
);
```

(VB)

```
routes.MapRoute( _
    "Product2", _
    "Product/{action}/{id}", _
    New With {.controller = "Product"} _
)
```

This route requires a URL to have three segments, and the URL /Product/Details has only two segments (two forward slashes).

NOTE

The URL requested is not required to have the same number of segments as a route's URL parameter. When a `route` parameter has a default value, a segment is optional. For example, the URL /Home/Index matches a route that has the URL pattern `{controller}/{action}/{id}` when the `id` parameter has a default value.

If you want to match a URL, regardless of the number of segments in the URL, you need to create something called a `catch-all` parameter. Here's an example of a route that uses a catch-all parameter:

(C#)

```
routes.MapRoute(
    "SortRoute",
    "Sort/{*values}",
    new {controller = "Sort", action = "Index"}
);
```

(VB)

```
routes.MapRoute( _
```

```
    "SortRoute", _
    "Sort/{*values}", _
    New With {.controller = "Sort", .action = "Index"} _
)
```

Notice that the route parameter named values has a star (*) in front of its name. The star marks the parameter as a catch-all parameter. This route matches any of the following URLs:

/Sort

/Sort/a/b/d/c

/Sort/Women/Fire/Dangerous/Things

All the segments after the first segment are captured by the catch-all parameter.

NOTE

A catch-all parameter must appear as the last parameter. Think of a catch-all parameter as a parameter array.

The Sort controller in Listing 9.6 illustrates how you can retrieve the value of a catch-all parameter within a controller action.

LISTING 9.6   Controllers\SortController.cs (C#)

```csharp
using System;
using System.Web.Mvc;

namespace MvcApplication1.Controllers
{
    public class SortController : Controller
    {

        public string Index(string values)
        {
            var brokenValues = values.Split('/');
            Array.Sort(brokenValues);
            return String.Join(", ", brokenValues);
        }

    }
}
```

LISTING 9.6   Controllers\SortController.vb (VB)

```vb
Imports System
Imports System.Web.Mvc

Public Class SortController
    Inherits Controller

    Public Function Index(ByVal values As String) As String
        Dim brokenValues = values.Split("/"c)
        Array.Sort(brokenValues)
        Return String.Join(", ", brokenValues)
    End Function

End Class
```

Notice that the catch-all parameter is passed to the Index() action as a string. (You *cannot* pass the value as an array.) The Index() method simply sorts the values contained in the catch-all parameter and returns a string with the values in alphabetical order (see Figure 9.8).

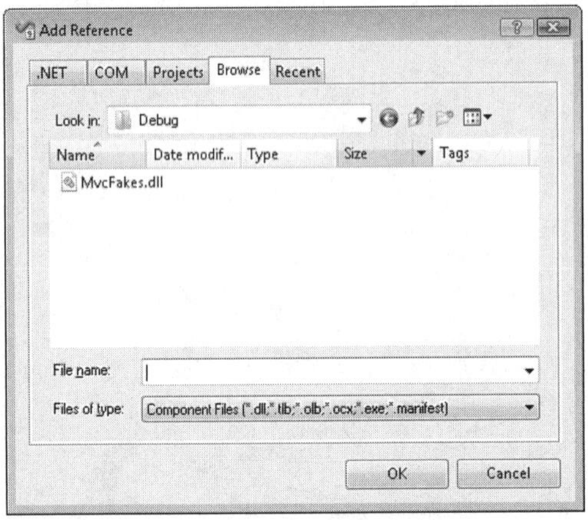

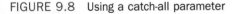

FIGURE 9.8   Using a catch-all parameter

Testing Routes

Every feature of the ASP.NET MVC framework was designed to be highly testable and URL routing is no exception. In this section, I describe how you can unit test both your routes and your route constraints.

Why would you want to build unit tests for your routes? If you build route unit tests, you can detect whether changes in your application break existing functionality automatically. For example, if your existing routes are covered by unit tests, you know immediately whether introducing a new route prevents an existing route from ever being called.

Using the MvcFakes and RouteDebugger Assemblies

To unit test your custom routes, I recommend that you add references to two assemblies: the RouteDebugger and the MvcFakes assemblies.

If you want to test your routes by name, you need to add a reference to the RouteDebugger assembly. The RouteDebugger assembly replaces the anonymous routes in your MVC application with named routes. That way, you can build tests that check whether a particular route is called by name.

I also recommend that you add a reference to the MvcFakes assembly. The MvcFakes assembly contains a set of fake objects that you can use in your unit tests. For example, MvcFakes includes a `FakeHttpContext` object. You can use the `FakeHttpContext` object to fake every aspect of a browser request.

Both of these assemblies are included with the code that accompanies this book. You can add references to these assemblies to your test project by selecting the menu option Project, Add Reference, selecting the Browse tab, and browsing to the following two assemblies (see Figure 9.9): RouteDebugger.dll and MvcFakes.dll.

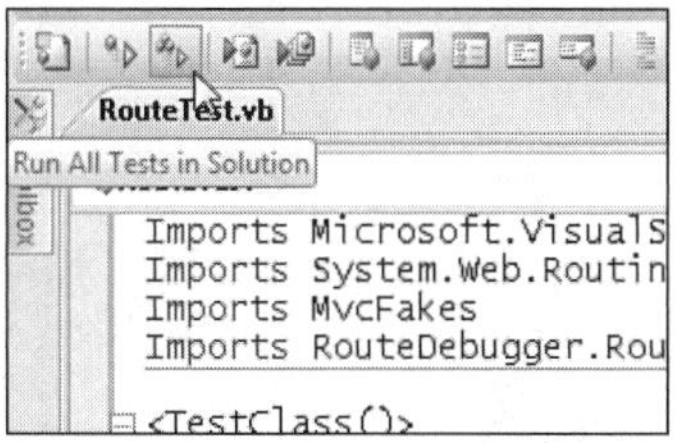

FIGURE 9.9   Adding a reference to an assembly

Testing If a URL Matches a Route

Let's start with a basic but useful unit test. Let's create a unit test that verifies that a particular URL matches a particular route. The unit test is contained in Listing 9.7.

LISTING 9.7   Routes\RouteTest.cs (C#)

```
using Microsoft.VisualStudio.TestTools.UnitTesting;
using System.Web.Routing;
using MvcFakes;
using RouteDebugger.Routing;

namespace MvcApplication1.Tests.Routes
{
    [TestClass()]
    public class RouteTest
    {
        [TestMethod]
```

```
    public void DefaultRouteMatchesHome()
    {
        // Arrange
        var routes = new RouteCollection();
        MvcApplication.RegisterRoutes(routes);

        // Act
        var context = new FakeHttpContext("~/Home");
        var routeData = routes.GetRouteData(context);

        // Assert
        var matchedRoute = (NamedRoute)routeData.Route;
        Assert.AreEqual("Default", matchedRoute.Name);
    }

  }
}
```

LISTING 9.7   Routes\RouteTest.vb (VB)

```
Imports Microsoft.VisualStudio.TestTools.UnitTesting
Imports System.Web.Routing
Imports MvcFakes
Imports RouteDebugger.Routing

<TestClass()> _
Public Class RouteTest

    <TestMethod()> _
    Public Sub DefaultRouteMatchesHome()
        ' Arrange
        Dim routes = New RouteCollection()
        MvcApplication.RegisterRoutes(routes)

        ' Act
        Dim context = New FakeHttpContext("~/Home")
        Dim routeData = routes.GetRouteData(context)

        ' Assert
        Dim matchedRoute = CType(routeData.Route, NamedRoute)
        Assert.AreEqual("Default", matchedRoute.Name)
    End Sub

End Class
```

You can add the unit test in Listing 9.7 to a Test project by selecting the menu option Project, Add New Test and selecting the Unit Test template. Remember to add the assembly references discussed in the previous section or the unit test won't compile.

WARNING

Don't select the Unit Test Wizard. Also, don't select the tempting menu option Project, Add New Unit Test. Either option launches the Unit Test Wizard. The Unit Test Wizard creates a unit test that launches a web server. (We don't want to do that.) Instead, always pick the menu option Project, Add New Test and select the Unit Test template.

After you create the unit test in Listing 9.7, you can run it by entering the keyboard combination Ctrl+R, A. Alternatively, you can click the Run All Tests in Solution button contained on the Test toolbar (see Figure 9.10).

The test in Listing 9.7 verifies that the URL ~/Home matches the route named Default. The unit test consists of three parts.

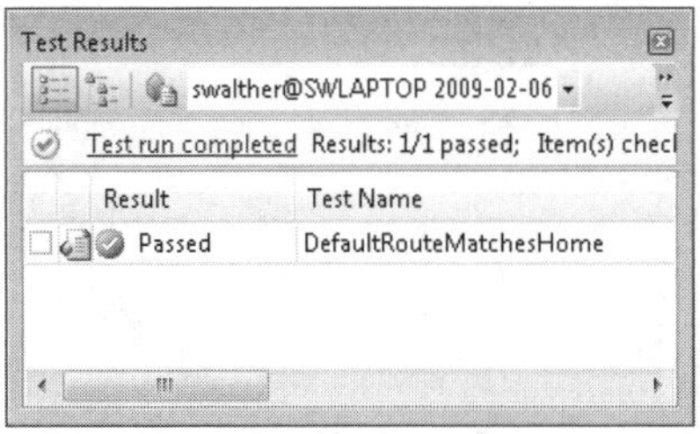

FIGURE 9.10 Running all tests in the solution

The first part, the Arrange part, sets up the routes by creating a new route collection and passing the route collection to the `RegisterRoutes()` method exposed by the Global.asax file. (Notice that you use the `MvcApplication` class to refer to the class exposed by Global.asax.)

The second part, the Act part, sets up the fake `HttpContext` that represents the browser request for ~/Home. The `FakeHttpContext` object is part of the MvcFakes project. The `FakeHttpContext` object is passed to the `GetRouteData()` method. This method takes an `HttpContext` and returns a `RouteData` object that represents information about the route matched by the `HttpContext`.

Finally, the Assert part verifies that the RouteData represents a route named Default. At this point, the unit test either succeeds or fails. If it succeeds, you get the test results in Figure 9.11.

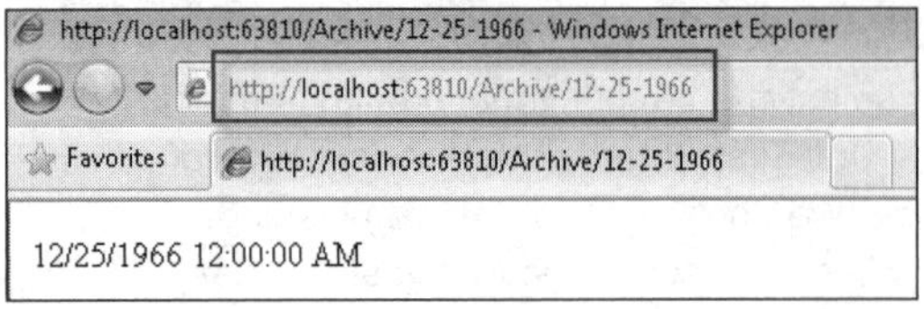

FIGURE 9.11   The test results

Testing Routes with Constraints

Let's try testing a slightly more complicated route. Earlier in this chapter, we discussed the HttpMethodConstraint that you can use to match a route only when the right HTTP method is used. For example, the following route should only match a browser request performed with an HTTP POST operation:

(C#)

```
routes.MapRoute(
    "ProductInsert",
    "Product/Insert",
     new  {controller = "Product", action = "Insert"},
     new  {method = new HttpMethodConstraint("POST")}
);
```

(VB)

```
routes.MapRoute( _
    "ProductInsert", _
    "Product/Insert", _
    New With {.controller = "Product", .action = "Insert"}, _
    New With {.method = New HttpMethodConstraint("POST")} _
)
```

The HttpMethodConstraint restricts this route to match only POST requests. This is the intention; how do you test it? Easy, fake the HTTP operation with the FakeHttpContext object.

The unit test in Listing 9.8 contains two unit tests. The first test verifies that the ProductInsert route is matched when performing a POST operation. The second test verifies that the ProductInsert route is not matched when performing a GET operation.

LISTING 9.8   Routes\RouteTest.cs (with ProductInsert tests) (C#)

```csharp
[TestMethod]
public void ProductInsertMatchesPost()
{
    // Arrange
    var routes = new RouteCollection();
    MvcApplication.RegisterRoutes(routes);

    // Act
    var context = new FakeHttpContext("~/Product/Insert", "POST", false, null);
    var routeData = routes.GetRouteData(context);

    // Assert
    var matchedRoute = (NamedRoute)routeData.Route;
    Assert.AreEqual("ProductInsert", matchedRoute.Name);
}


[TestMethod]
public void ProductInsertDoesNotMatchGet()
{
    // Arrange
    var routes = new RouteCollection();
    MvcApplication.RegisterRoutes(routes);

    // Act
    var context = new FakeHttpContext("~/Product/Insert", "GET", false, null);
    var routeData = routes.GetRouteData(context);

    // Assert
    if (routeData != null)
    {
        var matchedRoute = (NamedRoute)routeData.Route;
        Assert.AreNotEqual("ProductInsert", matchedRoute.Name);
    }
}
```

LISTING 9.8   Routes\RouteTest.vb (with ProductInsert tests) (VB)

```vb
<TestMethod()> _
Public Sub ProductInsertMatchesPost()
    ' Arrange
    Dim routes = New RouteCollection()
    MvcApplication.RegisterRoutes(routes)
```

```vb
    ' Act
    Dim context = New FakeHttpContext("~/Product/Insert", "POST", False, Nothing)

    Dim routeData = routes.GetRouteData(context)

    ' Assert
    Dim matchedRoute = CType(routeData.Route, NamedRoute)
    Assert.AreEqual("ProductInsert", matchedRoute.Name)
End Sub

<TestMethod()> _
Public Sub ProductInsertDoesNotMatchGet()
    ' Arrange
    Dim routes = New RouteCollection()
    MvcApplication.RegisterRoutes(routes)

    ' Act
    Dim context = New FakeHttpContext("~/Product/Insert", "GET", False, Nothing)
    Dim routeData = routes.GetRouteData(context)

    ' Assert
    If routeData IsNot Nothing Then
        Dim matchedRoute = CType(routeData.Route, NamedRoute)
        Assert.AreNotEqual("ProductInsert", matchedRoute.Name)
    End If
End Sub
```

The second parameter passed to the constructor for the FakeHttpContext object determines the HTTP operation that the FakeHttpContext object represents.

Summary

In this chapter, you learned how to control how browser requests map to controllers and controller actions by taking advantage of ASP.NET Routing. We started by discussing the standard parts of a route.

You also learned how to debug the routes contained in the Global.asax file by taking advantage of the RouteDebugger assembly. We took advantage of the Route Debugger when building our custom routes.

We also discussed how you can use route constraints to limit the routes that match a browser request. In particular, you learned how to use regular expression route constraints, HttpMethod route constraints, and custom route constraints.

Finally, you learned how to build unit tests for your custom routes. You learned how to take advantage of the FakeHttpContext object to fake different browser requests and test the routes that are matched.

Understanding View Master Pages and View User Controls

Creating a consistent page layout is important for a professional web application. In this chapter, you learn how to create a common page layout for the pages in your web application by taking advantage of *view master pages*. You learn how to create both view master pages and view content pages. You also learn how to pass data from a controller to a view master page.

Next, we discuss how you can create partial views (partials) by creating *view user controls*. You can use view user controls to display the same content in multiple pages. You learn how to create view user controls and how you can use a view user control as a template when displaying database data.

Understanding View Master Pages

View master pages enable you to create a common layout for the pages in your ASP.NET MVC application. For example, you can place standard navigational elements, such as a menu or tab strip, in a master page so that the navigation elements appear on every page in your application.

Creating a View Master Page

Normally, to make the master page available to all views, you create a master page in the \Views\Shared folder. Right-click the \Views\Shared folder and select the menu option Add, New Item. Select the Web\MVC category, select the MVC View Master Page template, and click the Add button (see Figure 10.1).

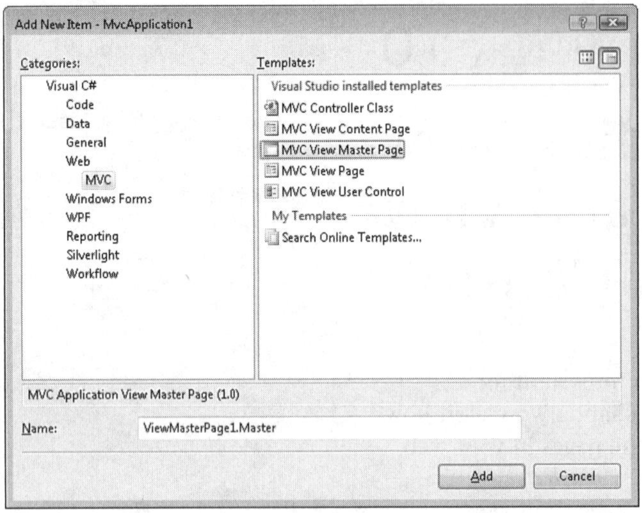

FIGURE 10.1   Adding a master page to a project

NOTE

When you create a new ASP.NET MVC project, you get a master page named Site.master automatically. You can modify this master page to fit your needs or delete it and start from scratch.

The master page in Listing 10.1, named MyMaster.master, is the default master page that you get when you create a new master page from the Visual Studio MVC View Master Page template.

LISTING 10.1   \Views\Shared\MyMaster.master

```
<%@ Master Language="C#" Inherits="System.Web.Mvc.ViewMasterPage" %>


<!DOCTYPE html PUBLIC "-//W3C//DTD XHTML 1.0 Transitional//EN"
➥"http://www.w3.org/TR/xhtml1/DTD/xhtml1-transitional.dtd">


<html xmlns="http://www.w3.org/1999/xhtml" >
<head runat="server">
    <title><asp:ContentPlaceHolder ID="TitleContent" runat="server" /></title>
</head>
<body>
    <div>
        <asp:ContentPlaceHolder ID="MainContent" runat="server">

        </asp:ContentPlaceHolder>
```

```
    </div>
</body>
</html>
```

A master page looks like a standard ASP.NET MVC view. It can contain both HTML and script. Notice that it contains the standard opening and closing <html>, <head>, <title>, and <body> tags.

However, unlike a standard view, a master page contains one or more <asp:ContentPlaceHolder> tags. The <asp:ContentPlaceHolder> tags mark the areas of the master page that can be overridden in particular view content pages.

You can add as many <asp:ContentPlaceHolder> tags to a master page as you want. Each <asp:ContentPlaceHolder> tag marks another area that can be customized in a content page.

You can add default content inside of the <asp:ContentPlaceHolder> tag. If the <asp:ContentPlaceHolder> tag is not overridden in a view content page, the default content contained in the <asp:ContentPlaceHolder> tag appears.

You can even nest <asp:ContentPlaceHolder> tags. Nesting <asp:ContentPlaceHolder> tags is useful when you want to have the option of overriding smaller or greater areas in the master page from the view content page.

For example, the view master page in Listing 10.2 creates a two-column layout. Each column contains one <asp:ContentPlaceHolder> tag. Notice that the master page also contains navigational links and a banner advertisement (see Figure 10.2). Anything that you want to appear in multiple views in your application, you put in a view master page.

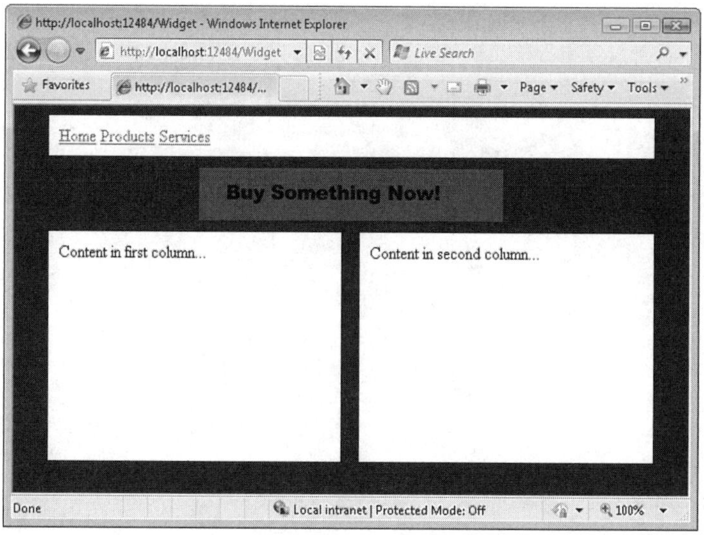

FIGURE 10.2   A page rendered by the TwoColumn.master master page

LISTING 10.2   Views\Shared\TwoColumn.master

```
<%@ Master Language="C#" Inherits="System.Web.Mvc.ViewMasterPage" %>
<!DOCTYPE html PUBLIC "-//W3C//DTD XHTML 1.0 Transitional//EN"
➥"http://www.w3.org/TR/xhtml1/DTD/xhtml1-transitional.dtd">
<html xmlns="http://www.w3.org/1999/xhtml" >
<head id="Head1" runat="server">
    <title></title>
    <style type="text/css">
    html
    {
        background-color: Blue;
    }

    .main
    {
        width: 600px;
        margin: auto;
    }

    .header
    {
        padding: 10px;
        background-color: White;
        border: 1px solid black;
    }

    .menu, .menu li
    {
        padding:0px;
        margin: 0px;
        display:inline;
    }

    .banner
    {
        margin: 10px 150px;
    }

    .column
    {
        width: 45%;
        min-height: 200px;
        border: solid 1px black;
        padding: 10px;
        background-color:White;
```

```
        }

        .left
        {
            float:left;
        }

        .right
        {
            float:right;
        }

    </style>
</head>
<body>
<div class="main">

    <div class="header">
        <ul class="menu">
            <li><a href="/master/">Home</a></li>
            <li><a href="/master/">Products</a></li>
            <li><a href="/master/">Services</a></li>
        </ul>
    </div>

    <img
        class="banner"
        src="/Content/BannerAd.png"
        alt="Buy Something" />

    <div class="column left">
        <asp:ContentPlaceHolder ID="ContentPlaceHolder1" runat="server">
        </asp:ContentPlaceHolder>
    </div>

    <div class="column right">
        <asp:ContentPlaceHolder ID="ContentPlaceHolder2" runat="server">
        </asp:ContentPlaceHolder>
    </div>

</div>
</body>
</html>
```

Creating a View Content Page

After you create a view master page, you can create one or more view content pages based on the master page. A view content page fills in the holes in the master page template.

Imagine that you have created the controller in Listing 10.3.

LISTING 10.3   Controllers\WidgetController.cs (C#)

```csharp
using System.Web.Mvc;


namespace MvcApplication1.Controllers
{
    public class WidgetController : Controller
    {
        public ActionResult Index()
        {
            return View();
        }


    }
}
```

LISTING 10.3   Controllers\WidgetController.vb (VB)

```vb
Public Class WidgetController
    Inherits System.Web.Mvc.Controller

    Function Index() As ActionResult
        Return View()
    End Function

End Class
```

The Index() action in Listing 10.3 returns a view located at \Views\Widget\Index.aspx. You can create a view content page for this view by right-clicking the Index() action in the source code editor and selecting the menu option Add View (see Figure 10.3).

Selecting Add View opens the Add View dialog. From within this dialog, you can select a view master page and enter the name of the primary ContentPlaceHolder tag from the master page. For example, you can select the TwoColumn.master view master page and enter ContentPlaceHolder1 (see Figure 10.4).

When you click Add, the view content page in Listing 10.4 is created.

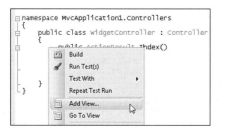

```
namespace MvcApplication1.Controllers
{
    public class WidgetController : Controller
    {
        public ActionResult Index()
```

	Build
	Run Test(s)
	Test With ▶
	Repeat Test Run
	Add View...
	Go To View

FIGURE 10.3   Opening the Add View dialog

LISTING 10.4   \Views\Widget\Index.aspx

```
<%@ Page Title="" Language="C#" MasterPageFile="~/Views/Shared/TwoColumn.Master"
➥Inherits="System.Web.Mvc.ViewPage" %>


<asp:Content ID="Content1" ContentPlaceHolderID="ContentPlaceHolder1"
➥runat="server">

    <h2>Index</h2>

</asp:Content>

<asp:Content ID="Content2" ContentPlaceHolderID="ContentPlaceHolder2"
➥runat="server">
</asp:Content>
```

The view content page in Listing 10.4 consists of two <asp:Content> tags. The
<asp:Content> tags are associated with the <asp:ContentPlaceHolder> tags in the master
page through the <asp:Content> tag's ContentPlaceHolderID attributes.

You cannot place any content outside of these <asp:Content> tags. You create the content
for a view content page by adding content within the <asp:Content> tags.

By placing content inside of the <asp:Content> tags, you can override the corresponding
area of the master page. You can place any content that you want inside of the
<asp:Content> tag including HTML and script.

The view content page in Listing 10.4 is associated with its master page through the <%@
Page %> directive MasterPageFile attribute. You can convert existing views into view
content pages by adding the MasterPageFile attribute to the view and moving all the
view's content into <asp:Content> controls.

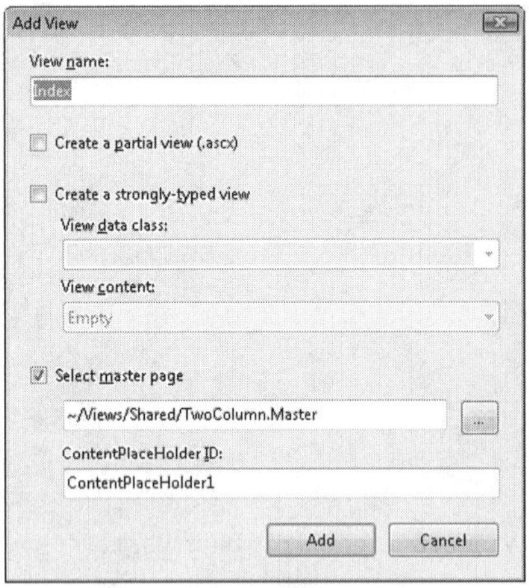

FIGURE 10.4   Selecting a view master page

Setting the Master Page from the Controller

The ASP.NET MVC framework provides you with an alternative method of associating a view content page with a master page. Instead of associating a view content page with a master page by using the MasterPageFile attribute, you can associate a view content page with a master page when you return a view from a controller action.

> **NOTE**
>
> The master page specified in a controller overrides the master page specified with a content view page. In other words, the controller takes precedence over the MasterPageFile attribute.

Why would you want to use this second method of setting the master page? One advantage of this second method is that you can select a master page dynamically at runtime.

Imagine, for example, that you decide to enable the users of your web application to skin the application. In other words, you want to allow visitors to pick their favorite color scheme and page layout. In that case, you can serve different master pages for each user by specifying the master page in the controller action.

The controller in Listing 10.5 illustrates how you can dynamically set the master page at runtime. The Index() action randomly selects either the Dynamic0.master or Dynamic1.master view master page.

LISTING 10.5   Controllers\DynamicController.cs (C#)

```
using System;
using System.Web.Mvc;
```

```
namespace MvcApplication1.Controllers
{
    public class DynamicController : Controller
    {
        public ActionResult Index()
        {
            // Randomly select master page
            var rnd = new Random();
            var masterPage = "Dynamic" + rnd.Next(2);

            // Return view with master page
            return View("Index", masterPage);
        }


    }
}
```

LISTING 10.5   Controllers\DynamicController.vb (VB)

```
Public Class DynamicController
    Inherits Controller

    Public Function Index() As ActionResult
        ' Randomly select master page
        Dim rnd = New Random()
        Dim masterPage = "Dynamic" & rnd.Next(2)

        ' Return view with master page
        Return View("Index", masterPage)
    End Function

End Class
```

Depending on the master page that is randomly selected, the view has a different color scheme and layout (see Figure 10.5).

Setting the Master Page Title

You don't want every page in a web application to share the same page title. For one thing, that would make bookmarking pages difficult.

The default master page includes the <asp:ContentPlaceHolder> tag named TitleContent for the page title (see Listing 10.6). Therefore, if you want to customize the title of a page, you can provide the <asp:Content> tag that corresponds to this ContentPlaceHolder in a view content page (see Listing 10.7).

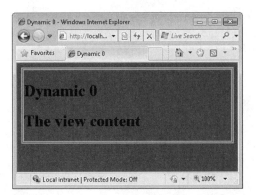

FIGURE 10.5   Selecting a master page dynamically

LISTING 10.6   Views\Shared\Site.master

```
<%@ Master Language="C#" Inherits="System.Web.Mvc.ViewMasterPage" %>


<!DOCTYPE html PUBLIC "-//W3C//DTD XHTML 1.0 Strict//EN"
➥"http://www.w3.org/TR/xhtml1/DTD/xhtml1-strict.dtd">
<html xmlns="http://www.w3.org/1999/xhtml">
<head runat="server">
    <title><asp:ContentPlaceHolder ID="TitleContent" runat="server" /></title>
    <link href="../../Content/Site.css" rel="stylesheet" type="text/css" />
</head>

<body>
    <div class="page">

        <div id="header">
            <div id="title">
                <h1>My MVC Application</h1>
            </div>

            <div id="logindisplay">
                <% Html.RenderPartial("LogOnUserControl"); %>
            </div>

            <div id="menucontainer">

                <ul id="menu">
                    <li><%= Html.ActionLink("Home", "Index", "Home")%></li>
                    <li><%= Html.ActionLink("About", "About", "Home")%></li>
```

```
            </ul>

        </div>
      </div>

      <div id="main">
          <asp:ContentPlaceHolder ID="MainContent" runat="server" />

          <div id="footer">
          </div>
      </div>
    </div>
</body>
</html>
```

LISTING 10.7   Views\Title\Index.aspx

```
<%@ Page Title="" Language="C#" MasterPageFile="~/Views/Shared/Site.Master"
➥Inherits="System.Web.Mvc.ViewPage" %>

<asp:Content ID="Content1" ContentPlaceHolderID="TitleContent" runat="server">
    I Am The Page Title!
</asp:Content>

<asp:Content ID="Content2" ContentPlaceHolderID="MainContent" runat="server">

    <h2>Index</h2>

</asp:Content>
```

When the Index view in Listing 10.7 is rendered to a browser, the title *I Am The Page Title!* is displayed (see Figure 10.6).

FIGURE 10.6   Changing the view master page title

Nested Master Pages

Most websites have multiple sections with different page layouts. Some pages might contain a single column, and some pages might contain multiple columns.

Typically, however, certain elements of the website design are constant. Every page has the same outer chrome consisting of navigation links, website logo, banner advertisements, and footer text.

You can nest one master page within another master page. Master pages can be nested infinitely deep. The outer master page can contain the standard content that you want to display on all pages in your application. The interior master page can contain particular page layouts. In this way, your website can have multiple page layouts but keep some elements constant.

The master page in Listing 10.8 is the outer master page. Notice that it is just a normal master page that contains one <asp:ContentPlaceHolder> tag—nothing special about it.

LISTING 10.8   Views\Shared\Outer.master

```
<%@ Master Language="C#" Inherits="System.Web.Mvc.ViewMasterPage" %>
<!DOCTYPE html PUBLIC "-//W3C//DTD XHTML 1.0 Transitional//EN"
"http://www.w3.org/TR/xhtml1/DTD/xhtml1-transitional.dtd">
<html xmlns="http://www.w3.org/1999/xhtml" >
<head id="Head1" runat="server">
    <title>Outer Master</title>
</head>
<body>
    <div>
        <h1>Outer Master</h1>
        <asp:ContentPlaceHolder
            ID="MainContent"
            runat="server" />
    </div>
</body>
</html>
```

The master page in Listing 10.9 is the nested master page. Notice that it has a MasterPageFile attribute that points to the Outer.master master page from Listing 10.8. The nested master page contains both <asp:Content> tags and <asp:ContentPlaceHolder> tags.

LISTING 10.9   Inner.master

```
<%@ Master Language="C#" MasterPageFile="Outer.master"
➡Inherits="System.Web.Mvc.ViewMasterPage" %>
```

```
<asp:Content ContentPlaceHolderID="MainContent" runat="server">
    <h1>Inner Master</h1>
    <asp:ContentPlaceHolder
        ID="MainContent"
        runat="server" />
</asp:Content>
```

Finally, the view in Listing 10.10 has a `MasterPageFile` attribute that points to the master page in Listing 10.9. When the view in Listing 10.10 is returned by a controller, the outer master page, the inner master page, and the Index view are merged and rendered to the browser (see Figure 10.7).

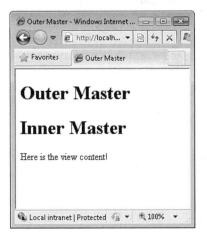

FIGURE 10.7   A view within a nested master page

LISTING 10.10   \Views\NestedMaster\Index.aspx

```
<%@ Page Title="" Language="C#" MasterPageFile="~/Views/Shared/Inner.Master"
➥Inherits="System.Web.Mvc.ViewPage" %>


<asp:Content ID="Content1" ContentPlaceHolderID="MainContent" runat="server">

    Here is the view content!

</asp:Content>
```

Passing View Data to Master Pages

Imagine that you want to show some data that you have retrieved from the database in your website master page. For example, if you create a Movie Database application, you might want to display a list of movie category links on your master page and retrieve the categories from a database table.

You pass data to a view by taking advantage of view data. How do you pass data to a master page?

You also can use view data to pass data to a master page. However, you should not add the data required by the master page in each controller action. Instead, you should create a base class for all your controllers—an Application controller—and modify the view data in the Application controller class. That way, you can avoid violating the DRY Principle (Don't Repeat Yourself), which makes your code more maintainable.

Listing 10.11 contains an abstract (MustInherit) class named ApplicationController. Notice that the class inherits from the Controller base class just like any standard ASP.NET MVC controller. However, because the ApplicationController is an abstract class, you can't actually use the class as a controller.

LISTING 10.11   \Controllers\ApplicationController.cs (C#)

```csharp
using System.Linq;
using System.Web.Mvc;
using MvcApplication1.Models;

namespace MvcApplication1.Controllers
{
    public abstract class ApplicationController : Controller
    {
        private MoviesDBEntities _entities = new MoviesDBEntities();

        public ApplicationController()
        {
            ViewData["categories"] = _entities.MovieCategorySet.ToList();
        }

    }
}
```

LISTING 10.11   \Controllers\ApplicationController.vb (VB)

```vb
Public MustInherit Class ApplicationController
    Inherits System.Web.Mvc.Controller
```

```
    Private _entities As New MoviesDBEntities()

    Sub New()
        ViewData("categories") = _entities.MovieCategorySet.ToList()
    End Sub

End Class
```

The constructor in the ApplicationController class modifies the view data. A list of movie categories is retrieved from the database and added to the view data dictionary with the key *categories*.

The controller in Listing 10.12 inherits from the ApplicationController class. Because the controller inherits from the base ApplicationController class, the list of movie categories is added to the controller's view data automatically.

LISTING 10.12   \Controllers\MovieController.cs (C#)

```csharp
using System.Web.Mvc;

namespace MvcApplication1.Controllers
{
    public class MovieController : ApplicationController
    {
        public ActionResult Index()
        {
            return View();
        }

    }
}
```

LISTING 10.12   \Controllers\MovieController.vb (VB)

```vb
Public Class MovieController
    Inherits ApplicationController

    Function Index() As ActionResult
        Return View()
    End Function

End Class
```

Finally, the master page in Listing 10.13 displays the list of movie categories by retrieving the list from view data (see Figure 10.8).

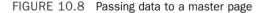

FIGURE 10.8   Passing data to a master page

LISTING 10.13   \Views\Shared\MovieMaster.master (C#)

```
<%@ Master Language="C#" Inherits="System.Web.Mvc.ViewMasterPage" %>
<%@ Import Namespace="MvcApplication1.Models" %>
<!DOCTYPE html PUBLIC "-//W3C//DTD XHTML 1.0 Transitional//EN"
➥"http://www.w3.org/TR/xhtml1/DTD/xhtml1-transitional.dtd">

<html xmlns="http://www.w3.org/1999/xhtml" >
<head runat="server">
    <title><asp:ContentPlaceHolder ID="TitleContent" runat="server" /></title>
</head>
<body>
    <div>
        <ul>
        <% foreach (var category in (List<MovieCategory>)ViewData["categories"])
           { %>

            <li><%= category.Name %></li>

        <% } %>
        </ul>
```

```
                <asp:ContentPlaceHolder ID="MainContent" runat="server" />
        </div>
</body>
</html>
```

LISTING 10.13   \Views\Shared\MovieMaster.master (VB)

```
<%@ Master Language="VB" Inherits="System.Web.Mvc.ViewMasterPage" %>
<!DOCTYPE html PUBLIC "-//W3C//DTD XHTML 1.0 Transitional//EN"
➡"http://www.w3.org/TR/xhtml1/DTD/xhtml1-transitional.dtd">

<html xmlns="http://www.w3.org/1999/xhtml" >
<head id="Head1" runat="server">
    <title><asp:ContentPlaceHolder ID="TitleContent" runat="server" /></title>
</head>
<body>
    <div>
        <ul>
        <% For Each category In ViewData("categories")%>

            <li><%= category.Name %></li>

        <% Next%>
        </ul>

        <asp:ContentPlaceHolder ID="MainContent" runat="server" />
    </div>
</body>
</html>
```

To summarize, if you need to display data in a sitewide master page, you should inherit all the controllers in your application from a base ApplicationController class. That way, you can modify the view data in just the ApplicationController to modify the view data returned by all your controller actions.

Understanding View User Controls

A view user control represents a partial view. In other words, user controls give you a method to encapsulate visual content so that the same content can be displayed in multiple views. A user control can contain (X)HTML and script.

Imagine, for example, that you want to display a list of featured products. If you want to display the list of featured products on every page, you can add the list of featured products to a master page. However, if you want to display the list of featured products only on certain pages and not others, it makes more sense to create a user control.

Typically, you want to add a user control to the \Views\Shared folder because you use a user control across multiple views. Right-click the \Views\Shared folder and select the menu option Add, View. Give your user control a name, check the check box labeled Create a Partial View (.ascx), and click the Add button (see Figure 10.9). Notice that you do not select a master page in the case of a partial.

FIGURE 10.9   Creating a new view user control

The user control in Listing 10.14 contains a list of news items. This user control contains static content.

LISTING 10.14   \Views\Shared\News.ascx

```
<%@ Control Language="C#" Inherits="System.Web.Mvc.ViewUserControl" %>
<div style="border:double 4px red;padding:10px">
<h3>What's New?</h3>
<ul>
    <li>
    See our store section for a selection
    of great new products!
    </li>
    <li>
    Visit our new help pages to learn more
```

```
        about navigating our poorly designed
        website!
        </li>
    </ul>
</div>
```

After you create a user control, you can add the user control to a view by calling the `Html.RenderPartial()` method in the view. The view in Listing 10.15 uses the `News` user control to display news items.

LISTING 10.15   \Views\Magazine\Index.aspx (C#)

```
<%@ Page Title="" Language="C#" MasterPageFile="~/Views/Shared/Site.Master"
➡Inherits="System.Web.Mvc.ViewPage" %>


<asp:Content ID="Content2" ContentPlaceHolderID="MainContent" runat="server">

    <h1>Welcome to the home page of our website!</h1>

    <% Html.RenderPartial("News"); %>

</asp:Content>
```

LISTING 10.15   \Views\Magazine\Index.aspx (VB)

```
<%@ Page Title="" Language="VB" MasterPageFile="~/Views/Shared/Site.Master"
➡Inherits="System.Web.Mvc.ViewPage" %>
<asp:Content ID="Content2" ContentPlaceHolderID="MainContent" runat="server">

    <h1>Welcome to the home page of our website!</h1>

    <% Html.RenderPartial("News")%>

</asp:Content>
```

WARNING

The `Html.RenderPartial()` method does not return a string. Therefore, use the `<% %>` script delimiters instead of the `<%= %>` delimiters when calling this method.

When the Index view in Listing 10.15 is rendered to the browser, the news user control is rendered as well (see Figure 10.10).

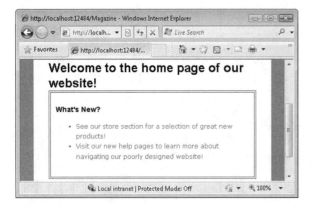

FIGURE 10.10   View containing news user control

Passing View Data to User Controls

The user control discussed in the previous section contained static content. However, you often want to display content that you have retrieved from a database within a user control. For example, you might want to display a list of featured products in a user control (see Figure 10.11).

How do you pass data from a controller to a user control? If you know that you want to add a user control to more than one view, it makes sense to create an action filter that adds the data required by the user control to view data.

The user control in Listing 10.16 displays a list of featured products. The user control accesses the ViewData.Model property to get the list of featured products.

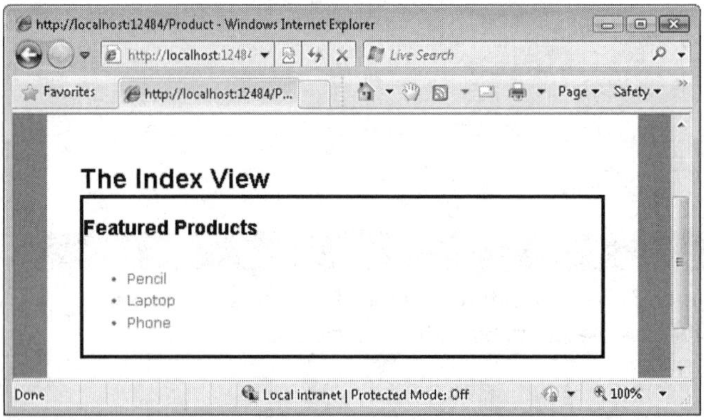

FIGURE 10.11   Displaying featured products with a user control

LISTING 10.16   \Views\Shared\Featured.ascx (C#)

```
<%@ Control Language="C#" Inherits="System.Web.Mvc.ViewUserControl<List<Product>>" %>
<%@ Import Namespace="MvcApplication1.Models" %>

<div style="border:solid 3px black">
<h2>Featured Products</h2>
<ul>
    <% foreach (var product in Model)
       { %>

        <li><%= product.Name %></li>

    <% } %>
</ul>
</div>
```

LISTING 10.16   \Views\Shared\Featured.ascx (VB)

```
<%@ Control Language="VB" Inherits="System.Web.Mvc.ViewUserControl(Of IEnumerable
➥(Of MvcApplication1.Product))" %>

<div style="border:solid 3px black">
<h2>Featured Products</h2>
<ul>
    <% For Each product In Model%>

        <li><%= product.Name %></li>

    <% Next%>
</ul>
</div>
```

The `featured` user control in Listing 10.16 is a *typed* user control. Just like a view, a user control can be typed. The `Inherits` attribute causes the `Model` property to be cast to a list of products.

The `Index` view in Listing 10.17 uses the `featured` user control to display a list of featured products.

LISTING 10.17   \Views\Product\Index.aspx (C#)

```
<%@ Page Title="" Language="C#" MasterPageFile="~/Views/Shared/Site.Master"
➥Inherits="System.Web.Mvc.ViewPage" %>
```

```
<asp:Content ID="Content2" ContentPlaceHolderID="MainContent" runat="server">

    <h1>The Index View</h1>

    <% Html.RenderPartial("Featured", ViewData["featured"]); %>

</asp:Content>
```

LISTING 10.17   \Views\Product\Index.aspx (VB)

```
<%@ Page Title="" Language="VB" MasterPageFile="~/Views/Shared/Site.Master"
➥Inherits="System.Web.Mvc.ViewPage" %>

<asp:Content ID="Content2" ContentPlaceHolderID="MainContent" runat="server">

    <h1>The Index View</h1>

    <% Html.RenderPartial("Featured", ViewData("featured"))%>

</asp:Content>
```

Notice that two values are passed to the `Html.RenderPartial()` method. The first value represents the name of the `featured` user control. The second value is a value from view data. The value of the featured item from view data is assigned to the `ViewData.Model` property of the `featured` user control.

We can add the featured products to view data by taking advantage of an action filter. The `FeaturedProduct` action filter is contained in Listing 10.18.

NOTE

We discussed action filters in Chapter 7, "Understanding Model Binders and Action Filters."

LISTING 10.18   \CustomActionFilters\FeaturedProductActionFilter.cs (C#)

```
using System;
using System.Collections.Generic;
using System.Linq;
using System.Web.Mvc;
using MvcApplication1.Models;
```

```csharp
namespace MvcApplication1.CustomActionFilters
{
    public class FeaturedProductAttribute: ActionFilterAttribute
    {
        private ProductsDBEntities _entities = new ProductsDBEntities();

        public override void OnResultExecuting(ResultExecutingContext filterContext)
        {
            var viewData = filterContext.Controller.ViewData;
            viewData["featured"] = GetRandomProducts();
        }

        private IList<Product> GetRandomProducts()
        {
            var rnd = new Random();
            var allProducts = _entities.ProductSet.ToList();
            var featuredProducts = new List<Product>();
            for (int i = 0; i < 3; i++)
            {
                var product = allProducts[rnd.Next(allProducts.Count)];
                allProducts.Remove(product);
                featuredProducts.Add(product);
            }
            return featuredProducts;
        }

    }
}
```

LISTING 10.18   \CustomActionFilters\FeaturedProductActionFilter.vb (VB)

```vb
Public Class FeaturedProductAttribute
    Inherits ActionFilterAttribute

    Private _entities As New ProductsDBEntities()

    Public Overrides Sub OnResultExecuting(ByVal filterContext As
➡ResultExecutingContext)
        Dim viewData = filterContext.Controller.ViewData
        viewData("featured") = GetRandomProducts()
    End Sub

    Private Function GetRandomProducts() As IList(Of Product)
        Dim rnd = New Random()
        Dim allProducts = _entities.ProductSet.ToList()
```

```
        Dim featuredProducts = New List(Of Product)()
        For i As Integer = 0 To 2
            Dim product = allProducts(rnd.Next(allProducts.Count))
            allProducts.Remove(product)
            featuredProducts.Add(product)
        Next
        Return featuredProducts
    End Function

End Class
```

The action filter in Listing 10.18 overrides the base `ActionFilterAttribute`'s
`OnResultExecuting()` method. This method executes before the controller action result
executes. This action filter adds a new item to view data that represents a list of featured
products.

The action filter calls the `GetRandomProducts()` method to get a list of three randomly
selected products from the database. This list of random products is assigned to an item
named featured in view data.

The controller in Listing 10.19 illustrates how you can use the `featured` action filter to
add the featured products view data to some actions, but not others.

LISTING 10.19   \Controllers\ProductController.cs (C#)

```csharp
using System.Web.Mvc;
using MvcApplication1.CustomActionFilters;

namespace MvcApplication1.Controllers
{
    public class ProductController : Controller
    {

        [FeaturedProduct]
        public ActionResult Index()
        {
            return View();
        }

        [FeaturedProduct]
        public ActionResult Details()
        {
            return View();
        }


        public ActionResult About()
```

```
    {
        return View();
    }

  }
}
```

LISTING 10.19   \Controllers\ProductController.vb (VB)

```
Public Class ProductController
    Inherits Controller

    <FeaturedProduct()> _
    Public Function Index() As ActionResult
        Return View()
    End Function

    <FeaturedProduct()> _
    Public Function Details() As ActionResult
        Return View()
    End Function

    Public Function About() As ActionResult
        Return View()
    End Function

End Class
```

The controller in Listing 10.19 has three action methods: Index(), Details(), and
About(). Only the first two action methods are decorated with the featured action filter.
Therefore, the list of featured products is added only to the view data when one of the
first two action methods is invoked.

Using a View User Control as a Template

You can use a view user control as a template when displaying a set of database records.
For example, when displaying a set of database records in an HTML table, you can use a
view user control as a template for each row.

The controller in Listing 10.20 returns a set of movies in view data.

LISTING 10.20   Controllers\TheaterController.cs (C#)

```
using System.Linq;
using System.Web.Mvc;
```

```csharp
using MvcApplication1.Models;

namespace MvcApplication1.Controllers
{
    public class TheaterController : Controller
    {
        private MoviesDBEntities _entities = new MoviesDBEntities();

        public ActionResult Index()
        {
            return View(_entities.MovieSet.ToList());
        }


    }
}
```

LISTING 10.20   Controllers\TheaterController.vb (VB)

```vbnet
Public Class TheaterController
    Inherits Controller

    Private _entities As New MoviesDBEntities()

    Public Function Index() As ActionResult
        Return View(_entities.MovieSet.ToList())
    End Function

End Class
```

The view in Listing 10.21 renders the set of movies in an HTML table by looping through the view data model.

LISTING 10.21   Views\Theater\Index.aspx (C#)

```
<%@ Page Title="" Language="C#" MasterPageFile="~/Views/Shared/Site.Master"
➥Inherits="System.Web.Mvc.ViewPage<IEnumerable<MvcApplication1.Models. Movie>>" %>

<asp:Content ID="Content2" ContentPlaceHolderID="MainContent" runat="server">

    <h2>Index</h2>

    <table>
        <tr>
            <th>
```

```
                Title
            </th>
            <th>
                Director
            </th>
            <th>
                DateReleased
            </th>
        </tr>

    <% foreach (var item in Model) { %>

        <% Html.RenderPartial("MovieTemplate", item); %>

    <% } %>

    </table>

</asp:Content>
```

LISTING 10.21   Views\Theater\Index.aspx (VB)

```
<%@ Page Title="" Language="VB" MasterPageFile="~/Views/Shared/Site.Master"
➥Inherits="System.Web.Mvc.ViewPage(Of IEnumerable (Of MvcApplication1.Movie))" %>

<asp:Content ID="Content2" ContentPlaceHolderID="MainContent" runat="server">

    <table>
        <tr>
            <th>
                Title
            </th>
            <th>
                Director
            </th>
            <th>
                DateReleased
            </th>
        </tr>

    <% For Each item In Model%>

        <% Html.RenderPartial("MovieTemplate", item)%>
```

```
    <% Next%>
    </table>
```

```
</asp:Content>
```

Notice that the `Html.RenderPartial()` method is called to render each table row. A user control named `MovieTemplate` is used to render each movie row. The `MovieTemplate` is contained in Listing 10.22.

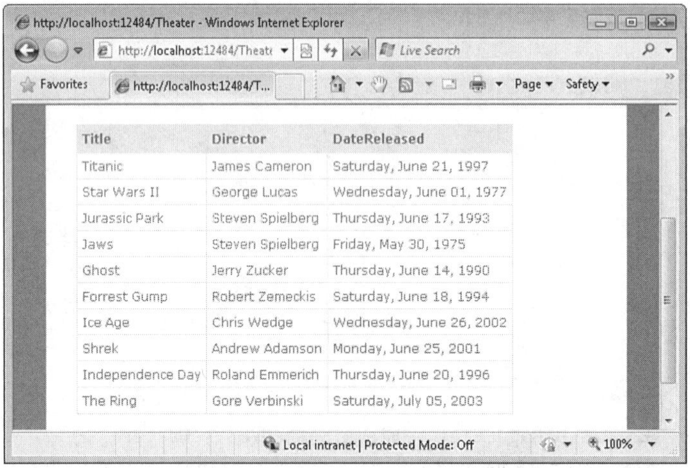

FIGURE 10.12   Rendering a table of movies with a template

LISTING 10.22   Views\Theater\MovieTemplate.ascx (C#)

```
<%@ Control Language="C#" Inherits="System.Web.Mvc.ViewUserControl
➥<MvcApplication1.Models.Movie>" %>
<tr>
    <td><%= Model.Title %></td>
    <td><%= Model.Director %></td>
    <td><%= Model.DateReleased.ToString("D") %></td>
</tr>
```

LISTING 10.22   Views\Theater\MovieTemplate.ascx (VB)

```
<%@ Control Language="VB" Inherits="System.Web.Mvc.ViewUserControl(Of
➥MvcApplication1.Movie)" %>
```

```
<tr>
    <td><%= Model.Title %></td>
    <td><%= Model.Director %></td>
    <td><%= Model.DateReleased.ToString("D") %></td>
</tr>
```

The `MovieTemplate` user control acts as a template for each row of data (see Figure 10.12). Splitting a single view into a separate view and user control can make a view more manageable.

Summary

In this chapter, you learned two methods of sharing visual content across multiple pages in an ASP.NET MVC application. First, you learned how to use view master pages to give the pages a common layout. You learned how to create both view master pages and view content pages. You also learned how to pass data from an application controller to a view master page.

In the second part of this chapter, we discussed view user controls (partials). You learned how to use a view user control to display the same visual content on multiple pages. Finally, you learned how to use a view user control as a template when displaying database data.

CHAPTER 11

Better Performance with Caching

The best way to improve the performance of an ASP.NET MVC application is by caching. The slowest operation that you can perform in an ASP.NET MVC application is database access. The best way to improve the performance of your data access code is to avoid accessing the database at all. Caching enables you to avoid accessing the database by keeping frequently accessed data in memory.

This chapter is devoted to the topic of improving the performance of your ASP.NET MVC applications through caching. You learn how to cache the results of controller actions, create cache profiles, and work with the cache API. We also discuss how you can test whether caching is enabled and whether data is properly stored in the cache.

Using the `OutputCache` Attribute

The easiest way to cache your views is to apply the `OutputCache` attribute to either an individual controller action or an entire controller class. For example, the controller in Listing 11.1 exposes two actions: `Index()` and `IndexCached()`. The `IndexCached()` action caches the view that it returns for 15 seconds.

LISTING 11.1 Controllers\HomeController.cs (C#)

```csharp
using System.Linq;
using System.Web.Mvc;
using MvcApplication1.Models;

namespace MvcApplication1.Controllers
{
```

```csharp
[HandleError]
public class HomeController : Controller
{
    private MoviesDBEntities _entities = new MoviesDBEntities();
    public ActionResult Index()
    {
        var movies = _entities.MovieSet.ToList();
        return View("Index", movies);
    }

    [OutputCache(Duration=15, VaryByParam="None")]
    public ActionResult IndexCached()
    {
        var movies = _entities.MovieSet.ToList();
        return View("Index", movies);
    }

}
}
```

LISTING 11.1   Controllers\HomeController.vb (VB)

```vb
<HandleError()> _
Public Class HomeController
    Inherits Controller

    Private _entities As New MoviesDBEntities()

    Public Function Index() As ActionResult
        Dim movies = _entities.MovieSet.ToList()
        Return View("Index", movies)
    End Function

    <OutputCache(Duration:=15, VaryByParam:="None")> _
    Public Function IndexCached() As ActionResult
        Dim movies = _entities.MovieSet.ToList()
        Return View("Index", movies)
    End Function

End Class
```

Both controller actions return the same view: the Index view. The Index view is contained in Listing 11.2. This view simply displays the current time and the list of movies returned by the controller actions (see Figure 11.1).

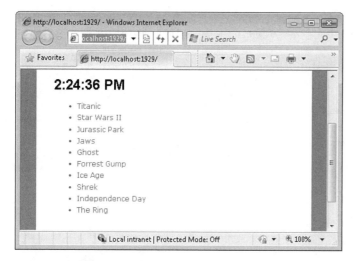

FIGURE 11.1   The Index view

LISTING 11.2   Views\Home\Index.aspx (C#)

```
<%@ Page Title="" Language="C#" MasterPageFile="~/Views/Shared/Site.Master"
➡Inherits="System.Web.Mvc.ViewPage<IEnumerable<MvcApplication1.Models. Movie>>" %>


<asp:Content ID="Content2" ContentPlaceHolderID="MainContent" runat="server">


    <h1><%= DateTime.Now.ToString("T") %></h1>

    <ul>
    <% foreach (var movie in Model)
        {%>

    <li><%= movie.Title%></li>

    <% } %>
    </ul>

</asp:Content>
```

LISTING 11.2   Views\Home\Index.aspx (VB)

```
<%@ Page Title="" Language="VB" MasterPageFile="~/Views/Shared/Site.Master"
➡Inherits="System.Web.Mvc.ViewPage(Of IEnumerable (Of MvcApplication1.Movie))" %>
```

```
<asp:Content ID="Content2" ContentPlaceHolderID="MainContent" runat="server">

    <h1><%= DateTime.Now.ToString("T") %></h1>

    <ul>
    <% For Each movie In Model%>

    <li><%= movie.Title%></li>

    <% Next%>
    </ul>

</asp:Content>
```

Each time that the Index view is returned by the Index() action, the view displays a new time. When the Index view is returned by the IndexCached() action, on the other hand, the time is not updated until at least 15 seconds pass. (You must keep hitting Refresh on your browser over and over again for 15 seconds to see a change.)

The OutputCache attribute enables you to dramatically improve the performance of your ASP.NET MVC applications. When you invoke the IndexCached() action, the movie records are not retrieved from the database on each request. Instead, the view is cached in memory, and your database can rest quietly.

> **NOTE**
>
> In this chapter, I focus on using the OutputCache attribute to cache views. However, the OutputCache attribute caches any type of response returned by a controller action. For example, you can also use the OutputCache attribute to cache a JsonResult.

If your data does not change often, you can set the cache duration to a really high number. Get out your calculator and do some math. You would set the duration to the value 3600 seconds to cache a view for 1 hour. You would set the duration to the value 86400 to cache a view for 1 day.

> **NOTE**
>
> There is no guarantee that a view will be cached for the amount of time that you specify. When memory resources become low, the ASP.NET framework evicts items from the cache automatically.

WARNING

Experienced developers from the ASP.NET Web Forms world are familiar with the *page* <%@ OutputCache %> directive. Don't use the <%@ OutputCache %> directive in a view. The OutputCache directive leaked into the MVC world from the Web Forms world. Pretend that it is not there.

You can apply the OutputCache attribute to an individual controller action or an entire controller. For example, the modified Home controller in Listing 11.3 has an OutputCache attribute applied to the controller class itself. Every action exposed by this controller is cached for 30 seconds.

LISTING 11.3   Controllers\HomeController.cs (C#)

```csharp
using System.Linq;
using System.Web.Mvc;
using MvcApplication1.Models;

namespace MvcApplication1.Controllers
{
    [OutputCache(Duration = 30, VaryByParam = "None")]
    public class HomeController : Controller
    {
        private MoviesDBEntities _entities = new MoviesDBEntities();

        public ActionResult Index()
        {
            var movies = _entities.MovieSet.ToList();
            return View("Index", movies);
        }

        public ActionResult IndexCached()
        {
            var movies = _entities.MovieSet.ToList();
            return View("Index", movies);
        }

    }
}
```

LISTING 11.3   Controllers\HomeController.vb (VB)

```vb
<OutputCache(Duration:=30, VaryByParam:="None")> _
Public Class HomeController
```

```
Inherits Controller

Private _entities As New MoviesDBEntities()

Public Function Index() As ActionResult
    Dim movies = _entities.MovieSet.ToList()
    Return View("Index", movies)
End Function

Public Function IndexCached() As ActionResult
    Dim movies = _entities.MovieSet.ToList()
    Return View("Index", movies)
End Function

End Class
```

Don't Cache Private Data

Caching a page that contains private user data is extremely dangerous. When a page is cached on the server, the same page is served to all users. So, if you cache a page that displays a user credit card number, everyone can see the credit card number (not good!).

The same page is cached for all users even when you require authorization. Imagine, for example, that you create a financial services website and the website includes a page that displays all a user's investments. The page displays the amount of money that a user has invested in a set of stocks, bonds, and mutual funds.

Because this information is private, you require the user to log in before seeing the page. In other words, each user must be authorized before the user can view the page.

To improve the performance of the financial services page, you decide to enable caching for the page. You add the OutputCache attribute to the controller action that returns the page.

Don't do that! If you cache the controller action that returns the financial services pages, the private financial data for the first person to request the page will be shared among every subsequent visitor to the application.

In general, adding the OutputCache and Authorize attribute to the same controller action opens a security hole. Avoid doing this:

(C#)

```
[OutputCache(Duration=999, VaryByParam="None")]
[Authorize]
public ActionResult Index()
{
    var investments = _entities.InvestmentSet.ToList();
    return View(investments);
}
```

(VB)

```
<OutputCache(Duration:=999, VaryByParam:="None"), Authorize> _
Public Function Index() As ActionResult
    Dim investments = _entities.InvestmentSet.ToList()
    Return View(investments)
End Function
```

There are a couple of exceptions to this rule. First, it makes sense to cache a page when a group of people needs to view the same cached data. For example, if you create an online magazine site that only authorized members can view, and everyone sees the exact same articles, it makes sense to cache the pages. In other words, if you authorize users by role and the content can be viewed only by members of a particular role, it makes sense to cache the content viewed by members of that role.

Second, if you don't cache the data on the server and you only cache the data on the client, you can cache the data without sharing the data among multiple users. In the "Setting the Cache Location" section, we discuss how you can specify exactly where data gets cached. Be warned that data is cached on the server by default.

What Gets Cached?

The `OutputCache` attribute caches the response from a controller action. When a controller action returns a view, the entire rendered output of the view—everything that you see when you select View Source in your web browser—is cached. This content is cached in memory. Every user who makes the same browser request, not only the current user, gets the same cached version of the page.

When a view is cached on the server, ASP.NET application events such as the `BeginRequest`, `AuthenticateRequest`, `AuthorizeRequest`, and `EndRequest` events are still executed. This fact can be demonstrated with the Global.asax handlers contained in Listing 11.4.

LISTING 11.4   Global.asax.cs (C#)

```
public void Application_BeginRequest()
{
    Debug.WriteLine("Application_BeginRequest");
}

public void Application_AuthenticateRequest()
{
    Debug.WriteLine("Application_AuthenticateRequest");
}

public void Application_AuthorizeRequest()
```

```
{
    Debug.WriteLine("Application_AuthorizeRequest");
}

public void Application_EndRequest()
{
    Debug.WriteLine("Application_EndRequest");
}
```

LISTING 11.4   Global.asax.vb (VB)

```
Public Sub Application_BeginRequest()
    Debug.WriteLine("Application_BeginRequest")
End Sub

Public Sub Application_AuthenticateRequest()
    Debug.WriteLine("Application_AuthenticateRequest")
End Sub

Public Sub Application_AuthorizeRequest()
    Debug.WriteLine("Application_AuthorizeRequest")
End Sub

Public Sub Application_EndRequest()
    Debug.WriteLine("Application_EndRequest")
End Sub
```

In Listing 11.4, several application events are handled and logged to the Visual Studio Console window. When the /Home/IndexCached controller action is invoked, all these events are still raised (see Figure 11.2).

> **NOTE**
>
> If a page is cached on the client (the browser), the server application events won't be raised. If a page can be retrieved from the browser cache then there is no need to query the server for the page. If you press Refresh in Internet Explorer, you can bypass the client cache.

During the `Application.ResolveRequestCache` event, the caching module checks if the current request can be served from the cache. If the request can be served from the cache, the normal request handler is not executed.

Because the normal request handler is not executed when a request is handled by the cache, the controller action associated with the request never gets executed. When a controller action result is cached, the controller logic is not executed until the response rendered by the controller expires from the cache.

```
Output
Show output from: Debug                    ▾ │ 🔍 │ 🔍 🔍 │ 🔍 🔍
Application_BeginRequest
Application_AuthenticateRequest
Application_AuthorizeRequest
Application_EndRequest
Application_BeginRequest
Application_AuthenticateRequest
Application_AuthorizeRequest
Application_EndRequest
```

FIGURE 11.2   Application events raised when cache-enabled

Furthermore, any action filters associated with the controller action never get executed after the action result has been added to the cache. If you have assigned any custom action filters to a cached controller action, these action filters will be executed only when the controller is first called. The action filters won't be executed when the controller response can be served from the cache.

Setting the Cache Location

By default, when you use the `OutputCache` attribute to cache a controller action, the view returned by a controller is cached on the browser, on the server, and on every proxy server in between.

You can control exactly where a view gets cached by setting the `Location` property on the `OutputCache` attribute. This property accepts the following values:

- ▶ Any (default)—The view is cached on the server, any proxy servers, and the client.

- ▶ Client—The view is cached only on the client.

- ▶ Downstream—The view is cached on any proxy servers and the client.

- ▶ Server—The view is cached only on the server.

- ▶ None—The view is not cached.

- ▶ ServerAndClient—The view is cached on the server and the client but not any proxy servers.

Why would you want to change the cache location? There might be several reasons.

First, if you want to cache personalized user data, you can change the value of the `Location` property to Client. That way, the personalized data will be cached on the browser but not on any proxy servers or the web server. Because the view is not cached on the server, the personalized information won't be shared with other users.

NOTE

The OutputCache attribute includes a NoStore property. When you set the NoStore property to the value true, a permanent copy of the data cached is not stored on any proxy servers or browsers. Setting NoStore is a good idea when you cache sensitive data on the client.

For example, the controller in Listing 11.5 displays the current user's name. However, because the Location property is set to the value Client, the username is not cached on the server, and the same username is not displayed to multiple users. (Each user sees his own username instead of seeing the username of the first person to invoke the controller action).

LISTING 11.5   Controllers\UserController.cs (C#)

```
using System.Web.Mvc;
using System.Web.UI;

namespace MvcApplication1.Controllers
{
    public class UserController : Controller
    {
        [OutputCache(Duration=9999, VaryByParam="None", Location=
➥OutputCacheLocation.Client)]
        public string Index()
        {
            return User.Identity.Name;
        }

    }
}
```

LISTING 11.5   Controllers\UserController.cs (VB)

```
Public Class UserController
    Inherits Controller

    <OutputCache(Duration:=9999, VaryByParam:="None", Location:=
➥OutputCacheLocation.Client)> _
    Public Function Index() As String
        Return User.Identity.Name
    End Function

End Class
```

Modifying the OutputCache Location property also makes sense when you want to control exactly when content is removed from the cache. If you want complete control over when the cache is updated, it makes sense to cache the content only on the server. In the "Removing Items from the Output Cache" section, you learn how to programmatically remove content from the output cache.

Varying the Output Cache by Parameter

One important issue that you quickly encounter when using caching is the issue of master/detail views. Imagine that you are creating an auction website. You want to create a Details view that displays details on different auction items. When you pass different product IDs to the Details view, you want to display information on different auction items.

Here's the problem. If you cache the Details page, the information for only one action item will cache. The first auction item requested caches, and details for later auction items will never be shown.

In particular, if the first auction item requested is an auction for the Wingless Quackers the Duck Beanie Baby (the most valuable Beanie Baby of all time), every time someone requests the Details view, everyone sees the details for the Quackers the Duck Beanie Baby auction item.

There is a simple way to solve this problem. The OutputCache attribute supports a VaryByParam property. This property accepts the following values:

▶ None—Create only one cached version of the page

▶ *—Creates different cached versions of the page when different query string or form parameters are passed to the page

▶ Comma-separated list of form or query string parameter names

The Details() action exposed by the controller in Listing 11.6 displays details for different movies. When you pass different IDs to the Details action, by passing different values for the MovieID query string parameter, different cached versions of the Details view are created.

LISTING 11.6   Controllers\MovieController.cs (C#)

```csharp
using System.Linq;
using System.Web.Mvc;
using MvcApplication1.Models;

namespace MvcApplication1.Controllers
{
    public class MovieController : Controller
    {
        private MoviesDBEntities _entities = new MoviesDBEntities();
```

```
        [OutputCache(Duration=9999, VaryByParam="movieId")]
        public ActionResult Details(int movieId)
        {
            var result = (from movie in _entities.MovieSet
                        where movie.Id == movieId
                        select movie).FirstOrDefault();
            return View(result);
        }


    }
}
```

LISTING 11.6   Controllers\MovieController.vb (VB)

```
Public Class MovieController
    Inherits Controller

    Private _entities As New MoviesDBEntities()

    <OutputCache(Duration:=9999, VaryByParam:="movieId")> _
    Public Function Details(ByVal movieId As Integer) As ActionResult
        Dim result = (From movie In _entities.MovieSet _
                    Where movie.Id = movieId _
                    Select movie).FirstOrDefault()
        Return View(result)
    End Function

End Class
```

If you invoke the Details() action with different values for the MovieId parameter, you get details for different movies. For example, you can invoke the Details() action by requesting the following URLs:

/Movie/Details?MovieId=1

/Movie/Details?MovieId=2

The first URL returns details on the movie *Titanic,* and the second URL returns details on the movie *Star Wars.* The Details view returned by the Details controller action displays the time (see Figure 11.3). You can use the time to determine when the view was cached.

It is important to understand that using VaryByParam results in more cached versions of a view and not less. Each time that you pass another value for the MovieId parameter, more server memory is devoted to caching a new version of the Details view. The time displayed by the Details view does not change when you refresh your browser because you get a cached version of the view.

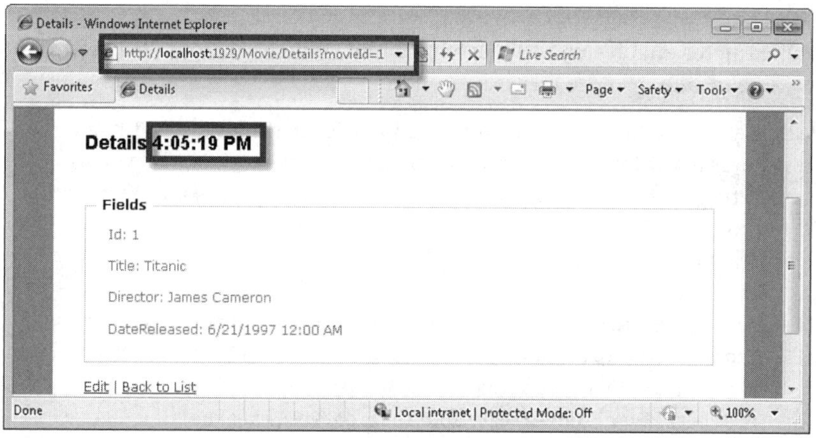

FIGURE 11.3   The Details view

NOTE

Different URLs always result in different cached versions of a page. If a parameter is extracted from a URL, different cached versions of a page are created automatically. For example, the default route extracts an `Id` parameter from the URL. When you invoke a controller action with different values for the `Id` parameter, different cached versions of the page are generated automatically. Therefore, when using the default route, you never need to use the `VaryByParam` property with the `Id` parameter.

Varying the Output Cache

In the previous section, you learned how the `VaryByParam` property enables you to create different cached versions of a view when there is a difference in a query string or `form` parameter passed to the view. There are additional types of parameters that you can use when creating different cached versions of the same view.

The `OutputCache` attribute supports the following properties:

- ▶ `VaryByHeader`—Enables you to create different cached versions of a view depending on the value of a browser header.

- ▶ `VaryByContentEncoding`—Enables you to cache both a compressed and uncompressed version of a view. Useful when used with Internet Information Services 7.0 compression (gzip or deflate).

- ▶ `VaryByCustom`—Enables you to specify a custom algorithm for when different cached versions of a view should be created. Accepts the special value browser that indicates that a different cached version of a view should be created when the type or major version of the browser varies.

Using `VaryByHeader`

The `VaryByHeader` parameter enables you to create different cached versions of a view depending on the value of one or more browser headers.

Whenever a browser makes a request to a website, the browser includes a set of headers in the request. These headers are different depending on the type of browser, the version of the browser, your operating system, and the software you installed. For example, when I use Microsoft Internet Explorer 7.0 to make a request from my personal laptop, the following headers are included in the request:

```
Accept: image/gif, image/x-xbitmap, image/jpeg, image/pjpeg, application/x-ms-
application, application/vnd.ms-xpsdocument, application/xaml+xml, application/x-ms-
xbap, application/x-shockwave-flash, application/x-
silverlight, application/x-silverlight-2-b2, application/vnd.ms-excel,
application/vnd.ms-powerpoint,
application/msword, */*
Accept-Language: en-us
UA-CPU: x86
Accept-Encoding: gzip, deflate
User-Agent: Mozilla/4.0 (compatible; MSIE 7.0; Windows NT 6.0; Mozilla/4.0
(compatible; MSIE 6.0; Windows NT 5.1; SV1) ; SLCC1; .NET CLR 2.0.50727; .NET CLR
1.1.4322; Tablet PC 2.0; .NET CLR 3.5.21022; MS-RTC LM 8; InfoPath.2; .NET CLR
3.5.30729; .NET CLR 3.0.30618)
Cookie: user-id=PTRAL92YG3P7; shopId=E0dUSqezrSvCf3nlDRxqwXQ
```

Notice that the browser headers include the Accept-Language header that represents my preferred language (United States English). If my website generates different language versions of the same view, I could use this header to vary the cached version of the page by language.

The browser headers also include the User-Agent header that represents information about the computer performing the browser request. Notice that the header contains information about the version of the .NET framework (.NET CLR) installed on my machine.

Imagine that some of your views contain different content depending on the type of browser used to invoke the controller action that returned the view. You could use the User-Agent header to create different cached versions of the view depending on the type of browser. However, the User-Agent header is too fine-grained. Small variations in the User-Agent header result in unnecessary caching of different versions of the same view.

Using `VaryByCustom`

A better option to handle browser differences is to take advantage of the `VaryByCustom` property. The `VaryByCustom` property accepts the magic value *browser*. When `VaryByCustom` has the value browser, only the type of browser and the major version of the browser is taken into consideration when creating different cached versions of a page.

For example, the controller action in Listing 11.7 returns the User-Agent header. The value returned by this action is cached. You get different cached versions of the action result when the action is invoked with Microsoft Internet Explorer and Mozilla Firefox. You also get different cached versions of the action result depending on whether the action is invoked by Internet Explorer 7 or Internet Explorer 8. (Browser differences other than the type or major version are ignored.)

LISTING 11.7   Controllers\BrowserController.cs (C#)

```csharp
using System;
using System.Web.Mvc;

namespace MvcApplication1.Controllers
{
    public class BrowserController : Controller
    {
        [OutputCache(Duration=999, VaryByParam="None", VaryByCustom="Browser")]
        public string Index()
        {
            return DateTime.Now.ToString("T") + ":" + Request.UserAgent;
        }

    }
}
```

LISTING 11.7   Controllers\BrowserController.vb (VB)

```vb
Public Class BrowserController
    Inherits Controller

    <OutputCache(Duration:=999, VaryByParam:="None", VaryByCustom:="Browser")> _
    Public Function Index() As String
        Return DateTime.Now.ToString("T") & ":" & Request.UserAgent
    End Function

End Class
```

The property is called the VaryByCustom property for a reason. You can create a custom function in the Global.asax file that determines when different cached versions of a view are created. You can use any criteria for creating different cached versions of the page that you want (the time of day, a random number generator, the weather).

For example, the controller action in Listing 11.8 returns different views depending on the capabilities of the browser invoking the action. If the browser making the request supports JavaScript, one view is returned. If the browser does not support JavaScript, another view is returned.

LISTING 11.8   Controllers\VaryCustomController.cs (C#)

```csharp
using System.Web.Mvc;

namespace MvcApplication1.Controllers
{
    public class VaryCustomController : Controller
    {
        [OutputCache(Duration=9999, VaryByParam="None", VaryByCustom="JS")]
        public ActionResult Index()
        {
            if (Request.Browser.EcmaScriptVersion.Major > 0)
                return View("IndexJS");

            return View("Index");

        }

    }
}
```

LISTING 11.8   Controllers\VaryCustomController.vb (VB)

```vbnet
Public Class VaryCustomController
    Inherits Controller

    <OutputCache(Duration:=9999, VaryByParam:="None", VaryByCustom:="JS")> _
    Public Function Index() As ActionResult
        If Request.Browser.EcmaScriptVersion.Major > 0 Then
            Return View("IndexJS")
        End If

        Return View("Index")

    End Function

End Class
```

The controller in Listing 11.8 takes advantage of the GetVaryByCustomString() method defined in the Global.asax file in Listing 11.9. The VaryByCustomString() method determines when the Index() controller action generates different cached versions of the view.

LISTING 11.9   Global.asax.cs (C#)

```csharp
public override string GetVaryByCustomString(HttpContext context, string custom)
{
    if (custom == "JS")
        return Request.Browser.EcmaScriptVersion.ToString();
    return base.GetVaryByCustomString(context, custom);
}
```

LISTING 11.9   Global.asax.vb (VB)

```vb
Public Overrides Function GetVaryByCustomString(ByVal context As HttpContext, ByVal
➥custom As String) As String
    If custom = "JS" Then
        Return Request.Browser.EcmaScriptVersion.ToString()
    End If
    Return MyBase.GetVaryByCustomString(context, custom)
End Function
```

Removing Items from the Output Cache

You can remove items from the cache programmatically, with one important qualification. Only items from the server cache can be removed programmatically. You can't reach out to the web browser through your application code and remove data that has been cached on the browser.

Imagine that you need to display a product catalog in your web application. You cache the product catalog to improve performance. Your website includes an administrative page that enables employees to add new products the catalog. You want to remove the catalog from the cache whenever the catalog is updated.

You can remove an item from the output cache programmatically by calling the shared HttpResponse.RemoveOutputCacheItem() method. Again, this method deletes the item only from the server cache and not the browser cache.

For example, the Time() action in Listing 11.10 returns a view that displays the current time and two links labeled Reload and Clear (see Figure 11.4). When you click the first link, the view is displayed again. Because the view is cached, the time displayed in the view does not change.

The second link invokes the Clear() action. This action invokes the HttpResponse.RemoveOutputCacheItem() method. As the name of the method suggests, this method removes a particular item from the output cache. You designate the item to remove by supplying a URL.

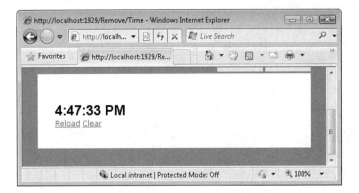

FIGURE 11.4 The Time view

LISTING 11.10 Controllers\RemoveController.cs (C#)

```csharp
using System.Web;
using System.Web.Mvc;
using System.Web.UI;

namespace MvcApplication1.Controllers
{
    public class RemoveController : Controller
    {
        [OutputCache(Duration=9999, VaryByParam="None", Location=
➥OutputCacheLocation.Server)]
        public ActionResult Time()
        {
            return View();
        }

        public ActionResult Clear()
        {
            HttpResponse.RemoveOutputCacheItem("/Remove/Time");
            return RedirectToAction("Time");
        }

    }
}
```

LISTING 11.10 Controllers\RemoveController.vb (VB)

```vbnet
Public Class RemoveController
    Inherits Controller
```

```
    <OutputCache(Duration:=9999, VaryByParam:="None", Location:=
➥OutputCacheLocation.Server)> _
    Public Function Time() As ActionResult
        Return View()
    End Function

    Public Function Clear() As ActionResult
        HttpResponse.RemoveOutputCacheItem("/Remove/Time")
        Return RedirectToAction("Time")
    End Function

End Class
```

Notice that the Time() action includes an OutputCache attribute with a Location property set to the value Server. The item can be removed from the cache because the item is not cached beyond the server.

Using Cache Profiles

A cache profile represents a set of cache settings. Cache profiles provide you with a convenient mechanism for managing cache settings for your controller actions in one centralized location. You define cache profiles in the web configuration (web.config) file. After you define a profile, you can apply the profile to one or more controllers or controller actions.

You create a cache profile by adding the profile to the system.web\caching\outputCacheSettings\outputCacheProfiles element of the web.config file. For example, you can add the contents of Listing 11.11 to the <system.web> section of an MVC application's web.config file.

LISTING 11.11   Cache Profiles

```
<caching>
<outputCacheSettings>
    <outputCacheProfiles>
        <add
            name="Profile1"
            duration="300"
            varyByParam="None"
            location="Server"/>
    </outputCacheProfiles>
</outputCacheSettings>
</caching>
```

The cache profile in Listing 11.11 is named Profile1. This profile represents a cache duration of 300 seconds (5 minutes) and a server-only cache.

The Index() action in Listing 11.12 uses the Profile1 cache profile.

LISTING 11.12   Controllers\ProfileController.cs (C#)

```csharp
using System;
using System.Web.Mvc;

namespace MvcApplication1.Controllers
{
    public class ProfileController : Controller
    {
        [OutputCache(CacheProfile="Profile1")]
        public string Index()
        {
            return DateTime.Now.ToString("T");
        }

    }
}
```

LISTING 11.12   Controllers\ProfileController.cs (C#)

```vbnet
Public Class ProfileController
    Inherits Controller

    <OutputCache(CacheProfile:="Profile1")> _
    Public Function Index() As String
        Return DateTime.Now.ToString("T")
    End Function

End Class
```

Using the Cache API

If you prefer, you can control the cache programmatically instead of declaratively. Controlling the cache through code takes more work but provides you with finer-grain control over the cache. There are two classes that you can manipulate to modify how controller responses are cached: the System.Web.HttpCachePolicy class and the System.Web.Caching.Cache class.

Using the **HttpCachePolicy** Class

The HttpCachePolicy class enables you to manipulate the cache related HTTP headers sent with a response. When controlling how a response is cached, there are several important HTTP headers that you need to be concerned about.

First, you can use the following two headers to specify how long a response should be cached on proxy servers and browsers:

▶ Cache-Control—The HTTP 1.1 method to specify how a response gets cached

▶ Expires—The HTTP 1.0 method to specify the expiration date and time of the response

And you can use the following two headers to indicate whether a resource has already expired in response to a browser request:

▶ Last-Modified—The HTTP 1.0 and HTTP 1.1 method to indicate the date and time when the resource was last modified.

▶ ETag—The HTTP 1.1 Entity Tag header enables you to associate a unique version key with a resource.

> **NOTE**
>
> When you get into how caching is implemented at the level of HTTP, things get messy because of differences between the HTTP 1.0 and HTTP 1.1 protocols. If you want to learn more, start by reading RFC 2616 at www.w3.org/Protocols/rfc2616/rfc2616-sec14.html.

If you want to modify the Cache-Control header to control how proxy servers and browsers cache a response, you can take advantage of the HttpCachePolicy.SetCacheability() method. The Index() action in Listing 11.13 caches a response for 10 seconds.

LISTING 11.13   CacheControlController.cs (C#)

```csharp
using System;
using System.Web;
using System.Web.Mvc;

namespace MvcApplication1.Controllers
{
    public class CacheControlController : Controller
    {
        public string Index()
```

```
        {
            Response.Cache.SetCacheability(HttpCacheability.Private);
            Response.Cache.SetMaxAge(TimeSpan.FromSeconds(10));
            return DateTime.Now.ToString("T") + " <a href=
➥'/CacheControl/Index'>link</a>";
        }


    }
}
```

LISTING 11.13   CacheControlController.vb (VB)

```
Public Class CacheControlController
    Inherits Controller

    Public Function Index() As String
        Response.Cache.SetCacheability(HttpCacheability.Private)
        Response.Cache.SetMaxAge(TimeSpan.FromSeconds(10))
        Return DateTime.Now.ToString("T") & " <a href=
➥'/CacheControl/Index'>link</a>"
    End Function

End Class
```

The SetCacheability() method sets the Cache-Control header to private. When the Cache-Control header has the value private, a response is not cached in any shared caches. (The cached response cannot be shared with multiple people.) Typically, the response is cached only within the browser cache.

The SetMaxAge() method caches the response for 10 seconds. If you link to this page, the content on the page is updated every 10 seconds. You can test this functionality by clicking the link that the Index() method renders (see Figure 11.5).

The Index() action does not cache the response on the server. If you press the Reload button on your browser, the response is regenerated from the server from scratch. Each time you click Reload, you get a new time.

NOTE

You can view the HTTP headers transmitted between web server and browser by using a tool such as Firebug or Fiddler:

http://GetFirebug.com

www.Fiddler2.com

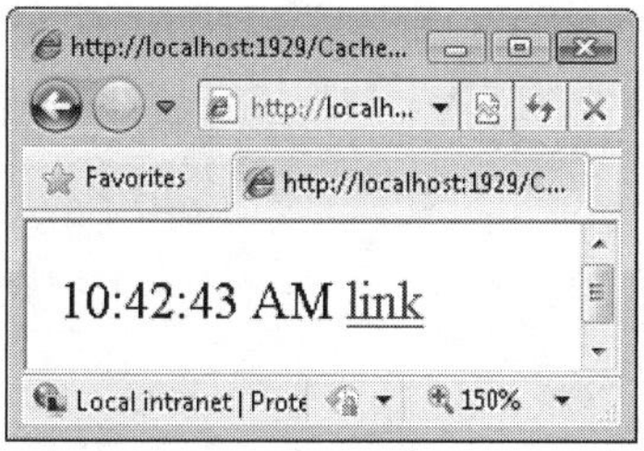

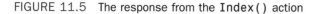

FIGURE 11.5   The response from the Index() action

Using the Cache Class

In the previous section, you learned how to use the HttpCachePolicy class to manipulate how responses get cached on proxy servers and browsers. In this section, we discuss the System.Web.Caching.Cache class. This class represents the server cache.

The Cache class works like a dictionary. You add key and item pairs to the Cache class. When you add an item to the Cache class, the item is cached on the server.

For example, imagine that you create a data repository to represent the Movies database table. Instead of caching the movies in your controller, you want to cache the movies in the repository. The MovieRepository in Listing 11.14 uses the server cache to cache the movies.

LISTING 11.14   Models\MovieRepository.cs (C#)

```csharp
using System.Collections.Generic;
using System.Linq;
using System.Web;
using System.Web.Caching;

namespace MvcApplication1.Models
{

    public class MovieRepository : MovieRepositoryBase
    {
        private MoviesDBEntities _entities = new MoviesDBEntities();
        private Cache _cache;

        public MovieRepository()
        {
            _cache = HttpContext.Current.Cache;
        }
```

```csharp
    public override IEnumerable<Movie> ListMoviesCached()
    {
        var movies = (IEnumerable<Movie>)_cache["movies"];
        if (movies == null)
        {
            movies = ListMovies();
            _cache["movies"] = movies;
        }
        return movies;
    }

    public override IEnumerable<Movie> ListMovies()
    {
        return _entities.MovieSet.ToList();
    }

    public override void CreateMovie(Movie movieToCreate)
    {
        _entities.AddToMovieSet(movieToCreate);
        _entities.SaveChanges();
        _cache.Remove("movies");
    }
  }
}
```

LISTING 11.14   Models\MovieRepository.vb (VB)

```vbnet
Public Class MovieRepository
    Inherits MovieRepositoryBase

    Private _entities As New MoviesDBEntities()
    Private _cache As Cache

    Public Sub New()
        _cache = HttpContext.Current.Cache
    End Sub

    Public Overrides Function ListMoviesCached() As IEnumerable(Of Movie)
        Dim movies = CType(_cache("movies"), IEnumerable(Of Movie))
        If movies Is Nothing Then
            movies = ListMovies()
            _cache("movies") = movies
        End If
        Return movies
    End Function
```

```
Public Overrides Function ListMovies() As IEnumerable(Of Movie)
    Return _entities.MovieSet.ToList()
End Function

Public Overrides Sub CreateMovie(ByVal movieToCreate As Movie)
    _entities.AddToMovieSet(movieToCreate)
    _entities.SaveChanges()
    _cache.Remove("movies")
End Sub
End Class
```

> **NOTE**
>
> You can test the MovieRepository class by using the MovieRepositoryController class included in the code on the book's website (www.informit.com/title/9780672329982).

A reference to the Cache object is assigned to a private field named _cache in the constructor. The Cache object is exposed by the static (shared) HttpContext.Current property.

The MovieRepository exposes three public methods named CreateMovie(), ListMoviesCached(), and ListMovies(). The CreateMovie() method inserts a new movie into the database. When a new movie is created, the current movies stored in the cache are removed. That way, when the ListMoviesCached() method is called, the new movie will be added to the cache.

The ListMoviesCached() method attempts to return all the movies from the cache. If the movies can't be retrieved from the cache because the cache is empty, the movies are retrieved from the database by calling the ListMovies() method.

> **WARNING**
>
> Make sure you call ToList() before assigning the results of a LINQ query to the cache. If you neglect to call ToList(), the query expression, and not the results of the query, will be assigned to the cache.

There are several reasons why the movies might not be successfully retrieved from the cache. If this is the first time the ListMoviesCached() method has been invoked, the cache will be empty. Second, if the CreateMovie() method has just been called, the movies will have been explicitly removed from the cache. Finally, an ASP.NET application scavenges items from the cache automatically. When memory resources become low, items are evicted from the cache automatically.

> **WARNING**
>
> Whenever you retrieve an item from the cache, it is important that you immediately check whether you were successful. There is no guarantee that an item will remain in the cache. If server memory resources get low, items are evicted from the cache automatically.

By default, when you add an item to the cache, the item is cached indefinitely. That means that the item remains in the cache until memory resources become low, the item is explicitly removed, or the application is restarted.

If you want more control over how an item is cached, you can use one of the various overloads of the Cache.Insert() method. This method accepts the following parameters:

- key—The key used to refer to the cached item.
- value—The item added to the cache.
- dependencies—One or more cache dependencies. You can create file dependencies, key dependencies, SQL cache dependencies, aggregate dependencies, or custom dependencies.
- absoluteExpiration—An absolute date and time when an item should be expired from the cache.
- slidingExpiration—An interval of time after which an item should be expired from a cache.
- priority—When memory resources becomes low, this value determines which items get evicted first.
- onRemoveCallback—Enables you to specify a method that is called when an item is removed from the cache.

Notice that there are two ways that you can specify when an item added to the cache should expire. You can supply either an absolute expiration date and time, or you can specify a sliding expiration date.

Providing an absolute expiration date and time is useful when you know when new data will be available. For example, if you know that your product catalog is updated in the database once every day at midnight, it makes sense to expire the product catalog from the cache at midnight.

A sliding expiration is useful when you have too many items to cache. Imagine, for example, that the Movies database table contains information on billions of movies. You can't cache all the movie data because there is just too much of it. In that case, you can take advantage of a sliding expiration to keep the most frequently requested movies in the cache.

You specify a sliding expiration by supplying a particular time span such as 10 minutes. Just as long as a movie keeps being requested within a 10-minute interval, the movie won't be expired from the cache. But, when more than 10 minutes pass without the movie requested, the movie will be removed from the cache. In this way, frequently requested items stay in the cache.

The controller in Listing 11.15 illustrates how you can use a sliding expiration cache policy.

LISTING 11.15   Controllers\SlidingController.cs (C#)

```csharp
using System;
using System.Diagnostics;
using System.Linq;
using System.Web.Caching;
using System.Web.Mvc;
using MvcApplication1.Models;

namespace MvcApplication1.Controllers
{
    public class SlidingController : Controller
    {
        private MoviesDBEntities _entities = new MoviesDBEntities();

        public ActionResult Details(int id)
        {
            var cache = this.HttpContext.Cache;
            var key = GetMovieCacheKey(id);
            var movie = (Movie)cache[key];

            if (movie != null)
            {
                Debug.WriteLine("Got movie from cache");
            }
            else
            {
                Debug.WriteLine("Getting movie from database");
                movie = (from m in _entities.MovieSet
                        where m.Id == id
                        select m).FirstOrDefault();
                cache.Insert(key, movie, null, Cache.NoAbsoluteExpiration,
➥TimeSpan.FromMinutes(10));
            }

            return View(movie);
        }
```

```csharp
        private string GetMovieCacheKey(int movieId)
        {
            return "movie" + movieId.ToString();
        }
    }
}
```

LISTING 11.15   Controllers\SlidingController.vb (VB)

```vb
Public Class SlidingController
    Inherits Controller

    Private _entities As New MoviesDBEntities()

    Public Function Details(ByVal id As Integer) As ActionResult
        Dim cache = Me.HttpContext.Cache
        Dim key = GetMovieCacheKey(id)
        Dim movie = CType(cache(key), Movie)

        If movie IsNot Nothing Then
            Debug.WriteLine("Got movie from cache")
        Else
            Debug.WriteLine("Getting movie from database")
            movie = (From m In _entities.MovieSet _
                    Where m.Id = id _
                    Select m).FirstOrDefault()
            cache.Insert(key, movie, Nothing, cache.NoAbsoluteExpiration,
➥TimeSpan.FromMinutes(10))
        End If

        Return View(movie)
    End Function

    Private Function GetMovieCacheKey(ByVal movieId As Integer) As String
        Return "movie" & movieId.ToString()
    End Function

End Class
```

In Listing 11.15, the movie details are kept in the cache just as long as no more than 10 minutes pass without the movie being requested. The Debug class writes to the Visual Studio Console window. You can examine the Console window to determine when an item is retrieved from the cache or when the item is retrieved from the database (see Figure 11.6).

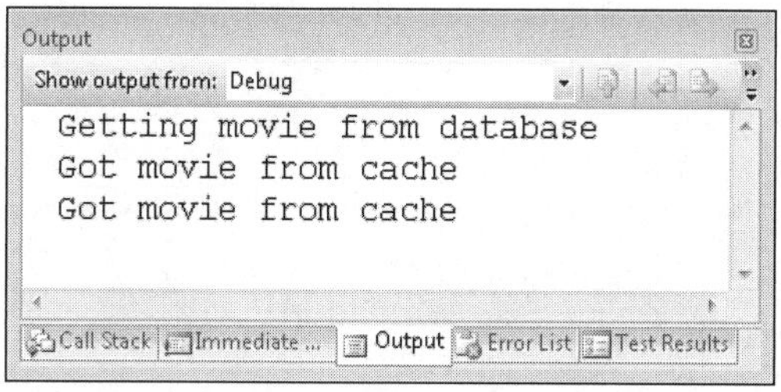

FIGURE 11.6   Seeing when an item is retrieved from the cache

Testing the Cache

There are two types of unit tests that you might be interested in creating when testing caching. First, you might simply want to make sure that a controller action is decorated with the OutputCache attribute. In other words, you might want to make sure that attribute is present on all the controller actions that you expect.

Alternatively, if you are using the Cache object in your code, you might want to test whether data is saved in the cache. In that case, you need to fake the cache so that you can test whether data is successfully added to the cache.

Testing the OutputCache Attribute

Testing the presence of the OuputCache attribute is straightforward. You can take advantage of the .NET framework GetCustomAttributes() method to get a list of attributes defined on a method. You can check if one of the attributes is the OutputCache attribute. Furthermore, you can check whether the right properties are set on this attribute.

For example, the Simple controller in Listing 11.16 includes a Time() action that returns the current time. This action method is decorated with an OutputCache attribute that caches the action result for 5 seconds.

LISTING 11.16   Controllers\SimpleController.cs (C#)

```csharp
using System;
using System.Web.Mvc;

namespace MvcApplication1.Controllers
{
    public class SimpleController : Controller
    {
        [OutputCache(Duration=5,VaryByParam="none")]
        public string Time()
        {
            return DateTime.Now.ToString("T");
```

```
        }

    }

}
```

LISTING 11.16   Controllers\SimpleController.vb (VB)

```vb
Public Class SimpleController
    Inherits Controller

    <OutputCache(Duration:=5, VaryByParam:="none")> _
    Public Function Time() As String
        Return DateTime.Now.ToString("T")
    End Function

End Class
```

The unit test in Listing 11.17 uses the GetCustomAttributes() method to verify that the OutputCache attribute is present. Next, the unit test verifies that the Duration property is set to the value 5 seconds.

LISTING 11.17   Controllers\SimpleControllerTests.cs (C#)

```csharp
using System.Web.Mvc;
using Microsoft.VisualStudio.TestTools.UnitTesting;
using MvcApplication1.Controllers;

namespace MvcApplication1.Tests.Controllers
{
    [TestClass]
    public class SimpleControllerTests
    {

        [TestMethod]
        public void TimeIsCached()
        {
            // Arrange
            var timeMethod = typeof(SimpleController).GetMethod("Time");
            var outputCacheAttributes = timeMethod. GetCustomAttributes(typeof
➥(OutputCacheAttribute), true);

            // Assert
            Assert.IsTrue(outputCacheAttributes.Length > 0);
```

```
        foreach (OutputCacheAttribute att in outputCacheAttributes)
            Assert.AreEqual(5, att.Duration);
    }


    }
}
```

LISTING 11.17   Controllers\SimpleControllerTests.vb (VB)

```
Imports Microsoft.VisualStudio.TestTools.UnitTesting
Imports System.Web.Mvc

<TestClass()> _
Public Class SimpleControllerTests

    <TestMethod()> _
    Public Sub TimeIsCached()
        ' Arrange
        Dim timeMethod = GetType(SimpleController).GetMethod("Time")
        Dim outputCacheAttributes = timeMethod. GetCustomAttributes(GetType
➥(OutputCacheAttribute), True)

        ' Assert
        Assert.IsTrue(outputCacheAttributes.Length > 0)
        For Each att As OutputCacheAttribute In outputCacheAttributes
            Assert.AreEqual(5, att.Duration)
        Next att
    End Sub

End Class
```

Notice that the unit test in Listing 11.17 loops through a collection of OutputCache attributes. Several OutputCache attributes might be applied to the same controller action.

Testing Adding Data to the Cache

Imagine that you create an application that contains a repository and service layer. You want to cache the data retrieved from the repository in the service layer. In that case, you might want to build unit tests to verify that the database data is actually getting cached.

Let's get concrete. The repository is contained in Listing 11.18. This repository class exposes one method named ListMovies() that returns all the movies from the database.

LISTING 11.18   Models\SimpleMovieRepository.cs (C#)

```csharp
using System.Collections.Generic;
using System.Linq;

namespace MvcApplication1.Models
{
    public class SimpleMovieRepository : ISimpleMovieRepository
    {
        private MoviesDBEntities _entities = new MoviesDBEntities();

        public IEnumerable<Movie> ListMovies()
        {
            return _entities.MovieSet.ToList();
        }


    }
}
```

LISTING 11.18   Models\SimpleMovieRepository.vb (VB)

```vb
Public Class SimpleMovieRepository
    Implements ISimpleMovieRepository

    Private _entities As New MoviesDBEntities()

    Public Function ListMovies() As IEnumerable(Of Movie) Implements
➥ISimpleMovieRepository.ListMovies
        Return _entities.MovieSet.ToList()
    End Function

End Class
```

The service is contained in Listing 11.19. This service has two methods named ListMovies()
and ListMoviesCached(). The ListMoviesCached() contains the caching logic.

LISTING 11.19   Models\SimpleMovieService.cs (C#)

```csharp
using System.Collections.Generic;
using System.Web;
using MvcFakes;

namespace MvcApplication1.Models
```

```
{
    public class SimpleMovieService : ISimpleMovieService
    {
        private ISimpleMovieRepository _repository;
        private ICache _cache;

        public SimpleMovieService()
            : this(new SimpleMovieRepository(), new CacheWrapper
➥(HttpContext.Current.Cache)) {}

        public SimpleMovieService(ISimpleMovieRepository repository, ICache cache)
        {
            _repository = repository;
            _cache = cache;
        }

        public IEnumerable<Movie> ListMoviesCached()
        {
            var movies = (IEnumerable<Movie>)_cache["movies"];
            if (movies == null)
            {
                movies = ListMovies();
                _cache["movies"] = movies;
            }
            return movies;
        }

        public IEnumerable<Movie> ListMovies()
        {
            return _repository.ListMovies();
        }

    }
}
```

LISTING 11.19   Models\SimpleMovieService.cs (C#)

```
Imports MvcFakes


Public Class SimpleMovieService
    Implements ISimpleMovieService

    Private _repository As ISimpleMovieRepository
    Private _cache As ICache
```

```vb
    Public Sub New()
        Me.New(New SimpleMovieRepository(), New CacheWrapper
➥(HttpContext.Current.Cache))
    End Sub

    Public Sub New(ByVal repository As ISimpleMovieRepository, ByVal cache As ICache)
        _repository = repository
        _cache = cache
    End Sub

    Public Function ListMoviesCached() As IEnumerable(Of Movie) Implements
➥ISimpleMovieService.ListMoviesCached
        Dim movies = CType(_cache("movies"), IEnumerable(Of Movie))
        If movies Is Nothing Then
            movies = ListMovies()
            _cache("movies") = movies
        End If
        Return movies
    End Function

    Public Function ListMovies() As IEnumerable(Of Movie)
        Return _repository.ListMovies()
    End Function

End Class
```

Finally, the controller in Listing 11.20 uses the movie service to retrieve the movies from the database.

LISTING 11.20   Controllers\SimpleMovieController.cs (C#)

```csharp
using System.Web.Mvc;
using MvcApplication1.Models;

namespace MvcApplication1.Controllers
{
    public class SimpleMovieController : Controller
    {
        private ISimpleMovieService _service;

        public SimpleMovieController()
            : this(new SimpleMovieService()) { }
```

```csharp
        public SimpleMovieController(ISimpleMovieService service)
        {
            _service = service;
        }

        public ActionResult Index()
        {
            return View(_service.ListMoviesCached());
        }
    }
}
```

LISTING 11.20   Controllers\SimpleMovieController.vb (VB)

```vb
Public Class SimpleMovieController
    Inherits Controller

    Private _service As ISimpleMovieService

    Public Sub New()
        Me.New(New SimpleMovieService())
    End Sub

    Public Sub New(ByVal service As ISimpleMovieService)
        _service = service
    End Sub

    Public Function Index() As ActionResult
        Return View(_service.ListMoviesCached())
    End Function

End Class
```

Theoretically, the Index() action in Listing 11.20 should be retrieving the movies from the cache. To increase our confidence that everything works in the way that we expect, we need a test.

To test the cache, we need to fake the Cache object. The MVC Fakes project that accompanies this book includes two classes and an interface that you can employ when faking the Cache:

▶ ICache—This interface contains the methods and properties exposed by the CacheWrapper and the FakeCache classes.

▶ CacheWrapper—This class is a wrapper class around the normal Cache class that implements the ICache interface. When you call any methods of the CacheWrapper class, the calls are delegated to the normal Cache class.

▶ FakeCache—This class is a fake version of the normal Cache class. You can use this class in your unit tests as a stand-in for the real Cache.

NOTE

Why fake the Cache class? After all, the real Cache class has a public constructor. Why not just use the actual Cache class in your unit tests? The problem is that the actual Cache class has dependencies on the HTTP runtime. You get a null reference exception when you try to create a new instance of the Cache class.

Listing 11.21 contains two tests named IndexAddsMoviesToCache() and IndexRetrievesMoviesFromCache(). The first test verifies that invoking the controller Index() action adds the movies to the cache. The second test verifies that the Index() action returns results from the cache.

LISTING 11.21   Controllers\SimpleMovieControllerTests.cs (C#)

```csharp
using System;
using System.Collections.Generic;
using System.Web.Mvc;
using Microsoft.VisualStudio.TestTools.UnitTesting;
using MvcApplication1.Controllers;
using MvcApplication1.Models;
using MvcApplication1.Tests.Fakes;
using MvcFakes;

namespace MvcApplication1.Tests.Controllers
{
    [TestClass]
    public class SimpleMovieControllerTests
    {

        [TestMethod]
        public void IndexAddsMoviesToCache()
        {
            // Arrange
            var cache = new FakeCache();
            var service = new SimpleMovieService(new FakeSimpleMovieRepository(),
➥cache);
            var controller = new SimpleMovieController(service);
```

```
            // Act
            controller.Index();

            // Assert
            Assert.IsInstanceOfType(cache["movies"], typeof(IEnumerable<Movie>));
        }

        [TestMethod]
        public void IndexRetrievesMovieFromCache()
        {
            // Arrange movies
            var movies = new List<Movie>();
            movies.Add(Movie.CreateMovie(1, "Star Wars", "Lucas",
➥DateTime.Parse("1/1/1977")));

            // Arrange cache
            var cache = new FakeCache();
            cache["movies"] = movies;

            // Arrange controller
            var service = new SimpleMovieService(new FakeSimpleMovieRepository(),
➥cache);
            var controller = new SimpleMovieController(service);

            // Act
            var results = (ViewResult)controller.Index();

            // Assert
            var movieResults = (List<Movie>)results.ViewData.Model;
            CollectionAssert.AreEqual(movies, movieResults);
        }

    }
}
```

LISTING 11.21   Controllers\SimpleMovieControllerTests.vb (VB)

```
Imports Microsoft.VisualStudio.TestTools.UnitTesting
Imports System.Web.Mvc
Imports MvcFakes

<TestClass()> _
 Public Class SimpleMovieControllerTests

    <TestMethod()> _
```

```vb
    Public Sub IndexAddsMoviesToCache()
        ' Arrange
        Dim cache = New FakeCache()
        Dim service = New SimpleMovieService(New FakeSimpleMovieRepository(), cache)
        Dim controller = New SimpleMovieController(service)

        ' Act
        controller.Index()

        ' Assert
        Assert.IsInstanceOfType(cache("movies"), GetType(IEnumerable(Of Movie)))
    End Sub

    <TestMethod()> _
    Public Sub IndexRetrievesMovieFromCache()
        ' Arrange movies
        Dim movies = New List(Of Movie)()
        movies.Add(Movie.CreateMovie(1, "Star Wars", "Lucas",
➥DateTime.Parse("1/1/1977")))

        ' Arrange cache
        Dim cache = New FakeCache()
        cache("movies") = movies

        ' Arrange controller
        Dim service = New SimpleMovieService(New FakeSimpleMovieRepository(), cache)
        Dim controller = New SimpleMovieController(service)

        ' Act
        Dim results = CType(controller.Index(), ViewResult)

        ' Assert
        Dim movieResults = CType(results.ViewData.Model, List(Of Movie))
        CollectionAssert.AreEqual(movies, movieResults)
    End Sub

End Class
```

NOTE

When I originally wrote the controller in Listing 11.19, I accidentally called the ListMovies() method instead of the ListMoviesCached() method. In other words, by mistake, I was not using the cache. When I ran the test in Listing 11.20, and it failed, I discovered my mistake. This is proof that tests do make a difference!

Summary

This chapter was divided into three parts. In the first part, you learned how to use the `OutputCache` attribute with MVC controller actions. We discussed how you can use the `OutputCache` attribute to cache controller responses for a particular duration of time and avoid requesting the same data from the database over and over again.

We also discussed the underlying cache API. You learned to control how proxy servers and browsers cache responses by manipulating cache headers. You also learned how to work directly with the `Cache` object in your data access code.

Finally, we tackled the ever-important topic of testing. You learned how to test whether the `OuputCache` attribute has been applied to a controller action. You also learned how to fake the cache in your unit tests.

CHAPTER 12

Authenticating Users

In this chapter, you learn how to add security to your ASP.NET MVC application. You learn how to password protect controllers and controller actions. You also learn how to register new users.

We also investigate how you can configure different types of authentication and Membership to use with an ASP.NET MVC application. For example, you learn how to authenticate users using Windows authentication and Forms authentication.

Finally, you learn how to create tests for controller actions that use authentication. You learn how to verify that only the right users can invoke a controller action.

Creating Users and Roles

Before we do anything else, we should start by creating some users and roles. We can use these users and roles in the remainder of the chapter to verify that we provide access to only the right users in the right roles. There are two ways that we can create new users: We can use the Web Site Administration Tool or use the Account controller.

Using the Web Site Administration Tool

You can take advantage of the Web Site Administration Tool to quickly create new users and roles. You can launch the Web Site Administration Tool from Visual Studio by selecting the menu option Project, ASP.NET Configuration.

Alternatively, you can click the scary icon of the hammer hitting the world that appears at the top of the Solution Explorer window (see Figure 12.1).

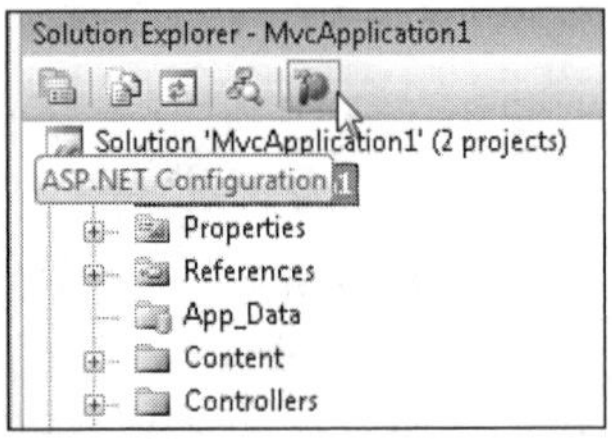

FIGURE 12.1   Launching the Web Site Administration Tool

WARNING

Before launching the Web Site Administration Tool, make sure that you have built your application at least once. Otherwise, you get the error message Could Not Load Type 'MvcApplication1.MvcApplication' when you click the Security tab.

The Web Site Administration Tool is implemented as an ASP.NET Application. If you are curious, you can take a look at the source for this application in the following folder:

C:\Windows\Microsoft.NET\Framework\v2.0.50727\ASP.NETWebAdminFiles

After you launch the Web Site Administration Tool, you can create new users and roles by clicking the Security tab. For example, I created two new users named Jack and Jill that I used to test the sample code in this chapter. (They both have the password secret.)

You also can enable roles and create roles. I created a role named Manager and added Jill to the role (see Figure 12.2).

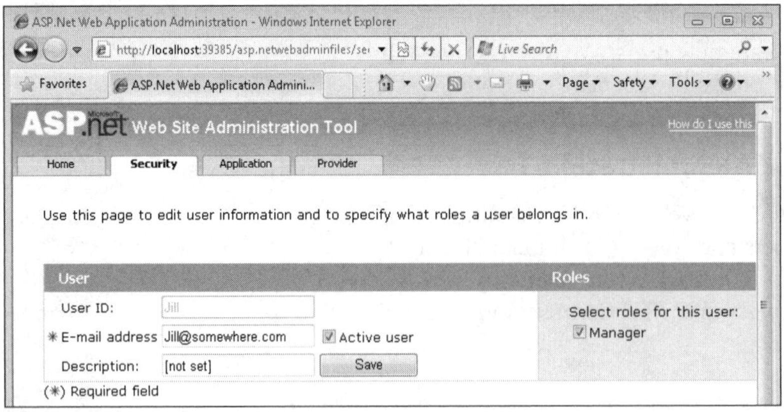

FIGURE 12.2   Adding Jill to the Manager role

WARNING

You can't run the Web Site Administration over the web (remotely).

Using the Account Controller

If you need to create users (but not roles), you can use the Account controller included with the default Visual Studio ASP.NET MVC template. Follow these steps:

1. Create a new ASP.NET MVC application and run it. (Press F5.)
2. Click the [Log On] link (see Figure 12.3).

FIGURE 12.3   Click the Log On link

3. Click the Register link.
4. Complete the registration form to create a new user (see Figure 12.4).

The Account controller is located in the Controllers folder just like any other controller. The Account controller exposes the following actions:

▶ LogOn()—Enables you to display a LogOn view

▶ LogOn(userName, password, rememberMe, returnUrl)—Enables you to authenticate

▶ LogOff()—Enables you to log off from the website

▶ Register()—Enables you to display the registration form

▶ Register(userName, email, password, confirmPassword)—Enables you to register a new user account

▶ ChangePassword()—Enables you to display the ChangePassword view

▶ ChangePassword(currentPassword, newPassword, confirmPassword)—Enables you to change a password

▶ ChangePasswordSuccess()—Enables you to display the ChangePasswordSuccess view

Notice that the Account controller exposes actions for changing a password. The sample ASP.NET MVC site does not provide you with a way to navigate to the ChangePassword

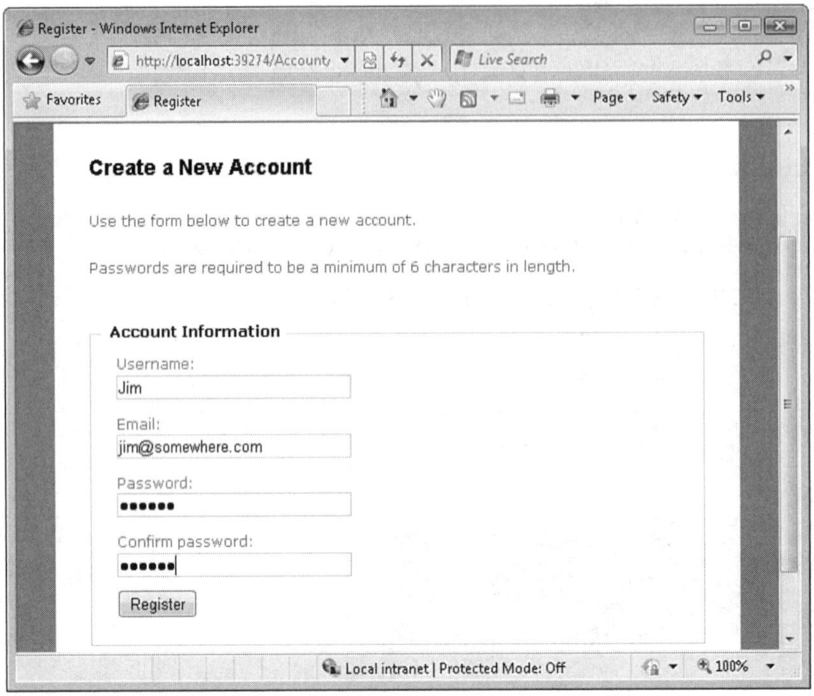

FIGURE 12.4   Registering a new user

view. (There is no link to this view.) You can get to the ChangePassword view by entering the following address into your browser address bar:

/Account/ChangePassword

You must be authenticated to navigate to the ChangePassword view. After you log on, you can use the ChangePassword view to change your password (see Figure 12.5).

Authorizing Users

If you want to allow only certain users, or only users in certain roles, to access a controller action, you need to specify the users or roles that are authorized to invoke the controller action. There are two ways that you can specify authorization: You can specify authorization declaratively, or you can specify authorization programmatically. We explore both approaches in the following sections.

Using the Authorize Attribute

You can decorate a controller action, or an entire controller class, with the Authorize attribute. If you use this attribute without specifying any additional properties, the attribute prevents any anonymous users from invoking the action.

For example, the Secrets() action in Listing 12.1 is decorated with the Authorize attribute.

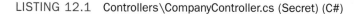

FIGURE 12.5   Changing your password

LISTING 12.1   Controllers\CompanyController.cs (Secret) (C#)

```csharp
using System.Web.Mvc;

namespace MvcApplication1.Controllers
{
    public class CompanyController : Controller
    {
        [Authorize]
        public ActionResult Secrets()
        {
            return View();
        }

    }
}
```

LISTING 12.1   Controllers\CompanyController.vb (Secret) (VB)

```vb
Public Class CompanyController
    Inherits Controller
```

```
<Authorize()> _
Public Function Secrets() As ActionResult
    Return View()
End Function

End Class
```

If you attempt to invoke the Secrets() action, and you are not logged in, you are redirected to the Account controller Login() action automatically. This action displays the Login view.

If, on the other hand, you are logged in, you can see the Secrets view in Figure 12.6.

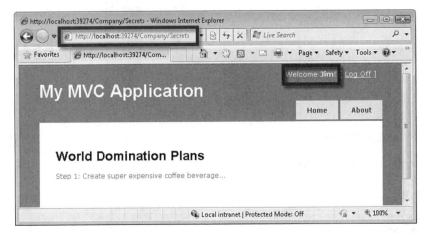

FIGURE 12.6   Company Secrets

Authorizing Particular Users

If you want to authorize only certain users to invoke a controller action, you can use the Users property when applying the Authorize attribute to an action. The Users property accepts a comma-separate list of users.

For example, the SuperSecrets() action in Listing 12.2 can be invoked only by Jack or Jill. If Jim attempts to invoke this action, he will be redirected to the LogOn view.

LISTING 12.2   Controllers\CompanyController.cs (SuperSecrets) (C#)

```
[Authorize(Users="Jack,Jill")]
public ActionResult SuperSecrets()
{
    return View();
}
```

LISTING 12.2   Controllers\CompanyController.vb (SuperSecrets) (VB)

```vb
<Authorize(Users:="Jack,Jill")> _
Public Function SuperSecrets() As ActionResult
  Return View()
End Function
```

If either Jack or Jill invoke the SuperSecrets() action, they see the view in Figure 12.7.

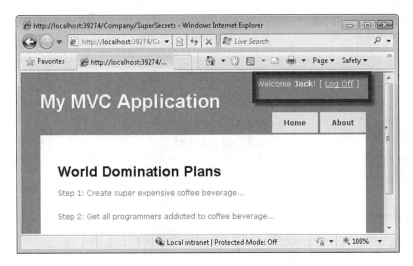

FIGURE 12.7   Super Secret World Domination Plans

Authorizing Particular Roles
You also can restrict access to a controller action by role. For example, you might want to enable only users in the Manager role to invoke a controller action.

The Authorize attribute includes a Roles property. You can assign a comma-separate list of roles to this attribute. For example, the SuperSuperSecret() controller action in Listing 12.3 can be invoked only by members of the Manager role.

LISTING 12.3   Controllers\CompanyController.cs (SuperSuperSecret) (C#)

```csharp
[Authorize(Roles = "Manager")]
public ActionResult SuperSuperSecrets()
{
    return View();
}
```

LISTING 12.3   Controllers\CompanyController.vb (SuperSuperSecret) (VB)

```vb
<Authorize(Roles:="Manager")> _
Public Function SuperSuperSecrets() As ActionResult
  Return View()
End Function
```

Because Jill is a member of the Manager role, she can successfully invoke the
SuperSuperSecrets() action (see Figure 12.8). However, when anyone who is not a
member of the Manager role attempts to invoke the action, that person is redirected to the
Account controller LogOn() action.

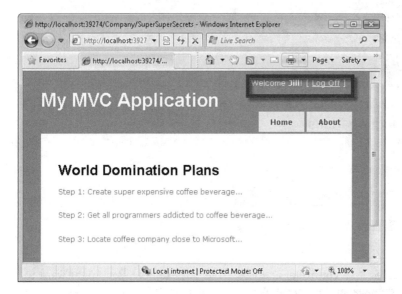

FIGURE 12.8   Super Super Secret Plans for World Domination

Using the User Property

If you prefer, you can implement authorization programmatically rather than declaratively. Instead of using the Authorize attribute, you can use the User property.

The User property is a property of the Controller class. The User property implements
the IPrincipal interface and, therefore, it exposes the following method and property:

▶ IsInRole(role)—Returns true if the current user is a member of the specified role

▶ Identity—Return an object that implements the IIdentity interface that represents the current user

The expression User.Identity returns an object that represents the current user. The User.Identity object has three properties:

▶ AuthenticationType—Returns a string that represents the authentication type such as *Forms* or *NTLM*. This property returns an empty string when the user is not authenticated.

▶ IsAuthenticated—Returns true when the user is authenticated.

▶ Name—Returns the username.

The controller in Listing 12.4 illustrates how you can use these methods and properties. The Secrets() action returns different views to different users.

LISTING 12.4   Controllers\UserController.cs (C#)

```csharp
using System.Web.Mvc;
using System;

namespace MvcApplication1.Controllers
{
    public class UserController : Controller
    {

        public ActionResult Index()
        {
            // Show ManagerView view to members of Manager role
            if (User.IsInRole("Manager"))
                return View("ManagerView");

            // Show JackView to Jack (and no one else)
            if (string.Equals(User.Identity.Name, "Jack",
➥StringComparison.CurrentCultureIgnoreCase))
                    return View("JackView");

            // Show AuthenticatedView to non-anonymous visitors
            if (User.Identity.IsAuthenticated)
                return View("AuthenticatedView");

            // Otherwise, redirect to LogOn action
            return RedirectToAction("LogOn", "Account");
        }
```

```
        }
    }
```

LISTING 12.4   Controllers\UserController.vb (VB)

```vb
Public Class UserController
    Inherits Controller

    Public Function Index() As ActionResult
        ' Show ManagerView view to members of Manager role
        If User.IsInRole("Manager") Then
            Return View("ManagerView")
        End If

        ' Show JackView to Jack (and no one else)
        If String.Equals(User.Identity.Name, "Jack",
➡StringComparison.CurrentCultureIgnoreCase) Then
            Return View("JackView")
        End If

        ' Show AuthenticatedView to non-anonymous visitors
        If User.Identity.IsAuthenticated Then
            Return View("AuthenticatedView")
        End If

        ' Otherwise, redirect to LogOn action
        Return RedirectToAction("LogOn", "Account")
    End Function

End Class
```

If you invoke the Index() action, and you are a member of the Manager role, you see the ManagerView. If your username happens to be Jack, you see the JackView. If you are an authenticated user, you see the AuthenticatedView. Finally, if you are an anonymous user, you are redirected to the Account controller LogOn action so that you can log in to the website.

Configuring Membership

In this section, you learn how to configure membership. For example, you learn how to specify where user account information is stored. You also learn how to configure membership with different password requirements.

Configuring the Membership Database

You might be curious about where user account information is stored. By default, user names and passwords are stored in a SQL Express database named ASPNETDB.mdf located in your application's App_Data folder. You can see this database in the Solution Explorer window if you click the Show All Files button at the top of the Solution Explorer window (see Figure 12.9).

FIGURE 12.9   The ASPNETDB.mdf database

Using the ASPNETDB.mdf database is fine (and convenient) when you develop a new application. However, when you are ready to release the application into production, you need to store your user information in your production database.

NOTE

You can use ASP.NET membership with Microsoft SQL Server version 2000 or above. You can't use membership with another type of database—for example, an Oracle database—without creating a custom membership provider.

If you want to store user account information in an alternative database, you need to complete the following three steps:

1. Configure your database.
2. Configure your application.
3. Configure database permissions.

You can complete the first step, configuring your database, by using the aspnet_regsql.exe command line tool. From the Start menu, navigate to All Programs, Microsoft Visual Studio 2008, Visual Studio Tools, Visual Studio 2008 Command Prompt. Type `aspnet_regsql.exe` into the command prompt to launch the ASP.NET SQL Server Setup Wizard (see Figure 12.10).

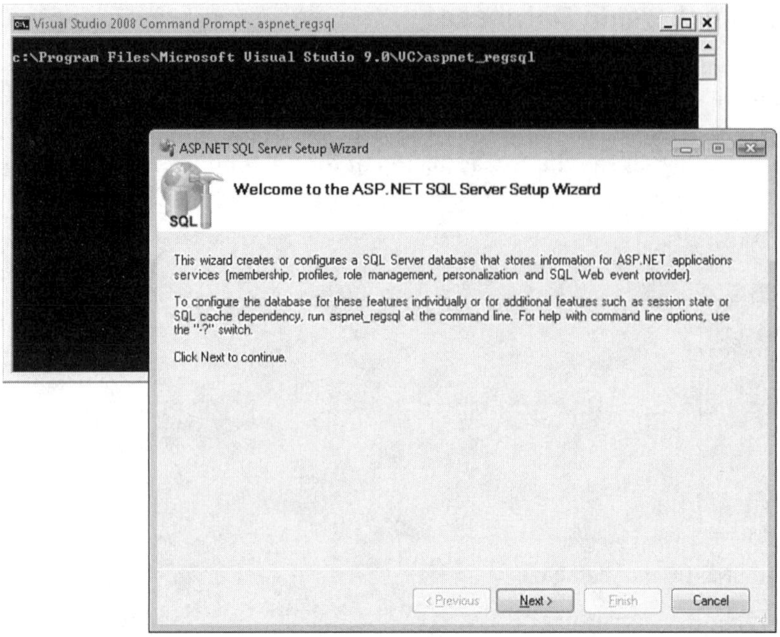

FIGURE 12.10   Launching the ASP.NET SQL Server Setup Wizard

WARNING

Your Windows account must have sufficient permissions to create the new objects in the database. The ASP.NET SQL Server Setup Wizard fails if you launch the tool while logged in to Windows without the necessary database permissions.

You use the ASP.NET SQL Server Setup Wizard to connect to a database (anywhere on your network) and create the necessary database objects. For example, the wizard creates the aspnet_Membership, aspnet_Users, aspnet_Roles, and aspnet_UsersInRoles table to store user and role information.

NOTE

If you don't want to use the ASP.NET SQL Server Setup Wizard, you can find SQL scripts for adding the application services database objects in the following folder: C:\Windows\Microsoft.NET\Framework\v2.0.50727.

After you create the necessary database objects, you need to modify the database connection used by your MVC application. Modify the ApplicationServices connection string in your web configuration (web.config) file so that it points to the production database. For example, the modified connection in Listing 12.5 points to a database named MyTestDB (the original `ApplicationServices` connection string has been commented out).

LISTING 12.5   Web.config

```
<connectionStrings>
    <!--<add name="ApplicationServices" connectionString="data source=.\
➥SQLEXPRESS;Integrated Security=SSPI;AttachDBFilename=¦DataDirectory¦aspnetdb.mdf;
➥User Instance=true" providerName="System.Data.SqlClient"/>-->
    <add name="ApplicationServices" connectionString="data source=localhost;
➥Integrated Security=SSPI;Initial Catalog=MyTestDB" />
</connectionStrings>
```

Finally, if you use Integrated Security to connect to your database, you need to add the correct Windows user account as a login to your database. The correct account depends on whether you use the ASP.NET Development Server or Internet Information Services as your web server. The correct user account also depends on your operating system.

If you use the ASP.NET Development Server (the default web server used by Visual Studio), your application executes within the context of your Windows user account. In that case, you need to add your Windows user account as a database server login.

Alternatively, if you use Internet Information Services, you need to add either the ASPNET account or the NT AUTHORITY/NETWORK SERVICE account as a database server login. If you use Windows XP, add the ASPNET account as a login to your database. If you use a more recent operating system, such as Windows Vista or Windows Server 2008, add the NT AUTHORITY/NETWORK SERVICE account as the database login.

You can add a new user account to your database by using Microsoft SQL Server Management Studio (see Figure 12.11).

FIGURE 12.11   Creating a new Microsoft SQL Server login

After you create the required login, you need to map the login to a database user with the right database roles. Double-click the login and select the User Mapping tab. Select one or more application services database roles. For example, to authenticate users, you need to enable the aspnet_Membership_BasicAccess database role. To create new users, you need to enable the aspnet_Membership_FullAccess database role (see Figure 12.12).

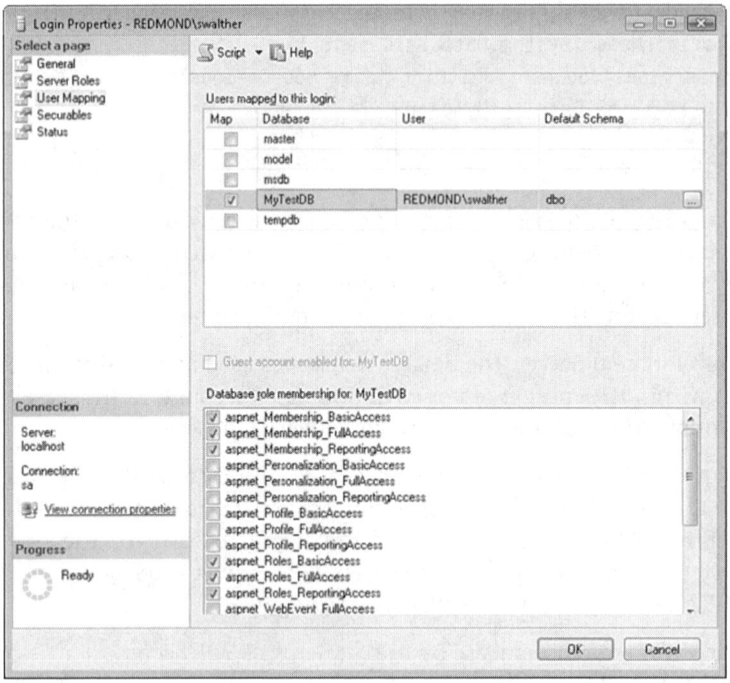

FIGURE 12.12   Adding Application Services database roles

After you complete all these steps, your user account information will be stored in your production database. If you want to verify that everything is set up correctly, you can create a new user account within your ASP.NET MVC application and check whether the new user is added to the aspnet_Users table (see Figure 12.13).

Configuring Membership Settings

By default, ASP.NET MVC uses the SQL membership provider. This provider exposes several configuration settings that you can use to customize the behavior of the provider:

▶ ApplicationName—The name of the ASP.NET application associated with the membership information.

▶ Description—The description of the provider that is displayed in administrative tools.

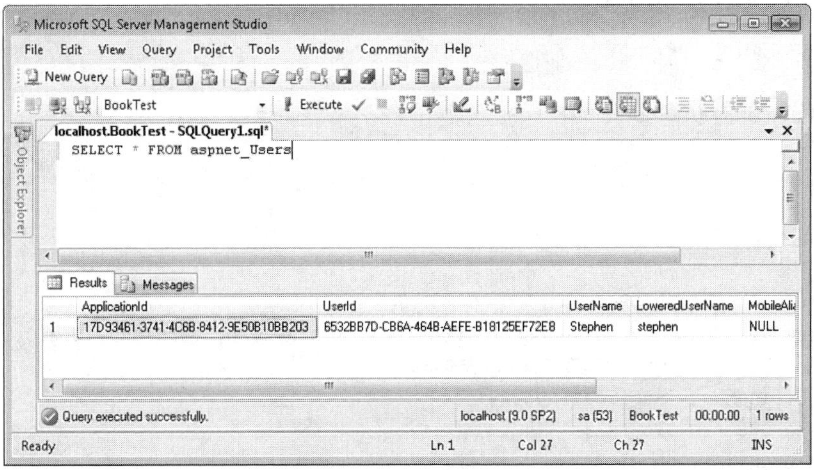

FIGURE 12.13   Adding a user to the production database

▶ EnablePasswordReset—When true, users can reset their password to a random password.

▶ EnablePasswordRetrieval—When true, users can recover their password.

▶ MaxInvalidPasswordAttempts—An integer that represents the number of log on attempts after which the user account is locked.

▶ MinRequiredNonalphanumericCharacters—The minimum number of characters other than an alphabetic or numeric character that must appear in a password (for example, #%).

▶ MinRequiredPasswordLength—An integer that represents the minimum length of a valid password.

▶ Name—The friendly name for this provider.

▶ PasswordAttemptWindow—An integer that represents an interval in minutes. If you enter the wrong password more than the MaxInvalidPasswordAttempts within this interval, your account is locked.

▶ PasswordFormat—Determines how passwords are stored in the database. The three possible values are Clear, Encypted, and Hashed.

▶ PasswordStrengthRegularExpression—A regular expression that a valid password must match.

▶ RequiresQuestionAndAnswer—When true, you must answer a question before you can retrieve or reset your password.

▶ RequiresUniqeEmail—When true, you cannot create two accounts with the same email address.

The membership provider is configured with the settings in Listing 12.6 in the root web configuration (web.config) file.

LISTING 12.6   Web.config (membership)

```
<membership>
  <providers>
    <clear/>
    <add
      name="AspNetSqlMembershipProvider"
      type="System.Web.Security.SqlMembershipProvider, System.Web, Version=2.0.0.0,
➥Culture=neutral, PublicKeyToken=b03f5f7f11d50a3a"
      connectionStringName="ApplicationServices"
      enablePasswordRetrieval="false"
      enablePasswordReset="true"
      requiresQuestionAndAnswer="false"
      requiresUniqueEmail="false"
      passwordFormat="Hashed"
      maxInvalidPasswordAttempts="5"
      minRequiredPasswordLength="6"
      minRequiredNonalphanumericCharacters="0"
      passwordAttemptWindow="10"
      passwordStrengthRegularExpression=""
      applicationName="/"/>
  </providers>
</membership>
```

You can toughen the requirements for a valid password by modifying these default settings. For example, if you want to require a password to be at least 10 characters and contain at least 1 nonalphanumeric characters, you can change the minRequiredPasswordLength and minRequiredNonalphanumericCharacters settings.

Notice the passwordFormat setting. By default, passwords are hashed with a one-way hash before stored in the database. When a user logs on, the password is hashed and compared against the hashed value in the database. So the actual user passwords are not stored anywhere.

The advantage of hashing passwords is that if your database server is ever compromised by an evil hacker, the hacker can't steal any of your website user passwords. The disadvantage of hashing passwords is that you can never recover a forgotten password. If a user forgets a password, the password must be reset.

You also can set the passwordFormat setting to the value Clear or Encrypted. When a password is stored with passwordFormat Clear, the password is stored as plain text. When stored with ENCRYPTED, the password is encrypted before being stored in the database.

Using the Membership and Role Manager API

Under the covers, the Account controller uses the Membership API to authenticate and create users. You can work directly with the Membership API in your code.

The Membership API consists of two main classes: the Membership class and the MembershipUser class.

The Membership class exposes a number of useful methods including the following:

```
CreateUser()

DeleteUser()

FindUsersByEmail()

FindUsersByName()

GeneratePassword()

GetAllUsers()

GetNumberOfUsersOnline()

GetUser()

GetUserNameByEmail()

UpdateUser()

ValidateUser()
```

Several of these methods return either an individual MembershipUser or a collection of MembershipUser objects. The MembershipUser class has the following methods:

```
ChangePassword()

ChangePasswordQuestionAndAnswer()

GetPassword()

ResetPassword()

UnlockUser()
```

The MembershipUser class also has several useful properties:

```
Comment

CreationDate

Email

IsApproved

IsLockedOut

IsOnline

LastActivityDate
```

LastLockoutDate

LastLoginDate

LastPasswordChangedDate

PasswordQuestion

UserName

The ASP.NET framework includes a Roles class that you can use to programmatically work with user roles. This Roles class has the following methods:

AddUsersToRole()

AddUsersToRoles()

AddUserToRole()

AddUserToRoles()

CreateRole()

DeleteCookie()

FindUsersInRole()

GetAllRoles()

GetRolesForUser()

GetUsersInRole()

IsUserInRole()

RemoveUserFromRole()

RemoveUserFromRoles()

RemoveUsersFromRole()

RemoveusersFromRoles()

RoleExists()

Let's look at a concrete sample of how you can use one of these classes. We create a lookup form in which you can search for a user by name. The results display whether each user is currently online.

The Lookup controller is contained in Listing 12.7.

LISTING 12.7   Controllers\LookupController.cs (C#)

```
using System.Web.Mvc;
using System.Web.Security;

namespace MvcApplication1.Controllers
{
    public class LookupController : Controller
    {
```

```
public ActionResult Index(string search)
{
    MembershipUserCollection users = new MembershipUserCollection();
    if (!string.IsNullOrEmpty(search))
        users = Membership.FindUsersByName("%" + search + "%");

    return View(users);
}

}
}
```

LISTING 12.7   Controllers\LookupController.vb (VB)

```
Public Class LookupController
    Inherits Controller

    Public Function Index(ByVal search As String) As ActionResult
        Dim users As New MembershipUserCollection()
        If Not String.IsNullOrEmpty(search) Then
            users = Membership.FindUsersByName("%" & search & "%")
        End If

        Return View(users)
    End Function

End Class
```

The controller has a single action named Index(). The Index() action retrieves all the users that match the search parameter passed to the action. Notice that the FindUsersByName() accepts the % wildcard.

The Index view is contained in Listing 12.8. Notice that it uses the IsOnline property to display whether each user is currently online (see Figure 12.14).

FIGURE 12.14   Lookup form for users

LISTING 12.8   Views\Lookup\Index.aspx (C#)

```
<%@ Page Title="" Language="C#" MasterPageFile="~/Views/Shared/Site.Master"
➥Inherits="System.Web.Mvc.ViewPage<MembershipUserCollection>" %>
<asp:Content ID="Content2" ContentPlaceHolderID="MainContent" runat="server">

    <% using (Html.BeginForm())
       { %>

       <%= Html.TextBox("Search") %>
       <input type="submit" value="Search" />

    <% } %>

    <ul>
        <% foreach (MembershipUser user in Model)
           { %>
        <li>
           <%= user.UserName%>
           <%= user.IsOnline ? "[Online]" : "[Offline]"%>
        </li>
        <% } %>
    </ul>

</asp:Content>
```

LISTING 12.8   Views\Lookup\Index.aspx (VB)

```
<%@ Page Title="" Language="VB" MasterPageFile="~/Views/Shared/Site.Master"
➥Inherits="System.Web.Mvc.ViewPage(Of MembershipUserCollection)" %>

<asp:Content ID="Content2" ContentPlaceHolderID="MainContent" runat="server">

    <% Using Html.BeginForm()%>

       <%= Html.TextBox("Search") %>
       <input type="submit" value="Search" />

    <% End Using%>

    <ul>
        <% For Each User As MembershipUser In Model%>
        <li>
            <%= user.UserName%>
```

```
            <%=IIf(User.IsOnline, "[Online]", "[Offline]")%>
        </li>
        <% Next%>
    </ul>

</asp:Content>
```

Using Windows Authentication

By default, an ASP.NET MVC application is configured to use Forms authentication and the SQL membership provider. If you want to authenticate your users against their Windows credentials, you can use Windows authentication.

In the following sections, you learn how to configure Windows authentication and use Windows authentication to authorize Windows users and groups.

> **NOTE**
>
> Another option, which we don't discuss in this book, is to use the Active Directory membership provider. You can use the Active Directory membership provider with Forms authentication to authenticate users against Active Directory.

Configuring Windows Authentication

You can switch from Forms authentication to Windows authentication by changing the authentication section in your application root web configuration (web.config) file. You need to modify the authentication section so that it looks like Listing 12.9.

LISTING 12.9   Web.config (Enabling Windows Authentication)

```
<authentication mode="Windows">
</authentication>
```

After you switch to Windows authentication, you delegate responsibility for authenticating users to your web server. In other words, the ASP.NET Development Server or Internet Information Services is responsible for authenticating users.

First, while developing an MVC application, you use the ASP.NET Development Web Server included with Visual Studio. By default, the ASP.NET Development Web Server executes all pages in the context of the current Windows account (whatever account you used to log in to Windows).

The ASP.NET Development Web Server also supports NTLM authentication. You can enable NTLM authentication by right-clicking the name of your project in the Solution Explorer window and selecting Properties. Next, select the Web tab and check the NTLM check box (see Figure 12.15).

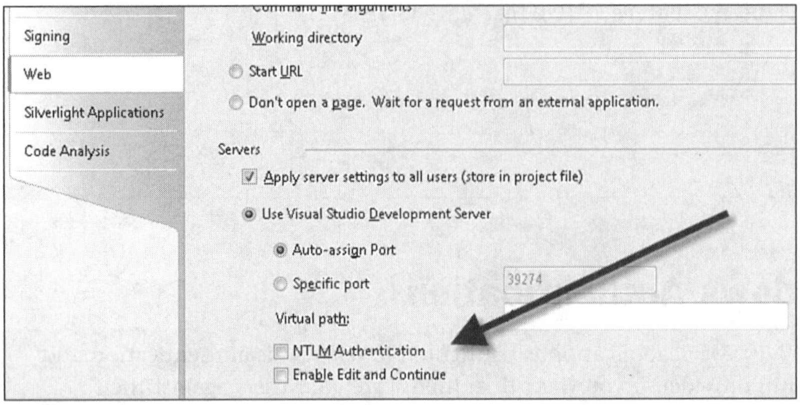

FIGURE 12.15   Enabling NTLM authentication for the ASP.NET Development Web Server

For a production web application, on the other hand, you use IIS as your web server. IIS supports several types of authentication including the following:

▶ **Basic authentication**—Defined as part of the HTTP 1.0 protocol. Sends user names and passwords in clear text (Base64 encoded) across the Internet.

▶ **Digest authentication**—Sends a hash of a password, instead of the password itself, across the internet.

▶ **Integrated Windows (NTLM) authentication**—The best type of authentication to use in intranet environments using windows.

▶ **Certificate authentication**—Enables authentication using a client-side certificate. The certificate maps to a Windows user account.

You can use Internet Information Services Manager to enable a particular type of authentication. Be aware that all types of authentication are not available in the case of every operating system. Furthermore, if you use IIS 7.0 with Windows Vista, you need to enable the different types of Windows authentication before they appear in the Internet Information Services Manager. Open Control Panel, Programs, Programs and Features; Turn Windows features on or off; and expand the Internet Information Services node (see Figure 12.16).

Using Internet Information Services, you can enable or disable different types of authentication. For example, Figure 12.17 illustrates disabling anonymous authentication and enabling Integrated Windows (NTLM) authentication when using IIS 7.0.

Authenticating Windows Users and Groups

After you enable Windows authentication, you can authorize Windows users and groups in the same way as you authorize users and roles when using Forms authentication.

When Windows authentication is enabled, the Authorize attribute works against Windows users and groups. For example, the controller in Listing 12.10 prevents anyone from accessing the Index() action except for the user with the account redmond\swalther.

FIGURE 12.16   Enabling Windows IIS features

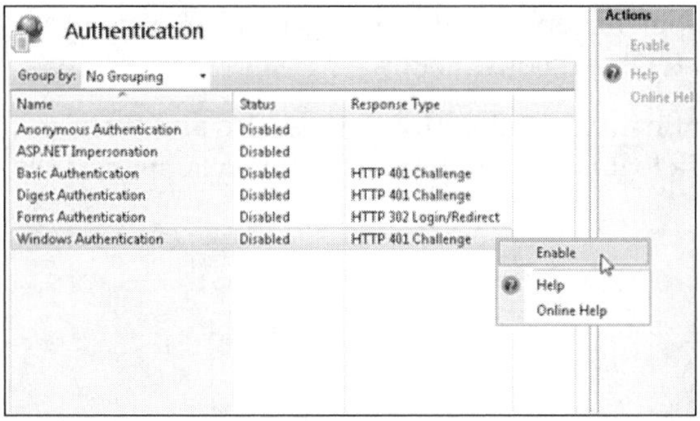

FIGURE 12.17   Enabling integrated Windows authentication

LISTING 12.10   Controllers\WindowsController.cs (C#)

```csharp
using System.Web.Mvc;

namespace MvcApplication1.Controllers
{
    public class WindowsController : Controller
    {
        [Authorize(Users="redmond\\swalther")]
        public ActionResult Index()
        {
            ViewData["userName"] = User.Identity.Name;
            return View();
        }


    }
}
```

LISTING 12.10   Controllers\WindowsController.vb (VB)

```vb
Public Class WindowsController
    Inherits Controller

    <Authorize(Users:="redmond\swalther")> _
    Public Function Index() As ActionResult
        ViewData("userName") = User.Identity.Name
        Return View()
    End Function

End Class
```

Exactly what happens when a user attempts to access a controller action and the user is not authorized depends on the type of authentication enabled in the web server. For example, when using the ASP.NET Development Server, you simply get a blank page. The page is served with a 401 Not Authorized HTTP Response Status.

If, on the other hand, you use IIS with Anonymous authentication disabled and Basic authentication enabled, you keep getting a login dialog prompt each time you request the protected page (see Figure 12.18).

FIGURE 12.18   Basic authentication login dialog

You also can use the Authorize attribute with Windows groups. That way, you can prevent an action from being invoked by anyone who is not the member of the right group.

Before you can use Windows groups, you need to enable the Windows token role provider. You can enable this provider by modify the roleManager section in your root web configuration (web.config) file to look like Listing 12.11.

LISTING 12.11   Web.Config (roleManager)

```
<roleManager enabled="true" defaultProvider="AspNetWindowsTokenRoleProvider">
    <providers>
        <clear/>
        <add connectionStringName="ApplicationServices" applicationName="/"
➡name="AspNetSqlRoleProvider" type="System.Web.Security.SqlRoleProvider, System.Web,
➡Version=2.0.0.0, Culture=neutral, PublicKeyToken=b03f5f7f11d50a3a"/>
        <add applicationName="/" name="AspNetWindowsTokenRoleProvider" type=
➡"System.Web.Security.WindowsTokenRoleProvider, System.Web, Version=2.0.0.0,
➡Culture=neutral, PublicKeyToken=b03f5f7f11d50a3a"/>
    </providers>
</roleManager>
```

In Listing 12.11, the roleManager element has been modified with a defaultProvider attribute that points at the Windows token role provider.

After you make this change, you can use the Authorize attribute with Windows groups. For example, the SalesFigures() action in Listing 12.12 can be invoked only by members of the Windows Managers group.

LISTING 12.12   Controllers\WindowsController.cs (SalesFigures) (C#)

```csharp
[Authorize(Roles = "Managers")]
public ActionResult SalesFigures()
{
    ViewData["userName"] = User.Identity.Name;
    return View();
}
```

LISTING 12.12   Controllers\WindowsController.vb (VB)

```vb
    <Authorize(Roles:="Managers")> _
    Public Function SalesFigures() As ActionResult
        ViewData("userName") = User.Identity.Name
        Return View()
    End Function
```

You also can programmatically verify a user's group. This approach is taken in the SecretStuff() action in Listing 12.13.

LISTING 12.13   Controllers\WindowsController.cs (SecretStuff) (C#)

```csharp
public ActionResult SecretStuff()
{
    if (User.IsInRole("Managers"))
        return View();

    return new HttpUnauthorizedResult();
}
```

LISTING 12.13   Controllers\WindowsController.vb (SecretStuff) (VB)

```vb
Public Function SecretStuff() As ActionResult
  If User.IsInRole("Managers") Then
    Return View()
  End If

  Return New HttpUnauthorizedResult()
End Function
```

> **NOTE**
>
> Because of Windows User Account Control (UAC), when working with Windows Vista or Windows Server 2008, the local Administrators group behaves differently than other groups. The [Authorize] attribute won't correctly recognize a member of the local Administrators group unless you modify your computer's UAC settings.

Testing Authorization

In this final section, we discuss two methods for testing authentication and authorization. In particular, you learn how to test that only the right user or right role has access to a controller action.

Testing for the `Authorize` Attribute

If you are using the `Authorize` attribute to protect controller actions, the easiest way to test authorization is to simply check for this attribute. For example, the controller in Listing 12.14 uses the `Authorize` attribute. The `Authorize` attribute prevents anyone except for Jack from invoking the `Index()` action.

LISTING 12.14   Controllers\JackController.cs (C#)

```csharp
using System.Web.Mvc;

namespace MvcApplication1.Controllers
{
    public class JackController : Controller
    {
        [Authorize(Users="Jack")]
        public ActionResult Index()
        {
            return View();
        }

    }
}
```

LISTING 12.14   Controllers\JackController.vb (VB)

```vbnet
Public Class JackController
    Inherits Controller

    <Authorize(Users:="Jack")> _
    Public Function Index() As ActionResult
        Return View()
    End Function

End Class
```

If you want to verify that the Authorize attribute is present on the Index() action, you can use the test in Listing 12.15. This test verifies that there is, in fact, an Authorize attribute on the Index() action and the Authorize attribute has a Users property set to the value "Jack".

LISTING 12.15   Controllers\JackControllerTests.cs (C#)

```csharp
using System.Web.Mvc;
using Microsoft.VisualStudio.TestTools.UnitTesting;
using MvcApplication1.Controllers;

namespace MvcApplication1.Tests.Controllers
{
    [TestClass]
    public class JackControllerTests
    {

        [TestMethod]
```

```
        public void JackCanAccessIndex()
        {
            // Arrange
            var controller = new CompanyController();
            var indexAction = typeof(JackController).GetMethod("Index");
            var authorizeAttributes=indexAction.GetCustomAttributes(typeof
➥(AuthorizeAttribute), true);

            // Assert
            Assert.IsTrue(authorizeAttributes.Length > 0);
            foreach (AuthorizeAttribute att in authorizeAttributes)
                Assert.AreEqual("Jack", att.Users);
        }
    }
}
```

LISTING 12.15   Controllers\JackControllerTests.vb (VB)

```
Imports Microsoft.VisualStudio.TestTools.UnitTesting
Imports System.Web.Mvc

<TestClass()> _
Public Class JackControllerTests

    <TestMethod()> _
    Public Sub JackCanAccessIndex()
        ' Arrange
        Dim controller As New CompanyController()
        Dim indexAction = GetType(JackController).GetMethod("Index")
        Dim authorizeAttributes = indexAction.GetCustomAttributes(GetType
➥(AuthorizeAttribute), True)

        ' Assert
        Assert.IsTrue(authorizeAttributes.Length > 0)
        For Each att As AuthorizeAttribute In authorizeAttributes
            Assert.AreEqual("Jack", att.Users)
        Next att
    End Sub
End Class
```

Personally, I find something unsatisfying about this test. The test does not actually capture our requirement. We want to test that only Jack is authorized to access the Index action. However, the test simply verifies that there is an Authorize attribute on the action.

Testing with the User Model Binder

In this section, we explore an alternative method of testing authorization. Instead of testing for the Authorize attribute, we use a custom model binder.

In Chapter 7, "Understanding Model Binders and Action Filters," we created a custom model binder named the user model binder. The user model binder enables you to pass a user (an IPrincipal object) as a parameter to a controller action.

You register the user model binder in an application by adding the line of code to the Global.asax file contained in Listing 12.16.

LISTING 12.16   Global.asax (C#)

```
protected void Application_Start()
{
    RegisterRoutes(RouteTable.Routes);

    ModelBinders.Binders.Add(typeof(IPrincipal), new UserModelBinder());
}
```

LISTING 12.16   Global.asax (VB)

```
Sub Application_Start()
   RegisterRoutes(RouteTable.Routes)
   ModelBinders.Binders.Add(GetType(IPrincipal), New UserModelBinder())
End Sub
```

After you register the user model binder, you can add an additional IPrincipal parameter to any controller action. For example, the controller action in Listing 12.17 displays the Index view only when the current user is Jill.

LISTING 12.17   Controllers\JillController.cs (C#)

```
using System.Security.Principal;
using System.Web.Mvc;

namespace MvcApplication1.Controllers
{
    public class JillController : Controller
    {

        public ActionResult Index(IPrincipal user)
        {
```

```
        if (user.Identity.Name != "Jill")
            return new HttpUnauthorizedResult();

        return View();
    }

  }
}
```

LISTING 12.17   Controllers\JillController.vb (VB)

```vb
Imports System.Security.Principal

Public Class JillController
    Inherits Controller

    Public Function Index(ByVal user As IPrincipal) As ActionResult
        If user.Identity.Name <> "Jill" Then
            Return New HttpUnauthorizedResult()
        End If

        Return View()
    End Function

End Class
```

The controller action in Listing 12.17 is easy to test. The test class in Listing 12.18 contains two tests. The first test verifies that Jill can invoke the Index() action, and the second test verifies that Jack cannot invoke the controller action. Jill gets a view and Jack gets an HTTP Unauthorized result.

LISTING 12.18   Controllers\JillControllerTests.cs (C#)

```csharp
using System.Web.Mvc;
using Microsoft.VisualStudio.TestTools.UnitTesting;
using MvcApplication1.Controllers;

namespace MvcApplication1.Tests.Controllers
{
    [TestClass]
    public class JillControllerTests
    {

        [TestMethod]
```

```csharp
public void JillCanAccessIndex()
{
    // Arrange
    var controller = new JillController();
    var principal = new FakePrincipal("Jill");

    // Act
    var result = controller.Index(principal);

    // Assert
    Assert.IsInstanceOfType(result, typeof(ViewResult));

}

[TestMethod]
public void JackCannotAccessIndex()
{
    // Arrange
    var controller = new JillController();
    var principal = new FakePrincipal("Jack");

    // Act
    var result = controller.Index(principal);

    // Assert
    Assert.IsInstanceOfType(result, typeof(HttpUnauthorizedResult));

}

    }

}
```

LISTING 12.18   Controllers\JillControllerTests.vb (VB)

```vb
Imports Microsoft.VisualStudio.TestTools.UnitTesting
Imports System.Web.Mvc

<TestClass()> _
Public Class JillControllerTests

    <TestMethod()> _
    Public Sub JillCanAccessIndex()
        ' Arrange
        Dim controller = New JillController()
```

```vbnet
        Dim principal = New FakePrincipal("Jill")

        ' Act
        Dim result = controller.Index(principal)

        ' Assert
        Assert.IsInstanceOfType(result, GetType(ViewResult))
    End Sub

    <TestMethod()> _
    Public Sub JackCannotAccessIndex()
        ' Arrange
        Dim controller = New JillController()
        Dim principal = New FakePrincipal("Jack")

        ' Act
        Dim result = controller.Index(principal)

        ' Assert
        Assert.IsInstanceOfType(result, GetType(HttpUnauthorizedResult))
    End Sub

End Class
```

When you run the tests in Listing 12.18, both tests pass. This should give you some confidence that only Jill can invoke the Index action (see Figure 12.19).

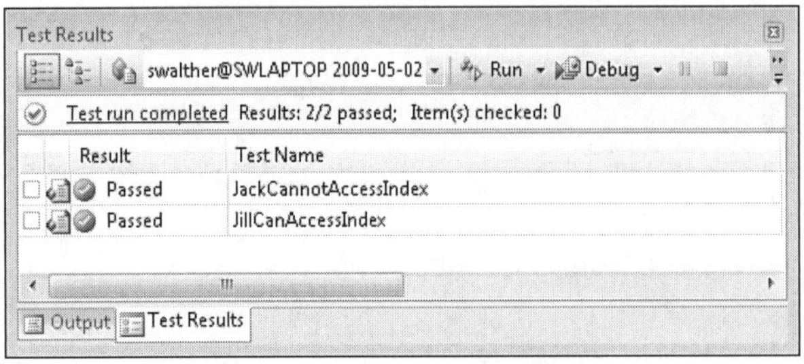

FIGURE 12.19   Passing authorization tests

The tests in Listing 12.18 make use of a FakePrincipal class. This (extremely simple) class is contained in Listing 12.19.

LISTING 12.19   Models\FakePrincipal.cs (C#)

```csharp
using System.Security.Principal;
using System;
using MvcApplication1.Tests.Models;

public class FakePrincipal : IPrincipal
{
    private string _name;

    public FakePrincipal(string name)
    {
        _name = name;
    }

    #region IPrincipal Members

    public IIdentity Identity
    {
        get { return new FakeIdentity(_name); }
    }

    public bool IsInRole(string role)
    {
        throw new NotImplementedException();
    }

    #endregion
}
```

LISTING 12.19   Models\FakePrincipal.vb (VB)

```vbnet
Imports System.Security.Principal

Public Class FakePrincipal
    Implements IPrincipal

    Private _name As String

    Public Sub New(ByVal name As String)
        _name = name
    End Sub
```

```
#Region "IPrincipal Members"

    Public ReadOnly Property Identity() As IIdentity Implements IPrincipal.Identity
        Get
            Return New FakeIdentity(_name)
        End Get
    End Property

    Public Function IsInRole(ByVal role As String) As Boolean Implements
➥IPrincipal.IsInRole
        Throw New NotImplementedException()
    End Function

#End Region
End Class
```

The FakePrincipal class uses a FakeIdentity class. For the sake of completeness, this class is included in Listing 12.20.

LISTING 12.20   Models\FakeIdentity.cs (C#)

```csharp
using System;
using System.Security.Principal;

namespace MvcApplication1.Tests.Models
{
    public class FakeIdentity : IIdentity
    {
        private string _name;

        public FakeIdentity(string name)
        {
            _name = name;
        }

        #region IIdentity Members

        public string AuthenticationType
        {
            get { throw new NotImplementedException(); }
        }

        public bool IsAuthenticated
        {
            get { throw new NotImplementedException(); }
```

```
        }

        public string Name
        {
            get { return _name; }
        }

        #endregion
    }
}
```

LISTING 12.20   Models\FakeIdentity.vb (VB)

```
Imports System.Security.Principal

Public Class FakeIdentity
    Implements IIdentity

    Private _name As String

    Public Sub New(ByVal name As String)
        _name = name
    End Sub

#Region "IIdentity Members"

    Public ReadOnly Property AuthenticationType() As String Implements
➥IIdentity.AuthenticationType
        Get
            Throw New NotImplementedException()
        End Get
    End Property

    Public ReadOnly Property IsAuthenticated() As Boolean Implements
➥IIdentity.IsAuthenticated
        Get
            Throw New NotImplementedException()
        End Get
    End Property

    Public ReadOnly Property Name() As String Implements IIdentity.Name
        Get
            Return _name
        End Get
```

```
    End Property

#End Region

End Class
```

Summary

In this chapter, you learned how to control access to controller actions. In the first section, you learned how to use the Web Site Administration Tool and the `Account` controller to create users and roles.

Next, you learned how to authorize users both declaratively and programmatically. You learned how to decorate controller actions with the `Authorize` attribute. You also learned how to take advantage of the `User` property.

Next, you learned how to configure membership. You learned how to configure a database and your application to store user accounts in a production database server.

We also explored the topic of Windows authentication. You learned how to enable Windows authentication so that you can authorize Windows users and groups.

Finally, we tackled the topic of testing. We examined two ways of testing authorization.

CHAPTER 13

Deploying ASP.NET MVC Applications

This chapter is devoted to the topic of deploying your ASP.NET MVC application to a web server and getting the application to work. In the first section, you learn how to configure Internet Information Services to work with ASP.NET MVC. In particular, you learn how to get ASP.NET MVC to work with Internet Information Services 7.0 and earlier versions of Internet Information Services.

Next, you learn how to use ASP.NET MVC with an existing Web Forms application. You are provided with a step-by-step guide to converting an existing Web Forms application into an application that supports both Web Forms and MVC.

Finally, you learn how you can deploy an ASP.NET MVC application to a hosting company that does not have the ASP.NET MVC framework installed. You learn how to take advantage of bin deployment.

Configuring IIS for ASP.NET MVC

The ASP.NET MVC framework depends on ASP.NET Routing to route browser requests to controller actions. To take advantage of ASP.NET Routing, you might have to perform additional configuration steps on your web server. It all depends on the version of Internet Information Services (IIS) and the request-processing mode for your application.

Table 13.1 summarizes the different versions of IIS, whether special configuration is required, and which version of Windows the IIS version is included with.

TABLE 13.1   IIS Configurations

IIS Version	Special Configuration Required to Use ASP.NET Routing?	Windows Version
IIS 7.0 (integrated mode)	No	Windows Server 2008; any version of Vista except Home Basic
IIS 7.0 (classic mode)	Yes	Windows Server 2008; any version of Vista except Home Basic
IIS 6.0	Yes	Windows Server 2003 (You cannot upgrade to IIS 7.0 with Windows Server 2003.)
IIS 5.1	Yes	Windows XP Professional
IIS 5.0	Yes	Windows 2000 and Windows 2000 Professional

Integrated Versus Classic Mode

IIS 7.0 can process requests using two different request-processing modes: integrated and classic. Integrated mode provides better performance and more features. Classic mode is included for backward compatibility with earlier versions of IIS.

The request-processing mode is determined by the application pool. You can determine which processing mode is used by a particular web application by determining the application pool associated with the application. Follow these steps:

1. Launch the Internet Information Services Manager.

2. In the Connections window, select an application.

3. In the Actions window, click the Basic Settings link to open the Edit Application dialog box (see Figure 13.1).

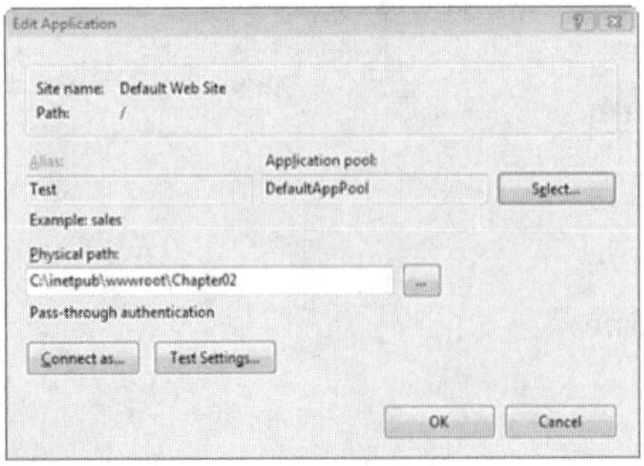

FIGURE 13.1   Detecting the request-processing mode

4. Take note of the application pool selected.

By default, IIS is configured to support two application pools: DefaultAppPool and Classic .NET AppPool. If DefaultAppPool is selected, your application is running in integrated request-processing mode. If Classic .NET AppPool is selected, your application runs in classic request-processing mode.

Notice that you can modify the request-processing mode within the Edit Application dialog. Click the Select button and change the application pool associated with the application. Realize that there are compatibility issues when changing an ASP.NET application from classic to integrated mode.

If an ASP.NET application is using the DefaultAppPool, you don't need to perform any additional steps to get ASP.NET Routing (and therefore ASP.NET MVC) to work. However, if the ASP.NET application is configured to use the Classic .NET AppPool, keep reading; you have more work to do.

Using ASP.NET MVC with Older Versions of IIS

If you need to use ASP.NET MVC with a version of IIS older than IIS 7.0, or you need to use IIS 7.0 in classic mode, you have two options. First, you can modify the route table to use file extensions. For example, instead of requesting a URL like /Store/Details, you can request a URL like /Store.aspx/Details.

The second option is to create something called a *wildcard script map*. A wildcard script map enables you to map every request into the ASP.NET framework.

If you don't have access to your web server (for example, your ASP.NET MVC application is hosted by an Internet service provider), you need to use the first option. If you don't want to modify the appearance of your URLs, and you have access to your web server, you can use the second option.

We explore each option in detail in the following sections.

Adding Extensions to the Route Table

The easiest way to get ASP.NET Routing to work with older versions of IIS is to modify your route table in the Global.asax file. The default and unmodified Global.asax file in Listing 13.1 configures one route named the Default route.

LISTING 13.1   Global.asax (Unmodified) (C#)

```
using System;
using System.Collections.Generic;
using System.Linq;
using System.Web;
using System.Web.Mvc;
using System.Web.Routing;

namespace MvcApplication1
{
```

```
    public class GlobalApplication : System.Web.HttpApplication
    {
        public static void RegisterRoutes(RouteCollection routes)
        {
            routes.IgnoreRoute("{resource}.axd/{*pathInfo}");

            routes.MapRoute(
                "Default",  // Route name
                "{controller}/{action}/{id}", // URL with parameters
                new { controller = "Home", action = "Index", id = "" }  //
➥Parameter defaults
            );

        }

        protected void Application_Start()
        {
            RegisterRoutes(RouteTable.Routes);
        }
    }
}
```

LISTING 13.1   Global.asax (Unmodified) (VB)

```
Public Class MvcApplication
    Inherits System.Web.HttpApplication

    Shared Sub RegisterRoutes(ByVal routes As RouteCollection)
        routes.IgnoreRoute("{resource}.axd/{*pathInfo}")

        ' MapRoute takes the following parameters, in order:
        ' (1) Route name
        ' (2) URL with parameters
        ' (3) Parameter defaults
        routes.MapRoute( _
            "Default", _
            "{controller}/{action}/{id}", _
            New With {.controller = "Home", .action = "Index", .id = ""} _
        )

    End Sub

    Sub Application_Start()
        RegisterRoutes(RouteTable.Routes)
    End Sub
End Class
```

The Default route configured in Listing 13.1 enables you to route URLs that look like this:

/Home/Index

/Product/Details/3

/Product

Unfortunately, older versions of IIS won't pass these requests to the ASP.NET framework. Therefore, these requests won't get routed to a controller. For example, if you make a browser request for the URL /Home/Index, you get the error page in Figure 13.2.

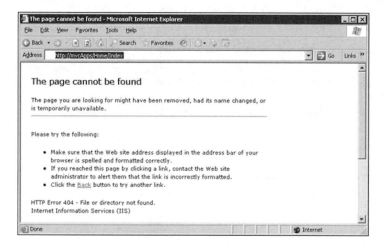

FIGURE 13.2   Receiving a 404 Not Found error

Older versions of IIS map only certain requests to the ASP.NET framework. The request must be for a URL with the right file extension. For example, a request for /SomePage.aspx gets mapped to the ASP.NET framework. However, a request for /SomePage.htm does not.

Therefore, to get ASP.NET Routing to work, we must modify the Default route so that it includes a file extension that is mapped to the ASP.NET framework.

When you install the ASP.NET MVC framework, a script named registermvc.wsf is added to the following folder:

C:\Program Files\Microsoft ASP.NET\ASP.NET MVC\Scripts

Executing this script registers a new .mvc extension with IIS. After you register the .mvc extension, you can modify your routes in the Global.asax file so that the routes use the .mvc extension.

The modified Global.asax file in Listing 13.2 works with older versions of IIS.

LISTING 13.2   Global.asax (Modified with Extensions) (C#)

```csharp
using System;
using System.Collections.Generic;
using System.Linq;
using System.Web;
using System.Web.Mvc;
using System.Web.Routing;

namespace MvcApplication1
{

    public class MvcApplication : System.Web.HttpApplication
    {
        public static void RegisterRoutes(RouteCollection routes)
        {
            routes.IgnoreRoute("{resource}.axd/{*pathInfo}");

            routes.MapRoute(
                "Default",
                "{controller}.mvc/{action}/{id}",
                new { action = "Index", id = "" }
              );

            routes.MapRoute(
                "Root",
                "",
                new { controller = "Home", action = "Index", id = "" }
            );

        }

        protected void Application_Start()
        {
            RegisterRoutes(RouteTable.Routes);
        }
    }
}
```

LISTING 13.2   Global.asax (Modified with Extensions) (VB)

```vb
Public Class MvcApplication
    Inherits System.Web.HttpApplication

    Shared Sub RegisterRoutes(ByVal routes As RouteCollection)
```

```
    routes.IgnoreRoute("{resource}.axd/{*pathInfo}")

    ' MapRoute takes the following parameters, in order:
    ' (1) Route name
    ' (2) URL with parameters
    ' (3) Parameter defaults
    routes.MapRoute( _
        "Default", _
        "{controller}.mvc/{action}/{id}", _
        New With {.controller = "Home", .action = "Index", .id = ""} _
    )

    routes.MapRoute( _
        "Root", _
        "", _
        New With {.controller = "Home", .action = "Index", .id = ""} _
    )

End Sub

Sub Application_Start()
    RegisterRoutes(RouteTable.Routes)
End Sub
End Class
```

WARNING

Important: Remember to build your ASP.NET MVC application again after changing the Global.asax file.

There are two important changes to the Global.asax file in Listing 13.2. There are now two routes defined in the Global.asax. The URL pattern for the Default route, the first route, now looks like this:

{controller}.mvc/{action}/{id}

The addition of the .mvc extension changes the type of files that the ASP.NET Routing module intercepts. With this change, the ASP.NET MVC application now routes requests like the following:

/Home.mvc/Index/

/Product.mvc/Details/3

/Product.mvc/

The second route, the Root route, is new. This URL pattern for the Root route is an empty string. This route is necessary for matching requests made against the root of your application. For example, the Root route matches a request that looks like this:

> http://www.YourApplication.com/

After making these modifications to your route table, you need to make sure that all of the links in your application are compatible with these new URL patterns. In other words, make sure that all your links include the .mvc extension. If you use the `Html.ActionLink()` helper method to generate your links, you should not need to make any changes.

WARNING

Instead of using the registermvc.wcf script, you can add a new extension to IIS that is mapped to the ASP.NET framework by hand. When adding a new extension yourself, make sure that the check box labeled Verify That File Exists is not checked.

Hosted Server

You don't always have access to your web server. For example, if you host your ASP.NET MVC application using an Internet hosting provider, you won't necessarily have access to IIS.

In that case, you should use one of the existing file extensions that are mapped to the ASP.NET framework. Examples of file extensions mapped to ASP.NET include the .aspx, .axd, and .ashx extensions.

For example, the modified Global.asax file in Listing 13.3 uses the .aspx extension instead of the .mvc extension.

LISTING 13.3   Global.asax (Modified with .aspx Extensions) (C#)

```csharp
using System;
using System.Collections.Generic;
using System.Linq;
using System.Web;
using System.Web.Mvc;
using System.Web.Routing;

namespace MvcApplication1
{

    public class MvcApplication : System.Web.HttpApplication
    {
        public static void RegisterRoutes(RouteCollection routes)
        {
```

```
        routes.IgnoreRoute("{resource}.axd/{*pathInfo}");

        routes.MapRoute(
            "Default",
            "{controller}.aspx/{action}/{id}",
            new { action = "Index", id = "" }
          );

        routes.MapRoute(
          "Root",
          "",
          new { controller = "Home", action = "Index", id = "" }
        );

    }

    protected void Application_Start()
    {
        RegisterRoutes(RouteTable.Routes);
    }
  }
}
```

LISTING 13.3   Global.asax (Modified with .aspx Extensions) (VB)

```
Public Class MvcApplication
    Inherits System.Web.HttpApplication
    Shared Sub RegisterRoutes(ByVal routes As RouteCollection)
        routes.IgnoreRoute("{resource}.axd/{*pathInfo}")

        ' MapRoute takes the following parameters, in order:
        ' (1) Route name
        ' (2) URL with parameters
        ' (3) Parameter defaults
        routes.MapRoute( _
            "Default", _
            "{controller}.aspx/{action}/{id}", _
            New With {.controller = "Home", .action = "Index", .id = ""} _
        )

        routes.MapRoute( _
            "Root", _
            "", _
```

```
            New With {.controller = "Home", .action = "Index", .id = ""} _
        )

    End Sub

    Sub Application_Start()
        RegisterRoutes(RouteTable.Routes)
    End Sub
End Class
```

The Global.asax file in Listing 13.3 is exactly the same as the previous Global.asax file except for the fact that it uses the .aspx extension instead of the .mvc extension. You don't have to perform any setup on your remote web server to use the .aspx extension.

Creating a Wildcard Script Map

If you don't want to modify the URLs for your ASP.NET MVC application, and you have access to your web server, you have an additional option. You can create a wildcard script map that maps all requests to the web server to the ASP.NET framework. That way, you can use the default ASP.NET MVC route table with IIS 7.0 (in classic mode) or IIS 6.0.

Be aware that this option causes IIS to intercept every request made against the web server. This includes requests for images, classic ASP pages, and HTML pages. Therefore, enabling a wildcard script map to ASP.NET does have performance implications.

Here's how you enable a wildcard script map for IIS 7.0:

1. Select your application in the Connections window.
2. Make sure that the Features view is selected.
3. Double-click the Handler Mappings button.
4. Click the Add Wildcard Script Map link (see Figure 13.3).
5. Enter the path to the aspnet_isapi.dll file. (You can copy this path from the PageHandlerFactory script map.)
6. Enter the name MVC.
7. Click the OK button.

Follow these steps to create a wildcard script map with IIS 6.0:

1. Right-click a website and select Properties.
2. Select the Home Directory tab.
3. Click the Configuration button.

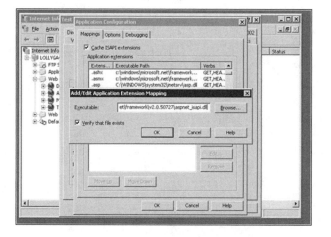

FIGURE 13.3   Creating a wildcard script map with IIS 7.0

4. Select the Mappings tab.
5. Click the Insert button (see Figure 13.4).

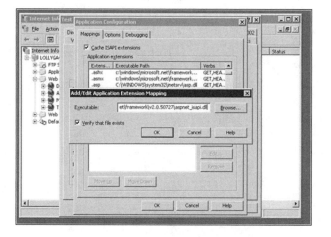

FIGURE 13.4   Creating a wildcard script map with IIS 6.0

6. Paste the path to the aspnet_isapi.dll into the Executable field. (You can copy this path from the script map for .aspx files.)
7. Uncheck the check box labeled Verify That File Exists.
8. Click the OK button.

After you enable wildcard script maps, you need to modify the route table in the Global.asax file so that it includes a Root route. Otherwise, you get the error page in

Figure 13.5 when you make a request for the root page of your application. You can use the modified Global.asax file in Listing 13.4.

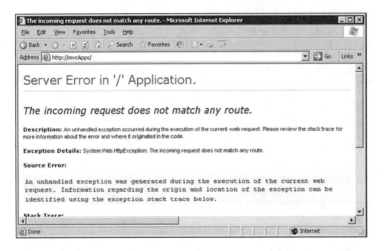

FIGURE 13.5   Missing Root Route error

LISTING 13.4   Global.asax (Modified with Root Route) (C#)

```
using System;
using System.Collections.Generic;
using System.Linq;
using System.Web;
using System.Web.Mvc;
using System.Web.Routing;

namespace MvcApplication1
{

    public class MvcApplication : System.Web.HttpApplication
    {
        public static void RegisterRoutes(RouteCollection routes)
        {
            routes.IgnoreRoute("{resource}.axd/{*pathInfo}");

            routes.MapRoute(
                "Default",
                "{controller}/{action}/{id}",
                new { action = "Index", id = "" }
              );

            routes.MapRoute(
```

```
            "Root",
            "",
            new { controller = "Home", action = "Index", id = "" }
        );

    }

    protected void Application_Start()
    {
        RegisterRoutes(RouteTable.Routes);
    }
}
}
```

LISTING 13.4   Global.asax (Modified with Root Route) (VB)

```vb
Public Class MvcApplication
    Inherits System.Web.HttpApplication

    Shared Sub RegisterRoutes(ByVal routes As RouteCollection)
        routes.IgnoreRoute("{resource}.axd/{*pathInfo}")

        ' MapRoute takes the following parameters, in order:
        ' (1) Route name
        ' (2) URL with parameters
        ' (3) Parameter defaults
        routes.MapRoute( _
            "Default", _
            "{controller}/{action}/{id}", _
            New With {.controller = "Home", .action = "Index", .id = ""} _
        )

        routes.MapRoute( _
            "Root", _
            "", _
            New With {.controller = "Home", .action = "Index", .id = ""} _
        )

    End Sub

    Sub Application_Start()
        RegisterRoutes(RouteTable.Routes)
    End Sub
End Class
```

After you enable a wildcard script map for either IIS 7.0 or IIS 6.0, you can make requests that work with the default route table that look like this:

```
/

/Home/Index

/Product/Details/3

/Product
```

Mixing ASP.NET Web Forms and ASP.NET MVC

Microsoft provides two major frameworks built on the ASP.NET framework: ASP.NET Web Forms and ASP.NET MVC. If you have already invested years of development effort into building an ASP.NET Web Forms application, you might not want to throw the existing application out and start over.

> **NOTE**
>
> You could argue that Microsoft actually provides four frameworks built on ASP.NET: ASP.NET Web Forms, ASP.NET MVC, ASP.NET AJAX, and Dynamic Data.

Fortunately, you can mix ASP.NET Web Forms and ASP.NET MVC. You can build parts of your application using ASP.NET Web Forms and parts of your application using ASP.NET MVC. This provides you with a gradual migration path from ASP.NET Web Forms to ASP.NET MVC.

In this section, you learn how to modify an existing ASP.NET Web Forms application so that it supports ASP.NET MVC. There are four steps:

1. Modify the Visual Studio Project file.
2. Add the required assemblies.
3. Modify the web configuration files.
4. Modify the Global.asax file.

> **WARNING**
>
> ASP.NET MVC is compatible with web application projects and not websites. If your existing ASP.NET Web Forms application is a website instead of a web application project, you need to first convert your Web Forms application into a web application project.

The quickest way to determine whether you have a website or web application is to look at the Visual Studio menu bar. If you see Website in the menu bar, you have a website. If you see Project, you have a web application project.

Modifying the Visual Studio Project File

If you want to take advantage of Visual Studio menu options such as Add Controller or Add View, you need to modify your Visual Studio project file. Follow these steps:

1. Close Visual Studio.

2. Navigate to the location of your Visual Studio project and open the .csproj or .vbproj file.

3. Find the ProjectTypeGuids element and change it using Notepad so that it includes the additional GUID for MVC applications.

(Web Forms C#)

```
<ProjectTypeGuids>{349c5851-65df-11da-9384-00065b846f21};{fae04ec0-301f-
➥11d3-bf4b-00c04f79efbc}</ProjectTypeGuids>
```

(Web Forms VB)

```
<ProjectTypeGuids>{349c5851-65df-11da-9384-00065b846f21};{F184B08F-C81C-
➥45F6-A57F-5ABD9991F28F}</ProjectTypeGuids>
```

(MVC C#)

```
<ProjectTypeGuids>{603c0e0b-db56-11dc-be95-000d561079b0};{349c5851-65df-
➥11da-9384-00065b846f21};{fae04ec0-301f-11d3-bf4b-00c04f79efbc}
➥</ProjectTypeGuids>
```

(MVC VB)

```
<ProjectTypeGuids>{603c0e0b-db56-11dc-be95-000d561079b0};{349c5851-65df-
➥11da-9384-00065b846f21};{F184B08F-C81C-45F6-A57F-5ABD9991F28F}
➥</ProjectTypeGuids>
```

Notice that there is one additional GUID in the case of the MVC ProjectTypeGuids.

Adding the Required Assemblies

The first step in using ASP.NET MVC with an existing Web Forms application is to add the assemblies (DLL files) required by the ASP.NET MVC framework. The ASP.NET MVC requires the following three assemblies:

- ▶ **System.Web.Routing**—This assembly contains the classes used by ASP.NET routing.

- ▶ **System.Web.Mvc**—This assembly contains all the core classes of the ASP.NET MVC framework.

- ▶ **System.Web.Abstractions**—This assembly contains wrappers around the intrinsic ASP.NET classes such as the HttpContext class.

Follow these steps to add these assemblies:

1. Select the menu option Project, Add Reference.

2. In the Add Reference dialog, select the .NET tab (see Figure 13.6).

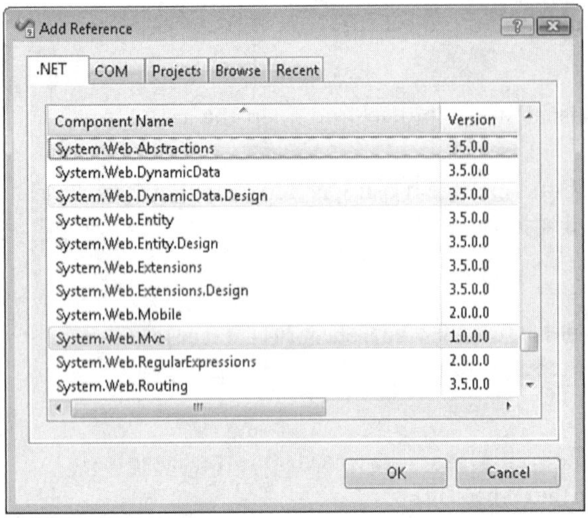

FIGURE 13.6   Adding assemblies

3. From the list box, select the System.Web.Routing, System.Web.Mvc, and System.Web.Abstractions assemblies.

4. Click the OK button.

There is an additional step related to assemblies when your project is a VB project. You must import the necessary namespaces for your application. Right-click your project in the Solution Explorer window and select the Properties menu option. Select the References tab. Under Imported Namespaces, import the System.Web.Mvc, System.Web.Mvc.Html, System.Web.Mvc.Ajax, and System.Web.Routing (see Figure 13.7).

FIGURE 13.7   Importing the necessary namespaces

Modifying the Web Configuration File

The next step—and this is the most difficult step—is to change the configuration of your application. You need to modify the existing root web configuration file and create a new web configuration file located in the Views folder.

First, you need to modify the web.config file located in the root of your application. Here are the (important) places in which the default Web Forms configuration file differs from the default MVC configuration file:

(Web Forms)

```
  <assemblies>
    <add assembly="System.Core, Version=3.5.0.0, Culture=neutral,
➡PublicKeyToken=B77A5C561934E089"/>
    <add assembly="System.Data.DataSetExtensions, Version=3.5.0.0,
➡Culture=neutral,PublicKeyToken=B77A5C561934E089"/>
    <add assembly="System.Web.Extensions, Version=3.5.0.0, Culture=neutral,
➡PublicKeyToken=31BF3856AD364E35"/>
    <add assembly="System.Xml.Linq, Version=3.5.0.0, Culture=neutral,
➡PublicKeyToken=B77A5C561934E089"/>
  </assemblies>
```

(MVC)

```
  <assemblies>
    <add assembly="System.Core, Version=3.5.0.0, Culture=neutral,
➡PublicKeyToken=B77A5C561934E089"/>
    <add assembly="System.Web.Extensions, Version=3.5.0.0, Culture=neutral,
➡PublicKeyToken=31BF3856AD364E35"/>
    <add assembly="System.Web.Abstractions, Version=3.5.0.0, Culture=neutral,
➡PublicKeyToken=31BF3856AD364E35"/>
    <add assembly="System.Web.Routing, Version=3.5.0.0, Culture=neutral,
➡PublicKeyToken=31BF3856AD364E35"/>
    <add assembly="System.Web.Mvc, Version=1.0.0.0, Culture=neutral,
➡PublicKeyToken=31BF3856AD364E35"/>
    <add assembly="System.Data.DataSetExtensions, Version=3.5.0.0,
➡Culture=neutral,PublicKeyToken=B77A5C561934E089"/>
    <add assembly="System.Xml.Linq, Version=3.5.0.0, Culture=neutral,
➡PublicKeyToken=B77A5C561934E089"/>
    <add assembly="System.Data.Linq, Version=3.5.0.0, Culture=neutral,
➡PublicKeyToken=B77A5C561934E089" />
  </assemblies>
```

The assemblies section of the web configuration file determines which assemblies are available to use in your .aspx files:

(Web Forms)

```
  <pages>
    <controls>
      <add tagPrefix="asp" namespace="System.Web.UI" assembly="System.Web.
➡Extensions, Version=3.5.0.0, Culture=neutral, PublicKeyToken=31BF3856AD364E35"/>
```

```
        <add tagPrefix="asp" namespace="System.Web.UI.WebControls" assembly=
➡"System.Web.Extensions, Version=3.5.0.0, Culture=neutral,
➡PublicKeyToken=31BF3856AD364E35"/>
      </controls>
    </pages>
```

(MVC)

```
<pages>
  <controls>
    <add tagPrefix="asp" namespace="System.Web.UI" assembly="System.Web.
➡Extensions,Version=3.5.0.0, Culture=neutral, PublicKeyToken=31BF3856AD364E35"/>
    <add tagPrefix="asp" namespace="System.Web.UI.WebControls"
➡assembly="System.Web.Extensions, Version=3.5.0.0, Culture=neutral,
➡PublicKeyToken=31BF3856AD364E35"/>
  </controls>

  <namespaces>
    <add namespace="System.Web.Mvc"/>
    <add namespace="System.Web.Mvc.Ajax"/>
    <add namespace="System.Web.Mvc.Html"/>
    <add namespace="System.Web.Routing"/>
    <add namespace="System.Linq"/>
    <add namespace="System.Collections.Generic"/>
  </namespaces>
</pages>
```

(Web Forms)

```
  <httpHandlers>
    <remove verb="*" path="*.asmx"/>
    <add verb="*" path="*.asmx" validate="false"
type="System.Web.Script.Services.ScriptHandlerFactory, System.Web.Extensions,
➡Version=3.5.0.0, Culture=neutral, PublicKeyToken=31BF3856AD364E35"/>
    <add verb="*" path="*_AppService.axd" validate="false"
type="System.Web.Script.Services.ScriptHandlerFactory, System.Web.Extensions,
➡Version=3.5.0.0, Culture=neutral, PublicKeyToken=31BF3856AD364E35"/>
    <add verb="GET,HEAD" path="ScriptResource.axd" type="System.Web.Handlers.
➡ScriptResourceHandler, System.Web.Extensions, Version=3.5.0.0, Culture=neutral,
➡PublicKeyToken=31BF3856AD364E35" validate="false"/>
  </httpHandlers>
```

(MVC)

```
<httpHandlers>
  <remove verb="*" path="*.asmx"/>
```

```
  <add verb="*" path="*.asmx" validate="false"
➥type="System.Web.Script.Services.ScriptHandlerFactory, System.Web.Extensions,
➥Version=3.5.0.0, Culture=neutral, PublicKeyToken=31BF3856AD364E35"/>
  <add verb="*" path="*_AppService.axd" validate="false"
➥type="System.Web.Script.Services.ScriptHandlerFactory, System.Web.Extensions,
➥Version=3.5.0.0, Culture=neutral, PublicKeyToken=31BF3856AD364E35"/>
  <add verb="GET,HEAD" path="ScriptResource.axd" type="System.Web.Handlers.
➥ScriptResourceHandler, System.Web.Extensions, Version=3.5.0.0, Culture=neutral,
➥PublicKeyToken=31BF3856AD364E35" validate="false"/>
  <add verb="*" path="*.mvc" validate="false" type="System.Web.Mvc.MvcHttpHandler,
➥System.Web.Mvc, Version=1.0.0.0, Culture=neutral,
➥PublicKeyToken=31BF3856AD364E35"/>
</httpHandlers>
```

Notice that the MVC handlers section includes a *.mvc handler:

(Web Forms)

```
  <httpModules>
    <add name="ScriptModule" type="System.Web.Handlers.ScriptModule,
➥System.Web.Extensions, Version=3.5.0.0, Culture=neutral,
➥PublicKeyToken=31BF3856AD364E35"/>
  </httpModules>
```

(MVC)

```
<httpModules>
  <add name="ScriptModule" type="System.Web.Handlers.ScriptModule,
➥System.Web.Extensions, Version=3.5.0.0, Culture=neutral,
➥PublicKeyToken=31BF3856AD364E35"/>
  <add name="UrlRoutingModule" type="System.Web.Routing.UrlRoutingModule,
➥System.Web.Routing, Version=3.5.0.0, Culture=neutral,
➥PublicKeyToken=31BF3856AD364E35" />
</httpModules>
```

If you want to deploy your MVC application on IIS 7.0, you need to make the following changes:

(Web Forms)

```
    <modules>
      <remove name="ScriptModule" />
      <add name="ScriptModule" preCondition="managedHandler"
➥type="System.Web.Handlers.ScriptModule, System.Web.Extensions, Version=3.5.0.0,
➥Culture=neutral, PublicKeyToken=31BF3856AD364E35"/>
    </modules>
    <handlers>
```

```
        <remove name="WebServiceHandlerFactory-Integrated"/>
        <remove name="ScriptHandlerFactory" />
        <remove name="ScriptHandlerFactoryAppServices" />
        <remove name="ScriptResource" />
        <add name="ScriptHandlerFactory" verb="*" path="*.asmx"
➥preCondition="integratedMode"
            type="System.Web.Script.Services.ScriptHandlerFactory,
➥System.Web.Extensions, Version=3.5.0.0, Culture=neutral,
➥PublicKeyToken=31BF3856AD364E35"/>
        <add name="ScriptHandlerFactoryAppServices" verb="*"
➥path="*_AppService.axd"preCondition="integratedMode"
            type="System.Web.Script.Services.ScriptHandlerFactory,
➥System.Web.Extensions, Version=3.5.0.0, Culture=neutral,
➥PublicKeyToken=31BF3856AD364E35"/>
        <add name="ScriptResource" preCondition="integratedMode" verb="GET,HEAD"
➥path="ScriptResource.axd" type="System.Web.Handlers.ScriptResourceHandler,
➥System.Web.Extensions, Version=3.5.0.0, Culture=neutral,
➥PublicKeyToken=31BF3856AD364E35" />
    </handlers>
```

(MVC)

```
<modules runAllManagedModulesForAllRequests="true">
  <remove name="ScriptModule" />
  <remove name="UrlRoutingModule" />
  <add name="ScriptModule" preCondition="managedHandler"
➥type="System.Web.Handlers.ScriptModule, System.Web.Extensions, Version=3.5.0.0,
➥Culture=neutral, PublicKeyToken=31BF3856AD364E35"/>
  <add name="UrlRoutingModule" type="System.Web.Routing.UrlRoutingModule,
➥System.Web.Routing, Version=3.5.0.0, Culture=neutral,
➥PublicKeyToken=31BF3856AD364E35" />
</modules>

    <handlers>
      <remove name="WebServiceHandlerFactory-Integrated"/>
      <remove name="ScriptHandlerFactory" />
      <remove name="ScriptHandlerFactoryAppServices" />
      <remove name="ScriptResource" />
      <remove name="MvcHttpHandler" />
      <remove name="UrlRoutingHandler" />
      <add name="ScriptHandlerFactory" verb="*" path="*.asmx" preCondition="
➥integratedMode"
            type="System.Web.Script.Services.ScriptHandlerFactory, System.Web.
➥Extensions, Version=3.5.0.0, Culture=neutral, PublicKeyToken=31BF3856AD364E35"/>
      <add name="ScriptHandlerFactoryAppServices" verb="*" path="*_AppService.axd"
➥preCondition="integratedMode"
```

```
        type="System.Web.Script.Services.ScriptHandlerFactory, System.Web.
➥Extensions, Version=3.5.0.0, Culture=neutral, PublicKeyToken=31BF3856AD364E35"/>
      <add name="ScriptResource" preCondition="integratedMode" verb="GET,HEAD"
➥path="ScriptResource.axd" type="System.Web.Handlers.ScriptResourceHandler,
➥System.Web.Extensions, Version=3.5.0.0, Culture=neutral,
➥PublicKeyToken=31BF3856AD364E35" />
      <add name="MvcHttpHandler" preCondition="integratedMode" verb="*"
➥path="*.mvc" type="System.Web.Mvc.MvcHttpHandler, System.Web.Mvc, Version=1.0.0.0,
➥Culture=neutral, PublicKeyToken=31BF3856AD364E35"/>
      <add name="UrlRoutingHandler" preCondition="integratedMode" verb="*"
➥path="UrlRouting.axd" type="System.Web.HttpForbiddenHandler, System.Web,
➥Version=2.0.0.0, Culture=neutral, PublicKeyToken=b03f5f7f11d50a3a" />
    </handlers>
```

After you make all these changes to the root web configuration, you need to add a new web configuration file to your project. Create a new folder named Views and create a web configuration file with the contents in Listing 13.5.

NOTE

I recommend copying the configuration file in Listing 13.5 from an ASP.NET MVC project instead of typing it.

LISTING 13.5   Views\Web.config

```
<?xml version="1.0"?>
<configuration>
    <system.web>
        <httpHandlers>
            <add path="*" verb="*"
                type="System.Web.HttpNotFoundHandler"/>
        </httpHandlers>

        <!--
        Enabling request validation in view pages would cause validation to occur
        after the input has already been processed by the controller. By default
        MVC performs request validation before a controller processes the input.
        To change this behavior apply the ValidateInputAttribute to a
        controller or action.
        -->
        <pages
            validateRequest="false"
            pageParserFilterType="System.Web.Mvc.ViewTypeParserFilter,
➥System.Web.Mvc, Version=1.0.0.0, Culture=neutral, PublicKeyToken=31BF3856AD364E35"
            pageBaseType="System.Web.Mvc.ViewPage, System.Web.Mvc, Version=1.0.0.0,
➥Culture=neutral, PublicKeyToken=31BF3856AD364E35"
```

```
                userControlBaseType="System.Web.Mvc.ViewUserControl, System.Web.Mvc,
➥Version=1.0.0.0, Culture=neutral, PublicKeyToken=31BF3856AD364E35">
            <controls>
                <add assembly="System.Web.Mvc, Version=1.0.0.0, Culture=neutral,
➥PublicKeyToken=31BF3856AD364E35" namespace="System.Web.Mvc" tagPrefix="mvc" />
            </controls>
        </pages>
    </system.web>

    <system.webServer>
        <validation validateIntegratedModeConfiguration="false"/>
        <handlers>
            <remove name="BlockViewHandler"/>
            <add name="BlockViewHandler" path="*" verb="*" preCondition=
➥"integratedMode" type="System.Web.HttpNotFoundHandler"/>
        </handlers>
    </system.webServer>
</configuration>
```

Modify the Global.asax File

The last step is to modify the Global.asax file so that your application includes the default
ASP.NET MVC routes. If your Web Forms application does not already have a Global.asax
file, create one. Modify the Global.asax file so that it looks like the file in Listing 13.6.

LISTING 13.6   Global.asax.cs (C#)

```csharp
using System;
using System.Collections.Generic;
using System.Linq;
using System.Web;
using System.Web.Mvc;
using System.Web.Routing;

namespace WebApplication1
{
    // Note: For instructions on enabling IIS6 or IIS7 classic mode,
    // visit http://go.microsoft.com/?LinkId=9394801

    public class MvcApplication : System.Web.HttpApplication
    {
        public static void RegisterRoutes(RouteCollection routes)
        {
            routes.IgnoreRoute("{resource}.axd/{*pathInfo}");
```

```
        routes.MapRoute(
            "Default",    // Route name
            "{controller}/{action}/{id}", // URL with parameters
            new { controller = "Home", action = "Index", id = "" }  //
➥Parameter defaults
        );

    }

    protected void Application_Start()
    {
        RegisterRoutes(RouteTable.Routes);
    }
  }
}
```

LISTING 13.6   Global.asax.vb (VB)

```
' Note: For instructions on enabling IIS6 or IIS7 classic mode,
' visit http://go.microsoft.com/?LinkId=9394802

Public Class MvcApplication
    Inherits System.Web.HttpApplication

    Shared Sub RegisterRoutes(ByVal routes As RouteCollection)
        routes.IgnoreRoute("{resource}.axd/{*pathInfo}")

        ' MapRoute takes the following parameters, in order:
        ' (1) Route name
        ' (2) URL with parameters
        ' (3) Parameter defaults
        routes.MapRoute( _
            "Default", _
            "{controller}/{action}/{id}", _
            New With {.controller = "Home", .action = "Index", .id = ""} _
        )

    End Sub

    Sub Application_Start()
        RegisterRoutes(RouteTable.Routes)
    End Sub
End Class
```

You need to modify the markup in the Global.asax file to refer to the right class. Right-click the Global.asax file in the Solution Explorer window and select the menu option View Markup. Change the Inherits attribute so that it matches the namespace and name of your global application class. For example

(C#)

```
Inherits="WebApplication1.MvcApplication"
```

(VB)

```
Inherits="WebApplication1.MvcApplication"
```

Using Web Forms and MVC

After you make all the changes previously described to your Web Forms application, you can start adding controllers and views to the application just like you would in a normal ASP.NET MVC application. You also can continue to add Web Form pages.

The default routes configured in the previous section enable you to request Web Form pages. For example, if you request the page MyPage.aspx, the MyPage.aspx is executed.

Bin Deploying an ASP.NET MVC Application

You can deploy an ASP.NET MVC application to a web server that does not have the ASP.NET MVC framework installed. For example, if your Internet hosting company does not yet support ASP.NET MVC, you can still deploy ASP.NET MVC applications to your hosting company.

The only requirement for using ASP.NET MVC is that your hosting company supports ASP.NET 3.5. The ASP.NET MVC framework requires ASP.NET 3.5.

NOTE

If your hosting company supports ASP.NET 3.5 Service Pack 1, you do not need to deploy the System.Web.Routing and System.Web.Abstractions assemblies. These assemblies are included in Service Pack 1.

The assemblies required by the ASP.NET MVC framework are *bin deployable*. This means that you can copy the required assemblies—System.Web.Mvc, System.Web.Abstrations, and System.Web.Routing—to your host when you deploy the rest of your application.

You need to do only one special thing to deploy the necessary assemblies when you deploy your application. You need to create local copies of the assemblies.

In a C# project, you can indicate that you want a local copy of an assembly by selecting the assembly in the References folder and assigning the value True to the Copy Local property in the Properties sheet (see Figure 13.8). You need to do this for the System.Web.Mvc, System.Web.Abstractions, and System.Web.Routing assemblies.

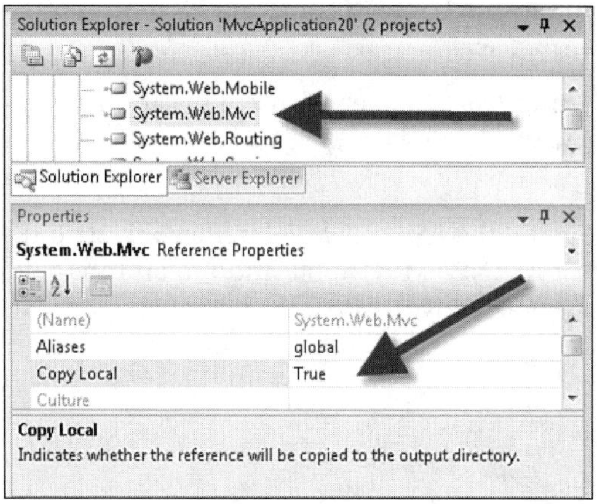

FIGURE 13.8   Enabling Copy Local in a C# project

In a VB project, you need to right-click your project in the Solution Explorer and select Properties. Next, select the References tab and find the System.Web.Mvc, System.Web.Abstractions, and System.Web.Routing assemblies. Double-click on each assembly to open the Properties sheet. Assign the value True to the Copy Local property (see Figure 13.9).

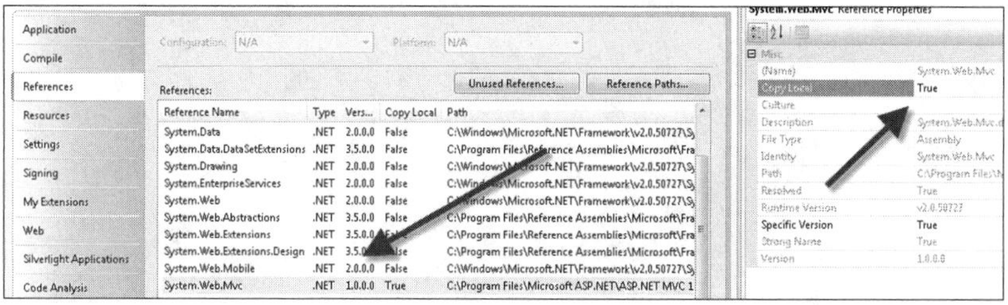

FIGURE 13.9   Enabling Copy Local in a VB project

After you make these changes, you can copy your website to your hosting company using your favorite method. For example, you can use the Visual Studio Build, Publish menu option, or you can use FTP. After the assemblies are copied local, they are present in the Bin folder so that they can be copied with everything else.

Summary

In this chapter, you learned how to overcome various challenges associated with deploying an ASP.NET MVC application. In the first section, you learned how to configure IIS to support ASP.NET MVC. (Or more accurately, you learned how to configure IIS to support ASP.NET Routing.)

Next, you learned how you can modify an existing ASP.NET Web Forms application so that it supports ASP.NET MVC. You learned how you can mix ASP.NET MVC controllers and views with ASP.NET Web Forms pages.

Finally, you learned how the assemblies required by the ASP.NET MVC framework are bin deployable. You learned how you can deploy an ASP.NET MVC application to an Internet hosting provider that supports ASP.NET 3.5, but not ASP.NET MVC.

Working with Ajax

Ajax (Asynchronous JavaScript and XML) enables you to avoid requesting an entire HTML page every time you want to get new content from the web server. When you perform an Ajax request, you retrieve only the content that you need.

Ajax applications are better than normal applications because Ajax applications are more responsive. When you interact with an Ajax application, you spend less time starting at a loading page. You are not required to reload an entire page whenever you need to update any of the content displayed by the page.

In this chapter, you learn one approach to using Ajax within the context of an ASP.NET MVC application. You learn how to take advantage of the Ajax helpers to perform asynchronous requests against the web server.

Using the Ajax Helpers

Before you can use the Ajax helpers, you must first include two JavaScript libraries in your page: the MicrosoftAjax.js library and the MicrosoftMvcAjax.js library. Both of these libraries are included in the default Visual Studio ASP.NET MVC template within the Scripts folder.

WARNING

The JavaScript libraries must be included in the right order. Also, the libraries must be included before any Ajax helper method is called.

The Scripts folder includes two debug versions of these libraries named MicrosoftAjax.debug.js and MicrosoftMvcAjax.debug.js. When developing your application, you should use the debug versions of the libraries because the debug versions return more detailed error messages. However, in production, don't use the debug versions because these libraries are significantly larger (and take longer to download) than the release versions. For example, the MicrosoftAjax.debug.js library is 304KB while Microsoft the MicrosoftAjax.js is just 98KB.

If you plan to use Ajax in multiple pages within your application, you should consider including the two JavaScript libraries within a master page instead of including the libraries in individual views. That way, you need to include only the libraries once for your entire application. Furthermore, you can easily switch between the debug and release versions of the libraries by changing the libraries in one location within the master page.

> **NOTE**
>
> If you receive the JavaScript error message Sys Is Undefined or Type Is Undefined when attempting to use an Ajax helper, you have forgotten to include the JavaScript libraries.

Debugging Ajax

If something goes wrong on the server when you perform an Ajax request, you will never see the error message. When working with Ajax, you need to take advantage of a debugging tool that enables you to monitor the request and response traveling between the browser and server.

I use two tools to debug my Ajax applications. First, I use a free tool named Fiddler, which enables you to view the request and response traffic (see Figure 14.1). You can use Fiddler with any web browser including Internet Explorer and Firefox. Fiddler can be downloaded from the following location: www.fiddler2.com/fiddler2/.

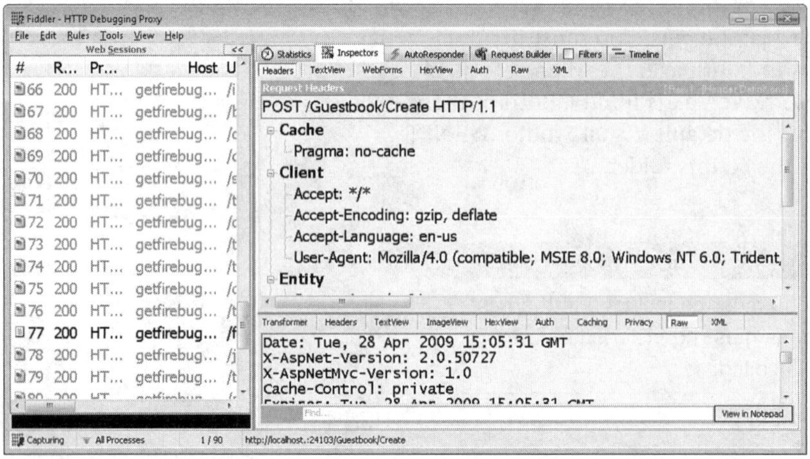

FIGURE 14.1   Using Fiddler to inspect traffic

NOTE

When using Fiddler to inspect requests made against localhost, you need to add a period in the browser address bar after localhost. For example, the following request will not be captured by Fiddler:

http://localhost:24103/Guestbook

The following request will be captured by Fiddler:

http://localhost.:24103/Guestbook

The other tool that I use extensively when debugging Ajax applications is Firebug. Because Firebug is a Firefox extension, it works only with the Firefox browser. You can download Firebug from the following location:

http://getfirebug.com/

NOTE

Firebug does much more than just displaying requests and responses. For example, Firebug enables you to inspect DOM elements and CSS rules.

Like Fiddler, you can use Firebug to inspect requests and responses. Firebug has a Net tab that enables you to inspect all traffic between the browser and the server. You also can pick the XHR subtab to filter the traffic to only Ajax requests and responses (see Figure 14.2). You can expand any result in the list to see the content of the request and response.

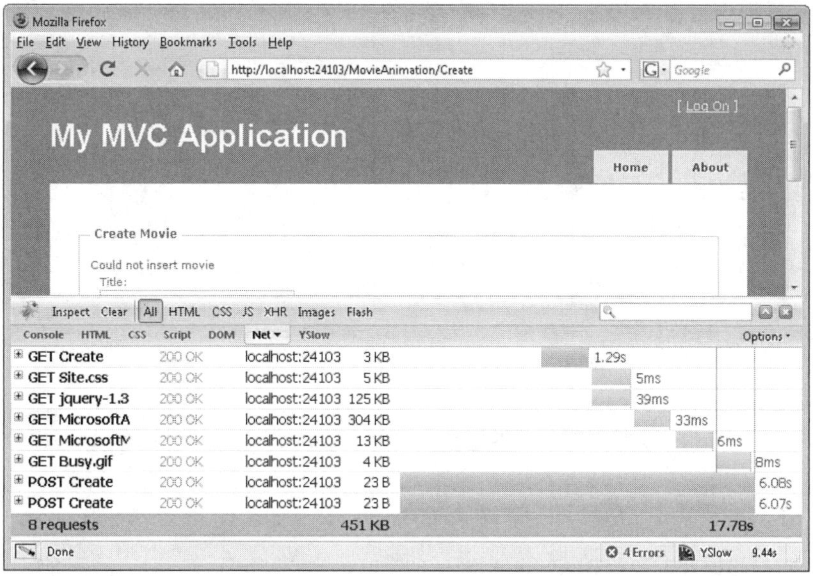

FIGURE 14.2   Using Firebug to inspect Ajax requests

Posting a Form Asynchronously

Normally, when you post an HTML form to the web server, you need to post the entire HTML page that contains the form. By taking advantage of the Ajax.BeginForm() helper, you can post a form asynchronously.

Imagine that you have created the controller in Listing 14.1. This controller has three actions named Index(), Create(), and Create(). The Index() action returns a view that displays a set of movies. The first Create() method displays a form for creating a new movie, and the second Create() method actually inserts the new movie into the database.

LISTING 14.1   Controllers\MovieController.cs (C#)

```csharp
using System.Linq;
using System.Web.Mvc;
using MvcApplication1.Models;

namespace MvcApplication1.Controllers
{
    public class MovieController : Controller
    {
        private MoviesDBEntities _entities = new MoviesDBEntities();

        // GET: /Movie/

        public ActionResult Index()
        {
            return View(_entities.MovieSet.ToList());
        }

        // GET: /Movie/Create

        public ActionResult Create()
        {
            return View();
        }

        // POST: /Movie/Create

        [AcceptVerbs(HttpVerbs.Post)]
        public string Create(Movie movieToCreate)
        {

            {
                _entities.AddToMovieSet(movieToCreate);
                _entities.SaveChanges();
```

```
            return "Inserted new movie " + movieToCreate.Title;
        }
        catch
        {
            return "Could not insert movie " + movieToCreate.Title;
        }
    }

}
}
```

LISTING 14.1   Controllers\MovieController.vb (VB)

```
Public Class MovieController
    Inherits Controller

    Private _entities As New MoviesDBEntities()

    ' GET: /Movie/

    Public Function Index() As ActionResult
        Return View(_entities.MovieSet.ToList())
    End Function

    ' GET: /Movie/Create

    Public Function Create() As ActionResult
        Return View()
    End Function

    ' POST: /Movie/Create

    <AcceptVerbs(HttpVerbs.Post)> _
    Public Function Create(ByVal movieToCreate As Movie) As String
        Try
            _entities.AddToMovieSet(movieToCreate)
            _entities.SaveChanges()
            Return "Inserted new movie " & movieToCreate.Title
        Catch
            Return "Could not insert movie " & movieToCreate.Title
        End Try
    End Function
End Class
```

Notice that the second `Create()` action returns a string. If the movie is successfully inserted into the database, a success message string is returned. Otherwise, a failure message string is returned.

You can add the `Create` view to your project in the normal way: Right-click the `Create()` action in the code editor and select the menu option Add View. In the Add View dialog, create a strongly typed `Create` view that creates a new movie (see Figure 14.3).

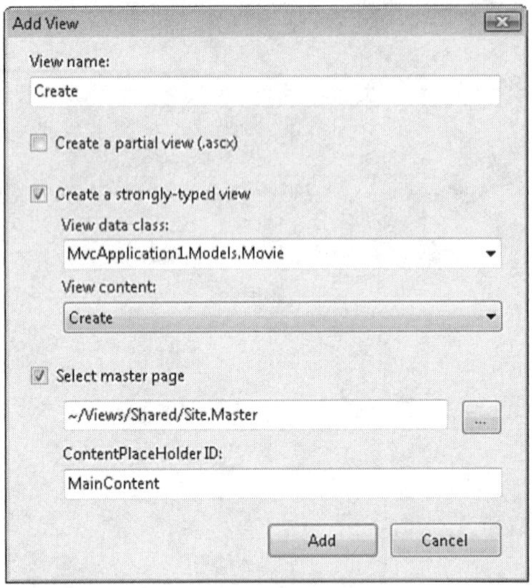

FIGURE 14.3   Adding the `Create` view

The `Create` view generated by Visual Studio does not perform an Ajax post of the form data. By default, a `Create` view performs a normal form post. You need to modify the view so that it looks like the view in Listing 14.2.

LISTING 14.2   Views\Movie\Create.aspx (C#)

```
<%@ Page Title="" Language="C#" MasterPageFile="~/Views/Shared/Site.Master"
➥Inherits="System.Web.Mvc.ViewPage<MvcApplication1.Models.Movie>" %>
<asp:Content ID="Content2" ContentPlaceHolderID="MainContent" runat="server">

    <script ssrc="../../Scripts/MicrosoftAjax.debug.js"
type="text/javascript"></script>
    <script src="../../Scripts/MicrosoftMvcAjax.debug.js"
type="text/javascript"></script>

    <script type="text/javascript">

        function createSuccess(context)
        {
```

```
            alert( context.get_data());
        }

    </script>

    <%= Html.ValidationSummary("Create was unsuccessful. Please correct the errors
➥and try again.") %>

    <% using (Ajax.BeginForm(new AjaxOptions {OnSuccess="createSuccess"}))
       {%>

        <fieldset>
            <legend>Create Movie</legend>
            <p>
                <label for="Title">Title:</label>
                <%= Html.TextBox("Title")%>
                <%= Html.ValidationMessage("Title", "*")%>
            </p>
            <p>
                <label for="Director">Director:</label>
                <%= Html.TextBox("Director")%>
                <%= Html.ValidationMessage("Director", "*")%>
            </p>
            <p>
                <label for="DateReleased">DateReleased:</label>
                <%= Html.TextBox("DateReleased")%>
                <%= Html.ValidationMessage("DateReleased", "*")%>
            </p>
            <p>
                <input type="submit" value="Create" />
            </p>
        </fieldset>

    <% } %>

    <div>
        <%=Html.ActionLink("Back to List", "Index") %>
    </div>

</asp:Content>
```

LISTING 14.2   Views\Movie\Create.aspx (VB)

```
<%@ Page Title="" Language="VB" MasterPageFile="~/Views/Shared/Site.Master"
➥Inherits="System.Web.Mvc.ViewPage(Of MvcApplication1.Movie)" %>
```

```
<asp:Content ID="Content2" ContentPlaceHolderID="MainContent" runat="server">

    <script src="../../Scripts/MicrosoftAjax.debug.js"
➥type="text/javascript"></script>
    <script src="../../Scripts/MicrosoftMvcAjax.debug.js"
➥type="text/javascript"></script>

    <script type="text/javascript">

        function createSuccess(context)
        {
            alert( context.get_data());
        }

    </script>

    <%= Html.ValidationSummary("Create was unsuccessful. Please correct the errors
➥and try again.") %>

    <% Using Ajax.BeginForm(New AjaxOptions With {.OnSuccess = "createSuccess"})%>

        <fieldset>
            <legend>Create Movie</legend>
            <p>
                <label for="Title">Title:</label>
                <%= Html.TextBox("Title")%>
                <%= Html.ValidationMessage("Title", "*")%>
            </p>
            <p>
                <label for="Director">Director:</label>
                <%= Html.TextBox("Director")%>
                <%= Html.ValidationMessage("Director", "*")%>
            </p>
            <p>
                <label for="DateReleased">DateReleased:</label>
                <%= Html.TextBox("DateReleased")%>
                <%= Html.ValidationMessage("DateReleased", "*")%>
            </p>
            <p>
                <input type="submit" value="Create" />
            </p>
        </fieldset>

    <% End Using%>

    <div>
```

```
    <%=Html.ActionLink("Back to List", "Index") %>
</div>

</asp:Content>
```

Notice that instead of calling `Html.BeginForm()`, the view in Listing 14.2 contains a call to `Ajax.BeginForm()`. Calling `Ajax.BeginForm()` performs an asynchronous post.

Notice, furthermore, that an instance of the `AjaxOptions` class is passed to the `Ajax.BeginForm()` helper method. The JavaScript `createSuccess()` method is called after the post is successful.

In Listing 14.2, the `createSuccess()` method displays whatever string that the `Create()` controller returns. If a new movie titled *Star Wars* is added to the database successfully, the message Inserted New Movie Star Wars appears (see Figure 14.4).

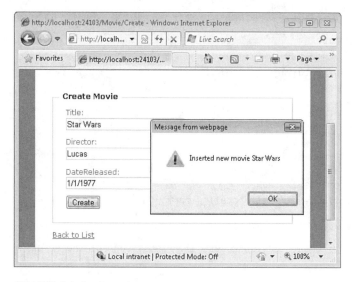

FIGURE 14.4   Inserting a new movie

Displaying Progress

Normally, when you post an HTML form to the server, the browser provides feedback on the progress of the post. The busy indicator spins, and you know that something is happening. When performing an Ajax post, in contrast, the browser does not provide any indication of progress.

When building Ajax applications, it is a good idea to provide some indicator of progress. Otherwise, a user might conclude that nothing is actually happening.

In this section, we explore two methods of displaying progress. You learn how to display a busy wait picture. You also learn how to display a jQuery animation during an Ajax post.

The `AjaxOptions` class includes a property named `LoadingElementId`. If you assign the name of an element in the page to this property, the `Ajax.BeginForm()` helper displays this element while performing an asynchronous post.

For example, the view in Listing 14.3 contains a DIV element with the Id divLoading. The divLoading element is assigned to the `LoadingElementId` property.

LISTING 14.3   Views\MovieProgress\Create.aspx (C#)

```
<%@ Page Title="" Language="C#" MasterPageFile="~/Views/Shared/Site.Master"
➥Inherits="System.Web.Mvc.ViewPage<MvcApplication1.Models.Movie>" %>
<asp:Content ID="Content2" ContentPlaceHolderID="MainContent" runat="server">

    <script src="../../Scripts/MicrosoftAjax.debug.js"
➥type="text/javascript"></script>
    <script src="../../Scripts/MicrosoftMvcAjax.debug.js"
➥type="text/javascript"></script>

    <script type="text/javascript">

        function createSuccess(context)
        {
            alert( context.get_data());
        }

    </script>

    <div id="divLoading" style="display:none">
        <image src="../Content/Busy.gif" alt="posting form" />
    </div>

    <%= Html.ValidationSummary("Create was unsuccessful. Please correct the errors
➥and try again.") %>

    <% using (Ajax.BeginForm(new AjaxOptions {OnSuccess="createSuccess",
➥LoadingElementId="divLoading"}))
        {%>

        <fieldset>
            <legend>Create Movie</legend>
            <p>
                <label for="Title">Title:</label>
                <%= Html.TextBox("Title")%>
                <%= Html.ValidationMessage("Title", "*")%>
            </p>
            <p>
```

```
            <label for="Director">Director:</label>
            <%= Html.TextBox("Director")%>
            <%= Html.ValidationMessage("Director", "*")%>
        </p>
        <p>
            <label for="DateReleased">DateReleased:</label>
            <%= Html.TextBox("DateReleased")%>
            <%= Html.ValidationMessage("DateReleased", "*")%>
        </p>
        <p>
            <input type="submit" value="Create" />
        </p>
    </fieldset>

<% } %>

<div>
    <%=Html.ActionLink("Back to List", "Index") %>
</div>

</asp:Content>
```

LISTING 14.3   Views\MovieProgress\Create.aspx (VB)

```
<%@ Page Title="" Language="VB" MasterPageFile="~/Views/Shared/Site.Master"
➥Inherits="System.Web.Mvc.ViewPage(Of MvcApplication1.Movie)" %>
<asp:Content ID="Content2" ContentPlaceHolderID="MainContent" runat="server">

    <script src="../../Scripts/MicrosoftAjax.debug.js"
➥type="text/javascript"></script>
    <script src="../../Scripts/MicrosoftMvcAjax.debug.js"
➥type="text/javascript"></script>

    <script type="text/javascript">

        function createSuccess(context)
        {
            alert( context.get_data());
        }

    </script>

    <div id="divLoading" style="display:none">
        <image src="../Content/Busy.gif" alt="posting form" />
    </div>
```

```
    <%= Html.ValidationSummary("Create was unsuccessful. Please correct the errors
➥and try again.") %>

    <% Using Ajax.BeginForm(New AjaxOptions With {.OnSuccess = "createSuccess",
➥.LoadingElementId = "divLoading"})%>

        <fieldset>
            <legend>Create Movie</legend>
            <p>
                <label for="Title">Title:</label>
                <%= Html.TextBox("Title")%>
                <%= Html.ValidationMessage("Title", "*")%>
            </p>
            <p>
                <label for="Director">Director:</label>
                <%= Html.TextBox("Director")%>
                <%= Html.ValidationMessage("Director", "*")%>
            </p>
            <p>
                <label for="DateReleased">DateReleased:</label>
                <%= Html.TextBox("DateReleased")%>
                <%= Html.ValidationMessage("DateReleased", "*")%>
            </p>
            <p>
                <input type="submit" value="Create" />
            </p>
        </fieldset>

    <% End Using%>

    <div>
        <%=Html.ActionLink("Back to List", "Index") %>
    </div>

</asp:Content>
```

The divLoading tag in Listing 14.3 contains an image that displays an animated progress indicator (see Figure 14.5). Notice that the element has a style property that hides the element by default. The element is displayed only during the asynchronous post.

NOTE

I downloaded the busy wait image from www.AjaxLoad.info.

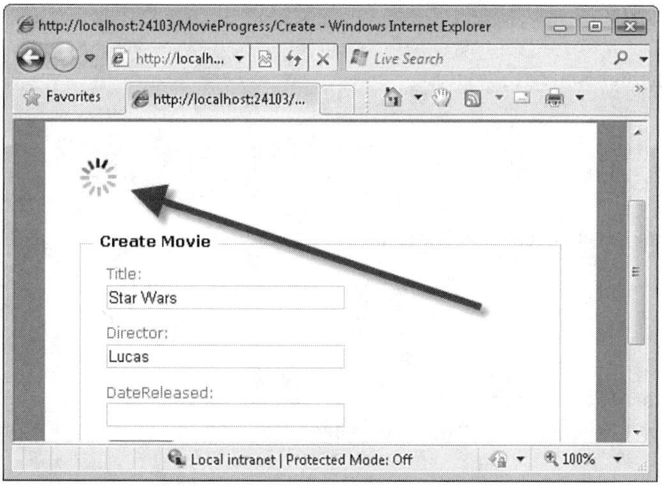

FIGURE 14.5   Showing a busy wait image

As an alternative to displaying a busy indicator during an Ajax post, you can display an animation. The AjaxOptions class includes an OnBegin and OnComplete property. You can use the OnBegin property to start the animation and the OnComplete property to end the animation.

For example, the view in Listing 14.4 displays a jQuery animation during an Ajax form post.

LISTING 14.4   Views\MovieAnimation\Create.aspx (C#)

```
<%@ Page Title="" Language="C#" MasterPageFile="~/Views/Shared/Site.Master"
➥Inherits="System.Web.Mvc.ViewPage<MvcApplication1.Models.Movie>" %>
<asp:Content ID="Content2" ContentPlaceHolderID="MainContent" runat="server">

    <script src="../../Scripts/jquery-1.3.2.js" type="text/javascript"></script>
    <script src="../../Scripts/MicrosoftAjax.debug.js"
➥type="text/javascript"></script>
    <script src="../../Scripts/MicrosoftMvcAjax.debug.js"
➥type="text/javascript"></script>

    <script type="text/javascript">

        function createBegin()
        {
            $("#movieForm").slideUp("slow");
        }
```

```
    function createComplete()
    {
        $("#movieForm").slideDown("slow");
    }

    function createSuccess(context)
    {
        $get("result").innerHTML = context.get_data();
    }

</script>

<div id="divLoading" style="display:none">
    <image src="../Content/Busy.gif" alt="posting form" />
</div>

<%= Html.ValidationSummary("Create was unsuccessful. Please correct the errors
➥and try again.") %>

<% using (Ajax.BeginForm(new AjaxOptions {OnSuccess="createSuccess",
➥OnBegin="createBegin", OnComplete="createComplete"}))
    {%>

    <fieldset id="movieForm">
        <legend>Create Movie</legend>
        <div id="result" style="color:red"></div>
        <p>
            <label for="Title">Title:</label>
            <%= Html.TextBox("Title")%>
            <%= Html.ValidationMessage("Title", "*")%>
        </p>
        <p>
            <label for="Director">Director:</label>
            <%= Html.TextBox("Director")%>
            <%= Html.ValidationMessage("Director", "*")%>
        </p>
        <p>
            <label for="DateReleased">DateReleased:</label>
            <%= Html.TextBox("DateReleased")%>
            <%= Html.ValidationMessage("DateReleased", "*")%>
        </p>
        <p>
            <input type="submit" value="Create" />
        </p>
    </fieldset>
```

```
    <% } %>

    <div>
        <%=Html.ActionLink("Back to List", "Index") %>
    </div>

</asp:Content>
```

LISTING 14.4   Views\MovieAnimation\Create.aspx (VB)

```
<%@ Page Title="" Language="VB" MasterPageFile="~/Views/Shared/Site.Master"
➡Inherits="System.Web.Mvc.ViewPage(Of MvcApplication1.Movie)" %>
<asp:Content ID="Content2" ContentPlaceHolderID="MainContent" runat="server">

    <script src="../../Scripts/jquery-1.3.2.js" type="text/javascript"></script>
    <script src="../../Scripts/MicrosoftAjax.debug.js"
➡type="text/javascript"></script>
    <script src="../../Scripts/MicrosoftMvcAjax.debug.js"
➡type="text/javascript"></script>

    <script type="text/javascript">

        function createBegin()
        {
            $("#movieForm").slideUp("slow");
        }

        function createComplete()
        {
            $("#movieForm").slideDown("slow");
        }

        function createSuccess(context)
        {
            $get("result").innerHTML = context.get_data();
        }

    </script>

    <div id="divLoading" style="display:none">
        <image src="../Content/Busy.gif" alt="posting form" />
    </div>

    <%= Html.ValidationSummary("Create was unsuccessful. Please correct the errors
➡and try again.") %>
```

```
<% Using Ajax.BeginForm(New AjaxOptions With {.OnSuccess = "createSuccess",
➥.OnBegin = "createBegin", .OnComplete = "createComplete"})%>

        <fieldset id="movieForm">
            <legend>Create Movie</legend>
            <div id="result" style="color:red"></div>
            <p>
                <label for="Title">Title:</label>
                <%= Html.TextBox("Title")%>
                <%= Html.ValidationMessage("Title", "*")%>
            </p>
            <p>
                <label for="Director">Director:</label>
                <%= Html.TextBox("Director")%>
                <%= Html.ValidationMessage("Director", "*")%>
            </p>
            <p>
                <label for="DateReleased">DateReleased:</label>
                <%= Html.TextBox("DateReleased")%>
                <%= Html.ValidationMessage("DateReleased", "*")%>
            </p>
            <p>
                <input type="submit" value="Create" />
            </p>
        </fieldset>

    <% End Using%>

    <div>
        <%=Html.ActionLink("Back to List", "Index") %>
    </div>

</asp:Content>
```

Notice that the view in Listing 14.4 includes the jQuery library. The jQuery library is
included in the Scripts folder in the default ASP.NET MVC Visual Studio template.

The OnBegin property points at a JavaScript method named createBegin(). This method
performs a jQuery slideUp animation on the movie form. The OnComplete property points
at a JavaScript method named createComplete(). This method returns the movie form to
its original state.

Updating Content After Posting

You can use the `UpdateTargetId` property to update page content after an Ajax post. For example, imagine that you create a simple guest book application, (Yes, I know that no one has created a guest book application since the late '90s—but we are pretending here.) When you enter a new name and message, you want the list of entries to be updated automatically (see Figure 14.6).

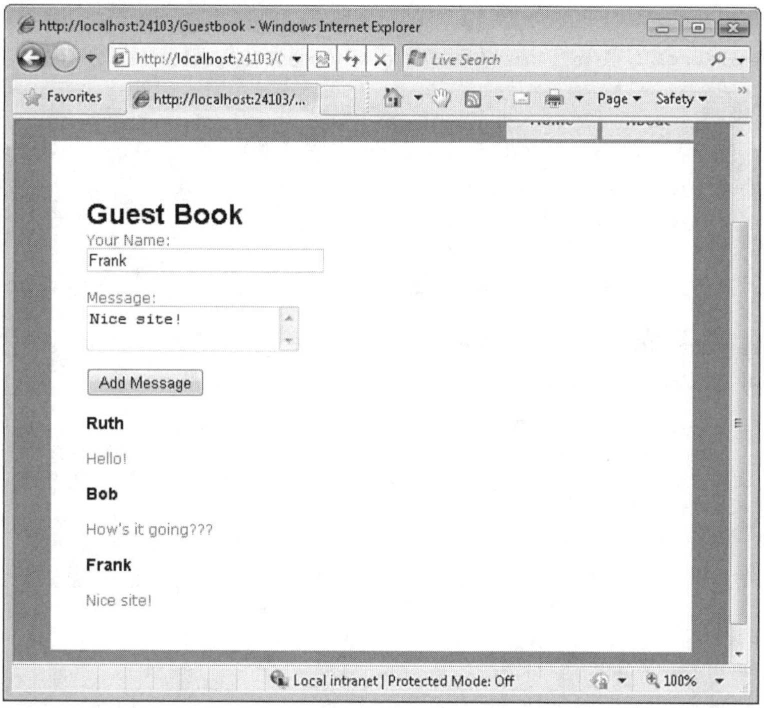

FIGURE 14.6   Updating content after an Ajax post

The view in Listing 14.5 uses the `Ajax.BeginForm()` helper to render a form that performs an Ajax post. Notice that the `AjaxOptions` include an `UpdateTargetId` property that is assigned the value `divMessages`. The divMessages DIV tag encircles a call to `Html.RenderPartial()` that renders the `Guests` partial.

LISTING 14.5   Views\GuestBook\Index.aspx (C#)

```
<%@ Page Title="" Language="C#" MasterPageFile="~/Views/Shared/Site.Master"
➥Inherits="System.Web.Mvc.ViewPage<IEnumerable<MvcApplication1.Models.Guest>>" %>
```

```
<asp:Content ID="Content2" ContentPlaceHolderID="MainContent" runat="server">

    <script src="../../Scripts/MicrosoftAjax.debug.js"
➥type="text/javascript"></script>
    <script src="../../Scripts/MicrosoftMvcAjax.debug.js"
➥type="text/javascript"></script>

    <h1>Guest Book</h1>

    <% using (Ajax.BeginForm("Create", new AjaxOptions {UpdateTargetId=
➥"divMessages" }))
       { %>

        <label for="Name">Your Name:</label>
        <br /><%= Html.TextBox("Name")%>

        <br /><br />

        <label for="Message">Message:</label>
        <br /><%= Html.TextArea("Message")%>

        <br /><br />

        <input type="submit" value="Add Message" />

    <% } %>

    <div id="divMessages">
        <% Html.RenderPartial("Guests"); %>
    </div>

</asp:Content>
```

LISTING 14.5   Views\GuestBook\Index.aspx (VB)

```
<%@ Page Title="" Language="VB" MasterPageFile="~/Views/Shared/Site.Master"
➥Inherits="System.Web.Mvc.ViewPage(Of IEnumerable (Of MvcApplication1.Guest))" %>
<asp:Content ID="Content2" ContentPlaceHolderID="MainContent" runat="server">

    <script src="../../Scripts/MicrosoftAjax.debug.js"
➥type="text/javascript"></script>
    <script src="../../Scripts/MicrosoftMvcAjax.debug.js"
➥type="text/javascript"></script>
```

```
<h1>Guest Book</h1>

<% Using Ajax.BeginForm("Create", New AjaxOptions With {.UpdateTargetId =
➥"divMessages"})%>

        <label for="Name">Your Name:</label>
        <br /><%= Html.TextBox("Name")%>

        <br /><br />

        <label for="Message">Message:</label>
        <br /><%= Html.TextArea("Message")%>

        <br /><br />

        <input type="submit" value="Add Message" />

    <% End Using%>

    <div id="divMessages">
        <% Html.RenderPartial("Guests")%>
    </div>

</asp:Content>
```

The Guests partial (see Listing 14.6) renders the list of messages. When you post a new message, then Ajax.BeginForm() helper updates the list of messages with the help of the Guests partial.

LISTING 14.6   Views\GuestBook\Guests.ascx (C#)

```
<%@ Control Language="C#" Inherits="System.Web.Mvc.ViewUserControl<IEnumerable
➥<MvcApplication1.Models.Guest>>" %>

<% foreach (var item in Model) { %>
    <div>
        <h3><%= Html.Encode(item.Name) %></h3>

        <%= Html.Encode(item.Message) %>
    </div>
<% } %>
```

LISTING 14.6   Views\GuestBook\Guests.ascx (VB)

```vb
<%@ Control Language="VB" Inherits="System.Web.Mvc.ViewUserControl(Of IEnumerable
➥(Of MvcApplication1.Guest))" %>
<%  For Each item In Model%>
    <div>
        <h3><%= Html.Encode(item.Name) %></h3>

        <%= Html.Encode(item.Message) %>
    </div>
<% Next%>
```

The controller used by the guest book application is contained in Listing 14.7. Notice that the `Create()` action returns a partial `view` result. The partial `view` result returns a fragment of HTML rendered with the help of the `Guests` partial.

LISTING 14.7   Controllers\GuestBookController.cs (C#)

```csharp
using System.Linq;
using System.Web.Mvc;
using MvcApplication1.Models;

namespace MvcApplication1.Controllers
{
    public class GuestBookController : Controller
    {
        private GuestBookDBEntities _entities = new GuestBookDBEntities();

        // GET: /GuestBook/

        public ActionResult Index()
        {
            return View(_entities.GuestSet.ToList());
        }
        // POST: /GuestBook/Create

        public ActionResult Create(Guest guestToCreate)
        {
            _entities.AddToGuestSet(guestToCreate);
            _entities.SaveChanges();

            return PartialView("Guests", _entities.GuestSet.ToList());
        }
    }
}
```

LISTING 14.7   Controllers\GuestBookController.vb (VB)

```vb
Public Class GuestBookController
    Inherits Controller

    Private _entities As New GuestBookDBEntities()

    ' GET: /GuestBook/

    Public Function Index() As ActionResult
        Return View(_entities.GuestSet.ToList())
    End Function

    ' POST: /GuestBook/Create

    Public Function Create(ByVal guestToCreate As Guest) As ActionResult
        _entities.AddToGuestSet(guestToCreate)
        _entities.SaveChanges()

        Return PartialView("Guests", _entities.GuestSet.ToList())
    End Function
End Class
```

Performing Validation

Normally, you need to validate form data when you submit the data to the server. For example, you might want to make a particular form field required and display an error message when the required field does not have a value. In this section, you learn how to display validation error messages when performing an Ajax post.

The view in Listing 14.8 contains a partial named GuestBook. This partial contains most of the content of the view including the HTML form and the list of guest book entries.

LISTING 14.8   Views\ServerValidate\Index.aspx (C#)

```aspx
<%@ Page Title="" Language="C#" MasterPageFile="~/Views/Shared/Site.Master"
➡Inherits="System.Web.Mvc.ViewPage<IEnumerable<MvcApplication1.Models.Guest>>" %>


<asp:Content ID="Content2" ContentPlaceHolderID="MainContent" runat="server">

    <script src="../../Scripts/MicrosoftAjax.debug.js"
➡type="text/javascript"></script>
    <script src="../../Scripts/MicrosoftMvcAjax.debug.js"
➡type="text/javascript"></script>
```

```
    <h1>Guest Book</h1>

    <% using (Ajax.BeginForm("Create", new AjaxOptions {UpdateTargetId=
➡"divMessages" }))
        { %>

        <div id="divMessages">
            <% Html.RenderPartial("GuestBook"); %>
        </div>

    <% } %>

</asp:Content>
```

LISTING 14.8   Views\ServerValidate\Index.aspx (VB)

```
<%@ Page Title="" Language="VB" MasterPageFile="~/Views/Shared/Site.Master"
➡Inherits="System.Web.Mvc.ViewPage(Of IEnumerable (Of MvcApplication1.Guest))" %>


<asp:Content ID="Content2" ContentPlaceHolderID="MainContent" runat="server">

    <script src="../../Scripts/MicrosoftAjax.debug.js"
➡type="text/javascript"></script>
    <script src="../../Scripts/MicrosoftMvcAjax.debug.js"
➡type="text/javascript"></script>

    <h1>Guest Book</h1>

    <% Using Ajax.BeginForm("Create", New AjaxOptions With
➡{.UpdateTargetId="divMessages" }) %>

        <div id="divMessages">
            <% Html.RenderPartial("GuestBook") %>
        </div>

    <% End Using %>

</asp:Content>
```

The GuestBook partial is contained in Listing 14.9. Notice that it contains calls to the server-side Html.ValidateMessage() helper method. This method renders a validation error message on the server side.

LISTING 14.9   Views\ServerValidate\GuestBook.ascx (C#)

```
<%@ Control Language="C#" Inherits="System.Web.Mvc.ViewUserControl<IEnumerable
➥<MvcApplication1.Models.Guest>>" %>


<label for="Name">Your Name:</label>
<br /><%= Html.TextBox("Name")%>
<%= Html.ValidationMessage("Name") %>

<br /><br />

<label for="Message">Message:</label>
<br /><%= Html.TextArea("Message")%>
<%= Html.ValidationMessage("Message") %>

<br /><br />

<input type="submit" value="Add Message" />

<hr />

<% foreach (var item in Model) { %>
    <div>
        <h3><%= Html.Encode(item.Name) %></h3>

        <%= Html.Encode(item.Message) %>
    </div>
<% } %>
```

LISTING 14.9   Views\ServerValidate\GuestBook.ascx (VB)

```
<%@ Control Language="VB"  Inherits="System.Web.Mvc.ViewUserControl(Of IEnumerable
➥(Of MvcApplication1.Guest))" %>
<label for="Name">Your Name:</label>
<br /><%= Html.TextBox("Name")%>
<%= Html.ValidationMessage("Name") %>

<br /><br />

<label for="Message">Message:</label>
<br /><%= Html.TextArea("Message")%>
<%= Html.ValidationMessage("Message") %>
```

```
<br /><br />

<input type="submit" value="Add Message" />

<hr />

<% For Each item In Model%>
    <div>
        <h3><%= Html.Encode(item.Name) %></h3>

        <%= Html.Encode(item.Message) %>
    </div>
<% Next%>
```

The controller used by this modified guest book application is contained in Listing 14.10. The Create() action returns the GuestBook partial.

LISTING 14.10   Controllers\ServerValidateController.cs (C#)

```
using System.Linq;
using System.Web.Mvc;
using MvcApplication1.Models;

namespace MvcApplication1.Controllers
{
    public class ServerValidateController : Controller
    {
        private GuestBookDBEntities _entities = new GuestBookDBEntities();

        // GET: /GuestBook/

        public ActionResult Index()
        {
            return View(_entities.GuestSet.ToList());
        }

        // POST: /GuestBook/Create

        public ActionResult Create([Bind(Exclude="Id")]Guest guestToCreate)
        {
            if (guestToCreate.Name.Trim().Length == 0)
                ModelState.AddModelError("Name", "Name is required.");
            if (guestToCreate.Message.Trim().Length == 0)
                ModelState.AddModelError("Message", "Message is required.");
```

```
        if (ModelState.IsValid)
        {
            _entities.AddToGuestSet(guestToCreate);
            _entities.SaveChanges();
        }

        return PartialView("GuestBook", _entities.GuestSet.ToList());
    }
  }
}
```

LISTING 14.10   Controllers\ServerValidateController.vb (VB)

```
Public Class ServerValidateController
    Inherits Controller

    Private _entities As New GuestBookDBEntities()

    ' GET: /GuestBook/

    Public Function Index() As ActionResult
        Return View(_entities.GuestSet.ToList())
    End Function
    ' POST: /GuestBook/Create

    Public Function Create(<Bind(Exclude:="Id")> ByVal guestToCreate As Guest) As
➥ActionResult
        If guestToCreate.Name.Trim().Length = 0 Then
            ModelState.AddModelError("Name", "Name is required.")
        End If
        If guestToCreate.Message.Trim().Length = 0 Then
            ModelState.AddModelError("Message", "Message is required.")
        End If

        If ModelState.IsValid Then
            _entities.AddToGuestSet(guestToCreate)
            _entities.SaveChanges()
        End If

        Return PartialView("GuestBook", _entities.GuestSet.ToList())
    End Function
End Class
```

If there are validation errors, the error messages will be rendered by the `Html.ValidateMessage()` helper within the `GuestBook` partial. Because the contents of the HTML form are updated when performing a form post, any validation messages will appear after the form post (see Figure 14.7).

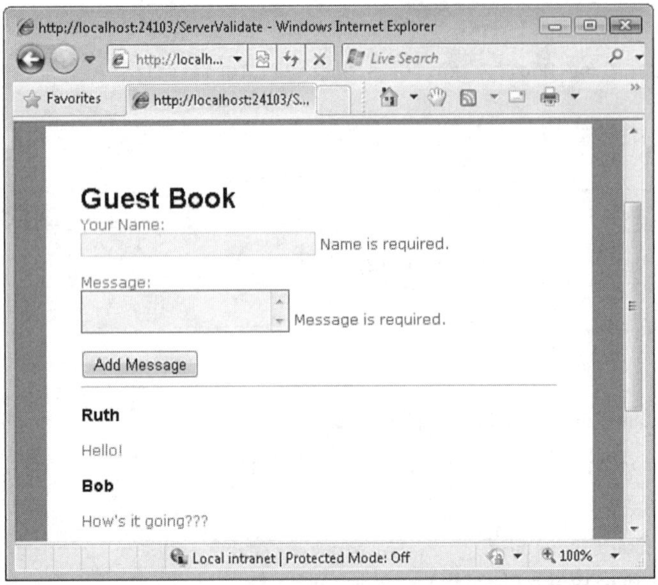

FIGURE 14.7 Server-side validation after an Ajax post

NOTE

The disadvantage of server-side validation is that the entire form must be passed across the wire every time that you do an Ajax form post. If you want to avoid transmitting this big chunk of HTML, you can use client-side validation. We discuss client-side validation in Chapter 15, "Using jQuery."

Providing Downlevel Browser Support

By taking advantage of Ajax, you can create a web application that provides a better user experience. However, what happens when someone attempts to use your application with a browser that does not support JavaScript?

You can design your application so that it works with both JavaScript enabled and JavaScript disabled. In other words, you can provide both an uplevel and downlevel user experience.

The controller in Listing 14.11 contains a `Create()` action that works with both uplevel and downlevel browsers. When the `Create()` action is invoked by a downlevel browser, an entire `view` is returned to the browser. When the `Create()` action is invoked by an uplevel browser, a partial `view` is returned.

LISTING 14.11   Controllers\DownlevelController.cs (C#)

```csharp
using System.Linq;
using System.Web.Mvc;
using MvcApplication1.Models;

namespace MvcApplication1.Controllers
{
    public class DownlevelController : Controller
    {
        private GuestBookDBEntities _entities = new GuestBookDBEntities();

        public ActionResult Index()
        {
            return View(_entities.GuestSet.ToList());
        }

        public ActionResult Create([Bind(Exclude = "Id")]Guest guestToCreate)
        {
            // validation
            if (guestToCreate.Name.Trim().Length == 0)
                ModelState.AddModelError("Name", "Name is required.");
            if (guestToCreate.Message.Trim().Length == 0)
                ModelState.AddModelError("Message", "Message is required.");

            if (ModelState.IsValid)
            {
                _entities.AddToGuestSet(guestToCreate);
                _entities.SaveChanges();
            }

            if (Request.IsAjaxRequest())
                return PartialView("GuestBook", _entities.GuestSet.ToList());

            return View("Index", _entities.GuestSet.ToList());
        }

    }
}
```

LISTING 14.11   Controllers\DownlevelController.vb (VB)

```vb
Public Class DownlevelController
    Inherits Controller
```

```
    Private _entities As New GuestBookDBEntities()

    Public Function Index() As ActionResult
        Return View(_entities.GuestSet.ToList())
    End Function

    Public Function Create(<Bind(Exclude:="Id")> ByVal guestToCreate As Guest)
➥As ActionResult
        ' validation
        If guestToCreate.Name.Trim().Length = 0 Then
            ModelState.AddModelError("Name", "Name is required.")
        End If
        If guestToCreate.Message.Trim().Length = 0 Then
            ModelState.AddModelError("Message", "Message is required.")
        End If

        If ModelState.IsValid Then
            _entities.AddToGuestSet(guestToCreate)
            _entities.SaveChanges()
        End If

        If Request.IsAjaxRequest() Then
            Return PartialView("GuestBook", _entities.GuestSet.ToList())
        End If

        Return View("Index", _entities.GuestSet.ToList())
    End Function

End Class
```

The Create() action uses the IsAjaxRequest() method to determine whether the action is invoked within the context of an Ajax request. If the IsAjaxRequest() method returns true, the partial view is returned. Otherwise, the full view is returned.

The easiest way to verify that the controller works with both downlevel and uplevel browsers is to turn off JavaScript in your browser. For example, you can disable JavaScript in Firefox by selecting the menu option Tools, Options and selecting the Content tab (see Figure 14.8).

Retrieving Content Asynchronously

The second Ajax helper included in the ASP.NET MVC framework is the Ajax.ActionLink() helper. This helper enables you to render a link that retrieves content from the web server asynchronously.

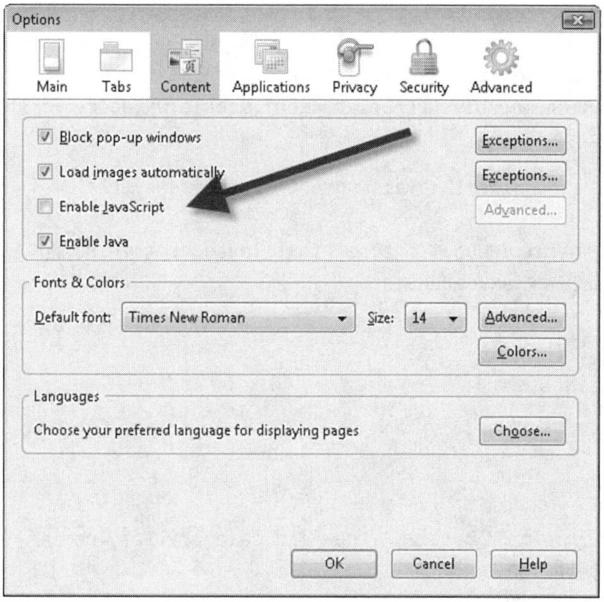

FIGURE 14.8   Disabling JavaScript in Firefox

The `Ajax.ActionLink()` helper is valuable when you want to create master/detail pages and you don't want to rerender the entire page every time someone selects a master record. You can use the `Ajax.ActionLink()` to limit the update to the details section only, and not the entire page, when you click a link.

For example, the `view` in Listing 14.12 displays a master/detail page that lists product categories and matching products (see Figure 14.9). When you click a category, the list of matching products is retrieved from the server through an Ajax request.

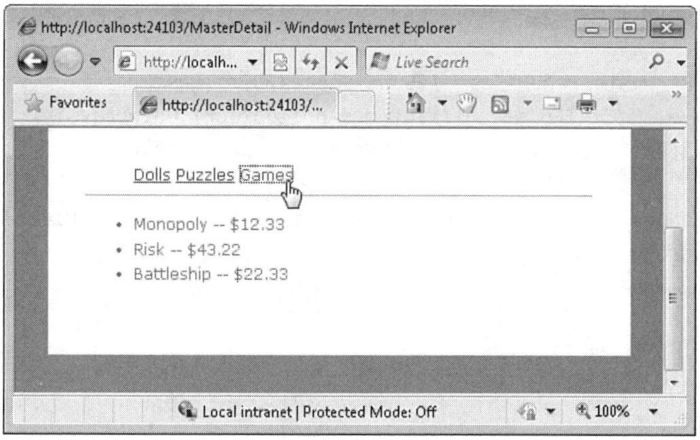

FIGURE 14.9   Displaying a master/detail page

LISTING 14.12   Views\MasterDetail\Index.aspx (C#)

```
<%@ Page Title="" Language="C#" MasterPageFile="~/Views/Shared/Site.Master"
➥Inherits="System.Web.Mvc.ViewPage<IEnumerable<MvcApplication1.Models.Category>>" %>


<asp:Content ID="Content2" ContentPlaceHolderID="MainContent" runat="server">

<script src="../../Scripts/MicrosoftAjax.debug.js" type="text/javascript"></script>
<script src="../../Scripts/MicrosoftMvcAjax.debug.js"
➥type="text/javascript"></script>

<ul style="display:inline">
<% foreach (var category in Model)
    { %>

    <li style="display:inline">
        <%= Ajax.ActionLink(category.Name, "Details", new {id=category.Id}, new
➥AjaxOptions {UpdateTargetId="divDetails"}) %>
    </li>

<% } %>
</ul>

<hr />

<div id="divDetails"></div>

</asp:Content>
```

LISTING 14.12   Views\MasterDetail\Index.aspx (VB)

```
<%@ Page Title="" Language="VB" MasterPageFile="~/Views/Shared/Site.Master"
➥Inherits="System.Web.Mvc.ViewPage(Of IEnumerable (Of MvcApplication1.Category))" %>
<asp:Content ID="Content2" ContentPlaceHolderID="MainContent" runat="server">

<script src="../../Scripts/MicrosoftAjax.debug.js" type="text/javascript"></script>
<script src="../../Scripts/MicrosoftMvcAjax.debug.js"
➥type="text/javascript"></script>

<ul style="display:inline">
<%  For Each category In Model%>

    <li style="display:inline">
```

```
        <%=Ajax.ActionLink(category.Name, "Details", New With {.id = category.Id},
➡New AjaxOptions With {.UpdateTargetId = "divDetails"})%>
    </li>

<% Next%>
</ul>

<hr />

<div id="divDetails"></div>

</asp:Content>
```

Notice the call to the Ajax.ActionLink() helper. Three parameters are passed to the helper: the link text, the action to invoke, and AjaxOptions. The UpdateTargetId property of the AjaxOptions class specifies the HTML element to update with the results of the Ajax request.

The master detail page uses the controller in Listing 14.13. This controller has two actions. The Index() action is invoked when the page is first requested. The Details() action is invoked when you click a category link rendered by the Ajax.ActionLink() helper. The Details() action is invoked only within the context of an Ajax request.

LISTING 14.13   Controllers\MasterDetailController.cs (C#)

```csharp
using System.Collections.Generic;
using System.Linq;
using System.Web.Mvc;
using MvcApplication1.Models;

namespace MvcApplication1.Controllers
{

    public class MasterDetailController : Controller
    {
        private ProductsDBEntities _entities = new ProductsDBEntities();

        public ActionResult Index()
        {
            return View(_entities.CategorySet.ToList());
        }

        public ActionResult Details(int id)
        {
```

```
                var products = from p in _entities.ProductSet
                            where p.CategoryId == id
                            select p;
                return PartialView("Details", products);
            }

    }
}
```

LISTING 14.13   Controllers\MasterDetailController.vb (VB)

```vb
Public Class MasterDetailController
    Inherits Controller

    Private _entities As New ProductsDBEntities()

    Public Function Index() As ActionResult
        Return View(_entities.CategorySet.ToList())
    End Function

    Public Function Details(ByVal id As Integer) As ActionResult
        Dim products = From p In _entities.ProductSet _
                        Where p.CategoryId = id _
                        Select p
        Return PartialView("Details", products)
    End Function

End Class
```

Notice that the Details() action returns a partial view result named Details. The Details partial is contained in Listing 14.14. This partial renders a set of products in a bulleted list.

LISTING 14.14   Views\MasterDetail\Details.ascx (C#)

```
<%@ Control Language="C#" Inherits="System.Web.Mvc.ViewUserControl<IEnumerable
➥<MvcApplication1.Models.Product>>" %>


<ul>
<% foreach (var product in Model)
    { %>

    <li>
        <%= product.Name %> -- <%= product.Price.ToString("c") %>
```

```
    </li>

<% } %>
</ul>
```

LISTING 14.14   Views\MasterDetail\Details.ascx (VB)

```
<%@ Control Language="VB" Inherits="System.Web.Mvc.ViewUserControl(Of IEnumerable
➡(Of MvcApplication1.Product))" %>

<ul>
<% For Each product In Model%>

    <li>
        <%= product.Name %> -- <%= product.Price.ToString("c") %>
    </li>

<% Next%>
</ul>
```

Highlighting the Selected Link

Typically, when you select a link in a master/detail page, you want to highlight the link
selected. For example, if you click a category to view a list of matching products, you want
to highlight the selected category (see Figure 14.10).

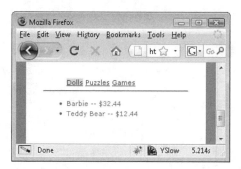

FIGURE 14.10   Highlighting the selected link

The easiest way to highlight a link is to use jQuery. The Index view in Listing 14.15
changes the background color of the selected link to yellow.

NOTE

We discuss jQuery in detail in the next chapter.

LISTING 14.15   Views\Selected\Index.aspx (C#)

```
<%@ Page Title="" Language="C#" MasterPageFile="~/Views/Shared/Site.Master"
➥Inherits="System.Web.Mvc.ViewPage<IEnumerable<MvcApplication1.Models.Category>>" %>

<asp:Content ID="Content2" ContentPlaceHolderID="MainContent" runat="server">

<script src="../../Scripts/jquery-1.3.2.js" type="text/javascript"></script>
<script src="../../Scripts/MicrosoftAjax.debug.js" type="text/javascript"></script>
<script src="../../Scripts/MicrosoftMvcAjax.debug.js"
➥type="text/javascript"></script>

<script type="text/javascript">

    $(pageReady);

    function pageReady()
    {
        $("#categories a").click( selectLink );
    }

    function selectLink()
    {
        $("#categories a.selected").removeClass("selected");
        $(this).addClass("selected");
    }


</script>

<ul id="categories" style="display:inline">
<% foreach (var category in Model)
    { %>

    <li style="display:inline">
        <%= Ajax.ActionLink(category.Name, "Details", new {id=category.Id}, new
➥AjaxOptions {UpdateTargetId="divDetails"}) %>
    </li>

<% } %>
</ul>
```

```
<hr />

<div id="divDetails"></div>

</asp:Content>
```

LISTING 14.15   Views\Selected\Index.aspx (VB)

```
<%@ Page Title="" Language="VB" MasterPageFile="~/Views/Shared/Site.Master"
➥Inherits="System.Web.Mvc.ViewPage(Of IEnumerable (OfMvcApplication1.Category))" %>
<asp:Content ID="Content2" ContentPlaceHolderID="MainContent" runat="server">

<script src="../../Scripts/jquery-1.3.2.js" type="text/javascript"></script>
<script src="../../Scripts/MicrosoftAjax.debug.js" type="text/javascript"></script>
<script src="../../Scripts/MicrosoftMvcAjax.debug.js"
➥type="text/javascript"></script>

<script type="text/javascript">

    $(pageReady);

    function pageReady()
    {
        $("#categories a").click( selectLink );
    }

    function selectLink()
    {
        $("#categories a.selected").removeClass("selected");
        $(this).addClass("selected");
    }


</script>
<ul id="categories" style="display:inline">
<%  For Each category In Model%>
    <li style="display:inline">
        <%=Ajax.ActionLink(category.Name, "Details", New With {.id = category.Id},
➥New AjaxOptions With {.UpdateTargetId = "divDetails"})%>
    </li>

<% Next%>
</ul>
```

```
<hr />

<div id="divDetails"></div>

</asp:Content>
```

The `pageReady()` JavaScript function is called after the HTML page is ready (after the DOM is loaded). The `pageReady` function associates a click handler with each of the category links. When you click a category link, the `selectLink()` method is called.

The `selectLink()` method returns a CSS class named *selected* from the currently selected category link. Next, the method adds the selected class to the link that was clicked.

The selected CSS class is defined in the Site.css file like this:

```
.selected {background-color:yellow;}
```

Creating a Delete Link

You also can use the `Ajax.ActionLink()` helper to render a delete link. Even better, you can use the `Ajax.ActionLink()` to render a delete link that performs a proper HTTP `DELETE`.

The HTTP protocol supports the following HTTP operations:

▶ `OPTIONS`—Returns information about the communication options available (idempotent)

▶ `GET`—Returns whatever information is identified by the request (idempotent)

▶ `HEAD`—Performs the same operation as `GET` without returning the message body (idempotent)

▶ `POST`—Posts new information or updates existing information (not idempotent)

▶ `PUT`—Posts new information or updates existing information (idempotent)

▶ `DELETE`—Deletes information (idempotent)

▶ `TRACE`—Performs a message loop back (idempotent)

▶ `CONNECT`—Used for SSL tunneling

These operations are defined as part of the HTTP 1.1 standard that you can read about at www.w3.org/Protocols/rfc2616/rfc2616-sec9.html.

HTML supports only `GET` and `POST` operations. When you click a link, you perform a `GET` operation against the web server and when you submit an HTML form, you can perform either a `GET` or a `POST` operation. The other HTTP operations are not supported.

If you want to perform an HTTP operation other than a `GET` or `POST`, you need to use JavaScript. One easy way to generate the necessary JavaScript is to use an `Ajax.ActionLink()` helper.

For example, for security reasons, you should not perform an HTTP GET when you click a delete link. If you allow a GET operation to result in the deletion of a record from your website, you open your website to cross-site scripting attacks.

The controller in Listing 14.16 exposes three Delete() actions. This first Delete() action can be invoked only in the context of an HTTP DELETE operation.

LISTING 14.16   Controllers\DeleteController.cs (C#)

```csharp
using System.Linq;
using System.Web.Mvc;
using MvcApplication1.Models;

namespace MvcApplication1.Controllers
{
    public class DeleteController : Controller
    {
        private MoviesDBEntities _entities = new MoviesDBEntities();

        public ActionResult Index()
        {
            return View(_entities.MovieSet.ToList());
        }

        [AcceptVerbs(HttpVerbs.Delete)]
        public ActionResult Delete(int id)
        {
            var movieToDelete = (from m in _entities.MovieSet
                                 where m.Id == id
                                 select m).FirstOrDefault();
            _entities.DeleteObject(movieToDelete);
            _entities.SaveChanges();
            return PartialView("Movies", _entities.MovieSet.ToList());
        }

        [ActionName("Delete")]
        public ActionResult Delete_GET(int id)
        {
            var movieToDelete = (from m in _entities.MovieSet
                                 where m.Id == id
                                 select m).FirstOrDefault();
            return View(movieToDelete);
        }

        [AcceptVerbs(HttpVerbs.Post)]
        [ActionName("Delete")]
```

```
        public ActionResult Delete_POST(int id)
        {
            var movieToDelete = (from m in _entities.MovieSet
                                     where m.Id == id
                                     select m).FirstOrDefault();
            _entities.DeleteObject(movieToDelete);
            _entities.SaveChanges();
            return RedirectToAction("Index");
        }

    }
}
```

LISTING 14.16   Controllers\DeleteController.vb (VB)

```
Public Class DeleteController
    Inherits Controller

    Private _entities As New MoviesDBEntities()

    Public Function Index() As ActionResult
        Return View(_entities.MovieSet.ToList())
    End Function

    <AcceptVerbs(HttpVerbs.Delete)> _
    Public Function Delete(ByVal id As Integer) As ActionResult
        Dim movieToDelete = (From m In _entities.MovieSet _
                                Where m.Id = id _
                                Select m).FirstOrDefault()
        _entities.DeleteObject(movieToDelete)
        _entities.SaveChanges()
        Return PartialView("Movies", _entities.MovieSet.ToList())
    End Function

    <ActionName("Delete")> _
    Public Function Delete_GET(ByVal id As Integer) As ActionResult
        Dim movieToDelete = (From m In _entities.MovieSet _
                                Where m.Id = id _
                                Select m).FirstOrDefault()
        Return View(movieToDelete)
    End Function

    <AcceptVerbs(HttpVerbs.Post), ActionName("Delete")> _
    Public Function Delete_POST(ByVal id As Integer) As ActionResult
        Dim movieToDelete = (From m In _entities.MovieSet _
```

```
                          Where m.Id = id _
                          Select m).FirstOrDefault()
        _entities.DeleteObject(movieToDelete)
        _entities.SaveChanges()
        Return RedirectToAction("Index")
    End Function

End Class
```

NOTE

The Delete_GET() and Delete_POST() actions provide downlevel browser support. If
a browser does not support JavaScript, the DELETE_GET() action displays a delete
confirmation form. When you submit the delete confirmation form to the
Delete_POST() action, the corresponding movie record is deleted. The downlevel
Delete() actions are also immune from cross-site scripting attacks because they
require an HTTP POST operation.

The view returned by the Index() action is contained in Listing 14.17. Nothing much
happens within this view. The view simply renders the partial contained in Listing 14.18.

LISTING 14.17   Views\Delete\Index.aspx (C#)

```
<%@ Page Title="" Language="C#" MasterPageFile="~/Views/Shared/Site.Master"
➡Inherits="System.Web.Mvc.ViewPage<IEnumerable<MvcApplication1.Models.Movie>>" %>


<asp:Content ID="Content2" ContentPlaceHolderID="MainContent" runat="server">

    <script src="../../Scripts/MicrosoftAjax.debug.js"
➡type="text/javascript"></script>
    <script src="../../Scripts/MicrosoftMvcAjax.debug.js"
➡type="text/javascript"></script>

    <h2>Movies</h2>

    <div id="divMovies">
        <% Html.RenderPartial("Movies"); %>
    </div>

</asp:Content>
```

LISTING 14.17   Views\Delete\Index.aspx (VB)

```
<%@ Page Title="" Language="VB" MasterPageFile="~/Views/Shared/Site.Master"
➥Inherits="System.Web.Mvc.ViewPage(Of IEnumerable (Of MvcApplication1.Movie))" %>


<asp:Content ID="Content2" ContentPlaceHolderID="MainContent" runat="server">

    <script src="../../Scripts/MicrosoftAjax.debug.js"
➥type="text/javascript"></script>
    <script src="../../Scripts/MicrosoftMvcAjax.debug.js"
➥type="text/javascript"></script>

    <h2>Movies</h2>

    <div id="divMovies">
        <% Html.RenderPartial("Movies")%>
    </div>

</asp:Content>
```

LISTING 14.18   Views\Delete\Movies.ascx (C#)

```
<%@ Control Language="C#" Inherits="System.Web.Mvc.ViewUserControl<IEnumerable
➥<MvcApplication1.Models.Movie>>" %>


<ul>
    <% foreach (var movie in Model)
        { %>

        <li>
            <%= movie.Title %>
            <%= Ajax.ActionLink("Delete", "Delete", new {id=movie.Id},
➥new AjaxOptions {HttpMethod="DELETE", Confirm="Delete record?",
➥UpdateTargetId="divMovies" })%>
        </li>

    <% } %>

</ul>
```

LISTING 14.18   Views\Delete\Movies.ascx (VB)

```
<%@ Control Language="VB" Inherits="System.Web.Mvc.ViewUserControl(Of IEnumerable
➥(Of MvcApplication1.Movie))" %>
```

```
<ul>
    <% For Each movie In Model%>

        <li>
            <%= movie.Title %>
            <%=Ajax.ActionLink("Delete", "Delete", New With {.id = movie.Id},New
➥AjaxOptions With {.HttpMethod = "DELETE", .Confirm = "Delete record?",
➥.UpdateTargetId = "divMovies"})%>
        </li>

    <% Next%>

</ul>
```

The Ajax.ActionLink(), in Listing 14.18, displays a delete link next to each movie record (see Figure 14.11). This helper method has five parameters: the link text, the action, the route values, the AjaxOptions, and the UpdateTargetId.

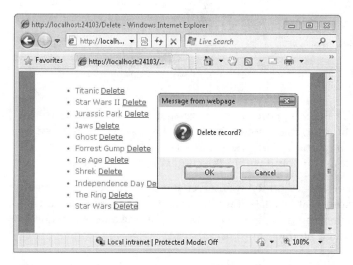

FIGURE 14.11   Displaying a delete confirmation

The AjaxOptions specifies the type of HTTP operation to perform when you click the link. The Ajax.ActionLink() in Listing 14.18 performs an HTTP DELETE operation.

The AjaxOptions includes a Confirm property. When you assign a string value to the Confirm property, clicking the link pops up a JavaScript confirmation dialog (see Figure 14.11).

Providing Downlevel Browser Support

The Ajax.ActionLink() helper is compatible with both uplevel and downlevel browsers. When you click on the link rendered by the Ajax.ActionLink() helper, an uplevel browser—a browser that supports JavaScript—performs an Ajax request. A downlevel browser—a browser that does not support JavaScript or that has JavaScript disabled—performs a normal request.

For example, you can use the Ajax.ActionLink() helper to create a master/detail page that works with both downlevel and uplevel browsers (see Figure 14.12).

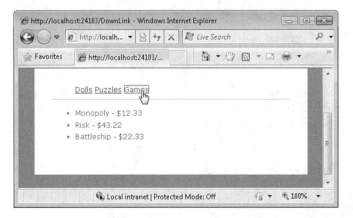

FIGURE 14.12   A master/detail form that works for both uplevel and downlevel browsers

The Details() action in Listing 14.19 supports both uplevel and downlevel browsers. When invoked by an uplevel browser, the action returns a partial view. When invoked by a downlevel browser, the action returns a normal view. The IsAjaxRequest() method is used to detect whether the action is invoked within the context of an Ajax request.

Notice that less work must be performed on the web server and database server during an Ajax request. Notice, furthermore, that less data must be pushed across the wire. During an Ajax request, only the matching products must be retrieved. During a normal request, in context, both the categories and products must be retrieved.

LISTING 14.19   Controllers\DownLinkController.cs (C#)

```csharp
using System.Collections.Generic;
using System.Linq;
using System.Web.Mvc;
using MvcApplication1.Models;

namespace MvcApplication1.Controllers
{
```

```
public class ProductsVDM
{
    public ProductsVDM(IEnumerable<Category> categories, IEnumerable<Product>
➥products)
    {
        this.Categories = categories;
        this.Products = products;
    }

    public IEnumerable<Category> Categories { get; set; }
    public IEnumerable<Product> Products { get; set; }
}

public class DownLinkController : Controller
{
    private ProductsDBEntities _entities = new ProductsDBEntities();

    public ActionResult Index()
    {
        var categories = _entities.CategorySet.ToList();
        var products = new List<Product>();
        return View(new ProductsVDM(categories, products));
    }

    public ActionResult Details(int id)
    {
        var products = from p in _entities.ProductSet
                       where p.CategoryId == id
                       select p;

        if (Request.IsAjaxRequest())
        {
            return PartialView("Details", products);
        }
        else
        {
            var categories = _entities.CategorySet.ToList();
            return View("Index", new ProductsVDM(categories, products));
        }

    }

}
}
```

LISTING 14.19   Controllers\DownLinkController.vb (VB)

```vb
Public Class ProductsVDM


    Private _categories As IEnumerable(Of Category)
    Private _products As IEnumerable(Of Product)

    Public Sub New(ByVal categories As IEnumerable(Of Category), ByVal products As
➡IEnumerable(Of Product))
        _categories = categories
        _products = products
    End Sub

    Public ReadOnly Property Categories() As IEnumerable(Of Category)
        Get
            Return _categories
        End Get
    End Property

    Public ReadOnly Property Products() As IEnumerable(Of Product)
        Get
            Return _products
        End Get
    End Property
End Class

Public Class DownLinkController
    Inherits Controller

    Private _entities As New ProductsDBEntities()

    Public Function Index() As ActionResult
        Dim categories = _entities.CategorySet.ToList()
        Dim products = New List(Of Product)()
        Return View(New ProductsVDM(categories, products))
    End Function

    Public Function Details(ByVal id As Integer) As ActionResult
        Dim products = From p In _entities.ProductSet _
                       Where p.CategoryId = id _
                       Select p

        If Request.IsAjaxRequest() Then
            Return PartialView("Details", products)
```

```
        Else
            Dim categories = _entities.CategorySet.ToList()
            Return View("Index", New ProductsVDM(categories, products))
        End If

    End Function

End Class
```

The Index() action returns the view in Listing 14.20. This view displays the list of categories and calls the Html.RenderPartial() helper method to display the list of products.

LISTING 14.20   Views\DownLink\Index.aspx (C#)

```
<%@ Page Title="" Language="C#" MasterPageFile="~/Views/Shared/Site.Master"
➥Inherits="System.Web.Mvc.ViewPage<MvcApplication1.Controllers.ProductsVDM>" %>


<asp:Content ID="Content2" ContentPlaceHolderID="MainContent" runat="server">

<script src="../../Scripts/MicrosoftAjax.debug.js" type="text/javascript"></script>
<script src="../../Scripts/MicrosoftMvcAjax.debug.js"
type="text/javascript"></script>

<ul style="display:inline">
<% foreach (var category in Model.Categories)
   { %>

   <li style="display:inline">
       <%= Ajax.ActionLink(category.Name, "Details", new {id=category.Id},
➥new AjaxOptions {UpdateTargetId="divDetails"}) %>
   </li>

<% } %>
</ul>

<hr />

<div id="divDetails">
    <% Html.RenderPartial("Details", Model.Products); %>
</div>

</asp:Content>
```

LISTING 14.20   Views\DownLink\Index.aspx (VB)

```
<%@ Page Title="" Language="VB" MasterPageFile="~/Views/Shared/Site.Master"
➥Inherits="System.Web.Mvc.ViewPage(Of MvcApplication1.ProductsVDM)" %>


<asp:Content ID="Content2" ContentPlaceHolderID="MainContent" runat="server">

<script src="../../Scripts/MicrosoftAjax.debug.js" type="text/javascript"></script>
➥<script src="../../Scripts/MicrosoftMvcAjax.debug.js"
type="text/javascript"></script>

<ul style="display:inline">
<%  For Each category In Model.Categories%>

    <li style="display:inline">
        <%=Ajax.ActionLink(category.Name, "Details", New With {.id = category.Id},
➥New AjaxOptions With {.UpdateTargetId = "divDetails"})%>
    </li>

<% Next%>
</ul>

<hr />

<div id="divDetails">
    <% Html.RenderPartial("Details", Model.Products)%>
</div>

</asp:Content>
```

The Details partial is contained in Listing 14.21. This partial is responsible for rendering the list of movies.

LISTING 14.21   Views\DownLink\Details.aspx (C#)

```
<%@ Control Language="C#" Inherits="System.Web.Mvc.ViewUserControl<IEnumerable
➥<MvcApplication1.Models.Product>>" %>


<ul>
<% foreach (var product in Model)
   { %>

    <li>
        <%= product.Name %> - <%= product.Price.ToString("c") %>
```

```
        </li>

<% } %>
</ul>
```

LISTING 14.21   Views\DownLink\Details.aspx (VB)

```
<%@ Control Language="VB" Inherits="System.Web.Mvc.ViewUserControl(Of IEnumerable
➥(Of MvcApplication1.Product))" %>


<ul>
<%  For Each product In Model%>

    <li>
        <%= product.Name %> - <%= product.Price.ToString("c") %>
    </li>

<% Next%>
</ul>
```

Using the AcceptAjax Attribute

In the previous section, we used the IsAjaxRequest() method within a controller to detect whether the action was invoked by an Ajax request. Using the IsAjaxRequest() method in a controller action can result in controller actions that are difficult to maintain. The controller action is given multiple responsibilities. The same action must handle both Ajax and non-Ajax requests.

Instead of using the IsAjaxRequest() method, you can use the AcceptAjax attribute. That way, you can create separate controller actions to handle Ajax requests and normal requests.

Unfortunately, the AcceptAjax attribute is not part of the standard Microsoft ASP.NET MVC framework. This attribute—currently—is included in ASP.NET MVC Futures, and it might be included in future versions of the official ASP.NET MVC framework.

NOTE

You can download the ASP.NET MVC Futures project from the www.ASP.net/mvc website that is the official Microsoft ASP.NET MVC website.

Fortunately, the AcceptAjax attribute is a simple attribute to create. The source code for this attribute is contained in Listing 14.22.

LISTING 14.22   CustomSelectors\AcceptAjaxAttribute.cs (C#)

```csharp
using System;
using System.Web.Mvc;
using System.Reflection;
public sealed class AcceptAjaxAttribute : ActionMethodSelectorAttribute

{
    public override bool IsValidForRequest(ControllerContext
➥controllerContext, MethodInfo methodInfo)
    {
        if (controllerContext == null)
        {
            throw new ArgumentNullException("controllerContext");
        }
        return controllerContext.HttpContext.Request.IsAjaxRequest();
    }
}
```

LISTING 14.22   CustomSelectors\AcceptAjaxAttribute.vb (VB)

```vbnet
Imports System.Reflection


Public NotInheritable Class AcceptAjaxAttribute
    Inherits ActionMethodSelectorAttribute

    Public Overrides Function IsValidForRequest(ByVal controllerContext As
➥ControllerContext, ByVal methodInfo As MethodInfo) As Boolean
        If controllerContext Is Nothing Then
            Throw New ArgumentNullException("controllerContext")
        End If
        Return controllerContext.HttpContext.Request.IsAjaxRequest()
    End Function

End Class
```

The controller in Listing 14.23 illustrates how you can use the AcceptAjax attribute.
Notice that there are two Details() actions. One action has the AcceptAjax attribute, and
it can be invoked only within the context of an Ajax request.

LISTING 14.23   Controllers\SelectorController.cs (C#)

```csharp
using System.Collections.Generic;
using System.Linq;
using System.Web.Mvc;
using MvcApplication1.Models;

namespace MvcApplication1.Controllers
{

    public class SelectorController : Controller
    {
        private ProductsDBEntities _entities = new ProductsDBEntities();

        public ActionResult Index()
        {
            var categories = _entities.CategorySet.ToList();
            var products = new List<Product>();
            return View(new ProductsVDM(categories, products));
        }


        [AcceptAjax]
        [ActionName("Details")]
        public ActionResult Details_Uplevel(int id)
        {
            var products = from p in _entities.ProductSet
                           where p.CategoryId == id
                           select p;

            return PartialView("Details", products);
        }


        [ActionName("Details")]
        public ActionResult Details_Downlevel(int id)
        {
            var categories = _entities.CategorySet.ToList();
            var products = from p in _entities.ProductSet
                           where p.CategoryId == id
                           select p;

            return View("Index", new ProductsVDM(categories, products));
        }


    }
}
```

LISTING 14.23   Controllers\SelectorController.vb (VB)

```vb
Public Class SelectorController
    Inherits Controller

    Private _entities As New ProductsDBEntities()

    Public Function Index()
        Dim categories = _entities.CategorySet.ToList()
        Dim products = New List(Of Product)()
        Return View(New ProductsVDM(categories, products))
    End Function

    <AcceptAjax(), ActionName("Details")> _
    Public Function Details_Uplevel(ByVal id As Integer) As ActionResult
        Dim products = From p In _entities.ProductSet _
                       Where p.CategoryId = id _
                       Select p

        Return PartialView("Details", products)
    End Function

    <ActionName("Details")> _
    Public Function Details_Downlevel(ByVal id As Integer) As ActionResult
        Dim categories = _entities.CategorySet.ToList()
        Dim products = From p In _entities.ProductSet _
                       Where p.CategoryId = id _
                       Select p

        Return View("Index", New ProductsVDM(categories, products))
    End Function

End Class
```

Compare the controller in Listing 14.23 with the controller (that does the same thing) in Listing 14.19. The controller that uses the AcceptAjax attribute is easier to understand and maintain.

Summary

In this chapter, you learned how to use the two Ajax helpers included with the ASP.NET MVC framework. In the first part of this chapter, you learned how to use the Ajax.BeginForm() helper to post an HTML form asynchronously. We discussed how you can display progress using an animated GIF or a jQuery animation during the form post operation. You also learned how to support both uplevel and downlevel browsers.

In the second part of this chapter, you learned how to use the `Ajax.ActionLink()` helper to retrieve content from the web server asynchronously. You learned how to use the `Ajax.ActionLink()` helper to create master/detail pages. Finally, we discussed how you can provide both uplevel and downlevel browser support when using the `Ajax.ActionLink()` helper.

In the next chapter, you learn how to use jQuery to perform Ajax calls from pure JavaScript.

CHAPTER 15

Using jQuery

The chapter is devoted to the topic of using the jQuery JavaScript library. The jQuery library provides you with a framework that makes it easier to perform common JavaScript tasks. In this chapter, you learn how to use jQuery to select elements from a page, display animations, perform Ajax requests, and use plug-ins.

Overview of jQuery

jQuery is not a Microsoft product. The jQuery library was created by John Resig, who released jQuery under both the MIT and GPL open source licenses. The official jQuery website is located at jQuery.com (see Figure 15.1).

Although jQuery is not a Microsoft product, Microsoft is including the jQuery library in future versions of the ASP.NET framework (both ASP.NET MVC and ASP.NET Web Forms). The jQuery library is included in the Scripts folder of the Visual Studio ASP.NET MVC template.

Why is Microsoft including jQuery with the ASP.NET framework? jQuery is an extremely popular JavaScript library. It is used by several major websites including Dell, Netflix, and Technorati. Furthermore, jQuery has a passionate and active developer community.

To make it easier to use this popular JavaScript library, the members of the Microsoft ASP.NET team decided to embrace jQuery and treat it much like any other Microsoft product. Microsoft provides "best-effort" product support for jQuery. This means that if you encounter an issue when using jQuery, you can call Microsoft product support and get help.

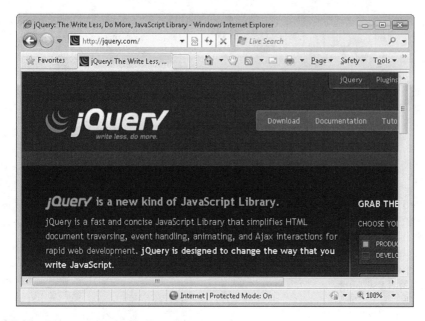

FIGURE 15.1   The jQuery.com website

Including the jQuery Library

Before you can use jQuery in your ASP.NET MVC views, you must reference the jQuery library. The Scripts folder includes two versions of the jQuery library:

▶ jQuery-1.3.2.js

▶ jQuery-1.3.2.min.js

The first version of the jQuery library is the debug version, and the second version is the release version. The release version is minified; all insignificant whitespace and comments have been stripped to reduce the size of the file. The debug version of the jQuery library is 125KB whereas the release version is (an astoundingly small) 58KB.

While in the process of developing an ASP.NET MVC, you should use the debug version of jQuery to make it easier to find errors. When you are ready to release your application to the world, make sure that you use the release version of the jQuery library.

The view in Listing 15.1 illustrates how you can include the debug version of the jQuery library. The jQuery library is included with the `<script src="..."></script>` tag.

LISTING 15.1   Views\Home\Index.aspx

```
<%@ Page Language="C#" MasterPageFile="~/Views/Shared/Site.Master" Inherits=
➥"System.Web.Mvc.ViewPage" %>

<asp:Content ID="indexContent" ContentPlaceHolderID="MainContent" runat="server">

    <script src="../../Scripts/jquery-1.3.2.js" type="text/javascript"></script>
    <script type="text/javascript">

        $(pageReady);

        function pageReady()
        {
            $("#title").css("background-color", "green");
        }

    </script>

    <h2 id="title">I like jQuery</h2>

</asp:Content>
```

TIP

The easiest way to add a script to a view is to simply drag it from the Solution Explorer window onto the code editor.

If you plan to use the jQuery library in multiple views within your ASP.NET MVC application, you should include jQuery within your view master page. That way, you don't need to add jQuery to each content view individually.

jQuery and Visual Studio Intellisense

Visual Studio is a good JavaScript development environment. When you write JavaScript code in the Visual Studio code editor, you get (partial) Intellisense. This is an amazing accomplishment because JavaScript, unlike languages such as C# or VB.NET, is not a statically typed language.

For example, if you assign a string to a variable, Visual Studio provides Intellisense for all the JavaScript string methods when you use the variable (see Figure 15.2).

FIGURE 15.2   JavaScript Intellisense

Visual Studio not only can provide Intellisense for JavaScript code, Visual Studio also can provide Intellisense for jQuery code. Before you can take advantage of jQuery Intellisense, you need to install a Hotfix for Visual Studio 2008. You can download the required patch from the following location:

http://code.msdn.microsoft.com/KB958502/Release/ProjectReleases.aspx?ReleaseId=1736

The patch modifies Visual Studio so that it retrieves the information required to display Intellisense from either a –vsdoc.js file or a .debug.js file. The –vsdoc.js or .debug.js file must be located in the same folder as the JavaScript library.

For example, if you create a JavaScript library named MyLibrary.js, Visual Studio attempts to retrieve Intellisense information from a file named MyLibrary-vsdoc.js. If the MyLibrary-vsdoc.js file cannot be found, Visual Studio attempts to retrieve Intellisense information from a file named MyLibrary.debug.js. Finally, if neither of these files can be found, Visual Studio retrieves Intellisense information from the actual MyLibrary.js file.

The Scripts folder includes both a jquery-1.3.2-vsdoc.js file and a jquery-1.3.2.min-vsdoc.js file. One file provides Intellisense information for the debug version of jQuery, and one file provides Intellisense information for the release version of jQuery (the minified version).

After you apply the Hotfix, and include the jQuery library in a view, you get Visual Studio Intellisense (see Figure 15.3).

You can download the jQuery -vsdoc.js file from jQuery.com. When there is a new version of jQuery, you need to download the new version of the -vsdoc.js file to get updated Intellisense.

Using jQuery Selectors

One of the most appealing features of jQuery is that most developers, without realizing it, already know how to use jQuery. It transfers the concept of selectors from Cascading Style Sheets into the JavaScript world.

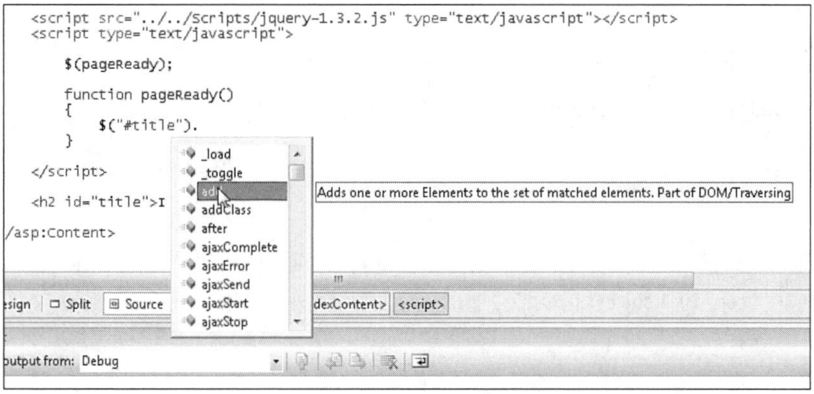

FIGURE 15.3   jQuery Intellisense in Visual Studio

You use selectors in Cascading Style Sheets to select elements from a document and apply a *style* to the elements. You use selectors in jQuery to select elements from a document and apply a *behavior* to the elements.

Let's look at some concrete examples. The following selector retrieves all the DIV tags from a document:

```
$("div")
```

The following selector retrieves all the DIV tags that have a CSS class named article:

```
$("div.article")
```

And, the following selector retrieves the single element that has an ID of mainContent:

```
$("#mainContent")
```

The jQuery library includes additional selectors that you might not be familiar with. For example, jQuery enables you to use filter selectors such as :first, :last, :even, and :odd. The view in Listing 15.2 illustrates how you can use the :odd selector to highlight odd rows in an HTML table to create a banding effect (see Figure 15.4).

LISTING 15.2   Views\Odd\Index.aspx

```
<%@ Page Title="" Language="C#" MasterPageFile="~/Views/Shared/Site.Master"
➥Inherits="System.Web.Mvc.ViewPage<IEnumerable<MvcApplication1.Models.Movie>>" %>


<asp:Content ID="Content2" ContentPlaceHolderID="MainContent" runat="server">

    <script src="../../Scripts/jquery-1.3.2.js" type="text/javascript"></script>
    <script type="text/javascript">

        $(pageReady);
```

```
        function pageReady()
        {
            $("tr:odd").css("background-color", "#eeeeee");
        }

    </script>

    <table>
    <% foreach (var item in Model) { %>

        <tr>
            <td>
                <%= Html.Encode(item.Title) %>
            </td>
            <td>
                <%= Html.Encode(item.Director) %>
            </td>
        </tr>

    <% } %>

    </table>

</asp:Content>
```

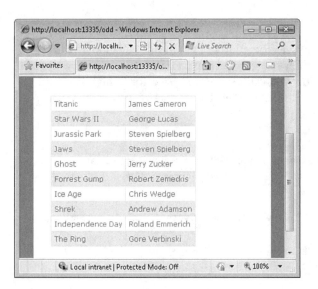

FIGURE 15.4   Using the :odd selector

> **NOTE**
>
> Notice the statement $(pageReady) in Listing 15.2. This statement causes the pageReady() method to execute after the entire document is loaded. If you attempted to execute the code in the pageReady() method before the document had loaded, the code would not work because the HTML table would not have been rendered.

jQuery also supports form selectors like the input, text, password, submit, and button selectors. The view in Listing 15.3 illustrates how you can highlight all the text boxes (input type="text") in a page with a yellow background.

LISTING 15.3   Views\Text\Index.aspx

```
<%@ Page Title="" Language="C#" MasterPageFile="~/Views/Shared/Site.Master"
➥Inherits="System.Web.Mvc.ViewPage<MvcApplication1.Models.Movie>" %>


<asp:Content ID="Content2" ContentPlaceHolderID="MainContent" runat="server">

    <script src="../../Scripts/jquery-1.3.2.js" type="text/javascript"></script>
    <script type="text/javascript">

        $(pageReady);

        function pageReady()
        {
            $("input:text").css("background-color", "yellow");
        }

    </script>

    <% using (Html.BeginForm()) {%>

        <fieldset>
            <legend>Create Movie</legend>
            <p>
                <label for="Title">Title:</label>
                <%= Html.TextBox("Title") %>
            </p>
            <p>
                <label for="Director">Director:</label>
                <%= Html.TextBox("Director") %>
            </p>
```

```
        <p>
            <label for="DateReleased">DateReleased:</label>
            <%= Html.TextBox("DateReleased") %>
        </p>
        <p>
            <input type="submit" value="Create" />
        </p>
    </fieldset>

<% } %>

</asp:Content>
```

You also can use attributes in a selector by using a selector such as [attribute] or
[attribute=value]. The view in Listing 15.4 illustrates how you can retrieve all the anchor
tags in a page that point to an external website and add a target="_blank" attribute. (In
other words, it forces all links to another website to open a new browser window.)

LISTING 15.4   Views\External\Index.aspx

```
<%@ Page Title="" Language="C#" MasterPageFile="~/Views/Shared/Site.Master"
➥Inherits="System.Web.Mvc.ViewPage" %>

<asp:Content ID="Content2" ContentPlaceHolderID="MainContent" runat="server">

    <script src="../../Scripts/jquery-1.3.2.js" type="text/javascript"></script>
    <script type="text/javascript">

        $(pageReady);

        function pageReady()
        {
            $("a[href^='http']").append(" [external]");
        }

    </script>

    <h2>Resources</h2>

    <ul>
        <li>
        <a href="http://www.ASP.net/mvc">Official ASP.NET MVC website</a>
        </li>
```

```
        <li>
        <a href="/articles">Articles</a>
        </li>
        <li>
        <a href="/videos">Videos</a>
        </li>
    </ul>

</asp:Content>
```

In Listing 15.4, the ^= operator is used to match an attribute value that starts with a particular value.

> **NOTE**
>
> There are more jQuery selectors than described here. You can view the full selector documentation at the jQuery.com website.

Adding Event Handlers

The jQuery library also makes it easy to add event handlers to a set of selected elements. You can use methods like `blur()`, `click()`, `dblclick()`, `focus()`, `hover()`, and `submit()` to create an event handler.

For example, the view in Listing 15.5 contains a menu created with a bulleted list. The `hover()` method highlights the particular menu item under the mouse.

LISTING 15.5   Views\Hover\Index.aspx

```
<%@ Page Title="" Language="C#" MasterPageFile="~/Views/Shared/Site.Master"
➡Inherits="System.Web.Mvc.ViewPage" %>


<asp:Content ID="Content2" ContentPlaceHolderID="MainContent" runat="server">

    <script src="../../Scripts/jquery-1.3.2.js" type="text/javascript"></script>
    <script type="text/javascript">

        $(pageReady);

        function pageReady()
        {
            $("#myMenu a").hover(highlight, lowlight);
        }
```

```
function highlight()
{
    $(this).css("background-color", "yellow");
}

function lowlight()
{
    $(this).css("background-color", "");
}

</script>

<ul id="myMenu">
    <li>
        <%= Html.ActionLink("Home", "Home") %>
    </li>
    <li>
        <%= Html.ActionLink("Products", "Products") %>
    </li>
    <li>
        <%= Html.ActionLink("Products", "Services") %>
    </li>
</ul>
```

```
</asp:Content>
```

The view in Listing 15.5 uses the hover() method to set up a function that is called when your mouse moves over a link and when your mouse moves off a link. The functions add and remove a yellow background color (see Figure 15.5).

FIGURE 15.5   Highlighting menu item

Using jQuery Animations

The jQuery library includes three built-in animation effects:

- ▶ show() and hide()
- ▶ slideDown() and slideUp()
- ▶ fadeIn() and fadeOut()

One situation in which these animations are particularly useful is when you need to show progress during an Ajax request. For example, the view in Listing 15.6 contains a link rendered with the Ajax.ActionLink() helper that fetches an updated list of movies. The jQuery slideUp() and slideDown() animation effects are used at the beginning and end of the request.

LISTING 15.6   Controllers\Slide\Index.aspx (C#)

```
<%@ Page Title="" Language="C#" MasterPageFile="~/Views/Shared/Site.Master"
➡Inherits="System.Web.Mvc.ViewPage<IEnumerable<MvcApplication1.Models.Movie>>" %>


<asp:Content ID="Content2" ContentPlaceHolderID="MainContent" runat="server">
    <script src="../../Scripts/MicrosoftAjax.js" type="text/javascript"></script>
    <script src="../../Scripts/MicrosoftMvcAjax.js"
➡type="text/javascript"></script>
    <script src="../../Scripts/jquery-1.3.2.js" type="text/javascript"></script>
    <script type="text/javascript">

        function beginFetch()
        {
            $("#divMovies").slideUp("slow");
        }

        function completeFetch()
        {
            $("#divMovies").slideDown("slow");
        }

    </script>

    <%= Ajax.ActionLink("Refresh Movies", "Refresh", new AjaxOptions
➡{OnBegin="beginFetch", OnComplete="completeFetch", UpdateTargetId="divMovies"}) %>

    <div id="divMovies">
```

```
        <% Html.RenderPartial("Movies"); %>
    </div>

</asp:Content>
```

LISTING 15.6   Controllers\Slide\Index.aspx (VB)

```
<%@ Page Title="" Language="VB" MasterPageFile="~/Views/Shared/Site.Master"
➥Inherits="System.Web.Mvc.ViewPage(Of IEnumerable (Of MvcApplication1.Movie))" %>
<asp:Content ID="Content2" ContentPlaceHolderID="MainContent" runat="server">

    <script src="../../Scripts/MicrosoftAjax.js" type="text/javascript"></script>
    <script src="../../Scripts/MicrosoftMvcAjax.js"
➥type="text/javascript"></script>
    <script src="../../Scripts/jquery-1.3.2.js" type="text/javascript"></script>
    <script type="text/javascript">

        function beginFetch()
        {
            $("#divMovies").slideUp("slow");
        }
        function completeFetch()
        {
            $("#divMovies").slideDown("slow");
        }

    </script>

    <%=Ajax.ActionLink("Refresh Movies", "Refresh", New AjaxOptions With {.OnBegin
➥= "beginFetch", .OnComplete = "completeFetch", .UpdateTargetId = "divMovies"})%>

    <div id="divMovies">
        <% Html.RenderPartial("Movies")%>
    </div>

</asp:Content>
```

The view in Listing 15.6 renders a link and a grid of movies (see Figure 15.6). When you click the link, the jQuery slideUp() animation is invoked. When the Ajax request completes, the jQuery slideDown() animation is invoked.

Notice that the constant "slow" is used with the slideUp() method. You can use the constants "slow", "normal", "fast". Alternatively, you can also supply a millisecond value.

FIGURE 15.6   Click the link to see the animation.

> **NOTE**
>
> There are an additional set of animations that you can download from the jQuery.com website. The additional animations are part of a separate project named jQuery UI that contains animations with names like Explode, Shake, and Bounce.

jQuery and Ajax

The jQuery library has several methods that you can use to perform Ajax requests:

- ▶ ajax()—Performs an Ajax request. This low-level method provides you with the most options for performing an Ajax request, but it is more difficult to use than the other methods.

- ▶ load()—Loads HTML and injects the HTML into an element.

- ▶ get()—Loads HTML by performing an HTTP GET request.

- ▶ getJSON()—Loads JSON by performing an HTTP GET request.

- ▶ getScript()—Loads and executes a script.

- ▶ post()—Loads HTML by performing an HTTP POST request.

You normally perform an Ajax request to get either a fragment of HTML from the server or JSON data from the server. The jQuery library enables you to easily perform either type of request.

For example, the view in Listing 15.7 updates a news item every 3 seconds (see Figure 15.7). The news item is retrieved with the jQuery load() method.

FIGURE 15.7   Random news item

LISTING 15.7   Views\News\Index.aspx

```
<%@ Page Title="" Language="C#" MasterPageFile="~/Views/Shared/Site.Master"
➥Inherits="System.Web.Mvc.ViewPage" %>


<asp:Content ID="Content2" ContentPlaceHolderID="MainContent" runat="server">

    <script src="../../Scripts/jquery-1.3.2.js" type="text/javascript"></script>
    <script type="text/javascript">

        $(pageReady);

        function pageReady()
        {
            window.setInterval(refreshNews, 3000);
        }

        function refreshNews()
        {
            $("#divNews").load("/News/Refresh");
        }

    </script>
```

```
<h2>Index</h2>

<div id="divNews"></div>

</asp:Content>
```

In Listing 15.7, the jQuery `load()` method invokes the `Refresh` action of the `News` controller by requesting the URL /News/Refresh. The `News` controller is contained in Listing 15.8.

LISTING 15.8   Controllers\NewsController.cs (C#)

```csharp
using System;
using System.Web.Mvc;

namespace MvcApplication1.Controllers
{
    public class NewsController : Controller
    {

        public ActionResult Index()
        {
            return View();
        }

        public ActionResult Refresh()
        {
            var partial = "";
            var rnd = new Random();
            switch (rnd.Next(2))
            {
                case 0:
                    partial = "News/News1";
                    break;
                case 1:
                    partial = "News/News2";
                    break;
            }
            return PartialView(partial);
        }
    }
}
```

LISTING 15.8   Controllers\NewsController.vb (VB)

```vb
Public Class NewsController
    Inherits Controller

    Public Function Index() As ActionResult
        Return View()
    End Function

    Public Function Refresh() As ActionResult
        Dim newsPartial = ""
        Dim rnd = New Random()
        Select Case rnd.Next(2)
            Case 0
                newsPartial = "News/News1"
            Case 1
                newsPartial = "News/News2"
        End Select

        Return PartialView(newsPartial)
    End Function

End Class
```

The News controller Refresh() action randomly returns one of two partials. The Refresh() action either returns the News1 or the News2 partial. Each partial contains a different news item. For example, the News1 partial is contained in Listing 15.9.

LISTING 15.9   Views\News\News\News1.ascx

```aspx
<%@ Control Language="C#" Inherits="System.Web.Mvc.ViewUserControl" %>


<div style="background-color:yellow;padding:10px">

    <h1>Aliens attack the moon!</h1>
</div>
```

The view in Listing 15.7 uses jQuery to retrieve a fragment of HTML across the wire. Instead of using jQuery to return a fragment of HTML, you can use jQuery to return JSON data.

For example, the view in Listing 15.10 displays a random set of movie records from the movie database table (see Figure 15.8). The movie records are retrieved with the help of the jQuery getJSON() method.

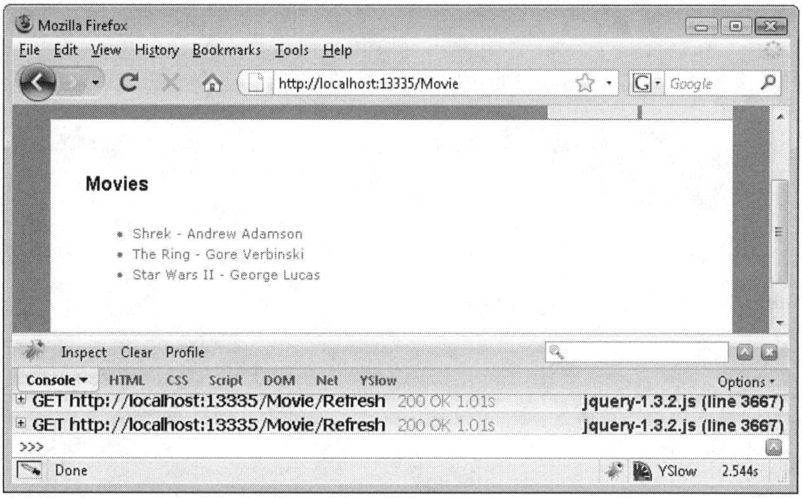

FIGURE 15.8   Displaying random movies with Ajax

LISTING 15.10   Views\Movie\Index.aspx

```
<%@ Page Title="" Language="C#" MasterPageFile="~/Views/Shared/Site.Master"
➡Inherits="System.Web.Mvc.ViewPage" %>


<asp:Content ID="Content2" ContentPlaceHolderID="MainContent" runat="server">

    <script src="../../Scripts/jquery-1.3.2.js" type="text/javascript"></script>
    <script type="text/javascript">

        $(pageReady);

        function pageReady()
        {
            $.ajaxSetup({cache:false});
            window.setInterval(refreshMovies, 3000);
        }

        function refreshMovies()
        {
            $.getJSON("/Movie/Refresh", showMovies);
        }

        function showMovies(movies)
```

```
        {
            var frag = "<ul>";
            for (var i = 0; i < movies.length; i++)
            {
                frag += "<li>" + movies[i].Title + " - " + movies[i].Director +
➥"</li>";
            }
            frag += "</ul>";

            $("#divMovies").html(frag);
        }

    </script>

    <h2>Movies</h2>

    <div id="divMovies"></div>

</asp:Content>
```

WARNING

Notice that the jQuery ajaxSetup() method is called in the pageReady() method to
disable browser caching. If you do not disable browser caching, Internet Explorer
always displays the exact same news items.

The getJSON() method invokes the controller action mapped to the URL /Movie/Refresh
and, after the data is returned, the method calls the showMovies() method. The
showMovies() method creates a bulleted list of the movies returned from the server. The
bulleted list is assigned to a DIV tag named divMovies.

The movies are retrieved from the Refresh action exposed by the Movie controller in
Listing 15.11.

LISTING 15.11   Controllers\MovieController.cs (C#)

```csharp
using System;
using System.Collections.Generic;
using System.Linq;
using System.Web.Mvc;
using MvcApplication1.Models;
using System.Collections;


namespace MvcApplication1.Controllers
```

```csharp
{
    public class MovieController : Controller
    {
        MoviesDBEntities _entities = new MoviesDBEntities();

        public ActionResult Index()
        {
            return View();
        }

        public ActionResult Refresh()
        {
            return Json( GetThreeMovies() );
        }

        private IEnumerable GetThreeMovies()
        {
            var rnd = new Random();
            var allMovies = _entities.MovieSet.ToList();
            var selectedMovies = new List<Movie>();

            for (int i = 0; i < 3; i++)
            {
                var selected = allMovies[rnd.Next(allMovies.Count)];
                allMovies.Remove(selected);
                selectedMovies.Add(selected);
            }

            var results = from m in selectedMovies
                          select new {Title=m.Title, Director=m.Director};

            return results;
        }

    }
}
```

LISTING 15.11   Controllers\MovieController.vb (VB)

```vb
Public Class MovieController
    Inherits Controller

    Private _entities As New MoviesDBEntities()

    Public Function Index() As ActionResult
```

```
        Return View()
    End Function


    Public Function Refresh() As ActionResult
        Return Json(GetThreeMovies())
    End Function


    Private Function GetThreeMovies() As IEnumerable
        Dim rnd = New Random()
        Dim allMovies = _entities.MovieSet.ToList()
        Dim selectedMovies = New List(Of Movie)()

        For i As Integer = 0 To 2
            Dim selected = allMovies(rnd.Next(allMovies.Count))
            allMovies.Remove(selected)
            selectedMovies.Add(selected)
        Next i

        Dim results = From m In selectedMovies _
                        Select New With {Key .Title = m.Title, Key .Director =
➥m.Director}

        Return results
    End Function

End Class
```

The Refresh() method returns a set of three movies randomly retrieved from the
movies database table. The Json() method is used to return a JSON result. The JSON
result looks like this:

```
{"Title":"The Ring","Director":"Gore Verbinski"},{"Title":"Jurassic
➥Park","Director":"Steven Spielberg"
},{"Title":"Ghost","Director":"Jerry Zucker"}
```

The advantage of using JSON over fragments of HTML is that JSON enables you to represent information much more compactly. In other words, in most cases, using JSON results
in better performance.

Using jQuery Plug-Ins

The jQuery library was designed to be small. It contains only the essentials for building
JavaScript applications. You don't want the users of your website to wait while downloading a JavaScript library that contains functionality that is never used.

If you want to do something more specialized, you can download a jQuery plug-in. There are hundreds of plug-ins available for download from the jQuery.com website (see Figure 15.9). These plug-ins enables you to accomplish an amazing variety of programming tasks, including plug-ins that display light boxes for images, plug-ins that render fancy menus, and plug-ins that enable you to copy data to the clipboard. You can download these plug-ins from http://plugins.jQuery.com.

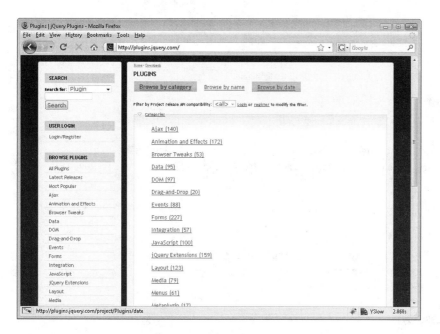

FIGURE 15.9   jQuery plug-ins available for download

The jQuery library was designed to make it easy to use plug-ins. In this section, we discuss how you can use something called the `tablesorter` plug-in. This plug-in enables you to sort the columns of an HTML table.

NOTE

You can download the `tablesorter` plug-in from http://tablesorter.com. The tablesorter plug-in is also included in the Visual Studio project that corresponds to this chapter. The tablesorter plug-in is dual licensed under the MIT and GPL open source licenses.

The view in Listing 15.12 uses the `tablesorter` plug-in. When you click one of the table headers—Id, Title, Director, DateReleased—the rows in the table are sorted by that column (see Figure 15.10). If you click the same header more than once, the sort order is reversed.

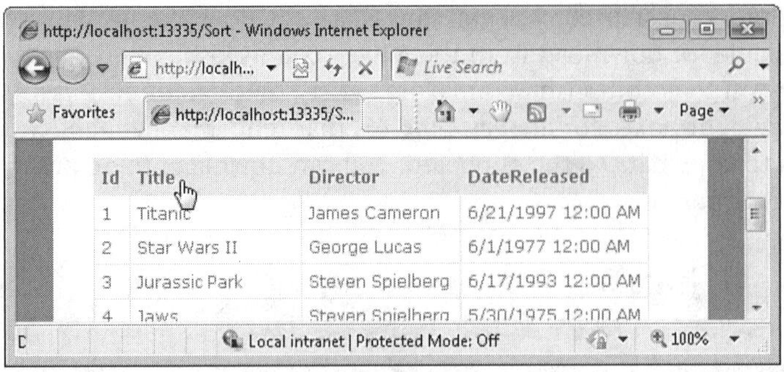

FIGURE 15.10   Using the tablesorter plug-in

LISTING 15.12   Views\Sort\Index.aspx

```
<%@ Page Title="" Language="C#" MasterPageFile="~/Views/Shared/Site.Master"
➥Inherits="System.Web.Mvc.ViewPage<IEnumerable<MvcApplication1.Models.Movie>>" %>


<asp:Content ID="Content2" ContentPlaceHolderID="MainContent" runat="server">

    <script src="../../Scripts/jquery-1.3.2.js" type="text/javascript"></script>
    <script src="../../Scripts/jquery.tablesorter.js"
➥type="text/javascript"></script>
    <script type="text/javascript">

        $(pageReady);

        function pageReady()
        {
            $("#movieTable").tablesorter();
        }

    </script>

    <table id="movieTable">
    <thead style="cursor:hand">
        <tr>
            <th>
                Id
            </th>
            <th>
                Title
            </th>
            <th>
```

```
            Director
        </th>
        <th>
            DateReleased
        </th>
    </tr>
</thead>
<tbody>
<% foreach (var item in Model) { %>

    <tr>
        <td>
            <%= Html.Encode(item.Id) %>
        </td>
        <td>
            <%= Html.Encode(item.Title) %>
        </td>
        <td>
            <%= Html.Encode(item.Director) %>
        </td>
        <td>
            <%= Html.Encode(String.Format("{0:g}", item.DateReleased)) %>
        </td>
    </tr>

<% } %>
</tbody>
</table>

</asp:Content>
```

To use the tablesorter plug-in, you need to do only two things. First, you need to include the tablesorter plug-in in the page. In Listing 15.12, the tablesorter is included with the second `<script src=""></script>` tag.

Second, you need to call the `tablesorter()` method on the table, or tables, that you want to sort. In Listing 15.12, the `tablesorter()` method is called in the `pageReady()` method.

WARNING

The `tablesorter` plug-in will work only with an HTML table that includes `<thead>` and `<tbody>` tags. The HTML table generated by the Visual Studio scaffolding does not include these tags. Therefore, you must add the `<thead>` and `<tbody>` tags by hand.

Summary

In this chapter, you were introduced to the jQuery JavaScript library. You learned how to use the jQuery library to select elements, create event handlers, display animations, and make Ajax calls. You also learned how to use jQuery plug-ins to extend the functionality of the base jQuery library.

PART II

Walkthrough: Building the Unleashed Blog Application

IN THIS PART

CHAPTER 16

Overview of the Application

In the following five chapters, we build the beginnings of a real-world ASP.NET MVC application—we build a simple blog application. I was motivated to build the blog application to satisfy two goals.

First, I want to demonstrate how you can use the features of the ASP.NET MVC framework in the context of building a real-world application. In the previous chapters of this book, we focused on particular features of the ASP.NET MVC framework. In the following chapters, you learn how all these features work together.

Second, I want to illustrate and promote a particular design methodology for building software applications called *test-driven development*. One of the primary goals of the ASP.NET MVC framework is to make it easy to practice test-driven development when building ASP.NET applications.

In this chapter, I provide you with a brief introduction to test-driven development. In particular, I explain why you might consider using test-driven development when building your own applications.

What Is Test-Driven Development?

When practicing test-driven development, you develop an application by performing these steps over and over again:

1. Create a failing test.
2. Write just enough code to pass the test.
3. Refactor your code to improve its design.

This process is called Red/Green/Refactor because a unit testing framework displays a red bar for a failing test and a green bar for a passing test.

When practicing test-driven development, the first step is always to create a failing test. You use the test to express how you want your code to behave.

For example, in our blog application, we start by writing a test that verifies whether you can retrieve a list of blog entries. We create this test before we write any application code.

After you create a failing test, you can allow yourself to write application code. However, you should allow yourself to write only enough code to cause the test to pass (to go green).

Finally, every once in a while, you take a step back from your code and consider how to improve the overall design of the code. You consider how you can *refactor* your code to have a better design. Because you have the safety net of tests, you can fearlessly refactor your code. Your tests immediately tell you if you have broken existing functionality.

> **NOTE**
>
> Refactoring refers to the process of rewriting code to improve its design without changing its behavior. Refactoring was popularized by Martin Fowler in his book *Refactoring: Improving the Design of Existing Code.*

Why Do Test-Driven Development?

Test-driven development is, first and foremost, a software design methodology. The primary goal of test-driven development is not to create a *well-tested* application. Instead, the goal is to create a *well-designed* application.

A well-designed software application is an application that can be easily maintained and extended over time. The claim is that test-driven development leads to better designed applications because the methodology forces you to continuously focus on design.

> **NOTE**
>
> The word *test* in test-driven development is misleading. Many people have suggested that the word test should be dropped from the name of test-driven development because the word confuses so many people about the goals of test-driven development. For example, proponents of behavior-driven development (a spin-off of test-driven development) avoid using the word *test*. Instead, they use the word *specification* in place of the word *test*. See the entry on behavior-driven development at Wikipedia.org (http://en.wikipedia.org/wiki/Behavior_driven_development).
>
> Other people who practice test-driven development, on the other hand, are happy with the word *test*.

The KISS and YAGNI Principles

Test-driven development enforces something called the KISS Principle (Keep It Simple Stupid) and the YAGNI Principle (You Ain't Gonna Need It). After you write a failing test, you should allow yourself to write only enough application code to pass the test and nothing more.

A developer feels the constant temptation to write more code than is needed in the current situation. I've been involved in many projects in which a team of developers developed a vast library of functions that ended up never being used. These giant libraries are a sad waste of many hundreds of hours of developer time.

Test-driven development forces you to concentrate on what you need to write to satisfy the requirements of the customer. You can think of a test as a mini-specification. By creating a criterion of success upfront that is expressed with a test, you can prevent yourself from wandering into the woods and writing code that no one will ever use.

Waterfall Versus Evolutionary Design

Test-driven development grew out of agile development, which grew out of a reaction to waterfall development. One important goal of test-driven development is what Kent Beck calls *incremental design* and what Martin Fowler calls *evolutionary design*. Instead of designing an application all at once and upfront, an application is designed incrementally test-by-test.

Waterfall design is modeled on the disciplines of electrical engineering or civil engineering. In civil engineering, there is a sharp distinction between the architect of a bridge and the workers who actually build the bridge. A highly educated and highly paid architect prepares a comprehensive design for a bridge. Only after the design is completed do the low-paid workers go out and start building the bridge brick-by-brick or girder-by-girder.

Waterfall development in software follows the same model. A highly paid software architect creates a comprehensive architectural design for a software application and then hands the design off to a team of lower-paid developers who implement the design. There is a sharp separation between the process of designing an application and the process of developing the application.

Proponents of test-driven development reject this analogy between software engineering and civil engineering. Instead, proponents of test-driven development claim that *the software is the design*. In other words, every developer is an architect and every developer should constantly be thinking about design. The developer is responsible for designing the application, and the compiler is responsible for building the application.

Test-driven development makes design central to the process of building software. Instead of trying to design an entire application upfront, proponents of test-driven development advocate that every developer participates in the continuous design of an application.

Test-driven development sharply separates the process of developing software into three separate stages. You have a different perspective on your code during each stage.

When you write a test, you are actively designing your code by taking the perspective of someone who will use the code. Creating a test forces you to think about the best way to build the public interface for your application.

After you write a test, you shift perspectives. You move from the perspective of someone who is designing the software to someone who is implementing the software. You shift from being a highly paid architect to a lowly paid laborer.

And, finally, in the refactor stage, you take a more global perspective on your application. During the refactor stage, you concentrate on improving the overall design of your application instead of an individual part.

TDD Tests Are Not Unit Tests

It is common to use the expression *unit test* for the type of test used in the context of test-driven development. Strictly speaking, however, the tests that you write within the context of test-driven development are related to unit tests, but not the same. Although you use a Unit Testing Framework, such as NUnit or Visual Studio Test, to build both TDD tests and unit tests, TDD tests have a very different purpose than unit tests.

Creating unit tests for an application is valuable. You can use unit tests to determine whether an application behaves in the way that you intend it to behave. Because a unit test tests a unit of code in isolation, you can use unit tests to quickly find defects in your code. In other words, unit tests are extremely useful in *regression testing*.

In contrast to unit tests, you do not create TDD tests to test your application. Instead, you use TDD tests to drive the development and design of your application. TDD tests work like mini-specifications or mini-acceptance tests.

Kent Beck, in his book *Test-Driven Development by Example*, is careful to refer to the tests that he uses in test-driven development as "small-scale tests" instead of unit tests because "they don't match the accepted definition of unit tests very well." Again, it would be more accurate to think of tests used in the context of test-driven development more as mini-specifications than unit tests.

> **NOTE**
>
> A useful side-effect or artifact of test-driven development can be unit tests. However, creating lots of unit tests for your code is not the main motivation behind test-driven development.

Tests Flow from User Stories

When practicing agile development, you always start with a list of user stories. The user stories are nontechnical descriptions of the ways in which your customers want to interact with an application. Typically, a user story consists of no more than two or three sentences.

When developing our blog application, we always start with a list of user stories written on a napkin. We use the user stories to create the initial set of tests. The tests are intended to capture the intentions behind the user stories. In other words, the tests work as (mini) customer acceptance tests.

User stories are written for the benefit of customers. The tests, in contrast, are written for the benefit of the developer. We use the tests to concentrate on the next task that needs to be accomplished. The tests act as automated success indicators.

Unit Testing Frameworks

There are several Unit Testing Frameworks that you can use when building an ASP.NET MVC application. The most popular Unit Testing Framework in the Microsoft .NET world is NUnit. The NUnit framework is maintained by Charlie Poole. You can use NUnit with both Microsoft Visual Studio and Microsoft Visual Web Developer.

In the following chapters, we use the built-in Unit Testing Framework included with Visual Studio called Visual Studio Test. To use this framework, you need the full version of Visual Studio. If you use Visual Web Developer, I recommend that you use NUnit, which you can download for free from the following location: http://NUnit.org.

Bibliography of Test-Driven Development

Test-driven development is a controversial topic. Within the test-driven development movement, there are many conflicting voices. I recommend that you read the source material. Here are some of the resources that I have found particularly valuable:

- ▶ *Test-Driven Development by Example* by Kent Beck. This book is the foundational book for test-driven development. It includes an extensive walkthrough of building a money converter library through test-driven development.

- ▶ *What Is Software Engineering?* by Jack Reeves (www.bleading-edge.com/Publications/ C++Journal/Cpjour2.htm). This article is one of the foundational articles of the agile movement. In this article, Jack Reeves claims that all developers are architects.

- ▶ *Working Effectively with Legacy Code* by Michael Feathers. This book focuses on using test-driven development with code that is not covered by tests. The title of this book is misleading. This is an excellent book on the topic of test-driven development in general.

- ▶ *Agile Principles, Patterns, and Practices in C#* by Robert and Micah Martin. This is a great book, which discusses test-driven development and addresses several topics beyond test-driven development.

- ▶ *Is Design Dead?* by Martin Fowler (http://martinfowler.com/articles/designDead. html). In this article, Martin Fowler advocates evolutionary design. He argues that design is not dead and that design is compatible with test-driven development.

▶ *Mocks Aren't Stubs* by Martin Fowler (http://martinfowler.com/articles/mocksArentStubs.html). In this article, Martin Fowler distinguishes between state verification tests and behavior verification tests and distinguishes between classical test-driven development and Mockist test-driven development.

▶ *Test-Driven Development in Microsoft .NET* by James Newkirk and Alexei Vorontsov. Unfortunately, this book is getting a little dated because it was written for an earlier version of the .NET framework. However, it is still the best book for learning about test-driven development in the Microsoft world.

Summary

The purpose of this chapter was to introduce you to the goals of test-driven development. In this chapter, you learned that test-driven development is first and foremost an application design methodology. By practicing test-driven development, you can build applications that can better withstand the tests of time.

In the following chapters, you learn how to use test-driven development in the context of building a real-world application. We start with the first test and move on from there.

Database Access

In this chapter, we start building our Unleashed Blog application. We start with the list of user stories written on the napkin in Figure 17.1.

As you can read on the napkin, in this chapter, we focus on implementing the data access code for our blog application.

These stories get converted into the following rough requirements:

1. Can show list of new blog entries
2. Can create new blog entries

But, before we can do anything else, we need to create our ASP.NET MVC application in Visual Studio.

Creating the Unleashed Blog Project

Create a new ASP.NET MVC application by launching Visual Studio 2008 and selecting the menu option File, New Project (see Figure 17.2). Select the ASP.NET MVC Web Application project template and give the new application the name UnleashedBlog.

After you click the OK button, the Create Unit Test Project dialog in Figure 17.3 appears. Select the option to create a unit test project and click the OK button.

After you complete these steps, your solution contains two projects named UnleashedBlog and UnleashedBlog.Tests (see Figure 17.4). The UnleashedBlog project contains all the code for the ASP.NET MVC application. The UnleashedBlog.Tests project contains all the tests for the application.

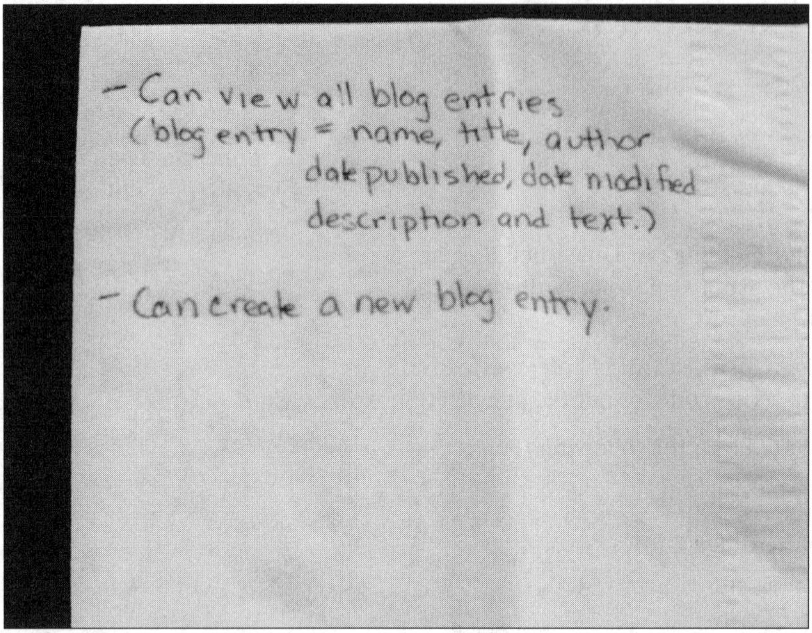

FIGURE 17.1   User stories for database access

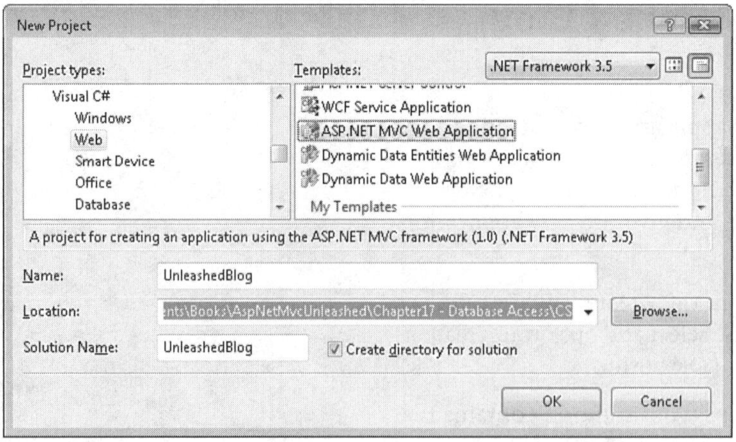

FIGURE 17.2   Creating a new ASP.NET MVC web application

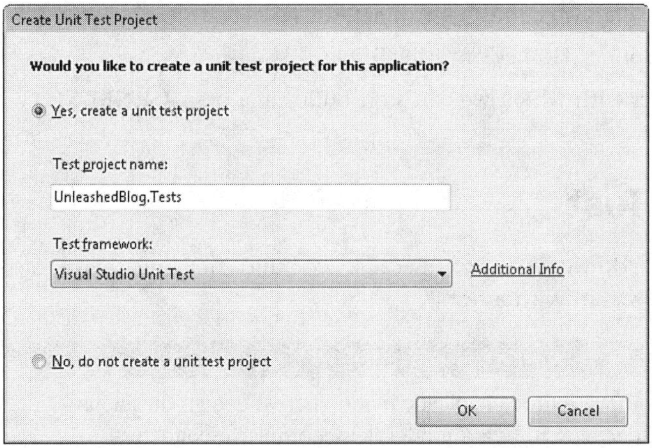

FIGURE 17.3 Creating a unit test project

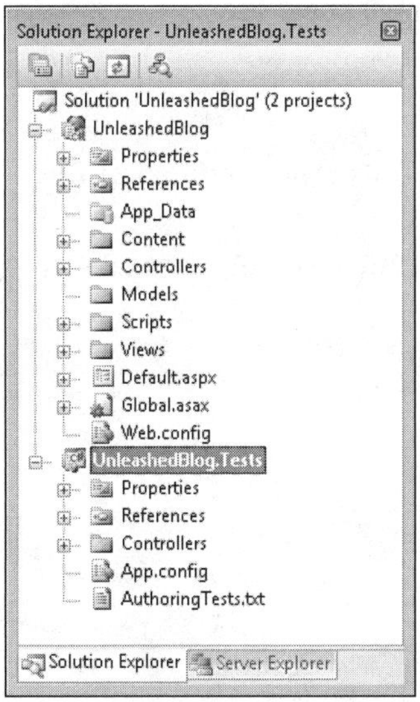

FIGURE 17.4 The UnleashedBlog and UnleashedBlog.Tests projects

When you create a new ASP.NET MVC project in Visual Studio, you get several sample files automatically. Because we want to start with a clean slate, we need to delete these sample files. Delete the following files and folders from the Solution Explorer window:

1. UnleashedBlog\Controllers\AccountController.cs
2. UnleashedBlog\Controllers\HomeController.cs
3. UnleashedBlog\Views\Account
4. UnleashedBlog\Views\Home

5. UnleashedBlog.Tests\Controllers\AccountControllerTest.cs

6. UnleashedBlog.Tests\Controllers\HomeControllerTest.cs

Now, we have a nice clean project with which we can start building a new ASP.NET MVC application.

Creating Our First Test

So, where do we start? What code do we write first? Because we build the Unleashed Blog using test-driven development, we start with a test.

> **NOTE**
>
> Before we write our first test, we have already implicitly made several design decisions. For example, we have made the decision to use a model-view-controller architecture. We also make the assumption that we should start with the controller and data access. (Someone else might decide to start with the domain model.) The general interaction of the model, view, and controller are already defined by the framework in which we work. But still, we can use test-driven development to fill in the details.

Follow these steps to add our first test:

1. Right-click the Controllers folder in the UnleashedBlog.Tests project and select the menu option Add, New Test.

2. In the Add New Test dialog (see Figure 17.5), select the Unit Test template and give your test the name BlogControllerTests.cs.

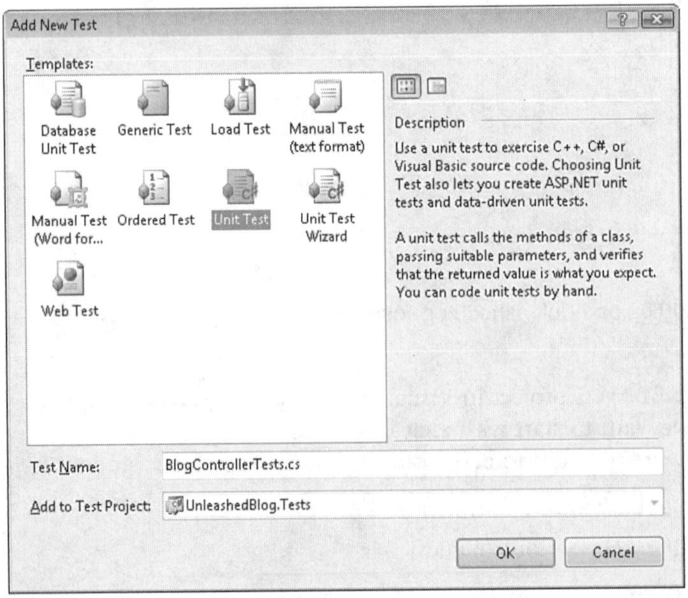

FIGURE 17.5   Adding a new unit test

3. Modify the BlogControllerTests.cs file so that it contains the test code in Listing 17.1.

WARNING

When adding tests, *do not* select the menu option Add, Unit Test. Selecting this option launches the Create Unit Tests Wizard that adds the wrong type of tests to your test project.

The wizard generates a unit test that spins up the web server. Because we are practicing test-driven development, and our tests need to run fast, we want to run our tests independently of the web server.

LISTING 17.1   UnleashedBlog.Tests\Controllers\BlogControllerTests.cs (C#)

```csharp
using System;
using System.Text;
using System.Collections.Generic;
using System.Linq;
using Microsoft.VisualStudio.TestTools.UnitTesting;
using System.Web.Mvc;
using System.Collections;

namespace UnleashedBlog.Tests.Controllers
{
    [TestClass]
    public class BlogControllerTests
    {

        [TestMethod]
        public void ShowNewBlogEntries()
        {
            // Arrange
            var controller = new BlogController();

            // Act
            var result = (ViewResult)controller.Index();

            // Assert
            CollectionAssert.AllItemsAreInstancesOfType((ICollection)
➥result.ViewData.Model, typeof(BlogEntry));
        }


    }
}
```

LISTING 17.1   UnleashedBlog.Tests\Controllers\BlogControllerTests.cs (VB)

```vb
Imports System
Imports System.Text
Imports System.Collections.Generic
Imports Microsoft.VisualStudio.TestTools.UnitTesting
Imports System.Web.Mvc

<TestClass()> Public Class BlogControllerTests

    <TestMethod()> _
    Public Sub ShowNewBlogEntries()
        ' Arrange
        Dim controller = New BlogController()

        ' Act
        Dim result As ViewResult = controller.Index()

        ' Assert
        CollectionAssert.AllItemsAreInstancesOfType(result.ViewData.Model,
➥GetType(BlogEntry))
    End Sub


End Class
```

The test class in Listing 17.1 contains a test named ShowNewBlogEntries. This test verifies that the Blog controller returns a list of BlogEntry objects from its Index() method.

The test has three sections named Arrange, Act, and Assert. In the Arrange section, an instance of the Blog controller class is created. In the Act section, the Blog controller Index() action is invoked. Finally, in the Assert section, the CollectionAssert class is used to verify that the view data returned by the Index() action represents a list of BlogEntry objects.

> **NOTE**
>
> The three A's of testing—Arrange, Act, and Assert—were invented by Bill Wake.

> **NOTE**
>
> When practicing test-driven development, I strongly recommend that you disable automatic statement completion in Visual Studio. Otherwise, you will be constantly fighting against Visual Studio whenever you type the names of classes that don't exist. Select the menu option Tools, Options. Under Text Editor, C# or Text Editor, Basic, uncheck the option Auto List Members.

After you write this test, you get the red squiggly warnings under the `BlogController` and `BlogEntry` classes (see Figure 17.6). This reaction of the Visual Studio editor is not surprising given that we have not created these classes yet.

```
[TestMethod]
public void ShowNewBlogEntries()
{
    // Arrange
    var controller = new BlogController();
```

FIGURE 17.6   Error messages resulting from nonexistent classes

Our test project won't even build at this point. Our test fails to even fail as a test.

Before we can even get our test to fail, we need to create the `BlogController` and `BlogEntry` classes to make the red squiggles go away. The `BlogEntry` class is contained in Listing 17.2 and the `BlogController` class is contained in Listing 17.3.

LISTING 17.2   UnleashedBlog\Models\BlogEntry.cs (C#)

```csharp
namespace UnleashedBlog.Models
{
    public class BlogEntry
    {
    }
}
```

LISTING 17.2   UnleashedBlog\Models\BlogEntry.vb (VB)

```vbnet
Public Class BlogEntry

End Class
```

LISTING 17.3   UnleashedBlog\Controllers\BlogController.cs (C#)

```csharp
using System.Collections.Generic;
using System.Web.Mvc;
using UnleashedBlog.Models;

namespace UnleashedBlog.Controllers
{
    public class BlogController : Controller
    {
        //
        // GET: /Blog/
```

```
        public ActionResult Index()
        {
            return null;
        }


    }
}
```

LISTING 17.3   UnleashedBlog\Controllers\BlogController.vb (VB)

```
Public Class BlogController
  Inherits Controller

  ' GET: /Blog/

  Public Function Index() As ActionResult
    Return Nothing
  End Function

End Class
```

You can add the BlogEntry class in Listing 17.2 to your project by right-clicking the UnleashedBlog\Models folder and selecting the menu option Add, Class. You can add the controller in Listing 17.3 by right-clicking the Controllers folder and selecting the menu option Add, Controller (see Figure 17.7).

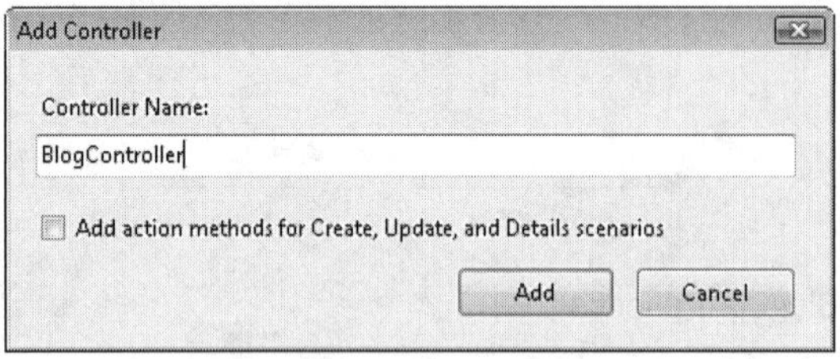

FIGURE 17.7   Adding a new controller

You might be disappointed with the code for the BlogEntry and BlogController classes. The BlogEntry represents a blog entry. However, it currently doesn't contain any properties. For example, it does not contain a property for the blog title or text.

Furthermore, the Index() action in the BlogController class simply returns null (nothing). We know that we haven't written enough code to make our test pass, but that is a good thing because we want to experience a failing test before we reach green (see Figure 17.7A).

> **NOTE**
>
> After you create the `BlogEntry` and `BlogController` classes, you need to import several namespaces before you can compile the test contained in Listing 17.1. The fastest way to import a necessary namespace is to click any class that has a red bar in the code editor and hit the keyboard combination Ctrl+. (hold the Control key while pressing the period key). This keyboard combination prompts you to add the necessary namespace.

You can run the failing test by entering the keyboard combination Ctrl+R, A. This keyboard combination runs all the tests in your solution.

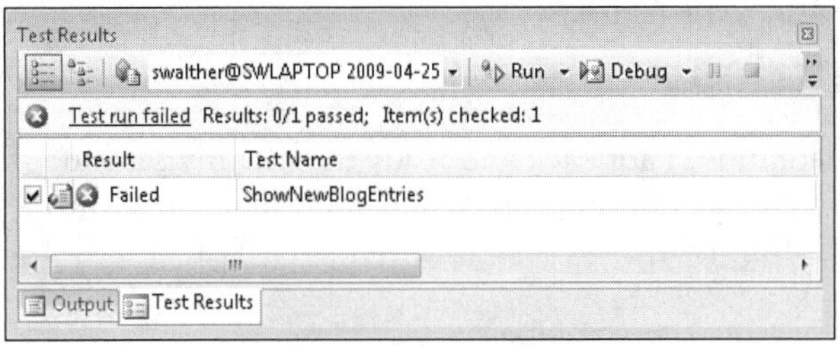

FIGURE 17.7A   A successfully failing test

Now that we have a failing test, we can allow ourselves to start writing code in earnest. Let's try revising our `Blog` controller `Index()` action so that it looks like this:

(C#)

```
public ActionResult Index()
{
    return View(new List<BlogEntry>());
}
```

(VB)

```
Public Function Index() As ActionResult
    Return View(New List(Of BlogEntry)())
End Function
```

We've modified the `Index()` action so that it returns a collection of `BlogEntry` classes. This might not seem like a huge improvement (we still aren't retrieving the blog entries from the database) but it is enough of a change to pass the test (see Figure 17.8).

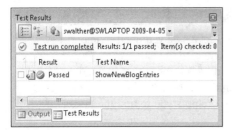

FIGURE 17.8   Passing our first test

So, it is time to celebrate! We created our first test and wrote enough application code (and only enough application code) to pass our first test. Yippee!

Creating New Blog Entries

After a long night of partying and celebration, I am back and ready to write my second test. We want to express the requirement that a person can create a new blog entry with a test. Our second test is contained in Listing 17.4.

LISTING 17.4   UnleashedBlog.Tests\Controllers\BlogControllerTests.cs (C#)

```csharp
[TestMethod]
public void CreateBlogEntry()
{
    // Arrange
    var controller = new BlogController();
    var blogEntryToCreate = new BlogEntry();

    // Act
    controller.Create(blogEntryToCreate);
    var result = (ViewResult)controller.Index();

    // Assert
    var firstEntry = ((IList)result.ViewData.Model)[0];
    Assert.AreSame(blogEntryToCreate, firstEntry);
}
```

LISTING 17.4   UnleashedBlog.Tests\Controllers\BlogControllerTests.vb (VB)

```vbnet
<TestMethod()> _
Public Sub CreateBlogEntry()
    ' Arrange
    Dim controller = New BlogController()
```

```
        Dim blogEntryToCreate = New BlogEntry()

        ' Act
        controller.Create(blogEntryToCreate)
        Dim result As ViewResult = controller.Index()

        ' Assert
        Dim firstEntry = result.ViewData.Model(0)
        Assert.AreSame(blogEntryToCreate, firstEntry)
    End Sub
```

The test in Listing 17.4 verifies that, after you create a new blog entry by invoking the
Create() action, the new blog entry can be retrieved by invoking the Index() action.

The test has three sections. In the Arrange section, a Blog controller and BlogEntry class is
created. Next, in the Act section, two actions of the Blog controller are invoked. First, the
Create() action is invoked and then the Index() action is invoked. Finally, in the Assert
section, the assertion is made that the new blog entry is the first item returned by the
Index() action.

After you add the test in Listing 17.4 to your project, your project won't even build. Your
project won't build because the Blog controller does not have a Create() method (see
Figure 17.9).

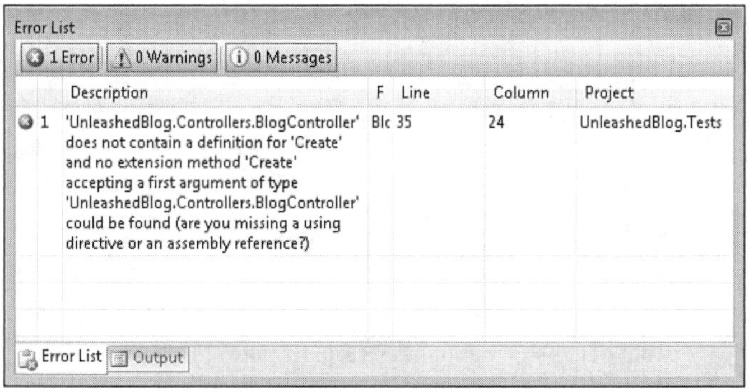

FIGURE 17.9   Test that does not build

The fact that the project won't build means that we, once again, failed to create a failing
test. Before we can even compile the test, we need to add a Create() action that accepts a
blog entry parameter to our Blog controller like this:

(C#)

```
public ActionResult Create(BlogEntry blogEntryToCreate)
{
    return null;
}
```

(VB)

```vb
Public Function Create(ByVal blogEntryToCreate As BlogEntry) As ActionResult
    Return Nothing
End Function
```

After we add this `Create()` action, our test successfully compiles and fails. If you press the Ctrl+R, A keyboard combination, you can witness the test fail (see Figure 17.9A). We have successfully created another failing test. Now, we can focus on writing the code required to go green.

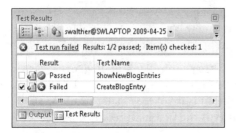

FIGURE 17.9A   A failing test for the `Create()` action

The updated `Blog` controller is contained in Listing 17.5.

LISTING 17.5   UnleashedBlog\Controllers\BlogController.cs (C#)

```csharp
using System.Collections.Generic;
using System.Web.Mvc;
using UnleashedBlog.Models;

namespace UnleashedBlog.Controllers
{
    public class BlogController : Controller
    {
        private List<BlogEntry> _blogEntries = new List<BlogEntry>();

        public ActionResult Index()
        {
            return View(_blogEntries);
        }


        public ActionResult Create(BlogEntry blogEntryToCreate)
        {
            _blogEntries.Add(blogEntryToCreate);
```

```
        return RedirectToAction("Index");
    }
  }
}
```

LISTING 17.5   UnleashedBlog\Controllers\BlogController.vb (VB)

```vb
Public Class BlogController
    Inherits System.Web.Mvc.Controller

    Private _blogEntries As New List(Of BlogEntry)

    Public Function Index() As ActionResult
        Return View(_blogEntries)
    End Function


    Public Function Create(ByVal blogEntryToCreate As BlogEntry) As ActionResult
        _blogEntries.Add(blogEntryToCreate)

        Return RedirectToAction("Index")
    End Function

End Class
```

The new version of the Blog controller in Listing 17.5 has a class level field named _blogEntries that represents a collection of blog entries. When you invoke the Create() action with a new blog entry, the new blog entry is added to this collection. When you invoke the Index() action, the blog entries are retrieved from this collection.

We've written just enough code to pass our test. If you enter the keyboard combination Ctrl+R, A then you can see that we pass all of our tests (see Figure 17.10). Filled with a sense of accomplishment, I'm done with work for today—I'm going to go see a movie.

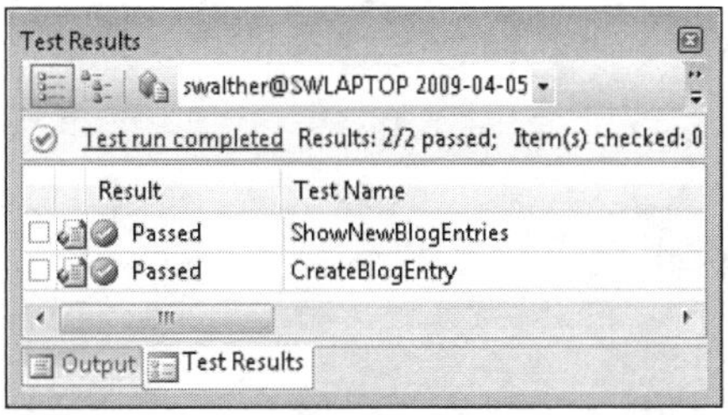

FIGURE 17.10   Passing the CreateBlogEntry() test

Refactoring to Use the Repository Pattern

At this point, we created two tests and built enough application code to pass the tests. We can list blog entries and create new blog entries.

This is a good point to consider refactoring our code. Right now, the Blog controller is storing and retrieving blog entries from an in-memory collection. However, we know that we need to store the blog entries in a database eventually.

We want to use a database to store our blog entries, but we want to test our application code without accessing a database. We want our application to use an in-memory database when the application is tested. However, we want our application to use a real database when the application is used in production.

> **WARNING**
>
> In general, when practicing test-driven development, you don't want to access a database when running tests. Executing tests against a database is slow. Because you might need to run hundreds, or even thousands, of tests each and every time you modify your code, your tests cannot be slow or you will never get any work done.

We need to refactor our blog application to use something called the *Repository pattern*. When you use the Repository pattern, you create an interface or abstract class that describes all the methods for retrieving and storing objects from a repository. Then, you can implement the interface or abstract class in multiple ways.

We create a repository base class that describes the methods for storing and retrieving blog entries. Next, we implement the repository base class in two different ways. We create both a fake blog repository that stores blog entries in memory and a real blog repository that stores blog entries in a database.

The first iteration of our repository base class is contained in Listing 17.6. This base class has three abstract (must inherit) methods named ListBlogEntries(), CreateBlogEntry(), and QueryBlogEntries().

LISTING 17.6   UnleashedBlog\Models\BlogRepositoryBase.cs (C#)

```
using System.Collections.Generic;
using System.Linq;

namespace UnleashedBlog.Models
{
    public abstract class BlogRepositoryBase
    {
        // Blog Entry Methods
        public abstract List<BlogEntry> ListBlogEntries();
        public abstract void CreateBlogEntry(BlogEntry blogEntryToCreate);
```

```
    protected abstract IQueryable<BlogEntry> QueryBlogEntries();
  }
}
```

LISTING 17.6   UnleashedBlog\Models\BlogRepositoryBase.vb (VB)

```
Imports System.Collections.Generic
Imports System.Linq

Public MustInherit Class BlogRepositoryBase

    ' Blog Entry Methods
    Public MustOverride Function ListBlogEntries() As List(Of BlogEntry)
    Public MustOverride Sub CreateBlogEntry(ByVal blogEntryToCreate As BlogEntry)
    Protected MustOverride Function QueryBlogEntries() As IQueryable(Of BlogEntry)

End Class
```

The Blog controller in Listing 17.7 has been refactored to use the BlogRepositoryBase class. Notice that it has a constructor that requires a repository that inherits from the BlogRepositoryBase class. The two actions exposed by the Blog controller use the base class.

LISTING 17.7   UnleashedBlog\Controllers\BlogController.cs (C#)

```
using System.Collections.Generic;
using System.Web.Mvc;
using UnleashedBlog.Models;

namespace UnleashedBlog.Controllers
{
    public class BlogController : Controller
    {
        private BlogRepositoryBase _repository;

        public BlogController(BlogRepositoryBase repository)
        {
            _repository = repository;
        }
        public ActionResult Index()
        {
            return View(_repository.ListBlogEntries());
        }

        public ActionResult Create(BlogEntry blogEntryToCreate)
```

```
        {
            _repository.CreateBlogEntry(blogEntryToCreate);

            return RedirectToAction("Index");
        }
    }
}
```

LISTING 17.7   UnleashedBlog\Controllers\BlogController.vb (VB)

```vb
Public Class BlogController
    Inherits System.Web.Mvc.Controller

    Private _repository As BlogRepositoryBase

    Public Sub New(ByVal repository As BlogRepositoryBase)
        _repository = repository
    End Sub


    Public Function Index() As ActionResult
        Return View(_repository.ListBlogEntries())
    End Function


    Public Function Create(ByVal blogEntryToCreate As BlogEntry) As ActionResult
        _repository.CreateBlogEntry(blogEntryToCreate)

        Return RedirectToAction("Index")
    End Function

End Class
```

Creating a Fake Blog Repository

A concrete implementation of the BlogRepositoryBase class is contained in Listing 17.8.
This class represents a fake blog repository—an in-memory version of the blog repository
that we use in our tests.

LISTING 17.8   UnleashedBlog.Tests\Models\FakeBlogRepository.cs (C#)

```csharp
using System.Collections.Generic;
using System.Linq;
```

```csharp
using UnleashedBlog.Models;
namespace UnleashedBlog.Tests.Models
{
    public class FakeBlogRepository : BlogRepositoryBase
    {
        private List<BlogEntry> _blogEntries = new List<BlogEntry>();

        protected override IQueryable<BlogEntry> QueryBlogEntries()
        {
            return _blogEntries.AsQueryable();
        }

        public override List<BlogEntry> ListBlogEntries()
        {
            return QueryBlogEntries().ToList();
        }

        public override void CreateBlogEntry(BlogEntry blogEntryToCreate)
        {
            _blogEntries.Add(blogEntryToCreate);
        }
    }
}
```

LISTING 17.8   UnleashedBlog.Tests\Models\FakeBlogRepository.vb (VB)

```vb
Imports System.Collections.Generic
Imports System.Linq

Public Class FakeBlogRepository
    Inherits BlogRepositoryBase

    Private _blogEntries As New List(Of BlogEntry)

    Protected Overrides Function QueryBlogEntries() As IQueryable(Of BlogEntry)
        Return _blogEntries.AsQueryable
    End Function


    Public Overrides Function ListBlogEntries() As List(Of BlogEntry)
        Return _blogEntries.AsQueryable.ToList()
    End Function

    Public Overrides Sub CreateBlogEntry(ByVal blogEntryToCreate As BlogEntry)
        _blogEntries.Add(blogEntryToCreate)
```

```
     End Sub
End Class
```

Notice that the repository class in Listing 17.8 inherits from the `BlogRepositoryBase` class. This implementation of the base class stores and retrieves blog entries from a collection stored in memory.

We can use the fake blog repository in our tests. A refactored version of the `Blog` controller tests is contained in Listing 17.9.

LISTING 17.9   UnleashedBlog.Tests\Controllers\BlogControllerTests.cs (C#)

```csharp
using System.Collections;
using System.Web.Mvc;
using Microsoft.VisualStudio.TestTools.UnitTesting;
using UnleashedBlog.Controllers;
using UnleashedBlog.Models;
using UnleashedBlog.Tests.Models;

namespace UnleashedBlog.Tests.Controllers
{
    [TestClass]
    public class BlogControllerTests
    {

        [TestMethod]
        public void ShowNewBlogEntries()
        {
            // Arrange
            var repository = new FakeBlogRepository();
            var controller = new BlogController(repository);

            // Act
            var result = (ViewResult)controller.Index();

            // Assert
CollectionAssert.AllItemsAreInstancesOfType((ICollection)result.ViewData.Model,
➥typeof(BlogEntry)));
        }


        [TestMethod]
        public void CreateBlogEntry()
        {
            // Arrange
            var repository = new FakeBlogRepository();
```

```csharp
            var controller = new BlogController(repository);
            var blogEntryToCreate = new BlogEntry();

            // Act
            controller.Create(blogEntryToCreate);
            var result = (ViewResult)controller.Index();

            // Assert
            var firstEntry = ((IList)result.ViewData.Model)[0];
            Assert.AreSame(blogEntryToCreate, firstEntry);
        }

    }
}
```

LISTING 17.9   UnleashedBlog.Tests\Controllers\BlogControllerTests.vb (VB)

```vb
Imports System
Imports System.Text
Imports System.Collections.Generic
Imports Microsoft.VisualStudio.TestTools.UnitTesting
Imports System.Web.Mvc

<TestClass()> Public Class BlogControllerTests

    <TestMethod()> _
    Public Sub ShowNewBlogEntries()
        ' Arrange
        Dim repository As New FakeBlogRepository()
        Dim controller = New BlogController(repository)

        ' Act
        Dim result As ViewResult = controller.Index()

        ' Assert
        CollectionAssert.AllItemsAreInstancesOfType(result.ViewData.Model,
➥GetType(BlogEntry))
    End Sub


    <TestMethod()> _
    Public Sub CreateBlogEntry()
        ' Arrange
        Dim repository As New FakeBlogRepository()
        Dim controller = New BlogController(repository)
```

```
    Dim blogEntryToCreate = New BlogEntry()

    ' Act
    controller.Create(blogEntryToCreate)
    Dim result As ViewResult = controller.Index()

    ' Assert
    Dim firstEntry = result.ViewData.Model(0)
    Assert.AreSame(blogEntryToCreate, firstEntry)
End Sub

End Class
```

Notice that both tests in Listing 17.9 use the fake blog repository. An instance of the fake blog repository is created in the Arrange section of both tests and passed to the constructor of the Blog controller.

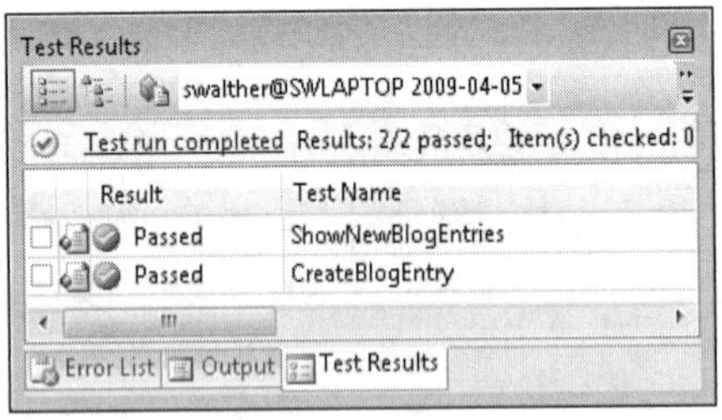

FIGURE 17.11   Tests still pass after refactoring.

We rewrote a lot of code in this section. However, we can rewrite our code fearlessly because it is covered by tests. If we press the keyboard combination Ctrl+R, A then all of our tests still pass (see Figure 17.11).

Creating an Entity Framework Repository

In this final section, we make everything real by implementing an Entity Framework blog repository. Unlike the fake blog repository, the Entity Framework blog repository actually stores the blog entries in a database.

To create an Entity Framework blog repository, we need to complete each of the following steps:

1. Create a database that contains a BlogEntries table.
2. Create an Entity Framework data model.
3. Implement the Entity Framework blog repository class.

Creating the Database Objects

We use SQL Server Express for our database. This database is free, and it can be downloaded with Visual Studio or Visual Web Developer. Follow these steps to create a new SQL Server Express database and database table:

1. Right-click the App_Data folder and select the menu option Add, New Item. Select the SQL Server Database template, name the database BlogDB.mdf, and click the Add button (see Figure 17.12).

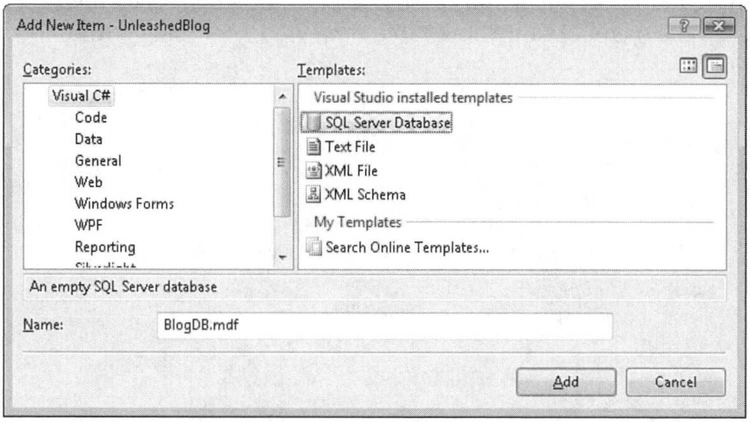

FIGURE 17.12   Creating a new database

2. Double-click the BlogDB.mdf file in the App_Data folder to open the Server Explorer window.
3. Right-click the Tables folder and select the menu option Add New Table.
4. Enter the columns in Table 17.1.

TABLE 17.1   BlogEntries Table Columns

Column Name	Data Type	Allow Nulls
Id	int	False
Name	nvarchar(500)	False
Author	nvarchar(100)	False
DatePublished	DateTime	False
DateModified	DateTime	True
Title	nvarchar(500)	False
Description	nvarchar(max)	True
Text	nvarchar(max)	False

5. Mark the Id column as a primary key column by selecting the Id column and clicking the button with the icon of a key.

6. Mark the Id column as an Identity column by expanding the Identity Specification property under Column properties and assigning the value Yes to the (Is Identity) property.

7. Click the Save button (the button with an icon of a floppy disk) and give the new table the name BlogEntries.

After you create the new database, you should add some fake blog entries to the database so that you have something to look at when you run the application. Right-click the BlogEntries table and select the menu option Show Table Data. Add a few blog entries to the table (see Figure 17.13).

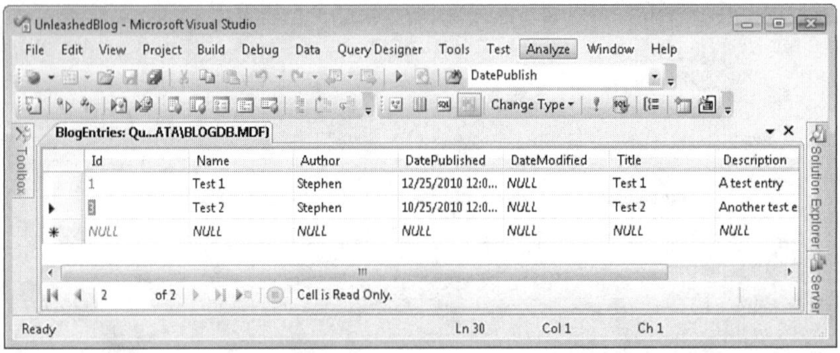

FIGURE 17.13   Adding blog entries to the BlogEntries table

Creating the Entity Framework Data Model

Next, we need to create the data model. In other words, we need to create a set of C# or VB.NET classes that represents our database in our ASP.NET MVC application.

Follow these steps to create a data model using the Microsoft Entity Framework:

1. Add a new folder to the Models folder named EntityFramework.

2. Right-click the Models\EntityFramework folder and select the menu option Add, New Item.

3. Select the Data category and the ADO.NET Entity Data Model template. Name your data model DataModel.edmx and click the Add button (see Figure 17.14).

After you complete these steps, the ADO.NET Entity Data Model Wizard launches. Complete the following wizard steps:

1. In the Choose Model Contents step, select the Generate from Database option.

2. In the Choose Your Data Connection step, select BlogDB.mdf for the data connection and BlogDBEntities for the entity connection settings.

3. In the Choose Your Database Objects step, select the BlogEntries database table. Enter the namespace UnleashedBlog.Models.EntityFramework for the model namespace.

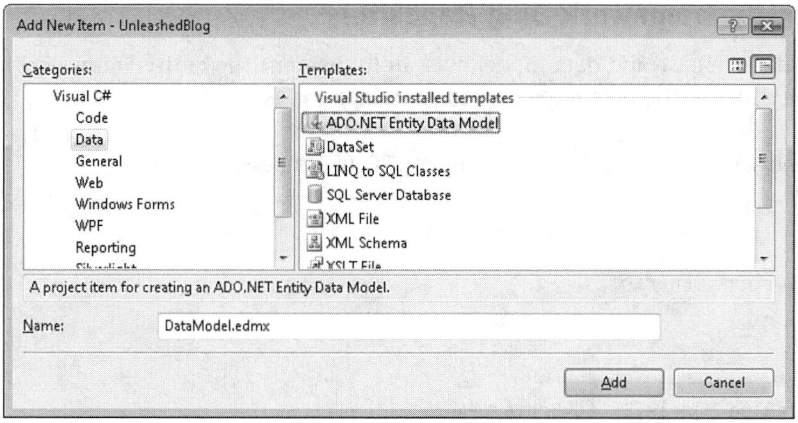

Add New Item - UnleashedBlog

Categories:

Visual C#
 Code
 Data
 General
 Web
 Windows Forms
 WPF
 Reporting

Templates:

Visual Studio installed templates

ADO.NET Entity Data Model
DataSet
LINQ to SQL Classes
SQL Server Database
XML File
XML Schema
XSLT File

A project item for creating an ADO.NET Entity Data Model.

Name: DataModel.edmx

Add   Cancel

FIGURE 17.14   Adding a Entity Framework data model

4. Click the Finish button to complete the wizard.

After you complete these steps, the Entity Framework Designer opens. The designer displays a class that corresponds to the BlogEntries database table.

We have one last step to complete. We need to rename the entity from BlogEntries to BlogEntryEntity. Right-click the BlogEntries entity in the designer and select the menu option Rename. Give the entity the name `BlogEntryEntity` (see Figure 17.15).

FIGURE 17.15   The Entity Framework Designer

Why do we name the entity BlogEntryEntity instead of BlogEntry? Our application will have both a `BlogEntry` and `BlogEntryEntity` class. The `BlogEntry` class is used in our application code. The `BlogEntryEntity` class will be encapsulated within our Entity Framework repository class. That way, we avoid introducing any dependency on the Entity Framework outside of our Entity Framework repository.

Creating the Entity Framework Blog Repository

Now that we created a database and data model, we can implement the Entity Framework blog repository. The code for the new repository is contained in Listing 17.15.

LISTING 17.15   UnleashedBlog\Models\EntityFramework\EntityFrameworkBlog
➡Repository.cs (C#)

```csharp
using System;
using System.Collections.Generic;
using System.Linq;
using System.Web;

namespace UnleashedBlog.Models.EntityFramework
{
    public class EntityFrameworkBlogRepository : BlogRepositoryBase
    {
        private BlogDBEntities _entities = new BlogDBEntities();

        private BlogEntryEntity ConvertBlogEntryToBlogEntryEntity(BlogEntry entry)
        {
            var entity = new BlogEntryEntity();

            entity.Id = entry.Id;
            entity.Author = entry.Author;
            entity.Description = entry.Description;
            entity.Name = entry.Name;
            entity.DatePublished = entry.DatePublished;
            entity.Text = entry.Text;
            entity.Title = entry.Title;
            return entity;
        }

        protected override IQueryable<BlogEntry> QueryBlogEntries()
        {
            return from e in _entities.BlogEntryEntitySet
                   select new BlogEntry
                   {
                       Id = e.Id,
                       Author = e.Author,
                       Description = e.Description,
                       Name = e.Name,
                       DateModified = e.DateModified,
                       DatePublished = e.DatePublished,
                       Text = e.Text,
                       Title = e.Title
```

```
                };
        }

        public override List<BlogEntry> ListBlogEntries()
        {
            return QueryBlogEntries().ToList();
        }

        public override void CreateBlogEntry(BlogEntry blogEntryToCreate)
        {
            var entity = ConvertBlogEntryToBlogEntryEntity(blogEntryToCreate);

            _entities.AddToBlogEntryEntitySet(entity);
            _entities.SaveChanges();
        }

    }
}
```

LISTING 17.15   UnleashedBlog\Models\EntityFramework\EntityFrameworkBlog
➥Repository.vb (VB)

```
Public Class EntityFrameworkBlogRepository
    Inherits BlogRepositoryBase

    Private _entities As New BlogDBEntities()

    Private Function ConvertBlogEntryToBlogEntryEntity(ByVal entry As BlogEntry) As
➥BlogEntryEntity
        Dim entity = New BlogEntryEntity()

        entity.Id = entry.Id
        entity.Author = entry.Author
        entity.Description = entry.Description
        entity.Name = entry.Name
        entity.DatePublished = entry.DatePublished
        entity.Text = entry.Text
        entity.Title = entry.Title
        Return entity
    End Function

    Protected Overrides Function QueryBlogEntries() As IQueryable(Of BlogEntry)
        Return From e In _entities.BlogEntryEntitySet _
                Select New BlogEntry With {.Id = e.Id, _
                                            .Author = e.Author, _
```

```
                                    .Description = e.Description, _
                                    .Name = e.Name, _
                                    .DateModified = e.DateModified, _
                                    .DatePublished = e.DatePublished, _
                                    .Text = e.Text, _
                                    .Title = e.Title}
    End Function
    Public Overrides Function ListBlogEntries() As List(Of BlogEntry)
        Return QueryBlogEntries().ToList()
    End Function

    Public Overrides Sub CreateBlogEntry(ByVal blogEntryToCreate As BlogEntry)
        Dim entity = ConvertBlogEntryToBlogEntryEntity(blogEntryToCreate)

        _entities.AddToBlogEntryEntitySet(entity)
        _entities.SaveChanges()
    End Sub

End Class
```

The repository in Listing 17.15 exposes two public methods named ListBlogEntries() and CreateBlogEntry(). There are the two methods called within the Blog controller.

The Entity Framework blog repository converts back and forth from instances of the BlogEntry class to instances of the BlogEntryEntity class. These classes—the BlogEntry and the BlogEntryEntity classes—have an identical set of properties. Why do we need both classes?

> **NOTE**
>
> I updated the BlogEntry class so that it has the same set of properties as the BlogEntryEntity class. We take a shortcut here. If we were following strict test-driven development, we wouldn't add properties to the BlogEntry class until we had a test that required it. However, because updating the Entity Framework data model is time-consuming, we are going to cheat.

The BlogEntryEntity class is generated by the Entity Framework Designer automatically. Internally, the BlogEntryEntity class depends on the Microsoft Entity Framework. The BlogEntry class, in contrast, does not depend on the Microsoft Entity Framework.

Because we want to maintain a sharp separation of concerns in our blog application, we don't want to use the BlogEntryEntity class in the remainder of our application. We want to isolate our data access logic from the remainder of our application logic.

There are two benefits that result from maintaining this sharp separation of concerns. First, in the future, we can easily switch to some other technology for our data access logic. For example, we could implement a LINQ to SQL blog repository or an NHibernate blog repository without modifying the remainder of our application code.

Second, maintaining a sharp separation of concerns between our data access logic and the remainder of our application makes our application more testable. Because our tests interact with the BlogEntry class and never the BlogEntryEntity class, we do not need to add a reference to the Microsoft Entity Framework to our test project.

Using the Entity Framework Repository

We now are ready to try out our new Entity Framework blog repository class. First, we need to update our blog controller (see Listing 17.16).

LISTING 17.16   UnleashedBlog\Controllers\BlogController.cs (C#)

```
using System.Collections.Generic;
using System.Web.Mvc;
using UnleashedBlog.Models;
using UnleashedBlog.Models.EntityFramework;

namespace UnleashedBlog.Controllers
{
    public class BlogController : Controller
    {
        private BlogRepositoryBase _repository;


        public BlogController()
            : this(new EntityFrameworkBlogRepository()) { }

        public BlogController(BlogRepositoryBase repository)
        {
            _repository = repository;
        }

        public ActionResult Index()
        {
            return View(_repository.ListBlogEntries());
        }
```

```
    public ActionResult Create()
    {
        return View();
    }


    [AcceptVerbs(HttpVerbs.Post)]
    public ActionResult Create(BlogEntry blogEntryToCreate)
    {
        _repository.CreateBlogEntry(blogEntryToCreate);
        return RedirectToAction("Index");
    }
  }
}
```

LISTING 17.16   UnleashedBlog\Controllers\BlogController.vb (VB)

```
Public Class BlogController
    Inherits System.Web.Mvc.Controller

    Private _repository As BlogRepositoryBase

    Public Sub New()
        Me.New(New EntityFrameworkBlogRepository())
    End Sub


    Public Sub New(ByVal repository As BlogRepositoryBase)
        _repository = repository
    End Sub


    Public Function Index() As ActionResult
        Return View(_repository.ListBlogEntries())
    End Function


    Public Function Create()
        Return View()
    End Function

    <AcceptVerbs(HttpVerbs.Post)> _
    Public Function Create(ByVal blogEntryToCreate As BlogEntry) As ActionResult
        _repository.CreateBlogEntry(blogEntryToCreate)
```

```
        Return RedirectToAction("Index")
    End Function

End Class
```

Notice that the blog controller in Listing 17.16 has been modified so that it has two constructors. The first constructor—the parameterless constructor—is called when the application is used in production. This constructor creates a new instance of the Entity Framework blog repository and passes it to the second constructor.

The second constructor accepts an instance of the blog repository class. This second constructor is called in the tests. Within a test, an instance of the fake blog repository class is passed to this second constructor.

To run our blog application, we need to add two views to the application. Right-click the Index() action and select the menu option Add View (see Figure 17.16).

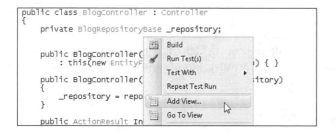

FIGURE 17.16   Adding the Index view

Check the check box labeled Create a Strongly-Typed View. For View Data Class, select the BlogEntry class. For View Content, select List. Click the Add button to generate the view.

WARNING

If nothing appears in the View Data Class drop-down list, verify that you can build the application. If there are build errors, the drop-down list will be empty.

Next, create a view for the Create() action by right-clicking the Create() action and selecting the menu option Add View. Create a strongly typed view that represents the BlogEntry class. For View Content, select Create (see Figure 17.17). Click the Add button to generate the Create view.

FIGURE 17.17   Adding the Create view

We need to make one last change before we can run the blog application. We need to modify the route table in the Global.asax file so that the default controller for our application is the Blog controller instead of the Home controller. Modify the Default route in the Global.asax file so that it looks like Listing 17.17.

LISTING 17.17   UnleashedBlog\Global.asax (C#)

```
routes.MapRoute(
    "Default",
    "{controller}/{action}/{id}",
    new { controller = "Blog", action = "Index", id = "" }
);
```

LISTING 17.17   UnleashedBlog\Global.asax (VB)

```
routes.MapRoute( _
  "Default", _
  "{controller}/{action}/{id}", _
  New With {.controller = "Blog", .action = "Index", .id = ""} _
)
```

You can run the blog application by pressing F5 (or by selecting the menu option Debug, Start Debugging). The page in Figure 17.18 appears in your browser. If you click the Create New link, you can add a new blog entry. (Warning: We haven't added any validation to the Create form yet.)

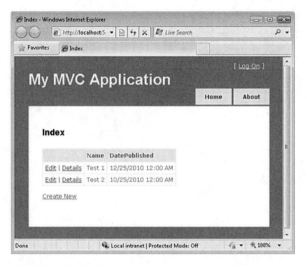

FIGURE 17.18   The page rendered by the Index view

Summary

So, we are off to a good start. In this chapter, we created the first iteration of our Unleashed Blog application. We can list blog entries and we can create new blog entries.

In this chapter, we stuck to good test-driven development practices. We started by writing a failing test. Then we wrote just enough code to satisfy the requirements expressed by the test.

We also took advantage of the Repository pattern. The Repository pattern enables us to maintain a sharp separation of concerns. By following the Repository pattern, we also made our application code more testable. We implemented two concrete blog repositories: a fake repository and an Entity Framework repository.

Creating the Routes

In this chapter, we modify the Unleashed Blog application so that it supports retrieving archived blog entries. In other words, we modify the blog application so that it supports the user stories displayed in Figure 18.1.

We need to create a new Archive controller; however, because we practice test-driven development, we start with the tests.

We need to add two types of tests. First, we need to create tests that verify that the Archive controller behaves in the way that we expect. We also need to create tests for the routes that we define in the Global.asax file.

Creating the Controller Tests

According to a careful reading of the napkin, we need to retrieve archived blog entries by date or name. For example, any of the following browser requests should return a list of blog entries:

/Archive/2010—Returns all blog entries from the year 2010

/Archive/2010/12—Returns all blog entries from December 2010

/Archive/2010/12/25—Returns all blog entries from Christmas 2010

/Archive/2010/12/25/Aliens-Attack—Returns the blog entry with the name Aliens Attack from Christmas 2010

We can express all these requirements with the set of tests in Listing 18.1.

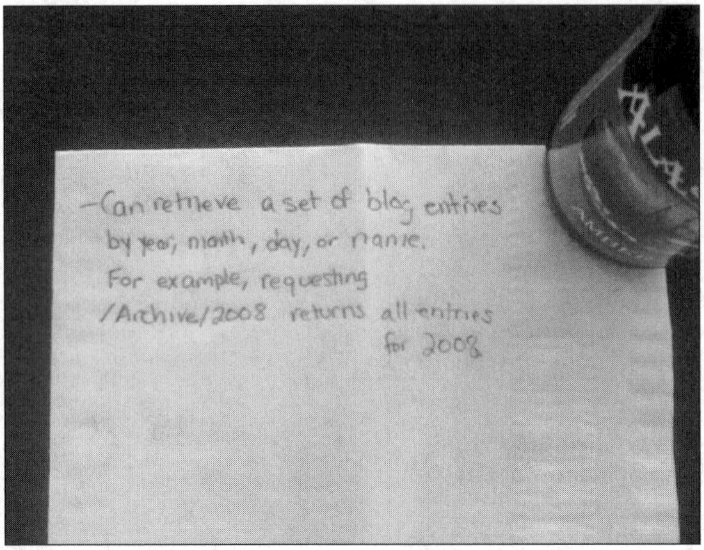

FIGURE 18.1   User stories

LISTING 18.1   UnleashedBlog.Tests\Controller\ArchiveControllerTests.cs (C#)

```
using System;
using System.Collections.Generic;
using System.Web.Mvc;
using Microsoft.VisualStudio.TestTools.UnitTesting;
using UnleashedBlog.Controllers;
using UnleashedBlog.Models;
using UnleashedBlog.Tests.Models;

namespace UnleashedBlog.Tests.Controllers
{
    [TestClass]
    public class ArchiveControllerTests
    {

        [TestMethod]
        public void IndexReturnsBlogEntriesByYear()
        {
            // Arrange
            var repository = new FakeBlogRepository();
            var blogController = new BlogController(repository);
            var archiveController = new ArchiveController(repository);
```

```
            blogController.Create(new BlogEntry { Name = "Test-1", DatePublished =
➥new DateTime(2010, 11, 25) });
            blogController.Create(new BlogEntry { Name = "Test-2", DatePublished =
➥new DateTime(2010, 12, 25) });
            blogController.Create(new BlogEntry { Name = "Test-3", DatePublished =
➥new DateTime(2011, 12, 26) });

        // Act
        var result = (ViewResult)archiveController.Index(2010, null, null, null);

        // Assert
        var blogEntries = (IList<BlogEntry>)result.ViewData.Model;
        Assert.AreEqual(2, blogEntries.Count);
    }


    [TestMethod]
    public void IndexReturnsBlogEntriesByMonth()
    {
        // Arrange
        var repository = new FakeBlogRepository();
        var blogController = new BlogController(repository);
        var archiveController = new ArchiveController(repository);


            blogController.Create(new BlogEntry { Name = "Test-1", DatePublished =
➥new DateTime(2010, 11, 25) });
            blogController.Create(new BlogEntry { Name = "Test-2", DatePublished =
➥new DateTime(2010, 12, 25) });
            blogController.Create(new BlogEntry { Name = "Test-3", DatePublished =
➥new DateTime(2010, 12, 26) });

        // Act
        var result = (ViewResult)archiveController.Index(2010, 12, null, null);

        // Assert
        var blogEntries = (IList<BlogEntry>)result.ViewData.Model;
        Assert.AreEqual(2, blogEntries.Count);
    }

    [TestMethod]
    public void IndexReturnsBlogEntriesByDay()
    {
        // Arrange
```

```
            var repository = new FakeBlogRepository();
            var blogController = new BlogController(repository);
            var archiveController = new ArchiveController(repository);


            blogController.Create(new BlogEntry { Name = "Test-1", DatePublished =
➥new DateTime(2010, 12, 25) });
            blogController.Create(new BlogEntry { Name = "Test-2", DatePublished =
➥new DateTime(2010, 12, 25) });
            blogController.Create(new BlogEntry { Name = "Test-3", DatePublished =
➥new DateTime(2010, 12, 26) });

            // Act
            var result = (ViewResult)archiveController.Index(2010, 12, 25, null);

            // Assert
            var blogEntries = (IList<BlogEntry>)result.ViewData.Model;
            Assert.AreEqual(2, blogEntries.Count);
        }



        [TestMethod]
        public void IndexReturnsBlogEntryByName()
        {
            // Arrange
            var repository = new FakeBlogRepository();
            var blogController = new BlogController(repository);
            var archiveController = new ArchiveController(repository);

            blogController.Create(new BlogEntry { Name = "Test-1", DatePublished =
➥new DateTime(2010, 12, 25) });
            blogController.Create(new BlogEntry { Name = "Test-2", DatePublished =
➥new DateTime(2010, 12, 25) });

            // Act
            var result = (ViewResult)archiveController.Index(null, null, null,
➥"Test-2");

            // Assert
            var blogEntries = (IList<BlogEntry>)result.ViewData.Model;
            Assert.AreEqual(1, blogEntries.Count);
            Assert.AreEqual("Test-2", blogEntries[0].Name);
        }
```

```
        }
}
```

LISTING 18.1   UnleashedBlog.Tests\Controller\ArchiveControllerTests.vb (VB)

```vb
Imports Microsoft.VisualStudio.TestTools.UnitTesting
Imports System.Web.Mvc

<TestClass()> _
    Public Class ArchiveControllerTests

    <TestMethod()> _
    Public Sub IndexReturnsBlogEntriesByYear()
        ' Arrange
        Dim repository = New FakeBlogRepository()
        Dim blogController = New BlogController(repository)
        Dim archiveController = New ArchiveController(repository)


        blogController.Create(New BlogEntry With {.Name = "Test-1", .DatePublished
➥= New DateTime(2010, 11, 25)})
        blogController.Create(New BlogEntry With {.Name = "Test-2", .DatePublished
➥= New DateTime(2010, 12, 25)})
        blogController.Create(New BlogEntry With {.Name = "Test-3", .DatePublished
➥= New DateTime(2011, 12, 26)})

        ' Act
        Dim result As ViewResult = archiveController.Index(2010, Nothing, Nothing,
➥Nothing)

        ' Assert
        Dim blogEntries As IList(Of BlogEntry) = result.ViewData.Model
        Assert.AreEqual(2, blogEntries.Count)
    End Sub


    <TestMethod()> _
    Public Sub IndexReturnsBlogEntriesByMonth()
        ' Arrange
        Dim repository = New FakeBlogRepository()
        Dim blogController = New BlogController(repository)
        Dim archiveController = New ArchiveController(repository)
```

```
        blogController.Create(New BlogEntry With {.Name = "Test-1", .DatePublished
➥= New DateTime(2010, 11, 25)})
        blogController.Create(New BlogEntry With {.Name = "Test-2", .DatePublished
➥= New DateTime(2010, 12, 25)})
        blogController.Create(New BlogEntry With {.Name = "Test-3", .DatePublished
➥= New DateTime(2010, 12, 26)})

        ' Act
        Dim result As ViewResult = archiveController.Index(2010, 12, Nothing,
➥Nothing)

        ' Assert
        Dim blogEntries As IList(Of BlogEntry) = result.ViewData.Model
        Assert.AreEqual(2, blogEntries.Count)
    End Sub

    <TestMethod()> _
    Public Sub IndexReturnsBlogEntriesByDay()
        ' Arrange
        Dim repository = New FakeBlogRepository()
        Dim blogController = New BlogController(repository)
        Dim archiveController = New ArchiveController(repository)


        blogController.Create(New BlogEntry With {.Name = "Test-1", .DatePublished
➥= New DateTime(2010, 12, 25)})
        blogController.Create(New BlogEntry With {.Name = "Test-2", .DatePublished
➥= New DateTime(2010, 12, 25)})
        blogController.Create(New BlogEntry With {.Name = "Test-3", .DatePublished
➥= New DateTime(2010, 12, 26)})

        ' Act
        Dim result As ViewResult = archiveController.Index(2010, 12, 25, Nothing)

        ' Assert
        Dim blogEntries As IList(Of BlogEntry) = result.ViewData.Model
        Assert.AreEqual(2, blogEntries.Count)
    End Sub

    <TestMethod()> _
    Public Sub IndexReturnsBlogEntryByName()
        ' Arrange
        Dim repository = New FakeBlogRepository()
        Dim blogController = New BlogController(repository)
        Dim archiveController = New ArchiveController(repository)
```

```
            blogController.Create(New BlogEntry With {.Name = "Test-1", .DatePublished
➡= New DateTime(2010, 12, 25)})
            blogController.Create(New BlogEntry With {.Name = "Test-2", .DatePublished
➡= New DateTime(2010, 12, 25)})

        ' Act
        Dim result As ViewResult = archiveController.Index(2010, 12, 25, "Test-1")

        ' Assert
        Dim blogEntries As IList(Of BlogEntry) = result.ViewData.Model
        Assert.AreEqual(1, blogEntries.Count)
        Assert.AreEqual("Test-1", blogEntries(0).Name)
    End Sub
```

```
End Class
```

For example, the first test in Listing 18.1 verifies that the Archive controller returns a list of blog entries that match a particular year. The test has an Arrange, Act, and Assert section.

In the Arrange section, an instance of the fake repository, Blog controller, and Archive controller are created. Three blog entries are created. Two of the blog entries have the year 2010 for their publication date, and one of the blog entries has the year 2011.

Next, in the Act section, the Archive controller Index() action is invoked with the value 2010 for the year.

Finally, in the Assert section, an assertion is made that two blog entries are returned from the Index() action. In other words, only the two blog entries with a publication date of 2010 should be returned, and the blog entry with a publication date of 2011 should not be returned.

When you create the tests in Listing 18.1, Visual Studio displays a red squiggly error message below every reference to the ArchiveController class. This class does not yet exist. We can't compile the tests because the Archive controller does not exist.

Before we do anything else, we should start by writing just enough application code to get our solution back into a state in which we can do a successful build. To build our application, we need to create the controller class in Listing 18.1A.

LISTING 18.1A   Controllers\ArchiveController.cs (C#)

```csharp
using System.Web.Mvc;
using UnleashedBlog.Models;

namespace UnleashedBlog.Controllers
{
```

```
public class ArchiveController : Controller
{
    public ArchiveController(BlogRepositoryBase repository)
    {
    }

    public ActionResult Index(int? year, int? month, int? day, string name)
    {
        return null;
    }

}
}
```

LISTING 18.1A   Controllers\ArchiveController.vb (VB)

```
Public Class ArchiveController
    Inherits Controller

    Public Sub New(ByVal repository As BlogRepositoryBase)
    End Sub

    Public Function Index(ByVal year As Integer?, ByVal month As Integer?, ByVal
➥day As Integer?, ByVal name As String) As ActionResult
        Return Nothing
    End Function

End Class
```

The Archive controller in Listing 18.1A gives us enough code to successfully compile our application. However, if we run our tests, the tests fail (see Figure 18.1A). That's good because we always want to start with a failing test. (We need to see the red before we see the green).

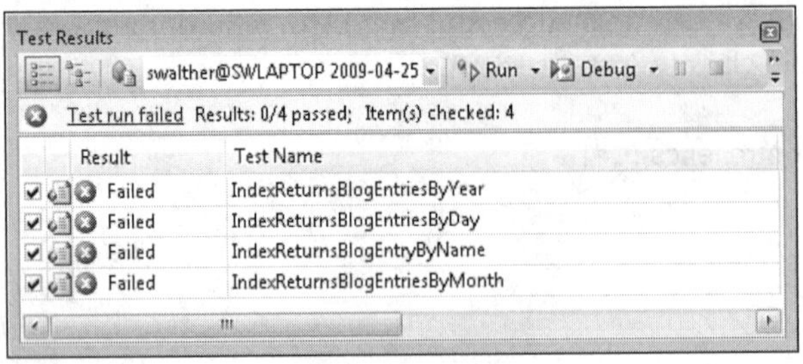

FIGURE 18.1A   Failing Archive controller tests

Because we have a set of failing tests, we can allow ourselves to write some application code. An updated Archive controller is contained in Listing 18.2.

LISTING 18.2   UnleashedBlog\ArchiveController.cs (C#)

```csharp
using System.Web.Mvc;
using UnleashedBlog.Models;
using UnleashedBlog.Models.EntityFramework;
namespace UnleashedBlog.Controllers
{
    public class ArchiveController : Controller
    {
        private BlogRepositoryBase _repository;

        public ArchiveController()
            : this(new EntityFrameworkBlogRepository()) { }

        public ArchiveController(BlogRepositoryBase repository)
        {
            _repository = repository;
        }

        public ActionResult Index(int? year, int? month, int? day, string name)
        {
            return View(_repository.ListBlogEntries(year, month, day, name));
        }

    }
}
```

LISTING 18.2   UnleashedBlog\ArchiveController.vb (VB)

```vbnet
Public Class ArchiveController
    Inherits Controller

    Private _repository As BlogRepositoryBase

    Public Sub New()
        Me.New(New EntityFrameworkBlogRepository())
    End Sub

    Public Sub New(ByVal repository As BlogRepositoryBase)
        _repository = repository
    End Sub
```

```
   Public Function Index(ByVal year As Integer?, ByVal month As Integer?, ByVal
➥day As Integer?, ByVal name As String) As ActionResult
       Return View(_repository.ListBlogEntries(year, month, day, name))
   End Function

End Class
```

The Archive controller exposes one action named Index(). The Index() action calls the ListBlogEntries() method on the repository class. The BlogRepositoryBase class in Listing 18.3 has been updated to include this new method.

LISTING 18.3   UnleashedBlog\Models\BlogRepositoryBase.cs (C#)

```
using System.Collections.Generic;
using System.Linq;

namespace UnleashedBlog.Models
{
    public abstract class BlogRepositoryBase
    {
        // Blog Entry Methods
        public abstract List<BlogEntry> ListBlogEntries();
        public abstract void CreateBlogEntry(BlogEntry blogEntryToCreate);
        protected abstract IQueryable<BlogEntry> QueryBlogEntries();

        public virtual List<BlogEntry> ListBlogEntries(int? year, int? month, int?
➥day, string name)
        {
            var query = this.QueryBlogEntries();
            if (year.HasValue)
                query = query.Where(e => e.DatePublished.Year == year.Value);
            if (month.HasValue)
                query = query.Where(e => e.DatePublished.Month == month.Value);
            if (day.HasValue)
                query = query.Where(e => e.DatePublished.Day == day.Value);
            if (!string.IsNullOrEmpty(name))
                query = query.Where(e => e.Name == name);

            return query.ToList();
        }
    }
}
```

LISTING 18.3   UnleashedBlog\Models\BlogRepositoryBase.vb (VB)

```vb
Imports System.Collections.Generic
Imports System.Linq

Public MustInherit Class BlogRepositoryBase

    ' Blog Entry Methods
    Public MustOverride Function ListBlogEntries() As List(Of BlogEntry)
    Public MustOverride Sub CreateBlogEntry(ByVal blogEntryToCreate As BlogEntry)
    Protected MustOverride Function QueryBlogEntries() As IQueryable(Of BlogEntry)

    Public Overridable Function ListBlogEntries(ByVal year As Integer?, ByVal month
➡As Integer?, ByVal day As Integer?, ByVal name As String) As List(Of BlogEntry)
        Dim query = Me.QueryBlogEntries()
        If year.HasValue Then
            query = query.Where(Function(e) e.DatePublished.Year = year.Value)
        End If
        If month.HasValue Then
            query = query.Where(Function(e) e.DatePublished.Month = month.Value)
        End If
        If day.HasValue Then
            query = query.Where(Function(e) e.DatePublished.Day = day.Value)
        End If
        If Not String.IsNullOrEmpty(name) Then
            query = query.Where(Function(e) e.Name = name)
        End If
        Return query.ToList()
    End Function

End Class
```

The ListBlogEntries() method in Listing 18.1 contains the application logic required to filter the list of blog entries by year, month, day, and name. This logic is used by both the fake repository and the Entity Framework repository.

After making these changes, the new set of Archive controller tests pass (see Figure 18.2).

Creating the Route Tests

To use the Archive controller, we need to add new routes to the route table defined in the Global.asax file. Right now, the Global.asax file contains a single Default route that maps incoming browser requests to the Blog controller. We need to map the right requests to the Archive controller.

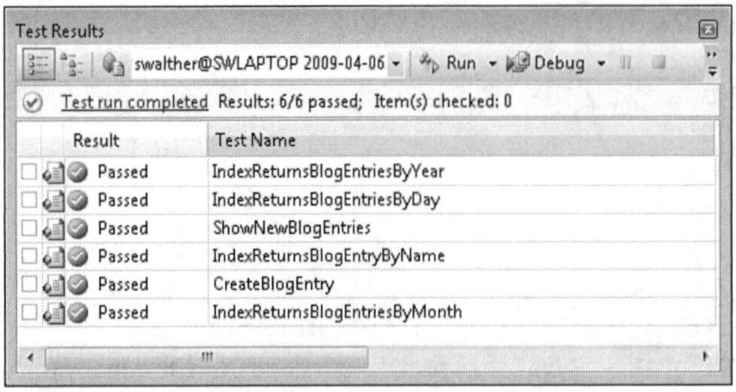

FIGURE 18.2   Passing the `Archive` controller tests

Because our route table starts to become complicated, we should build tests. We want to make sure that the right requests match the right route. We can use a set of tests in Listing 18.4 to test our routes.

LISTING 18.4   UnleashedBlog.UnitTests\Routes\RouteTests.cs (C#)

```
using System.Web.Routing;
using Microsoft.VisualStudio.TestTools.UnitTesting;
using MvcFakes;
using RouteDebugger.Routing;

namespace UnleashedBlog.Tests.Routes
{
    [TestClass]
    public class RouteTests
    {

        [TestMethod]
        public void DefaultRoute()
        {
            // Arrange
            var routes = new RouteCollection();
            MvcApplication.RegisterRoutes(routes);

            // Act
            var context = new FakeHttpContext("~/");
            var routeData = routes.GetRouteData(context);

            // Assert
            var matchedRoute = (NamedRoute)routeData.Route;
            Assert.AreEqual("Default", matchedRoute.Name);
        }
```

```csharp
[TestMethod]
public void ArchiveYear()
{
    // Arrange
    var routes = new RouteCollection();
    MvcApplication.RegisterRoutes(routes);

    // Act
    var context = new FakeHttpContext("~/Archive/2008");
    var routeData = routes.GetRouteData(context);

    // Assert
    var matchedRoute = (NamedRoute)routeData.Route;
    Assert.AreEqual("ArchiveYear", matchedRoute.Name);
    Assert.AreEqual("2008", routeData.Values["year"]);
}


[TestMethod]
public void ArchiveYearMonth()
{
    // Arrange
    var routes = new RouteCollection();
    MvcApplication.RegisterRoutes(routes);

    // Act
    var context = new FakeHttpContext("~/Archive/2008/12");
    var routeData = routes.GetRouteData(context);

    // Assert
    var matchedRoute = (NamedRoute)routeData.Route;
    Assert.AreEqual("ArchiveYearMonth", matchedRoute.Name);
    Assert.AreEqual("2008", routeData.Values["year"]);
    Assert.AreEqual("12", routeData.Values["month"]);
}

[TestMethod]
public void ArchiveYearMonthDay()
{
    // Arrange
    var routes = new RouteCollection();
    MvcApplication.RegisterRoutes(routes);

    // Act
    var context = new FakeHttpContext("~/Archive/2008/12/25");
```

```
        var routeData = routes.GetRouteData(context);

        // Assert
        var matchedRoute = (NamedRoute)routeData.Route;
        Assert.AreEqual("ArchiveYearMonthDay", matchedRoute.Name);
        Assert.AreEqual("2008", routeData.Values["year"]);
        Assert.AreEqual("12", routeData.Values["month"]);
        Assert.AreEqual("25", routeData.Values["day"]);
    }


    [TestMethod]
    public void ArchiveYearMonthDayName()
    {
        // Arrange
        var routes = new RouteCollection();
        MvcApplication.RegisterRoutes(routes);

        // Act
        var context = new FakeHttpContext("~/Archive/2008/12/25/Test");
        var routeData = routes.GetRouteData(context);

        // Assert
        var matchedRoute = (NamedRoute)routeData.Route;
        Assert.AreEqual("ArchiveFull", matchedRoute.Name);
        Assert.AreEqual("2008", routeData.Values["year"]);
        Assert.AreEqual("12", routeData.Values["month"]);
        Assert.AreEqual("25", routeData.Values["day"]);
        Assert.AreEqual("Test", routeData.Values["name"]);
    }



    }
}
```

LISTING 18.4   UnleashedBlog.UnitTests\Routes\RouteTests.vb (VB)

```
Imports Microsoft.VisualStudio.TestTools.UnitTesting
Imports MvcFakes
Imports System.Web.Routing
Imports RouteDebugger.Routing

<TestClass()> _
    Public Class RouteTests
```

```vb
<TestMethod()> _
Public Sub DefaultRoute()
    ' Arrange
    Dim routes = New RouteCollection()
    MvcApplication.RegisterRoutes(routes)

    ' Act
    Dim context = New FakeHttpContext("~/")
    Dim routeData = routes.GetRouteData(context)

    ' Assert
    Dim matchedRoute = CType(routeData.Route, NamedRoute)
    Assert.AreEqual("Default", matchedRoute.Name)
End Sub


<TestMethod()> _
Public Sub ArchiveYear()
    ' Arrange
    Dim routes = New RouteCollection()
    MvcApplication.RegisterRoutes(routes)

    ' Act
    Dim context = New FakeHttpContext("~/Archive/2008")
    Dim routeData = routes.GetRouteData(context)

    ' Assert
    Dim matchedRoute = CType(routeData.Route, NamedRoute)
    Assert.AreEqual("ArchiveYear", matchedRoute.Name)
    Assert.AreEqual("2008", routeData.Values("year"))
End Sub


<TestMethod()> _
Public Sub ArchiveYearMonth()
    ' Arrange
    Dim routes = New RouteCollection()
    MvcApplication.RegisterRoutes(routes)

    ' Act
    Dim context = New FakeHttpContext("~/Archive/2008/12")
    Dim routeData = routes.GetRouteData(context)

    ' Assert
    Dim matchedRoute = CType(routeData.Route, NamedRoute)
```

```vbnet
        Assert.AreEqual("ArchiveYearMonth", matchedRoute.Name)
        Assert.AreEqual("2008", routeData.Values("year"))
        Assert.AreEqual("12", routeData.Values("month"))
    End Sub


    <TestMethod()> _
    Public Sub ArchiveYearMonthDay()
        ' Arrange
        Dim routes = New RouteCollection()
        MvcApplication.RegisterRoutes(routes)
        ' Act
        Dim context = New FakeHttpContext("~/Archive/2008/12/25")
        Dim routeData = routes.GetRouteData(context)

        ' Assert
        Dim matchedRoute = CType(routeData.Route, NamedRoute)
        Assert.AreEqual("ArchiveYearMonthDay", matchedRoute.Name)
        Assert.AreEqual("2008", routeData.Values("year"))
        Assert.AreEqual("12", routeData.Values("month"))
        Assert.AreEqual("25", routeData.Values("day"))
    End Sub


    <TestMethod()> _
    Public Sub ArchiveYearMonthDayName()
        ' Arrange
        Dim routes = New RouteCollection()
        MvcApplication.RegisterRoutes(routes)

        ' Act
        Dim context = New FakeHttpContext("~/Archive/2008/12/25/Test")
        Dim routeData = routes.GetRouteData(context)

        ' Assert
        Dim matchedRoute = CType(routeData.Route, NamedRoute)
        Assert.AreEqual("ArchiveFull", matchedRoute.Name)
        Assert.AreEqual("2008", routeData.Values("year"))
        Assert.AreEqual("12", routeData.Values("month"))
        Assert.AreEqual("25", routeData.Values("day"))
        Assert.AreEqual("Test", routeData.Values("name"))
    End Sub


End Class
```

The test class in Listing 18.4 contains the following five tests:

1. DefaultRoute—Verifies that a request for ~/ matches the Default route.
2. ArchiveYear—Verifies that a request for ~/Archive/2008 matches the ArchiveYear route.
3. ArchiveYearMonth—Verifies that a request for ~/Archive/2008/12 matches the ArchiveYearMonth route.
4. ArchiveYearMonthDay—Verifies that a request for ~/Archive/2008/12/25 matches the ArchiveYearMonthDay route.
5. ArchiveYearMonthDayName—Verifies that a request for ~/Archive/2008/12/25/Test matches the ArchiveYearMonthDayName route.

Each route passes different information to the controller. For example, the ArchiveYearMonthDay route passes values for the year, month, and day parameters to the controller.

Before you can use the test class in Listing 18.4, you need to add references to the MvcFakes.dll and the RouteDebugger.dll assemblies:

▶ Add a reference to the MvcFakes.dll assembly to the UnleashedBlog.Tests project by selecting the UnleashedBlog.Tests project. Select the Project, Add Reference menu option and browse to the MvcFakes.dll assembly in the MvcFakes project in the sample code (available on the book's website, www.informit.com/title/ 9780672329982) (see Figure 18.3).

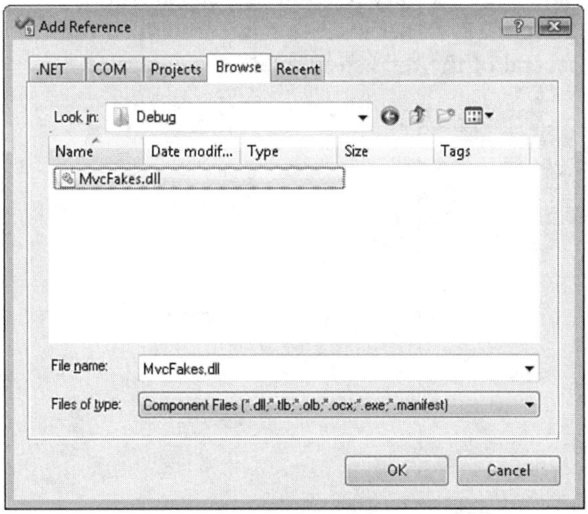

FIGURE 18.3   Browsing to the MvcFakes.dll assembly

▶ Add a reference to the RouteDebugger.dll assembly to both the UnleashedBlog project and the UnleashedBlog.Tests project. Select the Project, Add Reference menu option and browse to the RouteDebugger.dll assembly in the RouteDebugger project in the sample code on the website (see Figure 18.4).

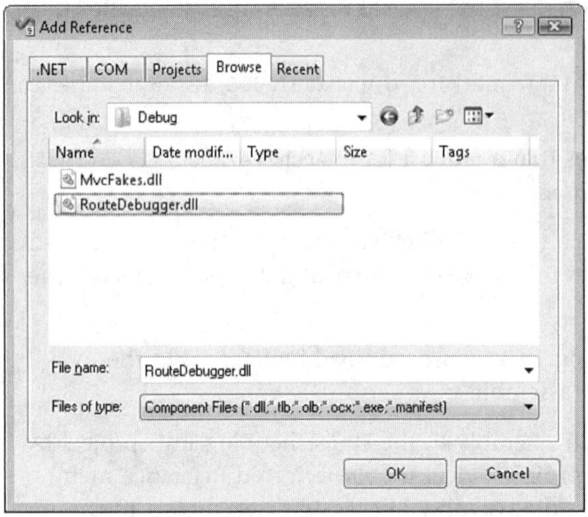

FIGURE 18.4 Browsing to the RouteDebugger.dll assembly

After you create the route tests, and you add the necessary references, you can run the tests by pressing the keyboard combination Ctrl+R, A. Because we have not added the necessary routes to the Global.asax file, several of the tests should fail (see Figure 18.5).

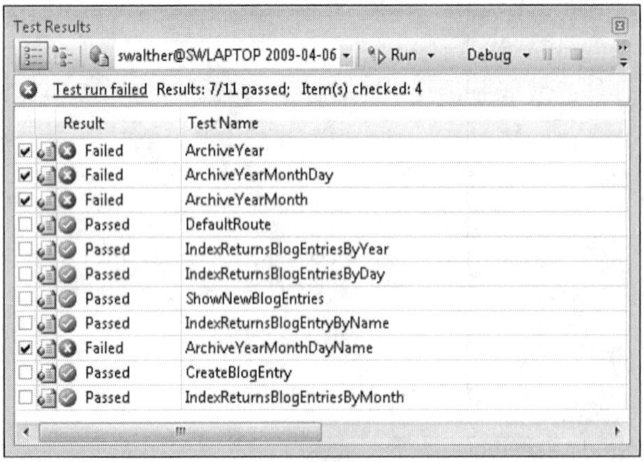

FIGURE 18.5 Failing route tests

In the next section, we modify the Unleashed Blog application so that it contains the necessary routes to pass these tests.

Creating the Archive Routes

We need to add the right routes to the route table created in the Global.asax file. We need to pass the right parameters, such as the year, month, day, and name, to the controller that matches the route.

The modified Global.asax file is contained in Listing 18.5.

LISTING 18.5   UnleashedBlog\Global.asax.cs (C#)

```csharp
using System;
using System.Collections.Generic;
using System.Linq;
using System.Web;
using System.Web.Mvc;
using System.Web.Routing;

namespace UnleashedBlog
{
    // Note: For instructions on enabling IIS6 or IIS7 classic mode,
    // visit http://go.microsoft.com/?LinkId=9394801

    public class MvcApplication : System.Web.HttpApplication
    {
        public static void RegisterRoutes(RouteCollection routes)
        {
            routes.IgnoreRoute("{resource}.axd/{*pathInfo}");

            routes.MapRoute(
                "ArchiveFull",
                "archive/{year}/{month}/{day}/{name}",
                new { controller = "Archive", action = "Index" }
            );


            routes.MapRoute(
                "ArchiveYearMonthDay",
                "archive/{year}/{month}/{day}",
                new { controller = "Archive", action = "Index" }
            );


            routes.MapRoute(
                "ArchiveYearMonth",
                "archive/{year}/{month}",
                new { controller = "Archive", action = "Index" }
```

```
            );


        routes.MapRoute(
            "ArchiveYear",
            "archive/{year}",
            new { controller = "Archive", action = "Index" }
        );


        routes.MapRoute(
            "Default",
            "{controller}/{action}/{id}",
            new { controller = "Blog", action = "Index", id = "" }
        );


    }

    protected void Application_Start()
    {
        RegisterRoutes(RouteTable.Routes);
    }
  }
}
```

LISTING 18.5   UnleashedBlog\Global.asax.vb (VB)

```
' Note: For instructions on enabling IIS6 or IIS7 classic mode,
' visit http://go.microsoft.com/?LinkId=9394802

Public Class MvcApplication
    Inherits System.Web.HttpApplication

    Shared Sub RegisterRoutes(ByVal routes As RouteCollection)
        routes.IgnoreRoute("{resource}.axd/{*pathInfo}")

        routes.MapRoute( _
            "ArchiveFull", _
            "archive/{year}/{month}/{day}/{name}", _
            New With {Key .controller = "Archive", Key .action = "Index"})


        routes.MapRoute( _
            "ArchiveYearMonthDay", _
            "archive/{year}/{month}/{day}", _
```

```
                New With {Key .controller = "Archive", Key .action = "Index"})


            routes.MapRoute( _
                "ArchiveYearMonth", _
                "archive/{year}/{month}", _
                New With {Key .controller = "Archive", Key .action = "Index"})


            routes.MapRoute( _
                "ArchiveYear", _
                "archive/{year}", _
                New With {Key .controller = "Archive", Key .action = "Index"})


            routes.MapRoute("Default", "{controller}/{action}/{id}", New With {Key
➡.controller = "Blog", Key .action = "Index", Key .id = ""})

        End Sub

        Sub Application_Start()
            RegisterRoutes(RouteTable.Routes)
        End Sub
    End Class
```

If you update the Global.asax file with the new routes and you rerun the tests in your test project by pressing Ctrl+R, A, all the tests pass (see Figure 18.6).

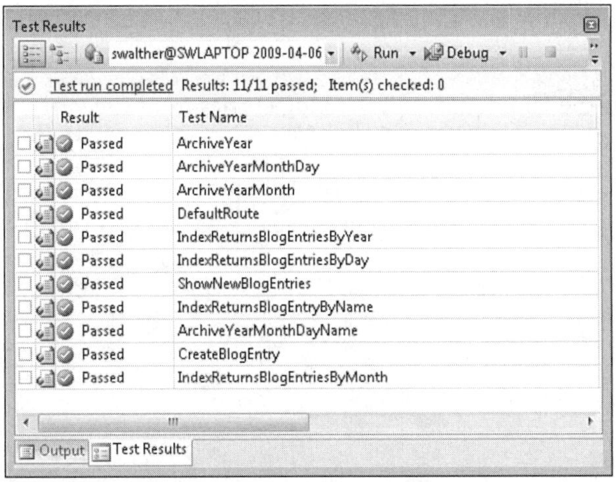

FIGURE 18.6   Passing the route tests

Trying Out the Archive Controller

You can try out the Archive controller by adding a new view to the UnleashedBlog project. Open the Archive controller, right-click the Index() action, and select the menu option Add View. Create a new strongly typed view with a BlogEntry view class and a List view content (see Figure 18.7).

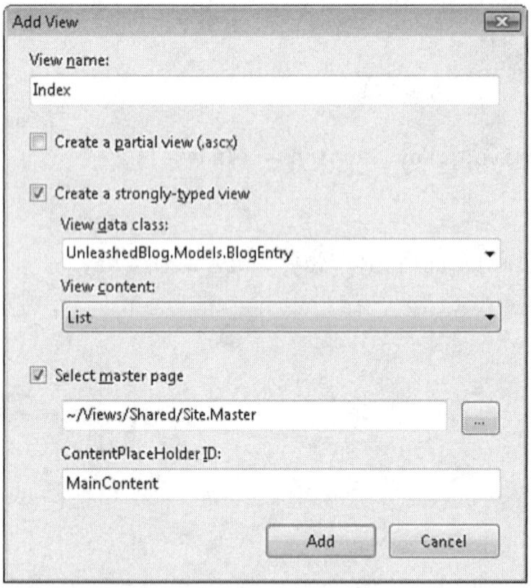

FIGURE 18.7   Adding an Archive controller Index view

After you add the Index view for the Archive controller, you can invoke the Archive controller by using a URL like the following:

/Archive/2008

Invoking the Archive controller with the URL returns all the blog entries from the year 2008 (see Figure 18.8).

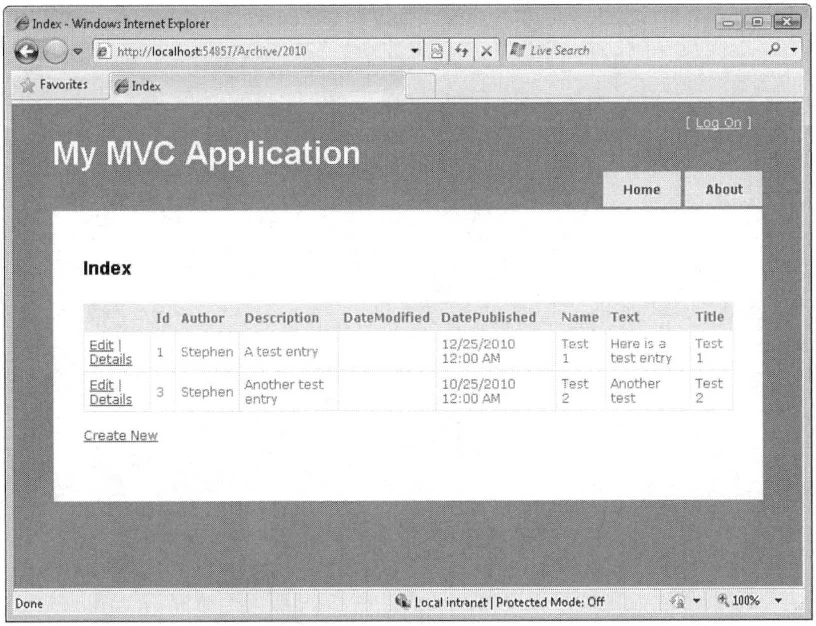

FIGURE 18.8   The page rendered by the `Archive` controller

Summary

In this chapter, we added support to the Unleashed Blog application for retrieving archived blog entries. First, we created a new set of tests to test the `Archive` controller. We created the `Archive` controller and modified the `blog` repository to satisfy these tests.

Next, we created a new set of tests to tests our routes. To use these tests, we need to add references to the MvcFakes.dll assembly and the RouteDebugger.dll assembly.

Finally, we tested out the new `Archive` controller by adding a new view to our blog application. We can filter archived blog entries by year, month, day, or name.

CHAPTER **19**

Adding Validation

In this chapter, we tackle adding validation and business rules to our blog application. As always, we begin with a set of stories (see Figure 19.1).

We need to implement the following stories:

▶ If a user submits a blog entry without a title, the validation error message "Title Is Required" displays.

▶ If a user submits a blog entry with a title longer than 500 characters, the validation error message "Title Is Too Long" displays.

▶ If a user submits a blog entry without text, the validation error message "Text Is Required" displays.

▶ Blog entry names should be encoded in an easy-to-understand way automatically. For example, the blog entry name "My Summer Vacation" should be encoded `"My-Summer-Vacation"`.

▶ If a user submits a blog entry with a title but not a name, the name is retrieved from the title.

Performing Validation in the Simplest Possible Way

First, we want to prevent a user from a submitting a blog entry when the user does not include a title for the blog entry. We can capture this requirement with the test in Listing 19.1.

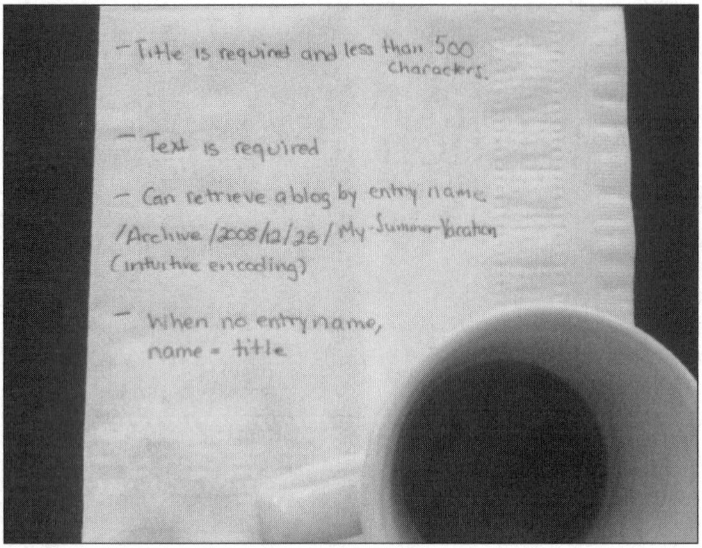

FIGURE 19.1   User stories

LISTING 19.1   UnleashedBlog.Tests\Controllers\BlogControllerTests.cs (C#)

```csharp
[TestMethod]
public void CreateTitleRequired()
{
    // Arrange
    var repository = new FakeBlogRepository();
    var controller = new BlogController(repository);
    var blogEntryToCreate = new BlogEntry
        {
            Title = string.Empty
        };

    // Act
    var result = (ViewResult)controller.Create(blogEntryToCreate);

    // Assert
    var titleState = result.ViewData.ModelState["Title"];
    Assert.IsTrue(HasErrorMessage(titleState, "Title is required."));
}

private bool HasErrorMessage(ModelState modelState, string errorMessage)
{
    foreach (var error in modelState.Errors)
    {
        if (error.ErrorMessage == errorMessage)
```

```
            return true;
    }
    return false;
}
```

LISTING 19.1   UnleashedBlog.Tests\Controllers\BlogControllerTests.vb (VB)

```vb
<TestMethod()> _
Public Sub CreateTitleRequired()
    ' Arrange
    Dim repository = New FakeBlogRepository()
    Dim controller = New BlogController(repository)
    Dim blogEntryToCreate = New BlogEntry With {.Title = String.Empty}

    ' Act
    Dim result As ViewResult = controller.Create(blogEntryToCreate)

    ' Assert
    Dim titleState = result.ViewData.ModelState("Title")
    Assert.IsTrue(HasErrorMessage(titleState, "Title is required."))
End Sub

Private Function HasErrorMessage(ByVal modelState As ModelState, ByVal
➥errorMessage As String) As Boolean
    For Each modelError In modelState.Errors
        If modelError.ErrorMessage = errorMessage Then
            Return True
        End If
    Next
    Return False
End Function
```

The test in Listing 19.1 creates a blog entry without a title and invokes the `Blog` controller `Create()` action. If the model state does not include the specific error "Title Is Required," the test fails.

Notice that the test makes use of a utility method named `HasErrorMessage()` that iterates through all the error messages in model state to perform a match. The `HasErrorMessage()` method is also included in Listing 19.1.

If you run this new test, it fails (see Figure 19.2). The test fails because we have not yet implemented any validation logic. Now that we have a failing test, we can modify the application code for our blog application.

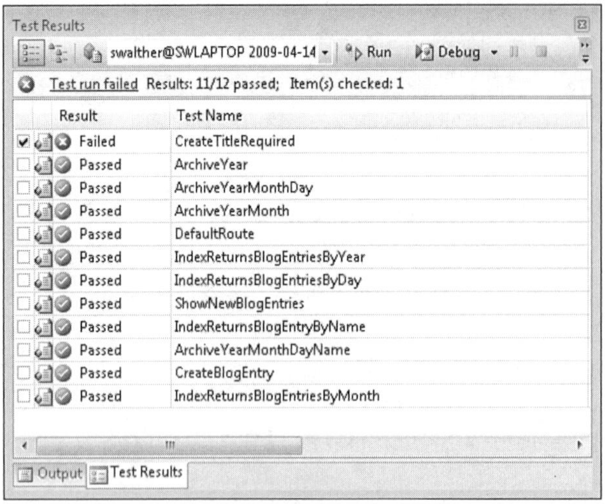

FIGURE 19.2   `CreateTitleRequired()` test fails.

The simplest way to get the test in Listing 19.1 to pass is to add the required validation logic directly to the `Create()` action of the `Blog` controller. The modified `Create()` action in Listing 19.2 includes a new validation section that verifies that the `Title` property is not empty.

LISTING 19.2   Controllers\BlogController.cs (C#)

```csharp
[AcceptVerbs(HttpVerbs.Post)]
public ActionResult Create(BlogEntry blogEntryToCreate)
{
    // validation
    if (blogEntryToCreate.Title.Trim().Length == 0)
        ModelState.AddModelError("Title", "Title is required.");

    if (!ModelState.IsValid)
        return View();

    _repository.CreateBlogEntry(blogEntryToCreate);
    return RedirectToAction("Index");
}
```

LISTING 19.2   Controllers\BlogController.vb (VB)

```vb
<AcceptVerbs(HttpVerbs.Post)> _
Public Function Create(ByVal blogEntryToCreate As BlogEntry) As ActionResult
```

```
    ' validation
    If blogEntryToCreate.Title.Trim().Length = 0 Then
        ModelState.AddModelError("Title", "Title is required.")
    End If
    If Not ModelState.IsValid Then
        Return View()
    End If

    ' Data access
    _repository.CreateBlogEntry(blogEntryToCreate)

    Return RedirectToAction("Index")
End Function
```

After you modify the Blog controller, our new test passes (see Figure 19.3). Time to cele-brate? Unfortunately, if you look again at Figure 19.3, you notice that several tests that previously passed are now failing. We have introduced a change that broke other code in our application.

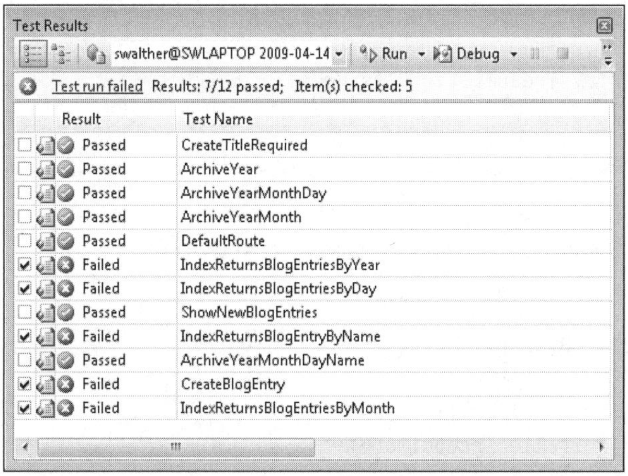

FIGURE 19.3 CreateTitleRequired() passes.

In this particular case, there is nothing wrong with our application code. The problem is with our existing test code. None of the tests that we previously wrote passed a value for the Title property. Because we just made the Title property required, all these existing tests now fail.

For example, Listing 19.3 contains the IndexReturnsBlogEntriesByYear() test. Before we made the Title property into a required property, this test passed. Now, this test fails because when the test creates new blog entries, the test does not create a value for the Title property.

LISTING 19.3   UnleashedBlog.Tests\Controllers\ArchiveControllerTests.cs (C#)

```csharp
[TestMethod]
public void IndexReturnsBlogEntriesByYear()
{
    // Arrange
    var repository = new FakeBlogRepository();
    var bController = new BlogController(repository);
    var aController = new ArchiveController(repository);


    bController.Create(new BlogEntry { Name = "Test-1", DatePublished = new
➥DateTime(2010, 11, 25) });
    bController.Create(new BlogEntry { Name = "Test-2", DatePublished = new
➥DateTime(2010, 12, 25) });
    bController.Create(new BlogEntry { Name = "Test-3", DatePublished = new
➥DateTime(2011, 12, 26) });

    // Act
    var result = (ViewResult)aController.Index(2010, null, null, null);

    // Assert
    var blogEntries = (IList<BlogEntry>)result.ViewData.Model;
    Assert.AreEqual(2, blogEntries.Count);
}
```

LISTING 19.3   UnleashedBlog.Tests\Controllers\ArchiveControllerTests.vb (VB)

```vb
<TestMethod()> _
Public Sub IndexReturnsBlogEntriesByYear()
    ' Arrange
    Dim repository = New FakeBlogRepository()
    Dim bController = New BlogController(repository)
    Dim aController = New ArchiveController(repository)


    bController.Create(New BlogEntry With {.Name = "Test-1", .DatePublished =
➥New DateTime(2010, 11, 25)})
    bController.Create(New BlogEntry With {.Name = "Test-2", .DatePublished =
➥New DateTime(2010, 12, 25)})
    bController.Create(New BlogEntry With {.Name = "Test-3", .DatePublished =
➥New DateTime(2011, 12, 26)})

    ' Act
    Dim result As ViewResult = aController.Index(2010, Nothing, Nothing, Nothing)
```

```
    ' Assert
    Dim blogEntries As IList(Of BlogEntry) = result.ViewData.Model
    Assert.AreEqual(2, blogEntries.Count)
End Sub
```

An easy fix to this problem would be to simply modify all our tests so that they include the required blog entry `Title` property. However, this approach to solving the problem is not a good solution. The next time that we introduce a new property or modify an existing property, we would need to modify all our tests again.

The real problem is that our test code is too brittle. We need to consider how we can make our test code more resilient to change. In other words, this is a good time to consider how we can refactor our test code to improve its design.

Refactoring the Test Code

You need to tend to the design of your test code as much as you tend to the design of your application code. In this section, we improve our test code so that it is more resilient to change.

The problem with our test code right now is that we create blog entries everywhere. We need to create a single location in our code where we create our blog entries (a single point of failure). That way, if we need to change the properties of the blog entry class, we don't need to make that change everywhere.

Listing 19.4 contains a new class named `BlogEntryFactory`. This class exposes a static method named `Get()` that returns a valid blog entry with all its properties in a valid state. In addition, the `BlogEntryFactory` class exposes a `GetWithDatePublished()` method that enables you to easily return a blog entry with a particular publication date.

LISTING 19.4   UnleashedBlog.Tests\Factories\BlogEntryFactory.cs (C#)

```csharp
using System;
using UnleashedBlog.Models;

namespace UnleashedBlog.Tests
{
    public class BlogEntryFactory
    {

        public static BlogEntry Get()
        {
            var blogEntry = new BlogEntry();
            blogEntry.Title = "Test Entry";
            blogEntry.Name = "Test Entry";
```

```
        blogEntry.DatePublished = new DateTime(2010, 12, 25);
        return blogEntry;
    }

    public static BlogEntry GetWithDatePublished(DateTime datePublished)
    {
        var blogEntry = Get();
        blogEntry.DatePublished = datePublished;
        return blogEntry;
    }


    }
}
```

LISTING 19.4   UnleashedBlog.Tests\Factories\BlogEntryFactory.vb (VB)

```
Public Class BlogEntryFactory


    Public Shared Function [Get]() As BlogEntry
        Dim blogEntry = New BlogEntry()
        blogEntry.Title = "Test Entry"
        blogEntry.Name = "Test Entry"
        blogEntry.DatePublished = New DateTime(2010, 12, 25)
        Return blogEntry
    End Function

    Public Shared Function GetWithDatePublished(ByVal datePublished As DateTime)
➡As BlogEntry
        Dim blogEntry = [Get]()
        blogEntry.DatePublished = datePublished
        Return blogEntry
    End Function


End Class
```

Now that we have a BlogEntryFactory class, we can use this class within our test code to create our blog entries. For example, the test in Listing 19.5 has been refactored to use the BlogEntryFactory class GetWithDatePublished() method.

LISTING 19.5 UnleashedBlog.Tests\Controllers\BlogControllerTests.cs (C#)

```csharp
[TestMethod]
public void IndexReturnsBlogEntriesByYear()
{
    // Arrange
    var repository = new FakeBlogRepository();
    var bController = new BlogController(repository);
    var aController = new ArchiveController(repository);


    bController.Create( BlogEntryFactory.GetWithDatePublished(new DateTime(2010,
➥11, 25) ));
    bController.Create( BlogEntryFactory.GetWithDatePublished(new DateTime(2010,
➥12, 25) ));
    bController.Create( BlogEntryFactory.GetWithDatePublished(new DateTime(2011,
➥12, 26) ));

    // Act
    var result = (ViewResult)aController.Index(2010, null, null, null);

    // Assert
    var blogEntries = (IList<BlogEntry>)result.ViewData.Model;
    Assert.AreEqual(2, blogEntries.Count);
}
```

LISTING 19.5 UnleashedBlog.Tests\Controllers\BlogControllerTests.vb (VB)

```vbnet
    <TestMethod()> _
    Public Sub IndexReturnsBlogEntriesByYear()
        ' Arrange
        Dim repository = New FakeBlogRepository()
        Dim bController = New BlogController(repository)
        Dim aController = New ArchiveController(repository)

        bController.Create(BlogEntryFactory.GetWithDatePublished(New
➥DateTime(2010, 11, 25)))
        bController.Create(BlogEntryFactory.GetWithDatePublished(New
➥DateTime(2010, 12, 25)))
        bController.Create(BlogEntryFactory.GetWithDatePublished(New
➥DateTime(2011, 12, 26)))
        ' Act
        Dim result As ViewResult = aController.Index(2010, Nothing, Nothing, Nothing)

        ' Assert
        Dim blogEntries As IList(Of BlogEntry) = result.ViewData.Model
        Assert.AreEqual(2, blogEntries.Count)
    End Sub
```

After the test code is updated, all the tests run successfully (see Figure 19.4).

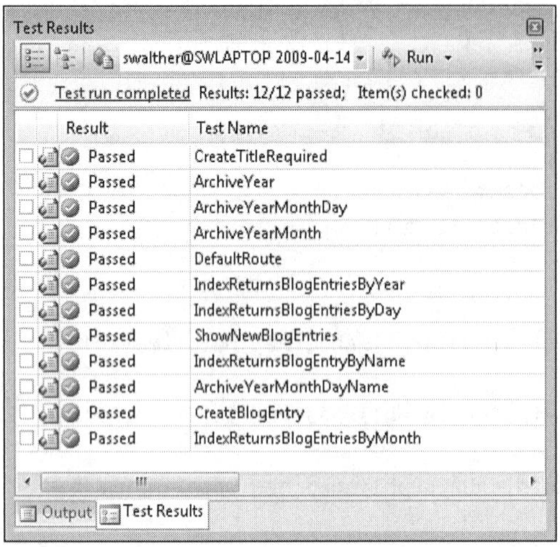

FIGURE 19.4   All green

Validating the Length of a Property

According to the next user story in our list, we need to verify that a user cannot submit a blog entry Title that contains more than 500 characters. This story will be easy to implement.

First, we create the test in Listing 19.6. This test creates a blog entry with a title that is too long and passes the blog entry to the Blog controller Create() method. The test verifies that the validation error message "Title Is Too Long" is added to model state.

LISTING 19.6   UnleashedBlog.Tests\Controllers\BlogControllerTests.cs (C#)

```
[TestMethod]
public void CreateTitleMaximumLength500()
{
    // Arrange
    var repository = new FakeBlogRepository();
    var controller = new BlogController(repository);
    var blogEntryToCreate = BlogEntryFactory.GetWithTitle("a".PadRight(501));

    // Act
    var result = (ViewResult)controller.Create(blogEntryToCreate);
```

```
// Assert
var titleState = result.ViewData.ModelState["Title"];
Assert.IsTrue(HasErrorMessage(titleState, "Title is too long."));
}
```

LISTING 19.6   UnleashedBlog.Tests\Controllers\BlogControllerTests.vb (VB)

```
<TestMethod()> _
Public Sub CreateTitleMaximumLength500()
    ' Arrange
    Dim repository = New FakeBlogRepository()
    Dim controller = New BlogController(repository)
    Dim blogEntryToCreate = BlogEntryFactory.GetWithTitle("a".PadRight(501))

    ' Act
    Dim result As ViewResult = controller.Create(blogEntryToCreate)

    ' Assert
    Dim titleState = result.ViewData.ModelState("Title")
    Assert.IsTrue(HasErrorMessage(titleState, "Title is too long."))
End Sub
```

If you run the test in Listing 19.6, the test fails (see Figure 19.5). We want the test to fail so that we can allow ourselves to write new application code.

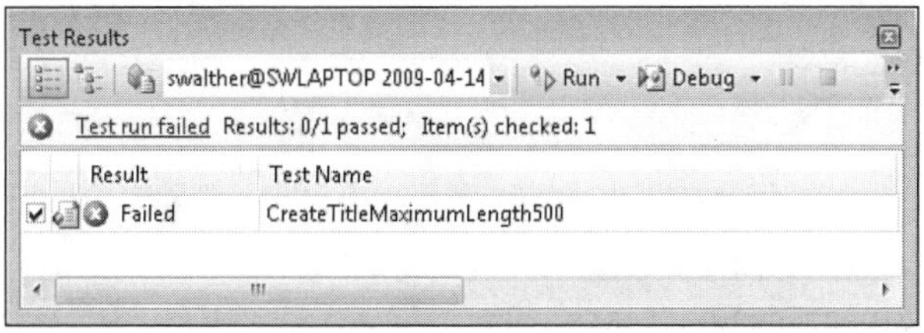

FIGURE 19.5   Failing CreateTitleMaximumLength500 test

The Blog controller Create() action in Listing 19.7 has been updated with the necessary code to pass the test. The modified Create() action adds an error to model state when the Title property is longer than 500 characters. At this point, if you run the tests again, we are back to green.

LISTING 19.7   UnleashedBlog\Controllers\BlogController.cs (C#)

```
[AcceptVerbs(HttpVerbs.Post)]
public ActionResult Create(BlogEntry blogEntryToCreate)
```

```
{
    // validation
    if (blogEntryToCreate.Title.Trim().Length == 0)
        ModelState.AddModelError("Title", "Title is required.");
    if (blogEntryToCreate.Title.Length > 500)
        ModelState.AddModelError("Title", "Title is too long.");


    if (!ModelState.IsValid)
        return View();


    _repository.CreateBlogEntry(blogEntryToCreate);
    return RedirectToAction("Index");
}
```

LISTING 19.7   UnleashedBlog\Controllers\BlogController.vb (VB)

```
<AcceptVerbs(HttpVerbs.Post)> _
Public Function Create(ByVal blogEntryToCreate As BlogEntry) As ActionResult

    ' Validation
    If blogEntryToCreate.Title.Trim().Length = 0 Then
        ModelState.AddModelError("Title", "Title is required.")
    End If
    If blogEntryToCreate.Title.Length > 500 Then
        ModelState.AddModelError("Title", "Title is too long.")
    End If
    If Not ModelState.IsValid Then
        Return View()
    End If

    ' Data access
    _repository.CreateBlogEntry(blogEntryToCreate)

    Return RedirectToAction("Index")
End Function
```

A Web Browser Sanity Check

Every once in a while, it is a good idea to actually run the ASP.NET MVC application that you build and view it in a web browser. The final goal, after all, is to create a working blog application.

If you run the blog application—by selecting the menu option Debug, Start Debugging or pressing F5—and you click the Create New link, you get the form for creating a new blog entry. If you attempt to submit the form without entering any values in the form fields, you get the validation error messages illustrated in Figure 19.6.

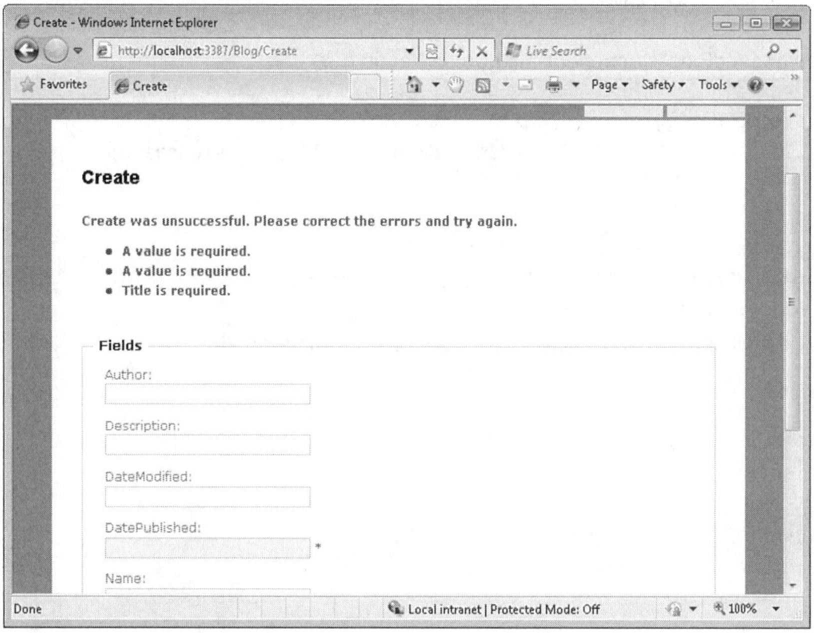

FIGURE 19.6   Validation errors

Notice that there are three validation error messages. We can account for the error associated with the `Title` property. We modified the `Blog` controller to add this error to model state when the `Title` property is empty.

However, there are two "A Value Is Required" errors. Where do these errors come from?

We can easily account for one of the "A Value Is Required." errors. One of these errors corresponds to the `DatePublished` property. The `DatePublished` property is a `DateTime` property, and a `DateTime` property cannot accept an empty value. Therefore, the ASP.NET MVC framework adds an error message to model state automatically. (In particular, the default model binder adds this error message to model state.)

But, there is still one validation error message left. This last error is mysterious because it does not correspond to any of the fields in the HTML form.

The final validation error message corresponds to the blog entry `Id` property. The `Id` property is an `integer` property. Like the `DatePublished` property, you cannot assign an empty value to the `Id` property.

However, we want the ASP.NET MVC framework to ignore the Id property because this property gets its value from the database. The Id property corresponds to an Identity column in the database.

To make the validation error message go away, we need to modify the Create() action so that it ignores the Id property when creating an instance of a blog entry from the HTML form fields. A modified Create() action is contained in Listing 19.8.

LISTING 19.8   UnleashedBlog\Controllers\BlogController.cs (C#)

```csharp
[AcceptVerbs(HttpVerbs.Post)]
public ActionResult Create([Bind(Exclude="Id")]BlogEntry blogEntryToCreate)
{
    // validation
    if (blogEntryToCreate.Title.Trim().Length == 0)
        ModelState.AddModelError("Title", "Title is required.");
    if (blogEntryToCreate.Title.Length > 500)
        ModelState.AddModelError("Title", "Title is too long.");


    if (!ModelState.IsValid)
        return View();

    _repository.CreateBlogEntry(blogEntryToCreate);
    return RedirectToAction("Index");
}
```

LISTING 19.8   UnleashedBlog\Controllers\BlogController.vb (VB)

```vb
    <AcceptVerbs(HttpVerbs.Post)> _
    Public Function Create(<Bind(Exclude:="Id")> ByVal blogEntryToCreate As
➥BlogEntry) As ActionResult

        ' Validation
        If blogEntryToCreate.Title.Trim().Length = 0 Then
            ModelState.AddModelError("Title", "Title is required.")
        End If
        If blogEntryToCreate.Title.Length > 500 Then
            ModelState.AddModelError("Title", "Title is too long.")
        End If
        If Not ModelState.IsValid Then
            Return View()
        End If

        ' Data access
```

```
        _repository.CreateBlogEntry(blogEntryToCreate)

        Return RedirectToAction("Index")
    End Function
```

Notice that the `blog entry` parameter in Listing 19.8 is decorated with a `Bind` attribute. This attribute excludes the `Id` property from the set of properties bound to the HTML form fields submitted to the server.

Refactoring to Use a Service Layer

Our validation code works, but it is not pretty. We are violating the Single Responsibility Principle (SRP) by mixing our validation logic into our controller logic. In general, you want each layer of your application to assume a single responsibility.

The software design principles exist for a reason. Mixing together different types of logic makes an application more difficult to maintain and modify over time. We need to clean up our code. *A place for everything and everything in its place.*

In this section, we refactor our code to migrate our validation logic to a separate service layer. We can fearlessly refactor our application to improve its design because our application is well covered by tests. The tests act as our safety net for change.

Listing 19.9 contains a new `blog service` class that acts as our service layer. This class contains all the validation logic that was previously located in the `blog controller` class.

LISTING 19.9   UnleashedBlog\Models\BlogService.cs (C#)

```csharp
using System;
using System.Web.Mvc;
using UnleashedBlog.Models.EntityFramework;
using System.Collections.Generic;

namespace UnleashedBlog.Models
{
    public class BlogService : BlogServiceBase
    {

        public BlogService(ModelStateDictionary modelState)
            : base(modelState, new EntityFrameworkBlogRepository()) { }

        public BlogService(ModelStateDictionary modelState, BlogRepositoryBase
➥blogRepository)
            : base(modelState, blogRepository) { }
```

```csharp
        public override IEnumerable<BlogEntry> ListBlogEntries()
        {
            return _blogRepository.ListBlogEntries();
        }


        public override IEnumerable<BlogEntry> ListBlogEntries(int? year, int?
➥month, int? day, string name)
        {
            return _blogRepository.ListBlogEntries(year, month, day, name);
        }


        public override bool CreateBlogEntry(BlogEntry blogEntryToCreate)
        {
            // validation
            if (blogEntryToCreate.Title.Trim().Length == 0)
                _modelState.AddModelError("Title", "Title is required.");
            if (blogEntryToCreate.Title.Length > 500)
                _modelState.AddModelError("Title", "Title is too long.");
            if (blogEntryToCreate.Text.Trim().Length == 0)
                _modelState.AddModelError("Text", "Text is required.");
            if (_modelState.IsValid == false)
                return false;

            // Data access
            _blogRepository.CreateBlogEntry(blogEntryToCreate);
            return true;
        }

    }
}
```

LISTING 19.9   UnleashedBlog\Models\BlogService.vb (VB)

```vb
Public Class BlogService
    Inherits BlogServiceBase

    Public Sub New(ByVal modelState As ModelStateDictionary)
        MyBase.New(modelState, New EntityFrameworkBlogRepository())
    End Sub

    Public Sub New(ByVal modelState As ModelStateDictionary, ByVal blogRepository
➥As BlogRepositoryBase)
```

```vbnet
        MyBase.New(modelState, blogRepository)
    End Sub


    Public Overrides Function ListBlogEntries() As IEnumerable(Of BlogEntry)
        Return _blogRepository.ListBlogEntries()
    End Function


    Public Overrides Function ListBlogEntries(ByVal year As Nullable(Of Integer),
➥ByVal month As Nullable(Of Integer), ByVal day As Nullable(Of Integer), ByVal name
➥As String) As IEnumerable(Of BlogEntry)
        Return _blogRepository.ListBlogEntries(year, month, day, name)
    End Function


    Public Overrides Function CreateBlogEntry(ByVal blogEntryToCreate As
➥BlogEntry) As Boolean
        ' validation
        If blogEntryToCreate.Title.Trim().Length = 0 Then
            _modelState.AddModelError("Title", "Title is required.")
        End If
        If blogEntryToCreate.Title.Length > 500 Then
            _modelState.AddModelError("Title", "Title is too long.")
        End If
        If blogEntryToCreate.Text.Trim().Length = 0 Then
            _modelState.AddModelError("Text", "Text is required.")
        End If
        If _modelState.IsValid = False Then
            Return False
        End If

        ' Data access
        _blogRepository.CreateBlogEntry(blogEntryToCreate)
        Return True
    End Function
End Class
```

The CreateBlogEntry() method validates the properties of the blog entry passed to the method. If there are any validation errors, the method returns the value false. Otherwise, the CreateBlogEntry() method calls the CreateBlogEntry() method on the blog repository class to add the new blog entry to the database and returns the value true.

We need to modify the `Blog` controller and `Archive` controller to use the blog service instead of the blog repository. The modified `Blog` controller is contained in Listing 19.10.

LISTING 19.10   UnleashedBlog\Controllers\BlogController.cs (C#)

```csharp
using System.Collections.Generic;
using System.Web.Mvc;
using UnleashedBlog.Models;
using UnleashedBlog.Models.EntityFramework;

namespace UnleashedBlog.Controllers
{
    public class BlogController : Controller
    {
        private BlogServiceBase _blogService;

        public BlogController()
        {
            _blogService = new BlogService(this.ModelState);
        }

        public BlogController(BlogRepositoryBase blogRepository)
        {
            _blogService = new BlogService(this.ModelState, blogRepository);
        }

        public ActionResult Index()
        {
            return View(_blogService.ListBlogEntries());
        }


        public ActionResult Create()
        {
            return View();
        }

        [AcceptVerbs(HttpVerbs.Post)]
        public ActionResult Create([Bind(Exclude="Id")]BlogEntry blogEntryToCreate)
        {
            if (_blogService.CreateBlogEntry(blogEntryToCreate) == false)
                return View();

            return RedirectToAction("Index");
        }
    }
}
```

LISTING 19.10   UnleashedBlog\Controllers\BlogController.vb (VB)

```vb
Public Class BlogController
    Inherits Controller

    Private _blogService As BlogServiceBase

    Public Sub New()
        _blogService = New BlogService(Me.ModelState)
    End Sub

    Public Sub New(ByVal blogRepository As BlogRepositoryBase)
        _blogService = New BlogService(Me.ModelState, blogRepository)
    End Sub

    Public Function Index() As ActionResult
        Return View(_blogService.ListBlogEntries())
    End Function


    Public Function Create() As ActionResult
        Return View()
    End Function

    <AcceptVerbs(HttpVerbs.Post)> _
    Public Function Create(<Bind(Exclude:="Id")> ByVal blogEntryToCreate As
➥BlogEntry) As ActionResult
        If Not _blogService.CreateBlogEntry(blogEntryToCreate) Then
            Return View()
        End If

        Return RedirectToAction("Index")
    End Function
End Class
```

Notice that an instance of the blog service is created in the blog controller constructors. Previously, the blog controller interacted directly with the blog repository. The new version of the blog controller interacts with the blog service and the blog service interacts with the blog repository.

These changes provide us with a clean separation of concerns. Our controller logic is kept in the controller layer, our validation logic is kept in our service layer, and our database logic is kept in our repository layer.

Because we have the safety net of our tests, we can refactor fearlessly. After these massive changes to the architecture of our application, our original tests continue to pass (see Figure 19.7).

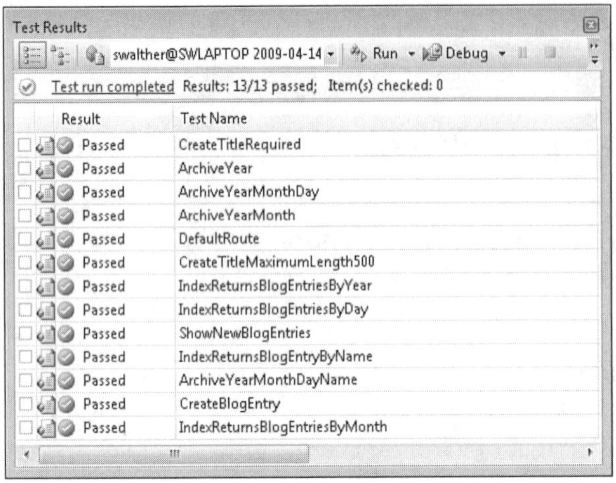

FIGURE 19.7   Refactored tests pass

Adding Business Rules

Before we can end this chapter, there are two final stories that we need to implement. Both of these stories relate to business rules concerning a blog entry name:

▶ Blog entry names should be encoded in an easy-to-understand way automatically. For example, the blog entry name "My Summer Vacation" should be encoded like `"My-Summer-Vacation"`.

▶ If a user submits a blog entry with a title but not a name, the name is retrieved from the title.

What's the difference between the title and name of a blog entry? The name of a blog entry is used when retrieving a blog entry. For example, you can retrieve a blog entry named "My Summer Vacation" by requesting the following URL:

www.MyBlog.com/2010/12/25/My-Summer-Vacation.

The title of a blog entry, on the other hand, is the title that is displayed for the blog entry in a page and in the RSS feed. For example, My Summer Vacation.

A blog entry name can only contain valid characters for a URL. According to the official standards (RFC 1738), a URL can contains only alphanumeric characters and a limited number of special characters. In particular, a name cannot contain spaces.

Let's start with a test for the first story. We need to create a test that verifies that any special characters in a blog entry name get encoded automatically. The test in Listing 19.11 uses a regular expression to verify that a set of blog entry names get encoded correctly.

LISTING 19.11   UnleashedBlog.Tests\Controllers\BlogControllerTests.cs (C#)

```csharp
[TestMethod]
public void CreateNameIsValid()
{
    // Arrange
    _blogController.Create( BlogEntryFactory.GetWithName("My Summer Vacation") );
    _blogController.Create( BlogEntryFactory.GetWithName("$&+,/:;=?@") );
    _blogController.Create( BlogEntryFactory.GetWithName("He said \"what?\""));

    // Act
    var result = (ViewResult)_blogController.Index();

    // Assert
    var blogEntries = (IList<BlogEntry>)result.ViewData.Model;
    foreach (var entry in blogEntries)
    {
        StringAssert.DoesNotMatch(entry.Name, new Regex("[\"$&+,/:;=?@]"));
    }
}
```

LISTING 19.11   UnleashedBlog.Tests\Controllers\BlogControllerTests.vb (VB)

```vb
<TestMethod()> _
Public Sub CreateNameIsValid()
    ' Arrange
    _blogController.Create(BlogEntryFactory.GetWithName("My Summer Vacation"))
    _blogController.Create(BlogEntryFactory.GetWithName("$&+,/:;=?@"))
    _blogController.Create(BlogEntryFactory.GetWithName("He said ""what?"""))

    ' Act
    Dim result As ViewResult = _blogController.Index()

    ' Assert
    Dim blogEntries = CType(result.ViewData.Model, IList(Of BlogEntry))
    For Each entry In blogEntries
        StringAssert.DoesNotMatch(entry.Name, New Regex("[""$&+,/:;=?@]"))
    Next entry
End Sub
```

To pass the test in Listing 19.11, we need to modify the blog service so that it encodes the blog entry Name property. The updated blog service in Listing 19.12 correctly encodes the Name property.

LISTING 19.12   UnleashedBlog\Models\BlogService.cs (C#)

```csharp
public override bool CreateBlogEntry(BlogEntry blogEntryToCreate)
{
    // validation
    if (blogEntryToCreate.Title.Trim().Length == 0)
        _modelState.AddModelError("Title", "Title is required.");
    if (blogEntryToCreate.Title.Length > 500)
        _modelState.AddModelError("Title", "Title is too long.");
    if (blogEntryToCreate.Text.Trim().Length == 0)
        _modelState.AddModelError("Text", "Text is required.");
    if (_modelState.IsValid == false)
        return false;

    // Business Rules
    blogEntryToCreate.Name = blogEntryToCreate.Name.Replace(" ", "-");
    blogEntryToCreate.Name = Regex.Replace(blogEntryToCreate.Name,
➥"[\"$&+,/:;=?@]", string.Empty);


    // Data access
    _blogRepository.CreateBlogEntry(blogEntryToCreate);
    return true;
}
```

LISTING 19.12   UnleashedBlog\Models\BlogService.vb (VB)

```vb
    Public Overrides Function CreateBlogEntry(ByVal blogEntryToCreate As
➥BlogEntry) As Boolean
        ' validation
        If blogEntryToCreate.Title.Trim().Length = 0 Then
            _modelState.AddModelError("Title", "Title is required.")
        End If
        If blogEntryToCreate.Title.Length > 500 Then
            _modelState.AddModelError("Title", "Title is too long.")
        End If
        If blogEntryToCreate.Text.Trim().Length = 0 Then
            _modelState.AddModelError("Text", "Text is required.")
        End If
        If _modelState.IsValid = False Then
            Return False
        End If

        ' Business Rules
```

```
        blogEntryToCreate.Name = blogEntryToCreate.Name.Replace(" ", "-")
        blogEntryToCreate.Name = Regex.Replace(blogEntryToCreate.Name,
➡"[""$&+,/:;=?@]", String.Empty)

        ' Data access
        _blogRepository.CreateBlogEntry(blogEntryToCreate)
        Return True
    End Function
```

One last story. If a user supplies a blog entry title, but not a name, we should get the name from the title automatically. We can express this requirement with the test in Listing 19.13.

LISTING 19.13   UnleashedBlog.Tests\Controllers\BlogController.cs (C#)

```csharp
[TestMethod]
public void CreateNameFromTitle()
{
    // Arrange
    var blogEntryToCreate = BlogEntryFactory.Get();
    blogEntryToCreate.Title = "TheTitle";
    blogEntryToCreate.Name = string.Empty;

    var aController = _controllerFactory.GetArchiveController();


    // Act
    _blogController.Create(blogEntryToCreate);
    var result = (ViewResult)aController.Index(null, null, null, "TheTitle");

    // Assert
    var blogEntries = (IList<BlogEntry>)result.ViewData.Model;
    Assert.AreEqual(1, blogEntries.Count);
}
```

LISTING 19.13   UnleashedBlog.Tests\Controllers\BlogController.vb (VB)

```vb
    <TestMethod()> _
    Public Sub CreateNameFromTitle()
        ' Arrange
        Dim blogEntryToCreate = BlogEntryFactory.Get()
        blogEntryToCreate.Title = "TheTitle"
```

```
        blogEntryToCreate.Name = String.Empty

        Dim aController = _controllerFactory.GetArchiveController()

        ' Act
        _blogController.Create(blogEntryToCreate)
        Dim result As ViewResult = aController.Index(Nothing, Nothing, Nothing,
➡"TheTitle")

        ' Assert
        Dim blogEntries = CType(result.ViewData.Model, IList(Of BlogEntry))
        Assert.AreEqual(1, blogEntries.Count)
    End Sub
```

The test in Listing 19.13 verifies that when a blog entry is created with a title, but not a
name, that the name is retrieved from the title. The modified CreateBlogEntry() method
in Listing 19.14 causes this test to pass.

LISTING 19.14 UnleashedBlog\Models\BlogService.cs (C#)

```csharp
public override bool CreateBlogEntry(BlogEntry blogEntryToCreate)
{
    // validation
    if (blogEntryToCreate.Title.Trim().Length == 0)
        _modelState.AddModelError("Title", "Title is required.");
    if (blogEntryToCreate.Title.Length > 500)
        _modelState.AddModelError("Title", "Title is too long.");
    if (blogEntryToCreate.Text.Trim().Length == 0)
        _modelState.AddModelError("Text", "Text is required.");
    if (_modelState.IsValid == false)
        return false;

    // Business Rules
    if (String.IsNullOrEmpty(blogEntryToCreate.Name))
        blogEntryToCreate.Name = blogEntryToCreate.Title;
    blogEntryToCreate.Name = blogEntryToCreate.Name.Replace(" ", "-");
    blogEntryToCreate.Name = Regex.Replace(blogEntryToCreate.Name,
"[\"$&+,/:;=?@]", string.Empty);

    // Data access
    _blogRepository.CreateBlogEntry(blogEntryToCreate);
    return true;
}
```

LISTING 19.14   UnleashedBlog\Models\BlogService.vb (VB)

```
    Public Overrides Function CreateBlogEntry(ByVal blogEntryToCreate As
➡BlogEntry) As Boolean
        ' validation
        If blogEntryToCreate.Title.Trim().Length = 0 Then
            _modelState.AddModelError("Title", "Title is required.")
        End If
        If blogEntryToCreate.Title.Length > 500 Then
            _modelState.AddModelError("Title", "Title is too long.")
        End If
        If blogEntryToCreate.Text.Trim().Length = 0 Then
            _modelState.AddModelError("Text", "Text is required.")
        End If
        If _modelState.IsValid = False Then
            Return False
        End If

        ' Business Rules
        If String.IsNullOrEmpty(blogEntryToCreate.Name) Then
            blogEntryToCreate.Name = blogEntryToCreate.Title
        End If
        blogEntryToCreate.Name = blogEntryToCreate.Name.Replace(" ", "-")
        blogEntryToCreate.Name = Regex.Replace(blogEntryToCreate.Name,
➡"[""$&+,/:;=?@]", String.Empty)

        ' Data access
        _blogRepository.CreateBlogEntry(blogEntryToCreate)
        Return True
    End Function
```

Summary

In this chapter, we added validation and business rules to our blog application. We started by adding the validation rules in the simplest way possible; we added the validation rules directly to our controller class.

After we successfully passed our tests, it was time to refactor our application to have a better design. We refactored our validation code into a separate service layer.

Finally, we implemented two business rules related to blog entry names. We verified that blog entry names are valid. We also implemented a business rule that causes the Name property to be retrieved from the Title property when no name is supplied.

CHAPTER 20

Paging, Views, and Ajax

In this chapter, we focus on the user interface. In the first part of this chapter, we add support for paging through blog entries. Next, we create the views for our blog application. Finally, we modify our blog application to take advantage of Ajax.

We have only two user stories that we need to implement (see Figure 20.1). One story for paging and one story for Ajax.

Adding Paging Support

Our first user story concerns paging. We don't want users of the blog application to get overwhelmed with too many blog entries displayed in a page at one time. According to the user story:

No more than five blog entries should be displayed on a page at a time. When there are more than five entries, the user should navigate to earlier entries.

In Chapter 6, "Understanding HTML Helpers," we implemented a simple paging framework. We can take advantage of that framework here in our blog application.

In the paging framework, we use the class in Listing 20.1 to represent a page of items.

FIGURE 20.1   The user stories

LISTING 20.1   UnleashedBlog\Paging\PageList.cs (C#)

```csharp
using System;
using System.Collections.Generic;

namespace Paging
{
    public class PagedList<T> : List<T>
    {
        public PagedList(IEnumerable<T> items, int pageIndex, int pageSize, int
➥totalItemCount, string sortExpression)
        {
            this.AddRange(items);
            this.PageIndex = pageIndex;
```

```
        this.PageSize = pageSize;
        this.SortExpression = sortExpression;
        this.TotalItemCount = totalItemCount;
        this.TotalPageCount = (int)Math.Ceiling(totalItemCount /
➥(double)pageSize);
    }

    public int PageIndex { get; set; }
    public int PageSize { get; set; }
    public string SortExpression { get; set; }
    public int TotalItemCount { get; set; }
    public int TotalPageCount { get; private set; }

  }
}
```

LISTING 20.1   UnleashedBlog\Paging\PageList.vb (VB)

```
Public Class PagedList(Of T)
    Inherits List(Of T)

    Private _pageIndex As Integer
    Private _pageSize As Integer
    Private _sortExpression As String
    Private _totalItemCount As Integer
    Private _totalPageCount As Integer

    Public Sub New(ByVal items As IEnumerable(Of T), ByVal pageIndex As Integer,
➥ByVal pageSize As Integer, ByVal totalItemCount As Integer, ByVal sortExpression
➥As String)
        Me.AddRange(items)
        Me.PageIndex = pageIndex
        Me.PageSize = pageSize
        Me.SortExpression = sortExpression
        Me.TotalItemCount = totalItemCount
        Me.TotalPageCount = CInt(Fix(Math.Ceiling(totalItemCount / CDbl(pageSize))))
    End Sub

    Public Property PageIndex() As Integer
        Get
            Return _pageIndex
        End Get
        Set(ByVal value As Integer)
            _pageIndex = value
        End Set
    End Property
    Public Property PageSize() As Integer
        Get
```

```
            Return _pageSize
        End Get
        Set(ByVal value As Integer)
            _pageSize = value
        End Set
    End Property

    Public Property SortExpression() As String
        Get
            Return _sortExpression
        End Get
        Set(ByVal value As String)
            _sortExpression = value
        End Set
    End Property
    Public Property TotalItemCount() As Integer
        Get
            Return _totalItemCount
        End Get
        Set(ByVal value As Integer)
            _totalItemCount = value
        End Set
    End Property
    Public Property TotalPageCount() As Integer
        Get
            Return _totalPageCount
        End Get
        Private Set(ByVal value As Integer)
        _totalPageCount = value
        End Set
    End Property

End Class
```

The nice thing about the PagedList class in Listing 20.1 is that it represents not only a
page of items, but it also represents additional properties such as the total page count and
the page size.

We want to modify our blog application to use this paging framework. However, before we
can start rewriting our application code, we first need to create some tests.

Here's what we want to test:

1. The Index() action should accept a page parameter.
2. The Index() action exposed by the Blog controller should return an instance of the
   PagedList class that corresponds to the page parameter.

3. The PagedList returned by the Blog Index() action should never contain more than five blog entries.

4. The PageList returned by the Blog Index() action should order the blog entries by date (latest blog entry first).

This list gives us the four tests that are contained in Listing 20.2.

LISTING 20.2   UnleashedBlog.Tests\Controllers\BlogControllerTests.cs (C#)

```csharp
[TestMethod]
public void IndexAcceptsPage()
{
    // Act
    var result = (ViewResult)_blogController.Index(0);
}


[TestMethod]
public void IndexReturnsPagedListForPage()
{
    // Arrange
    CreateBlogEntries(50);

    // Act
    var result = (ViewResult)_blogController.Index(2);

    // Assert
    var page = (PagedList<BlogEntry>)result.ViewData.Model;
    Assert.AreEqual(2, page.PageIndex);
}

[TestMethod]
public void IndexReturnsLessThan6BlogEntries()
{
    // Arrange
    CreateBlogEntries(20);

    // Act
    var result = (ViewResult)_blogController.Index(0);

    // Assert
    var page = (PagedList<BlogEntry>)result.ViewData.Model;
    Assert.IsTrue(page.Count < 6);
}
```

```
[TestMethod]
public void IndexReturnsBlogEntriesInOrderOfDatePublished()
{
    // Arrange
    var blogEntry1 = BlogEntryFactory.GetWithDatePublished(new
➡DateTime(2005, 12, 25));
        _blogController.Create(blogEntry1);
    var blogEntry2 = BlogEntryFactory.GetWithDatePublished(new
➡DateTime(2005, 12, 26));
        _blogController.Create(blogEntry2);

    // Act
    var result = (ViewResult)_blogController.Index(0);

    // Assert
    var page = (PagedList<BlogEntry>)result.ViewData.Model;
    Assert.AreSame( blogEntry2, page[0]);
}


private void CreateBlogEntries(int count)
{
    for (int i=0;i<count;i++)
    {
        var name = "Blog Entry " + i.ToString();
        var blogEntryToCreate = BlogEntryFactory.GetWithName(name);
        _blogController.Create(blogEntryToCreate);
    }
}
```

LISTING 20.2   UnleashedBlog.Tests\Controllers\BlogControllerTests.vb (VB)

```
<TestMethod()> _
Public Sub IndexAcceptsPage()
    ' Act
    Dim result = CType(_blogController.Index(0), ViewResult)
End Sub


<TestMethod()> _
Public Sub IndexReturnsPagedListForPage()
    ' Arrange
    CreateBlogEntries(50)

    ' Act
```

```vb
        Dim result = CType(_blogController.Index(2), ViewResult)

        ' Assert
        Dim page = CType(result.ViewData.Model, PagedList(Of BlogEntry))
        Assert.AreEqual(2, page.PageIndex)
    End Sub


    <TestMethod()> _
    Public Sub IndexReturnsLessThan6BlogEntries()
        ' Arrange
        CreateBlogEntries(20)

        ' Act
        Dim result = CType(_blogController.Index(0), ViewResult)

        ' Assert
        Dim page = CType(result.ViewData.Model, PagedList(Of BlogEntry))
        Assert.IsTrue(page.Count < 6)
    End Sub


    <TestMethod()> _
    Public Sub IndexReturnsBlogEntriesInOrderOfDatePublished()
        ' Arrange
        Dim blogEntry1 = BlogEntryFactory.GetWithDatePublished(New DateTime(2005, _
➥12, 25))
        _blogController.Create(blogEntry1)
        Dim blogEntry2 = BlogEntryFactory.GetWithDatePublished(New DateTime(2005, _
➥12, 26))
        _blogController.Create(blogEntry2)

        ' Act
        Dim result = CType(_blogController.Index(0), ViewResult)

        ' Assert
        Dim page = CType(result.ViewData.Model, PagedList(Of BlogEntry))
        Assert.AreSame(blogEntry2, page(0))
    End Sub


    Private Sub CreateBlogEntries(ByVal count As Integer)
        For i As Integer = 0 To count - 1
            Dim name = "Blog Entry " & i.ToString()
```

```
            Dim blogEntryToCreate = BlogEntryFactory.GetWithName(name)
            _blogController.Create(blogEntryToCreate)
        Next i
    End Sub
```

When we first attempt to run the tests in Listing 20.2, they fail. The tests won't even build because the `Blog` controller `Index()` action does not currently accept a `page` parameter (see Figure 20.2).

	Description	File	Line	Column	Project
Error List					
⊗ 4 Errors ⚠ 0 Warnings ⓘ 0 Messages					
⊗ 1	No overload for method 'Index' takes '1' arguments	BlogContr	166	38	UnleashedBlog.Tests
⊗ 2	No overload for method 'Index' takes '1' arguments	BlogContr	177	38	UnleashedBlog.Tests
⊗ 3	No overload for method 'Index' takes '1' arguments	BlogContr	192	38	UnleashedBlog.Tests
⊗ 4	No overload for method 'Index' takes '1' arguments	BlogContr	208	38	UnleashedBlog.Tests

FIGURE 20.2 New tests fail because of a missing page parameter.

Before we do anything else, we need to write just enough code so that our solution compiles. We need to modify the `Blog` controller `Index()` action so that it accepts a page parameter and returns a `PagedList`. The modified `Index()` action is contained in Listing 20.3.

LISTING 20.3 UnleashedBlog\BlogController.cs (C#)

```csharp
public ActionResult Index(int? page)
{
    return View(_blogService.ListBlogEntries());
}
```

LISTING 20.3 UnleashedBlog\BlogController.vb (VB)

```vb
Public Function Index(ByVal page As Integer?) As ActionResult
    Return View(_blogService.ListBlogEntries())
End Function
```

Unfortunately, modifying the `Index()` action introduces new problems with our test code. Three tests that passed before now fail because we have modified our `Index()` action (see Figure 20.3).

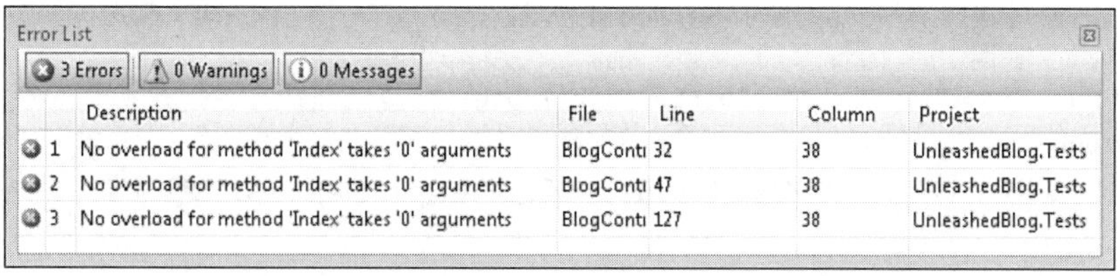

FIGURE 20.3   Old tests fail because of a new page parameter.

This problem is easy enough to fix. We just need to update the old tests so that the tests pass a NULL value when calling the Index() action. After we make this change to the test code, the first of our four new tests pass.

To get the next test to pass, we need to modify our application code so that the Index() action returns a PagedList. However, it cannot be just any PagedList. The PagedList must represent the set of blog entries that correspond to the page passed to the Index() action.

The modified Index() action in Listing 20.4 passes the page parameter to the ListBlogEntries() method.

LISTING 20.4   UnleashedBlog\Controllers\BlogController.cs (C#)

```csharp
public ActionResult Index(int? page)
{
    return View(_blogService.ListBlogEntries(page));
}
```

LISTING 20.4   UnleashedBlog\Controllers\BlogController.vb (VB)

```vb
Public Function Index(ByVal page As Integer?) As ActionResult

    Return View(_blogService.ListBlogEntries(page))
End Function
```

We need to modify the ListBlogEntries() method so that it accepts a page parameter (see Listing 20.5).

LISTING 20.5   UnleashedBlog\Models\BlogService.cs (C#)

```csharp
public override PagedList<BlogEntry> ListBlogEntries(int? page)
{
    return _blogRepository.ListBlogEntries(page, null, null, null, null);
}
```

LISTING 20.5   UnleashedBlog\Models\BlogService.vb (VB)

```vb
    Public Overrides Function ListBlogEntries(ByVal page As Integer?) As
➡PagedList(Of BlogEntry)
        Return _blogRepository.ListBlogEntries(page, Nothing, Nothing, Nothing,
➡Nothing)
    End Function
```

Finally, we need to modify the Blog repository so that it returns the records that correspond to a particular page. The updated Blog repository ListBlogEntries() method is contained in Listing 20.6.

LISTING 20.6   UnleashedBlog\Models\BlogRepositoryBase.cs (C#)

```csharp
        public virtual PagedList<BlogEntry> ListBlogEntries(int? page, int? year,
➡int? month, int? day, string name)
        {
            var query = this.QueryBlogEntries();
            if (year.HasValue)
                query = query.Where(e => e.DatePublished.Year == year.Value);
            if (month.HasValue)
                query = query.Where(e => e.DatePublished.Month == month.Value);
            if (day.HasValue)
                query = query.Where(e => e.DatePublished.Day == day.Value);
            if (!string.IsNullOrEmpty(name))
                query = query.Where(e => e.Name == name);

            return query.ToPagedList(page, 5);
        }
```

LISTING 20.6   UnleashedBlog\Models\BlogRepositoryBase.vb (VB)

```vb
    Public Overridable Function ListBlogEntries(ByVal page As Integer?, ByVal year
➡As Integer?, ByVal month As Integer?, ByVal day As Integer?, ByVal name As String)
➡As PagedList(Of BlogEntry)
        Dim query = Me.QueryBlogEntries()
        If year.HasValue Then
            query = query.Where(Function(e) e.DatePublished.Year = year.Value)
        End If
        If month.HasValue Then
            query = query.Where(Function(e) e.DatePublished.Month = month.Value)
        End If
        If day.HasValue Then
```

```
            query = query.Where(Function(e) e.DatePublished.Day = day.Value)
        End If
        If Not String.IsNullOrEmpty(name) Then
            query = query.Where(Function(e) e.Name = name)
        End If
        Return query.ToPagedList(page, 5)
    End Function
```

In Listing 20.6, the `ListBlogEntries()` method has been modified to return a `PagedList` class. Notice the final statement. The final statement calls the `ToPagedList()` extension method (defined in the `PagingLinqExtensions` class) to return a `PagedList` from a query.

After we make all these changes, all our tests pass except for one (see Figure 20.4). Unfortunately, our blog entries are not returned in the right order. We want to display the blog entry with the latest publication date first.

We need to make one last change to our `Blog` repository `ListBlogEntries()` method. We need to order the blog entries by the date published. We can do this by calling the

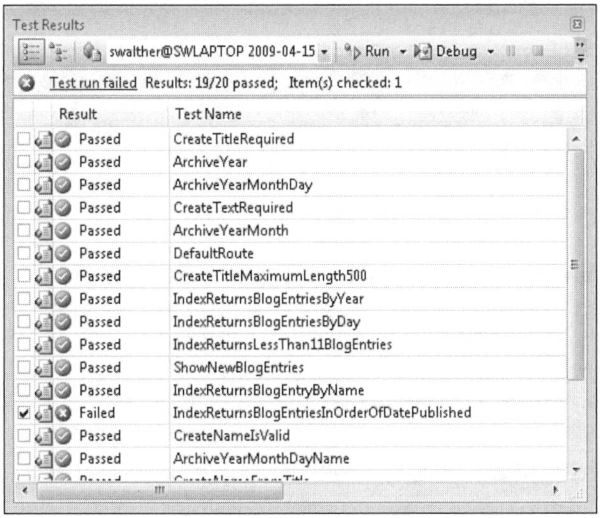

FIGURE 20.4   Blog entries are returned in the wrong order.

`OrderByDescending()` LINQ method on our query (see Listing 20.7). Finally, all the tests pass (see Figure 20.5).

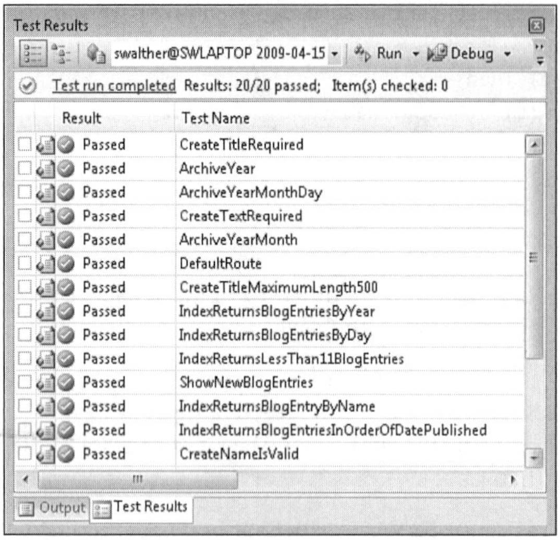

FIGURE 20.5   All tests pass!

LISTING 20.7   UnleashedBlog\Models\BlogRepositoryBase.cs (C#)

```csharp
        public virtual PagedList<BlogEntry> ListBlogEntries(int? page, int? year,
➥int? month, int? day, string name)
        {
            var query = this.QueryBlogEntries();
            if (year.HasValue)
                query = query.Where(e => e.DatePublished.Year == year.Value);
            if (month.HasValue)
                query = query.Where(e => e.DatePublished.Month == month.Value);
            if (day.HasValue)
                query = query.Where(e => e.DatePublished.Day == day.Value);
            if (!string.IsNullOrEmpty(name))
                query = query.Where(e => e.Name == name);

            return query.OrderByDescending(e => e.DatePublished).ToPagedList (page,
➥5);
        }
```

LISTING 20.7   UnleashedBlog\Models\BlogRepositoryBase.vb (VB)

```vb
Imports System.Collections.Generic
Imports System.Linq


Public MustInherit Class BlogRepositoryBase
```

```
' Blog Entry Methods
Public MustOverride Function ListBlogEntries() As List(Of BlogEntry)
Public MustOverride Sub CreateBlogEntry(ByVal blogEntryToCreate As BlogEntry)
Protected MustOverride Function QueryBlogEntries() As IQueryable(Of BlogEntry)

Public Overridable Function ListBlogEntries(ByVal page As Integer?, ByVal year
➥As Integer?, ByVal month As Integer?, ByVal day As Integer?, ByVal name As String)
➥As PagedList(Of BlogEntry)
      Dim query = Me.QueryBlogEntries()
      If year.HasValue Then
          query = query.Where(Function(e) e.DatePublished.Year = year.Value)
      End If
      If month.HasValue Then
          query = query.Where(Function(e) e.DatePublished.Month = month.Value)
      End If
      If day.HasValue Then
          query = query.Where(Function(e) e.DatePublished.Day = day.Value)
      End If
      If Not String.IsNullOrEmpty(name) Then
          query = query.Where(Function(e) e.Name = name)
      End If
      Return query.OrderByDescending(Function(e)
➥e.DatePublished).ToPagedList(page, 5)
   End Function

End Class
```

Adding the Views

It is finally time to improve the appearance of our blog application. In this section, we create the views and partials for our blog.

Let's start with the default page—the page generated by the view returned by the Blog controller Index() action. This view displays the list of blog entries (see Figure 20.6).

Because we changed the view data model returned by the Blog controller Index() action, we need to delete the existing Index view and re-create it with the correct view data model class. Replace the existing Index view with the Index view in Listing 20.8.

LISTING 20.8   UnleashedBlog\Views\Blog\Index.aspx (C#)

```
<%@ Page Title="" Language="C#" MasterPageFile="~/Views/Shared/Site.Master"
➥Inherits="System.Web.Mvc.ViewPage<Paging.PagedList<UnleashedBlog.
➥Models.BlogEntry>>" %>
```

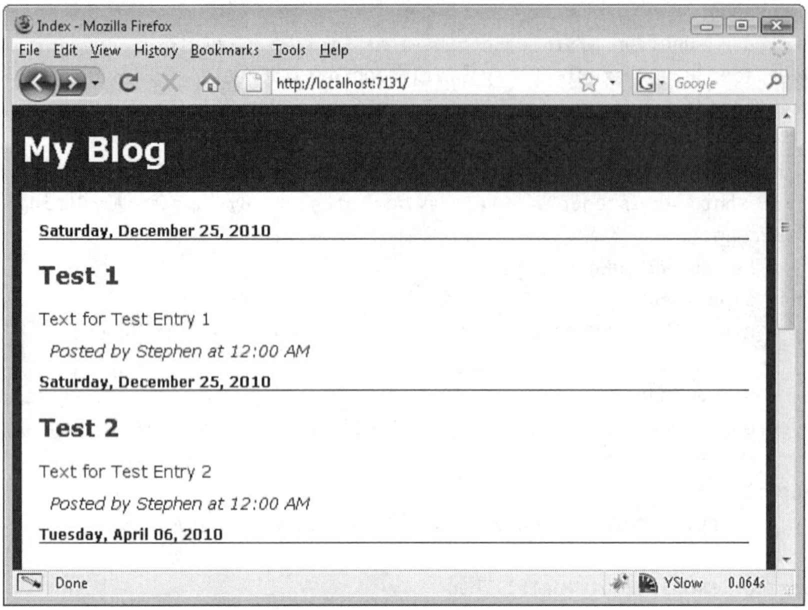

FIGURE 20.6   The Blog Index view

```
<asp:Content ID="Content1" ContentPlaceHolderID="TitleContent" runat="server">
    Index
</asp:Content>

<asp:Content ID="Content2" ContentPlaceHolderID="MainContent" runat="server">

    <% Html.RenderPartial("BlogEntries"); %>

</asp:Content>
```

LISTING 20.8   UnleashedBlog\Views\Blog\Index.aspx (VB)

```
<%@ Page Title="" Language="VB" MasterPageFile="~/Views/Shared/Site.Master"
➥Inherits="System.Web.Mvc.ViewPage(Of UnleashedBlog.PagedList (Of
➥UnleashedBlog.BlogEntry))" %>

<asp:Content ID="Content1" ContentPlaceHolderID="TitleContent" runat="server">
    Index
</asp:Content>

<asp:Content ID="Content2" ContentPlaceHolderID="MainContent" runat="server">
```

```
<% Html.RenderPartial("BlogEntries")%>
```

```
</asp:Content>
```

Notice that the view in Listing 20.8 has an `Inherits` attribute that causes the view data model to be cast to a `PagedList<BlogEntry>` class.

The `Index` view delegates all its blog entry rendering work to a partial named `BlogEntries`. The `BlogEntries` partial renders all the blog entries and the pager user interface.

The `BlogEntries` partial is used by both the `Blog` Index view and the `Archive` Index view. By creating a separate partial, we've eliminated duplicate user interface content among the views in our application.

The `BlogEntries` partial is contained in Listing 20.9.

LISTING 20.9   UnleashedBlog\Views\Shared\BlogEntries.ascx

```
<%@ Control Language="C#" Inherits="System.Web.Mvc.ViewUserControl
➥<Paging.PagedList<UnleashedBlog.Models.BlogEntry>>" %>


<% foreach (var entry in Model)
   { %>

    <div class="blogEntryContainer">

        <h2 class="blogEntryDatePublished"><%= entry.DatePublished.ToString ("D")
➥%></h2>
        <h3 class="blogEntryTitle"><%= Html.BlogLink(entry) %></h3>

        <div class="blogEntryText">
            <%= entry.Text %>
        </div>

        <div class="blogEntryFooter">
            Posted by <%= entry.Author %> at <%= entry.DatePublished.
➥ToString("t") %>
        </div>

    </div>

<% } %>

<div id="pager">
    <%= Html.BlogPager(Model) %>
</div>
```

LISTING 20.9   UnleashedBlog\Views\Shared\BlogEntries.ascx (VB)

```
<%@ Control Language="VB" Inherits="System.Web.Mvc.ViewUserControl(Of
➥UnleashedBlog.PagedList (Of UnleashedBlog.BlogEntry))" %>


<%  For Each entry In Model%>

    <div class="blogEntryContainer">

        <h2 class="blogEntryDatePublished"><%= entry.DatePublished. ToString("D")
➥%>></h2>
        <h3 class="blogEntryTitle"><%= Html.BlogLink(entry) %></h3>

        <div class="blogEntryText">
            <%= entry.Text %>
        </div>

        <div class="blogEntryFooter">
            Posted by <%= entry.Author %> at <%= entry.DatePublished.
➥ToString("t") %>
        </div>

    </div>

<% Next%>

<div id="pager">
    <%= Html.BlogPager(Model) %>
</div>
```

Notice that the `BlogEntries` partial uses two custom HTML helpers. First, the
`Html.BlogLink()` helper renders a link to a blog entry. This helper is contained in
Listing 20.10.

LISTING 20.10   UnleashedBlog\Helpers\BlogLinkHelper.cs

```
using System.Web.Mvc;
using System.Web.Mvc.Html;
using UnleashedBlog.Models;

namespace UnleashedBlog.Helpers
{
    public static class BlogLinkHelper
    {
        public static string BlogLink(this HtmlHelper helper, BlogEntry entry)
```

```
        {
            return helper.ActionLink(entry.Title, "Index", "Archive", new
➥{year=entry.DatePublished.Year, month=entry.DatePublished.Month,
➥day=entry.DatePublished.Day, name = entry.Name }, null);
        }
    }
}
```

LISTING 20.10   UnleashedBlog\Helpers\BlogLinkHelper.vb (VB)

```
Namespace Helpers


    Public Module BlogLinkHelper


        <System.Runtime.CompilerServices.Extension()> _
        Public Function BlogLink(ByVal helper As HtmlHelper, ByVal entry As
➥BlogEntry) As String
            Return helper.ActionLink(entry.Title, "Index", "Archive", New With {Key
➥.year = entry.DatePublished.Year, Key .month = entry.DatePublished.Month, Key .day
➥= entry.DatePublished.Day, Key .name = entry.Name}, Nothing)
        End Function


    End Module


End Namespace
```

NOTE

To avoid registering the namespace for the HTML helpers in every page in which I use
the helpers, I registered the namespace in the web.config file like this:

```
<pages>

<namespaces>

    <add namespace="UnleashedBlog.Helpers"/>

</namespaces>

</pages>
```

A second HTML helper renders the pager user interface (see Listing 20.11). This helper
renders an Older Entries link when there are older entries and a Newer Entries link when
there are newer entries. If there isn't more than a single page of blog entries, the helper
renders nothing at all.

LISTING 20.11   UnleashedBlog\Helpers\BlogPagerHelper.cs (C#)

```csharp
using System.Text;
using System.Web.Mvc;
using System.Web.Mvc.Html;
using System.Web.Routing;
using Paging;

namespace UnleashedBlog.Helpers
{
    public static class BlogPagerHelper
    {

        public static string BlogPager(this HtmlHelper helper, IPagedList pager)
        {
            // Don't display anything if not multiple pages
            if (pager.TotalPageCount == 1)
                return string.Empty;

            // Build route data
            var routeData = new RouteValueDictionary
➥(helper.ViewContext.RouteData.Values);

            // Build string
            var sb = new StringBuilder();

            // Render Newer Entries
            if (pager.PageIndex > 0)
            {
                routeData["page"] = pager.PageIndex - 1;
                sb.Append(helper.ActionLink("Newer Entries", "Index", routeData));
            }

            // Render divider
            if (pager.PageIndex > 0 && pager.PageIndex < pager.TotalPageCount - 1)
                sb.Append(" ¦ ");

            // Render Older Entries
            if (pager.PageIndex < pager.TotalPageCount - 1)
            {
                routeData["page"] = pager.PageIndex + 1;
                sb.Append(helper.ActionLink("Older Entries", "Index", routeData));
            }

            return sb.ToString();
        }
```

```
        }
}
```

LISTING 20.11   UnleashedBlog\Helpers\BlogPagerHelper.vb (VB)

```vb
Namespace Helpers

    Public Module BlogPagerHelper

        <System.Runtime.CompilerServices.Extension()> _
        Public Function BlogPager(ByVal helper As HtmlHelper, ByVal pager As
➥IPagedList) As String
            ' Don't display anything if not multiple pages
            If pager.TotalPageCount = 1 Then
                Return String.Empty
            End If

            ' Build route data
            Dim routeData = New RouteValueDictionary
➥(helper.ViewContext.RouteData.Values)

            ' Build string
            Dim sb = New StringBuilder()

            ' Render Newer Entries
            If pager.PageIndex > 0 Then
                routeData("page") = pager.PageIndex - 1
                sb.Append(helper.ActionLink("Newer Entries", "Index", routeData))
            End If

            ' Render divider
            If pager.PageIndex > 0 AndAlso pager.PageIndex < pager.TotalPageCount -
➥1 Then
                sb.Append(" ¦ ")
            End If

            ' Render Older Entries
            If pager.PageIndex < pager.TotalPageCount - 1 Then
                routeData("page") = pager.PageIndex + 1
                sb.Append(helper.ActionLink("Older Entries", "Index", routeData))
            End If

            Return sb.ToString()
```

```
        End Function
    End Module
End Namespace
```

Adding Ajax Support

I love my iPhone. The iPhone was designed to provide a great user experience. The iPhone has a number of user interface design innovations. One innovation concerns how paging is implemented.

Earlier in this chapter, we implemented a standard user interface for paging. We created `Older` Entries and `Newer` Entries links. When you first request the page, the first five blog entries display. When you click the `Older` Entries link, the first blog entries are replaced with the next blog entries.

In this section, we change our user interface for paging to take advantage of Ajax. Instead of displaying `Older` Entries and `Newer` Entries links, we only display a `More Entries` link. When you click the `More Entries` link, additional blog entries are appended to the first five blog entries. The list of blog entries grows instead of being replaced (see Figure 20.7).

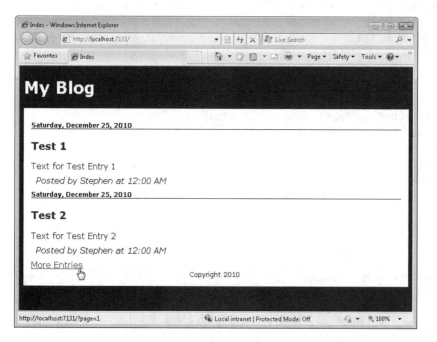

FIGURE 20.7   Growing list of blog entries

NOTE

Even after we implement Ajax paging, our blog application continues to work with JavaScript disabled. When JavaScript is disabled, the blog application does a normal post to the server to retrieve the next set of five blog entries.

In this section, we improve the user experience and responsiveness of our blog application by adding support for Ajax. We focus on implementing the following user story:

When there are more than five entries, a More Entries link displays. When you click the More Entries link, five more blog entries are appended to the list of blog entries (see Figure 20.8).

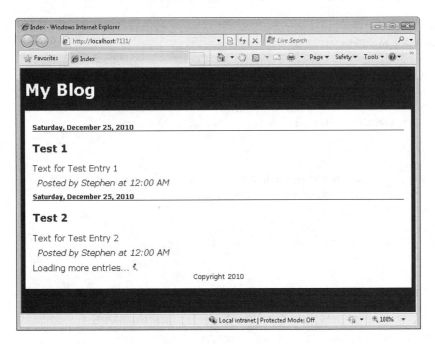

FIGURE 20.8   Appending the additional blog entries

As always, we start with a test. There are now two ways that we want to retrieve blog entries: with a normal page request and with an Ajax request. In the first case, we want to return a ViewResult, and in the second case we want to return a PartialViewResult. The test in Listing 20.12 verifies that we can invoke an action that returns a PartialViewResult.

LISTING 20.12   UnleashedBlog.Tests\ControllerTests\BlogControllerTests.cs (C#)

```csharp
[TestMethod]
public void Index_AjaxReturnsPartialViewResult()
{
    // Act
    var result = _blogController.Index_Ajax(0);

    // Assert
    Assert.IsInstanceOfType(result, typeof(PartialViewResult));
}
```

LISTING 20.12   UnleashedBlog.Tests\ControllerTests\BlogControllerTests.vb (VB)

```vbnet
<TestMethod()> _
Public Sub Index_AjaxReturnsPartialViewResult()
    ' Act
    Dim result = _blogController.Index_Ajax(0)

    ' Assert
    Assert.IsInstanceOfType(result, GetType(PartialViewResult))
End Sub
```

When we first attempt to run the test in Listing 20.12, it fails because the Blog controller does not have an Index_Ajax() action. Because we have a test, we can allow ourselves to add this new action (see Listing 20.13).

LISTING 20.13   UnleashedBlog\Controllers\BlogController.cs (C#)

```csharp
[AcceptAjax]
[ActionName("Index")]
public ActionResult Index_Ajax(int? page)
{
    return PartialView("BlogEntries", _blogService.ListBlogEntries(page));
}
```

LISTING 20.13   UnleashedBlog\Controllers\BlogController.vb (VB)

```vbnet
<AcceptAjax(), ActionName("Index")> _
Public Function Index_Ajax(ByVal page As Integer?) As ActionResult
    Return PartialView("BlogEntries", _blogService.ListBlogEntries(page))
End Function
```

The `Index_Ajax()` action in Listing 20.13 is exactly the same as the `Index()` action, except the `Index_Ajax()` action returns a `PartialViewResult` instead of a normal `ViewResult`.

Notice that the `Index_Ajax()` action is decorated with two attributes. The `AcceptAjax` attribute causes this action to be called only in the context of an Ajax request. This attribute is not a standard part of the ASP.NET MVC framework. We discussed this attribute in Chapter 14, "Working with Ajax."

The second attribute, the `ActionName` attribute, exposes the method as an action with a different name than the method name. This attribute causes the `Index_Ajax()` method to be exposed as the `Index()` action.

To take advantage of the new `Index_Ajax()` action, we need to modify our views. Listing 20.14 contains the updated `Blog` controller `Index` view.

LISTING 20.14   UnleashedBlog\Views\Blog\Index.aspx (C#)

```
<%@ Page Title="" Language="C#" MasterPageFile="~/Views/Shared/Site.Master"
➥Inherits="System.Web.Mvc.ViewPage<Paging.PagedList<UnleashedBlog. Models.
➥BlogEntry>>" %>


<asp:Content ID="Content1" ContentPlaceHolderID="TitleContent" runat="server">
    Index
</asp:Content>

<asp:Content ID="Content2" ContentPlaceHolderID="MainContent" runat="server">

  <div id="blogEntries">
    <% Html.RenderPartial("BlogEntries"); %>
  </div>

  <div id="loadingMoreEntries" style="display:none">
    Loading more entries...
    <img src="<%= Url.Content("~/Content/ajax-loader.gif") %>"
        alt="Loading more entries" />
  </div>

</asp:Content>
```

LISTING 20.14   UnleashedBlog\Views\Blog\Index.aspx (VB)

```
<%@ Page Title="" Language="VB" MasterPageFile="~/Views/Shared/Site.Master"
➥Inherits="System.Web.Mvc.ViewPage(Of UnleashedBlog.PagedList (Of
➥UnleashedBlog.BlogEntry))" %>
```

```
<asp:Content ID="Content1" ContentPlaceHolderID="TitleContent" runat="server">
    Index
</asp:Content>


<asp:Content ID="Content2" ContentPlaceHolderID="MainContent" runat="server">

  <div id="blogEntries">
    <% Html.RenderPartial("BlogEntries")%>
  </div>

  <div id="loadingMoreEntries" style="display:none">
    Loading more entries...
    <img src="<%= Url.Content("~/Content/ajax-loader.gif") %>"
        alt="Loading more entries" />
  </div>

</asp:Content>
```

Notice that the view in Listing 20.14 includes a `loadingMoreEntries` DIV element. The
contents of this DIV element display while the blog application waits for the results of an
Ajax request.

NOTE

I downloaded the busy wait image from www.ajaxload.info. This website enables you to
generate different types of busy wait images and use them in your applications for free.

The updated `BlogEntries` partial is contained in Listing 20.15.

LISTING 20.15   UnleashedBlog\Views\Shared\BlogEntries.ascx (C#)

```
<%@ Control Language="C#" Inherits="System.Web.Mvc.ViewUserControl
➥<Paging.PagedList<UnleashedBlog.Models.BlogEntry>>" %>


<% foreach (var entry in Model)
   { %>

   <div class="blogEntryContainer">

        <h2 class="blogEntryDatePublished"><%= entry.DatePublished.ToString("D")
➥%></h2>
        <h3 class="blogEntryTitle"><%= Html.BlogLink(entry) %></h3>

        <div class="blogEntryText">
           <%= entry.Text %>
```

```
            </div>

        <div class="blogEntryFooter">
            Posted by <%= entry.Author %> at <%= entry.DatePublished.ToString
➡("t") %>
        </div>

    </div>

<% } %>

<div id="pager">
    <%= Ajax.BlogPager(Model) %>

</div>
```

LISTING 20.15   UnleashedBlog\Views\Shared\BlogEntries.ascx (VB)

```
<%@ Control Language="VB" Inherits="System.Web.Mvc.ViewUserControl(Of
➡UnleashedBlog.PagedList (Of UnleashedBlog.BlogEntry))" %>

<%  For Each entry In Model%>

    <div class="blogEntryContainer">

        <h2 class="blogEntryDatePublished"><%= entry.DatePublished.ToString ("D")
➡%></h2>
        <h3 class="blogEntryTitle"><%= Html.BlogLink(entry) %></h3>

        <div class="blogEntryText">
            <%= entry.Text %>
        </div>

        <div class="blogEntryFooter">
            Posted by <%= entry.Author %> at <%= entry.DatePublished.ToString
➡("t") %>
        </div>

    </div>

<% Next%>

<div id="pager">
    <%= Ajax.BlogPager(Model) %>

</div>
```

Only one change has been made to the partial in Listing 20.15. The `BlogEntries` partial now uses an `Ajax.BlogPager()` instead of the `Html.BlogPager()`.

The `Ajax.BlogPager()` is contained in Listing 20.16.

LISTING 20.16   UnleashedBlog\Helpers\BlogPagerHelper.ascx (C#)

```csharp
public static string BlogPager(this AjaxHelper helper, IPagedList pager)
{
    // Don't display anything if not multiple pages or no more entries
    if (pager.TotalPageCount == 1 || pager.PageIndex ==
pager.TotalPageCount -1)
        return string.Empty;

    // Build route data
    var routeData = new RouteValueDictionary
(helper.ViewContext.RouteData.Values);

    // Build Ajax options
    var options = new AjaxOptions
        {
            UpdateTargetId = "blogEntries",
            InsertionMode=InsertionMode.InsertAfter,
            LoadingElementId="loadingMoreEntries",
            OnBegin= "function() {this.style.display='none';}"
        };

    // Render More Entries
    routeData["page"] = pager.PageIndex + 1;
    return helper.ActionLink("More Entries", "Index", routeData, options);
}
```

LISTING 20.16   UnleashedBlog\Helpers\BlogPagerHelper.ascx (VB)

```vb
<System.Runtime.CompilerServices.Extension()> _
Public Function BlogPager(ByVal helper As AjaxHelper, ByVal pager As
IPagedList) As String
        ' Don't display anything if not multiple pages or no more entries
        If pager.TotalPageCount = 1 OrElse pager.PageIndex =
pager.TotalPageCount - 1 Then
            Return String.Empty
        End If
```

```
            ' Build route data
            Dim routeData = New
➡RouteValueDictionary(helper.ViewContext.RouteData.Values)

            ' Build Ajax options
            Dim options = New AjaxOptions With {.UpdateTargetId = "blogEntries",
➡.InsertionMode = InsertionMode.InsertAfter, .LoadingElementId =
➡"loadingMoreEntries", .OnBegin = "function() {this.style.display='none';}"}

            ' Render More Entries
            routeData("page") = pager.PageIndex + 1
            Return helper.ActionLink("More Entries", "Index", routeData, options)
        End Function
```

The `Ajax.BlogPager()` calls the `Ajax.ActionLink()` helper method internally to render the More Entries link. An instance of the `AjaxOptions` class is created to specify the behavior of the `Ajax.ActionLink()`. The `AjaxOptions` class causes the link to update the `blogEntries` DIV tag with the results of the Ajax request.

After we make these changes, our blog application now supports Ajax. When we page through the blog entries by clicking the More Entries link, additional blog entries are appended to the existing page.

Summary

In this chapter, we focused on improving the user interface of our blog application. In the first part of this chapter, we added support for paging through blog entries. We took advantage of the paging framework that we created in Chapter 6.

Next, we rewrote the views and partials for our blog application. Our views share a single partial that displays the list of blog entries. That way, we can control the appearance of our blog entries by modifying a single file.

Finally, we added Ajax support to our blog application. We created an Ajax pager that enables us to continuously grow our page by appending new blog entries to the existing blog entries.

CHAPTER 21

Adding Comments

A blog application that enables only one-way communication is no fun. In this final chapter, we add support for comments to our blog application. We implement the set of user stories in Figure 21.1.

We have the following stories related to comments:

1. A user should be able to add a comment to a particular blog entry. A comment consists of a title, date published, URL, name, email, and text.

2. After a user adds a comment to a blog entry, the user should see the comment when viewing the blog entry.

3. The last comment posted should appear last in the list of comments.

4. The number of comments associated with each blog entry should appear next to each blog entry when a set of blog entries are listed.

This gives us enough to start writing tests. We tackle each of these requirements one-by-one.

Implementing Comments

According to the first user story, a user should be able to create a new comment. Furthermore, according to the story, a comment should consist of title, date published, URL, name, email, and text.

The test in Listing 21.1 captures the intention of the first user story.

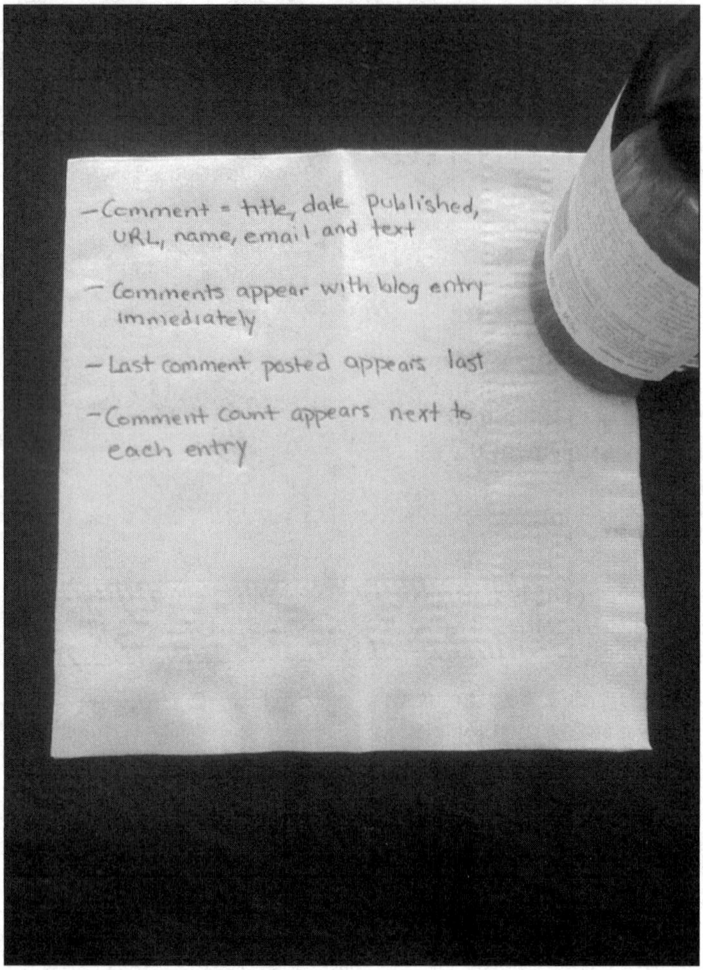

FIGURE 21.1   User stories

LISTING 21.1   UnleashedBlog.Tests\Controllers\CommentControllerTests.cs (C#)

```
[TestMethod]
public void CreateComment()
{
    // Arrange
    var controller = new CommentController();
    var commentToCreate = new Comment();
    commentToCreate.Title = "New Comment";
    commentToCreate.DatePublished = new DateTime(2010, 12, 25);
    commentToCreate.Url = "http://myblog.com";
    commentToCreate.Name = "Bob";
    commentToCreate.Email = "Bob@somewhere.com";
```

```
commentToCreate.Text = "Here is the comment";

// Act
controller.Create(commentToCreate);
}
```

LISTING 21.1   UnleashedBlog.Tests\Controllers\CommentControllerTests.vb (VB)

```
<TestMethod> _
Public Sub CreateComment()
    ' Arrange
    Dim controller = New CommentController()
    Dim commentToCreate = New Comment()
    commentToCreate.Title = "New Comment"
    commentToCreate.DatePublished = New DateTime(2010, 12, 25)
    commentToCreate.Url = "http://myblog.com"
    commentToCreate.Name = "Bob"
    commentToCreate.Email = "Bob@somewhere.com"
    commentToCreate.Text = "Here is the comment"

    ' Act
    controller.Create(commentToCreate)
End Sub
```

NOTE

The test in Listing 21.1 does not have an Assert section. An Assert section is not needed because the test is verifying that you can create a comment successfully and the comment has particular properties.

After you create the test, the application won't compile because we have not yet created a CommentController or a Comment class (see Figure 21.2). Therefore, the first thing that we need to do is to create these classes (see Listing 21.2 and Listing 21.3).

	Description	F	Line	Column	Project
1	The type or namespace name 'CommentController' could not be found (are you missing a using directive or an assembly reference?)	Co	17	34	UnleashedBlog.Tests
2	The type or namespace name 'Comment' could not be found (are you missing a using directive or an assembly reference?)	Co	18	39	UnleashedBlog.Tests

FIGURE 21.2   Failing CreateComment test

LISTING 21.2   UnleashedBlog\Models\Comment.cs (C#)

```csharp
using System;

namespace UnleashedBlog.Models
{
    public class Comment
    {
        public string Title { get; set; }
        public string Name { get; set; }
        public string Url { get; set; }
        public string Email { get; set; }
        public string Text { get; set; }
        public DateTime DatePublished { get; set; }
    }
}
```

LISTING 21.2   UnleashedBlog\Models\Comment.vb (VB)

```vb
Public Class Comment
    Private privateTitle As String
    Public Property Title() As String
        Get
            Return privateTitle
        End Get
        Set(ByVal value As String)
            privateTitle = value
        End Set
    End Property
    Private privateName As String
    Public Property Name() As String
        Get
            Return privateName
        End Get
        Set(ByVal value As String)
        privateName = value
        End Set
    End Property
    Private privateUrl As String
    Public Property Url() As String
        Get
        Return privateUrl
        End Get
        Set(ByVal value As String)
```

```vbnet
                privateUrl = value
            End Set
        End Property
        Private privateEmail As String
        Public Property Email() As String
            Get
                Return privateEmail
            End Get
            Set(ByVal value As String)
                privateEmail = value
            End Set
        End Property
        Private privateText As String
        Public Property Text() As String
            Get
                Return privateText
            End Get
            Set(ByVal value As String)
                privateText = value
            End Set
        End Property
        Private privateDatePublished As DateTime
        Public Property DatePublished() As DateTime
            Get
                Return privateDatePublished
            End Get
            Set(ByVal value As DateTime)
                privateDatePublished = value
            End Set
        End Property
    End Class
```

LISTING 21.3   UnleashedBlog\Controllers\CommentController.cs (C#)

```csharp
using System.Web.Mvc;
using UnleashedBlog.Models;

namespace UnleashedBlog.Controllers
{
    public class CommentController : Controller
    {
        public ActionResult Create(Comment commentToCreate)
        {
            return View();
```

```
        }

    }

}
```

LISTING 21.3   UnleashedBlog\Controllers\CommentController.vb (VB)

```vbnet
Public Class CommentController
    Inherits Controller

    Public Function Create(ByVal commentToCreate As Comment) As ActionResult
        Return View()
    End Function

End Class
```

After we add the `Comment` and `CommentController` classes, we are back in the green. All of our tests pass (see Figure 21.3).

FIGURE 21.3   `CreateComment` test passes.

The `Create()` action isn't actually doing anything. However, we want to write the minimum amount of code to get the test to pass and the test does, in fact, pass.

Next, we need to implement the user story related to viewing the comments. According to this user story, after you add a comment, you should see the comment when you retrieve the blog entry. The test in Listing 21.4 is intended to capture the intent of this story.

LISTING 21.4   UnleashedBlog.Tests\Controllers\CommentControllerTests.cs (C#)

```csharp
[TestMethod]
public void CreateAndThenGetComment()
{
    // Arrange
    var blogEntry = CreateBlogEntry();
    var comment1 = CreateComment(blogEntry, "Comment 1", new
➥DateTime(2010, 12, 25));

    // Act
    var archiveController = _controllerFactory.GetArchiveController();
    var result = (ViewResult)archiveController.Index
➥(blogEntry.DatePublished.Year, blogEntry.DatePublished.Month,
➥blogEntry.DatePublished.Day, blogEntry.Name);

    // Assert
    var comments = ((BlogEntry)result.ViewData.Model).Comments;
    Assert.AreEqual("Comment 1", comments[0].Title);
}

private BlogEntry CreateBlogEntry()
{
    var blogController = _controllerFactory.GetBlogController();
    var blogEntryToCreate = BlogEntryFactory.Get();
    blogController.Create(blogEntryToCreate);
    return blogEntryToCreate;
}

private Comment CreateComment(BlogEntry blogEntry, string commentTitle,
➥DateTime commentDatePublished)
{
    // Create comment
    var commentToCreate = CommentFactory.Get();
    commentToCreate.BlogEntryId = blogEntry.Id;
    commentToCreate.Title = commentTitle;
    commentToCreate.DatePublished = commentDatePublished;

    // Add to blog entry
    var commentController = _controllerFactory.GetCommentController();
    commentController.Create(commentToCreate);

    return commentToCreate;
}
```

LISTING 21.4   UnleashedBlog.Tests\Controllers\CommentControllerTests.cs (VB)

```vb
<TestMethod> _
Public Sub CreateAndThenGetComment()
    ' Arrange
    Dim blogEntry = CreateBlogEntry()
    Dim comment1 = CreateComment(blogEntry, "Comment 1", New DateTime(2010, 12, 25))

    ' Act
    Dim archiveController = _controllerFactory.GetArchiveController()
    Dim result As ViewResult = archiveController.Index
➥(blogEntry.DatePublished.Year, blogEntry.DatePublished.Month,
➥blogEntry.DatePublished.Day, blogEntry.Name)

    ' Assert
    Dim comments = (CType(result.ViewData.Model, BlogEntry)).Comments
    Assert.AreEqual("Comment 1", comments(0).Title)
    End Sub

    Private Function CreateBlogEntry() As BlogEntry
    Dim blogController = _controllerFactory.GetBlogController()
    Dim blogEntryToCreate = BlogEntryFactory.Get()
  blogController.Create(blogEntryToCreate)
    Return blogEntryToCreate
End Function

Private Function CreateComment(ByVal blogEntry As BlogEntry, ByVal commentTitle As
➥String, ByVal commentDatePublished As DateTime) As Comment
    ' Create comment
    Dim commentToCreate = CommentFactory.Get()
    commentToCreate.BlogEntryId = blogEntry.Id
    commentToCreate.Title = commentTitle
    commentToCreate.DatePublished = commentDatePublished

    ' Add to blog entry
    Dim commentController = _controllerFactory.GetCommentController()
    commentController.Create(commentToCreate)

    Return commentToCreate
End Function
```

Listing 21.4 contains one test method named CreateAndThenGetComment(). The test creates a blog entry, creates a comment associated with the blog entry, and retrieves the blog entry. If the comment can be retrieved, the test passes.

Notice that the test uses two helper methods named `CreateBlogEntry()` and
`CreateComment()`. These helper methods make the `CreateAndThenGetComment()` test
method more readable.

NOTE

In the solution in the code samples on the website (www.informit.com/title/
9780672329982), the `CreateBlogEntry()` and `CreateComment()` helper methods
have been moved into a separate helper class named `TestHelpers`.

This is not an easy test to pass. To pass this test, we need to modify several classes including the `CommentController`, the `BlogService`, and the `BlogRepository` class.

I won't include all the code that I had to modify to get the test to pass here. The application logic for retrieving comments is similar to the application logic that we wrote earlier
for retrieving blog entries.

Let's move to the next user story. According to the next user story, the last comment
posted to a blog entry should appear last when the comments display. The test in Listing
21.5 represents this user story.

LISTING 21.5   UnleashedBlog.Tests\Controllers\CommentControllerTests.cs (C#)

```
[TestMethod]
public void CommentsOrderByDatePublished()
{
    // Arrange
    var blogEntry = CreateBlogEntry();
    var comment1 = CreateComment(blogEntry, "Comment 1", new
➥DateTime(2009, 12, 25));
    var comment2 = CreateComment(blogEntry, "Comment 2", new
➥DateTime(2010, 12, 25));
    var comment3 = CreateComment(blogEntry, "Comment 3", new
➥DateTime(2007,12, 25));

    // Act
    var archiveController = _controllerFactory.GetArchiveController();
    var result = (ViewResult)archiveController.Index (blogEntry.
➥DatePublished.Year, blogEntry.DatePublished.Month, blogEntry.DatePublished.Day,
➥blogEntry.Name);

    // Assert
    var comments = ((BlogEntry)result.ViewData.Model).Comments;
```

```
        Assert.AreEqual("Comment 3", comments[0].Title);
        Assert.AreEqual("Comment 2", comments[2].Title);
    }
```

LISTING 21.5   UnleashedBlog.Tests\Controllers\CommentControllerTests.vb (VB)

```vb
<TestMethod> _
Public Sub CommentsOrderByDatePublished()
    ' Arrange
    Dim blogEntry = CreateBlogEntry()
    Dim comment1 = CreateComment(blogEntry, "Comment 1", New DateTime(2009, 12, 25))
    Dim comment2 = CreateComment(blogEntry, "Comment 2", New DateTime(2010, 12, 25))
    Dim comment3 = CreateComment(blogEntry, "Comment 3", New DateTime(2007, 12, 25))

    ' Act
    Dim archiveController = _controllerFactory.GetArchiveController()
    Dim result As ViewResult = archiveController.Index(blogEntry.
➥DatePublished.Year, blogEntry.DatePublished.Month, blogEntry.DatePublished.Day,
➥blogEntry.Name)

    ' Assert
    Dim comments = (CType(result.ViewData.Model, BlogEntry)).Comments
    Assert.AreEqual("Comment 3", comments(0).Title)
    Assert.AreEqual("Comment 2", comments(2).Title)
End Sub
```

Getting this test to pass is not as difficult as the previous test. We simply need to order the comments returned by the blog repository by DatePublished. After we make this change, all tests pass (see Figure 21.4).

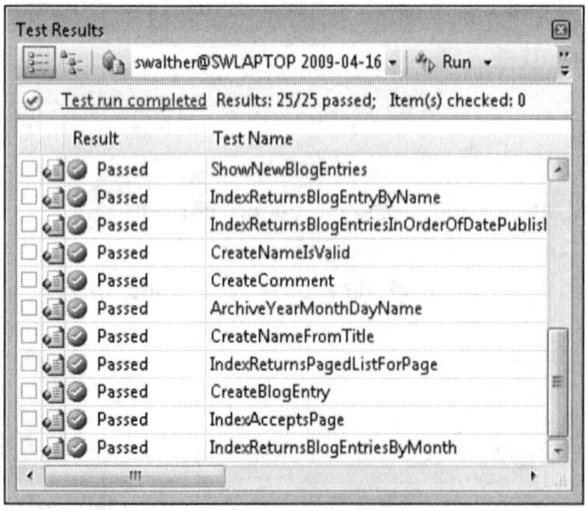

FIGURE 21.4   The first three comment tests pass.

Let's tackle the final user story concerning blog comments. According to the final user story, a count of the number of comments associated with a blog entry should appear next to each blog entry. The test in Listing 21.6 is intended to capture the intention behind this story.

LISTING 21.6   UnleashedBlog.Tests\Controllers\CommentControllerTests.cs (C#)

```csharp
[TestMethod]
public void BlogEntriesIncludeCommentCount()
{
    // Arrange
    var blogEntry = CreateBlogEntry();
    var comment1 = CreateComment(blogEntry, "Comment 1",
new DateTime(2009, 12, 25));
    var comment2 = CreateComment(blogEntry, "Comment 2",
new DateTime(2010, 12, 25));

    // Act
    var blogController = _controllerFactory.GetBlogController();
    var result = (ViewResult)blogController.Index(null);

    // Assert
    var entries = (List<BlogEntry>)result.ViewData.Model;
    Assert.AreEqual(2, entries[0].CommentCount);
}
```

LISTING 21.6   UnleashedBlog.Tests\Controllers\CommentControllerTests.vb (VB)

```vb
<TestMethod> _
Public Sub BlogEntriesIncludeCommentCount()
    ' Arrange
    Dim blogEntry = CreateBlogEntry()
    Dim comment1 = CreateComment(blogEntry, "Comment 1", New DateTime(2009, 12, 25))
    Dim comment2 = CreateComment(blogEntry, "Comment 2", New DateTime(2010, 12, 25))

    ' Act
    Dim blogController = _controllerFactory.GetBlogController()
    Dim result As ViewResult = blogController.Index(Nothing)

    ' Assert
    Dim entries = CType(result.ViewData.Model, List(Of BlogEntry))
    Assert.AreEqual(2, entries(0).CommentCount)
End Sub
```

The test in Listing 21.6 creates a blog entry with two comments. Next, the test invokes the Archive controller action method to retrieve all the blog entries. The test verifies that the first blog entry has a CommentCount of 2.

Unfortunately, the only way to get this test to pass is to modify the FakeBlogRepository class (see Listing 21.7). Because the application code in the FakeBlogRepository class is not executed when the application is run during production, testing any code in the FakeBlogRepository class does not test production code.

LISTING 21.7   UnleashedBlog.Tests\Models\FakeBlogRepository.cs (C#)

```
protected override IQueryable<BlogEntry> QueryBlogEntries()
{
    return from e in _blogEntries.AsQueryable()
            select new BlogEntry
                {
                    Id = e.Id,
                    Author = e.Author,
                    Description = e.Description,
                    Name = e.Name,
                    DateModified = e.DateModified,
                    DatePublished = e.DatePublished,
                    Text = e.Text,
                    Title = e.Title,
                    CommentCount = (from c in _comments.AsQueryable()
                                    where c.BlogEntryId == e.Id
                                    select c).Count()


                };
}
```

LISTING 21.7   UnleashedBlog.Tests\Models\FakeBlogRepository.vb (VB)

```
    Protected Overrides Function QueryBlogEntries() As IQueryable(Of BlogEntry)
        Return From e In _blogEntries.AsQueryable() _
                Select New BlogEntry With {.Id = e.Id, .Author = e.Author,
➥.Description = e.Description, .Name = e.Name, .DateModified = e.DateModified,
➥.DatePublished = e.DatePublished, .Text = e.Text, .Title = e.Title,
➥.CommentCount = (From c In _comments.AsQueryable() _
                Where c.BlogEntryId = e.Id Select c).Count()}
    End Function
```

However, the test in Listing 21.7 is not without value. For example, the test verifies the way the controller, service, and repository classes interact. The test verifies the behavior of all the application code around the repository even if the test does not verify the behavior of the repository itself.

At this point, we have passed all the tests related to comments. We have implemented the application logic for creating comments, retrieving comments, and displaying a comment count.

Adding Comments to the Database

To support comments, we need to update the database so that it includes a Comments database table. The Comments table contains the following columns (see Table 21.1).

TABLE 21.1   The Comments Database Table

Column Name	Data Type	Allow Nulls
Id	int	False
BlogEntryId	int	False
Title	nvarchar(100)	False
Name	nvarchar(100)	False
Email	nvarchar(500)	True
Url	nvarchar(500)	True
DatePublished	DateTime	False
Text	nvarchar(max)	False

The first column, the Id column, is an Identity and primary key column.

After we create the table, we need to update our data model. Follow these steps:

1. Open the Entity Framework Designer by double-clicking the DateModel.edmx file in the Solution Explorer window.
2. Right-click the designer surface and select the menu option Update Model from Database.
3. In the Update Wizard, select the Comments table from beneath the Add tab (see Figure 21.5).
4. Click Finish to close the wizard and add the table.
5. Rename the entity from Comments to CommentEntity (see Figure 21.6).

To use the new Comments database table, we need to update the EntityFrameworkBlogRepository. The updated EntityFrameworkBlogRepository in Listing 21.8 contains new or revised QueryBlogEntries(), QueryComments(), and CreateComment() methods.

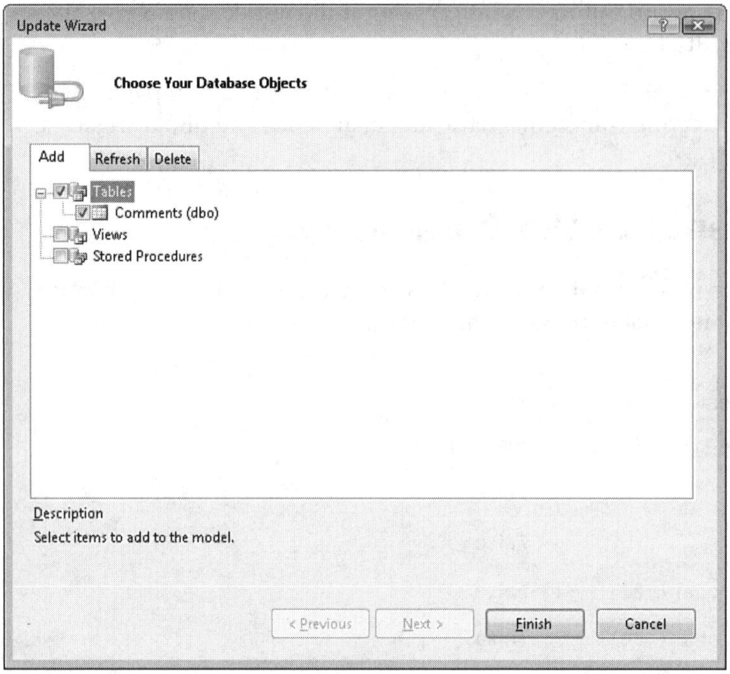

FIGURE 21.5   Selecting the Comments table in the Update Wizard

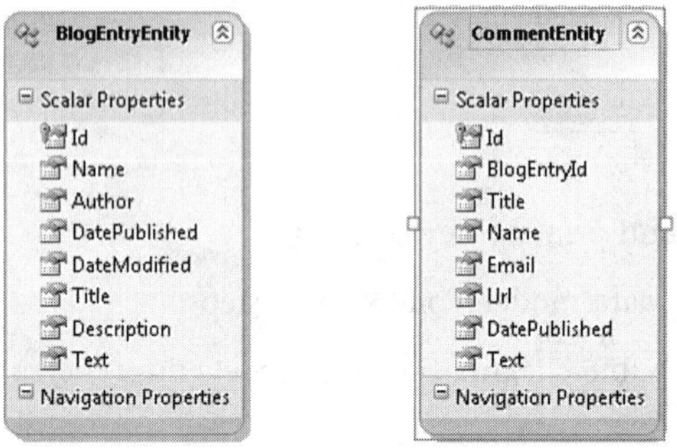

FIGURE 21.6   Renaming the Comments entity

LISTING 21.8   UnleashedBlog\Models\EntityFramework\EntityFramework
BlogRepository.cs (C#)

```csharp
    protected override IQueryable<BlogEntry> QueryBlogEntries()
    {
        return from e in _entities.BlogEntryEntitySet
               select new BlogEntry
               {
                   Id = e.Id,
                   Author = e.Author,
```

```
                        Description = e.Description,
                        Name = e.Name,
                        DateModified = e.DateModified,
                        DatePublished = e.DatePublished,
                        Text = e.Text,
                        Title = e.Title,
                        CommentCount = (from c in _entities.CommentEntitySet
                                        where c.BlogEntryId == e.Id
                                        select c).Count()
                };
}


private CommentEntity ConvertCommentToCommentEntity(Comment comment)
{
    var entity = new CommentEntity();

    entity.Id = comment.Id;
    entity.BlogEntryId = comment.BlogEntryId;
    entity.DatePublished = comment.DatePublished;
    entity.Email = comment.Email;
    entity.Name = comment.Name;
    entity.Text = comment.Text;
    entity.Title = comment.Title;
    entity.Url = comment.Url;
    return entity;
}


protected override IQueryable<Comment> QueryComments()
{
    return from c in _entities.CommentEntitySet
           select new Comment
           {
               Id = c.Id,
               BlogEntryId = c.BlogEntryId,
               DatePublished = c.DatePublished,
               Email = c.Email,
               Name = c.Name,
               Text = c.Text,
               Title = c.Title,
               Url = c.Url
           };
}


public override void CreateComment(Comment commentToCreate)
{
    var entity = ConvertCommentToCommentEntity(commentToCreate);
```

```
            _entities.AddToCommentEntitySet(entity);
            _entities.SaveChanges();
        }
```

LISTING 21.8   UnleashedBlog\Models\EntityFramework\EntityFramework
BlogRepository.vb (VB)

```
    Protected Overrides Function QueryBlogEntries() As IQueryable(Of BlogEntry)
        Return From e In _entities.BlogEntryEntitySet _
            Select New BlogEntry With {.Id = e.Id, .Author = e.Author,
➥.Description = e.Description, .Name = e.Name, .DateModified = e.DateModified,
➥.DatePublished = e.DatePublished, .Text = e.Text, .Title = e.Title,
➥.CommentCount = (From c In _entities.CommentEntitySet _
            Where c.BlogEntryId = e.Id Select c).Count()}
    End Function

    Private Function ConvertCommentToCommentEntity(ByVal comment As Comment) As
➥CommentEntity
        Dim entity = New CommentEntity()

        entity.Id = comment.Id
        entity.BlogEntryId = comment.BlogEntryId
        entity.DatePublished = comment.DatePublished
        entity.Email = comment.Email
        entity.Name = comment.Name
        entity.Text = comment.Text
        entity.Title = comment.Title
        entity.Url = comment.Url
        Return entity
    End Function

    Protected Overrides Function QueryComments() As IQueryable(Of Comment)
        Return From c In _entities.CommentEntitySet _
            Select New Comment With {.Id = c.Id, .BlogEntryId = c.BlogEntryId,
➥.DatePublished = c.DatePublished, .Email = c.Email, .Name = c.Name, .Text =
➥c.Text, .Title = c.Title, .Url = c.Url}
    End Function

    Public Overrides Sub CreateComment(ByVal commentToCreate As Comment)
        Dim entity = ConvertCommentToCommentEntity(commentToCreate)

        _entities.AddToCommentEntitySet(entity)
        _entities.SaveChanges()
    End Sub
```

Notice the `ConvertCommentToCommentEntity()` method. This method converts an instance of a `Comment` class to an instance of a `CommentEntity` class. We created the `Comment` class by hand, and we use the `Comment` class in our blog application. The `CommentEntity` class, on the other hand, was generated by the Microsoft Entity Framework. We convert back and forth between these two versions of the `Comment` class in our blog application.

> **NOTE**
>
> Why don't we use the Microsoft Entity Framework `CommentEntity` class everywhere? In other words, why do we perform the additional work of creating a separate `Comment` class? We want to use a POCO (Plain Old CLR Object) when writing our application logic. Otherwise, we cannot build our application through incremental design.

Displaying Comments and Comment Counts

We need to update our views to take advantage of comments. We don't want to display the list of comments associated with a blog entry on every page. We only want to display the list of comments on the page that displays a single blog entry.

I created a new view named `Details` that displays a single blog entry (see Figure 21.7). The `Details` view is contained in Listing 21.9.

LISTING 21.9   Views\Archive\Details.aspx (C#)

```
<%@ Page Title="" Language="C#" MasterPageFile="~/Views/Shared/Site.Master"
➥Inherits="System.Web.Mvc.ViewPage<UnleashedBlog.Models.BlogEntry>" %>


<asp:Content ID="Content1" ContentPlaceHolderID="TitleContent" runat="server">
    Details
</asp:Content>


<asp:Content ID="Content2" ContentPlaceHolderID="MainContent" runat="server">

    <% Html.RenderPartial("BlogEntry"); %>

    <div class="commentsContainer">
    <% foreach (var comment in Model.Comments)
        { %>
        <div class="commentContainer">
        <h3><%= Html.Encode( comment.Title ) %></h3>
        <div class="commentHeader">
        Posted by <%= Html.NameLink(comment) %>
        on <%= comment.DatePublished.ToString("D") %>
        </div>
```

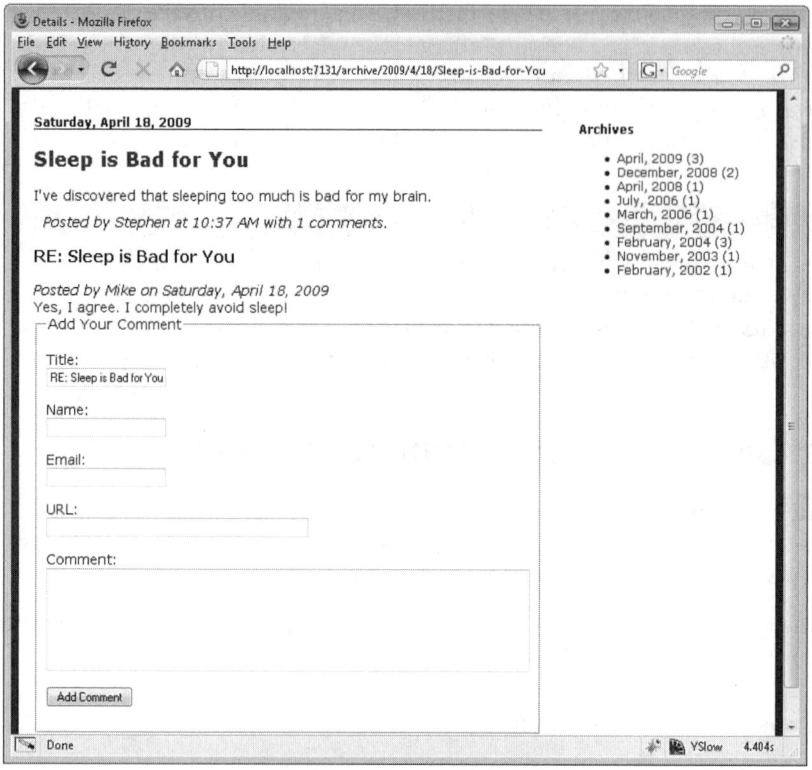

FIGURE 21.7   The page rendered by the Details view

```
        <div class="commentText">
            <%= Html.Encode( comment.Text ) %>
        </div>
        </div>
    <% } %>
    </div>


    <fieldset>
    <legend>Add Your Comment</legend>
    <%= Html.ValidationSummary("Create was unsuccessful. Please correct the errors
➥and try again.") %>

    <% using (Html.BeginForm("Create", "Comment"))
        { %>

        <%= Html.Hidden("Comment.BlogEntryId", Model.Id) %>
        <p>
            <label for="Comment.Title">Title:</label>
            <br /><%= Html.TextBox("Comment.Title", "RE: " + Model.Title)%>
```

```
            </p>
            <p>
                <label for="Comment.Name">Name:</label>
                <br /><%= Html.TextBox("Comment.Name")%>
            </p>
            <p>
                <label for="Comment.Email">Email:</label>
                <br /><%= Html.TextBox("Comment.Email")%>
            </p>
            <p>
                <label for="Url">URL:</label>
                <br /><%= Html.TextBox("Comment.Url", string.Empty, new { size = 50 })%>
                <%= Html.ValidationMessage("Comment.Url", "*")%>
            </p>
            <p>
                <label for="Comment.Text">Comment:</label>
                <br /><%= Html.TextArea("Comment.Text", new { cols = 60, rows = 5 })%>
            </p>
            <p>
                <input type="submit" value="Add Comment" />
            </p>
        <% } %>
        </fieldset>


</asp:Content>
```

LISTING 21.9   Views\Archive\Details.aspx (VB)

```
<%@ Page Title="" Language="vb" MasterPageFile="~/Views/Shared/Site.Master"
➥Inherits="System.Web.Mvc.ViewPage(Of UnleashedBlog.BlogEntry)" %>


<asp:Content ID="Content1" ContentPlaceHolderID="TitleContent" runat="server">
    Details
</asp:Content>


<asp:Content ID="Content2" ContentPlaceHolderID="MainContent" runat="server">

<%  Html.RenderPartial("BlogEntry")%>

    <div class="commentsContainer">
<%  For Each comment In Model.Comments%>
        <div class="commentContainer">
        <h3><%=Html.Encode(comment.Title)%></h3>
        <div class="commentHeader">
```

```
        Posted by <%=Html.NameLink(comment)%>
        on <%=comment.DatePublished.ToString("D")%>
        </div>
        <div class="commentText">
            <%=Html.Encode(comment.Text)%>
        </div>
        </div>
<%  Next%>
    </div>

    <fieldset>
    <legend>Add Your Comment</legend>
    <%=Html.ValidationSummary("Create was unsuccessful. Please correct the errors
➥and try again.")%>

<%  Using Html.BeginForm("Create", "Comment")%>

        <%=Html.Hidden("Comment.BlogEntryId", Model.Id)%>
        <p>
            <label for="Comment.Title">Title:</label>
            <br /><%=Html.TextBox("Comment.Title", "RE: " & Model.Title)%>
        </p>
        <p>
            <label for="Comment.Name">Name:</label>
            <br /><%=Html.TextBox("Comment.Name")%>
        </p>
        <p>
            <label for="Comment.Email">Email:</label>
            <br /><%=Html.TextBox("Comment.Email")%>
        </p>
        <p>
            <label for="Url">URL:</label>
            <br /><%=Html.TextBox("Comment.Url", String.Empty, New With {Key .size
➥= 50})%>
            <%=Html.ValidationMessage("Comment.Url", "*")%>
        </p>
        <p>
            <label for="Comment.Text">Comment:</label>
            <br /><%=Html.TextArea("Comment.Text", New With {Key .cols = 60, Key
➥.rows = 5})%>
        </p>
        <p>
            <input type="submit" value="Add Comment" />
        </p>
```

```
<% End Using%>
    </fieldset>

</asp:Content>
```

The Details view renders a single blog entry by rendering the BlogEntry partial. Next, the view renders all the comments associated with the view. Finally, the view displays a form for entering a new comment.

Adding a new Details view to our project required a modification to our route tests and route table. Our route tests class includes the new test in Listing 21.10 and the Global.asax file includes the new route in Listing 21.11.

LISTING 21.10   UnleashedBlog.Tests\Routes\RouteTests.cs (C#)

```
[TestMethod]
public void ArchiveYearMonthDayName()
{
    // Arrange
    var routes = new RouteCollection();
    MvcApplication.RegisterRoutes(routes);

    // Act
    var context = new FakeHttpContext("~/Archive/2008/12/25/Test");
    var routeData = routes.GetRouteData(context);

    // Assert
    var matchedRoute = (NamedRoute)routeData.Route;
    Assert.AreEqual("Details", matchedRoute.Name);
    Assert.AreEqual("2008", routeData.Values["year"]);
    Assert.AreEqual("12", routeData.Values["month"]);
    Assert.AreEqual("25", routeData.Values["day"]);
    Assert.AreEqual("Test", routeData.Values["name"]);
}
```

LISTING 21.10   UnleashedBlog.Tests\Routes\RouteTests.vb (VB)

```
<TestMethod()> _
Public Sub ArchiveYearMonthDayName()
    ' Arrange
    Dim routes = New RouteCollection()
    MvcApplication.RegisterRoutes(routes)
```

```vb
    ' Act
    Dim context = New FakeHttpContext("~/Archive/2008/12/25/Test")
    Dim routeData = routes.GetRouteData(context)

    ' Assert
    Dim matchedRoute = CType(routeData.Route, NamedRoute)
    Assert.AreEqual("Details", matchedRoute.Name)
    Assert.AreEqual("2008", routeData.Values("year"))
    Assert.AreEqual("12", routeData.Values("month"))
    Assert.AreEqual("25", routeData.Values("day"))
    Assert.AreEqual("Test", routeData.Values("name"))
End Sub
```

LISTING 21.11   UnleashedBlog\Global.asax.cs (C#)

```csharp
routes.MapRoute(
    "Details",
    "archive/{year}/{month}/{day}/{name}",
    new { controller = "Archive", action = "Details" }
);
```

LISTING 21.11   UnleashedBlog\Global.asax.vb (VB)

```vb
routes.MapRoute("Details", "archive/{year}/{month}/{day}/{name}", _
  New With {Key .controller = "Archive", Key .action = "Details"})
```

The test in Listing 21.11 verifies that requesting the URL ~/Archive/2008/12/25/Test matches a route named Details. Furthermore, the test verifies that the year, month, day, and name route parameters get correctly populated from the URL.

The route defined in Listing 21.11 satisfies the test. Adding this route causes all our tests to go green (see Figure 21.8).

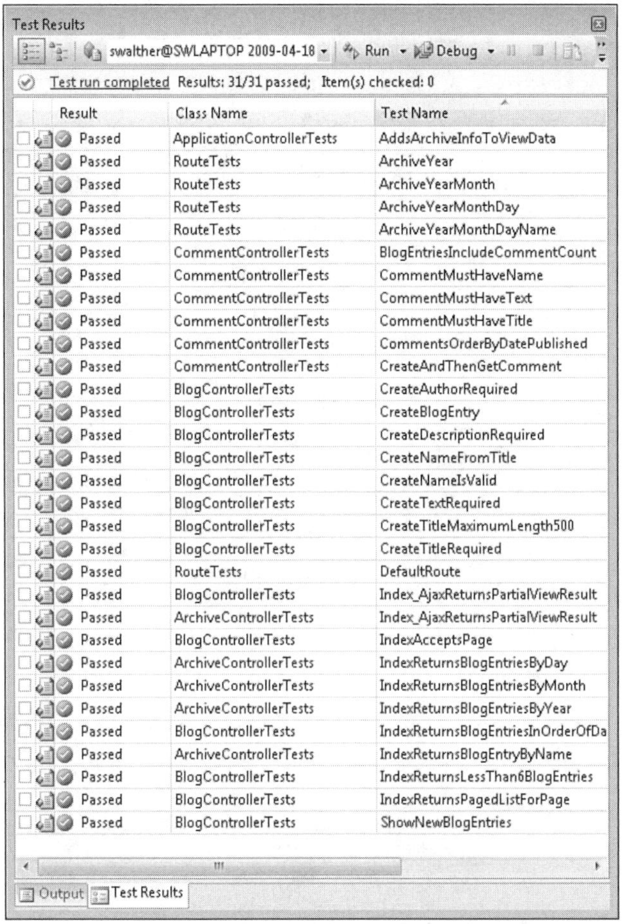

Result	Class Name	Test Name
Passed	ApplicationControllerTests	AddsArchiveInfoToViewData
Passed	RouteTests	ArchiveYear
Passed	RouteTests	ArchiveYearMonth
Passed	RouteTests	ArchiveYearMonthDay
Passed	RouteTests	ArchiveYearMonthDayName
Passed	CommentControllerTests	BlogEntriesIncludeCommentCount
Passed	CommentControllerTests	CommentMustHaveName
Passed	CommentControllerTests	CommentMustHaveText
Passed	CommentControllerTests	CommentMustHaveTitle
Passed	CommentControllerTests	CommentsOrderByDatePublished
Passed	CommentControllerTests	CreateAndThenGetComment
Passed	BlogControllerTests	CreateAuthorRequired
Passed	BlogControllerTests	CreateBlogEntry
Passed	BlogControllerTests	CreateDescriptionRequired
Passed	BlogControllerTests	CreateNameFromTitle
Passed	BlogControllerTests	CreateNameIsValid
Passed	BlogControllerTests	CreateTextRequired
Passed	BlogControllerTests	CreateTitleMaximumLength500
Passed	BlogControllerTests	CreateTitleRequired
Passed	RouteTests	DefaultRoute
Passed	BlogControllerTests	Index_AjaxReturnsPartialViewResult
Passed	ArchiveControllerTests	Index_AjaxReturnsPartialViewResult
Passed	BlogControllerTests	IndexAcceptsPage
Passed	ArchiveControllerTests	IndexReturnsBlogEntriesByDay
Passed	ArchiveControllerTests	IndexReturnsBlogEntriesByMonth
Passed	ArchiveControllerTests	IndexReturnsBlogEntriesByYear
Passed	BlogControllerTests	IndexReturnsBlogEntriesInOrderOfDa
Passed	ArchiveControllerTests	IndexReturnsBlogEntryByName
Passed	BlogControllerTests	IndexReturnsLessThan6BlogEntries
Passed	BlogControllerTests	IndexReturnsPagedListForPage
Passed	BlogControllerTests	ShowNewBlogEntries

FIGURE 21.8 All 31 of our tests pass.

Summary

This is the final chapter devoted to the Unleashed Blog and the final chapter of this book. The goal of this final part of this book was to demonstrate the process of building a real-world application using ASP.NET MVC and test-driven development. We implemented each feature of the blog application by starting with a user story and then capturing the intent of the user story with one or more tests. We did not write any application code until after we had a failing test.

Our blog application is not a full blog application. Our blog is missing major features such as support for tags and RSS. In other words, we still have some work to do!

However, you are in an excellent position to extend the blog application. Because we used test-driven development, our blog application code is covered by a set of 31 tests. Because the code is supported by the safety net of tests, you can fearlessly refactor and extend the blog application without worrying about breaking existing functionality.

PART III

Appendixes

IN THIS PART

APPENDIX A

C# and VB.NET Language Features

ASP.NET MVC takes advantage of many advanced features of the C# and VB.NET languages. Some of these features were not introduced into these languages until C# 3.0 and Visual Basic 9.0. This appendix provides you with a brief overview of these new language features.

Type Inference

Both C# and Visual Basic can infer the type of a variable when you create a local variable. For example, the following line of code creates a new string variable named `message` with the value "Hello World!":

(C#)

```
var message = "Hello World!";
```

(VB)

```
Dim message = "Hello World!"
```

Notice that you do not need to specify the type of the message variable. The compiler figures out the type from "Hello World!" automatically.

There are no performance drawbacks from using type inference. The type is inferred at compile time and not runtime. In particular, using type inference does not result in late binding.

Type inference is a good way to remove some of the redundancy in the C# language. Consider the following statement:

(C#)

```
ArrayList countries = new ArrayList();
```

(VB)

```
Dim countries As New ArrayList()
```

In the case of C#, the type of the *countries* variable is specified twice: on both sides of the = sign. Using type inference removes this redundancy with no drawbacks in performance:

(C#)

```
var countries = new ArrayList();
```

Object Initializers

Object initializers provide you with shorthand syntax for creating a new object and setting one or more properties on the object. Imagine, for example, that you want to create an instance of a Customer class and set the FirstName and LastName properties. Normally, you would have to write the following code:

(C#)

```
Customer customer1 = new Customer();
customer1.FirstName = "Scott";
customer1.LastName = "Guthrie";
```

(VB)

```
Dim customer1 As New Customer()
customer1.FirstName = "Scott"
customer1.LastName = "Guthrie"
```

By taking advantage of the new object initialize syntax, you can reduce the three lines of code to a single line:

(C#)

```
Customer customer1 = new Customer() { FirstName="Scott", LastName="Guthrie"};
```

(VB)

```
Dim customer1 As New Customer() With {.FirstName = "Scott", .LastName = "Guthrie"}
```

Anonymous Types

Anonymous types give you a compact way to define a new class and create a new instance of the new class at the same time. For example, the following line of code both creates a new type of class and instantiates an instance of the new class at the same time:

(C#)

```
var product1 = new { Name = "Netbook", Price = 344.99m };
```

(VB)

```
Dim product1 = New With {.Name = "Netbook", .Price = 344.99}
```

This single line of code is equivalent to first creating a new class:

(C#)

```
public class Product
{
    public string Name { get; set; }
    public decimal Price { get; set; }
```

(VB)

```
Public Class Product

    Private _name As String
    Private _price As Decimal

    Public Property Name() As String
        Get
            Return _name
        End Get
        Set(ByVal value As String)
            _name = value
        End Set
    End Property

    Public Property Price() As Decimal
        Get
            Return _price
        End Get
        Set(ByVal value As Decimal)
            _price = value
        End Set
    End Property
End Class
```

And then creating an instance of the new class:

(C#)

```
var product1 = new Product {Name="Netbook", Price=344.99m};
```

(VB)

```
Dim product1 = New Product With {.Name = "Netbook", .Price = 344.99}
```

Obviously, using anonymous types takes far, far less typing to accomplish the same work.

Two anonymous types that have the same properties, in the same order, are the same type. For example, product1 and product2 are the same type:

(C#)

```
var product1 = new { Name = "Netbook", Price = 344.99m };
var product2 = new { Name = "Comb", Price = 4.88m };
Debug.Write(product1.GetType() == product2.GetType());
```

(VB)

```
Dim product1 = New With {.Name = "Netbook", .Price = 344.99D}
Dim product2 = New With {.Name = "Comb", .Price = 4.88D}
Debug.Write(product1.GetType() Is product2.GetType())
```

However, sandwich1, sandwich2, and sandwich3 are all different types; the order of the properties is different in the case of sandwich1 and sandwich2:

(C#)

```
var sandwich1 = new { Name = "Dagwood", Bread = "Bun" };
var sandwich2 = new { Bread = "Bun", Name = "Dagwood" };
var sandwich3 = new { Name = "Dagwood", Bread = "Bun", HasLettuce=true };
```

(VB)

```
Dim sandwich1 = New With {.Name = "Dagwood", .Bread = "Bun"}
Dim sandwich2 = New With {.Bread = "Bun", .Name = "Dagwood"}
Dim sandwich3 = New With {.Name = "Dagwood", .Bread = "Bun", .HasLettuce = True}
```

Anonymous types are used extensively in the ASP.NET MVC framework. For example, you can specify a set of HTML attributes when using an HTML helper by using an anonymous type:

(C#)

```
<%= Html.TextArea("Comments", new {cols="50", rows="10"}) %>
```

(VB)

```
<%=Html.TextArea("Comments", New With {.cols = "50", .rows = "10"})%>
```

When this `Html.TextArea()` helper renders an HTML `textarea`, the `textarea` is rendered with `cols="50"` and `rows="10"` attributes.

> **NOTE**
>
> When creating anonymous types with Visual Basic, you can use the Key keyword to mark certain properties as key properties. A key property is used to determine when two instances of the same anonymous type are equal. If two instances of the same anonymous type have the same values for their key properties, then the two instances are equal.

Nullable Types

Reference types, such as a string, can accept the value `null` (`Nothing`). Value types, such as an `integer` or `DateTime`, normally cannot accept the value `null` (`Nothing`).

By taking advantage of nullable types, you can assign the value `null` to a value type like an `integer` or `DateTime`. For example, the following line of code creates a nullable `DateTime` named `dateReleased`:

(C#)

```
DateTime? dateReleased = null;
```

(VB)

```
Dim dateReleased As DateTime? = Nothing
```

The question mark indicates that the `dateReleased` variable represents a nullable type instead of a value type.

You can use nullable types with method parameters. For example, you can use a nullable type with an ASP.NET MVC action parameter like this:

(C#)

```
public ActionResult Index(int? id)
{
    Product product = null;
    if (id.HasValue)
```

```
        product = _repository.GetProduct(id.Value);
    return View(product);
}
```

(VB)

```
Function Index(ByVal id As Integer?) As ActionResult
    Dim product As Product = Nothing

    If id.HasValue Then
        product = _repository.GetProduct(id.Value)
    End If

    Return View(product)
Function
```

You can invoke this action using either of the following URLs:

/Home/Index

/Home/Index/22

Because the Index action accepts a nullable parameter, invoking the action without supplying a parameter does not result in an error.

Notice how the action uses the HasValue and Value properties. You use HasValue to determine if a nullable type has the value null (Nothing). You use the Value property to get the non-nullable type from the nullable type.

Extension Methods

Extension methods enable you to add new functionality to an existing class without deriving a new class. In other words, extension methods enable you to extend an existing class with new methods.

In the ASP.NET MVC framework, all the helper methods are implemented as extension methods. For example, the Html.TextBox() helper method is an extension method that extends the HtmlHelper class.

You create extension methods in different ways when using C# versus Visual Basic. When working with C#, you create an extension method by creating a static class with a static method.

(C#)

```csharp
using System;
using System.Web.Mvc;

namespace MvcApplication1.Helpers
{
    public static class ButtonHelpers
    {
        public static string Button(this HtmlHelper helper, string text)
        {
            return String.Format("<button>{0}</button>", text);
        }

    }
}
```

Notice that the first parameter is qualified by the this keyword. The this keyword indicates that the Button() extension method extends the HtmlHelper class. The Button() method becomes a method of the HtmlHelper class.

You create an extension method with Visual Basic by creating a module:

(VB)

```vb
Namespace Helpers
    Public Module ButtonHelpers

        <System.Runtime.CompilerServices.Extension()> _

        Public Function Button(ByVal helper As HtmlHelper, ByVal text As String) As
➥String
            Return String.Format("<button>{0}</button>", text)
        End Function

    End Module
End Namespace
```

Notice that the Button() method is decorated with the System.Runtime.CompilerServices.Extension attribute.

To use an extension method, you must remember to import the namespace of the extension method. For example, if you want to use the Html.Button() helper method in a view, then you must import the Helpers namespace in the view using the Import directive like this:

```
<%@ Import Namespace="MvcApplication1.Helpers" %>
```

After you import an extension method, the extension method appears in Intellisense just like any other method (see Figure A.1).

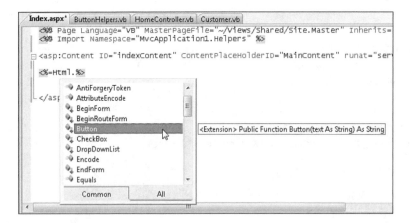

FIGURE A.1   Using the `Button()` extension method

Generics

A *generic* is a class, structure, interface, or method that accepts one or more type parameters. If you have worked with generic collections, you are already familiar with generics. For example, the generic `List` collection, which you can use to represent a list of items of a particular type, is a generic class:

(C#)

```csharp
var shoppingList = new List<string>();
```

(VB)

```vb
Dim shoppingList As New List(Of String)()
```

When you create a generic `List`, you specify the type of item that the list represents. In the preceding code, the `List` represents a list of strings.

Generics is another language feature that is used extensively in the ASP.NET MVC framework. For example, the `ViewPage` class—the base class for views—is a generic class. When you create a view, you supply a generic type parameter for the `ViewPage` class in the `<%@ Page %>` directive like this:

(C#)

```
<%@ Page Language="C#" Inherits="System.Web.Mvc.ViewPage<IEnumerable<TestCS.
➥Models.Product>>" %>
```

(VB)

```
<%@ Page Language="VB" Inherits="System.Web.Mvc.ViewPage(Of IEnumerable (Of
➥MvcApplication1.Product))" %>
```

In this case, we actually have two generic type parameters. Both the `ViewPage` class and the `IEnumerable` interface accept a generic type parameter.

The generic type parameter is used by the `ViewPage` class to cast the `Model` property to a particular type. In this case, the `Model` property is cast to a collection (`IEnumerable`) of `Product` items.

Lambda Expressions

A *lambda expression* provides you with a compact way to express a function. You can use a lambda expression to represent a function like this:

(C#)

```
x => x * 2
```

(VB)

```
Function(x) x * 2
```

This expression represents a function that accepts a parameter named x and times x by two. This lambda expression is equivalent to the following function:

(C#)

```
int TimesTwo(int x)
{
    return x * 2;
}
```

(VB)

```
Function TimesTwo(ByVal x As Integer) As Integer
   Return x * 2
End Function
```

> **NOTE**
>
> The C# => operator is pronounced as the "goes to" operator.

Lambda expressions are used most often with LINQ. See the next section to learn about LINQ.

LINQ

LINQ (Language INtegrated Query) enables you to perform operations on a set of objects. The objects could be a set of database records. By taking advantage of LINQ, you can write all your database logic within the C# or Visual Basic language, and you never need to write any SQL code again.

The System.Linq namespace contains two classes named `Enumerable` and `Queryable`. The `Enumerable` class contains a set of extension methods for the `IEnumerable<T>` interface. For example, the `Enumerable` class includes the following extension methods (this is not even close to being a complete list):

- ▶ Average()
- ▶ Count()
- ▶ First()
- ▶ Last()
- ▶ Max()
- ▶ Min()
- ▶ OrderBy()
- ▶ Select()
- ▶ Sum()
- ▶ Where()

Because these are extension methods on the `IEnumerable<T>` interface, you can use these methods on any class that implements the `IEnumerable<T>` interface including the generic List class:

(C#)

```
var products = new List<Product>();
products.Add(new Product { Name = "Laptop", Price=344.44m });
products.Add(new Product { Name = "Comb", Price = 2.99m });
products.Add(new Product { Name = "Chair", Price = 88.00m });

var results = products
    .Where(p => p.Price > 50.00m)
    .OrderBy(p => p.Name)
    .Select(p => p);
```

(VB)

```
Dim products As New List(Of Product)()
products.Add(New Product With {.Name = "Laptop", .Price = 344.44D})
products.Add(New Product With {.Name = "Comb", .Price = 2.99D})
```

```
products.Add(New Product With {.Name = "Chair", .Price = 88D})

Dim results = products _
    .Where(Function(p) p.Price > 50D) _
    .OrderBy(Function(p) p.Name) _
    .Select(Function(p) p)
```

This code creates a generic `List` class that represents a set of products. The `Enumerable` extension methods are used to retrieve a set of products where each product has a price greater than $50.00 and the products are ordered by name. Therefore, you get the following products in the following order: `Chair`, `Laptop`.

Notice that the LINQ methods use lambda expressions. For example, the `Where()` method accepts a lambda expression (a function) that returns a Boolean value. The lambda expression is used to filter the set of products.

The `Queryable` class contains a similar set of extension methods; however, these methods extend any class that implements the `IQueryable<T>` interface.

Both the Microsoft Entity Framework and Microsoft LINQ to SQL represent database tables with classes that implement the `IQueryable<T>` interface. That means that you can use these extension methods with either technology.

For example, here is how you would retrieve a set of database records by using the `Queryable` extension methods with the Microsoft Entity Framework:

(C#)

```
var entities = new MoviesDBEntities();
var results = entities.MovieSet
    .Where(m => m.Title.StartsWith("T"))
    .OrderBy(m => m.DateReleased)
    .Select(m => m);
```

(VB)

```
Dim entities = New MoviesDBEntities()
Dim results = entities.MovieSet _
    .Where(Function(m) m.Title.StartsWith("T")) _
    .OrderBy(Function(m) m.DateReleased) _
    .Select(Function(m) m)
```

The query retrieves all the movies that have a title that starts with the letter *T* and orders the results by the date the movie was released.

Instead of using the `Enumerable` or `Queryable` extension methods directly, you can use the new query syntax language features introduced into the C# and Visual Basic languages. In other words, there are two ways to execute a LINQ query: method syntax and query syntax.

The following code uses query syntax to retrieve the same set of movies that we retrieved earlier using method syntax:

(C#)

```
var entities = new MoviesDBEntities();
var results = from m in entities.MovieSet
              where m.Title.StartsWith("T")
              orderby m.DateReleased
              select m;
```

(VB)

```
Dim entities = New MoviesDBEntities()
Dim results = From m In entities.MovieSet _
    Where m.Title.StartsWith("T") _
    Order By m.DateReleased _
    Select m
```

You might find query syntax more readable than method syntax. There is no difference in performance. Your choice between method and query syntax is purely a preference issue.

When you use LINQ against a database, the query is translated into a SQL query and executed. When you retrieve a set of database records, the SQL query is not executed until you actually start iterating through the results (for example, by using a for each loop).

This is an important point: LINQ does not load an entire database table into memory and then perform operations on the loaded data. Instead, LINQ waits until the last possible moment to execute a query. Just before you start to iterate through the results of a query, LINQ analyzes your query and converts it into the most efficient SQL query possible and then executes the SQL query against the database.

APPENDIX B

Using a Unit Testing Framework

Throughout this book, we created tests for our ASP.NET MVC code. This appendix provides you with a brief introduction to unit testing frameworks.

Following are several popular unit testing frameworks for the .NET framework:

▶ **Visual Studio Unit Test**—Included with Visual Studio Professional and above

▶ **NUnit**—Open source testing framework available from NUnit.org

▶ **xUnit.net**—Open source testing framework available from xunit.CodePlex.com

This book uses the Visual Studio Unit Test framework because it is included with Visual Studio. In other words, using Visual Studio Unit Test does not require any special setup, and my goal is to keep things as simple as possible for you, the reader.

However, there are some significant drawbacks to using Visual Studio Unit Test. First, Visual Studio Unit Test is not included with the free version of Visual Studio: Visual Web Developer. To use Visual Studio Unit Test, you must purchase Visual Studio Professional or above.

Second, Visual Studio Test was not designed to make creating unit tests easy. Visual Studio Unit Test wants you to spin up a web server when you run tests against a web application. So, when using Visual Studio Unit Test, you must be careful to avoid doing what it tempts you into doing.

NOTE

I'm happy to report that Visual Studio 2010 includes an improved unit testing framework.

This chapter demonstrates how you can create and run unit tests by using two unit testing frameworks: the Visual Studio Unit Test framework and the NUnit framework.

Using Visual Studio Unit Test

When you create a new ASP.NET MVC application, you are prompted to create a new test project at the same time (see Figure B.1). The default unit testing framework is Visual Studio Unit Test.

Create Unit Test Project

Would you like to create a unit test project for this application?

◉ _Y_es, create a unit test project

Test _p_roject name:

    MvcApplication1.Tests

Test _f_ramework:

    Visual Studio Unit Test   ▾   Additional Info

○ _N_o, do not create a unit test project

    OK   Cancel

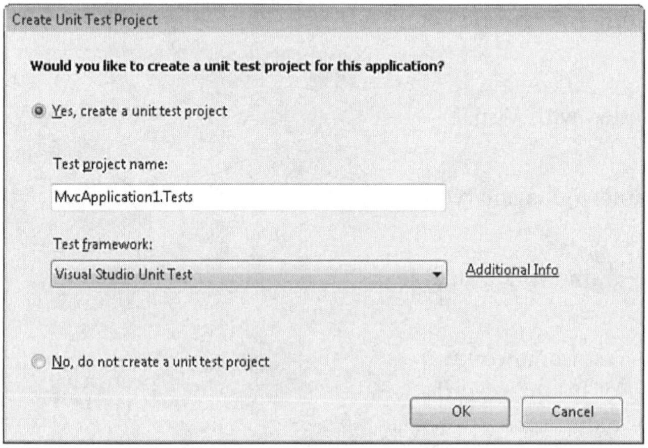

FIGURE B.1   Create Unit Test Project dialog

If you select the option Yes, Create a Unit Test Project (and you should always select this option), then Visual Studio adds two projects to your solution: the ASP.NET MVC Web Application project and the Unit Test project.

The Unit Test project contains a Controllers folder that contains sample unit tests for the Account controller and Home controller. If you want to create tests for additional controllers, you can add your unit tests to the Controllers folder.

There are two ways that you can create a new test. First, you can create a new unit test by following these steps:

1. Right-click the Controllers folder and select the menu option Add, New Test.

2. In the Add New Test dialog select Unit Test (see Figure B.2).

3. Enter a good name for your test. For example, if you create a test for the Product controller, create a test named ProductControllerTests.

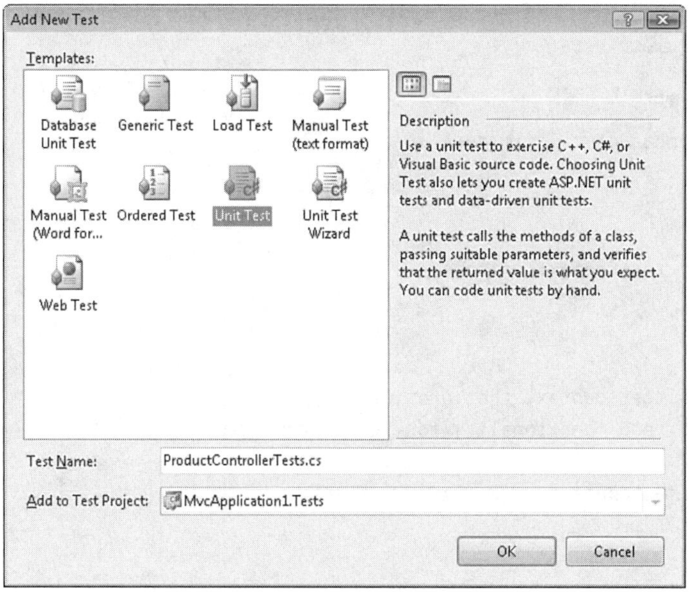

FIGURE B.2   Add New Test

4. Click the OK button to generate the test.

WARNING

Don't select the menu option Add, Unit Test. This option launches the Create Unit Tests dialog that generates tests that spin up a web server.

Completing these steps results in the test class in Listing B.1.

LISTING B.1   Controllers\ProductControllerTests.cs (C#)

```csharp
using System;
using System.Text;
using System.Collections.Generic;
using System.Linq;
using Microsoft.VisualStudio.TestTools.UnitTesting;

namespace MvcApplication1.Tests.Controllers
{
    /// <summary>
    /// Summary description for ProductControllerTests
    /// </summary>
    [TestClass]
    public class ProductControllerTests
```

```csharp
{
    public ProductControllerTests()
    {
        //
        // TODO: Add constructor logic here
        //
    }

    private TestContext testContextInstance;

    /// <summary>

    ///Gets or sets the test context that provides
    ///information about and functionality for the current test run.
    ///</summary>
    public TestContext TestContext
    {
        get
        {
            return testContextInstance;
        }
        set
        {
            testContextInstance = value;
        }
    }

    #region Additional test attributes
    //
    // You can use the following additional attributes as you write your tests:
    //
    // Use ClassInitialize to run code before running the first test in the class
    // [ClassInitialize()]
    // public static void MyClassInitialize(TestContext testContext) { }
    //
    // Use ClassCleanup to run code after all tests in a class have run
    // [ClassCleanup()]
    // public static void MyClassCleanup() { }
    //
    // Use TestInitialize to run code before running each test
    // [TestInitialize()]
    // public void MyTestInitialize() { }
    //
    // Use TestCleanup to run code after each test has run
    // [TestCleanup()]
    // public void MyTestCleanup() { }
```

```
        //
        #endregion

        [TestMethod]
        public void TestMethod1()
        {
            //
            // TODO: Add test logic     here
            //
        }
    }
}
```

LISTING B.1   Controllers\ProductControllerTests.vb (VB)

```
Imports System
Imports System.Text
Imports System.Collections.Generic
Imports Microsoft.VisualStudio.TestTools.UnitTesting

<TestClass()> Public Class ProductControllerTests

    Private testContextInstance As TestContext

    '''<summary>

    '''Gets or sets the test context that provides
    '''information about and functionality for the current test run.
    '''</summary>
    Public Property TestContext() As TestContext
        Get
            Return testContextInstance
        End Get
        Set(ByVal value As TestContext)
            testContextInstance = Value
        End Set
    End Property

#Region "Additional test attributes"
    '
    ' You can use the following additional attributes as you write your tests:
    '
    ' Use ClassInitialize to run code before running the first test in the class
```

```
    ' <ClassInitialize()> Public Shared Sub MyClassInitialize(ByVal testContext As
➥TestContext)
    ' End Sub
    '
    ' Use ClassCleanup to run code after all tests in a class have run
    ' <ClassCleanup()> Public Shared Sub MyClassCleanup()
    ' End Sub
    '
    ' Use TestInitialize to run code before running each test
    ' <TestInitialize()> Public Sub MyTestInitialize()
    ' End Sub
    '
    ' Use TestCleanup to run code after each test has run
    ' <TestCleanup()> Public Sub MyTestCleanup()
    ' End Sub
    '
#End Region

    <TestMethod()> Public Sub TestMethod1()
        ' TODO: Add test logic here
    End Sub

End Class
```

There is a lot of code in Listing B.1 that we don't need. After I create a new test, I always immediately remove all this unnecessary code so that the test class looks like Listing B.2.

LISTING B.2   Controllers\ProductController.cs (Cleaned Up) (C#)

```csharp
using Microsoft.VisualStudio.TestTools.UnitTesting;

namespace MvcApplication1.Tests.Controllers
{
    [TestClass]
    public class ProductControllerTests
    {
        [TestMethod]
        public void TestMethod1()
        {
        }
    }
}
```

LISTING B.2   Controllers\ProductController.cs (Cleaned Up) (VB)

```vb
Imports Microsoft.VisualStudio.TestTools.UnitTesting


<TestClass()> Public Class ProductControllerTests

    <TestMethod()> Public Sub TestMethod1()
    End Sub


End Class
```

The other method to create a test is to simply add a new class to your test project. Follow these steps:

1. Right-click the Controllers folder and select the menu option Add, Class.
2. In the Add New Item dialog, name your new class ProductControllerTests and click the Add button.
3. Modify the class so that the class is public.
4. Add a TestClass attribute to the new class.

When the red bar appears below the TestClass attribute, press the keyboard combination Ctrl+. (Control key and period) and import the Microsoft.VisualStudio.TestTools.UnitTesting framework (see Figure B.3) by pressing the Enter key.

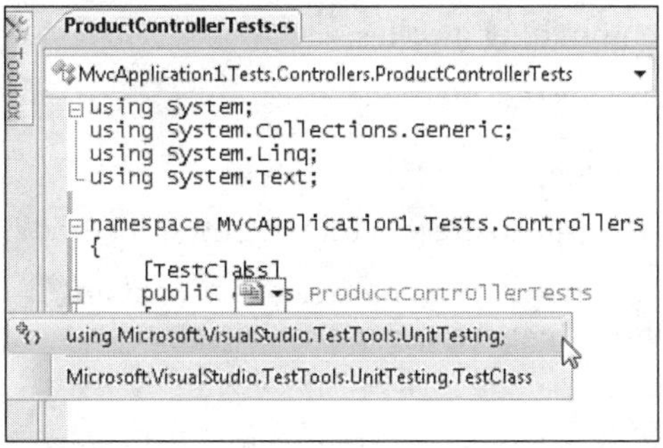

FIGURE B.3   Importing the UnitTesting namespace

After you complete these steps, you end up with the test class in Listing B.3.

LISTING B.3   Controllers\ProductControllerTests.cs (C#)

```csharp
using System;
using System.Collections.Generic;
```

```
using System.Linq;
using System.Text;
using Microsoft.VisualStudio.TestTools.UnitTesting;

namespace MvcApplication1.Tests.Controllers
{
    [TestClass]
    public class ProductControllerTests
    {

    }
}
```

LISTING B.3   Controllers\ProductControllerTests.cs (VB)

```
Imports Microsoft.VisualStudio.TestTools.UnitTesting

<TestClass()> _
Public Class ProductControllerTests

End Class
```

Understanding the Test Attributes

There are three main attributes that you use when building unit tests:

- ▶ TestClass—Marks a class as a class that contains test methods
- ▶ TestMethod—Marks a method as a test method
- ▶ TestInitialize—Marks a method that is run immediately before each test method

The Visual Studio test runner uses the TestClass attribute to find classes that contain unit tests. Next, the test runner executes each public method decorated with the TestMethod attribute.

You might want to perform some type of initialization before running each of your tests. For example, you might want to create a fake repository that contains a set of fake database records. In that case, you can mark a method with the TestInitialize attribute that contains the logic for initializing the fake repository.

For example, the test class in Listing B.4 contains tests for a MathUtility class that adds numbers.

LISTING B.4   Models\MathUtilityTests.cs (C#)

```csharp
using Microsoft.VisualStudio.TestTools.UnitTesting;
using MvcApplication1.Models;

namespace MvcApplication1.Tests.Models
{
    [TestClass]
    public class MathTests
    {
        private MathUtility _math;

        [TestInitialize]
        public void Initialize()
        {
            _math = new MathUtility();
        }

        [TestMethod]
        public void AddPositiveNumbers()
        {
            // Act
            var result = _math.AddNumbers(3, 2);

            // Assert
            Assert.AreEqual(5, result);
        }

        [TestMethod]
        public void AddNegativeNumbers()
        {
            // Act
            var result = _math.AddNumbers(-3, -2);

            // Assert
            Assert.AreEqual(-5, result);
        }

    }
}
```

LISTING B.4   Models\MathUtilityTests.vb (VB)

```vb
Imports Microsoft.VisualStudio.TestTools.UnitTesting


<TestClass()> _
Public Class MathTests

    Private _math As MathUtility

    <TestInitialize()> _
    Public Sub Initialize()
        _math = New MathUtility()
    End Sub

    <TestMethod()> _
    Public Sub AddPositiveNumbers()
        ' Act
        Dim result = _math.AddNumbers(3, 2)

        ' Assert
        Assert.AreEqual(5, result)
    End Sub

    <TestMethod()> _
    Public Sub AddNegativeNumbers()
        ' Act
        Dim result = _math.AddNumbers(-3, -2)

        ' Assert
        Assert.AreEqual(-5, result)
    End Sub

End Class
```

The test class contains two test methods named AddPositiveNumbers() and
AddNegativeNumbers(). The test class also contains an Initialize() method that initial-
izes the MathUtility component being tested. The Initialize() method re-creates the
MathUtility immediately before each test is run so that the results of each test are isolated.

You are not required to use the TestInitialize attribute. You could repeat your test setup
logic in each test; however, that would be ugly and would lead to un-maintainable test code.

Using Assertions

Tests normally end with an assertion. A test asserts that something is true.

NOTE

In this book, we concentrate on state verification tests. State verification tests end with assertions about the state of your application after a certain action. But other types of test, such as behavioral verification tests, don't necessarily make an assertion about state.

The Visual Studio Unit Test framework includes three types of classes that you can use to perform assertions:

- ▶ `Assert`—The main class for performing assertions.
- ▶ `CollectionAssert`—This class contains specialized assertion methods for collections of objects.
- ▶ `StringAssert`—This class contains specialized assertion methods for strings.

In most cases, you use the `Assert` class. For example, you use `Assert.AreEqual()` to assert that an actual value is equal to an expected value. You use `Assert.IsInstanceOfType()` to assert that a particular object is a certain type (an instance of a particular class).

If you are working with a collection, you can use the `CollectionAssert` class. For example, the `CollectionAssert.AreEqual()` method enables you to verify that two collections have the same items in the same order. The `CollectionAssert.AreEquivalent()` verifies that two collections have the same items, but not necessarily in the same order.

Finally, the `StringAssert` class enables you to make assertions about strings. For example, the `StringAssert.Contains()` method enables you to verify that a string has a particular substring. The `StringAssert.Matches()` enables you to verify that a string matches a particular regular expression pattern.

Running the Tests

Visual Studio provides you with four options for running tests:

- ▶ Run Tests in Current Context
- ▶ Run All Tests in Solution
- ▶ Debug Tests in Current Context
- ▶ Debug All Tests in Solution

The context is determined by the location of your cursor. For example, if you have clicked a test named VerifyUnitsInStock() and you select the option to run tests in the current context, then only the VerifyUnitsInStock() test runs. On the other hand, if you select an area of the test class outside any test method, then every test method in the test class runs.

Running tests in debug mode is useful when you need to set breakpoints in your test methods. Sometimes, just like any other application code, your test code fails to work for a mysterious reason. You can set breakpoints and run your tests in debug mode to try to figure out what is actually happening.

You can run your tests from the Test Tools toolbar (see Figure B.4). This toolbar should appear automatically when you have any file in your test project selected. If it does not appear, you can open this toolbar by selecting the menu option View, Toolbars, Test Tools.

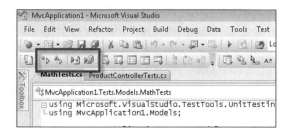

FIGURE B.4   The Test toolbar

A better option for running your unit tests is to use the keyboard. You can use the following keyboard combinations to run your unit tests:

- **Ctrl+R, T**—Run all tests in context
- **Ctrl+R, C**—Run all tests in class
- **Ctrl+R, N**—Run all tests in namespace
- **Ctrl+R, A**—Run all tests in solution
- **Ctrl+R, Ctrl+T**—Debug tests in context
- **Ctrl+R, Ctrl+C**—Debug tests in class
- **Ctrl+R, Ctrl+N**—Debug tests in namespace
- **Ctrl+R, Ctrl+A**—Debug tests in solution

The nice thing about using the keyboard to run your unit tests is that you do not need to be in your unit test project to use these keyboard combinations. You can run your tests using these keyboard combinations while you have a file from your ASP.NET MVC project open in the code editor.

When you run your tests, your tests appear in the Test Results window (see Figure B.5). You can double-click a test to view details on a particular test result. For example, if you run the test in debug mode, you can view a stack trace for a failing test.

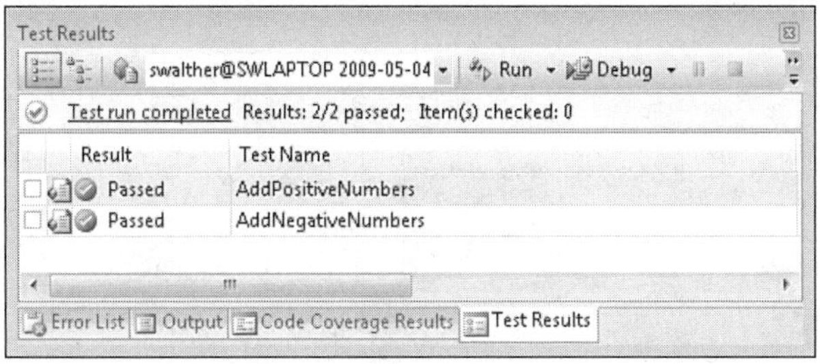

FIGURE B.5   Viewing test results

Limiting Visual Studio Test Results

By default, Visual Studio records and saves the results of up to 25 test runs. It saves the test results, and a copy of the assemblies being tested, in a folder named TestResults. This folder can get large (see Figure B.6).

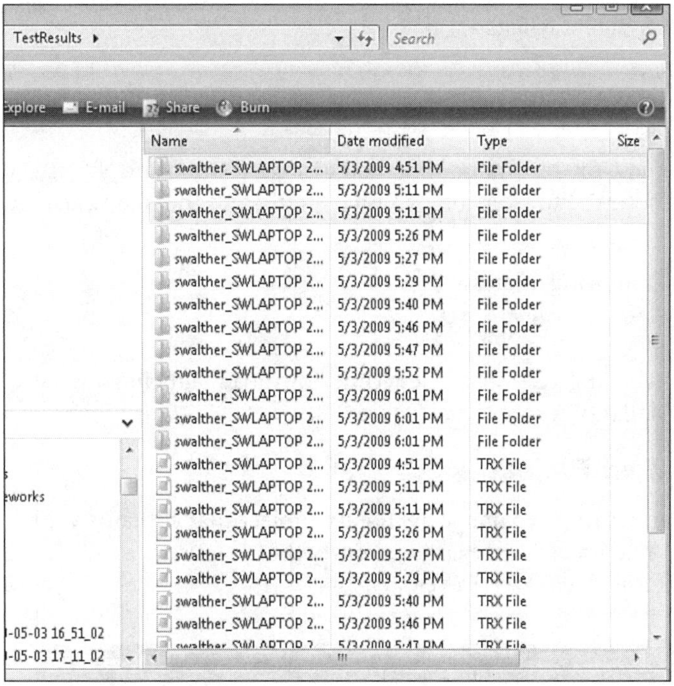

FIGURE B.6   Lots of test runs clogging my hard drive

There is a simple way that you can fix this problem. You can limit the number of test runs that Visual Studio records by selecting the menu option Tools, Options, Test Tools, Test Execution (see Figure B.7). Change the Limit Number of Old Test Results setting from 25 to 1. Modifying this setting causes Visual Studio to save only one test result. (Unfortunately, you can't set this property to zero.)

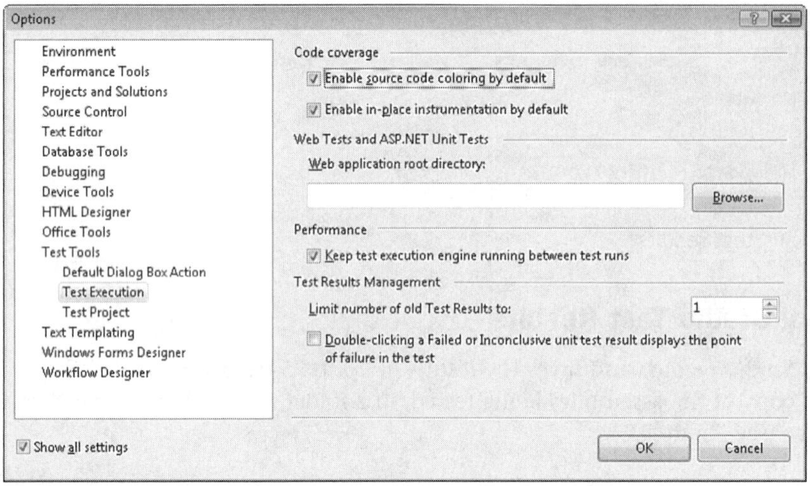

FIGURE B.7   Limiting the number of test results

Using NUnit

Instead of using the Visual Studio Unit Test framework, you can use NUnit. The NUnit framework is compatible with both the full version of Visual Studio and the free Visual Web Developer.

You download NUnit from the following address:

  http://NUnit.org

Installation is straightforward. The MSI version of the NUnit download launches a wizard that walks you through the installation process (see Figure B.8).

Creating an NUnit Unit Test Project

After you install NUnit, you can create a separate class library project that contains your unit tests. You can follow the same procedure regardless of whether you use the full version of Visual Studio or you use Visual Web Developer.

> **WARNING**
>
> You must have Visual Web Developer 2008 Service Pack 1 to create ASP.NET MVC applications and class library projects.

FIGURE B.8   Installing NUnit

Follow these steps:

1. Create a new ASP.NET MVC web application project.

2. Select the menu option File, Add, New Project.

3. Select the Windows project type and select the Class Library template (see Figure B.9).

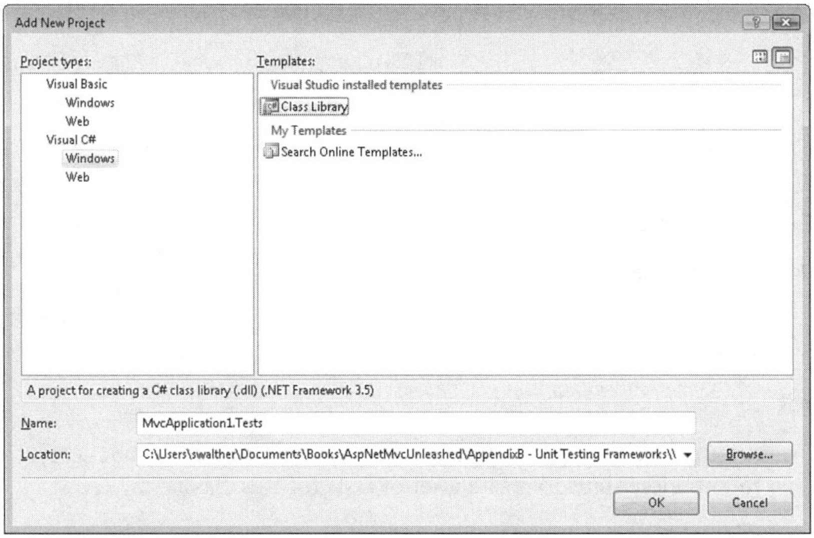

FIGURE B.9   Creating a class library project with Visual Web Developer

4. Provide a name for the class library (for example, MvcApplication1.Tests) and click the OK button.

After you create the test project, you need to add two references to the project. First, you need to add a reference for the ASP.NET MVC application to the test project. Follow these steps:

1. Select the menu option Project, Add Reference.

2. Select the Projects tab.

3. Click the OK button.

Next, you need to add a reference to NUnit. Follow these steps:

1. Select the menu option Project, Add Reference.

2. Select the Browse tab.

3. Navigate to the folder where you installed NUnit and select the NUnit assembly (for example, C:\Program Files\NUnit 2.5\bin\net-2.0\framework\nunit.framework.dll). See Figure B.10.

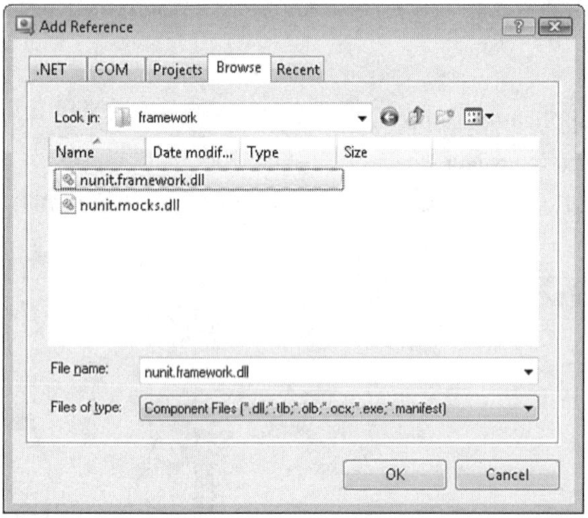

FIGURE B.10   Adding a reference to NUnit

4. Click the OK button.

Creating a Test

Imagine that you want to test a class in your ASP.NET MVC project named MathUtility. In that case, you can follow these steps to create a set of tests for this class:

1. Add a Models folder to your test project.

2. Add a class to your test project by right-clicking the Models folder and selecting Add, Class. Name the new class MathUtilityTests and click the OK button.

3. Enter the code in Listing B.5 into the new class.

4. Build your solution by selecting the menu option Build, Build Solution.

LISTING B.5   Models\MathUtilityTests.cs (C#)

```csharp
using MvcApplication1.Models;
using NUnit.Framework;

namespace MvcApplication1.Tests.Models
{
    [TestFixture]
    public class MathUtilityTests
    {
        private MathUtility _math;

        [SetUp]
        public void Setup()
        {
            _math = new MathUtility();
        }

        [Test]
        public void AddPositiveNumbers()
        {
            // Act
            var result = _math.AddNumbers(3, 2);

            // Assert
            Assert.AreEqual(5, result);
        }

        [Test]
        public void AddNegativeNumbers()
        {
            // Act
            var result = _math.AddNumbers(-3, -2);

            // Assert
            Assert.AreEqual(-5, result);
        }

    }
}
```

LISTING B.5   Models\MathUtilityTests.vb (VB)

```vb
Imports NUnit.Framework


<TestFixture()> _
Public Class MathUtilityTests

    Private _math As MathUtility

    <SetUp()> _
    Public Sub Setup()
        _math = New MathUtility()
    End Sub

    <Test()> _
    Public Sub AddPositiveNumbers()
        ' Act
        Dim result = _math.AddNumbers(3, 2)

        ' Assert
        Assert.AreEqual(5, result)
    End Sub

    <Test()> _
    Public Sub AddNegativeNumbers()
        ' Act
        Dim result = _math.AddNumbers(-3, -2)

        ' Assert
        Assert.AreEqual(-5, result)
    End Sub

End Class
```

The NUnit test class in Listing B.5 is similar to the Visual Studio Unit Test class in Listing B.4. The attributes have slightly different names, but they work the same. When creating an NUnit test, you typically use the following attributes:

▶ TestFixture—Marks a class as a class that contains test methods

▶ Test—Marks a method as a test method

▶ Setup—Marks a method that is run immediately before each test method

Running Tests

NUnit includes a GUI test runner that you can use to run your tests. You open the GUI test runner by selecting Start, All Programs, NUnit, NUnit (see Figure B.11).

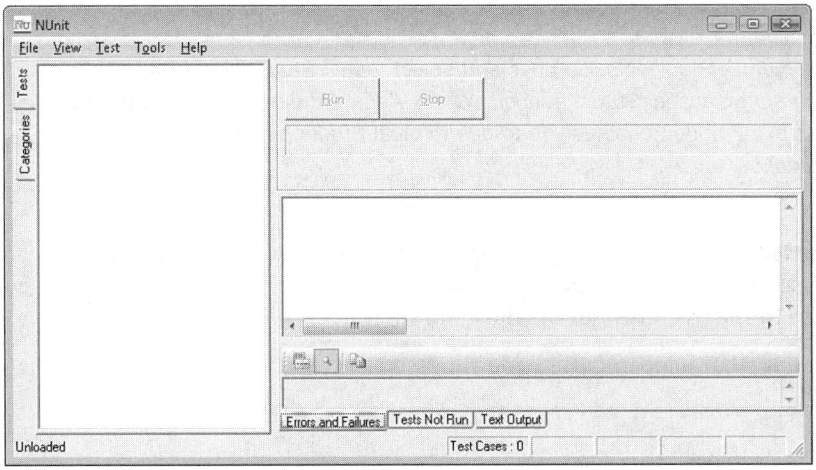

FIGURE B.11   The NUnit GUI test runner

After the program starts, you need to open the assembly (DLL file) generated by your test
project. Select the menu option File, Open Project and browse to the Bin\Debug folder of
your test project. Select the assembly generated by your test project—for example,
MvcApplication1.Tests.dll—and click the Open button (see Figure B.12).

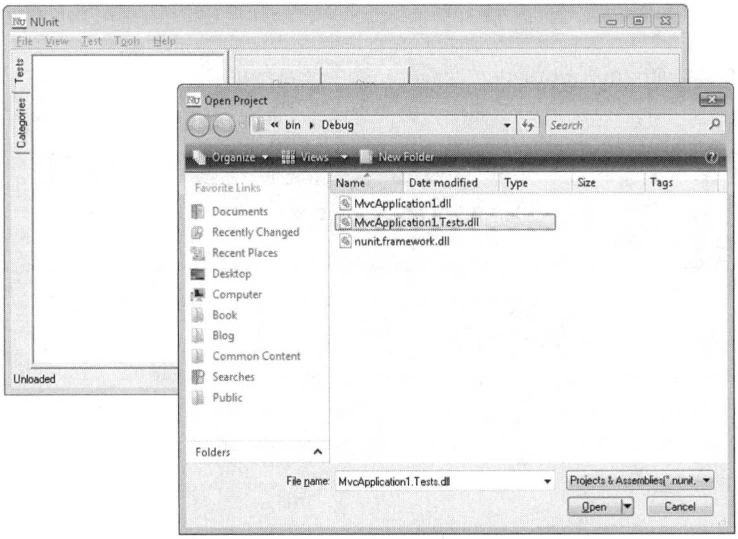

FIGURE B.12   Opening the test project assembly

> **NOTE**
>
> If you select the menu option Tools, Settings and select Visual Studio under IDE
> Support, you can enable Visual Studio support. When Visual Studio support is enabled,
> the Open Project menu option enables you to open Visual Studio projects and solutions
> instead of assemblies.

After you load the test project assembly, you can run your tests by clicking the Run
button. You can use the tree view to specify exactly which tests to run. For example, if you
select the top node in the tree, then all of your tests are run.

Figure B.13 illustrates what happens when you run two tests. The first test failed and the
second test passed.

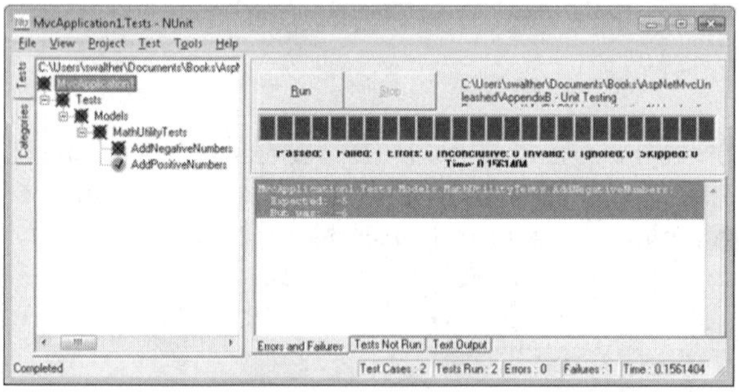

FIGURE B.13   Running tests with the GUI runner

> **NOTE**
>
> NUnit also includes a console test runner, named nunit-console.exe, which you can use
> to run tests from the command line.

Using a Mock Object Framework

The purpose of this appendix is to provide a brief overview of Mock Object Frameworks. Most classes that you want to test depend on multiple other classes. A Mock Object Framework makes it possible to isolate code so that it is testable.

You can use several popular Mock Object Frameworks with ASP.NET MVC including the following:

▶ **Moq**—An open source Mock Object Framework that is relatively new but already popular. The ASP.NET MVC used Moq. You can download Moq from http://code. google.com/p/moq.

▶ **Rhino Mocks**—The established open source Mock Object Framework. You can download Rhino Mocks from http://ayende.com/projects/rhinomocks/down-loads.aspx.

▶ **Typemock Isolator**—A commercial Mock Object Framework. Very powerful. You can learn more about Typemock Isolator from the company website at www. typemock.com.

In this appendix, I focus on describing Moq. The advantage of using Moq is that it is easy to understand. However, after you investigate Moq, I strongly encourage you to explore the other Mock Object Frameworks because each of the Mock Frameworks has its own strengths and weaknesses.

Understanding the Terminology

The terminology that surrounds Mock Object Frameworks can be confusing. Here is a brief glossary of terms:

▶ **Double**—This is the generic term for any object that you use as a replacement for a production object.

▶ **Stub**—A stub is an object that you use in place of a production object to make it easier to test your code. For example, you might create a stub for a repository class to make it easier to test a service class. You can generate stubs with a Mock Object Framework.

▶ **Mock**—A mock is a class that you use to test the interaction between objects in an application. When you create a mock object, you specify expectations about how other objects interact with the mock object. If the other objects do not interact with the mock object in the way that you expect, the test fails.

▶ **Fake**—A simplified version of a real production object. For example, a repository class that interacts with an in-memory database instead of an actual database. A fake is not created with a Mock Object Framework.

You can create two main types of objects with a Mock Object Framework: stubs and mocks. A *stub* is an object that you create to make it easier to perform a test. If one object depends on another object, you can stub the second object to make it possible to test the first object.

A *mock object*, in contrast, tests the interaction of the objects in your application. You create a mock of a production object to verify that the production object is called in the way that you expect. For example, you might want to verify the expectation that your service layer calls a particular method in your repository layer. In that case, you can mock the repository layer to verify this interaction.

In this appendix (and this book), I focus on using Mock Object Frameworks to create stubs and not mocks.

> **NOTE**
>
> This terminology is based on Gerard Meszaros's terminology from his book *xUnit Design Patterns: Refactoring Test Code*. Also see the following two articles by Martin Fowler at http://martinfowler.com/bliki/TestDouble.html and http://martinfowler.com/articles/mocksArentStubs.html.

Installing Moq

You can download Moq from the following location: http://code.google.com/p/moq.

> **NOTE**
>
> The latest version of Moq, at the time that I write this, is version 3.1.

After you download Moq, make sure that you unblock the archive by right-clicking the file, selecting Properties, and clicking the Unblock button (see Figure C.1).

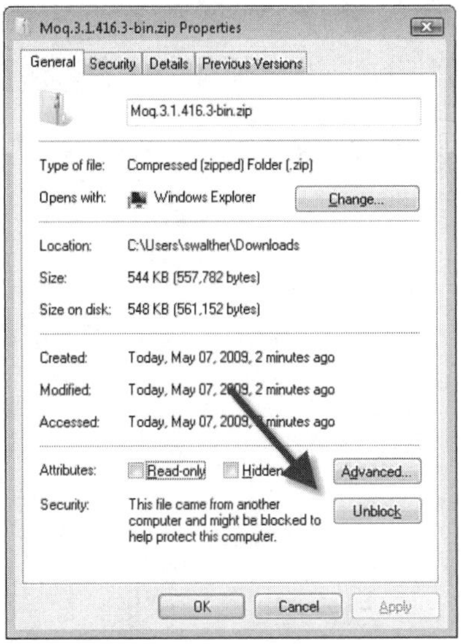

FIGURE C.1   Unblocking Moq

If you don't unblock Moq, Visual Studio generates mysterious security errors when you try to use Moq in your test project.

Before you can use Moq in a test project, you need to add a reference to the Moq assembly. Follow these steps:

1. After selecting your test project in the Solution Explorer window, select the menu option Project, Add Reference.

2. In the Add Reference dialog, click the Browse tab.

3. Browse to the folder where you download Moq and select the Moq.dll assembly (see Figure C.2).

4. Click the OK button.

After you complete these steps, use the Moq framework in your test project.

Using Moq to Create a Class from an Interface

Imagine that you want to create a Movie database application. Imagine, furthermore, that you have followed proper design patterns and divided your application logic into separate classes in which each class has a single responsibility.

You create a controller class, a service class, and a repository class. The controller class contains your controller logic, the service class contains your validation logic, and the repository class contains your data access logic.

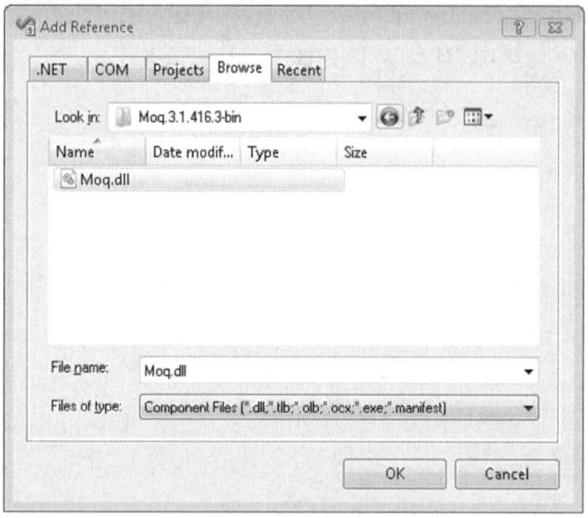

FIGURE C.2   Selecting the Moq assembly

The controller class is contained in Listing C.1.

LISTING C.1   Controllers\MovieController.cs (C#)

```csharp
using System.Linq;
using System.Web.Mvc;
using MvcApplication1.Models;

namespace MvcApplication1.Controllers
{
    public class MovieController : Controller
    {
        private IMovieService _service;


        public MovieController()
        {
            _service = new MovieService(this.ModelState);
        }

        public MovieController(IMovieService service)
        {
            _service = service;
        }

        public ActionResult Index()
        {
            return View(_service.ListMovies());
        }
```

```
    //
    // GET: /Movie/Create

    public ActionResult Create()
    {
        return View();
    }


    //
    // POST: /Movie/Create

    [AcceptVerbs(HttpVerbs.Post)]
    public ActionResult Create([Bind(Exclude = "Id")]Movie movieToCreate)
    {
        if (_service.CreateMovie(movieToCreate))
            return RedirectToAction("Index");
        return View();
    }


  }
}
```

LISTING C.1   Controllers\MovieController.vb (VB)

```
Public Class MovieController
    Inherits Controller

    Private _service As IMovieService

    Sub New()
        _service = New MovieService(Me.ModelState)
    End Sub

    Sub New(ByVal service As IMovieService)
        _service = service
    End Sub

    Function Index() As ActionResult
        Return View(_service.ListMovies())
    End Function

    ' GET: /Movie/Create
```

```
Function Create() As ActionResult
    Return View()
End Function


' POST: /Movie/Create

<AcceptVerbs(HttpVerbs.Post)> _
Function Create(<Bind(Exclude:="Id")> ByVal movieToCreate As Movie) As ActionResult
    If _service.CreateMovie(movieToCreate) Then
        Return RedirectToAction("Index")
    End If
    Return View()
End Function

End Class
```

And, the service class is contained in Listing C.2.

LISTING C.2   Models\MovieService.cs (C#)

```
using System.Collections.Generic;
using System.Web.Mvc;

namespace MvcApplication1.Models
{
    public class MovieService : IMovieService
    {
        private ModelStateDictionary _modelState;
        private IMovieRepository _repository;

        public MovieService(ModelStateDictionary modelState)
            :this(modelState, new MovieRepository()){}

        public MovieService(ModelStateDictionary modelState, IMovieRepository
➥repository)
        {
            _modelState = modelState;
            _repository = repository;
        }

        public IEnumerable<Movie> ListMovies()
        {
            return _repository.ListMovies();
        }
```

```csharp
        public bool CreateMovie(Movie movieToCreate)
        {
            // validate
            if (movieToCreate.Title.Trim().Length == 0)
                _modelState.AddModelError("Title", "Title is required.");
            if (movieToCreate.Title.IndexOf("r") > 0)
                _modelState.AddModelError("Title", "Title cannot contain the letter
➡r.");
            if (movieToCreate.Director.Trim().Length == 0)
                _modelState.AddModelError("Director", "Director is required.");
            if (!_modelState.IsValid)
                return false;

            _repository.CreateMovie(movieToCreate);
            return true;
        }
    }


    public interface IMovieService
    {
        IEnumerable<Movie> ListMovies();
        bool CreateMovie(Movie movieToCreate);
    }
}
```

LISTING C.2   Models\MovieService.vb (VB)

```vbnet
Public Class MovieService
    Implements IMovieService

    Private _modelState As ModelStateDictionary
    Private _repository As IMovieRepository

    Public Sub New(ByVal modelState As ModelStateDictionary)
        Me.New(modelState, New MovieRepository())
    End Sub

    Public Sub New(ByVal modelState As ModelStateDictionary, ByVal repository As
➡IMovieRepository)
        _modelState = modelState
        _repository = repository
    End Sub
```

```vbnet
    Public Function ListMovies() As IEnumerable(Of Movie) Implements
➥IMovieService.ListMovies
        Return _repository.ListMovies()
    End Function

    Public Function CreateMovie(ByVal movieToCreate As Movie) As Boolean Implements
➥IMovieService.CreateMovie
        ' validate
        If movieToCreate.Title.Trim().Length = 0 Then
            _modelState.AddModelError("Title", "Title is required.")
        End If
        If movieToCreate.Title.IndexOf("r") > 0 Then
            _modelState.AddModelError("Title", "Title cannot contain the letter r.")
        End If
        If movieToCreate.Director.Trim().Length = 0 Then
            _modelState.AddModelError("Director", "Director is required.")
        End If
        If (Not _modelState.IsValid) Then
            Return False
        End If

        _repository.CreateMovie(movieToCreate)
        Return True
    End Function
End Class


Public Interface IMovieService
    Function ListMovies() As IEnumerable(Of Movie)
    Function CreateMovie(ByVal movieToCreate As Movie) As Boolean
End Interface
```

And, the repository class is contained in Listing C.3.

LISTING C.3   Models\MovieRepository.cs (C#)

```csharp
using System;
using System.Collections.Generic;
using System.Linq;
using System.Web;

namespace MvcApplication1.Models
{
    public class MovieRepository : IMovieRepository
    {
```

```csharp
        private MoviesDBEntities _entities = new MoviesDBEntities();

        public IEnumerable<Movie> ListMovies()
        {
            return _entities.MovieSet.ToList();
        }

        public void CreateMovie(Movie movieToCreate)
        {
            _entities.AddToMovieSet(movieToCreate);
            _entities.SaveChanges();
        }
    }

    public interface IMovieRepository
    {
        IEnumerable<Movie> ListMovies();
        void CreateMovie(Movie movieToCreate);
    }
}
```

LISTING C.3   Models\MovieRepository.vb (VB)

```vb
Public Class MovieRepository
    Implements IMovieRepository

    Private _entities As New MoviesDBEntities()

    Public Function ListMovies() As IEnumerable(Of Movie) Implements
➥IMovieRepository.ListMovies
        Return _entities.MovieSet.ToList()
    End Function

    Public Sub CreateMovie(ByVal movieToCreate As Movie) Implements
➥IMovieRepository.CreateMovie
        _entities.AddToMovieSet(movieToCreate)
        _entities.SaveChanges()
    End Sub
End Class

Public Interface IMovieRepository
    Function ListMovies() As IEnumerable(Of Movie)
    Sub CreateMovie(ByVal movieToCreate As Movie)
End Interface
```

Now, imagine that you want to test the service class. You want to verify that if you pass a movie with a missing title to the service class `Create()` method, the method returns the value false.

Unfortunately, you can't just create the service class in your test code because it depends on two other classes. The service class depends on an instance of the `ModelStateDictionary` class and an instance of the `MovieRepository` class. You can see these dependencies by looking at the constructor for the service class.

The `ModelStateDictionary` class does not present a problem. The `ModelStateDictionary` is just a specialized collection class. We can simply create a new instance of this class in our test code.

The `MovieRepository` class, on the other hand, *does* present a problem. We don't want to create an instance of the actual `MovieRepository` class because the actual class interacts with a database. We need some way of creating a double for the actual `MovieRepository` class for the purposes of our test code.

NOTE

As an alternative to *stubbing* the `MovieRepository` class, we could *fake* the `MovieRepository` class. We could fake the `MovieRepository` class by implementing the `IMovieRepository` interface with a class that interacts with an in-memory database instead of the actual database. We explore this option in Chapter 5, "Understanding Models."

We can use the Moq framework to quickly and easily create a stub for our `MovieRepository` class. The test in Listing C.4 illustrates how you can generate a stub from the `IMovieRepository` interface.

LISTING C.4   Models\MovieServiceTests.cs (C#)

```
using System;
using System.Web.Mvc;
using Microsoft.VisualStudio.TestTools.UnitTesting;
using Moq;
using MvcApplication1.Models;

namespace MvcApplication1.Tests.Models
{
    [TestClass]
    public class MovieServiceTests
    {
        [TestMethod]
        public void CreateMovieWithEmptyTitleReturnsFalse()
        {
```

```
            // Arrange
            var modelState = new ModelStateDictionary();
            var repositoryStub = new Mock<IMovieRepository>();
            var service = new MovieService(modelState, repositoryStub.Object);
            var movieToCreate = Movie.CreateMovie(0, String.Empty, "Lucas",
➡DateTime.Parse("1/1/1977"));

            // Act
            var result = service.CreateMovie(movieToCreate);

            // Assert
            Assert.IsFalse(result);
        }

    }

}
```

LISTING C.4   Models\MovieServiceTests.vb (VB)

```
Imports Microsoft.VisualStudio.TestTools.UnitTesting
Imports System.Web.Mvc
Imports Moq

<TestClass()> _
    Public Class MovieServiceTests
    <TestMethod()> _
    Public Sub CreateMovieWithEmptyTitleReturnsFalse()
        ' Arrange
        Dim modelState As New ModelStateDictionary()
        Dim repositoryStub As New Mock(Of IMovieRepository)()
        Dim service As New MovieService(modelState, repositoryStub.Object)
        Dim movieToCreate = Movie.CreateMovie(0, String.Empty, "Lucas",
➡DateTime.Parse("1/1/1977"))

        ' Act
        Dim result = service.CreateMovie(movieToCreate)

        ' Assert
        Assert.IsFalse(result)
    End Sub

End Class
```

In Listing C.4, the stub for the MovieRepository class is created with this line of code:

(C#)

```
var repositoryStub = new Mock<IMovieRepository>();
```

(VB)

```
Dim repositoryStub As New Mock(Of IMovieRepository)()
```

Notice that the stub for the repository class is created from an interface: The stub is created from the IMovieRepository interface. (You also could create the stub from an abstract class.)

The repositoryStub variable does not represent the class that implements the IMovieRepository interface. You must use the expression repositoryStub.Object to get to the double for the MovieRepository. The responsitoryStub.Object class is the class that has the ListMovies() and CreateMovie() methods.

Returning Fake Values

In the previous section, you learned how you can test the Movie service class by creating a stub for the Movie repository class. By taking advantage of a Mock Object Framework, we isolated the Movie service class from the Movie repository class.

In this section, you learn how to return values from a stub object. In some situations, you need to make a stub class behave in a particular way to perform a test on the actual class being tested.

For example, imagine that you want to test the Movie controller class. This class is dependent on the Movie service class. To test the Movie class, we need to do more than simply stub the Movie service class. We need to fake values returned from calling methods on the Movie service class.

We want to test the controller logic in the Movie controller Create() action. The Create() action does one of two things depending on the value returned from calling the MovieService.CreateMovie() method. If CreateMovie() returns false—there is a validation error—then the Create() action should redisplay the form for creating a movie. On the other hand, if CreateMovie() returns true, then the Create() action should return a RedirectToAction result.

To test the Movie controller, we need to fake the value returned by the Movie service CreateMovie() method. We need to fake the value returned by the Movie service to fully test the Movie controller.

The two tests in Listing C.5 illustrate how you can fake the value returned by the CreateMovie() method.

LISTING C.5   Controllers\MovieControllerTests.cs (C#)

```csharp
using System.Web.Mvc;
using Microsoft.VisualStudio.TestTools.UnitTesting;
using Moq;
using MvcApplication1.Controllers;
using MvcApplication1.Models;

namespace MvcApplication1.Tests.Controllers
{
    [TestClass]
    public class MovieControllerTests
    {
        [TestMethod]
        public void CreateWithBadMovieReturnsView()
        {
            // Arrange
            var movieToCreate = new Movie();
            var serviceStub = new Mock<IMovieService>();
            serviceStub.Setup(s =>
➥s.CreateMovie(It.IsAny<Movie>())).Returns(false);
            var controller = new MovieController(serviceStub.Object);

            // Act
            var result = controller.Create(movieToCreate);

            // Assert
            Assert.IsInstanceOfType(result, typeof(ViewResult));
        }

        [TestMethod]
        public void CreateWithGoodMovieReturnsRedirect()
        {
            // Arrange
            var movieToCreate = new Movie();
            var serviceStub = new Mock<IMovieService>();
            serviceStub.Setup(s => s.CreateMovie(It.IsAny<Movie>())).Returns(true);
            var controller = new MovieController(serviceStub.Object);

            // Act
            var result = controller.Create(movieToCreate);

            // Assert
            Assert.IsInstanceOfType(result, typeof(RedirectToRouteResult));
        }
```

```
    }
}
```

LISTING C.5   Controllers\MovieControllerTests.vb (VB)

```vb
Imports Microsoft.VisualStudio.TestTools.UnitTesting
Imports Moq
Imports System.Web.Mvc

<TestClass()> _
    Public Class MovieControllerTests
    <TestMethod()> _
    Public Sub CreateWithBadMovieReturnsView()
        ' Arrange
        Dim movieToCreate As New Movie()
        Dim serviceStub As New Mock(Of IMovieService)()
        serviceStub.Setup(Function(s) s.CreateMovie(It.IsAny(Of Movie)
➥())).Returns(False)
        Dim controller = New MovieController(serviceStub.Object)

        ' Act
        Dim result = controller.Create(movieToCreate)

        ' Assert
        Assert.IsInstanceOfType(result, GetType(ViewResult))
    End Sub

    <TestMethod()> _
    Public Sub CreateWithGoodMovieReturnsRedirect()
        ' Arrange
        Dim movieToCreate = New Movie()
        Dim serviceStub = New Mock(Of IMovieService)()
        serviceStub.Setup(Function(s) s.CreateMovie(It.IsAny(Of
➥Movie)())).Returns(True)
        Dim controller = New MovieController(serviceStub.Object)

        ' Act
        Dim result = controller.Create(movieToCreate)

        ' Assert
        Assert.IsInstanceOfType(result, GetType(RedirectToRouteResult))
    End Sub

End Class
```

The CreateWithBadMovieReturnsView() test verifies that when the Movie service CreateMovie() method returns false, the Movie controller returns a view result. The CreateWithGoodMovieReturnsRedirect() test verifies that when the Movie service CreateMovie() method returns true, the Movie controller returns a redirect to route result. (The RedirectToAction() method returns a RedirectToRouteResult.)

The following line of code causes the Movie service CreateMovie() method to return the value true:

(C#)

```
serviceStub.Setup(s => s.CreateMovie(It.IsAny<Movie>())).Returns(true);
```

(VB)

```
serviceStub.Setup(Function(s) s.CreateMovie(It.IsAny(Of Movie)())).Returns(True)
```

When any movie parameter is passed to the CreateMovie() method, the CreateMovie() method returns the value true.

Index

Symbols

A

Q-R

T

X-Y-Z

W

How can we make this index more useful? Email us at indexes@sampublishing.com

UNLEASHED

Unleashed takes you beyond the basics, providing an exhaustive, technically sophisticated reference for professionals who need to exploit a technology to its fullest potential. It's the best resource for practical advice from the experts, and the most in-depth coverage of the latest technologies.

Microsoft Dynamics CRM 4 Integration Unleashed
ISBN-13: 9780672330544

OTHER UNLEASHED TITLES

ASP.NET 3.5 AJAX Unleashed
ISBN-13: 9780672329739

Windows Small Business Server 2008 Unleashed
ISBN-13: 9780672329579

Silverlight 2 Unleashed
ISBN-13: 9780672330148

Windows Communication Foundation 3.5 Unleashed
ISBN-13: 9780672330247

Windows Server 2008 Hyper-V Unleashed
ISBN-13: 9780672330285

LINQ Unleashed
ISBN-13: 9780672329838

C# 3.0 Unleashed
ISBN-13: 9780672329814

Ubuntu Unleashed 2008 Edition
ISBN-13: 9780672329937

Microsoft Expression Blend Unleashed
ISBN-13: 9780672329319

Windows PowerShell Unleashed
ISBN-13: 9780672329883

Microsoft SQL Server 2008 Analysis Services Unleashed
ISBN-13: 9780672330018

Microsoft SQL Server 2008 Integration Services Unleashed
ISBN-13: 9780672330322

Microsoft XNA Game Studio 3.0 Unleashed
ISBN-13: 9780672330223

SAP Implementation Unleashed
ISBN-13: 9780672330049

System Center Configuration Manager (SCCM) 2007 Unleashed
ISBN-13: 9780672330230

Microsoft SQL Server 2008 Reporting Services Unleashed
ISBN-13: 9780672330261

informit.com/sams

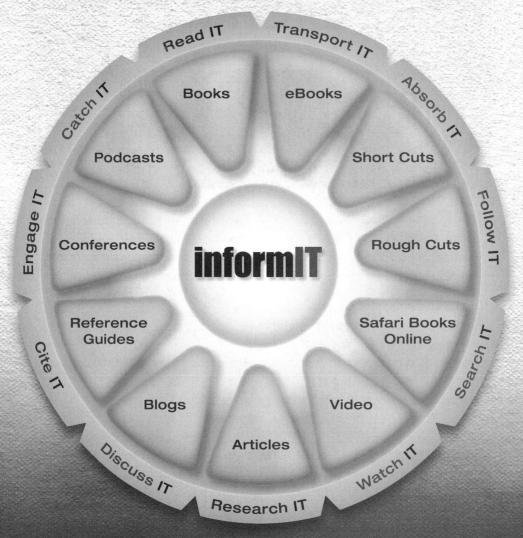

FREE Online Edition

Your purchase of **ASP.NET MVC Framework Unleashed** includes access to a free online edition for 45 days through the Safari Books Online subscription service. Nearly every Sams book is available online through Safari Books Online, along with more than 5,000 other technical books and videos from publishers such as Addison-Wesley Professional, Cisco Press, Exam Cram, IBM Press, O'Reilly, Prentice Hall, and Que.

SAFARI BOOKS ONLINE allows you to search for a specific answer, cut and paste code, download chapters, and stay current with emerging technologies.

Activate your FREE Online Edition at www.informit.com/safarifree

> **STEP 1:** Enter the coupon code: RNKPFDB.

> **STEP 2:** New Safari users, complete the brief registration form.
> Safari subscribers, just log in.

If you have difficulty registering on Safari or accessing the online edition, please e-mail customer-service@safaribooksonline.com